Deborah Case & Robert Lawrence, Editors

Press, an imprint of Cader Publishing, Ltd., Sterling Heights, Michigan

Whispers

Acknowledgements

We wish to thank Lisa Bommarito for her assistance in the preparation of the manuscript and production copy, Sharon Derderian for managing the judging, Machel Warner for proofing and editing, and (in alphabetical order) Andreya, Chris, Joy, Kelly, Kim, Melissa, Melissa, Tamara and Tracy for their efforts in book production and logistics.

Copyright © 1996 by Iliad Press, an imprint of Cader Publishing, Ltd. All rights reserved. No portion of this work may be reproduced, in whole or in part, without the prior written consent of the publisher and/or the author(s) of the individual works. Individual works copyright by author

Iliad Press sponsors four literary competitions per year. Each competition presents awards to 100 winners. Iliad Press offers a $1,000 grand prize and 99 other cash and/or merchandise prizes. Non-winning entries which are believed to be of particular note and merit are awarded an Honorable Mention. No purchase or entry fee is required for the first entry in the competition. Contest rules are subject to change without notice. All winners are selected by an independent panel of judges. Contests run continuously, four per year.

The address for Iliad Press is:

36915 Ryan Road
Sterling Heights, Michigan 48310
810-795-3635 Phone
810-795-9875 Fax

Printed and manufactured in the United States of America

ISBN:
1-885206-44-5

Library of Congress Catalog Number:
96-071186

Table of Contents

Special Note: The editors get frequent calls and letters about the typography and copy in our anthologies. Many of the contributors to *Whispers* take considerable "poetic license" with spelling, punctuation, grammar and word usage. Clear errors are corrected by the editors, however, many "errors" are returned to their original state by the authors. All selections are proofread and approved by the authors.

Chapter One
The Laureates of the Iliad Literary Awards
Spring 1996 Iliad Literary Award Winners..1

Chapter Two
Honorable Mention Awards
Judges' Honorable Mention Selections...25

Chapter Three
Youth Honorable Mention Awards
Honorable Mentions in the Youth Awards Program 79

Chapter Four
The Browning Competition
Winners and selected works from the VERSES Browning Competition 191

Chapter Five
The Haiku Competition
Winners and selected works from the VERSES Haiku Competition 195

Chapter Six
The Longfellow Competition
Winners and selected works from the VERSES Longfellow Competition 197

Chapter Seven
Dedications
Special dedications requested by participating authors...203

Chapter Eight
Whispers Around the World
Entries from competitors in the Spring Iliad Literary Awards Program..............207

Chapter Nine
About the Author
Biographies of selected authors and members of The National Authors Registry.................411

Index
Alphabetical Index by Author i

Whispers

Chapter One

The Laureates

Award winning verse & prose from the adult and youth winners of the
Spring 1996
Iliad Literary Awards Program.

Spring 1996 Iliad Literary Awards Program

Grand Prize Winner

The Ravens Know
by Patricia Kent

A baby lies
in umarked grave
at the old orphanage
somewhere out behind
the chickencoop
its little bones
frozen all these years
in ground that three feet down
does not thaw
even in July.

People came once
to look for their small one
but no cross
or stone
marks the place.

I think the ravens
know where baby sleeps.

Every afternoon
as if to pay respect
they glide over the field
in wide graceful arc.

 First Place Winner

Killer

by Jane E. Englehart

He saunters in, smelling like cheap
cologne and Luckystrikes.
His black hair is as smooth
as his dance moves
and his velvet voice
boasts of voluptuous babes
he's black booked.
He works the room, with his steel blue eyes,
preying on the innocent
and unfortunate.
Telling tales of untruth
never revealing himself.
His lips move, but not his mind,
for the story is always the same.
His laughter rolls off his tongue,
never feeling the smile.
The forced conversation is a ritual
practiced to perfection.
The ultimate goal, lies in wait
while he takes what he deserves.
Days unto nights, he prowls the streets
waiting for a seraph to work her gentle magic-
she never comes.
He continues on, robotic,
hardened by bitter truths,
walking past life,
never seeing his angel,
crying out to him.

 Second Place Winner

Ode To The Parrot Who Shrieked "I Love You" To Me In The Middle Of The Mall Of America
by Rachael Koch

All I know is that you are
red and green and blue.
Your name as well as your birthplace
escapes my memory.
But I want to thank you
all the same
for being so verbal
about your feelings for me.
If I were your type,
how long do you think we'd last?
Do you put the toilet seat down?
Does your mother make frequent visits?
I wonder if I would miss
my wingless homosapiens.
Because as I watch you devour that peanut
with the aid of your foot,
I realize that you don't have much in common
with them
save your table manners.

 Third Place Winner

Date From Hades
by Karen Williams

You raved about Asian women,
  ranking each country according to beauty.
You said my rambunctious child
  should be taken down a notch or two.
You said I had the wrong kind of life insurance,
  for gosh sakes.
You merely picked at the broccoli spaghetti
  I served for dinner.
{ Granted, it was akin to wallpaper paste.}
You barged ahead of me into the theater
  and elbowed me in the ribs during the movie's
  comic moments.

You seemed perplexed that I had to be home by 9:30
  to wash my hair.

I dashed off an indignant letter,
  demanding you never contact me again.

But now I try to remember our date with humor.

Anger burns when you hold it.

Spring 1996 Iliad Literary Youth Awards Program

 First Place Winner

Ode To Dusk (Afternoon Of Sorrow)
by Alissa Patrice Stone - age 17

I will bid you goodnight:
I will leave you
before you have the chance to tell me
all that you'll regret
and I'll close my eyes as though I never
wept.

I will not think of the pain- I bore
the icy stares traded
the green thoughts boiled
I'll only remember life's lessons taught and toil.

I'll forget the kindness and the joy,
the happy hearts---
whomever employed
-the tingling
jingling songs of bells,
that shook our dreams
into a fiery hell.
To not remember- which ever-
joy or pain
keeping not one for the sake of sane.

But...
if I slip a thought or two recognizing
that day renewed,
or thinking of things-
I might regret.
I'll turn my heart as though I never wept.

 Second Place Winner

Automaton
by Emily Farmer - age 17

the window on my car won't roll down,
i told her,
and you have to hit the seatbelt-
hard--
to make it latch
i have to flick the turn signal lever myself
because it's stopped clicking when i turn it on.
they laugh because i always park in the same spot
whether it's convenient or not
but it's something tangible
a pattern
and that's important on a rainy 7 am morning
or a dull 4pm afternoon
and when the key sticks hopelessly in the lock
i want to smile and cry
for i have become particular and cranky, just
like my car,
a mess of gadgetry and incomplete circuits
temperamental diodes and weak resistors
sure, anyone with the key
can drive my car
but only i know how to do it right

 Third Place Winner

Millington
by Anna Christopher - age 15

Welcome to Millington; population five hundred and fifty-
Somewhere near to Illinois river.
Not easy to find, but the farmer's fence posts,
Unevenly staked and crudely connected by haggard wire,
Lead you to the tired farm homes
With peeling pain and sagging steps and
Lazy dogs lying on lonely porches
Soaking in an afternoon's last sun rays,
Old cardboard signs rest in overgrown grass and
Read "Manure for sale" or "Pasture for rent"
Dead dandelion tufts whirl in the wind
Backdropped by a lagoon-blue sky.
A house on Sleepy Hollow Way
Bears a homemade sign:
"Fresh Eggs $.75;
A patch of velveteen violets
Grows below it. At the house's peak
An enduring iron weather vane
Waits for a breeze
And above the slapping screen door, a cross
Woven of twisting twigs faithfully hangs.
No trains roar here, no cars spit their exhaust,
No business meetings in tall steel buildings,
No suits and ties and pantyhose.
Only people in jeans and flannels
And things like fresh eggs and tired dogs
To make the days go by.

But I'm Wearing Green
by Rachel I. Aldrich - age 19

I want to wear red.
I want to wear red patent leather shoes
white bobbie sox, and an Annie dress.
I want red bows in my pony tails
that bounce and yell, "Look, look, look at me! I'm cute!"

I want to wear sharp, red, spiked heels,
I want long, curving, red fingernails
that could..."accidentally"
cut flesh with a click.
I want red leather with
zippers that warn:
"Don't get caught in me. I might hurt!"

I want to wear an ankle length,
sparkly red,
slit-to-the-hip gown
with red satin lining.
I want to reflect my sparkles
across a black baby grand.
I want to wear red lipstick
that reaches out to be kissed.
I want a plummeting neckline
that taunts:
"You want this? Prove it!"

But I'm wearing green.

Southern Emperors
by Dawn Austrom

      Crystalline flakes
      Land
        on a frigid
    and Shinning expanse.

    Howling, shrieking
        Storms
      Batter hooded
        Forms;
    Huddled for warmth.

    Tuxedoed clowns,
        Nigh,
    Outline the slate
        And
      Sinister sky.

      Dark royalty
        Pose
    In feathered suits
    With deep sympathy.

      Cold emperors
        Slide
      Along ancient
        And
      Capacious ice.

    Awkward grey chicks
        Dive
      Into icy
      Depths.
    Will they survive?

Remain
by Elizabeth Bahs - age 18

I don't like the sound
of my feet slapping linoleum.
I don't like the way I love.
I hate needing
to know what
only you feel.

Somtimes
I despise the nothing
that hangs on my shoulders,
the drawn out
remembering,
and the almost silence.

I don't want
a fairy godmother or
false affection,
only a friend eager
to adopt me back.

I like my yellow-white skin,
my arms that fold
under like wings,
and stories told
on a purple couch
at the Hilton.

When my devotion is
ignored
I don't leave--
just stay
silent
until you need me.

Turned Backs
by Brenda Beausoleil

Turned Backs
are an effective means
of communication -
done properly, of course.
No room for compromise
when the stiff neck
creaks into dismissal
emptying dreams with
a mere muscle flex
of condemnation.

To Dream of Deeper Things
by Patricia M. Crawford

I dreamt of green
    Cool shades of envy
        That whisper secrets to the wind
    Oceans of tall grass
        Rippling endlessly to shore
    Monoliths reaching
        To bleed green in gold making blue
    Did I make them so
        Invitingly alive because
I dreamt of green?

November Walk
by Vera Ogden Bakker

The patio is deserted now.
The last trace of barbecue
   and roses has been erased.
Dry grass crackles beneath my feet
   as shriveled strawberry plants
      huddle close to the earth.

Leftover flies stagger
   along the brick wall in
      fading warmth of the afternoon sun.
One robin, feathers ruffled,
   seeks shelter amid bare lilac twigs.
A box elder bug flattens itself
   into a crack in the bark.

The granite mountains have pulled
   heavy gray clouds over their shoulders.
An icy blast rips the last
   dry leaves from the apple tree.

I clutch my sweater tighter and hurry indoors
   having just witnessed the passing
      of another Autumn.

Mendocino
by Jim Barnes

A child in a yellow slicker
holds a red balloon on a string
and skips playfully past
the white and grey picket fences
in the slowly ebbing fog.
Homes whose builders long have passed,
of whose descendants still are here,
stand calmly, so serene,
in the waxing light of morning.
In the cool breeze she searches
the ocean's graying form
to see what hint of movement
there was that she had seen.
The gray whale goes by, secure,
unnoticed save by her,
and so she turns to hurry home
in the slowly ebbing fog
to tell her mother all about
red balloons and picket fences
and yet another whale.

Love
by Nicole Elliott - age 16

      Love is pure and sweet
  like the first drink of cool water.
The question is shall I drink the whole glass
     or take little sips.

Shall I dip into the ocean without any doubt.
  Or forbid myself to drink water at all.

    For I am very thirsty now...

The Hardware Store
by Helen F. Blackshear

I like the man-smell of a hardware store
odors of old leather,
fresh cut lumber, oiled machines,
limey smell of plaster and new paint.

I like the men who come to hardware stores,
men with calloused hands
in dirty jeans and sweaty shirts,
men who work.

I remember times we came together
for shingles to reproof the shed,
cement for the outdoor barbecue,
bricks for the patio.

Now I come alone and pause a moment
just inside the door.
Almost I see you there
beyond the ray of dust motes in the aisle.

So strong the sense of deja vu
I have to catch my breath
as if these old familiar smells
could bring you back from death.

Route 13
by Tiffany Bolz

He drives over potholes and roadkill and does not slow down.
Past the fire house and the Baptist church
on a two lane highway
with only one headlight working
on his battered pickup truck.
His cigarette makes an arc of orange sparks and he does not look back
as he rolls up the window and reaches for another beer.
Dim yellow eyes of the dashboard lights shine on
her crumpled bra, limp on the seat next to him and
torn panties hiding under this almost gone six-pack.
He reaches up to zigzag scratches underneath his eye
and on his neck. His shirt is torn.
The radio croons in and out of static country tunes
and he sings just a little.
He ignores the fence and the No Trespassing sign
as he slows to a stop and idles the truck.
He pulls her from the back by her hair and
she slumps in the hard packed dirt.
Her socks look almost holy,
stark white against her skin and his scuffed work boots.
He does not see the tiny bits of him left
underneath her fingernails or the bruises
on her neck and thighs.
He steps on her hand as he walks around the truck
to grab her bra. He drops it on the dirt next to her and
climbs back into the truck. His seat is still warm.
He does not look into his rear view mirror at her as he drives away.
She glows red in the tail lights for a moment
and then he is gone.

Oviraptor
by June Miller

For eighty million years!
she crouches brooding,
skeleton legs curving around--
naked claws clutching--
twenty eggs turned to stone.

Fossil bones of neck stretch
up and out, skull jaws gaping
wide and wider--O aeonic keening!
monster/mother, mother primeval--
mother of monsters--cry
for the children.

Growing Up
by Leslie Bourke - age 14

You no longer accept the fact that the sky is blue,
You want to know why.
The baby shoes are saved in boxes.
The night light is no longer kept on.
The monster under the bed disappears.
Baby blankets are stored away in the attic.
The little tales of Santa Claus, the Easter bunny, and the tooth fairy are shattered.

You grow taller and taller.
No more bed time stories.
No more being tucked into bed.

Years pass and your grade becomes higher and higher.
You old clothes are handed down to a little brother or sister.
Your little bike is replaced with a bigger 10 speed bike.
Hugs from your parents are very embarrassing.

You keep growing and growing,
until finally you are an adult who only has happy fading memories of when a sky was just blue.

Teddy Bear
by Adrienne Brand - age 13

Old, forlorn,
slouching in a
rickety old rocker
Remembering days
gone by,
Days full of
sunny gloom,
and the times which
were spent
smacking against a wiry pallet
of a bed in
ferocious tantrums
But most of all,
of all, of all,
those times together,
alone,
sitting, hugging,
sharing emotions,
BEING love... then
....years... going..by
And now,
no one left,
but the
dust.

Think
by April Brazee - age 17

A blazing red fire
With clouds of black and gray smoke
Engulfing one's home.
A black sky
And turning clouds
Spitting out flashes
of yellow.
A swift, hard wind
In a foreign, white
Wonderland
With invisible ice.
A clean, white shirt
Splattered with red
From a hole caused
By a bullet passing
Through one's skin.
These are the
Colors to worry about,
Not the color of one's skin.

Ending Metaphors
by Charity Brokaw - age 17

Poetry, smooth as chardonnay
rolling the body
swallowing the sliced, sculpted words
until it's trickling down your throat
through your veins
until you feel the rythym in the
thumping of your heart
until you savor the sweetness
of emotion soaked in vulnerability
salty, bitter, deep and bloody
smell it feel it touch it taste it
fondle it perceive it caress it
then die at the hands of the words
fly with the stanzas
drink with the darkness
hold the shadows to your soul and
taste the turbulence
but never stop until you're addicted
don't ever quit until you can't live
without it
until you smoother and suffocate into
the thickness of the mood
until you walk away changed
forever.

Untitled
by Dianne Brooks

In 1958 when I was twelve years old, only thirteen years had passed since
Cadaverous Jewish prisoners, finally free, hobbled from Dachau and
    Bergen-Belsen
And I wanted to swim in the crystalline water at the Country Club pool,
But they had a sign, "No Jews allowed."

In 1964 I was eighteen. I went to college and nineteen years had passed
    since
Gaping graves spilled Jewish bones in Auschwitz and Treblinka
And I wanted to join one of the dozen sororities with pristine houses high
    up on the hill
But there were only two for Jews
They said "Choose one of those two."

In 1969 when I was twenty-two and married, over twenty years had passed
    since
A handful of Jews had withstood the Nazi assault until their deaths in the
Warsaw Ghetto
And I wanted to go to Memphis to buy lox and bagels, hard to find in
Tennessee.
"They have them, though" is what they told me
"You'll find them in the Jewish ghetto."

In 1988 my eldest son applied to Harvard, and was it fifty years that passed
    since
Kristallnacht when broken Jewish glass shattered synagogues and lives
Not only in Berlin, and quotas filled up freight trains?
And was it twenty years or thirty since Harvard too had Jewish quotas?

Finally planned diversity might help a worthy Jewish boy.
Affirmative action, scholarships. Americans prize minorities.
"Yes" they said to darker skins and children come from Southern climes.
"Jews" they laughed.
Americans.
Assimilated every one.

The Good Ol' Boys
by Milt Carland

The old men straddle their stools at the bar,
Rummaging through the attics of their lives.
Aging bullfrogs splayed upon thier lily pads,
Chirping and burping in the fading light.

Whittle
by Gregory Case

Winds whistle against aspen,
Whistling forgotten melodies
Cemented in misplaced times.

Carvings are easy to chase
when carried off trunks
to dance in unknown wood.

Shavings make their own
noise
against clay and beer can
painted streams.

Enticed by sound,
I follow the whittled whisper
until lost in the music.

liquid life
by Kara Chiodo - age 18

the bright green plastic container
holds promise
64 ounces of childhood fun
multicolored in the light --
soap bubbles wait to come out

anyone may give birth to these beauties
skill is not required, only
chubby fingers to grasp the wand
puckered lips to blow and help
the liquid capture air

fragility is their nature
their short but happy lives end
at a touch, a breath
or a disturbance too small
for wide young eyes to see

Anew
by Shannon Churchey - age 19

Barren sky stretches endlessly,
gray and cold, pausing
before green sets itself
upon earth--briefly
illuminating every crevice
left uncovered by quilts
of snow, open to wind's
prying fingers which leave
fine ash in their wake--

Puffs of silver smoke
roll over slated roofs,
warming lives of desolate
inhabitants who witness etchings
of naked branches, who weep
at bitter reality of natures suspension
between loneliness
and rebirth, brief breath
air takes before warming,
trees takes before spawning
life takes before blooming
before earth shudders,
chisels away packed sod,
renews springs's memory
in a tiny green shoot.

The Dress Dilemma
by Susie Coffman - age 17

Hunting for the ultimate dress,
Through jungles of naked hangers.
The hunters insanely search for the prize,
Knocking down anyone in their path.

The girls unheedfully mouth at their mothers,
"Zip me."
"Unbutton me."
"Tie me."
"Snap me."
And the mothers eagerly do so,
And glance at their princess.

One dress after the other.
How can someone feel like a "princess"?
Velvet dress..l.
Too tight.
Sequins dress...
Too itchy.
The long red dress...
Look at the price!
The hunt becomes a vicious fight for time.

Through the reflection of the mirror
Stands a smile.
Ugliness forgotten.
A princess unveiled.
Beauty.
Charm.
Opulence.
Grace.
The winning dress.
Search has ended.

A flood of relief.

Hunting for the ultimate shoes...

American Romanticism
by Shawn Cote

Here I sit, imbibing romanticism.
Listen, Emerson, you Optimist--what about Hitler?
Are ponds the answer for everyone, Henry David--
you make good sense, you justify my indolence.
And Whitman, you are brave or a fool--you believe
in democracy, but what is that, at what price does
it come? Is it found in tar[a[er shacks or the
dust of Lincoln, long shadows of martyrdom?

There is something to be said for everything and
what is good without evil and where is John Wilkes now?
And Emerson, you Philosopher, will I know myself when I
rejoin the whole, can I take with me what was good in
this world and will Hitler and John Wilkes be there too
and must I share my good things with them?

Pheasant in the Snow
by Martha Crabtree

Snow deepens,
We spread their feast again.
There, beyond the window,
They peck at crusts and grain--
Winter's tiny mascots of brown and grey,
A few crested top-knots, but modest, they.
Sometimes a cardinal, flashing red;
Sometimes a bluejay
Snatching bread.

Always we look for the royal guest--
His stately pilgrimage we like best.
Up from the wood's rim
He prints a trail:
Brilliant his plumage, his wondrous tail;
Winter's sun gleams
In his golden eye,
Approaching, he pauses...
Will he pass by?
No--he will honor us--
See, for our bread,
Calmly he bows his magnificent head.

Reminder
by Sarah Cunningham - age 18

We are born imperfect, scarred,
each one of us bearing the mark
of our mother.

The middle of our physical existence
carries the human identification
first given by Eve.

Everyone could see, but no one notices
the significance of a single indentation
that only a fingertip may fill.

Not a mere decoration, as its name suggests,
or just a pierceable piece of flesh,
it once was a portal through which
our mother's blood flowed,
a link to the fountain of life
before we had middle names,
or our father's dark eyes.

Now just a small crevice
in our smooth expanse of belly
that might hold water
in the tub, or collect lint and dust
from lack of attention.

For us, it is only the shadow of a body part,
hidden under society's standards of decency,
lacking any function,

except to serve
as a reminder, a faint memory,
of life that supported us
before we even opened our mouths
to take in our first breath
of forgettable oxygen.

When the Rain Forgot August
by Cherisse Dilizio - age 16

The mock waterfall of a garden hose invented paradise in a drought
She cupped her hands over her hair that sparkled like gold fish scale in the apricot sun
Rusty water fell like a drippy spigot into her sun toasted hands, they separated like oil and vinegar
Releasing two tablespoons of crimson water that ran on her hair and rinsed her face
She spun like a top
Her orange tresses twirling like the hairs of a mop
Pretending to be sprinkler just so she could say it rained

When the rains came they fell like sifted water through cloudy colanders
but from where she stood no clouds withheld rain
After that dandelion of a sun was plucked
All there was to do was look at the sky
So she did
A tie-dye mix of a sunset of thistle pink blossoms and cornflower blue
Stars studded in the sky like pegs on a *lite bright*
On those nights
When the moon was new, she trusted her senses and knew it was there.

Memo
by Scott Dinho

Please don't pick the flowers from the vine.
Even though they may be exciting.
Let them be.
So that others may enjoy them.
So that bees may use them.
So they may bloom again tomorrow.

Take the fallen beauties from the ground.
Their demise is only a workbook away,
Pick them up.
So that you might enjoy them.
So that vases may use them.
So that they may bloom for you tomorrow.

We trust that with your cooperation, all will be served.

Restricted
by Lindsay Dozoretz - age 17

Restricted
By assignments, requirements, regulations
By practically, ignorance
By time

I was given a task: to simply draw a solitary cube.
"Why," I inquired of my renowned art professor, "can I not create
a flaming dragon to suddenly poke its head out of a side of this cube?"
"The cube is your limit." he replied with a smirk, his condescension mocking my naiveté,
"You have been given a restricted space for a purpose, not for some
    ridiculously fantastical creative outlet."

He stung my imagination as he spat out the words
and my psyche cowered in the corner of my mind
just beyond my reach--I could not touch it
But its booming voice spoke, proud and bitter, it said
"Color is freedom. Art is freedom. I am freedom...."

Silence echoed in deaf ears
And, restricted by expectations,
I sketched out a sterile box.

Spring 1996 Laureates

Night Sounds
by A. Katherine Earl

"Bases are loaded as Morgan comes to bat,
He's 0 for 3."

The oracle speaks through quiet night,
his single, shining eye of red giving life
to the small box in which he lives.

He speaks soothing words, without meaning,
to the fearful child who knows
that night has stalked into the silent house.

The lyrics blur into a sing-song lullaby,
while cicadae and cricket
play descant and arpeggios,
and the rise and fall of distant roaring voices
pound upon the shore of consciousness.

"He's out!"

Young Salvationist
by Thomas Reynolds

The cross stood on a hill, silent...
Two days before, the crowds had
screamed "King".
Then the sky turned like night.
And blood dripped from
a young man's head
staining the brow soil.
Blood from a thorn crown
tore his soft skin.
Struggling he lifted his head
while people screamed "Crucify Him!"
All was silent and he died...

for those who hung him there.

Jettisoned
by Larry Etue

Street corner preachers, street corner
sinners... the compatibility of rhinos
and tickbirds.
Sidewalk strollers, alley dwellers
all reflected in storefront
windows, mirroring society's
images in dirty glass...

Yesterday's bright future
among those, the
unshaven, unwashed,
uninhibited, unknown,
unscrewed from the
usual connections.

Wrappers, cigarette butts,
previous 'gotta haves,'
now form residue from earlier
pleasures jettisoned
as more useless than they are
by the 'uns' reading at
bus stop libraries
of the world of which
they are not and
which views them as...
not.

Mama
by Kimberly Faught

I watch as she eats
her heart.
Once I would have asked her
if she wanted some tabasco
to spice it up
and she would have laughed.

But she doesn't smile anymore
and I don't try to make her.
I used to sit for hours and talk.
I told her about Janey eating paste, and
the time when Eric cut off all of her hair.
One day I sat there and told her every dirty joke
that I could remember from college.
I tried everything. When she wouldn't laugh,
I tried to make her angry; and when
she wouldn't scream, I tried to make her cry.
I would have been thankful for a curse,
a moan, a sob.

But she stopped talking in August,
five days after the accident.
It was the day she signed the paper,
signed away her son,
my brother,
and she hasn't said a word since.

So I just sit
and stare, as she slowly slips
away; a suicide of sorts.

I Miss Missing You
by E.M. Short

Before, when we were apart
I used to go to bed hugging your picture
and crying into my pillow,
as if that somehow would bring
us closer together.

It wasn't very good for your picture;
the corners bent and you got a crease
in your face.

But now I can go for two hours
sometimes
without even thinking
about you.
I miss missing you.

A Hanger to Take Your Place
by Jennifer Simon - age 15

I have hung you
in the back of my closet,
To black you from
My thoughts.

You dangle from
a wiry metallica,
an askew pedestal
Vying for your place.

How I wish you were a
sleek garment;
Frequently abandoning
Such security
To fill the void
You've left
Heaping on the floor.

An Old Woman
by Miriam Inbar - age 15

Upon a splintered oaken chair she sits
An aged crone, frail bones baked brittle
Eyes near drowned in hollow fat rimmed pits
Weary limb sigh; she moves but little

Yet in my face her eyes find hold
Her shriveled vein wrought hands seek mine
A new leaf grown to replace the old
Torn by wind, tarnished by brine

In her languid eyes I am the past
The ever branching roads untred
The never broken pleasure fast
Eternal pages yet unread

Dreams and hopes dashed into pieces
Choices made both wrong and right
Arms and legs, head and faces
A perfect day, a sleepless night

All this she sees while one wish grew
Another chance to walk the road
To shut the book and star anew
To shed like skin the crushing load

To Laura Rothenberg:
by Natasha Grant - age 16

How wrong was I when I thought,
That because I was young I could live freely,
That my life ran untimed,
And that I'd been born with the right to a lifetime.
With a right to live untouched by death.
Immortal dream.
Naive hope.
Unrealistic.
Justice is not yet acquainted with this world,
And fate at any moment avariciously steals your ticket to life.
I hear each day of things unjustified.
Innocence corrupted by the reality of immortality.
I need to hear it ..... now I see you,
And I feel the pain of your evanescent life.

My Crystalnacht
by Jean Friedman

Following my mother's death
which came quite suddenly, after a long illness,
the ice storms came and left
ice-encrusted twigs and branches
that clicked against each other like bones.
That night was incredibly sharp and clear.
The light from street lamps and the moon
danced among the trees and surfaces of things ice-covered,
making haloes.
The icy air, like a surgical instrument, cut deeply
into my consciousness, through layers and layers of fuzziness
accumulated over the years like collectibles
and kept for no apparent reason.
We walked silently, my dog and I, through the
stillness of sharply defined shapes in a sterile winter landscape,
devastatingly beautiful, without choices, final.
So, this was the end of things,
a specimen of frozen time, encased in ice,
Crystalnacht. My night of glass
On the very day of my mother's funeral
a pure white gardenia, her favorite flower,
bloomed on a plant that hadn't bloomed
for two and a half years.

On Why I Love Trees
by Liz Fink

My father plants trees. Hundreds of them - pine, birch, oak, sumach - you name it. They are small and fragile. He tends them like children. In my lifetime, I guess he's planted over 2,000. Some are taller than houses now.

My father plants trees. His new project is a stand of oaks, but the squirrels keep digging up the seedlings for the acorns.

I remember as a kid I would spend hours in the yard with him. I was the youngest of six, and I had cracked the secret of how to get to know Dad: plant trees.

He would come home from work (he's a surgeon by trade) and open the fridge. He would grab the liverwurst or left-over meat loaf or just about anything, cut off a slab, and eat it with his hands. I watched with a mixture of revulsion and adoration as he poured ketchup on the food and his hand and vacuumed the whole mess up with his mouth.

Once he had refueled, he would walk upstairs and change into yard clothes. They were thick with dirt and sap from the night before. He slipped his "yard" pipe into his pocket and mysteriously appeared out back without getting caught by Mom for household issues.

I would watch him from the window-debating whether it was worth getting filthy for a little quality time. I'd slip on my Keds and work my way out to the "new site" where a cluster of saplings stood, waiting in their tubs for transplantation.

"Do you want some help?" I would ask awkwardly. He'd look up-smeared with dirt, mosquitos flattened on his forehead and cheeks. "Sure honey, why don't you run get the hose."

I knew I was perceived as an intrusion at first. He had a rhythm, an amazing sense of purposefulness to his yard work. It always took me a while to snap into the grove.

An hour or so would pass and we would hit team frequency and then we could talk.

"Do you ever get sad?" I would venture.

"Sure I do", he replied casually.

"Depressed?", I'd push on.

He's stop and look at me, sensing we had reached a level of intimacy.

"Sure I get depressed. I've been very depressed at times. Why do you ask?" And the conversation would flow. Like two shipwrecked sailors we would work and talk for hours. If we were really on a roll, we could sustain the connection through dinner and resume later.

My father plants trees. Thousands of them-still. Now he comes over to my place and plants them. Now we are openly friends and our connection is never broken. We talk about life and fears, regrets and dreams. Sometimes I feel like one of those trees.

In Love (and Vulnerable)
by Alan Frame

My love for you is my Achilles' heel;
Your beauty is my armor's only chink.
I can't control exactly how I feel;
You're truly so disarming, I can't think!
In front of you, my feelings are exposed--
So, therefore, they are open to attack.
These eyes that covet you are never closed,
Although they're watching you--and not my back!
Because my loving heart and soul are bared,
No shield can stop them both from being scarred.
Whenever you are near me, I am scared,
Because I'm too in love to be on guard.
You only have to bat your eyes of brown
To capture me with my defenses down.

Toy Soldiers
by Gabriel Garrido - age 19

A thousand soldiers stand dead on their feet,
arms and legs melting in the suns merciless heat,
the acrid smell of plastic hangs limp in the air,
but no one notices or even seems to care,
battalion upon battalion lined up by the dozen,
in a battle stance they are forever frozen,
eagerly awaiting the hands that will bring them to life once more,
and guide them through the tactics of their unfinished war,
their world exists in the mind of a child,
so the battle is never ending and the killing is wild,
a grenade will go off and kill four men,
but in another minute they're alive and fighting again,
silent gunfire rings in the child ears,
as the fighting continues for weeks and then years,
many are wounded and the casualties run high,
everyone mourns the losses and a few people cry,
the soldiers are placed in a box and then packed away,
destined to join the memories of a forgotten yesterday,
now they're about as useful as a broken cup
their battle is over...
...the child has grown up.

Nighttime in the Desert
by Carol L. Gautney, II

The desert sighs, painted in the moon's pale wash,
The cactus sleeps here in its prickly bed
While moonglow bleaches the bones of the dead,
And spills its milk over the crookneck-squash.

Furry prey scampers for a stone shadow,
A predator reels in soundless flight
And screeches triumph in the dead of night,
Along the banks of the Colorado.

Canyon mustangs dance in ceremony,
The ancient voices calling them to come,
Prancing to the rhythm of a phantom drum,
The land in hushed awe of these ghost ponies.

The souls of warriors rise from their graves
Like feathery visions in their moonlight bath,
Floating past echoes of an old warpath
Of antelope skulls brought down by their brave.

The desert breathes deep as the moon sinks low,
The cottontail flees from all-seeing eyes;
Somewhere a young ground squirrel curls up and dies,
As hues paint the sky to dawn the first glow.

Over 50
by Dawn R. Hill

Sexiest 57 year old
imaginable
zooms around town in his
little black car sunroof open
little red car full of bikes...
Sexiest 57 year old
imaginable
smells of baby powder and ivory soap
tastes like coffee and jelly beans.
Sexiest 57 year old
imaginable
tingles my toes
catches my breath.
I'm in love with the
sexiest 57 year old
imaginable.

Standing in the Gap
by Stephaine Givens

On her knees, bent down in prayer,
that's my sista prayin' there.
Her young shoulders quiver and shake,
as she calls upon God, for my own dear sake.
Her lips move, but no sound escapes,
but God hears her heart, that's all it takes.
Tears fall and spill right down her face,
but God will wipe them away, he'll leave not one trace.
Standin' in the gap.

The room is empty, silent and still,
the Lord's presence is there, strong enough to feel.
The room is empty, or is it seems,
but filling the church, are angels on their knees.
God is there, and he is not silent,
His angels will fight if demons get violent.
Standin' in the gap.

So if you think your prayer is not heard,
if you don't feel the Lord and you can't say a word.
find you a prayer closet, get down on your knees,
Cry to the lord Jesus, he always sees you.
Standin' in the gap.

Please Forgive Me
by Dianne Hamilton

My own tongue
has betrayed me,
unmistakably
uttering words
so mean and malicious,
they create a chasm
between us.

Your shocked silence
restores sensibility
more effectively
than a physical blow,
and I flinch with shame
at the malevolence
of my mind.

Those worded weapons,
though senselessly spoken,
have malignantly sown
seeds of self-doubt;
I see it in your eyes.
If my remorse
could wish words back...

Would you forgive me?

Dies Mortis
by Marjorie A. O'Donnell

Everything is over.
I flounder in a cacophonic sea
Grimly struggling to uplift my head.
No one must see the word slashes
Bleeding wounds from your vindictive leaving.
After all, it's not as if I'd know you for a lifetime
You were an interlude...
A simple prelude to a more harmonious union.
Now discordant cymbals hammer at my temples
Constant drums insinuate your rhythm
Until my groin cries out, release me.
Trombones moan your double-edged smile of pity
Grieving with me, are they also saying
Love was never meant to die this way?

The Edge of Heaven
by William J. Hiles

It was so long ago
That day of pride and wrath
Oh the tumbling, the falling--
(and the hatred and fear that followed)
Better to rule here than serve--
Oh our will was iron
But like rust, grief soon marred
And in my heart I knew--still know
One truth
I miss you

There is a distant light circling
This wounded home
And I know you are there
But They say you never think of me
And They say They never lie
(They with wings of fire and eyes of ice)
Yet I still cry out to you
And--though They would never admit it--
I know you hear me--your bound wings trembling

This love is a faith that transcends my life
Pierces the heart
Burns the eyes
Screams in a voice to shatter all doubt
A voice even They cannot avoid--in truth--
Or deny

One night, my love, I will rise
To the edge of Heaven
And kiss you
When God is sleeping...

Woodland Reverie
by Joan E. Hunt

Some day again,
I'm not sure when,
we'll walk together in the woods
on leaf-strewn path dappled with sun,
watch the birds flit through shafts of light,
hear their cries of warning.

We'll follow the pulsing rush of water
until we find the brook
and stop, again, to feel bright ripples
against our hands, to see
minnows dart through light,
then disappear in deepest dark.

Will riders come again,
white-jodpured, through the shadows,
sitting tall on their dark mounts?
We can watch the horses pick their way,
snorting at chill of water,
flicking tails against black flies.
Then they'll be gone
behind the screen of trees and shadows,
their clop-clop lost in bird calls
as the running brook
pulses through our hands,
your face blurring into mine,
like horse and rider,
flowing with the trees
and brook and birds
into gentle tapestry.

Night Light
by Nancy J. Huston

The silver of the moon gives up miserly portions tonight
The stars compensate by sharing connecting patterns
Looking into the vastness of it all, I wonder at the small treasures below
Orchids relentlessly drip their scent into night's soft blanket
My connection with the universe is potent now

You reach out with fingers of kindness, arms of compassion, words of love
To hold my tiny yellow speck of fear in your own hand,
Warming it, you turn it to golden remission
I discover an appreciation for the great orchestration
Of the music and dance of my own life

Willows weep no more for their beloved riverbanks
The long wolf chooses to walk the silent hills tonight
It is a time of awareness, it is a time of wonder
I would share with you the world,
And of course me

Love Quilts
by Amy Jones - age 19

I
Meticulously stretched over rays
of morning breeze
Needle, thread, eye-glasses -
spines curved over meadows of
labored cloth
Hours and hours - the old-fashioned
way
dressed and service designed
Their love quilts, their pioneer art

IV
In pools of blood she rests
On the crochet sweat of her
grandmother
The crystals dissolve
from her eyes
Mesmerized, the miracle, the wonder -
she is the dream - what quilts
she shall weave!

V
The sun awakens early
Pale and withered - cool to touch
Covers pulled from toe to chin
This great celebration - children
of children of children gather round
These patches, this design, so
eloquently done - hangs proud
and is now complete

Attic Lies
by Klaire L. Martin

In an attic a small girl hides
where pleasant odors of old
books linger, and words she can't
read yet, smell important.
She's discovered parts of life
meant to be hidden under Christmas
wrap, tinsel, a tree Santa sets up.
Her bright curious eyes spy
Easter baskets stashed
in a dark, dusty corner.
Strands of fake green grass cover
stale bits of nesting red and
black jelly-beans that awkward
fingers failed to capture.
Her mind begins to feel a lie,
through tears she whispers no.

The Road
by Gary M. Joy

A moccasin path
across the prairie
left unspoiled
in passing

            Sunset, sunrise

A rutted muddy road
traveled by Conestoga wagons
heading west

            Sunset, sunrise

A graveled rocky road
for farmers and ranchers
in rattling and creaking black cars
going to town

            Sunset, sunrise

A sleek vein of concrete and steel
connecting beating hearts
found in a land with many wounds
inflicted by multiple dreams

Sunrise
by Rex Kelly

Within the depths of an ancient mirror,
A story lingered too long and fell,
Spiraling down beyond the grasp of its child.
Wavering and weaving a lonely spell,
Of actions and fears -- of wind dried tears,
Leaving hands empty and frail.
I strain to touch verses,
        As they flee into birdsong.
Emotion trapped within this fading shell.

I will extend myself the dance of the sunset,
And I will listen, and I will feel.
As the canvass grows gray,
        And the warmth turns away,
Solitude shall cloak me and become all to real.

For in my world your voice was home,
And in your presence, all I have known.
Nothing shines, nothing sings...
With no one beside me.
I coaxed my soul into a song,
That together we could welcome the dawn,
Only silence, only sorrow
Witness it with me.

Cigarettes
by Grant Koo - age 20

I labor through an entanglement of limbs,
Careful to keep quiet,
Not to wake dreaming angels.
As I feel around for my shoes.
And piercing together clothes
That have grown too tight,
I finger the dark for cigarettes.

A memory should have some time to smoke.

It breaks my heart,
This slow cigarette burn,
I watch her toss and turn.
The room grows bright
With each sullen pull casting weird shadows
That shiver against milk warm thighs.

She looks like a sigh.

An evening wind
That taps against the window
Interrupts my reveries
To tell me it's time.
I rise with resignation
And fumble for the door.

But then she starts to dream out loud
Incoherent songs of sweet mythical nonsense.
Each inhale becoming a drawn out "and"
A promise of things to come.

I remain paralyzed,
Caught in the clutches
Of some siren's spell
And left to consider:
Can she really remember
Enough songs in her sleep
To keep me here forever?

6:00 Dinner Time
by Kellee Carene Krause

6:28 p.m. yellow headlights roaring down the gravel road
Rushed by with the whistle in the trees and an explosion of rocks and dirt
I climb back up the drive struggling with the wind whipping
    the hood of my jacket down

Wind so cold it burned my eyelids as I blindly searched for your tire dust
Cold like the gush from the kitchen faucet that slices my fingers as I snap

    the green leaves for dinner

I sit in our room balancing the clock at the top of my bent knees
It ticks at my stubbornness at never asking where you've been
I close the window only when the cold reminds me of you

Clawing in the garden only feeds my temper, when the weeds come back alive
I frantically pick at the black dirt wedged under my fingernails while I

    hear a faint clock buried under my pillow

Finally I pitch the beast glowing 8:42 p.m. against the picture wall
scattering plastic parts all over your pile of dirty clothes while the salad I

    made warms, browning and rotting in your place at the table

Winters Power
by Paul Lefever

The morning broke crisply and brightly across the mountainous horizon. The brilliant multicolored-orange of the sunrise layered ocean-blue sky, silhouetted by deep green, forested mountains.

As the glowing sun rose, blinding snow glistened across the valley like diamonds shining, thoroughly polished, lying in a sea of golden sand.

The silence of the morning was broken by the thumping of heavy snow falling to the white-cushioned ground from swollen pine branches, as whistling arctic winds meandered and occasionally surged through thick forested limbs.

The frosted breath of an aging rancher spread across the terrain like a fire-breathing dragon spewing his power, the puffy redness in his face shown through a woolen scarf like grease paint on a circus clown. White-tailed deer running through the willow-covered ravine, treaded the powdery snow like an alpine skier conquering a freshly covered, waist-deep sea of fluffy whiteness.

As the radiant sun drifted toward the frozen western terrain, darkened shadows began taming the glistening of crystal snowdrifts, turning the valleys to a crusty-gray blanket of frosty, rolling hills. The yellowish, fiery sun, sunken on the horizon, gave way to a rust-colored sunset. Eventually a bright winter moon spotlighted the wondrous scene. Its lantern glow illuminated the huge Douglas fir and long-needled pine trees with cones hanging like weighted Christmas ornaments.

The bitter cold of winter controlled the still mountains and valleys like the Roman army hovering over shivering, frightened Christians.

Mother
by Anita Leinen - age 16

With hands that have worked like a man's, cracked and
dry, she carefully writes.

Trying to fulfill her dreams.
Clenches her fists and watches as her hands betray her.
Blood drips from her knuckles
I'm sorry.

Her hands are an old farmer's hands
but her face is elegant.
Her hair is silver
her face tan and weatherworn.

Her nose is crooked
from an auto accident,
We didn't have the money to get it set properly.

She has lived the life of all her ancestors,
a hard working women.

She is aging before her time
With a disease that can be fixed, but won't be.

She works every day
-in pain,
depressed
her face is beautiful
her mind is full
and her heart is tired.

She is my mother.

The Tree
by Mary Jane Leisey

In the barren field,
a child in a red wool
jacket waited,

kicking the snow,
watching it dance
around him.

When it began to sleet
he headed toward a
lone tree near the road

but it provided neither
shelter, nor warmth.
When he pressed

closer to shield himself,
the dead trunk snapped,
pinning him beneath it.

A few passersby
caught a glimpse
of the crimson form,

nearly hidden in
the drifting snow,
but they drove on.

A Kiss Goodbye
by Maureen Williams - age 17

He runs his fingers across her lips
Looks deep in her eyes and sees her pain
To him it's all a childs game
Love is but a word to use
The female body, an object to abuse
And a kiss goodbye is all it takes
To break the promises he makes
To her it seems life is through
To him it's time for someone new
Between her sobs, and his laughter
Only one moment when they part
He takes with him a lightened heart
And she is left with nothing more
Than the tears she cries and the kiss goodbye.

From The Observation Car Of An Amtrak Rolling Through Desert State With Music In My Ears
by Carl Lenox - age 20

Arid tableaux unfurls,
all mesas at sunset,
dusty railroad junctions,
dry arroyos creasing red soil
cheap plastic sets set in rows, orange,
passengers stare blankly, helplessly
at the landscape flowing past plexiglass
a blur of sagebrush moments.
This silent, fair girl, face delicately carved
she sits beside me cold like a beautiful stone,
draped in white, shapeless dress folds
and her eyes are a tragedy.
Smell a greasy snack-bar food drifts close
rails rumble, clacking
beat resonates in the injection mold chair
trains motion, mirroring music in my ears
sun drops over dream colored tableland
And we streak, melancholy happy, lighted
Earthbound comet in the descending purple night.

Dive
by Steven Meyers

Dark noisy paradise,
The smell of beer & cheap perfume,
Cigarette smoke clouds the air.
Making no apologies,
Men revel in their madness
& ill-humored women
Look to rekindle the past.

We drank the wine.
Sweet wine.
We longed for trouble.

The wet bottom of an empty glass.
The dead silence that comes
With a roomful of people.

Tomorrow will no doubt be a haze.

My Father's Eyes
by Joy Lindsay

My father's eyes were as deep as midnight
Coming down over Mount Kilomanjaro
In them I saw the still of night
A distant ground
Talking drums
Jungle sound
Bungo come
Making music till it's light
Simple were my father's eyes
Tempered weary and tried
An ancient voice
Majestic skies
Yeah! Africa's songs were in my father's eyes

A flaming fire there burned for truth
   and yearned for right
A judgement call
A freedom fight...a warrior lived there in those eyes...
Set in silver and cut like a knife
They stained great straights in Maroon flight
Showed me ships and auction blocks
And stilled the stench of burning flesh that marked our stock

Simple were my father's eyes
Pained and patient...tempered weary and tried
But a man of solid gold stared from those eyes.

Circle
by Sarah Savage

The marsh reeds quiver
to the empty song
of the howling wolf.

The silver wolf
cries to answer
the cold wind
that skates across
the white caps
of the ocean surface.

And the wind races against Time
to find the lonely pebble
that endlessly,
and timelessly
rocks at the bottom
of the rolling sea.

Old Buildings
by George W. Martin

I walk in the projects at twilight,
And stare at the tired,
   crumbling tenements;
Their broken windows
Stare back like sad, accusing eyes.
"Why have you done this to us?"
They say.

Empty now, they are yet filled
With the hopes and dreams,
The sad tears, the fears
Of those who shared these walls
A little while and then moved on,
Empty eyed, to other tenements
In other projects
In other slums to be.

I stare at the buildings at twilight
And have no answer
To their dumb entreaty.

Old buildings,
Like old dogs and people,
Need love and caring,
And quiet, gentle touchings.

Leaving
by Jamie McKee - age 16

In the pervasive, quiet stillness of my darkening room,
As the squat, alarm clock tick-tocks a rhythmic drum,
As the ceiling fan whirls, revolves, rotates in flowing, patterned circles,
My gaze embraces material memories haunting the walls that encompass
   me.
All the pencil-marked yellow post-it stamps,
Dictating rigid reminders that ruled my life again and again,
All the dog-eared novels sitting proudly on my cluttered, white shelves,
Asking to come alive and be read once again,
All the ragged, but cherished stuffed animals - grinning, mahogany teddy
   bears,
Suggesting we play hide-and-go-seek in the crowded closet again,
All the tattered, old notebooks stuffed, brimming with countless reports
dressed
   in scarlet ink,
Demanding their hard earned grades be acknowledged again,
All the winsome dried flowers tied in faded, colored ribbons,
Whispering of the day when they will be fresh again,
All these precious memories, never forgotten, revived to be pondered,
Then put away once again.

His Sleep
by Robin E. Timm

His feet hang off the bed and he
sleeps with his arms all tangled about his head
and pillow
and my pillow
and sometimes I wake to find his sleeping hand
hanging grotesquely in my face
with twitching language and violent dreams and
I laugh because he
snores too loud and
talks too much, saying
"the air is tight in the barn"
and other such nonsense
which I make note to tell him but
always forget.

So I settle down into him
and form to his form and
giggle myself back to sleep.

Gone Fishing
by Norah Meadows

Walking the sod;
    Casting a rod.
Titillating the catfish,
    Making a fly twitch.
Rubber hip-boots,
    Remembering one's roots.
Unloading the boat;
    Hope it will float!
Motor in the water;
    Pulling on the starter.
Going for a saunter,
    Listening to a songster.
Looking for leeks,
    Careful of tiny beaks.
Cold fall nights,
    Warm spring sights.
Essence of the air,
    Blossoming bud fair.
An old black skillet,
    Sizzlin' silver fillet.
Camp fire flickering
    Creek bed trickling.
Telling of fish lore;
    Hearing rain pour.
Rough wood cabin,
    Fun worth havin'.

Mr. and Mrs. Jones
by Karen Medders - age 14

He knows her as perfectly as a human can.
He knows the depths of her eyes almost as well
As he knows the wrinkles in the corners of her mouth.
She calls them dimples.

She knows him for all that he was and is.
She knows his large, calloused, gentle hands
And the flab on his arms.
He calls them muscles.

He loves the small snort when she laughs.
He loves her hair as she washes it out.
He doesn't understand why she bothers with makeup.
He thinks she's beautiful without it.

She loves the tiny shaving nicks on his chin.
She loved his tears when their child was born.
She enjoys watching him snore at night,
She says it's her turn to change the baby when it's actually his.

He cries when he thinks she needs him to.
She asks for his help when she thinks his ego needs a boost.
In short, she is his world.
In short, he is her life.

Paper Flowers
by Christina Melnyk - age 17

Today while searching in my drawer, I found
A paper flower. I had forgotten
That it was there, but seeing that flower,
A red rose once, now just a pink bud,
Crushed against the wooden back of the drawer,
Stained and faded after years in hiding...
I remember his words like yesterday...
"I would give you a thousand red roses
One for each time I think of you each day.
But roses wilt, and roses fade and die.
So I give you this paper blossom
To remind you that my love will not fade...
I will be as eternal as that rose."

That was many years ago; time has passed,
And he is just a distant memory.
Looking at this rose I wonder at fate...
We had a love that should never have died,
Like the myth, linden and oak intertwined
Time passed, and he went with it to his end.
I guess he was right; as long as this rose
Is in my hand he will be eternal,
Because I have my memories right here,
And memories can never, ever die...

The Quilt
by Dara M. Meranus - age 16

Her mind is a patchwork of memories,
Sewn together by the years of her life.
As a whole, they are a magnificent creation,
A beautiful quilt rich in experience.
They are her smiles, her tears, her laughter, her heartache.

But the years of use have worn the quilt thin.
The stitching is coming loose,
And the bright colors have faded into dullness.
Anxiously, she tries to piece the patches back together,
To recreate the memories she once cherished.

But as she sews one back on, two more fall off.
The tears and heartache come loose first;
The smiles and laughter soon follow.
All too soon she puts down her needle and thread in defeat.
And as a teardrop falls from her eye, the beautiful quilt
Falls from her lap to be lost forever...

Mary Anne
by Heather Mihok

I studied my tables over and over
And backwards and forwards, too.
But I couldn't remember six times nine
And I didn't know what to do.

'Til my sister told me to play with my doll
And not to bother my head.
"If you call her 'Fifty-four' for awhile,
You'll learn it by heart," she said.

So, I took my most favorite Mary Anne
Though I thought 'twas as dreadful shame,
To give such a perfectly lovely child
Such a perfectly horrid name.
So I called her my dear little fifty-four
A hundred times 'til I knew,
The answer to six times nine, as well,
As the answer to two times two.

Next day, Elizabeth Wiggleworth,
Who always acts so proud,
Said "Six times nine is fifty-two,"
And I nearly laughed aloud.
But I wish I hadn't when teacher said,
"Now Dorothy, tell if you can."
So I thought of my doll and sakes alive,
I answered, "Mary Anne!"

Silent Child
by Lori Watson - age 14

    Your absent name at roll call was more present then you ever were. I thought of you and felt afraid. I trembled as I now scribbled a light penmark through the bold blackness of your typed name, getting darker with every pass over the letters. I stopped and paused, looking over across the room staring at the right empty corner, knowing that somewhere hidden in that seat was a young child that I barely had gotten to know. I sat up and walked toward the old black chalk board that you once touched. I lifted a bright shiny piece of yellow chalk and began writing. My E's and F's traveled over the old slate causing a squeak or two, and I remember that once in my class room, seated in a far corner, was a speechless child.

The Recital
by Valerie Mulvey - age 13

Standing on stage
all eyes upon you
You are alone.
The hot spotlight
shines down upon you.
Beads of sweat trickle down your face,
yet you are not scared.
The hush of the crowd is frightening,
yet so coaxing.
You bring your violin to your chin to play.
The notes waltz across the minds
of the unpredictable audience
and the bounce from wall to wall
in the magnificent auditorium.
Your notes of sadness cast a spell
on all who listen.
You feel the message you're sending,
trying to make the audience relate.
Your song of beauty comes to a soft ending.
You have a burning desire to know
the thoughts of the audience.
But wait no longer.
The crowd is in utter shock.
Each second of universe shattering applause
reassures you, in a delicate whisper,
"You will be remembered..."

Gems and Cotton Candy
by Lisa Marie Pellegrini

She sits upright,
straight, very straight,
like a soldier standing at attention.
Her apple-green orbs shine like semi-precious gems
as she squints up dreamily,
almost seductively,
asking for her dinner.
The shiny whiskers that grace her moon face
are long and thin like the threads of a spider's web.
And so she sits,
nestled in the warmth of her cotton candy fur.
Her chest fur spreads out like a fan,
as she sits and waits.
The little white spot in the center flashes,
like a diamond around a woman's neck.
And then,
as the smell of tuna wafts through the air,
her paws pitter-patter happily across the floor,
and she raises her bushy tail high,
as if to say, "Thank you!"

The River Kwai '96
by Elma Diel Photikarmbumrung

My lucky motorboat glides swiftly on a river
where souls have fallen from mother wars of long ago.
How rich the waters have become from crimson droplets
of bodies garbed in olive fatigues and leafy helmets,
how memories have floated and sparkled on wavelets
dancing in the sun. Yes,-memories tell of triumph and
defeat, with casualty as their common name. In either
case, courage did not falter or faint or get blown by
gusty winds of our time. It melted right here into water
molecules, transformed into prisms of freshness and beauty,
cleansed, diluted, but nevertheless, still fragrant.
The arching bridge close by resembles a discolored rainbow
as if some muddy rain had soaked and bathed its pools
and steel rims with debris, leaving discoloration marks
as permanent as scars on faces drawn by bayonets.

War came because leaders elsewhere failed to draw the peace.

Yonder at stone's throw on a shore, a mother elephant glides
with tusk curved gracefully, rolling logs wearily in the hot
sun and humid afternoon. Destined to take a break, she
plunges in the river to savor coolness and comfort. Then gently
rising, she emerges refreshed, - body and spirit altogether,
renewed.

Summertime
by Stephanie Porcaro - age 14

I remember fishing
Our topless bodies caked with Coppertone
Immersed hands resting under minnows.
Impatient quivering on my part,
Daddy's stillness-Don't move-
Ah Ha! A squirming black prize.

I remember the steep hill we drove to.
Warm night air alive with
Cicadas droning.
An electric mass below made
Stars stop shinning.

I remember my first music lessons
Taught on dads synthesizer.
His hairy hands plunked out chords
And he couldn't read a note.

Yearly visits a few days long, now.
It's amazing how things change.
Money in the mail,
Phone calls every few weeks, or
Whenever his schedule allows.

Not enough memories,
Not enough Daddy.

Books
by Kristy Shaw - age 13

A book is like a candy bar
waiting to be devoured,
like an unknown world,
waiting to be explored.
A book is like a closet,
go, choose your clothes.
Imagine a book, a roller coaster,
swirling up and down with events,
once you're on, you can't get off
until the ride is over.
Dive into the sea of books,
swim to your heart's content.
Devour the words like a hungry lion.
Explore new worlds, now horizons,
search beneath the words,
dig for the buried treasure
of meaning,
inside the leather-bound cover.

Pan
by Rochelle Theo Pienn

Sitting on this metal chair,
where it is still,
it is quiet, except
for the mile breeze, not quite humid,
and the Greek women arguing like
hagglers over sausages
and the old men smoking cigarettes
and winking with wandering eyes,
I remember you,
hooves kicking backward in the dust,
broad face scowling with indignation,
brainwaves devising revolutions.
And you had a jolliness, too--
rumbling like a steam engine picking up
speed, your mustache hiding
your plebeian smile.
You will be happier
when you come to your end,
all wealth desiccated to cigarettes
peeking from between your graying lips,
your eyes winking and wandering,
your ship drifting in the mist.

Prisonme
by Williams Robbins

Upon the cell's dreck laden floor
Sunlight's brush composes captivity's logo -
A white square ribbed by the shadows of bars.
Cockroaches stop to warm themselves in the sun
Before crawling off in search of food.
In the corner a prisoner dressed in sweat stained rags
Rises from a flea infested mattress
And staggers toward the door,
His dirt-caked bare feet
Crunching insects with each step.
Malfeasance's millstone too much to bear - he rattles the door.
But the jailer fails to appear.
Screaming, he utters a string of profane epithets,
But still the jailer fails to appear.
Defeated, he shuffles to a grimy basin,
Washing his face in it's rusty torpid liquid.
On the wall hangs the wedge of a mirror's remnant.
He stares and sobs at his bluntness,
Knowing that it is the only place,
The jailer will appear.

Los Angeles, 1992
by Loretta Ramseyer

Trumpets herald merger news.
Loyal ears listen with pride.
Makes them feel bigger inside.

Blindness of loyalty and reflexive emotions
Sense of elation and this is the key: A bigger corporation is a bigger me.
Lives long ago molded to corporate form
Illusions of security based on seniority
Betrayals delivered by those suited to kill.

Rank and choose. Break the news.
Tally the numbers. Act with fitness.
Mass executions minimize mess
Economies of scale; no time for bail.
The tap on the shoulder a prelude to death.

Reenigineer, restructure. Merge, redeploy.
Eliminate jobs and force out to the street.
Layoff lingo; gigolo jingle.
Somber tune for moving soon
Corporate shearing and human pruning.
Merger transition is not a cheap thrill
We all foot the bill.

Our House Is Crawling With Boys
by Chevin Ray - age 12

If you'd wish to visit me, I think I'd warn you first,
Just be prepared,
Don't be too scared,
Just expect the worst!
Our house is crawling with boys.

Be careful where you put your feet,
Because you never know,
You might just find a GI Joe,
Stuck between our toe!
Our house is crawling with boys.

If you decide to stay a while,
Be careful where you sit.
The chair you choose could be bad news,
With a big old glob of spit!
Our house is crawling with boys.

If you think that there is worse,
By George you are wrong!
Be prepared for a night so long,
That you'll be ready to burst!
Our house is crawling with boys.

Here and there and everywhere,
There's smelly socks and underwear,
And snakes and bugs and things that bite,
I think I've lost my appetite!
Our house is crawling with boys.

Sometimes I think that I'll just burst,
I feel I've been unfairly cursed,
Because it's just my mom and me,
Against this whole menagerie!
Our house is crawling with boys.

Song Of Myself
by Sally Reynolds - age 17

I stare through my reflection on the bottle at my side;
My own nakedness leaves me frightened.
I am the missing liquid that flows from your lips.
I alone fill the glass with broken words that hit the bottom hard.

I lay my head on the tingling blades of grass;
My neck laughs at their touch.
I am the reproductive underside of all the fences.
Spinning spores fall around me and I hold none captive.

I fold my hands to protect my protruding light source;
My fingers writhe like snakes moving through eachothers tongues.
I am the hidden spite that only the blind can see.
I can taste your endless capabilities that always fall just short of me.

I tear down the barricades that keep my emotions contained;
My insides twist and turn as the possession of each organ differs.
I am the fortress that sits underneath the battle.
I reach far from the center of the ring of fire;
My skin becomes a canvas for the ashes' painted dance.
I am the creator, smoldering still.
I hear your voice and drink up every word.

One Summer
by Susan Sanders

She found a haven
in those hills.
Your cabin in the woods
stood Deep
like a river passage
of the lines
in a logger's hand.

This lost girl
trembled in your arms
that rubbed
the strength back, believing
not only in the heart
but every bone.

After one summer's heat
her fingers ceased
to drum against the window sill,
finding their place by
tracing the edges of yours.

She was a candle
easy to light
with the right flick
of the tongue,
starting small fires

At the top
of the stairs.

from a student in AP English 12
by Cynthia Shih - age 17

You call yourself a poet, and yet
who the hell Cares whether you meant
A ball of clay that was really gold
Or the stars gazing from an infinite breath
Of ebony?

If the words meandered off your pen
And leaped past the pulsing irises of those who must read,
Then galoomphed about in their brains, mute, obstinate
While the one who wields the Red Pen says
       "two page essay on their dance."-

-perhaps better if they never galoomphed at all.

Mind you, I hold no grudge
Against images. I do not pin my lips against a smile
When one thanks You God for this most amazing
day:
And yet why dangle a chocolate éclair from a thread
To play Hades to our Tantalus?
You give us the gift in half-conjure only: you sneer from your pedestal
"Ah, you are not worthy, feeble mind, take English 30B!"

Words take flight with feathers so gleaming
That none (or few at most) will ever let them
Come to roost, comprehended.
Why let words fly on empty breezes, forlorn and admired,
Never stroked by a gentle and knowing hand?

The purpose was to communicate, was it not?

Speak To Me
by Dorothy Shriver

Speak to me - of little things
with downy fur and gossamer wings;
Of pearly shells that span the beach,
and grains of sand that sift my reach;
Dewdrops and rain, and flakes of snow
that fall upon the buds that grow
on sleeping wood, in violet spawn,
to greet with grace - the birth of dawn!

Speak to me - of quiet things;
The gentle brush of angel wings;
A fleet of stars in silent flight,
that sail across the Sea of Night.
And, towering, pinaceous trees
that reach to touch God's hand with ease,
and fold their emerald finger tips -
to whisper prayers from frosted lips.

Speak to me - of pretty things,
like buttercups and daisy rings;
Blue shadows in the foliage lace;
The rainbow, as it fuses space;
And floating clouds that kiss the cheeks
of coral crested lonely peaks,
capturing their tears that fall -
to weave them in a winter shawl!

Rebirth
by Jameson Tucker

She shook the cold from her breasts
breathed heavy and light
as it slid down her center
and out into the night.
She turned her shimmering nakedness
to the wind,
and sailed unswervingly
into the bulbous red glow
of the setting sun,
the dark and decay
falling effortlessly behind her
sliding from her form
like soiled linens
drifting far and away
on the rolling breeze.
What had been old felt new
the impending rot of death
a memory
her passion
newborn and fresh
her fluids pulsing with life
her fire
the lingering cold ember
of life past
blazing anew
renewed
released
into the sun.

Tchaikovsky
by A. Arwen Taylor - age 14

The oboe sings, a sorrowed note unwinds,
Rises in thick reverie and falls;
A trumpet sounds; a cello sings a sigh;
The flute, across the quiet, dances, calls.

The melody, so shatteringly sweet
Through silence whispers, eloquent as night
Of hate and anger, passion bittersweet;
Returns, then runs and leaps in frenzied flight.

Explosions burst through passion's saddest sea
Wild anger, dark emotions fly unleashed.
Among despairing floods of misery
Do battle in the remnants of their peace.

Majestic chords fly thick across the sky,
And dance and roll with grace as river long.
In desperate chant across the world they fly.
And ebb then having sung their only song.

As sadness once again recovers grief,
A pain in mem'ry far too great to tell,
And wandering through the shadows like a thief
The night will come and Death will toll his bell.

All fades and wanders back to silent state,
Expression such as this may n'er return.
To understand such yearning is to sate
The lonely pleading of Tchaikovsky's tune.

Alzheimer's
by Wanda Wilhelm-Norton

Slowly,
    inexorably,
        I am losing the pieces of my life.
I shed them, little by little,
    watching as they fall to the ground,
        lying silent and colorless about my feet,
        the petals of a beautiful rose
            slowly dying.
They cannot be replaced, these petals.
No miracle of man
    can restore their beauty.
And I, the vine, live painfully on
    not fully knowing what I've lost
        but feeling it all the same.
It seems forever since my youth-
    moments that were packed
        carefully away to be cherished,
        are now crushed,
            tiny fragments no longer
                recognizable.
I pass my friends,
    my eyes wide open, I do not know them.
But they, behind my bent back
    and silvered head,
        whisper platitudes of sorrow.
I know this and understand;
    in solitude I wait
        and pray for salvation
            against the coming night.

Boredom
by Devon Sprague - age 17

boredom sunk into my bones
like the thirsty ground
sucking in the rain
it made sloshy sounds
wetness
falling over my eyes
so that I see no options

I know that I was
alone on this day
strange how the colors
all blend, and fade
under the drumming
of a downpour

at least I am dry
and sour
soaking up the
just splendid view
from the window

At least the rain should
stop by tomorrow
and the colors and life
will all jump out at me
from their hidden corners
and boredom
will slither quietly into
the soggy ground.

Puzzling
by Gail Woods

The table stood in the middle of the room
oddly shaped pieces of cardboard scattered
    about
with multicolored faces and bits of wisdom
waiting to be put in some logical order.

They pick up the pieces and examine them
arranging small piles by cut and color
straight edges are sorted and connected
bringing continuity to the project.

The child chatters about school and other
    things
as she helps to reshape the pieces on the
    board
and grandmother listens intently to every
    word
offering encouragement and understanding.

In time the child will go and grandmother
    will return to her chores
but soon their heads will be together again
    searching and chattering
shaping the picture on the table and
    the young girls character

The Milk House Path
by Eddy Wilson

Gone
Long gone
Is the path
Worn through
The goose grass
Beside the red hand pump
Round the broad willow tree
From the barn to the milk house.

Once, when early dandelions bloomed
Scouting for spring's first honeybees
Uninterrupted
I traced back-and-forth
The path where I often heard,
"Comin' through. Don't stand in my way."

The dairy herd's gone to the tax man,
The willow's gone to a storm,
The son's gone off to school,
And the father's gone to his grave.

But still,
I could walk
The milk house path.
For a son's feet,
Know their father's way.

Whispers

Days In The Furrow
by Elmer Yee

wrinkled and faded
our hands now knotted and gnarled
we bowed in frail age
unable to support our own weight
the seasons have come and gone
and with them, all our children
leaving us alone
to stand silently over empty plots
to think that life once arose from the earth
but now the earth has reasserted its dominance
reestablishing the need to struggle
a wandering breath
caught the last wisps of our hair
reminding us how good it felt to be young
to have the sun bathe us in life
all we have now are a few wooden beads
relics of an intangible past
each day we force ourselves to take that slow walk
no longer expecting to hear children's voices
just peace of mind
that we won't have to walk anymore
or enter lonely rooms
free to reminisce about days gone by
still coursing through our veins
just two naked trees
under the obsidian moon

Epitaph for Grandfather
by Wesley Wordsmith

Red-leathered bones squat
On grey dust. Iron-black eyes
Turn slowly,
Squint from behind a native mask

Into the sunken sun
To watch a marsh hawk curve
Silently across
An indifferent sky.

    The hawk, carving an ever-narrowing
    Ovoid, follows the harvester until
    A harrowed creature bolts, choosing
    Open, fallow field for its swift death.

Ancient, windswept rumors
Ponder the old Indian,
Now motionless, seeing nothing
But the maelstrom.

    Salt peppers dust
    At the bare feet
    Of a young boy
    In the quiet

Still.

My Heritage
by Christine Young - age 12

As the sun set,
we all sat
like a circle of ridged,
wooden totem poles,
around the blazing ball
of fire.
We watched in silence,
as shadowy figures danced around us,
screeching,
chanting
sacred eagle cries,
the wind joining along,
whipping the flames of the fire,
with warm breath.
I am Cherokee,
born on mother earth,
and shined on every day,
by father sun.

Whispers

Chapter Two

Honorable Mentions

Honorable Mention Awards for Competitors in the Spring 1996 Iliad Literary Awards Program.

The Clown
by Diana R. Agbayani

the moon
casts
its shadow
a faint
glimmer
upon the empty
chairs...

take off
your masks
O, clown
bid laughter goodbye
gaiety is over now

and there's
only
this
vast
empty
room...

This Place
by Soili Alholinna

There is this place within my mind,
Where I can go to visit.
It is a place of happiness,
A refuge from my suffering.
But I dare not stay, too long to play,
For fear of not returning.

I can stop to rest awhile,
In this place, to where I travel.
Unload my suitcase full of woes
And sip a cup of peace.
But I dare not linger on, too long,
For fear of not returning.

Reflection Of The Fifties
by Robert Allen

It was Third Avenue
        complete with my ancient tenement,
The El, the corner bar,
        streets ripe with pent-up resentment;
It was Central Park
        complete with trees and breathable air,
Caged jungle cats,
        and a carousel ride (with the fare);
It was a routine school,
        low-paid teachers, a seat in the last row,
The Korean War,
                Captain Video and Marilyn Monroe.

Pictographs
by Vivian Allison

Where nature sparsely decorates the landscape,
And the scant greenery is adorned with needle-sharp spines,
I raced the storm though thorns turned torment,
Toward a cave in the canyon wall.

In the silence of late morning the sun developed
A hard steely gleam and shown deep inside,
Revealing black, rust, and red-orange figures,
Painted on top of each other, thy rise and collide.

Soaring humans aloft in rapture,
Crablike creatures scuttle through the ether,
A deer succumbs to a hunter's spear,
All hinting of a powerful, mystic religion.

Centering the strange mural a shaman levitates,
Arms extended waving weapons, face blank and featureless,
Hair standing on end.
And a strange prickly thing ornaments his wrist.

Drunk on the hallucigen, peyote,
He wrestled, confronted, and communed with gods.
Songs, dances and ritual robes have vanished,
Alien shapes, bizarre lines now crumbling to dust.

Life Flame
by B.J. Anderson

The pain seems overwhelming,
  like a swimmer far to tired to stroke,
    as a last ditch effort I float
      and pray somebody saves me.

Or sometimes it takes a different twist
  against myself turned,
    and I am filled with self disgust,
      such loathing, my belly burns.

So set the dial for self destruct,
  but slyly so no one guesses.
    I am just to tired to fight,
      need no proof that I am worthless.

Then comes the one I sometimes hate,
  'cause his eyes see what I am hiding.
    tosses a life line, wrapped in a dare
      Guaranteed to set my temper flaring.

For in me it is anger, properly stoked
      That keeps the life flame burning.

I Spy
by Evelyn Garrett-Bledsoe

Like a vulture circling
I eye the terrain.
Is this one stirring?
Does that one remain?

AHA! At last the prey is spied.
My chance to possess, to claim.
Out of the way, you tried!
But this parking spot has my name.

But I Always Send Her Flowers On Tuesday
by Donald Ankofski

I don't give her the time of day
& whenever she approaches me
I find an excuse to walk away
If she catches my eye I look down
& when she invites me to her parties
I always tell her I'll be out of town
but i always send her flowers on tuesday.

When she's feeling down I act like I don't know
yet everytime that happens
I just want to hold her & make her sadness go
I try to talk but I'm much too shy
& whenever she smiles at me
my smile comes out wry
but i always send her flowers on tuesday

She waves but I pretend not to see
she asks if I send the flowers
I shake my head & say "No, not me"
Her every "Good Morning" is followed by "What's New?"
& everyday I say; "Nothing"
But then whisper "Except that I still love you"
& i always send her flowers on tuesday.

Mercy
by James A. Anthony

Do you need any
Joyful surprises in life's
Grab bag of living

I saw a beggar
Who was in need of kindness
My pockets had none

My reflection cried
For the man wanting mercy
When I saw myself

More hours pass
And yet I have not enriched you
A cross I cannot bear

Did you hear them talk
Unsubstantiated vile
Insipid rumor

My valuables
Are free gifts from my beloved
I possess nothing

Crammed Brain
by Lisa Baker

There is pain on the other side of this brain.
As I seek relief from a Tylenol, I feel the blood drain.
It all adds up.
Pressure is overflowing its cup.

You wake me at 5a.m. each morning.
Already I'm looking forward to evening.
Throughout the day you feed me a light meal.
I get dizzy, I tell you! How do you expect me to feel?

You work me overtime.
I'm trying to solve everyone's situation.
I must listen to everyone whine.
I'm seeking help with your cooperation.

So, there it is!
I am crammed!
Either you go on with her way or his.
My reception signals are now jammed!

Comfort in the Night
by Susan Baldwin

It is quiet now.
My children sleep the innocent sleep of the young.
Now a great trouble treads fearfully in.
"Hush now, I'll see you in the morning,
there's the light.
Soon you will wake to a light
more frightening than a dark night could ever be imagined.
Day will surely break over you. Don't look eastward.
It will come, someone will be there.
Go to sleep now son, I love you."

The Window
by Vijaya Aruldass

A glasspane he is,
framed by fine wood
with him I see within myself...
A reflection of my being
a mirror of my inner core of thinking.

A glasspane he is,
a fiery molten liquid
cooled by hardness that can be broken
like the carefully adorned masks
I wear, that can be torn down
to reveal inner fragility.

A glasspane he is,
I stand before him,
my soul bared and naked
light streams in, enlightenment...
beyond, I fear to step
To see the loveliness, enjoy the pain
To watch the ugliness, to wallow in pleasure
but whispering in vain.

A glasspane he is,
a final realization of his role
a filter of feelings, of hurt and joy...
a push, a step, flattering at the brink
a warm misty print upon the polished glass
fades with the cold wind.
The opened panes are far behind...
a resolution of wood and glass.

Oneness
by Hong Dang Bui

Outside into the night, I stepped.
No, it was not dark,
The moon shone its caressing rays
Into the dancing clouds,
And onto the trees, some tall, some stout.
The breeze softly brought about a harmony of perfumes
From above to below.
Snails trod their way, silent and slow,
Crickets from nowhere sent their swift music show:
I realized I did not walk anymore
I did not know since when
Blended to all,
Part of all,
One with the immense peace.

Do You Know Who I Am?
by Rita Ashton

I swish about purple mountain peaks
I swish across lush green valleys and riffle the creeks
I dance at the rise of the sun in the East
I curl lazily down with the sun in the West
I am often times the world's unwelcome test
I am in the tree tops peeking at Harvest Moon
I am asleep during the sundial's slow turn at noon
I am the culprit who carries winter's bitter vest
I am a part of summer's sultry dress
I carry red and gold leaves to the ground in Fall
I am a child's hope as he tugs at a kite string in early Spring
Life is a story book, few people take the time to really look
At the wind
I am so glad you carried the notes of life for me as I sang my life's song
While others looked on
The who in this story is my friend
He is the whispering wind

An Anomous Request
by Dianne Atkinson

I want you to
plant yourself
Sturdy in the spring,
growing with each
rainfall or ray
of sun. Never lose
yourself in the fog.
Don't forget the lilacs.

I want you to
nature yourself
and spread your
roots deep, in the summer
heat. never
wither in the storm.
Cool yourself in the
evening.
Don't forget the roses.

I want you to
reflect your
beautiful colors in
a nearby lake
in autumn.
Smell the crisp
brown leaves, hear
them rustle.
Don't forget the wild flowers.

If you follow these
instructions you will rest
warmly in the cold,
remembering your seasons.

The Coloring Book
by Michele Burden

Color in the emotions of life with your crayolas of fate.
Bless this child's almighty hand that so christens this blank page.
Life is not what you dream it to be, but simply what you make.
Each of us, like a crisp, white sheet, will choose the colors of our name.

God's Promise
by Doris Hartsell Brewer

Rolling hills of thunder.
Nature's fiery show
raging winds of fury
across the hills did blow.
The clouds were dark and soaring.
The sunshine hid its face.
Lightning struck so boldly,
at a shrieking pace.
I thought God was angry,
with such a wild display.
My heart was filled with turmoil
and fearful dismay.
I bowed my head in reverence
and ask the reason why.
    Then
with awe and wonder, I saw a rainbow
stretched across the sky.

True Believers
by Thomas Atterberry

The rain fell upon Parker Wells,
for years now barren and lost.
Most had spread their wings to fly;
others had paid the cost.

A few remained with meager means;
every day they gathered to pout.
Old tales were told of days of gold
and years before the drought.

William Creek just a dusty bed;
now ran with water for sure.
Greek flats with a new lease on life;
somehow now would endure.
Almost ten years they had withered,
but those with a belief had stayed;
now with the rain still falling;
all their patience had been repaid.

Sacchaw
by Carlo Auguste

   Yesterday I dreamed, once again, of a nine year old girl named Saccaw whom I met last Christmas Eve. She was, on that cold day, sitting on the lat step of a building stairs at Beverly Road. She was there for hours, with a weary face showing the pathetic countenance of one exiled in her own country, the sorrowful image of one lost in her own house. She was there thinking about nothing but her misery, waiting for nobody in those dirty clothes she surely had not changed for days.
   "I want my parents back, that's all" was what she said in answer to my question about her expectation from that Christmas. And, it was as inconsolable a child as I have never seen, crying as I have never thought a human being capable of who showed me a wrinkled sheet of paper on which were written these words;

"Dear Santa Claus my daddy abandons me, and my mommy smokes crack. I need them to pamper me and kiss me good night as they used to. Please Santa, bring me back my parents."

   It was the prayer, she told me, that she had been saying day and night for five long years, with the faithful belief that Santa, Jesus and God would put their magical power together to make her dream come true.

It's Not My Fault
by Mary Tempest Bachtell

I have a good excuse this time.
It's really not my fault.
Listen, Please Miss Higgins,
I don't think you understand.
My homework was finished
But Wooly Joe was there.
      Who is Wooly Joe , you say?
Oh, he's my sheep dog
Who always loves to tease.
He leaped and lumped around the room
And bumped into my desk.
There was a bang, a clatter.
My notebook fell and whoosh,
Stamping on my notebook
With his broad and awkward feet,
He grabbed it in his drooling mouth
To rip and tear and munch and chomp.
      Oh, you say you have an answer
      For this sad catastrophe.
I'm a member of the team.
They need me for a pitcher.
There's no one else but me!
      You say you'll guard my homework
      As carefully as can be!
Oh, yes Miss Higgins.
I clearly understand.
You have a special "NO-Fault" class
For creative people like me!

Dear God
by B.A. "Babs" Barrick

I saw a bumper sticker today
"Kids need to pray" it said
It's the truth
We're a messed up bunch
But most of us don't know it
I'd just like to say
I tried
I used to pray
Things were okay I guess
It's easy to pray that way
You know what I mean?
When things get not okay
That's when you're tested
So I keep on praying
In the worst way
I prayed
Nothing happened
What did I expect?
What's going on?
What'd I do?
I'm not really that bad
No crimes against humanity
Nothing too bad
I can think of worse-
Maybe that's it

A Oneness With All
by Gregory M. Bedard

I like to sit on a high ridge
Of a canyon in the hills.
Away from life's dilemmas,
Unmindful of the bills.
I like to hear the wind's song
As played upon the trees.
And the merry babbling of the brook
As it tumbles toward the seas.
I like to watch the eagle
Soaring through the skies,
While a host of other creatures
Bring wonder to my eyes.
I like the way the earth smells
After a summer rain.
And the smells of trees and flowers
In a clean alpine domain.
I like to feel the solitude
And a oneness with it all.
A reminder - in spite of my import -
That I'm really very small.

Complacency
by Lacinda Beggs

      Sometimes
      When I look
      And stare
      At the walls
      In my room
      Which are bare
      Time seems to go by
      So slowly
      That I haven't
      A clue
      What I will do
      In the future
      And
      Would I care
      If I knew.

Fancy
by Sandra Boyette

On some fine mornings, I sit alone, firmly enabled with my coffee cup
The sands of sleep layered heavily within half-shuttered eyes
From my kitchen window, I see the clear blue dominion of the sky
And watch dawns' colors glow and change as the sun comes up
Feeling my souls' communion with the birds' early cries
A new day is born, while the old one dies

In the early hours, ones' imagination swoops and dives
With thoughts unfettered, I think and dream of things possible, but are yet to be
Unbounded time loses meaning in pleasant reverie
Weaving dreams molds the substance of future plans for better lives
Todays' plans are vague, forgotten; awash, and lost at sea
Superseded by backward looks called old memories

Free Fall
by Alfred Berger

I fell one hundred miles, free falling,
sitting in my chair, feet on the ground.
After that, a ton of bricks, on top of that.
There were no broken bones, no crushed body,
much worse, a broken heart.
My head exploded, the tears rolled
down my face, drip, drip,
I was speechless.
My heart raced uncontrollably,
needles pierced it from all angles.
shock struck me, breathing stopped,
the end had come.
The end of twenty-eight years, gone
in ten seconds, all gone.

The words were sudden and quick,
although I knew they would come,
I knew not when, but I knew.
A matter of time, it had been brewing,
first sizzling, then bubbling, then boiling,
and finally exploding into loud words at me.
The inevitable had arrived, the ultimatum was decreed,
that was it, no "if's, and's or but's!"
"You're our of here by December,
it's over, I want you out." were
her loud orders.
The shock has passed, time to think,
what to do, where to start.
The tension is now gone, feeling better
about myself, a new beginning.
Free again!

Untitled
by P.S. Brady

I feel your breath
    against my face
I hear your voice
    whisper in my ear
I see you beloved
    though you're not here.

But the wind is kind
    and touches my face
And the nightsong
    plays to my ear
Then the sweetest of dreams does come to me
    and once again you're near.

Perfect Package
by Martha Crabtree

So tiny
So new
And yet embracing all that is to come
In one perfect package.
The schoolgirl lives within you,
And the bride--
The loves, the hates, the dances and the songs
Have their beginnings here.
You hold the future in your baby hands,
The mystery of who you will become.

Think About It!!!
by Kari Bergeron

When a child is called upon to fulfill the role of a man,
And he ultimately looses his innocence in the ravages of war,
Isn't he still a child?
THINK ABOUT IT!!!

When a child becomes a man and he makes the ultimate sacrifice,
In an evil, immoral and unnecessary war,
Isn't he still a child?
THINK ABOUT IT!!!

has the status of his parents changed?
Is he still not their child?
Is he still not their son, although now deceased?
Their memories will long remain!

Therefore, isn't he still a child;
One who has been forced to mature in an accelerated
And unnatural manner?
THINK ABOUT IT?

Only to be a "Man", momentarily, and then to die as a child;
And then to die as a mere babe in the arms of violence.
Please...
Please! THINK ABOUT IT!

Love Me Tonight
by Jacqueline N. Cotman

    A princess set sail from akrotiri bay for ashdod
      I watched the sun set on cyprus-
      purple, orange, yellow, green cloud waves
        above two ranges of mountains

    Aphrodite's alluring call to midnight moon watches
      steep endowed cliffs splashed with a sea so blue
    Commandaria grapes on every fertile hill and plain
        drink a cup of friendship in love

      A beguiling sight of a star so close
      not over bethlehem this night but splendid
    so brilliant over a place between the cliffs
        in paphos... love me tonight

Circles of Light
by Lenore Cooper Clark

We speak of God as light, and yet we know
That darkness, too, is part of nature's plan.
The blazing sun that quickens plants to grow
Would scorch, if not for nighttime's darkened span.

The darkest winter ends; spring lights each bower.
The seed that sleeps within the tomb of earth
Cannot resist the sunlight's drawing power,
But struggles upward to another birth.

The infant, sleeping in the darkened womb,
Reacts to light's first touch with cries of fear.
When one we love is placed in earth's dark tomb,
We cry for loss of what we held most dear.

    But in our darkness, hope anew is born:
    We wait for light of resurrection's morn.

The King Of Nothing
by Ben Bessman

Some people have everything.
All I have are dreams.
For I am the King of Nothing,
 and Nothing is what it seems.

My throne, my only treasure.
Even my shadow, lost to me.
Willing to pain, for pleasure,
 knowing Nothing, is forever free.

Some people believe anything.
But I can not be deceived.
For I am the King of Nothing,
 and Nothing is what I believe

No one desires, my simple throne.
I am truly, without an heir.
Feeling trapped, cold and alone,
 knowing Nothing, keeps me from despair.

Some people say anything.
but I speak from the heart.
For I am the King of Nothing,
 and Nothing can tear you apart.

The final stone, hath been cast.
I am flooded, by stark, bleak sorrow.
Being forever, without a past,
 knowing Nothing, may grant me a tomorrow.

Some people have everything.
All I want is to be.
For I am the King of Nothing,
 and Nothing matters to me.

Caged With Clipped Wings
by Jennifer Ayn Buttler

Looking through the bars surrounding me,
Observing all those who pass by.
A glance my way-
All they see is the cage,
the bars.
Those who stop to admire
only see my feathers,
oh and my wings.
They can't see the spirit inside,
the energy being wasted.
Longing to fly,
the air I will never get to feel.
Craving freedom until I can
taste it in my water.
With my eyes closed, of course.
Wanting so much more than these 52 bars-
I have counted them,
but they do not know I can count-
I've certainly had the time to learn.
Do they ever wonder if I'm happy
in this cage?
Hasn't anyone ever wanted to open the door and
see what I'd do?
Even if they left it open,
Would fear stop me from trying to soar?
Would someone catch me if I were to fall?

The Garden of Stone
by Margaret Harucki-Brennan

**In memory of Frank J. Harucki 1922-1993
and his son, Francis W. Harucki 1945-1995**

As the families gather all around,
Together, and yet, alone.
Tears fill the eyes of all who visit
Here, in the Garden of Stone.

We're remembering the days gone by
And the happiness we had known.
Now, we walk with sadness in our hearts
Through the Garden of Stone.

The Flags are waving proudly;
But, at half-mast they are flown.
They wave for our quiet heroes
Within the Garden of stone.

They lived with the torment and nightmares
Of a non-ending violent storm.
They finally found peace within the walls
Of their personal Garden of Stone.

The years have left us fond memories,
But the emotions that are shown
Are mixed with our pride and, yet, bitterness
Due to the Garden of Stone.

The pain will remain within me.
No matter how much I have grown,
As I kneel beside my loved one, who
Lies in the Garden of Stone.

But a voice inside brings me comfort,
Saying that from the Garden of Stone,
God is leading our fallen heroes as
The soldiers make their final march Home.

**Dedicated to all the men and women who served in the
Armed Forces of The United States of America**

Life
by Katherine L. Bond

To a life where we all have to shift
and juggle.
To make something of one's self, is a
constant pull and uphill struggle.
To fulfill what one has always dreamed,
to search for meaning, as human beings.
to be educated and gain more knowledge,
we must apply ourselves, and go to
college.
To acquire and amass much, we must have
persistence, we must have guts.
To achieve marital bliss an monogamy
we must love, and keep harmony.
To procreate -- see ourselves mirrored
in our small.
Hopefully God will grant our seed to
sprout, thus growing tall.
To sit back in our easy chair, while
grandchildren we are allowed to share.
To feel blessed when all is through
that we had God who saw us thru.
To know before that final sleep, that
the Lord will watch -- our souls to
keep.

Spring 1996 Honorable Mentions

Time
by Lisa Marie Boone

Spinning,
Turning,
Burning,
Yearning,
Hours tick by.

Screaming,
Yelling,
Shouting,
Pouting,
Minutes tick by.

Laughing,
Crying,
Sighing,
Lying,
Seconds tick by.

Caring,
Feeling,
Touching,
Loving,
Time stands still.

Time
by Joseph Cartier

As a warm summer's breeze
turns quickly to an autumn sneeze,
and winter's snow blankets another year to sleep.

We remember and sigh
on just how fast time goes by,
for memories of spring seem like last week.

And to our children so young
who's time has just begun,
and thinks the year's past was unending.

We try to explain
but we know it's in vain,
For their memories of seasons are still pending.

hand-prints
by Alison Conley

I remember the tousle haired boy
    dropping by with flowers picked along the way,
      eager to share his wondrous world.
He blew through my days like a gust of wind,
    bringing the sweet sounds of laughter,
      handfuls of daisies and a tadpole or two.
When he completed kindergarten he rang the bell,
    diploma in hand to show me,
      and I poured Pepsi into wine glasses
    to toast the graduate.
The screen-door closed with a bang behind him,
    leaving silence in its wake,
      and I saw the hand-print on the wall
    where he stopped to fumble with his shoe.
Today when first I heard the news,
    I remembered that wall
      and all the hand-prints he left,
    dropping by.

Chiu-Wai Leung
by Cindy J. Brazil

My feet sink into the soft sand.
The icy waters of the Atlantic trickle into my unlaced shoes.
My toes feel its numbing effects.
I'm oblivious as I dream about a specific man.

I only know you from afar.
You are fading from my memory.
How can I capture your attention?
I can not sing, play the piano or guitar.

What I can do is write.
For it is you I write about, to capture on paper.
You've helped me to rediscover a talent almost lost.
I think of you and my emerald eyes shine bright.

My life has changed because of you.
Some have been good, bad, other changes yet to come.
What sacrifices have been made...
My determination is all I have to one day meet you.

Will you read of my cries in London or Hong Kong?
Casually over another movie script?
I pray to my angels that fate will bring us together.
May it not take long.

I stagger back to the fifty foot tall rickety stairs.
I hope someday you come across my work.
Maybe then you will be crying for me.
Maybe we could make a pretty pair?

All I had were dreams in becoming a writer.
Chiu-Wai, I want to thank you.
For you are my inspiration.
Tony, because of you I am a writer.

Winds of Time
by Greg Crosby

I heard a whisper in the winds of time
Or was it just an echo of years gone by
Years can blow by like a winter wind
Or linger like a summer breeze.

Time flows in my mind as a gentle stream
Or races like a raging river
Winds blow memories of younger days
Swift and sweet they drift in my minds eye

My life is but a speck in the winds of eternity
Yet I can find joy in the blink of an eye
Who can say what the winds of time will bring
I will let them carry me where they may

Untitled
by Nichole Falconer

Careless youth, careless days,
Careless action, and who pays?

Naked truth, naked lie,
Naked child begins to cry.

Stolen body, stolen mind,
Stolen pleasures rob me blind.

Broken trust, broken heart,
Broken spirit, from the start.

Empty promise, empty love,
Empty heaven, up above.

Grandma Rose
by Marilyn Brehm

She couldn't hear well
This Rose in full bloom
Through the years were kind and gentle
She got angry when her hands
Wouldn't kneed the bread or
Beat the cakes
And she loved to bake so
She'd Just sit and smile
On her old wooden rocker
Why! no one came to visit
At least enough
Dreaming of sweeter times
Loving times
When her family was young
And needed her so
Desperately clinging to pictures
Of a young Rose
With soft brown hair
Rushing about
Now she sits alone in her world
Waiting for something
To make it all better

My City
by Mark Carle

Look!
Out beyond this lake I swam
whose waters have since dried, due to the dam
They built it to stop the flow
Robbing me of what used to grow
I tried to fight it
This notion I've started
This emotion I've discarded

Look!
Out beyond the pasture's fence
Beyond what they call common sense
Dare to be the one to live
Dare to be the one to give
But don't even try
to get on by
This notion I've started
This emotion I've discarded

Nature's Fatal Overture
by Ronald Busse

The dangling branch weighs down heavy, lifeless,
burdened by dripping blankets of white, wintry slush.

A January storm always pack a wallop, but this
furious, unnumbered movement was being composed
during the first few bars of November.
For music has no era.

Though unusually surprising, unmercifully relentless..
A few brown, brittle leaves cling to life,
soon to snap- and fall; returning feebly
to fertilize Earth's quiet, niveous terrain.

Etched into memory of the weakening branch, a young
sapling, happier times...when newborn leaves,
rubberlike, vibrant, sang through the branch in
octaval unison; waving hello! to the world,
orchestrating a joyful overture in C major...

Succumbing to many years of weathering countless
beatings, the once mighty now aged limb
snapped- and fell. Amidst a free fall, the
lifeless branch heard the final chord
ring out - in F minor.

Untitled
by Elizabeth McNielly Carey

As an afterthought, I turned down the light
and left the door ajar.
The burnt August twilight rippled for miles
unconscious of the human flesh
that was eating up the sky.

The drip of leaves on the woods edge
inflamed the long grasses,
which like my slow hard tears
had become a stagnant growth.

My mouth blew hat shaped paper boats
that circled like an eyesore
disappearing in the black mud.
The cold water mirrored their silver sails
as the fluid accepted the new arrivals.

The tedious ceremony had soaked my tiny brain
producing only an empty vision of a sterile moth
traveling through the dark; aware of his solitude.;

I trampled across a gray wooden bridge
drawn towards the cry of dying dogs.
A solitary spirit with silver studded pockets
destined to hide my tears and stand alone.

Friendly Customer
by Joyce B. Carey

Our grassy lawn now bestows
a breath of spring.
I toss bird seed on this
green blanket every week.
Even with winter's fury, the birds
manage to find an ample supply.
One April afternoon, a lonely chick
arrives suddenly to taste of our
meager harvest.
He surveys me and our kingdom
with a glint in his eye.
Softly he prances around to partake
of this needed food, then satisfied,
dashes off into the blue horizon.
I pay homage often to the birds,
who keep me company on many a lonely day,
when society is busy with its usual
active routine.

Walls
by Andorrea Castro

Why can't they see me, see who I am?
They have built me a wall, and won't look around.
The graffiti on the wall, written bold and clear,
it says: shy, quiet, and submissive.
But the wall lies.

The wall I build is the one no one sees.
The graffiti on my wall is also bold and clear,
yet unnoticed it says: open, caring, and stubborn.
My wall tells the truth.

If I feel this way, there must be others.
Did they build you a wall also?
The wall built for me is not thick, I can break it down.
But yours, is it build all the way around?
If it is, I am truly sorry and wish you the best.
For once mine is gone, I will be able to rest.

Ecstasy/Fantasy
by Bettie Carney

"Ecstasy, Ecstasy" --- "Fantasy, Fantasy"
Could it not be?? It could not be.
Oh, the sunshine, the Spring, the birds that sing, all called out to me
"Ecstasy, Ecstasy!"
But a voice within me softly cried, "Fantasy, Fantasy".
How I longed to fulfil that dream, a dream of love forever lasting,
A dream of joy and beauty and passion, a touch of a hand that left me
    trembling,
The touch of lips that left me singing, "Ecstasy, Ecstasy!"
Oh, the warmth of the sun, the blossoms of Spring, the shades of Summer,
The starlit nights in a hillside slumber, all came together with an explosion
    of joy,
In the form of a man, who was emotionally, a boy.
Oh, joy, oh joy! A soulmate, an artist like me! "Ecstasy, ecstasy!"
With all the zeal of my creativity, I painted a vision of my beautiful fantasy.
But with the falling of the Autumn leaves, the vision began to fade,
As did the leaves of yellow from Summer's deep shades of jade.
Alas, the angst of my own reality, refused to unite with that of my fantasy.
The ending of Autumn was the end of the dream, the sunlight's rays no
longer gleamed,
The sunset walks down a country lane soon turned to cold December rains.
No longer would there be moonlight walks and, long searching, romantic
    talks,
No soothing words and gentle touch in the sweet, wee hours of morning's
    hush.
Truth finally won out; it could not be, I could not resurrect my fantasy.
But those joyous moments remain with me still, the fun-filled sojourns up
    a wooded hill,
The sounds of a distant crow in flight, the gently falling rain drops at
night,
The beautiful landscapes on that country farm where we walked for miles,
    arm in arm.
It could not be, it could not be, I could not have my fantasy.
But, remaining forever within my heart, is a feeling of ecstasy which will
    never depart.
Like William Blake, who advocates kissing the joy as it flies,
I plan on spending the rest of my life in the glow of eternities sunrise.

For my Grandfather
by R.J. St. Patrick

His face has more cracks and lines in it then the hardened and forgotten
        dirt
    of the same lonely road that he's traveled for years.
    He shuffles his feet now because he's gotten old,
        but my grandfather is a warrior,
            still fighting,
            still fighting.

    He carries an old pail to draw water from his pump.
        It is almost too heavy for him to carry.
            His body is tired
            and his eyes are dim,
        but my grandfather is a warrior,
            still fighting,
            still fighting.

            His hair is white,
            His skin is brown
            from too many days
            in the morning sun,
        but my grandfather is a warrior,
            still fighting,
            still fighting.

        His hands are twisted from trouble
            and times of hatred
                and pain.
        And though his back is bent,
            it is not bent from shame,
        because my grandfather is a warrior,
            still fighting,
            still fighting.

On Cross So Glorious Sonnet
by Stephanie Cedervall

On cross so glorious He extends His arms,
Outstretched to East, to West, to timeless throng,
And there a God-sent surge of heartbeat strong
Sustains our hopes and silences alarms.

On cross so glorious He reaches far
To North, to South, to timeless place...and Death,
Itself, soon dies...with metamorphic breath
Of life rekindled by His Heavenly Star.

On cross so glorious, opposing line
Is leaning toward another with respect,
At crucial point of crossing to detect
True love will bind the human and divine.

Like joyful butterflies now newly born,
We, too, can wing our way from worldly scorn.

Pantomime
by Bill Cibbarelli

The mind's pantomime
Once upon a time
Brought forward to the present
Miming a whispered hello
A nod
Desperate hugs tugging at the heart
Reaffirmation
Love is real
Neither dream nor illusion.
The pantomime
The soft caresses of cotton dresses
Running along my skin like feathers
Together
A carefree tickling touch
The once upon time
Not yesterday, today or tomorrow
Everyday.
The pantomime
Unconsciously performed
No convention. Fitting no norm
Being reborn everyday and every yesterday
For uncounted mornings to come

Synchronizer
by Sylvia Marie Cochran

            Time itself is but a span
            A breadth continuing
            Cessation from ancestral clan

            A moment is but the twinkle
            An instant flashing
            Mortality disguised as wrinkle

            Consequence is but an aftermath
            An insignificantly voiding
            Repeal of tranquil wrath

            The eternal One aligns and adjusts
            Planets, souls, minutes and life
            Twinned companion of dissent
            The temporal two not sure that He trusts
            Harmonious turmoil and strife
            Show single approval by crescent

Empty
by Tonya Mae

The walls show no life,
the curtains are drawn,
and everyone is gone.
The cupboards are bare,
and the closets have nothing to share.
The only sound is a slow drip coming
from the lonely faucet.
The shadows of old times linger here,
but the love, I'm afraid, isn't near.
The still house lays empty, except
for my quiet intruding thoughts.
I fight off the time that will lead me
another way.
The warm laughter haunts cold in my ear,
and I'm left alone to savior the empty tear.
Empty house, new memories will appear.
In some ways we're setting each other free,
at times you've held too much security.
Empty of the past.
Farewells to get us through,
you remained full as we emptied you.

Morning
by L. George Collins

The morning comes with blessings
Fielding sunrises, as arcs of light
Signal the dawning;as from dark night
Life form moving signal Now risings'.

From the heart the still Presence;
Somnolent stirrings of quiet peace.
Awakenings myriad left to release
Slumbering sensings; Beings' essence.

Waking dawn's iridescence:
Opening light comes color-streaking
Paintbrush hues of a day breaking:
Patterns forming sylph-shaping Presence.

Eyelids and heart-lids open to see.
Hearing and smelling mornings' flow
Of breathings and breezes on the lea.

The Accident
by Rhonda Constance

Waiting
for the visit
Never arrives
to see The Face
the Beauty of the Person
loved so dearly
Pain in my body
from not holding His
almost matches the Agony in my soul
Nagging
Wondering is the worst part
Separation is Temporary
yet Doubt persists
knowing it should be otherwise
but the heart needs to be sure
if it's otherwise
why is He so late
Anniversary = Hell
with No One
the knock on the door
Finally!!!
heart beating ready for love
'til the Stranger explains
putting Doubt to Shame
"there's been an Accident..."

Life of a Bird
by Dena Cowdrey

Over the raging waters
soaring above the sea
only birds may fly free.

Through the silky feathers
to the rounded wings
only the wind may bring
the wonders of these things.

As the sun may surely rise,
a bird always flies.

A sea or a tree
no difference it would make
just as long as it's not a fake.

The rise and fall
of a bird so small
in a world vast
he'll finally go at last.

Neurosis
by Melissa Cross-Zepernick

Darkness envelopes the bedroom,
allowing only a sliver of moonlight to seep in.

Influenced by fear,
the child is reluctant to even blink.
Infantile thoughts are created.
Touch the switch, not the floor.

Tears are now chasing one another.
Touch the switch, not the floor.
The child's legs uncurl,
and lower themselves to the floor.
She bolts to the light.

CLICK

The same darkness shines around her.
Her face radiates terror.
The child's piercing cry, so forceful, cannot be heard.

Knowing that gnarled fingers soon
will be tugging at her unslippered feet,
the child races to her bed.

Sheets tuck themselves under her neck.
She cautiously drifts into her dreams.

Vulnerable
by Rebecca Dalvesco

Suspended horizontally on a silken,
colorless cushion, the selfish coolness
begins to possess the innards of a six-foot body.
The pungent smell of carnations and
formaldehyde venture and grope through
the humid, dusty air, trying to find a
passage way to enter.

In the close distance, sharp, piercing
murmurs and restrained howls forcefully
bounce into the hard encasement,
trying to vibrate my musty lungs.

Unbroken rhythms from the vulture-like
shadows fly aimlessly across my face.
I am unable to escape their pitying
claw hands as they descend.

Helpless I lie, waiting for the soft,
white rose to turn hard and black
in the midst of my grip.

Pushing Through Life
by Don Davidson

Push me not brother
I will push you back,
What I do in life
Is no concern of yours
As is your life
Of no consequence to me,
Your path is walked by you,
I may join you
For a time
But, inevitably,
I go my own way,
Do as you will
Because I do as I will
But push me not brother
For I will, indeed,
Push you back

Source Unknown
by Teri Davids

Where does it come from,
    this emptiness
so vast, so chilling,
with no edges in sight
to cling to
in desperate hours
of thundering quiet,
where the shriek of silence
commands it's presence
    to be known?

Where does it come from,
    this strength
to make it through
another day,
where clocks
are the enemy,
calendars an affront,
mocking, marking
the loss of precious time
and dreams unfulfilled?

Where does it come from,
    this desire
        to carry on?

My Best Friend Luddy
by Julius J. Davis Jr.

My best friend Luddy lived down the block
In the big country mansion where music always played
I called him "Luddy" for short
He was stocky and fat
And his hair was always frayed.

His family was kinda weird, but Luddy was cool
We'd share lunches, and try to smoke Camels
without filters
Luddy could hear music and write it from his head
He also played great piano and ate lots of apple
fritters.

I figured it was my job to "funk" him up,
So when he would come to my house,
I put my old 45's on the record machine
Luddy dug the Temptations and Elvis
And he thought Aretha was really keen.

You know, it was me who taught Luddy how to dance
The jerk, the swim, the four corners
You shoulda seen him in my mama's kitchen
Doin' the robot and the funky chicken.

As we got older though, his taste in music changed
He started back to writing stuff that only
orchestras could play
But we would still "hook up" every so often
And remember those by-gone days.

Now my best friend Luddy is a superstar
Warner Brothers sighed him in '86
And when we get together these days,
He's still up to his musical tricks

Playin' in a country-western orchestra
He finally found his niche
My best friend Beethoven can really jam
His music heals and makes our souls rich.

Love Struck
by Dora Day

I close my eyes and feel
Your warm, moist lips
Searching for mine.
My heart pounds and
I can't get my breath.
Your strong arms encircle me,
Sliding down my extremities.
I breathe deeper. My body throbs
And my innards explode with excitement,
Awaiting your entrance.
I anticipate your next touch...
Strong and tight.
My heart sings, my lips curl up,
My eyes flash like stars.
My breathing now heavy and deliberate...
Rising and falling.
My mind remembers only you.
I'm so love struck,
I don't know what to do.

The Living Will
by John M. Denney

There comes a time in all our lives
    When we must go to sleep,
And even the strongest among us
    Will break down and cry and weep.

And though--up to a point==
    We still have satisfactions,
Eventually, we realize
    We can't control all our actions.

So...if the time comes soon
    That my vital signs grow weak
I only ask that you allow
    My soul to go to sleep.

September 6th
by Louise DePino

Can you recall, can you remember
That special 6th day in September
When you and I proclaimed I do.
And I walked hand in hand with you.

When we were joined man and wife
To spend our happy wedded life.
Can you believe how years passed by
When, all our kids, were just knee high.

And one by one they left our home
To have a family of their own
Do your remember as I remember
That happy 6th day of September

And now our hair, has strands of gray
And all those years, have slipped away
If you turn back the time and years
Some were joyous, some were tears

Can you remember as I recall
When we were young and had it all
Again, I'm sure as day is through
You'd marry me, I'd marry you.

Open Eyes
by Cindy Dietzman

The April wind teases the infant tree leaves
Like a child nudging a baby out of sleep.
See the golden daffodils' dancing sheathes
Bending down as if in delight to weep?

Scattering between the thick blades of green
Press out the dandelion and buttercup,
Spring beauty and blue violet bright and keen,
And maybe the four petaled clover of luck.

Thickly clustered above the blue heights
like pale pioneers trekking eastward
Tumble the cumulus clouds so light;
While here and there darts the wheeling buzzard.

Now zips the inquisitive bumble bee
circling my head like a satellite,
But no time in his flight to pause has he
And just as suddenly zooms out of sight.

Within this fond reverie do I melt,
My soul's hand enfolded by Mother Earth's;
My heart sings happily for what I've felt,
"You've opened my eyes to witness Spring's birth!
You've opened my eyes to witness Spring's birth!"

Captive Thoughts
by Marianne Dimmick

It's no rumor,
I have a tumor

People come into my room, then go,
some are familiar, others I don't know

No matter how hard I try to communicate,
I end up feeling like an expatriate

My thoughts are held captive within the confines of my mind,
I run around inside and even those words I do find,

I can't get them down to my mouth,
the damn thing is just too far south,

At times I hear an echo down deep somewhere,
as always, some obstacle keeps me from getting there

My brain will not allow me to write...
and NO it's not "all right."

Just once I would like to say, loud and clear:
"Hey you! I can't talk--but I sure can hear!"

The Circus Life Of A Working Housewife
by Molly Durante

Twenty-two years of juggling, keeping all my plates spinning -
evenly, fairly, balancing on such a tenuous high wire.

No circus clown could make me smile.
Or distract and divert me from my extra mile.

Given daily, given freely, nothing required in return,
as the hoops of fire grow higher and hotter,
I leap through them with seeming ease.

And when the last trapeze flyer drops gently into their net,
I fall fatigued - the aches and pains of my needs never quite met.

Dear Grandma
by Ann Dudley

"Today was the birds wedding day, and they were chirping and twittering, swooping and darting all over the lilac bushes and telephone wires."

I wrote that to my grandmother when I was ten years old. I wrote to her once, sometimes twice, a week and shared with her all my secret joys, dreams and heartaches. I described the first primrose of springtime, sometimes pressing it and enclosing it in my letter. I told her of sibling squabbles and complained of my mother's unfairness in meting out punishment. I sent her school papers, and I painted vivid word pictures of my adventures and misadventures, chronicling the delights of haymaking, of nutting and berrying in the woods around our village, and of bicycle rides to the seashore.

My grandmother encouraged me by sending me boxes of stationary- invitingly pristine paper with nice, square envelopes that made a resounding plop as they were dropped into the mailbox.

Writing was always rewarding. My compositions were often read aloud in class, and sometimes the teacher would ask ME to read them. I liked that because I read well. I read dramatically, with a great deal of expression, and I felt important and accomplished. It didn't matter then that I was pudgy, and hopeless at sports.

Another teacher wrote encouraging comments on my papers, and funny remarks, and invited me to tea, and his wife fed me cucumber sandwiches and Victoria Sponge cake. Neither batted an eye when I confided that one day I would be either a famous actress or writer.

Today I realize how fortunate I was to have a family that prized letter-writing, and teachers who were encouraging and who nurtured whatever abilities I had. Now I endeavor to do the same for my grandchildren - by E-Mail, of course!

Sanguine Feel
by David Forsyth

I chose not to mince words with you
my time is for the fray, for the dark-maned beasts of unmanned caves
the war i wage is against your tepid mediocrity
for you, i'll gather up the dust and blood of wyverns
because, that's the stuff of elaborate volumes for your empty shelves.

The Turkey
by H. Fitzgerald Durbin

Early one spring day farmer Jones, went out to plow his corn.
To be ready for anything, he took his gun along.
When he heard this Turkey Gobbler, gobble from the brush.
He grabbed his old shotgun, and took off in a rush.

When he got down to the creek, that ran across his land.
Farmer Jones could hardly wait, to get that turkey in his hand.
He followed him so stealthily, as he headed up the creek.
He swore he would get that turkey, if it took him a week.

He looked this way and that, as he followed the turkeys sound.
He was like a coonhound on the hunt, with his nose close to the ground.
He followed him across the creek, and then back again.
He could have shot a turkey many times, but he did not want a hen.

As he followed the gobbler up the creek, and then over the hill.
He kept mumbling to himself, "Boy! will this ever be a kill?"
All else was forgotten, as he kept steadily on the trail.
He said. "Nothing will stop me now, rain, snow, sleet, or hail!"

He finally saw him as he crossed, a bare spot of land.
He said, "He's bigger than I thought, Oh boy this is grand!"
He followed him around some brush, to the top of the hill.
He raised his shotgun and took aim, and there he made his kill.

He stood looking down on the bird with a most generous smile.
Then said, "Oh shucks I'll have to carry him, it must be nigh a mile."
He grasp his neck slung him on his back, and said, "Well I must go."
The wing tips as he carried the bird, plowed furrows in the snow.

To A. R. A Moth to the Flame
by Trevor D. Ebanks

I am a plain brown moth
You are the dazzling fire
I flit and I flutter
attracted by desire

Your beauty bids me closer
Commands me to draw near
Your warmth it entices me
And removes the cold of fear

And still I hover closer
Basking in your glow
I'm flirting with hell fire
The danger will I know

Let me come a little closer
and fan you with my wings
although you grow much hotter
And your heat, how it stings

And as you grow still brighter
I am quickly consumed
From the moment I saw you
I was already doomed

And as I turn to cinder
regrets are but a few
For one, brief, brilliant moment
I was one with you

Each Other's Keeper
by John Edwards

Sister
Sister

We are
Each other's keeper

As Cain said to God
Am I my brother's keeper?
You say to me
And I say to you
Sister
Sister
We are each other's keeper

How can I tell you
To be strong
When I'm not even fighting
The fight?
Sure both of us can
Talk the talk
But are we really willing to
Walk the walk?
Sure we both can understand
The weakness we have shared
But are we to
Stand by
And watch
Each other die?
No sister
Not

What Is Art?
by Duane Ellis

I feel that art is in the eyes
of a child,
It glitters and glows with light.
It lifts the wings of every bird,
And guides it through the night.
It fashions every female form,
Takes a boy and creates a man.
Lights the fire of two lovers,
Art can do what no one can,
To me, are is a gift from God
to mankind
An expression of love, A burning
fire
Art is life, the good and the bad,
That reveals our deepest desire.
Art is not here and is not there,
It has no specific place.
But nevertheless, Art can
Always be found,
In every person's face.

Shadows In The Dark
by Dave Enz

Shadows don't only exist in the reflections of light
That the sun cast all around
I know, met one the other night
Long past sun down
Strangely enough, it seemed to know about my life
Memories lost, were suddenly found

Your shadow is your ghost
Your ghost is your shadow
If it's spirits you fear the most
You have no idea of true horror

Met a man with no eye sight
Who could hear the slightest of sounds
He told me about the shades of twilight
Angels who are earth bound
To help make our's and their's wrongs, right
so they can rest in heaven's hallowed ground

Your ghost is your shadow
Your shadow is your ghost
In your steps it will follow
A celestial guest to which you host

For Grandpa
by Colleen Ford

These photos show the
Love in your eyes
Those chairs the
Pride of your work
Our memories tell of the
Joys and the pains
Of your full life
You're the father of
Three beautiful generations
And many more to come
You've loved so long
And worked so hard
that you will always be
Remembered in our stories
So rest now Grandpa
Rest
You're finally home again
Back in the arms that
Never really let you go.

Bias
by Cin Ezzell

There is but only one way.
To stop this ceaseless burning.
Be this a clandestine affair.
Of bodies, and hearts.
Pull me down passionately, to meet you.

I am ready, and waiting...
Wanting...

More than my heart can stand.

I can see only one path to take.
But in your arms, I am not afraid.
For I have never known such desire in my life.

All consuming...
my hands tremble.
I pledge my love for you.
Eternal...

My every breath, is for you.
My waking hours apart, torment.
finding only comfort, in coupling again.

Greeted by you at days end.
Is the entanglement of a lovers first kiss.
New, and fresh with giving, unleashed passion.

We giggle, softly with innocence.
Overwhelmed by new discovery.
Tumbling...
Fumbling atop the downy feathers.

I feel as though, I've no mind of my own.
Our souls have united.
Fragrant with loves afterglow...

MetalBeast
by Mike Fejes

Motionless it sits
at the end of a trail
of tread-like paw prints.
Massive metal body rests in a field,
sinking in the upturned earth.
Specks and flecks of mud
coupled with scratches
cover the MetalBeast's eyes,
forming a false, milky cataract.
Huge double jointed arm
arcs high overhead and ends
in a half-buried claw.
Shiny pistons look impossibly clean
against the rest of the filthy creature's body.
The MetalBeast's hide is
construction orange-yellow
that is interrupted only by
the bubbling, rust colored sores
of industrial leprosy.
The smell of the MetalBeast's sweat,
oil and grease,
mingles with the scent of fresh snow
as cotton ball sized flakes land then disappear.
The low growl that rises
to an angry, throaty howl
is absent as the Beast rests;
awaiting dawn when its
heart returns.

Reflections Of A Ruin
by Mary J. Fogarty

In my ruin I am desolate and sterile.
I have ceased to grow
those things upon which life must continue.

In my dreariness, only brief images emerge,
and my moments of feeling are few.
The pages of my mind are flipped by the winds,
and they crumble from the whipping sands.

The springs of my sexual emotion have been
strained and overused.

In my ruin I am surrounded by people whose
shallow pleasures seem sadder than their pains.
I see them performing labors that wear down their
souls and bring them no profit.

I see a world of shattered institutions,
strained nerves, and bankrupt ideals.
I am haunted by this wilderness that surrounds me,
for all I see are reflections of myself.

I long for the clear waters that exist
in the desert of my dreams.

An Alter By The Curb
by Nicholas Gardiner

The Laws of our City's nights,
are quick as flicker in the neon sign,
and as frail as smoker's glass.
It's her purse he wants,
not to take her Life,
but in a tiny moment passed,
something has gone wrong.
She's lying out on midnight ground,
in that sure shape of Death,
while in sneakers he runs away,
light patters, echoes failing fast.
They'll place tall candles out,
perhaps some family picture frames,
a dozen types of flowers,
here on yet another curb.
He'll buy a little rock,
the same thing once again,
the need will soon return,
and he'll be back out then.

Kansas No More
by Elizabeth Gray

The wild tornado whirls out of control like
    a washing machine filled with dirt.
The destruction it brings is devastating.
The houses are either blown away or destroyed.
Kansas just isn't Kansas anymore.

Music To Me
by Marianne Garvey

Slits of ice blue remedies swirling
Spinning, dancing fills my head
Boundless balance, like a rescue
Returns the gray again, to red.

Bringing passion back, the heart beats
Two guitars strumming as one
Filling power, stirring feeling
Warmth, the rays aim like the sun.

With the strumming of the G strings
With each caress, the master knows
Sparks set fire to the fingers
Shooting flames into the soul.

Pay me as you play me
A cautious, mellow price, this toll
Feel a soul dance through the fire
Feel the feel of ebbing whole.

Two guitars playing passion
A boundless balance for the head
Yours and mine, the long-lost lovers-
How passions play like sheets on beds.

My Heart - Listens
by H.S. Gilbert

I lay upon my side, one arm extended,
with the fingers of the hand just slightly curled,
as if awaiting - touch.

Soft breath of air wafts by,
and tendrils of the zephyr find emptiness,
my hand is dry and cool,
in space once filled with - warmth.

But see! a sheen of dampness,
glimmering faintly in my palm,
anticipating sweet - congress.

Caress once known, (I have been blessed),
I must still know, (and still be blessed),
your love enfolds me and I - smile.

Whisper to me gently, darling,
my heart - listens.

Momentum
by S.L. Givhan

The best talk shows day and night,
in the ring we win our fights.
Theaters have us on big screen,
Michael, Diana and Whitney say sing.
92 Olympics shinning through,
Black Enterprises business view.
Johnson's Ebony Fashion Fair,
Jet to Powell and Emerge with Blair.
Young sisters and brothers of Essence will be,
the new NAACP.
Push to excel in the defenders News,
Bud Billiken each year with greater review.
BET network, Doctors, Poets, Attorneys and
yes, even the highest court in the land.

Poet's Parterre
by G.G. Gilchrist

Arthritic fingers
    shriveled, palsied palms
      pluck no poet's quills, lightening rods;
Heart's hushed..still throbs with in-scored meters'
    echoings re-tuned, old Glad Tidings...
        Yet, pleased poet's paled; LOGOS
            of spirit, as willed, breathes...

Mindful of meanwhiles
    in humbled doldrums'
      wake-dreams fallowed, poet pauses...
prunes plied perceptions' private paintings
    from psyche: Poems? Acorns germinal
      in germander-gravities?
           Or, real oaks struggling skyward?

Vatic vague, unversed;
    insights inchoate,
    inconologies intimate,
    worn-inherent incoherencies?
Feelings', flashings, flit as fire flies
    through frozen fields, fling fantom
        along my soulscape's silence....

The Hardship Trail
by Elizabeth S. Gill

Down through the Connecticut Valley stubborn pioneers came
Thrown out of Massachusetts with very great shame.
For they thought when they sailed to this rugged new land
They could worship in peace; their own beliefs in hand.

Determined to make their new homes as they wanted,
They moved southeast to Rhode Island with courage undaunted.
The hardships were many, while the rewards were few;
But these brave men and women to their dreams remained true.

Their new shelters were tents and small cabins of wood
Built near rivers for fish and fresh water so good.
The Indians surrounded them; some soon became friends
Who taught them to hunt and to fish river bends.

They built houses of worship to practice their beliefs
And chose leaders among them to keep law as their chiefs.
They braved all kinds of weather to build a new life
Working and planting, each husband and his wife.

The children worked hard; they helped with all of the chores
Farming and gathering wood for the fireplace indoors.
Towns and cities stand today as a tribute to their foresight.
Their wisdom and commitment to God and country turned out right.

Nature
by Sheila Hamilton

The habits
Of rabbits
Are known to all:
They multiply.

It isn't wise
To criticize
They can't refrain
If they should try.

From the best to the very least,
It is the nature of the beast.

A Blind Man
by Howard Golley Jr.

A blind man has a special sense
That sighted folks do not know.
Making his movements very tense
He tries not to let them show.

Feelings are all trapped inside
Threatened by anxiety and fear.
Strange emotions can never hide
The embarrassment that is near.

He carries a vision in his mind
A disappointment in his heart.
Looking for a pleasure to find
So happiness will get a start.

He walks alone in the darkness
During the sunny part of a day.
Trying to conquer his blindness
Using a cane to guide his way.

Confusion fills his every need
Thank God for help he's given.
Without caring friends to lead
Life wouldn't be worth liven.

Intoxication
by Andrea Gonzalez

With salt on my lips
I drink you down
heedlessly
recklessly
without regard for the potency you unmercifully deliver

You weaken my senses
blur my reality
with delicious
heat rising
throughout my body
seeping
into every crevice

For a brief moment
I forget she is
there like always
ready to fill you
up again and again
craving
the taste of you

Emotions dulled
I slowly walk
away with you
on my mind and the bitterness
of lime still
pungent in my mouth

Waiting For The Bus
by Michael Goodman

I sip stale vending machine coffee
in the corner booth of the
Greyhound station. A styrofoam cup
left on the table becomes my ashtray,
as I drag on my cigarette to stay warm.
Intoxicating aromas cling to the shadows of
every passer-by, illing what senses I have left.

A full moon peaks in through the window, watching
me reach for the flask from inside my winter
parka. I glance up only to find a wrinkled old woman,
who had seen better times in better places, swollen
with red blotches breathing from her open pores. Barely
able to balance herself, she borrows the wobbly
table I occupy to lean against.

"Is there somthing I can do
for you?" exhales from my lips.

"How 'bout a sip of that there booze
in your jacket, kid? HACK!! Hack!! It sure
would help me beat this nasty cough," groans back.

"Why don't you just take the whole bottle,
I can find another one. And here's a fresh
pack of Marlboro Reds just opened, to keep warm."

Looking over her shoulder with
a paranoid twitch, she swipes up
my goods and dips out the back door. As
I sip vending machine coffee
in the corner booth of the
Greyhound station.

Unseen Thoughts
by Darius Keith Gordon

He thought of different ways to fix his problems
The idea of leaving life kicked in
He didn't know if he wanted to stay or go
The real problems in life set in

Wondering what the next day would bring
Life itself was very much like a dream
The world was mine in my own eyes
And everything revolved around me

The walk to the store was long and cold
My wife flashed before my eyes
I gave her an engagement ring today
A lifesaver, I wish I had one

Walking out of the store I paused
Took a deep breath and opened the door
Just as I thought on this day today
My life I will soon depart

The sound could be heard from miles around
And at the end the world seemed quiet
For now I lie in a pool of blood
Knowing that I am gone

Everything is left behind now
My wife & child both named DEE
I wanted to see him take his first steps
and turn the lifesaver into a gold ring

Well now it seems to late & I wish
I could've told my wife how I felt
If I had the chance I would apologize
for my faults & promise my love till death

The Spirit Of Christmas
by Mary Gordon

What is this spirit of Christmas
We hear mentioned every year?
Is it merely a time of decorations
With a christmas tree for cheer?
Is it the carols that we sing for the season
Or is it the look in the eyes of the children
As it gets closer to Christmas Eve Night?

Is it the sending of christmas cards
And the fun of the gift giving scene?
Or the renewing of old friendships
Tell me, is that all Christmas means?

What is the spirit of christmas
we hear mentioned every year?
It's all these things I've mentioned.
But more, much more, that's clear.
For you see, it's the celebration
Of god's gift to mankind for all time
It's the birthday of our Lord Jesus
And the acceptance of God's gift divine.

Untitled
by Heather Arlene Hall

Angels are discovered on the
roof tops of only exclusive homes.

Honored not for the abundance
or scarcity of material possessions
creating the physical beauty,
rather blessed for the overwhelming
presence of faith, love, and morality
bound within the walls.

A residence in which the vast
quantity and quality of heart
dwelling within penetrates and
inspires all who enter.

Only a structure of immeasurable
goodness is deserving of such
guardians.

Mengele Escapes
by Krista Greenberg

Catholic priests helped
guide
the Angel of Death
out of Europe.
A perversion
of the Jewish Passover
to cheat justice.
Lamb's blood
replaced by
the blood of twins
in the name of
genetic and racial purity.
Bold enough
not to use
an alias
on a passport
in Buenos Aires.

Fifty years later,
his name is on
the street sign and
the factory.
The people
are still
silent.

The Flame
by Grover W. Gregory II

Watching the flame of a candle
I began to think of life
And as it burned I wondered
How long will I see it's light?
A candle feeds upon itself
As does each of our lives
And continues forever forward
Until the flame dies
Some burn out sooner than others
Which seems strange to me
Because they don't burn faster
They just have less to be
Now this is set by the creator
How long the flame will last
And by the same decision
How much light will be cast
Some are very much needed
Some are just to enjoy
It doesn't really matter
As long as they aren't destroyed
So when the flame flickers
Remember the words I've said
And say a prayer for the flames
That have reached their candle's end

How It Is
by Bonnie Hayes

The marble is dusted.
The silver is polished.
I place it precisely so, and leave.
The door slams in noisy disrespect.

Outside the building
Someone sleeps in a doorway;
Or does he merely hide
Under his torn tarp and burlap bags?

Two different worlds
Existing a door and a street apart.

One man his mind on silver and show,
The other hiding lest his condition show.

Betrayal
by Linda Jose

"Is there someone else?" I asked,
And his lying lips said, "No,"
But my eyes and heart said, "Oh, yes, there is."
I loved him still so the "No" prevailed,
I was not ready for the heartbreak.

"Is he seeing someone else?" she asked.
Should I lie and say, "No,"
While her eyes and heart say, "Oh, yes, there is"?
I hesitate, just a second, but she already knows.

She cries, I cry, he bellows in rage at being caught.
I love him, she loves him, we are not ready for the heartbreak.
He leaves, adding my name to all the others who have betrayed him.
Is betraying a betrayer betrayal?
She has the right to know, and so did I.

Mantra In the Darkness
by Madonna N. Groom

The Spirit of Tesla
Borrowed by Marconi
Drifts along the midnight shadows

A mantra in the darkness...

The Taos hum?
A distant drum?
The Anasazi know

The mantra in the darkness...

Complexity fills new yearnings
With desire
To seek one's fortune

From the mantra in the darkness...

But how?
When, where?
The Chu'en Dynasty knows

About the mantra in the darkness...

For now you will have to
Close you eyes in the darkness
And join the mantra
To be one
With the one
That flows through you.

The Pianist
by Laura Gygi

    I watched with envy as her fingers flowed gently over the ivory keys. Her touch was soft and delicate. The sound of each note was choice. My mind danced as I heard the familiar tones of Franz Liszt's masterpiece, "Liebesträume." She played from memory on the ancient upright piano. Not one note was missed as she continued on.
    Her long, slender fingers arched out from her artistically rounded hand. She sat erect, in perfect posture, playing with magnificent dignity. She performed naturally, showing abundant emotion. Just watching her, I was moved by her talent- My talent-which I had been fortunate to inherit.
    Practice. It was a law by which she lived. I could recall all her stories. Practicing for hours without end to become a virtuoso pianist like her mother. And now I, too, was also striving towards that goal as each generation before me had.
    I gazed at her with admiration. The piece came to a close and she rose with a pleased expression. I seated myself where she had once been and sat up straight. I rounded my hands, arched my fingers, and began to play. I, the budding virtuoso, played elegantly, proud to continue the legacy of "Love Dreams."

A Testimony Of God's Love
by Estelle Kaczenas

My whole life has been a testimony of God's love--
    I must witness to it.

Through a lost childhood, He sustained me.
Through a loveless marriage, He supported me.
Through tragedies of sudden death, He comforted me.
Through poverty and hunger, He nourished me.
Through sordid circumstances, He uplifted me.
Through births of three children, He blessed me.
Through an enquiring mind, He enriched me.
Through a near-fatal stroke, He made me well.

A witness? Yes, with praise and prayer

Behind each of the above, there is a story--
    that someday I must tell.

The Mythic Virgin
by Laura L. Halfvarson

Where she stood,
Bare, luminous,
With glowing mass and curve,
Suffused with raptures of
The living light that
Dances by the constant
Touch of love,
A radiant tower
To be scaled;
A temple, just appearing
To be womankind,
Encircled by the fire
Laid acutely by her father's hand,
She waited.

Time mattered not,
For made was she
To meet with love
And search the heart's
Aspiring path
In jubilant eternity
With he who entered
Through the gate,
To storm the tower
On his knees,
And gain the temple,
Flashing swords
Of love, and laughing,
Lift her to the soaring life,
Rejoicing in the farthest stars.
He comes.

A Forgotten Face
by Lee Hamilton

Drunk on blissful sobering silence
Dissolved and crystallized in fathomless stillness
Gone to nothing, yet present as everything
How you let go into my eyes, outsmiling your disguise
Sparks trying to make sense out of the dark
Your mind in an unholy bliss
Lost in itself, twisted in pain
Never understanding why this sacred invitation
Knowing you are caught in a vortex you have created
Damned with the fertility of a lost body inside a twisted mind
Which takes you on a walk through hell

Lost within yourself conjuring up the demons
That invade your soul telling you worthless lies
Bound in a dungeon condemned in a hell
Brood in anger and held by self pity
Yet secretly looking for a way out

Turn loose the pawn and give way to desire
Stop treating your need like an unwanted child
Free your mind - open your eyes and remember
This energy you've forced into its drunken pain
You made in your hurt spun in a web of lost feelings

But looking to the now born
The frosty green swirl of unraveled longings
Drinking in the new horizons, filled with rebirth
Freed of black and white and transfixed on color
Gaze upon the reflection reunited in a smile
Lost in speech deep in silence you find...
It's only you

The Broken Agreement
by Lisa Hanebrink

When we started out, we both agreed it was just for fun.
Nothing serious, no mention of love, and no commitments.
Everything was just for a good time, and the here and now.
But, that was before all the Thursday nights we spent
cuddled together watching "Seinfield" and "ER":
The pink champagne in the hot tub, the
night on th steps, and the times
you made me laugh.
It soon became increasingly difficult to keep my promise
Don't be angry. I tried to not become attached.
To be a 90's woman and just enjoy the moment.
And to check my feeling at the door on the way out;
but I failed.
Did you know that I've caught myself staring out the window
and suddenly giggling, remembering a
funny antic of yours or moment we've shared?
Or that I sometimes wake up in the middle of the night longing
for your arms around me?
Yes, I admit I didn't keep my end of the bargain and that I broke all
the terms of our agreement.
I guess there is nothing left to say except...
What if the penalty for falling in love with you when
I promised not to?

The Game
by Dunya Michael Hanna

He is a poor pawn
always jumps to the next square
He doesn't turn right or left
not looks behind
He is moved by a fool queen
who passes throughout the board
holding trunks and cursing the bishops
She is a poor queen
moved by a hasty king
who counts the squares everyday
and claims they are incomplete
He prepares the knights and the castles
and dreams of a stubborn opponent
He is a poor king
moved by a skilled player
who loses his time
in an endless game
He is a poor player
moved by an empty life
that has no blackness neither whiteness
It is a poor life
moved by a bewildered god
who tried to play with clay
He is a poor God
He doesn't know how
to get rid of his dilemma

"Was That She?"
by Robert MacIntosh

I still think I see her.
She appears for fleeting moments in a crowd.
Smiling and happy, then,.. gone.
There was no time to get close to
the owner of, the imposter of that face.
To shout out loud, "Come back, my darling".
The noise of the crowd would smother my words,
And then my hopes,
And then my heart, once more,
As they did again today,
When she passed by the exit door
And quickly slipped away!

A Cry For Help...
by Lyn J. Hansen-Blizzard

Acid and Speed are bad they say
Claim the price will be hard to pay
Burns our minds out for all time
But look at me, I'm doin' fine

Tried everything on the streets and in school
Nothing but the best, buddy, I'm no fool
I may enjoy it but I'm no junkie's clown
I could stop if I wanted, I just fool around

Try it all at least once, my friend once said
Funny but that friend of mine, now is dead
Maybe there's something to stoppin' after all
Guess I'm gettin' tired of dodgin' the Law

Wonder who would help me if I really tried
Tried to talk to Mom once, she just cried
Guess she thinks she failed me and Dad does too
Doesn't really matter now, I'm lost and that's true

Screamin' out for mercy to a God they say does care
I can't see or hear Him, is He really there?
Can He really help me, is there a hope -
Or will I die a loser, hooked on dope?!

You Won't Come to Me
by Betty Jean Hill

I feel like writing a poem,
but one won't come to me.
If I could get it to come
out,
it would be as sad as
sad could be.
I long for you and
want you here
but you're just like this
thing.
I'm sad as sad can be,
and you won't come to me.

Flowers For Algernon
by Linda Harvey

Charlie Gordon was a simple man
Simply different, no knowledge at hand
He knew it was important to read and write
He also knew he wasn't so bright.

Algernon was the name of a mouse he met
Algernon is smart now Charlie's upset
Charlie begins to like Algernon
He watches the maze, he thinks this is fun.

Algernon's had an operation on his brain
So Charlie feels he'll have the same
The operation was closely guarded
Now Charlie is no longer retarded.

Charlie became so intelligent you see
Then realized he had no company
He had no friends, not even one
But then he thought about Algernon.

Charlie and Algernon went away
They knew they'd never be back someday
Algernon was slowly dying
Charlie knew he shouldn't be crying.

Charlie buries Algernon
And things to himself my last friend is gone
He's not worried, he knows he would cope
But what's the point, when there is no hope.

Dreams in Motion
by Paul A. Harville

A dream, a dream,
some what like the
waters of a stream.

As the water will come,
and the water will
flow,
with this motion,

Dreams will come,
and the
dreams will go.

My dreams live short,
then they die.
As the waters flow
I say goodbye.

But as I say good bye,
and touch the
water flow,
with you,

My heart will go

I'll Think About It Tomorrow
by Kathy Highley

My daughter is ten years old, and quite the little lady. Her main concern is that she will never get old enough to shave her legs, get her ears pierced or to wear a bra. Trivial matters these are to those of us with real problems like mortgages and the IRS. Right?

Wrong! When seen through the eyes of a little girl, the magnanimity of hairy legs sticking out from pink shorts while sitting next to a boy during school assembly could be overwhelming.

She is stuck between baby dolls she no longer plays with (but wants to) and puberty that she can only imagine (and dream of). She teeters between cleaning the entire house to surprise me and lounging on the couch for an entire day, oblivious to the clutter that surrounds her.

She smiles, hugs me warmly, and says, "I'll never get mad at you like Bubba does." I hug her back and say, "Thank, you, darling," although I realize that teen-hood is a struggle for every parent and child.

Mother wants her little girl to stay cute and sweet, and not make the same mistakes she did. Dad wants his little girl to stay cute and sweet in order to avoid facing beautiful and experienced.

I may read this again in a few years just to remind myself that I knew it was coming. I will wonder then as I do now with my son, "Why wasn't I better prepared?"

I will not be prepared, though, because I choose to push those gloomy forecasts into the clouds of tomorrow and enjoy the innocence of today. After all, with every trial God supplies a measure of grace, enough that we may bear it. I can wait.

The Blemish
by Lynne Hayes

It was just a blemish,
Or so I thought.
It never really went away,
But I forgot.

Life went on as usual,
Days flew by.
There was so much to do,
I don't know why.

Then one day I noticed it;
It grew quite big.
The doctor did a biopsy.
I'll need a wig.

And now the treatment's done at last.
It didn't work.
It won't be long now.
Just a quirk.

Now the pain's so bad
I could cry.
But I don't have the energy;
I die.

Star
by Cynthia Hayslette

Bright, shining star
Brightest among millions
Grant me the desires of my heart
Love, happiness and peace
O brilliant star
With your moonlight serenade
For so much have I prayed
So little do I need
Sparkling, twinkling star
So close and yet so far
As I strive to reach for you and beyond
O wondrous star
With your golden stardust
Give me your strength and your wisdom
So I may walk with my head held high
Bright, shining star
Grant me the dream of all dreams
That I may soar with the eagle
Rising higher and higher as I fly.

Through Love's Eyes
by Carolyn Heck

Love is like the ribbon
of a brand new day,
stretching across the land.
Or a child's christmas toy
all bright-eyed and shiny,
waiting to be opened.
Love is like the kupie doll
you win at the fair,
for only a quarter's share.
Love is seagulls stalking
the shore,
with me walking the empty stretch
knowing you are waiting.

For Me
by Janice Hernandez

Dark cloud - edge-lit
like midnight tissue
dipped in silver,
unfolds the opal moon
to spin it's soft gleam
across the sky
for me.

For me?
My eyes expand
to consume this gift.
My soul stretches beyond
the universal night,
accepting this offering
until it IS me.
Or I am it.

My grateful prayer
names my own senses bliss
for if I have
no moment more than this
I can attest eternally
it was enough
for me.

Quiet Rain
by N. Loy Higgins, R.A.

The sound of a quiet rain
In the midst of a hot summer's day.
So pleasant to hear
A song to the ear
Like sweet music, coming your way.

A cloudburst releases
Tiny droplets today.
Blossoms appear,
Renewed life is clear,
To all that had wilted away.

The sun now is shining,
The day crisp and bright.
Things seem refreshed,
As tho they'd been blessed.
A few remaining dewdrops delight.

The Hummingbirds
by Betty Hisaw

The flowers are blooming,
Spring is surely here.
It's time for the return
Of hummingbirds, dear.

Maybe they'll build a nest
In a nearby tree,
And lay some tiny eggs-
One, two; but not three.

The ruby - throated male,
Aggressive and bold,
Protects his family
As if it were gold.

From flower to flower
He hovers and darts.
Then flies away quickly
To other blooming parts.

Soon the flowers will fade.
The babies have grown,
Hummingbirds will hitch a ride-
My friend will be gone!

Untitled
by Darcy Holmes

Sparkling like sapphires
The ocean waves
The sand glistens like diamonds
Seagulls are in circled flight.
The wave recedes and the sand is wet.
Footprints are left,
With only memories,
To hold dear to your heart,
To treasure forever
The summer of passion.

God's Other Angel
by Marcie'a Hooley

God needed another angel
So he called one home today
And he shines down on us from Glory
So we can find our way

He's with loved ones who went before him
Where he'll never have to get old
The street he ran down this morning
Was paved with solid gold

He can play hard and be rotten
I'll bet he's having a blast
Where he's healthy and protected
Free from harm at last

He walks side by side with Jesus
And he doesn't have any pain
He anxiously waits for the day
That we'll all be together again

In Loving Memory of Our Little Angel,
KALEB NATHANIEL SORRELLS.

(Struck and killed by a tractor trailor.)

Remember...I Love You
by Linda Huggins

When my days are at an end
And my name is being called
When this life is at a finish
And I have to move along
Remember, wherever you are
How very much I love you.

When my soul escapes my body
And is free to roam at will
When I've entered another dimension
And my body is laid at rest
Remember, wherever you are
How very much I love you.

When I return to learn a lesson
What it be, I do not know
When I look to be another
I will not be far behind
Remember, wherever you are
How very much I love you.

When my breath is wiped away
And I've left without a kiss
When you feel life has no meaning
In your heart, I still exist
Remember, wherever you are
How very much I love you.

The Happiness Flower
by Heidi Huso

Did you ever find the happiness flower?
   It isn't so hard to find;
   It opens wide at the morning hour,

But sometimes it grows down in the fields
of perfect trust you always can find it
       There.

It's sweet as the nectar of the gods,
       Happiness Flower,
   Winter and summer the same
   on the difficult trails of lifes
       Trials and tribulations
It shines like a diamond sparkling in
       The sun.

If ever you find the happiness flower,
   And it isn't so hard to find
By the rainbows end in April shower,
Where the tears and smiles are as one,

May it flourish daily in your garden
       Ground,
And glisten with morning dew;
May the sunshine of love n happiness
   All the year round
Lie warm on your flower and you.

Magnolia Street
by Carolyn P. Hutcheson

Little black child with your runny nose
Why do you stand there and cry?
Don't you know the white Santa Claus
is gonna bring you joy?
Don't cry chile.
Don't you know yo' momma don't cry?
She down at the corner bar
Pickin' up de customers.
Hush up, boy. Here she come with
Santa Claus now.

Red Rose
by Marie-Catheline Jean-Francois

When I touched
The stem of the beautiful
Red rose you had given me,
Blood quickly broke free
From my finger
And spread itself over my torn skin.
What I did not see
Were the pyramid-shaped thorns
Which stood horizontally
Along the tall green stem.
If only I had taken notice
To the fact that you had neglected
To remove the pyramid-shaped thorns
Before you handed me that beautiful red rose,
I would have known that your love
Would eventually break through
The surface of my heart,
Rupturing it like a balloon
Filled with hot air.

A Little Thought To Ignore
by Dewaine Ibbotson

47 trees full of leaves
and a box full of nails
with the groundhogs near
and me and my little fear

neither can I say anymore
of the silent backdrop
the weary waves flee
and the little golden birds sing

every little thing here is
turning around too fast
and every little thing there is
better now that it's past

and we are all still living
on nature's fretful ignorance
but why complain
sleep now... It's starting to rain.

Keep On, Keep On
by Barbara Irgens

- Keep coming, he cried - slapping din
        Resolute - head up - no underlie
        Waves tossing - blinding veil -
                papery, ducky dim -
- Keep striding, he wailed - hold on
        Head high, grit gain
        Vexation, pique pain
        Piercing, biting, slapping, crushing
- Keep eyes direct, he bawled -
        - elude disorder - look onward
        Blinking, straining - rough, crude
        - squall gale
- Keep clutching, he howled - climbing, fighting
        Hold on, he heartened,
- Keep ahead, he roared - bantering Babel ravel
        Bear up, resolved - firm, precisioned, crowned
- Keep anchor - he bore sardonic snigger
        Triumphant, he grinned -
                Keep on - Keep on

the matter of poetry
by Josef Karst

        is because of the lies
            and lies
            and lies
        strange how it happened
          Henry Miller
            was bored
        masturbation wasn't fun
        impotence was everywhere
          and poetry was gay

Death Has A Name
by Melinda Kay Jacob

With a keen eye I walk
I walk with all sight,
never forgetting his face nor his fight.

Unrefined in his covet
it is I he wishes to claim,
For I am an inconstant women with no
further shame.

With my heart in deadlock
I set out for my day,
my journey yet to be started for around
the bend he stays.

I beg thee to withdraw me form his sword,
uncommonness is mine to behold
forsaken not the ingredient that draws
him to my florid face,
with cursive gowns I will flee this
place.

And with a short lived visit I invoke
your shadow to let me be.
Oblivious to all in power is he.

Overthrown elsewhere for this moment
in being,
I shall never again surmise
perhaps I have won this time
this game,
but be sure in the void he will again
come a calling
for death has a name.

Paisley
by Helen J. Jarvis

Do you remember paisley?
It's a great design.
I awoke from sleep,
With paisley on my mind!

Where did this design
Get it's great appeal?
I quickly arose and did find
Paisley, paisley with zeal!

Paisley blouses, dressed too
Soon I was searching,
It became an obsession
Then upon a box I was wrapping!

This was a special box,
For a special friend,
There it was in the closet
Waiting for this end!

Why didn't I use it when it was bought?
It was just waiting for this purpose,
When I needed a special design,
I awoke months before, with paisley on my mind.

Untitled
by Julienne Johnson

 I promise to
 put myself aside
 to bridge
 the gap
 that
 has grown
 so wide
 if
 you promise
 to provide
 some space
 to hide
 my melancholy face
 from
 all the lies
 I told my pride
 and please
 one empty room
 inside
 for
 all my feelings

In Search Of...
by Marsha A. Johnson

I looked to the sky
in search of answers
to questions only He could understand.

I wanted to know why
my life is so hard
and how I should play my hand.

So I spoke a little louder
in case He didn't hear
and I waited for most of the day.

But all that was there
was a sky of blue
and clouds that drifted away.

It took me a while
before I finally realized
the answers aren't His to give.

He is there for me
whenever I need Him
but I have my own life to live.

The questions I ask
are always the same
yet He listens without resistance.

And only time will tell
if I am to discover
the elusive answers of existence.

Brahma
by Vishnu P. Joshi

Human shadow and human light are the same;
If the slayer thinks he slays, or if the shadow thinks it is slain,
They know not my meaning.

The doubter and doubt in human mind,
The pleasure and pain in human heart, and the Tears and smiles
Running from the depth of human soul are truly my manifold creations.

In your dreams you create figures, as you most like it;
Different ones I create when you are awake;
In one you feel as a King, in the other a beggar.

When the birds fly, I am the wing.
When the warriors fight, I am the weapon.
I am Brahma, the doubter, and the doubt itself.

In war and in peace, and in tears and in smiles.
I rise and I fall, and I weave a living garment.

In this garment of flesh and bones,
Play thy part as per rules laid down in this universe;
Play the game of shadows and lights.

With birth and death, life aflame;
Behold your figure dancing in it,
And the whole world woven in this never ending dream.

Followed By A Shadow
by Demetra Kafantaris

 Submerged in cynicism
 Drowned in despair
 Overcome by fatalism
 Ruled by the unfair
 Expecting naught but misery
 Preparing for more hurt
 Dwelling in negativity
 With decay I do flirt

But optimism bright as day
threatens Shadow's stay
Chasing him to an end
where he has been fastened

So strong is he that no binds hold
his body nor his will
For Shadow causes frost and cold
and cracks all chains still

Thus Shadow's presence here
merges with mine, oh dear!
And now not body nor being
but image, shade and fleeing

 Entangled in duality
 Blinded in blackness
 Cheated of identity
 Branded with madness
 Striving for a new found hope
 Needing strength and will to cope
 Dreading the oncoming cloud
 Seeing, yet again, shade begin to crowd!

To Die In The Lord
by Darlene Kelley

Can I be one with the mountains?
Can my spirit join the sky?

Can I rise above my shackles,
peace within my bosom lie?

When my body surrenders to dust
and the wheat field bears my seed.

My soul returns to god
and I'm caressed by the trees.

With my identity in the earth,
in His creation I'm alive.

The wind will bear my voice
and with the Lord I'll abide.

Answers
by Rex Kelly

Restlessness my ever constant companion --
Pulls at my sleeve and billows it's sails in my chest.
The gift of flowing within the shadows -
Teasing starlights grasp,
        I have learned not to resist.

The unknown destinations promise,
        Always eluding --
Yet tonight it seems so real.
The constant of my heartbeat,
The grace of the quickened step,
This is power, this is purpose,
I have achieved what it is to feel.

At long last my journey has come to its end.
Shimmering silver wed to motionless Blacks.
Here truth in all things begins.
Peace is found, by the waters edge.
Her slender hands held up to caress -
Selfless affection to the spirit of the night.
Their magic flows into all the world.
Through gentle curves and perfect lines.
His nobility has shown throughout to the sun's eternity,
The faceless maidens name,
        ...Fulfilled destiny.

Inside Mother Outside Child
by Whitney Lyons

She is petite and strong-
Everyone says that she's
A beautiful song.
They fail to look within
At a heart that's badly skinned,
There, there is a sad child
Who hungers to be held awhile,
Deep with in her soul is a
Loving mother who struggles to bring
The babe's horrors to an end.
Deep within, this child is bold-
Where her heart can unfold.
The inside mother is a guide
To bring the hidden hungry child outside.

A Force of Light
by Bruce Nassiri Kermane

When I had watered well the plants
in the yard,
a single snail on a protruding leaf
caught my wayward eye.

Being an advocate of growth and green,
I picked the snail with measured moves,
but did not throw it far as I often do
unto the road,
but brought it into the house
and placed it with gentle care,
as if doing something rash,
deep in the kitchen container
beneath the trash.

This day's discarded salad leaves
and broken petals of flowers old
would keep the little creature fair,
until an inadvertent crush maybe
by supper time
would bring the end. I must allow
a greater plan to do the deed.
I could not be the one to smash
the intricate geometry of shock
and shell.

But not content to go along with schemes,
the snail within an hour's time
when I returned
had squirmed it's way atop a cardboard box,
was demanding to pick a fight
with the obtruding, omnipotent
ceiling light.

Attic of My Memories
by Joan A. Kimminau

As I wandered through the attic
        of my memories,
I found my childhood treasures,
        boats and dolls and keys.

But, then I found my family,
        a unicorn and friends,
the joy and love I've needed most,
        that will never end.

While I stumbled in the attic
        of my memories,
rainbows, clouds, and sun
        were shining just to please.

But, best of all I found your love
        with bittersweet recall.
Good and bad, the ups and downs,
        we've always had it all.

As the door closed to the attic
        of my memories,
I took with me a pegasus
        to use in all my dreams.

Sorrow And Hope Of The Blue-Eyed Indian
by Candyce King

I am the deer you killed, more for sport than for meat;
I am the wolf that you hunt down from planes in Alaska,
again just to slaughter and not to eat,
I am part Indian; I am of the earth;
so you can't hurt the earth without hurting me.
I am the one you kill at Christmas time to decorate your homes;
I am a Standing Person, a tree;
I love the animals; I hug the trees;
I grieve for them like family lost;
but no one sees.
I am the buffalo, who the Indians saw as an elder,
who taught wisdom to the medicine man.
And like the buffalo, you will kill me, just cause you can.
But I believe the spirits of the Indians and animals
and trees you slaughtered are still alive;
and like them, no matter what you do,
my spirit will always survive.

Letter to the Universe
by Kara Kneubuhler

I am the blue-green that
stands out in your night,
I am the one who has
seen wrong and right.
I have witnessed the birth of man,
I have witnessed his fight for land.
I knew a man who could
make the lame fly,
I was there when a
cross held Him high.
I control the mighty, dark sea,
I decide when volcanic
ash is set free.
I am the one who offered
a home to the winds,
but they are too restless-
do they run from their sins?
Don't run from your sins,
for our Maker believes:
If you ask forgiveness, you shall receive.
I know that all good things
must come to an end,
and this is why I write
this poem to send.
I am crying, I am calling,
I am dying, I am falling.
Please help me- I hold joy
beyond all exhilaration-
I am planet Earth,
headed toward annihilation.

The Truth of Me
by Daniel Kolb

The truth of me
Is the truth in me
I need your truth
To be true to me

The best of me
Is for you to see
The best of thee
You I truly see

To Madison
by Rachel Koch

I fell in love with your little blond head
and the way you tried to laugh and waddle
all at the same time.
And could you have possibly known
how it took my breath away
every time you fell asleep on my shoulder?
The love of a man could not compare
to your faithful hugs or sloppy kisses.
You would not let me out of your sight
to go to school or even down the hall
to get a drink of water.
How well I remember our conversations.
    "Who love you Maddie?"
    "Rachel loves me."
I could hold you forever
even now, though you will not permit it.
Being four means that
I cannot be your best friend.
That I mist watch you from a distance.
but is enough for me
to be in the same room
and to see your comical face peer at me
as if you sometimes still remember.

A Self Portrait
by Vitaly Korschow

Here sits a man
Two century too young
The world has changed
Without him
His body is in a world of crowds
With his soul in a world of wilderness
He is a prisoner of time,
An eighteenth century romantic soul
In a twentieth century body
In the same place at the same time
The soul wishes to go back to where it should be
With the body wanting to stay where it is
This has put him out of place with the world
Or has it put the world out of place with him

Why did it become
A body and soul two century apart
His contemporary mind
is part of three worlds
That of his mother Austria
His father Russia
And birthplace of America

So how come is he so happy
When he doesn't
know who he is
Or what he wants

The Band Of Gold
by Sharen L. Loucks

In love, they caress
one another.
Through life, they walk
down the winding path in
love's sweet hold.
Once unknown, now destined
for happiness in their hearts.
The band of gold upon
their fingers tells the
story of their love for
one another, of hearts
intertwined, by a lasting
bond of love.

Sisyphus Goes On A Drunk
by Lester C. LaFrentere

   Hmmm ... two-tone town of soap and tar ... up we stumble ... dumdadum ... here everybody hides inside ... buildings white and powdery soft ... scrape the sky with steeples high ... seemed so strong and young at first ... paint applied so long ago ... flakes fly down like seagull feathers ... buildings seemed so straight at first ... set to fall in on me now ... here's a hill ... now let it roll ...

   Here in this valley ... human sweat and muscatel ... soot, flesh, tobacco, tar ... no cologne and cool fresh air ... buildings smaller ... flatter too ... leaning in on one another ... doors all open ... holes inside ... people hurrying ... angry tongues ... feet walk up ... feet walk down ... buildings crumbling all around ... never stop swaying gently, slowly ...

   Strangest thing about this place ... two torn ends of a half-ass town ... so intensely symbiotic ... sewn together by somebody's hands ... who the hell could rip them apart ...

   Where the hell is that goddamn rock ... aaar ... let it roll ...

           let it roll...

The Butler Did It
by 'Rida Larche

You are a book...and I've read you before...
 and before that,
  and before that!

You're a lovely fantasy...
 Written in your own unique style,
But although the introduction
 is different,
 and the middle has its variations,
 the conflict is the same.

I wonder why I take the time to read you?
No matter how diversified
 the storyline may get,
  I already know the ending by heart!

The Struggle
by Brenda Maillet

Weary body, harboring a worn soul.
Roaring, silently in pain.
Alienated, my exceptance of self, denied.
I labor in vain.
The claws of depression dig deep into my inner flesh.
An affliction I find hard to shake free of.
I need to cleanse this contaminated soul.
If only tears could free me.
I struggle to continue, hour by hour.

Heart Monitor
by Jodi Leckbee

Her father told her about a man who was in cardiac rehab with him. He was 78 and had already had six bypass operations. "The nurses keep a close eye on him. We were riding the exercise bikes yesterday and a nurse came by to check his pulse. They make a big fuss over him. I told him if he keeled over dead to fall in the other direction because I didn't want anything to break my rhythm." Her father was himself again this way, speaking in stories with punch lines and awaited laughter. She always laughed at his stories. By laughing she was saying I love you. The words themselves her family never spoke aloud. What was it about the phrase that frightened them all so? She was driving, the doctor had warned him that driving could be too stressful for him so soon after his heart attack. So she moved the blazer carefully along the blacktop, letting big rigs pass by in a blur, conscious always of the speedometer drifting lazily on fifty-five. Every now and then he would comment on a defensive driving lesson he had learned at training seminars the company had paid for him to attend. She always looked over making eye contact, pretending she was taking his advice to heart. She felt he deserved that from her. At the next stop her brother argued that she was driving too slow,"I kept slowing down to forty-five to let you catch up with me, what is the problem?" His voice jumping eagerly over the sound of cars passing them in a buzz on the distant highway. She smiled at his impatience. Her father piped in, "Your going to have the next attack, if you not careful." The procession continued. Darren was leading the way to Austin. He lived there now and had volunteered to help move their sister Carri into her dorm. She was leaving home for the first time, moving ahead with Darren, a blur up ahead, small enough to touch with your finger. An hour later her father was asleep beside her, his arms crossed in a stubborn pose, a straw hanging out of his mouth. The straw was the doctor's suggestion to help him adjust life without a cigarette in his face and a screen of smoke to look through. She searched her brain for a memory of anyone other than her father driving on family trips, he was the expert, the person in charge, he knew the way without ever looking at a map. She wondered what he felt sitting beside her, letting her decide when to pass, how fast to drive, what exit to take. But even with him asleep her hands stayed frozen in the ten and two position and the speedometer never ventured above the appropriate level. She tried to move the blazer as smoothly as possible off the highway onto the exit, her eyes darting anxiously to her father's closed lids. "Don't wake up" she prayed to herself. She wanted him to sleep, to rest, the way she did as a child with the sound of the road beneath them, echoing the divisions of the payment with a slight thump, a steady, rolling heartbeat.

Restless
by Charles Lowry

  Fear envelopes feelings of mortality
  Fleeting moments of restless iniquity
  Darkness surrounds emotions unsure
  Of labors and trails yet to endure

   Lost, wasted, unused ability
  Quixotic battles things unseen
  Surrounded by foes, faces sublime
  Unstoppable seconds, vanishing time

   Standing against the intangible
  Fighting the battle without control
   Never knowing victory's gain
   Slashing away, giants lay slain

 Be still 'O kindred spirit, peace is upon you
Refreshing, revitalizing as early morning dew
  A ray of light amidst a violent storm
   Giving faith of the newly born
  Commandments of love calling to obey
  Strength and courage to face another day

Velvet Petals
by Anne Marie Legan

They stood in silent rows on the grassy slope of land.
The last speckled patches of sunlight silence jiggled across
The eroding slate headstones,
Making their inscriptions as clearly as the final judgment hand.

The last memorial of names, already forgotten.
Nothing now but a few words surmounted by a cross.
Once the glimmer of a memory they had in time, now loss.

Beneath the sod, only bones, their souls departed.
Their mute voices haunting the silence.

In her hand she clutched a single rose, now wilting.
Her heart aching as if a backbone of a whale
Pressed against it, heavy and sharp.

The wind curled along the path;
Swaying the weeds that had grown in the cracks.

Crouching low, her face pressed against the tombstone,
With half-closed eyes stinging with tears.
How long had it been? How many years?

Touching the small mound, her fingers ruffling across the grass,
As if it would tell her something of his past.

The pain and bitterness stroking her face, each limb, resting on her heart.
It was the burial plot of a man she never knew, long departed.

She laid down the velvet petals quite motionless
As she gazed
At her father's grave.

Madelyn
by Mary Jane Leisey

In the cafe at the train station she
looks at me from her chair, kneeling,
arms propped on it's back, resting
her chin, pondering my presence.

As I wave and smile to her, behind the
shield, curious but reticent, the 12 month
old child, is willing to bloom if she
decides I am deserving of her trust.

Symbolically she reaches for a connection
between her and my inner child, hand
outstretched, in awestruck wonderment
she smiles pure joy and babbles a greeting.

We play peek - a - boo until she's tired of it,
then she climbs off her chair and pushes
her stroller down the aisle, never looking
back, our fleeting connection gone.

Sweet Madelyn, you touch my life, let
me into yours, and I saw not my dandelions,
but beheld the beauty and essence of lilacs,
and felt the unconditional trust of innocence.

Springtime
by Gerree Leslie

Dawn gently nudges night-time out of her way ushering
in an efflorescent spring day.
Sunbeams play peek-a-boo with tousled leaves on the
trees, set in motion by a mischievous breeze.
Birds awaken, twitter, then burst into song.
An exuberant bee skips from daisy to tulip humming
along.
Multi-hued butterflies choreographed ballets in mid-air;
and spiders spin intricate webs with artistic flair.
Bushy-tailed squirrels scamper 'round a hollow tree
stump.
An army of ants declare war on an old rusty pump.
Wild flowers paint designs on a high grassy knoll.
Beyond a fence, a mare nurses her wobbly-legged foal.
A meandering brook mutters to every pebble and rock.
Tinkling bells herald a herder and his ovine flock.
Mother Nature ponders summer, winter, and fall, then
softly whispers; "spring is the most exciting season
of all!"

Reflections
by Daryl Lewis

With passing time upon me
I see my father's face
Reflected in the mirror
I've now taken his place

For once we were so different
Wild youth was part to blame
I often saw him so unjust
And now we are the same

With years I've gained maturity
And some knowledge about life
I've anguished over children
And seen the purpose of his strife

He was distanced from his father
Until the later years
Like I with him so much was lost
In the midst of proudly fears

We cried so when we lost him
But his heritage has not died
For I've now stepped up to take his place
And fill his shoes with pride

May I ever be so worthy
To provide security
With love and peace to those I love
As my lasting legacy.

The Beggar
by Steven Morrison

On a cold winter's day,
There he stands upon the street,
His image is seen through falling snow,
While strangers he stops to meet.
We all see him from time to time,
And our ancestors saw him too,
Like them we hear his plaintive speech,
On that cold street like an echo.
He cries out for a dime, a dollar,
As cup in hand he stands and speaks,
And although the snow obscures his image,
In our minds an image he wreaks.
He reminds us of that great blight,
That has plagued our present and past,
He walks the street as a symptom,
To show us poverty continues to last.

Longed for Places
by Joy Lindsay

I come from a place
Where beauty itself cascade
Down gigantic rocks
And nature paints the earth with colours
That could rival any spectrum...

I come from a place
where loveliness climbs up over... and
In cool shimmer upon blue Mountain dips down

Ah what island paradise
Oh how she gets caressed
Lulled from every side
By soft blue/green-aquamarine Caribbean waters

Yes I loved these longed for places
There ... where rainfall comes to patter
My sun drenched roof
And straining down in cooling falls
Upon my red veranda ...

Blow trade winds blow
and whistle me a melody
Let buttercups flutter like butterflies do
Like kernels of corn on the
Threshing floor - scattered - pretty
On the grass ... let them dance
In their places at last.

Ye ... I come from, and I long for this place
This piece of land where beauty knows no shame.
Is so fine, so undaunted ... and ... so forever vain.

Courage and Pies
by Carrol C. Lowe

Agnes C. graduated from the eighth grade, married, gave birth to seven children, and helped raise them to maturity during the "Great Depression." With the help of her children, she operated the family farm five days each week while her 40-year-old husband attended and graduated from college.

A few years later her husband left his position as minister to a four-church circuit and became an army chaplain. He was assigned to the European Theatre during the hectic days of World War II.

Agnes answered the plea of the parishioners by securing an "Exhorter's License" and filling the pulpits each Sunday morning. But first she had to learn to drive. The auto was under constant stress and dents appeared regularly. Agnes took the whole matter in stride. Her daughters were all in school and two of them were cheerleaders in high school. She appeared at ball games all over the area, and on Sunday morning continued to fill the pulpits. She also attended midweek services, church conferences, church socials, and various committee meetings at four churches. In her "spare time" she wrote countless letters to her three boys and husband, all in various war zones. She also wrote to friends, relatives, and parishioners in uniform everywhere.

At the end of World War II she turned the churches over to her returning husband. As a bonus, he also received a battered car and a group of undisciplined daughters. The parishioners had very little to say about her sermons. They were quite vocal, however, about the high quality of her pies and how they would be missed at the church suppers and ice cream socials!

Unknown Wonderer
by Bonnie Luna

As a child grows he learns, he knows,
Only what he sees and hears.
But the child who hears not a soul,
Learns through what he feels.

If what he feels is good and wise,
He'll grow a responsible man.
But if he falls along the line,
Who is to blame?
Might he know right from wrong?
Though he's never heard to tell.
Yet he steps in his friends steps,
Only to find he fell.

Can he find a place in this world,
Where others like him have failed?
Can people trust in what he sees?
Can he trust in what he feels?

Imani
by Robert Minnifield

She is
My heart and extension of my soul
Through her I may love again
Precious innocence,
I'm her Warrior in Life or Death
Virgin Emotions dance and
refresh in this angelic innocence
I'm humbled by the Miracle of life
May destiny be kind!!

The Wife's Story
by Bertha L. Mack

We started young, parenting six of our own.
He seemed to father me.
The work was hard
the hours were long
Yet wonderful in so many ways.

Could that house be a home?
We proved it could together
Never alone, side by side
Exhausted at day's end.

Tears and tempers entered our domain.
Comedic solace brought back reality
our comfort zone retained.

Love, a word used less in those early days.
No time given to walks in the meadows.
Holding hands calloused but kind.
Gentle love unspoken.

Children, held close in their cartoon world.
Visual images on a screen
while Mother cleans.

So quiet now, where are the voices?
warm climate our goal now our legacy.

We wait in silent rooms
an isthmus between us.
Inculpable as a child in our private world.

Love, is now our word.
On tethered pillows before repose.
Long days and night our anticipation.

One Tiny Step
by Carrie Maddux

I heard them softly say
I took one tiny step
Upon the double sea
Thinking life beautiful
Till it crushed about me

Crushed me to the earth
Burst my heart in twain
Scattered my faith asunder
Scorched my fevered brain

Causing me to regret
Days so short so few
Which gave a draught of evening
But none of morning dew

Take Time To Pray
by Joy Malcolm

Do you know the most important thing that you should do today?
It really isn't shopping, or finding a new game to play.
Too often we find, it's so easy to lose sight
Of what should be an every day practice and a pure delight.
If you really want to have a super good day,
Start every morning out right.
    Take time to pray.

When you have a day that starts out all wrong,
Nothing seems to go right the whole day long,
You get so frustrated, to the point of tears,
Yet you just keep jamming and grinding your gears.
Did you take time at the start of the day?
No, you probably didn't
    Take time to pray.

Our Lord is patiently waiting and is always there for you.
No matter what the trouble, he will see you through.
He died for your sins a long time ago.
But you must remember, you're gonna reap what you sew.
He's just waiting to guide you, through each and every day,
It is up to you to
    Take time to pray.

Where The Roses Never Fade
by Imo McGill

A home is just a dwelling
Unless there's love within
And lots of joy and laughter
As each new day begins

Built sturdy as an oak tree
Unbending in the wind
A shelter to protect us
A place to meet old friends

May the circle be unbroken
As we stand there face to face
If only in our memories
That time cannot erase

Our hearts entwined forever
Of dreams that we had made
Just our little piece of heaven
Where the roses never fade.

The White Feather
by Ann McCray

The white feather, oversized, ethereal,
its center vein, a sitting place, this white feather
rides invisible winds, and carries me.

I am not surprised by such friendship.
We fly together. I am a child with long, flowing hair.

Then, dream-turvy, Feather turns Horse,
sturdy, stout, snorting hello,
pacing, panting, pawing the ground.

He invites me to ride, to share
his magnificence again, pure delight.

I am weightless. My balance is perfect.

I have no agenda, no place to go,
only this one perfect moment,
sacred communion I cannot define.

We sail, as though today would not turn into tomorrow,
as though space were made only for such imaginary wanderings,
as if waking were not possible from such vision.

Slowly, slowly, Horse freezes into inanimate stick horse,
child's toy with more force than Feather or animal, together.

Stick Horse pulls a rickety cart,
old-fashioned, wood, red in color, spots.

The cart carries me, flitting, flying, we dart
up sheer facings, lush green mountains,
swooping down into meadowed-valleys,
my hair streaming gloriously, behind.

Forceful air pulls my face back, tight.
My eyes close against bright light.

Freedom.
Freedom.
Freedom!

Victory
by Corinne R. McGonagle

The cells are screaming
Her brow resigns in oppression,
suppressing the cries
with brutal force

The nut and shell melt together
but sustenance is still lacking.
The organs know
which ingredient will revive the army,
conquering the sickness]That lingers deep through the core.

Scarce and fragile
The nut is falling quickly
dangling over the cliff
The hungry ocean below...
The ground quivers.

The treks to be explored
other battles awaiting...
One must find the tree
in order to win the war.

The Land Still Lies
by Chris McKinnon

> stretched
> before my eyes
>
> itself pulled
> over a frame
> stretched
> cross a rack
>
> its own pain
> surmounted
> its bertillon eyes
> dulled
>
> its moue of mouth
> strung shut
>
> its arms bent back
> a bow
> its under girth
> beams a rainbow agony
>
> its tongue puffed
> hangs an overstuffed pillow
>
> no rain

Delage Adrift
Guy Delage swam the Atlantic
by Craig W. McLuckie

Days and days at sea
The monotony of water-horizon
Of endless sky lack of cloud
Of inhabiting the rubber-sealed self

Its emptiness its fear of what's there
Or not

Concession in the waterproofed fax
Communicant with critics first
With public euphoria next

Minute interruptions once fax is dead
Include the shooed away shark
The comic book "biff" on its snout

Bored with it
The 'swim' work life
I drift

Currents--nature's course--move
Me faster than my propulsion
Give ironic insight to pedant's plea
That my drifting float
Is technology on one side, man on th' other
In a singular duality which offers a gripping
Metaphor of contemporary western man.

Come on David le Breton!
Sociologist of valorized despair.
I floated from Cape Verde
A fifty-five-day cross-Atlantic
Drift to Barbados....

Heroic...
Only a demetaphorised ennui
With life was marked out there.

Untitled
by Robin McNeely

As these stagnant winter moments drift slowly by;
I marvel at each snowfall's ability to
    purify and caress this scarred land
The trees, barren now, asleep among the whiteness;
    await the warm April showers to
    stir the life within their branches.

In the frozen refuge, it was so easy
    to be touched by his genuine zeal'
    it enriched the newness and calmed
    the crisp, light winds.
As we trespassed across the trails,
    our conversation was a beacon;
    it guided the fresh, informal meeting

Each thawing effects the countryside
    trickling mud, and other debris;
    preparing the soil for more fruitful seasons to come
I reflect on change; on new directions and
    on our comfortable beginning
    fascinated by our relaxed discussions
    framed by the scenic white innocence.

Recently, springtime has teased us;
    with singing birds and sprouting perennials
    each eluding to Earth's annual rebirth
It's refreshing to meet a kindred spirit
    someone else seeking an inner-balance and
    who is also awed by the seasonal forces
We are weaving this new tapestry formed with
    gentle harmony threaded by instinct.

Dedicated to Bill

Runaway Mules
by Martha Mervish

Back in the 1920's and early 30's, my father always had a ribbon cane patch. When it was ready to be harvested, he and my brothers would strip, cut and stack the cane and haul it to the mill.

The old syrup mill sat in the woods, on a gentle sloping hill near a cool, spring water stream. The freshly cut, striped ribbon cane was fed into it by hand. A mule hitched to a wooden frame, turned the cogs that crushed the cone, by going in a circle around the mill. A long two-inch pipe or narrow trough carried the sweet juice down to the syrup pan, consisting of several compartments. Men worked from sunup to sundown, skimming the syrup and stoking the fire under the long, wide pan. When the juice was cooked into syrup, it was poured into gallon buckets and sealed. At our house, a pitcher of syrup was always on the table to be served with hot biscuits and freshly churned butter.

The men did not take time out to go home for dinner. The women would cook their dinner and take it to them. I remember when I was around 8 years old my sister Jessie Mae, age 16, came to the house to pick up their dinner. She was driving a wagon and a team of young mules. Mama had the dinner ready and packed to go. They put it in the wagon with a large water jug. My job was to hold the jug to keep it from bouncing around. I sat in the middle of the wagon bed. Mama sat in the back with her feet hanging out. We had to go down a long hill with a curve and a bridge at the bottom. When we started down the hill the mules spooked and started running away. Jessie Mae could not stop them, the brakes had failed. They went faster and faster. By the time they reached the curve at the bottom of the hill, they were going full speed. When they went around the curve, the bed of the wagon flipped off, throwing me to the side of the road into a grassburr patch. Jessie Mae was pinned underneath the wagon bed like a chicken in a coop. Mama jumped out when the mules started running. The dinner was scattered all over the road. The mules kept going over the bridge and over the next hill. When we didn't show up with the dinner, one of the men came looking for us. They lifted the wagon bed and let Jessie Mae out. It was a miracle that it landed over her instead of on her. We were thankful she survived.

I Sit Here Listening
by Melissa Miller

I sit here listening and the stab from your words rocks front to back with my body.
"I need you to understand what I'm saying to you. I know that this is hard on you, but I wish you could forgive him, just this once."
"Forgive him!" .....If I were to forgive him would it help my pain? You think because I love him. I should continue to hurt, or in some way, your words can erase his lies. This isn't about what I want, it's about his deceit, I have no control.
And if I allow time to reminisce, to smile, to cry? My thoughts will only intrude on my memories, never allowing me to relive the good.
I think of all that I should have been, or should have erased from my past, realizing I'm not at fault.
He was incredible to look at. One of the best looking of the many I had seen. Nobody could look at him and see the insecurity that stretched for miles. You did not know him in his angry mode, lashing out, over and over again-his manic state-the frame of which he is in now. Some of us have seen it, as I have, only now it is clear.
I pampered him. They say that is important. I was good to all of them, but for him, I tried perfection. I did all of the things the older women said were "right".

Space
by James E. Milstead

Drifting upon the surface.
Across the waves without a purpose.
A leaf passed silently by.
As the wind moans a tender sigh.

Nature's choir dedicates this dance.
As currents ponder love's chance.
Upon the ripples shall it stay.
Or as the sun, just fade away?

As the loon upon a barren sea.
Unto none a lonesome plea.
Alone and drifting to and fro.
For only the currents truly know.

Streams upon a rock trickles slowly down.
Without a whisper, without a sound.
A leaf waltzing this painful dance.
It's now up to fate, the final chance.

Still drifting upon a cold wet surface.
Across the ripples, but with a purpose.
A leaf passes silently by.
As the wind moans a compassionate cry...

A Young Willow
by Michael Mitchell

On the farthest island's shore is a young willow.
Quietly swaying in a breezy caress,
Her long green leaves give soft invitation
For the wind to abide on it's pillow.
Often birds cross the water and rest
On it's swaying limbs in peaceful meditation.

Oh that I were wind or wing
And I would cross that shore and sing
How willows weeping is only lore
For my young willow would weep no more.

Choices
by Debbie Minnema

Life has many traveled paths, so many roads to take.
Decisions overwhelm sometimes, but must be ours to make.
Sometimes we take a detour and it seems we're moving in reverse.
But would we appreciate rolling downhill, if uphill were not a curse?
We can always take the scenic route, like many people do.
For others there's the highway, if you prefer not to have a view.
If you can't see where you're going, perhaps you move a bit too fast.
We cannot move ahead sometimes unless we learn from what we've passed.
Some people always take a right turn at the intersection,
While others, time and time again, will go the wrong direction.
Life for some seems like a stroll through gardens in the park,
Others feel they're on a cliff-side road while driving in the dark.
Those who have gotten lost and stopped to take a nap
probably chose long ago to leave without a map.
Sometimes we feel so tired, like we're traveling alone.
We all take individual roads, but all are going home.
All roads join together and in this there is connection.
No matter which route we take we end up the same direction.
Whichever way we get home, there will be occasion to rejoice.
We all learn the same lessons; how we learn them is our choice.

Easter Days
by Joyce Morgan

I lift my arms wide open,
Heaping on worship and praise
For the Resurrection!
And all resurrections yet to come
To us.
I lift my arms wide open
In worship and praise
For all these Easter Days!
For all the roadside earthen vases filled
With wild dogwood, becandled pine!
Do you keep yours from one year to the
Next?
I was just wondering...
You know what I do with mine...
I scatter them in my daily valleys
And on my daily hillsides!

Oh, Resurrection I can hide in!
Oh, Easter Days where I can abide in
His warm arms of springtime color!

Raw Dawn
by Juli Morgan

Behold the raw dawn
    What have you for me today?
    Will this be the day I die?
We desire a clean slate
    How much will we pay?
    Can we loosen all ties?
Someday I'll have to let go
    But not today
    Perhaps not ever
Your skin is so sweet
    That each time I smell it
    I behold the raw dawn

Behold the new day
    Become lost in it's splendor
                White light; white noise
Build no walls
    like the ridges of the mountains
    It only blackens your soul
As the snow melts away
    Feel the warmth of our heart
    Open your minds
Behold the raw dawn

A Pen For My Thoughts
by Icie Moore

This ink is stealing my thoughts,
It's writing them all down.
If it doesn't stop soon,
My mind will run out,

Of silly things I want to say,
Things to think too.
Because this ink is telling,
Everything to you.

I've tried laying the pen down,
But my hand won't let go.
I think I have a plan,
Maybe I don't know.

I'll put my mind to rest,
By quickly falling to sleep.
Then my pen will have to fall,
For my hand will be tired and weak.

I'll wake up in the morning,
And read what this ink has said.
That without asking permission,
It snuck out of my head.

Reflections
by Mary Nagode

Upon the embers of life's dwindling fire
This mortal is delighted to reflect,
The grinding wheels of this worlds sweet empire,
And live again the glow in retrospect;
Delay the ticking clock up in the tower
And share again the joys that love can bring;
Delay the final striking of the hour
My thoughts echo a symphony of spring.

Come gather round and taste again the wine
The candle's glow still lingers where we dine,
There are as yet, so many binding ties,
Let us enjoy the flame before it dies;
Life's beauty touches once again this soul
Viewing the fragrant blossoms in the bowl.

Scents of Summer
by Sean Nyberg

Nose is aroused
By familiar smells
Scents of missed season
The smell of fresh cut grass
The odor of mosquito repellent
The scent of suntan lotion
For three seasons
They were not around
Today they return
Bringing pleasure
To nose, mind, heart, and body
In a few short months
They will disappear again

Stillness...
by Barbara Newton

Stillness...
And the only sound - a beating heart
As I wrap my arms around a tree trunk
And listen to the earth's song.
Rivers flow to keep him alive,
Slowly I kiss with swollen lips
As I bask in the glow of love;
His eyes open with a smile
And in return he wraps his
Branches around my tormented body
to soothe me with a tender caress of a breeze
And whisper like the wind sweet nothings.

This House
(Just spoke to Me)
by Jeffrey S. Minton

The curtains blew with the wind
and your ghost pirouetted through,
your smell was all about the room
and my soul took a dance with you.

I heard the ocean waves crash
as I walked around your room,
and I felt your tender hand
and your love and spirit exhumed.

You let me go, too soon,
as I walk about these rooms.
I can't forget your love, you see,
cause this house just spoke to me.

I walk the beach at night,
but my heart won't let you go.
Dreams are filled with nightmare lights,
I feel lost without a soul.

I finally shut my eyes,
I see your face and tender smile.
I take out your hand for me this time,
and we will sit and talk a while.

You let me go, too soon,
as I walk about these rooms.
I can't forget your love, you see,
cause this house just spoke to me.

When Old Roads Are Forgotten
by Joseph V. Novak

I think it best from time to time
to burn a bridge or two
To close the road behind us
and find one that is new.
Roads grow weary-developed ruts
when constantly back trodden
And new roads travel lighter
when old roads are forgotten.

When Unicorns Ran Free
by M.L. Moeller

In a land before time, under skies so blue
Unicorns ran free, two by two.
Shaking heads so proud, as they played,
Shaking off their horns, what a picture they made.

They ran through valleys and over steep hills.
They danced in summer warmth and winter's chills.
Fleet of foot, beautiful coats of purest snow;
Sparks turning to butterflies wherever they go.

It was said that evil would never have its day
As long as least one unicorn came to us to play.
And I remember in the golden grasses below
Watching them frolic, the silver horns aglow.

In the morning sun they travelled the breeze;
Through forests and rivers they crossed with ease.
Sometimes they would look up at my home
As I stood by my door in the afternoon alone.

Those were the years and I in my youth,
I took for granted I would always find truth.
For weren't the unicorns still running free.
That in itself could reassure me.

Then one day when my hair was white
I didn't see any unicorns as day turned night.
Where were they when we need them most.
No longer innocent could we boast.

It's been years since unicorns danced
In the meadows where once they pranced.
With them they took all of our hope,
For when innocence departs how do we cope?

Loving Someone
by Dena A. Morton

Like a bird taking to flight,
even if for the very first time;
like a duckling swimming downstream
in a strange new world;
loving someone never came so natural.

Like a mother giving birth to a child,
feeling complete as she watches him take his first breath;
like a child being dependent on their mother
for the first few years of life;
loving someone never felt so real.

Like touching for the first time
and being so excited you're speechless;
like a passionate kiss that you're unsure of,
but then hope it never ends;
loving someone never brought such joy.

Like falling asleep as it rains
listening to the pitter-patter of each drop;
like when our eyes meet
and it seems as though I've known you forever;
loving someone never came so easy.

Like gazing at the stars on a clear night
and wondering exactly how they were created;
like the exuberant flow of a waterfall
as it dashes against the rocks below;
loving someone never felt so magical.

Like when you caress my body ever so gently
and in return, I yours;
like waking with you by my side
knowing how much you mean to me;
loving someone never felt so right!

Forgotten
by Ronda Mullins

Left in a closet
on a dust covered shelf,
the hatbox sits precariously,
ready to fall.
Annoyed with age,
worn with time,
Darkened recess
fills the empty space,
its contents
spilled onto the floor,
tending a corner bare.
The weaver of straw and roses pink,
ambles the fashion trends
of baseball caps and visors,
the haughty strut in front of the mirror,
bargaining on the years past.
The mirror reflects
on relics old,
the little girl Mom
flicks the brim
of the cap she is wearing,
finger tracing the wrinkled lines
that flatter her T-shirt,
and she smiles, bounding from the room.

Life Is Like Sand
by Patrick Nate

Life is like sand that shifts, lures and blows,
and time as like grains of sand become too endless to test,
While the seasons enlist a time to be valued,
for that which falls through our days.

To give us meaning to the hours that meter out our lives,
until we must reckon our worth and purpose.
Whether now just, or jest, or jilted, or jaded,
these few sentiments must thus remain.

Here now we bear witness to the fault or the deed,
once done can not be put asunder.
Shadows cast nor the light of the past,
nor the tainted moment of its misspent deeds can ever fade.

Now we press our souls against the flowers of life's good earth,
to thus last taste of the sweetness twice remembered.
There now we stay until we slumber and dream but memories,
until life and the sands shift no more.

Devil's Time
by Hawani Negussie

I met a time, a devil's age
these times tricked my seconds to age.
God lent me time
where devils rhyme.
My time you see
doesn't watch thee.
My devils rhyme
,REPEAT,
　　it's time
,AGAIN,
　　you say
thy devil's way.
It never ends
time's devils friends.
So is this time
look at your watch,
your day turns night
while devils catch.

I have a rhyme,
where devils time.

The Flames of Love
by Kimberly A. Neuhauser

We used to love each other
with a special kind of flair
my heart use to flutter
whenever I saw you there

Lately our life is in turmoil
we're filled with anger and regret
we can't stop fighting
and refuse to forget

We fight about the dishes
the laundry, money and kids
we even fight over the TV remote
and who didn't put on the tooth paste lids

We can't stop hurting each other
even when we try
God knows how long we can hold out
till one of us says good bye

I pray that our love isn't over
it seems such ashame
to have shared so much together
to have it go down in flames

To My Companion
by Obie O'Brien

The silver veil of winter had not yet fully dissolved into the bright hues of springtime, when I took your hand in mine.

We walked down the pathways of life arm in arm, conscious of the beauty that God had provided for us to see, smell, taste, hear, feel and spiritually partake of.

We have enjoyed the blessings of this biological existence always loving one another.
We have at times felt the pain and grief that also comes with this life. I feel consolence in your sweet embrace at these times of despair.

Our children joined our trek for a time, then moved on their own pathways. Then our grandchildren and now our great grandchildren are here. Summer has been long over.
Autumn is nearing it's end. Already the forest that was ablaze with bright colors applied by the master's brush has begun to fade.

We know that as winter draws nigh, our time here grows shorter. Had our stay together been a thousand years we would judge it not long enough.

We know that inevitably out trek will take us to the end of this mortal life. That we will arrive at a veiled gate through which one of us will be called. The other one must remain for a time, waiting for another to call.

It is my sincere prayer that after we both arrive in that other land, I will be judged worthy to again take your dear sweet hand in mine and with you walk down those infinite pathways for time and all eternity.

"Poetry"
by Pauline O'Connor

To you a salutation, for your loyalty to me,
Ever since I contracted the virus H.I.V.
I only wish that others had the courage you possess,
You've really been a friend to me during my distress.

My sickness knows no prejudice in this society,
It's vicious as it takes away my pride and energy.
Thanks for understanding, I know you really care.
It's plain to see your love for me surpasses all your fears.

But if they had the understanding, about the way it's passed,
Then they might treat the victims with a little more class.
Some get it through behaviors that they know are bad,
And some have gotten it innocently, this my friend is sad.

Yet all in all the end result is not the way it came,
But that we are positive, and we are dying just the same.
At times I cannot help myself, I get weaker every day,
This disease takes away everything in a cold and tragic way.

And as it slowly does it also takes your pride,
and the way that people stare at you, you want to run and hide.
But I really try to understand the reasons why they are scared,
And then I realize a lack of knowledge always brought out fear.
They cannot catch it from me in casual contact,
I just yearn in my last days for the companionship I lack.
But you have been so wonderful this I realize,
So here's my "SALUTATION" before I close my eyes.

I am a man that's dying, and soon I will be gone,
But I pray for you my loyal friend a life that's very long.

Bitter Snow
by Cindy Odom
(special thanks to Kevin)

Junco, Snowbird.
Would do anything
to get the nefarious stuff,
Never seeming to get enough
...........he'd even sell his soul.

A disciple of his powder icon
(substitute for love.)
An advocate for his atropine,
Only to lose animation after
          a month
      a week
   a day
with the crystalline CZAR.

His life is up
   wasted
spent.
Consumed beyond any hope.

Then he is found face down in snow broth,
Without his sanctimonious snow.
Just another junkie
    friend
  lover
son, who will be glad to see him go?

Shrewdly, the idol snatches another
Neophyte to subdue.
Just another son
      lover
         friend
            junkie...........

Call Of The Wild
by Robin Osborne

I hear the call,
The beating of drums,
Stars winking to life,
I glide by,
Soaring to the beat,
The call I hear,

Wildly in flight,
far above the heavens,
The blackened sky,
Points of light,
So bright!

Hear the beat,
Winged friends,
To flight!

Answer the call,
Clearly heard,
Call of the wild,
So strong,
I fear to feel,
A winged beat,
To heal.

Baby Portals
by Reba Owen

The tracings farthest back,
Seem
As Persephone's year,
Only Spring,

Sweet salty smell of single roses,
Bridal veil,
Spirea,
White petals falling,
On big fat pink roses,
Along the gravel walk,
Where the mother
Salted
The gray rocks,
With extra pearls,
From the gold fish bowl.

Daphne whose scent,
Addicted all,
Before and after.
Bright poppies,
With dangerous, black centers.
White lilacs,
As ivory carvings,
Within ivory carvings,
Within ivory carvings.

And Fall remembered,

Periwinkle sky,
Maple leaves
Of butter.
Johnathans white as sugar,
Carmeled by the mother,
Every October 13th.

Being Battered Never Mattered
by Anita Pat Palmonari

Do you recall those wedding vows?
I think of them moreso, now

I am not grieving
for leaving
it was not right
for our children to see us fight.

However, my being battered
never mattered.

To hit without regret
is one thing I cannot forget.

As I grow old
and less bold
with just enough money
to milk or honey,
no car of mine
or dinners with wine.

Not only, my life was shattered,
my being battered never mattered.

Strength, somehow is being strong.
Strength, truly is admitting wrong.

Not all was forsaken,
or ever mistaken
that you should walk free
from what was done to me.

Without paying,
Without saying.

My being battered,
really did matter!

Sotto la luna
by Denise Pierson

Shower me in pools of blue
Beneath the moon
Surround only by you
Sweet words fall from your lips
flowing over me
The soft mist of your kiss caresses my skin
As I float around you but never with you
In an eternal sea of blue

Outing
by Stan Pelfrey

Paintings
Still-life windows
The snow fell
-How life is frozen!
Solids inside canvas,
Watching from outside,
I see this winter-landscape
from a reflection on glass.
Then I realize something
is reflecting in front of
the blowing snow, larger,
and full of life, Me,
remembering all the icy
days of the past.

I Am Your Leper
by Susan Paquette

I am the blind, the illiterate, the unwanted born child.
I am the birth defected, the retarded, the mentally ill.
I am the victim of a contagious disease with symptoms so mild.
I am a victim of AIDS with no curing pills.
I am the poor, an alcoholic, a drug addict, the emotionally weak.
I am the homeless, the raped, the sexually abused to scared to speak.

I am your father, you sister or brother.
I am your neighbor, your boss or grandmother.
I am your aunt, your uncle, your mother and many others.
I am alive all over the world, I am alive in large cities and small towns.
I am your leper who burdens and anchors you down.

I want understanding instead of ridicule.
I need love instead of hate.
I demand dignity within life and deaths view.
I like acceptance, not to be an object to humiliate.
I enjoy happiness not living in despair.
I will cherish peace with laughter and human bonding to share.
I expect independence where prejudice chains me on ruthless grounds.
I demand not to be your leper who burdens and anchors you down.

Aeneas
by Billy Joe Parker

Our man of clean water,
his honor a halo above Trojan hill
where the sweet river
cut through shining grass

and spilled into the Hellespont,
the olden world's great shipping lane.
Aeneas, soft hero,
his soul a peaceful meadow,

lit Roman lamps
that cast law-light
upon a darkened world.
In good, oar driven ships,

Aeneas came to behold
the mist encircled seven hills
to break the ice of ages
and establish Rome.

Guatemalan Terrain
by Carol Parker

So many tear at the truth
soiling this land.
So many corrupt their
sympathetic hand.
Too many fear the iron fist
tucked neatly below
propaganda's mist.

So silent could chill
are bones asleep in the hills.
A greed that sickens -
a sickness that kills.

Jungles where endangered
birds sing louder
than human cries.
Mountains where a culture
is weaved into lies.

The Man I Look Up To
by Quanah Parker

He grew up in a harder time
A time we cannot imagine
A time with milk and bread each meal.
Cruel, abusive, with no way out.

Now times have changed for the better
In his mind, they will never change
Misunderstood, he takes the rap
For all his careless words and deeds.

He knows no better, tactless soul
Suffering alone, he stays home
His den, a man's secret haven.
He's wired for sound, pictures too.

He seems happy in his late years
No one can see life through his eyes
No one knows of his joy or pain
we, the children, misunderstood.

We know not of the leaner years
The years of strife, hunger, the wars
His tactless honesty has hurt
His tainted decisions destroy.

Date With An Enchantress
by Kelly Lee Parsons

Alas, when we met...
Hazel, green flecked eyes,
Brown hair of velvet,
You could hypnotize
With a touch or glance.
Your love, a surprise...
(Thank God for romance!)
My first woman love...
We met, happenstance
And fit like a glove.
At Ember's I wait
With thanks to above
For my gorgeous date.
You're an enchantress.
Under your spell's fate
I will now confess;
From the very start,
I've craved your caress.
You've captured my heart.
From you, I'll n'ere part.

The Philosopher
by C.H. Pyka

His gaze lingered
on the rippling stream,

a young man
whose face held the majesty and strength
of Mt. McLoughlin...
....thoughts caught in the flowing
luster of the water.

Eons later he rose to turn from the passing flow.

A whiteness seemed to crown
the verdure of his being,
...or...was it but a reflection
of the snow-capped mount?

Rise To The Occasion
by Theodore Paster

The sea was calm no trade winds blew as moonlight filled my room.
Then with one sound my sleep was cut the sound was pending doom.
A watchman blew Danger Ahead on his pipe and then he thought,
The crew's asleep and down below a bad place to get caught.
This sound meant every hand on deck no need for explanation.
We all jumped to every man knew he'd rise to the occasion.

We moved too near our enemy and felt their cannons fire,
So if I heard that pipe again I knew what would transpire.
Our ship got ripped at mid-deck. The rigging fell right down.
Their guns were smashing steadily and then I heard that sound.
The pipe sounded Small Boats Away with simple resignation.
As brave men fought the Captain thought, who'll rise to the occasion?

The battle lost; defeat in sight, what sorrows will this bring?
I still saw cannon spitting out, still heard their shrapnel sing.
My shipmates fell most dead I Feared, there's not much I could do.
I saw the water pouring in. The end was near I knew.
The pipe then blew Abandon Ship, I filled with consternation,
That's when I cried to all that died "Please rise to the occasion".

But no man rose at my request they could not even hear.
The screams from other dying men drown out my voice I fear.
I helped young men and salty dogs a few I'd try to save.
By now the ship was sinking fast and would soon be my grave.
But as I sink, I hear; I think, the pipe of consecration.
This journey's done my reward's won.
I rise to the occasion.

Freedom
by Katarina Petrovic

We have built parks so that we can play in the sand
We have pleaded for nice weather because rain bothered us
We have begged the flowers to bloom
so that the air would smell sweet to us

And all that wasn't enough for us to be happy

We have built houses and made walls around them
We have made streets and cities
so that we wouldn't wander around the world
We have made children to have somebody to entertain us

And all that wasn't enough for us to be less lonely

We have closed our minds so that we can capture our thoughts
We have closed our eyes so that we wouldn't see anything but beauty
And we have listened only to what pleased our souls

But all that wasn't enough
for us to deceive our hearts
And all that wasn't enough
for us to be less lonely

That's why

We unlocked the gates of our souls
We let the rain fall
We let the flowers from the park
grow and wither when they like
We let the eyes see the ears hear the heart feel
We let Ugly to be equal with Beauty
We let agony be
the same as happiness and laughter
We knocked down all the fences
and cried from the inside

And in the middle of all that pain
Finally felt happy

Sharp Blue
by Susan Pelman

My knees weaken
and I am in flames
Consuming the ashes of my past
Swallowed into a disappearing age
I am left with a free hand
to touch your life
Solidified within a desire
to merge our histories
I open and close
Shut down
Shut off
I am stone
Drowning in water
Annihilated by fire
I cling to earth
Diving down beneath the ground
To Mother
To solitude
Darkness and safety
Suddenly
shot up to the sky
Breathing sharp blue air
into tarnished lungs
Finding you waiting with patient eyes
I offer my fingers and toes
Fragile into flowing hands

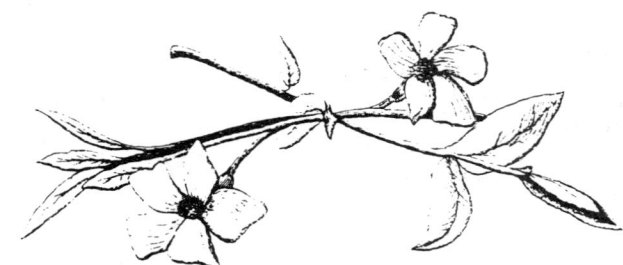

Sunflowers II
by Ms. Ronnie Peterson, RN, MS

SUNFLOWERS...

Enjoy the coolness of a spring rain.
Believing that from the rain,
Brings the promise of new life.

SUNFLOWERS...

Are flexible when the going gets rough.
Yet, remains supple enough to endure.

A SUNFLOWER'S

Roots are deeply planted.
Keeping them firmly in place, and close to the earth.

SUNFLOWERS...

Are admired by many.
They are imitated by many, but, reproduced by few.

SUNFLOWERS...

Add beauty to our world.
Appreciated by those in need and cherished by those who have.

SUNFLOWERS...

Bear seeds for all to enjoy.
Uses only what it needs and shares all that is left.

Don't you wish that people were more like sunflowers?

Literary Suicide
by Fred Phillips

Struggling alone with my absurdist
Fears,
Isolated without the soothing windsong of
Cheers,
Falling into a cool cascade of
Tears,
Spiraling in a raging whirlwind of
Fears,
Rotating without the knowledge of
Direction,
Naked and drowning, stripped of
Protection,
And suddenly, without the slightest
Warning,
The burning sun rises without the
Morning,
And all my order is surely
Dead,
Pure anarchy is loosed upon my
Head,
With surrealistic visions that I
Dread,
The metaphors pronounce me
Dead.

Eternal Fires
by Elma D. Photikarmbumrung

There is a spark in every darkness
that is constant and equated to a fire
continuously burning; the hopes remain
with dreams that never die.
The kindling stays forever on and gives
birth to more fires with heat that sears
the bones.

Youth brings to light the past
when you and I possess eternal fires
our precious hybrids now have borne.

There is a trace of youth in all of us
with open minds and hearts that still
beat to the tune of young emotions.
We strive to let this trace remain unfold.

For even in the after prime of life
We sing the songs and dance the dances
that at one time told us
We will swing and sway forever
And never ever grow old.

Prelude to a Tornado
by Gordon C. Pierce

The brooding sky suddenly separates
into parallel bands of color;
Like the curtains in a proscenium arch,
ready to drop in an instant.
The top curtain a foreboding jet black
with an uncertain bottom edge;
the center strand an indigo blue grey;
the bottom sheet a ghostly white;
contrasted with the brooding mountain range;
a stage waiting for the grand climax to occur.
It is truly a sky fraught with peril!
The top curtain descends,
the colors merge,
and the maelstrom ensues
of shrieking, swirling winds
admit complete utter darkness.
of a place unknown and undiscerned
with a future facing oblivion.

A Boy I Used To Know
by Deborah Podszus

I think that you remind me
Of a boy I used to know.
On a windy day he'd climb the roof
to feel the summer breeze.
On a winter's morn he'd walk to the park
To see the sparkling trees.
He'd ride his bike down by the creek
And try to find rare birds,
He'd run and laugh 'til evening came,
and make up secret words.
He'd lie in the grass beneath the stars
To find the constellations,
And wait to see a shooting star
With everlasting patience.
But no one else could feel the thrill
Of the wind blowing through their hair,
Or knew which birds were so unique,
Or have such fun with Truth-or-Dare.
And no one else made up crazy words,
Or knew where to find Orion,
Or made a wish on a falling star,
Or knew why I was crying.
No one else saw the serenity
Of the freshly fallen snow.
I know that you remind me
Of a boy I used to know.

The Wastelands
by Michael C. Pollard

the wastelands are wildly deceiving
Death is cheap
But mildly amusing
Scattered are the cards with his own breath
Patience is a virtue
Pounds his fists on the table
The house has blown in
The wolf has triumphed
For now
Who knows what tomorrow will bring
But the seer
He sees not the future
But spins a web of broken lies
Seeing through a dead man's eyes
He'll sit and wait for sweet release
Will it come
Does it ever come to those who wait
Will the flower bloom in winter's haste
Spreading seeds, though it's too late
The land is dead
Will always be
Will it
Will the wastelands now defeat
And take man back to savagery
The sun has set on a hateful day
Who knows what tomorrow will bring
Maybe the sun will come out again

Healing Hands
by Alma K. Pratt

Warm soothing little healing hands
so wonderfully free to massage
each aching body parts that brings comfort to me.
With tender hearts their message imparts
Loving message of caring and sharing
individually to contented sick hearts
joyfully promoting healing becomes their art.

Dear Bruria:
by Henry Pool

I'm sitting at the window
and look upon the street.
Through trees I see the wind blow,
the sun strike with its heat.

The mailman rounds the corner
and drops the letters quick.
But I feel like a mourner
whose sorrow makes him sick.

My little darling daughter
is far away from me.
I don't know what has caught her,
perhaps economy?

I'm waiting for a letter
from Princess Bee, my love.
My heart does nearly shatter,
my spirit's like a dove.

Though you are o'er the ocean,
oh child, forget me not.
Put now your hands in motion
and write me quite a lot!

The Juices of Hell
And The Beast Within
by Lori-Beth Porter

When the night falls you can hear the roar of the Devil
As he calls out to the man on the town;
He lures him into his clenches and feeds him a drink;
The man accepts with gratitude and drinks the hellish juice;
Down into his blood goes the juice;
Out of the man arises a beast;
With the Devils look in his eyes;
He runs off into the night;
Into the house he storms looking for his first victim;
There sits a woman of beauty and brevity;
With one blow of his evil words,
She is knocked down to her knees;
Without an ounce of care, he's off to his next victim;
Run! Run!--Hide! Hide!
Cry the children;
Its too late;
There's no escape;
Three down with one mighty blow;
One more left...
The beast sights her with his night owl vision;
Off he runs like a predator after his prey;
He darts off like a bat out of Hell into the night;
Only to arise the next nightfall.

No More Monsters in the Closet
by Sarah Sillin

Fear is like the thickest rope of gold,
Squeezing at your stomach,
With a power know only to Hercules.
Your brain is frozen,
Like all beings in the ice age.
So logic escapes you,
Your mind is only open to your imagination.
The iced brain lets you believe.
To overcome is to thaw the brain,
To let illusions slip away,
No more monsters in the closet.

The Clown
by Shiela Roark

His heart is heavy, but so what?
It's show time now, they say.
And so he dresses for his part.
He knows no other way.

The children came to see him,
No matter what his plight.
They want to see the clown perform
His act this Friday night.

And even though he wears a grin,
And acts the perfect clown,
His sadness grows inside him
And starts to wear him down.

I must remember I'm a clown.
I have to act the part.
Who ever heard of a circus clown
Who wears a broken heart?

Question
by Kathleen Rampton

I call myself
A daughter of Artemis

Yet I don't know
The name of the mustard-breasted

Birds, sitting on the branches
On my backyard apple tree.

Overlooking a landing strip
Studded with the radial symmetry
Of perfect dandelion puffs.

There are only 1,000 panda bears
Left in China, innocently chewing
On bamboo as the rivers and
Air around them turn to poison.

What machine are we feeding
Those of us who are living and dying

Why must so much be sacrificed
And in the name of what?

Thoughts Upon Visiting
A Funeral Home
by Charles Rathbun

They stand about bewildered
Icy hand holding icy hand
That dare not disturb the curtains
That separate
Room from room from room
And the cry of the bewidowed
Does not end too soon.

Ah, youth
Basking in the sunshine
Of the night
Let out a cry of delight
Like a bird with winged flight
Cascading across the sky,
And, yes, create another
That it too may die.

Sands of Time
by Glenda Ramsey

I gaze upon the sands of time,
remembering days gone by,
reliving each precious moment
with tear-stained eyes.

I think about my childhood,
the good times and the bad,
and of the happy years of love
since you and I first wed.

Our children brought such joy
and made our house a home,
but one by one, they have gone
to make lives of their own.

Now you, my love, have gone away
to that Heavenly home.
My heart yearns for yesterday
as I sit here all alone.

I gaze upon the sands of time,
beholding Heaven's door,
and dream about my life ahead
when this life is no more.

Nature Of Love
by Elizabeth Ray

Put your lips up to the wind
And kiss the chilly air.
Let the breeze carry you to me,
So I can feel you through my hair.
Raise your hands to the clouds
And imagine my skin to your touch.
Know with the softness that I'm with you
And missing you, oh, so much.
Open your mouth to the falling rain.
Can you taste the tears that I cry?
Speak softly to the leaves that blow,
And I'll catch them as they pass by.
I'll place them up to my ear
And listen to you speak
Those loving precious words
That leave me feeling weak.
We both reach out to the sun
So that with the beams we can embrace,
And in the reflection of the moon
I'll look for your smiling face.
No open road can keep us apart
With the wonder of nature we have here.
I'll use those wonders to keep you in my heart
Until I can have you near.

He's Awesome?
by Madeline Johnson Ridgway

Don't stand in awe, but respect you may.
Each person's a person made from clay.
Just like him, you're god's child's, too,
So don't let him intimidate you.

A man, a king, oh oh, my lad;
He wore his pants, same as your dad.
The king of England, he seemed to me
a man no less of the monarchy
brought down to size, so went the story;
A king's yet a man, in all of his glory.

Nature's Palette
by Melissa Ray

The wind whipped the garden, in a silent fury-
While the leaves of whispering trees - shook in the distance.
Only the inky sky was broken by the spell of dancing moonbeams...
As they chased away the angry, thunderous clouds!

As the stars left, one by one - they were slowly replaced by showering,
Amber hues of sunlight...cast in a soft, celestial glow.
The storm's luminous trail had left a brilliant pattern of crystal raindrops-
That carpeted the grass, like tiny jewels.

The garden awoke to the warmth of the summer sun,
slowly opening it sleepy eyes.
birds filled the air with their first sonnet-
while lively crickets joined in with their joyous songs!

Butterflies and bees began filling themselves with the sweet nectar
Of canopied flowers...rolled out before them, like quilted patchworks of color.
Above them, rose a spiraling rainbow...
A vision of peace - from the night's raging storm!

It was a myriad of sparkling colors that filtered in a high arc.
As its sprinkling rays touched the garden's floor -
The prism of the rainbow seemed to melt
into the ground, like liquid sunshine!

It illuminated a blanket of roses, standing proudly like a sentinel...
Their petals, softly kissed, by the morning dew.
In the quietness of this moment - we are awed
By the divine tranquility of 'nature's palette.'

Still Dancing With You
by Randy R. Reed

The tunnel of time is an amazing thing
Through it you can see things you used to say and do
And through this ever-present time tunnel
I'm still dancing with you

I've heard time can play tricks on a memory
Make people forget things they knew
But in my mind I see it as plain as day
I'm still dancing with you

I see your shining eyes and your smiling face
When I look back from this point of view
I feel your soft, gentle arms slip around me
And I'm still dancing with you

They say that hindsight is twenty-twenty
And from what I've seen, I'd say it's true
Because when I look back on yesterday
I'm still dancing with you

I see you turn and begin to walk toward me
And I'm reminded of how your love for me once grew
You smile as if you know what I'm thinking
And I'm still dancing with you

Today, as I look back at our years together
I can't see myself with someone new
Because when I look ahead to the future
I'm still dancing with you

Desert Storm Easter
by Mildred Bedinger Rhea

If you hit me, I'll hit you.
If you hit my brother, I'll hit you too!
Are you listening? Are you really listening?
Not a group of small boys ---
But the voice of world, and nations.
For the spirit of war is sweeping creation!

Are you listening? Can't you hear it?
Shrieking missiles, bombs deadly sound
Flung over earth, sea, sky and ground;
Sounds of wanton destruction of human life,
Of buildings, some centuries old, destruction
Of the oil we all covet, that liquid black gold!

Are you listening? Are you truly listening?
Hear those awesome terrified cries,
Flung out across miles of desert,
Raised to those dark, fearsome skies
Hoping that a God in His Heaven,
Somehow hears them and replies.
Then there's that quiet, quiet, quiet sound,
It's a very young soldier's heart, slowly
                    winding d-o-w-n.
Over it all hear that sad weary wailing?
Rising, ever rising, ever rising, never failing,
Over seas and skies, over sands running red;
Babies and children crying for parents, war dead.
So forget conniving, profiteering, face-saving,
Forget propaganda and even flag waving.
Listen to all those sounds, for one hour, one whole day;
Then this Easter season, pray, pray, pray!

Waiting For The Morning
by Paula Wiest Shannon

In a corner of the closet
She keeps staring at the door
Where she locked the world away
Like many times before.
"Please, don't find me,"
She whispers through the night.
"Please, don't hurt me,"
She shivers with the fright.
Too scared to fall asleep
She listens for a sound,
Too young to understand
The world all around.
A light creeps through the door then-
The dawning of a day.
She stands to face the world
As she wipes her tears away.

Surrender to the Sunrise
by Jenette St. George

His knowing lips
Rushed over hers like running fire.
Her heart
Melted like the snow in the early spring.
His sweet talk,
A singing fly in her ear,
Gave her a hollow mind.
Their love
Shattered by the sneaking sunrise.

I Am Whispering
by Virginia Riley

I am whispering feelings that I dare not say
Perhaps I'm feeling angry or simply dismayed

It's not that I lack courage, or feel so insecure
But whispering protects you from hostility I'm sure

Perhaps you have hurt me, forgetting I am here
and my whispers of speaking up, but you will never hear

That you have crushed my fragile heart
    or dashed a pretty dream
I'll almost tell you off my friend
    with whispers in a scream-

I'd never hurt you like you did
I'd never fluff you off
But I'll scream as loud as I can
with whispers that are soft

For the bleeding of emotions, can kill a happy heart
And no one knows the better, of how it even starts

I'd never want one mortal, to feel the pain they give
for when hurt is propagated, it destroys the way we live

Can you hear me whisper-Dear heart the things I say
I wish it wasn't necessary to whisper in this way

Darkness Enfold Me
by Vetta E. Steel

Darkness, enfold me,
wrap your loving arms around me.
I love your breath on my neck;
it makes me such a wreck.
I feel you longing for me.
Darkness, enfold me.
Kiss me all over,
and then let's roll in the clover.
I dream of you
in the morning dew.
Oh night,
I have lost my sight.
Enfold me
in your swirling sea.
Darkness,
I am yours.

The Listener
by Michael L. South

How will anyone know
When all they do is speak to those
Who have listened to years of life's stories
If only they would have listened instead of spoken
Looked into the eyes of those who hear
The darkness your pain has given them
For no one hears the listener speak
Until tomorrow the listener will hear
The unspoken meanings within the words
They have heard
Who could have known
The darkness within
The listeners eyes
Who will hear us now
Did we even hear your good-bye

Seasons Past, Seasons Come
by Robin Roberts

There are changes in the air
Fall comes to us in crisp shafts of sun
And sits on the lawn with it's foggy feet tucked under.
Hazy hills watching, waiting for the colder days
Behind the prickly grass
That crunches under foot.

Soon the winter evening will be among the trees
To pull the white sheets tight around their trunks
While they snuggle their toes in the warm earth.

Winter comes windless from the North
In slow, grey masses,
And the memory of skirting papers and balls of dust
In strewn streets, lingers
Like my mother's pie.

Frisbees are in flight again
Sharing their precious space
With footballs and loud shouts.
The boys bare their backs to the thin sun
And breathe clouds at ten in the morning.
They run on the slippery lawn and stumble,
Desperate not to fall

Thirty Lines For Jeremy
by Tamela Christensen-Rold

Words on a page
Are all I have of you
It has to be enough
Because it is all you have to give
I accept it so gratefully
Because it allows me in some small way
To be part of your life
Not a big part
But with every letter I know
You were for a few precious moments
Thinking of me
How can I feel so connected to someone I have never met?
I feel a bit silly at times
Counting you among my friends
Although your face has never been in front of mine
You have marked my soul
With each stroke of your pen
And changed the way I see the world
Because I know you're out there somewhere
In a country so different from mine
Living a life so separate from me
Yet so much is the same it carries us through
Because we both know
Friendship is not about collecting moments together
But of connecting lives
Which we have done in spite of distance
What we have between us is so special to me
I will cherish it for always
And hope we can continue to find new wonder in our world
Just by knowing each other.

Poem of the End
by Monica Rodriguez

This is the last poem I'll ever write to you
A poem of a deceived heart, a poem of truth

A poem that took time to take form or shape
For the hardest things to write about, are things of hurt and pain.

I know it was hard to deal with my lifestyle, my kids and all
But do you pull a good tree from its soil, strip it from its unripe fruit, and turn its wood to charcoal?

Or do you water it and let it grow, and cultivate its fruit?
And when the fruit is ready, don't you reap it, and isn't excellent the juice?!

Did you stay long enough to see how all would have turned out?
Did you give your love unconditionally, without hesitation or doubts?

Did you understand my human faults and offered full support?
Or did you criticize and put me down, when things didn't turn out as thought?

Tell me, did you hold me in your arms the many times I cried?
Or did you walk away, without a word...while I died inside?

I don't know how I loved you, or how much can I love again,
But I promised myself to forget you, that's why I named this poem The End.

Because it ends with the reminiscence of all the things left to say;
Feelings roaming in my heart, where they longer had no space.

So today I give them new dwellings, among some ink and paper and forever they shall serve as mirrors and reflectors
So I always may remember, how my heart was torn and trashed like an old, moth-eaten book or yesterday's paper.

And after you've read this poem, your lips will taste of remorse
And cowardice will tempt you to throw it out, but keep it will whisper some invisible force!
And trapped this way between the wall and sword, ultimately it will end up in some personal draw.

And you might not pick it up for a while, perhaps for many years
Maybe because it meant nothing, but most likely because you fear.

Because words may seem frozen on paper, like a spider seems harmless in her dreams
But the strength and power they both convey, can bring the biggest of men to his knees.

It's late, my little ones await me...even the one that this evening could have been untying your shoes after a hard day of work,
And anticipating that big kiss you would have given her, later tonight when you tucked her in bed.

And maybe one day some other love will stumble upon this poem, and amuse herself with the verses of genuine prow'ess
Never suspecting you are the deceiving man of this poem, and I am...the admired poet.

Untitled
by Cammie Trajceksi

Look for a rainbow
and count the colors ---
Because one day,
you might need that last color...
for your pot of gold.

When Dragons Roar
by Tony Salomone

On a hot still August night
I sat alone in the belly of my street-dragon
Her loud and steady rumbling thunder
Was a soothing sound, a melody of raw power
As each vibration passed through me
And with the dim lights from her gauges
She whispered to me
It's alright I'm here with you
When you call, I'll give all I have for you
Now feel me, love me, be one with me
Because she lives, she breathes, she wants
She is a beast of pure power
With an innocence that loved a gentle touch

Next to us the leviathan roared
Tense and ready
Breathing its own fiery rage and thunder
The two beasts were ready to do battle on the filed of honor
I looked ahead, she still spoke to me
Her amber eyes lighting the dark road ahead
With a high that no drug could match
My heart raced, my blood churned
My body became taunt as adrenalin filled my senses
While I tried to hold my cool stare
We charged into the emptiness of the night
Never wanting to stop, never stopping to want
Every move we made were as one flesh
while the roaring thunder broke through the hot still night

Slipping Through
by Sylvia Schuster

My eyes
live inside
the walls
of my old home.

Each time
I return
I watch
my father vanish
through the keyhole.

My mother
blindfolded
reaches out
for anyone...
and feels
the air
slip through her fingers.

The Storm
by Linda Saunders

Toe tickling water in puddles of blue all around,
Waving winds that seems to lift the heat from the ground,
Distant echoes of thunder like an approaching buffalo stampede,
As lightning flashes its warning, "Mankind, take heed".

The storm now takes its aim along its own path,
To show the world that even nature has wrath.
Creatures seek shelters in burrows and basements so still,
As the storm clouds move climbing every valley and hill.

Death defying quiet before the freight train's arrival,
Find the helpless ones searching for their very own survival.
Uprooting, flattening destruction, mark the brand of a twister,
One can still see smiles on the lucky ones that missed her.

Paintbox Morning
by Tami Sandlin

Deep black velvet blankets the land
The world is still sleeping.
When pale gold shatters the darkness at hand,
As Madam sunlight comes slowly creeping.

From the dark of the storm she has awakened,
Waving her magic wand.
Reveling in the beauty she is making,
She's come to paint the dawn.

She takes her paintbox from its shelf,
And prepares to roam
With colors she's borrowed from Nature herself,
And some she creates on her own.

Blending the gold with the orange and pink,
Splashing the colors about,
A bit of purple over there, she thinks,
Just beyond the clouds.

A dash of turquoise, periwinkle blue,
Amethyst, coral, and mauve,
Daffodil, primrose, and indigo, too,
Caressing the canvas above.

Then, just like magic, the colors fade,
Gone with little warning.
Madam sun hides her paintbrush away
And dreams of a paintbox morning.

A Letter To The Minister
by Christina Smith

Dear Minister, I came to church today to hear tell of God's love and wondrous ways, and how his life was spent during his last days.

I know I am a sinner, and I've strayed far from home, and this guilty conscience won't let me alone.

You preach in your sermon that hell has a wide road, and how some of us are not carrying enough of a load. But remember dear preacher you chose to follow your star, and without your intervention we won't go very far.

I know you love Jesus; otherwise there could never be such an outpouring of love for your parishioners and strangers you see.

The church doors are open both day and night for those who do wrong and those who do right. Your phoneline is open for all who call; for those who are "saved", and for those with their backs against the wall.

There is much to be said for your dedication and good deeds. You are not a god, but you help plant the seeds. So continue to lead us in prayer as you usually do and God will have a special blessing just for you.

Manasquan '75
by Louis Sellari

The Jersey shore, like no place on earth
Tan lines, kegs, sexual surround sound
A time for Lust and Love--all goodies in between
"Do you believe in summer love?" I'm just a harmless hound.

Herb, booze, Coppertone, ludes; filling my senses
Babes, bikinis, hard-ons in the sand
A whisper in my ear, drop your drawers!
Love for the night. Relax, I know where to put my hand!

Showers in the yards; no privacy; views galore
Girls struttin' down the boulevard,
Bouncing, free and at ease
Chatter, music box, pizza, onions, caress my nose, the grease
Yearning for a slice; Ospray calls;
Dance with a pretty tease.

Such a time, bottled forever in my mind
The scent of a woman's tan skin
Her expression tells of the deed just done
Manasquan '75, a history lesson in
Unadulterated Sin.

Innocence Lost
by Shaun Sellers

      Yea as I walk through the valley
        of the shadow of Death...
The battle is over
The Earth is quiet
The weapons of death and destruction
    have been silenced
Only the screams of the dying can be heard
The sky is a deep purplish red,
    as the fires of Hell
The blood is an eighth sea over the land
Bodies of the dead float on the surface,
    trying not to surrender to the fear,
    the fear of the unknown
The sea of blood shines with the
    colors of the rainbow;
    the colors of humankind
The acrid smell of gunpowder and burning flesh
    stink up the fresh air and joy of innocence
Up from the screams and the smoke comes Death
    on his pale horse,
    as he travels to the battlegrounds of the future,
    waiting to claim his next victims
No peace, or joy, or victory has been found
    on his day, only the agony and death
    of our fellow man.

Running
by Melissa Ann Vinneau

Gone through stones and twigs,
    feet bare and scraped,
    blood trails on the gravel,
    icy wind, sharp hail
against my ebony skin;
horizon dull and blurred,
    I do not stop,
I am a fugitive slave.

The Spot
by Kathleen Sgro

Wandering through the meadows,
    Skipping through the blades,
We embraced our spot,
    And there our home we made.

Examining the ladybug,
    Weaving green grass mats,
Serving acorn caps of tea,
    Waving away the gnats.

A bedroom off the living room,
    Lie down and take a nap,
Dreaming of our next task,
    A clover crown my cap.

Trekking home at dusk,
    Memories for a lifetime,
Imagining our tomorrows,
    Sisters speak in mime.

Days have all gone by,
    Our spot we visit no more,
But, behind my garden gate...
    Acorn tea caps I pour.

Primping Snapdragon earrings,
    On elephant ears we sat,
My grandchild finds her spot,
    Weaving iris blade placemats.

To my sister Mary Ann

To Be Free
by Tracie Shanahan

The eagle swooped down into the field
He stood there, majestic and proud
His white feathered cap and deep brown cape.

I watched him, from behind the barbed wire fence
And I was jealous
For he, the symbol of freedom, truly was.

Free to fly away
Where ever the winds may blow
The choice is yours
No barbed wire to stop nor cage
All you need do, is lift your wings.

you are not a prisoner
You are free
I, am earth bound
Never free.

Oh, to have wings and fly away
I am jealous
fly my friend
Be Free.

Web of Love
by Janet Addison Winslow

If I could weave a web of love
I'd keep you by my side
I'd be your favorite captor
My love I would not hide
I'd keep you in a secret place
From harm and injury
If I could weave a web of love
For all eternity.

Shadow Of The Falcon
by Gloria J. Smith

I am trapped in my shadow
as it streaks across the wall:
black and shapeless.

Its darkness ascends
to waver on the ceiling,
grotesque, bird-like.
My dark hidden self
holds me, naked in my fear.

We become a preying Falcon,
with wide flapping wings.
Fingers are earth roots
with curved talons,
growing larger
against the light.

Fierce Falcon anger
over-takes the shaking fear.
I claw, peck and suck
this black shadow
deep into my throat.

I return from this abyss
into the world of bright lights,
left with the taste
of blackness in my mouth.

But the darkness
of the Falcon will not
leave my mind.
I know we will again do battle,
where fear and love mate
within the shadow.

Your Funeral Memorial
by Dona K. Soler

You should have seen your Memorial;
    You'd have been delighted with the throng
Of friends gathered in the church
    To raise their voice in song . . .

All your favorite music
    And the whole choir was there
And your voice remembered
    With the only empty chair.

The flowers were just lovely;
    Every variety and hue . . .
A very special tribute
    To a dear one, such as you.

Many spoke of you in memory
    Of things you'd do or say
And between tears and laughter. . .
    It was really quite a day.

We had a nice brunch after;
    A connoisseur affair,
And it seemed a real shame. . .
    That everyone but you, was there . . .

Why these great ovations
    After one is dead . . . ?
You'd have enjoyed every minute
    And hearing what was said.

One Wild, One Tame
by Brenda Sorensen

    The river of no return
washed up over my toes.
It rumbled over and under
the huge gray-black
speckled boulders and stones
that lined it's shores.
    Ambling slowly down
the hill on the other
side of the water.
Came a dozen wild horses.
Their main and tails
swishing and swirling,
in graceful waves.
    They slipped into a small
grove of pine trees near the
water.
    Separated from man
by half a block of
swiftly flowing water.
    Both of us safe from the other
So we watched.
One wild,
One tame.
Neither of us could tell which.

Field of Dreams
by Daniel Spoor

A river runs without an end.
There's a path that's by its side.
They'll be together through the winds of change,
until the end of time.
You're the river that brings me life.
I'm the path that's by your side.
As long as you are watering me,
I'll live and grow with pride.
Run with me through a field of dreams.
Run where there is no pain.
Run with me through lengths of time
that only have one frame.
Flow with me through the mountains and plains,
through the fields of rich green grass.
I promise my love to stay by your side
as the seasons come and pass.
We've run by other rivers,
by lakes and streams so blue.
They've never gotten a second look,
cause I'm so in love with you.

The Little Spider
by Linda L. Stalts

I know a little spider,
Who was a crafty thing,
He'd always build his little home
Of things that looked like strings.

And everyday the maid would come
And wipe him off the wall,
And he'd have to build his home again
Away down the hall.

Then at night--when all was dark
He'd climb upon the wall,
And start to build his home again,
Away down the hall.

Armstrong The Mountain Climber
by Robert Stancampiano

I hear the banter of boys in humor,
    the bantering brawl of words unfit to scrawl.
I hear the giggling of girls mingling,
    the giggling gaiety in flowery dresses.

And over all I hear Armstrong,
    detailing his latest adventure
    in a drunken harangue,
    his voice booming like a church choir.

"...yes, the place they call the end of the earth,
    feels like you're dangling at the end of a wire...
...the place where doom sits back on it's haunches,
    smiles and patiently waits...
...a native girl with a tattoo on her, well...says it's her fate.
...the place where the moon is a battered whore,
    the sun is a liar..."

"Hah! Liar? Liar?...I think we know who the liar ith...
    you're drunk, go home and go to bed!"
Shouts Bernie Bridgetts, a coffee house lunatic
    with tourette's and a Cindy Brady lisp.

But Armstrong is still caught up in his story,
    "...and you know what the natives were chanting?
In sadness and in pain, the natives were dancing.
They love the drum of madness, the cry of disaster..."

"You've been telling the thame thstory thinths the thickthtieths."

"Yeah, shut up already," adds Mildred Drew, "We've heard it before."

And the rest of the party forces him out the door.

"Fine," says a drunken and suddenly dejected Armstrong,
    "they can't deep a good man down."
He goes home to sleep
    and in the morning he sets out for the nineties.

Racism
by Janet Nicholson Swann

A deadly spirit
That spreads itself around its victim unmercifully
It enters by way of the ear, then races to the darkened heart
Its tentacles quickly adhering themselves
It finds there no opponent
And ruthlessly grows
Spreading itself through the mouth
Carrying its victim on to disaster
A spirit that will not stop at one
For it breeds on numbers
It's strengthened through weakness and difficulty
The lower it can take its victim the better
It gives its beloved false strength
In some it entwines their very soul
Taking them on to new heights
One of imprisonment even death
Then laughs at their downfall
And forges on to yet another victim
Uncaring delighting in its power

Snowbound
by Marigo Stathis

After complaints of non-winter weather, the gods respond in synchrony,
New Year confettied epiphany:
    pearl-creamed, fleece, phantomed flakes,
    silverswanivory-dusted matter,
    crystaled here and there, mounded two or three feet high,

Sitting in the warmth, sheltered from piles that dwarf,
shivering, you resent everything you usually ignore:
    messy home, lazy husband, dying plants, unpaid bills.
Animate or not, also snowbound, they now scream: FACE US

Though the shovel promises paved path,
and boots might allow pilgrimage to Meccas of bars and grocery stores
wrath, at home, you might ration not just your food, but your fears.

    By the fireplace, do you feel the flickering cindering?:
    just as mortality is certain, uncertainty breathes immortal,...without prediction,
    flurrying or avalanching as under, at times,
    each blizzard bringing with it in the necessity of inclemency,
        to slow down what has been prematurely quickened,
    for the blurs of our racing, for our doppler effects.

Today, the master of winter once again brings us gentle micro-doilies,
    which, for our minds, could slowly melt or sublimate:
in each snow crystal, a simple design, another evaporating moment,
    begging to be grasped, before its dissolve.
When we wait, open-armed, the grace of water, nature's priestess,
    baptizes our vicissitudes whole.

From bedroom window, still ill-disposed, you curse frost juxtaposed on freshly buried car.
Too hasty to see that only the screen separates you from the scene,
    that the glass through which you peer, from another angle,
could reflect snowdrifted beauty into self-assessment,
    you scatter to the TV or the latest magazine,
quick in the brainwash of any naked image to escape the binding of the storm.

AIDS (A Father's Broken Heart)
by Judy Steele

When I open my eyes
I remember where I am
it seems the night before
is when my life began.

I wake to a feeling of dread
not wanting to get out of bed
happiness is not what I feel
surviving the day is what is real

I dream, I long, for existence
with my son. That would complete
my life and my family would be as one.

My son, my son, I will always weep
in my heart from your death and smile
from the memories of your life.

You filled the earth with pleasure
and light up the heavens with your soul.

You have not died in vain my son
the children will know of the pain
and agony that aids does bestow.

The Underground Railroad
by Benjamin Stevens

Listen!, the conductor calls in the deep of the night.
At the slave's cabin window in the moon by the light.
To the whispers in the darkness do apprehend.
"Welcome aboard, it's a friend of a friend!"

It's every captive's dream and familiar code.
A ticket to the station of the underground railroad.
To make this old life live up to par.
You are invited, indeed you are!

Torn between this state of time.
Running ahead, leaving families behind.
This way is hard and quite very far.
But follow your dreams, follow that star!

Don't listen to the distant gunfire sounds.
Or ferocious barks of the old bloodhounds.
But listen to the whistle of the train that calls.
It will carry you to freedom, it will carry you all!

Run to escape those who seek after!
Run from the master and the hired slave catchers!
Run by the moonlight so no one will see!
Run for your lives if you want to be free!

It will pay off for all that it's worth.
So follow that star to the way up north!
Arriving in Canada, you won't be alone.
Some friends and relatives will welcome you home.

So field hands, craftsmen and domestics be patient.
Look for the railroad to the underground station!
To be in captivity, whoever you are.
Follow your dreams, follow that star!

*Written in present tense to make more personal to the reader,
and to historically commemorate our ancestors in Southern Bondage.*

July 8, 1995
My Birthday Poem
by David Thomson

Summer, again, ambles by
glimpsed through dappled shade;
on the far side of the rugged hills
the river, yet, flows.

        What are these
        sentiments of new beginnings?
        Silver arching of growing moon?

Each day,
I must focus experience
through my tangled mind
to the finite point of my pen.

All,
and I mean all,
extraneous things must
of their own weight die.

        Each day I must do this
        --- win or lose.

The Magic Time
by Sarah Tolliver

When shakespeare dipped his quill
Into his ruddy ink, the magic time began;
He wrote what the muse willed;
But once
He dipped and dropped the tip
Differently; he knew where to find
A treasure full of time--magic--time--
And composed a map. He tucked the map inside a bottle,
Threw it into the running water on to the edge of the
Road. He watched as it meandered down to the forest
Where the streamlet
Dumped into a river.

Bottom and Titania were picnicking beside the water
Of the river when she hap'd to see the bottle.
"Wait most precious, let me get the thing and we'll
see what paper this is."

On their way to find the treasure, after looking at
The map, Bottom found the five stones laid
In a circle where the treasure chest
Was buried.

Sitting on the edge of a small gracelike hole was the chest;
Bottom took his hammer from his tool pouch and beat
The lock off. He looked into Titania's eyes, turned, and
Opened the lid. A giant hourglass, worth all the sand
At the bottom of it.

Titania took the glass and tipped it over;
She and bottom loved like neither ever
Had; then, the sand ran
Out, they fell apart, and time was everyday again;
She rose, picked up the glass, and turned it end for end.

"Together We Will Succeed"
by Jodi Uhrich

You are such a light,
Such a sweet burning candle,
In the dampness of life.
Deep within my soul
Can I touch you?
Are you real,
Or am I once again dreaming of perfection?

Through the heavy curtain of lifes blackened fog
You found me.
You placed your hand on my shoulder
And led me to the sun.

Within life's turmolic expressions,
We met in the middle and grasped hands.
As a bond of purity, honesty, and compassion
Wrapped it's arms around us
And enveloped our beings.

To say thank you is almost meaningless.
So instead I hold you.
And hope you feel who I am
And what I experience...
Surrounding you.

Together we will push through the challenges of life.
Together we will survive.
Together we will succeed.

Through a Child...
by Linda Van Camp

Through the voice of a child, the truth no longer can hide;
for we learn acceptance, where deception and faults are no longer masked by pride.

Through the eyes of a child, our innocence is restored;
for it is a world unknown that we see now with a grandness yet unexplored.

Through the mind of a child, we remember when uncommitted yet were our sins,
and learn of forgiveness and strength, and where honesty begins.

Through the heart of a child, we learn of a love not just given to few;
for where there is no hate, nor wrath, our true world comes into view.

Through the soul of a child, a life is reborn;
a life that brings peace, not a world apart torn.

A child can teach us in ways we've forgotten or ignore;
for it is through their patience and vision that our minds can soar

to reach those goals, to make a difference in our lives,
to grow, to learn, to for our dreams to strive.

Through a child we can mirror what we once wanted to be -
through that once protected soul now wanting to be free.

Through a child we can now see, we can speak with a new voice;
for that child shows that we always live with a choice.

For it is in freedom of mind, of heart and thought
that we learn through a child the special gifts our life has brought.

The Leaves Are Falling
by Jeannie Vaughn

The leaves are falling to the ground;
They are spinning and grinning as they fall all around.
Now the leaves are running across the street;
They are flying and dying as they stop at people's feet.
The leaves seem to be saying "please don't trample
    on us with your big feet."
The leaves would rather be put in a book where
    they can stay nice and neat.
The leaves are having fun with their last dying breath;
They're whirling, swirling and unfurling with their
    slow, unpainful death.
The leaves are remembering their life on a tree...
There is where they felt alive, warm and at liberty.
When the leaves were on the tree, they were flowing
    freely, fastened securely with their stem--
Blowing in the wind as fluids flowed through their veins.
The leaves began to remember when they began to
    change into different colors --
The leaves said,"Those were the days of glory my brother;
Where wither we goest now my dear leaves--
Now that we have fallen from the tree and no one grieves?"
All the leaves clutched each other in a big pile;
The biggest leaf replied,"We will be like this for a while...
Then we will disintegrate and renew the earth's soil;
We will come back again in a different form and then
    we shall not spoil."

Battle of the Soul
by Colleen D. Vanskiver

In life we have our mountains high, they take our souls soaring through the sky,
But, in the blink of an eye, we look beneath the clear blue sky,
And their are valleys dark and low that twist at our very soul,
From the day we are born the battle begins, we never know who will win...
To stand upon the Mountain peaks, that brush the deep blue sky,
To watch the soft white clouds, as they go rolling by,
To hear the rustle of the tallest trees, the quietness that puts your mind at ease,
The solitude and peace it brings to almost every living thing...
The feel of the cool crisp air, as it caresses your skin,
You know that this is the house that God lives in...
But, we turn around and before we know, the valley is calling from below,
For life does have it's mountain peaks, but it also has it's valleys deep.
And in this valley dark and green, I buried one of life's most precious dreams,
The sun still shines, the birds still sing,
I hear the words of the Minister ring, your son has gone to live with his king...
Now I am in this valley dark and low, a place I hoped I would never go...
The demons are at the door,
I hear someone whispering to me, life is not worth living anymore,
Now in my soul, the pain so deep I am trying hard to find that mountain peak...
My heart cries out to you sweet Lord, can't you hear my plea,
I need you here beside me, to set this broken heart free...
I am lost in a land deep in despair, I cannot find the door,
I need you Lord to help me, climb that mountain once more...
He hears my plea, he has come with his great love, to set this broken heart free...
He says to me, I will put your battered soul to rest,
My child when, you are lost and alone I am at my very best...
I hear your plea, now listen to me he whispers on the wind,
I too have lost a son, for mankinds sin...
Take my hand, together we will walk this land, this battle we will win...
For my heart to shares this loss and pain, and I will show you how to live again...

This poem is dedicated to my son Alex Vanskiver, whom I still love and miss very much.

Sign of The Times
by Harriette Vaughn

I walked down to the corner and the old drug store was gone,
I went to look for my dog of 15 years, only to find none,
Then my doctor, he tells me I'm getting old,
I think this is something I already know,
My car of 10 years is taking longer to start,
Then last year my poor mother did depart,
My house of 30 years is starting to leak,
And every day I notice my eyes are more weak,
My back seems to hurt all the time,
And I think that it's just a crime,
That every year I work for less each time,
but I guess you know, it's just a sign of the times.

Childhood Memories
by Dona Samson Zappone

A Strauss waltz
a Mozart sonata
taste for the classics
inherited from father
a shared loved
a passion for music
remembrance of things past.

A Damsel Remembers
by Layla B. Vaughn-Trader

Eyes of blue, and face of long ago
                last seen on battlefield.
        Wind blew through your hair --
        Your eyes looked toward heaven --
Never to look to me again.

Eternity has parted us. My special friend
                a lifetime ago.
        On that misty battlefield --
        your sword fell to the ground --
and how I remember it so well.

All of my life, haunted by images
                finally now, can I recall.
        Did we live before?
        Do I imagine too much?
You once told me I asked too many questions and we laughed.

I can still hear your voice.
                and your sad eyes of blue are
        closed forever on bloody battlefield.
        Will no one believe me when I say
"A Damsel remembers...I knew him then."

Left Behind
by Ricardo Villavicencio

The wicker basket left behind,
a pink vase for cut flowers
standing empty, a bath robe
hung behind the door.

The ring on the finger
of the pale porcelain hand
on the vanity where she once dressed.

Debris left behind by the storm,
scattered about in the whirlwind
created by her leaving.

A home left alone, with only
me and the relics
of what used to be.

The reminders collect dust,
hanging on to places
once warm and alive,
rendered quiet.

Time buries the past
with days and weeks,
they grow into months
and years.

The objects in this house
that made this place hers
were slowly gathered, stored away.

Memories have become distant,
like a dream recurring
with sweet scents and soft touches
from hands that long ago
turned the front doorknob
of this house left behind.

American Royalty
by Nuwatanka

Not long ago, I watched part of the auction of the estate of Jacqueline Kennedy. The newsperson, interviewing those who were fortunate enough to attend, asked one young lady, "What brought you here?"

"The Kennedys are like the American Royal Family. They are the only royalty we have," came the reply.

The existence of royalty in America is a fact known by few who are educated in the United States. Nonetheless, they existed. Kings and queens--descendants of alii and chiefs--reigned in Hawaii a century ago.

Who? Who held a king hostage until a treaty was signed? Who imprisoned a queen until a provisional government and statehood were achieved?

Who? The government of the United States.

As the state of Hawaii struggles under escalating financial burdens, tourists and foreigners are increasingly given priority over islands dwellers. Shall we, the other island dwellers, not soon follow the Hawaiian Trail of Tears?

The missionaries and the President of the United States have issued official apologies to the native Hawaiians.

Justice -- a nation within a nation--for Hawaiians under the blessing of the United States could be the beginning of a return to the aloha so quickly disappearing form these islands.

A recent article in the Wall Street Journal was critical of the Islands of Hawaii as a tourist destination. Could an attitude in state and national government--an attitude that puts the welfare of the residents and natives first--restore both the economy and the aloha?

The Hawaiians say, "Our life comes from the sea. We face the sea, our backs to the mountains. The sea is our mother. Our visitors come from the sea."

And may the sea grant honor to our true American royalty.

Our Worst Nightmare:
by Elizabeth L. Wangberg R.A.

The children and I, we live alone,
waiting, wondering, fearing that unknown.
Never sure, looking over our shoulder,
those feelings of frustration, getting colder.
It's a terrible thing to feel afraid,
dreading the day he passes by to invade.
The harassment and cruelty we've had to endure,
we have now come so close to our cure.
All that is now taunting our minds,
is the never ending nightmares he's left behind.
Oh why do we have to live this way,
being afraid to go out every day.
Feeling the eyes watching us try to go on,
we are so desperately trying to just belong.
To end our nightmares and close that door,
locking him out, so we hurt no more.
No one should have to live this way,
fearing to go out in your own yard to play.
How we wish and pray,
to get this man out of our hair,
this terrible man who causes;
Our Worst Nightmare.

A Child: A Gift From God
by Constance M. Weese

O LORD: don't ever let me forget that he is
    heaven sent.
So pleasant and so pure, so loving so dear.
It is hard for us to part from him whenever we are
    so near.
No one can ever take there place, there smile is so
    rare, the happiness that linger's there.
The joy that they have given us can never be
    replaced,
especially when you see that look upon their
    little face.
OH! thank you LORD for giving me your child
for a little while, because I know I have to guide
    him to you with a smile.
I love this child so dearly LORD, I know that he
    is mine.
I know I will have to give him back when ever
    it is mine.

Portents To 2012
by Barbara Weppener

A fingernail of silver
Scratched the eastern sky
Etching a channel
For the new moon's birth.
Celestial charts,
Disturbed by cosmic pressure,
Responded to the dissonance
Of the spheres.
Titan, Rhea and Dione gyrated
Within multi-colored rings
As Saturn moved in irregular convulsions.
Orion swung his flashing sword,
Tightening his reins on the Horsehead Nebula.
Cosmos and Earth reverberated
The time is coming-
Rebirth or death
Of the world as we know it.

Priority
by Rupert H.D. Westmaas

From what I hear and read and see
I wonder what it's going to be,
for on the land and sea and air
horrendous news we have to bear;
As round this globe we criss and cross
weaving a trail of human loss
and multiply financial greed
that's only matched by vehicle speed.

We often hear of planes near missed
as confusion reigns and cross is crissed,
yet we aspire to planets reach
while leaving earth with peace in breach
and lots of problems unsolved here;
Will we spread confusion there?

I hope that God, if He forbid
our effort to push off Heaven's lid,
would gently hold, then put us down
let each safely find his town;
Then all vehicles made for space
safely stayed to end the mad race,
'till we establish peace on Earth
before allowed a starward berth.

The Addict
by Phyllis White

There is a man I have loved
beyond reason and hope, enabling
the death knells tongued at my door:
dried roses, flat of fragrance, from
some distant war.

Now a tube connects life to
his frail determination while
white walls paraphrase, exact
each hoarse struggle
of his breath.

I look on, dry and myopic, distanced
from delusion. What subconscious path
corrupted him to follow Persephone's
abduction to Cerberus' gate?
Was it the intrigue of swollen lips, dark arcades?

Will Dawn dare reckon with him?
If in his soul She finds some morsel
of salvation, could broken bones mend?
Or will the candle flicker,
forever waiting the verdict?

If I could travel in time, a dream-machine,
Fate would not fall as sorry as this.
Now he lies in harsh homelessness,
crushed, driven over by a seedy seductress,
her face jaundiced, twisted by booze, perversed.

I am no Savior, just a time-waster,
a reluctant Madonna, nothing better to do.
The promise broken, the vows subterrealized:
new word, same dirt cast into the darkness
of his perennial tomb.

What A World We Live In Today
by Lisa Wikoff

    What a world we live in today,
Ravaged with the scenes of war
Whereever we look and whenever we watch t.v.
Innocent people terrorized everyday by the
Barbarians who say they are fighting for their rights.
    What a world we live in today,
When our elders can barely survive
On their fixed incomes, when the
Cost of living continues to increase
Day by day, year by year, with no end in sight.
Then, when we can no longer care for
Them ourselves, it is almost impossible
For us to find a good home that is
Reasonably priced and has the excellent
Care that is needed for those we love.
    The world we live in today
Is not the world our ancestors left for us.
    The world we live in today
Is a world we created ourselves through
Our recklessness and greed of businessmen
Who see fit to fire people that only make
Four dollars, twenty-five cents an hour
So that they can get richer, and the
Poor, well, can become poorer.
    This world we live in today is the world
Our children will inherit when we are gone
And will try to create a future for themselves.

Noble Thoughts While You're Down!
by Judi Wild-Becker

A donkey took a painful slip...
Landing greatly in the mud.
Whatever was the cause of this,
It created quite a thud!

An elf of tiny stature
Climbed high upon his tummy.
So uplifted, he was well inspired
To write words he thought were funny.

He attempted to capture humor,
Perhaps make the donkey sing --
Maybe stripes would fin'ly make him laugh...
This job was a monstrous thing!

The grandness of his efforts
Caused the elf to mull it over.
"Using aptitudes and enterprise
May enable <u>our</u> greatness and pow'r!"

As tough as living may seem,
Just 'being' might seem terrifying!
But seeing life as our work of art
Gives reason to keep right on trying!

Words Upon A Page
by Wanda Wilhelm-Norton

By day I live through other's lives,
    Plot their futures
        Without guidance of stars
            or heavenly beings.
They are all that I am not,
    but without me-
        they are nothing.
I gave birth to them,
    daily I breathe life into them
        and they in turn,
            bear their hearts and souls to me-
Who is the Creator
    and who is the Creation...
Sometimes I feel
    that they are more real than I;
        they live, love, laugh with abandon,
            sometimes depart-die...
    the pain of their death can be so real:
        They are, after all, my children.
Even as I spill their life-blood
    across the pages
        I weep for the ones who are no more.
Turn the page...
    It is night now,
        and time to put them carefully away.
Most sleep,
    content to wait until the morn,
        but one, impatient, dances through my dreams,
            begging me for more
than cold words upon a page.

Monotony
by Bill Willett

Forgiveness begins in the front pew --
Perfect, well-dressed, listless saints!
How is it true soldiers are so few,
When the voice of sorrow and sin kindly faints?
Whispers! Whispers! Back-biting tongues!

Forgiveness can bend a rainbow
Across the sky -- could heal thy scar,
But unspoken words from hearts aglow
Never taste the fruit of prayer.
Whispers! Whispers! But who really cares?

Burdened to death with their passion,
Their pedestals too high to reach,
Their heart and mind a loaded handgun,
Even now they do not care to teach.
Whispers! Whispers! The pain is too great!

Then, in broken spirit, I heard
    of thee, Christ --
        A man of compassion!
        A God of mercy!
        A Maker of silent pew watchers!

A Love For All
by Debra L. Yager

Love is all around us on this planet called earth.
It keeps us going by giving us a sense of worth.
Not limited by a specific set of rules or norms,
Love is found in many different shapes and forms.

Partnership love is between husbands and wives.
It is a commitment made 'til the end of their lives.
They will work through whatever is sent their way,
And their love, though tried, will grow with each day.

Passionate love is the fire between two lovers,
This love is a love that is not shared with others.
It causes their hearts to pound when they are alone.
It is the most physical side of love that is known.

Platonic love is the love that all friends share.
It is the type that shows that you really do care.
Love of this kind doesn't look at gender or race;
It's caring about a person you could never replace.

Parental love is the love that comes from mom and dad.
It thrives in all experiences, whether happy or sad.
It is given unconditionally, even before we are born.
We return to this love when others leave us forlorn.

Perfect love was shown when God willingly gave his Son,
And when Jesus bowed his head and said, "It is done."
This love is still alive and being offered to you.
You can accept or reject it; which one will you do?

The Wind Is In The Sail
by Pauline Williams

The wind is in the sail
Hear the sea gull cry o'head
See the skies in hues of red
With horizon dead ahead
Eyes are cast beyond the sea
And all worry tends to flee
While the wind in the sail

The wind is in the sail
See the whitecaps lap their way
To the shores around the bay
Luring creatures there to stay
So they swim along in glee
Sensing peace and harmony
While the wind is in the sail

The wind is in the sail
Rising moon shows birds in flight
Seeking home in fading light
Calling loved one in the night
Heaven's north star's guiding ray
Pilots ships along their way
While the wind is in the sail

In The Firmament
by Sharon Yoder

Water in the sky
And water beneath;
All over the earth,
Her powerful sea.
Beware the hideous power
Which hides beneath the
Still, peaceful face;
A rumbling sleep beneath
It's quiet pace.
From high and low a sudden burst
Of stormy rain upon the earth;
Forty days and forty nights
Saw the destruction of life
With all its force of might.
Nature echoes that event
Of long ago,
Remembering it's power
In the stream's flow.
Still a promise holds it back,
A bow in the rain to promise
The earth would not die this
Way again shining in the
Firmament above and below.

That Darn Cat
by Mary Anne Moseley

Once upon a morning sunny, as I ate my eggs all runny,
On a plate of china blue with toast to sop them up,
I daydreamed some - then came a clanging.
From outside something was banging, banging, and I
dropped my cup.
"What's that?" I cried as it fell to the floor.
The banging stopped, I ran to the door.
It's just the cat, and nothing more.

In he struts, so bold and brassy, smoothly moves his
golden chassis,
Rubs my leg and starts to purr.
A pretty cat - he looks so pleasing.
I pick him up and start in sneezing, wheezing as I pet his fur.
My eyes are tearing, so therefore,
The cat must go - back out the door.
I will not suffer - nevermore!!

Enlightener
by Wesley Wordsmith

That I, this stubborn, lonely man, could
Have been seduced, and so quickly and
Irretrievably, by this Lady
Of The Night! This Queen whose beauty is
So astonishing and so distant ---
This Ancient Woman whose charms have left
Me cold and aloof these many years.

By day, I seek relief under the
Cliffs in this perspiring wilderness
Awaiting her almost unwonted
Appearance. Each night she takes longer
To show herself, but then appears more
Radiant, and never once turning
Her back, she reveals a little more.

I remember the Aetolian,
Eastern shepherd, so solitary
And so far---an ancient lover---and
I feel a kindred closeness to him
In this belated sharing. Tonight,
Here among the paloverde, she
Is round and plump and her enchantment

Diminishes
All else.

Morning Glory
by Elmer Yee

in the midst of a field
stands a single morning glory
surrounded by a throng of dancing daffodils

star of the earthen stage

a glint of sun
and a lilting breeze
set the ballet in motion

on this solitary morn

clad in phoenician purple
with a crown of white
this child of nature sways

to the sound of daybreak

intoxicating to the eye
yet seen by none
this private theater endures

tribute to the heavens above

day begins anew
and the stage wakes with life
fueled by the passion of a dancer

the morning's glory
a single morning glory

Spring 1996 Honorable Mentions

Whispers

Chapter Three

**Youth Program
Honorable Mention Awards**

Competitors in the Spring 1996
Special Awards Program
for Competitors under the age of 21.

My Mind
by Amanda Acree - age 15

As I awake inside the night, my body dripping in cold sweat,
I try to go back to sleep. There is great despair in my life,
but I amuse myself with ambition. Everyone lives in fear, but
everyone has different fears of different things. Most do not
realize that they live in fear of themselves. I am greatly
feared by my mind. My curiosity runs wild with love and fear.
Sometimes when I wake I'm glad to be alive, but when I
lay down to sleep I want to die. My mind makes no sense. It's
odd how a mind can be so confused. But we live in a world that
is very confusing.
I usually deprive myself from love. Because love can cause
so much hunger and pain. But yet, I desire a companion to love
and cherish. But my mind might scare them away.
I live my life in the dark, because in the light you can see
more than you can have, but in the dark, it's only black.

Poem, Poema
by Debby J. Adams - age 12

Though always seeming tone,
the fact still is they're volcanoes inside,
waiting to explode, though often hidden in time.
Though sounding odd, out of place, or bizarre
these are words collected from their heart
and though poems this or poems that.
each one is special, because it contains love!
an unmeasurable gift to those who care,
belonging to poets anywhere,
the tamed, outraged courage inside
to spill on to paper where there's nothing to hide
though often rejected, one's words are one's words
but may it be a gift to each boy and girl.

Someday
by Stephanie Adamson - age 13

The gift that I would give the world
would be given lots of thought.
This gift would be specially made, not
manufactured, packaged, or bought.

This gift would be overflowing with
love, the love of one person, thats me!
But ever soon, the amount of that love
will increase to two or three.

The amount of love will get bigger each
day as more people realize what's going on,
And soon the war and prejudice in this
world will suddenly be gone.

Nobody would ever be hated again for
their culture, heritage, or race,
And I'm positively sure people will think the
world's a better place.

If everyone helps just a little with my
gift, in their own caring way,
Maybe, I think, my gift will be finished and
given to the world someday.

I Ask For Honesty
by Danielle Addeo - age 17

 Please don't bring me roses to
satisfy your guilt
 Just like broken promises, every
rose will wilt.
 Never stare into my eyes as you're
telling me a lie
 I'd rather you stay silent, than
have your honesty die
 Don't ever kiss my lips because you
think that you're supposed to
 I couldn't bare your embrace if
the feelings weren't true
 Please don't think that you should
have to call me every single night
 Only when you long to hear my
voice do you know the time is right
 Never make I love you part of
our routine
 I'd rather have that moment
turn out just like a dream
 Don't ever think of leaving me
before you say good-bye
 Tell me that you're going so I
don't sit alone and cry

Not The Same
by Joseph Adesso - age 17

Inbetween the real and surreal
Unsure about anything and everything
Something caught in the mind
Others locked away
Touching reality and not facing it
It is the beginning of the end
It is the end of the beginning
Confusion or distortion
A reflection or an image
A piece or none
Facing reality and lost
Forget it
Pleasure of pain and hurt
Killing all without knowing
The advantage, vulnerable
Sure about nothing

Finally
by Angela A. Aguon - age 13

Love wraps around me like
a warm blanket in the winter.
I welcome its warmth and
glimmer with joy.

I scream with happiness, blink
with excitement, and I twitch
with anxiety.

Finally, love has heard my
desperate cries.

Bitter Sweet Dream
by Michael Alcala - age 19

I once had a dream
One of beauty
And I would live that dream
No matter how far out of reach it would seem
At night was the only true happiness
Somehow I wanted to make the dream last
One day the dream came true
And by talking to you
My world was no longer blue
But reality has a way of diminishing dreams
For I had nothing you needed by no means
But I went to my dream that night
And still couldn't stop the dream
Even though I put up a fight
I one had a dream
One of you
And I would live that dream
Even though I knew it wouldn't come true

High Mountain
by Angela Aldrich - age 13

Beyond this deep, dark valley
Over the hill somewhere,
I know there is a mountain,
Where people seem to care.
The shadows of the darkness
Will all be cast away
By the light that shines upon us
As though it's always day.
The loneliness that makes us cry.
Will be comforted by friends,
And all our crooked unknown paths
Will be straightened at the bends.
So beyond this deep dark valley
Over the hill somewhere
I'll find that one high mountain,
And the happiness I'll share.

My Love For You
by Lia-Maria Alfonsi - age 16

Like a blooming flower lying in a meadow you look prettier than you ever have.
If you give a piece of your heart to me, I'll add it on to my heart to make it complete; My love for you is like an ocean of water, nothing can come between us,
I'll make the vow and say I do, if that's what it takes to be with you.

Dancer of the Night
by Kara Alicakos - age 13

She dances with the arts of emotion,
Glides around like a leaf in a warm
　breeze.
Her dress sculptures her body's every
　movement.
Her dance is like a spell,
Binding every move with mystery.
She mixes in with the brightness
　of dark.
Until the rays of light dies.
And she is left standing,
In a pool of darkness.

A Single Leaf
by Nicole Allen - age 16

A single leaf
quickly blows off it's protecting branch,
and soars through the sky-
refusing the guidance of the wind.
It travels past the other leaves
that are still connected to the branch
of the hovering mother-tree.
The leaf yearns a life of it's own,
and to experience joys and sorrows
that the winds of change may bring.

Summer
by Ashlee Almeida - age 17

I see heaven in the summer
When daylight never ends
And the sun and moon
Shine together
All day long
The iridescent sky
Offers lustrous stars
For wish-making
And the overwhelming heat
Burns like passion
And sweat gushes from your pores
Like an internal desire
Forcing it's way
To the surface
Summer love blooms
Among the daisies,
Blossoms with the roses
The pansies, and the daffodils
Decorate the emerald earth
With the exquisite beauty
Of the endless summer.

Winter Carnival
by Kristina Almquist - age 16

Today,
as unrelated to you as it was,
my father was relieved
your parents were the ones
who were picking me up tonight.
Today,
I thought of how
we sat in your house.
How we cleaned
and smiled and loved.
Today, I remembered
it's in that drawer
that you keep the forks...
and in that one
that you keep the cooking spoons.
Today,
I tried to rest,
to get you off my mind...
Only to dream of you,
as platonic as that moment was,
smiling in the snow.
Today, my friend,
I shivered with fear
at the thought that
I may never hold you again.
My stomach was sick when
I thought of how we loved
and let it pass.

Loneliness
by Denise Alonso - age 13

As I stare out into the sea,
A strange feeling comes over me.
Dark clouds cover the once blue sky,
The cold winds rush on by.
Loneliness in side of me.

All I see is a fading sun,
No flowers blooming, not even one.
Shadows covering my smiles,
That used to run for miles and miles.
Loneliness around me.

No more friends, just strangers around,
A cold, dark world I have found.
Alone in the world I once knew,
That has now turned my spirits blue.
Loneliness...That is me.

Love
by Maria Ambion - age 15

The brownest leaf in autumn...
The whitest of all the snow,
A timeless treasure...
That a savage could never know,
Various emotions...
That are all felt in one;
A sudden desire...
To chase the obscured sun,
Tears of hope...
Emerging from the walls of despair;
A fallen petal of a rose...
Being careful not to tear,
A silhouette of dreams...
Against the lightness of day.
Something so close to the heart...
Yet so very far away;
An echo of laughter...
When things are going so wrong,
An enemy of weakness...
The strength behind all who are strong;
An undefined word...
That only takes a second to say,
Something that would surely take...
A lifetime to portray.

"I Saw"
by Heather Amos - age 19

I saw your perfect face again
Those eyes that remind me of all that might have been
I saw those arms that used to hold me
They seem so weak now that I'm no longer lonely
I saw the hands that once clasped mine
Held me in another place and time
I saw you reflected in the glass
Shadows of the present, future, past
I saw the reasons that made me say goodbye
I saw you today and for once didn't cry

Who Is God?
by Stout Anawati - age 14

Sometimes I take time to think,
think about life.
It helps to have time to myself;
I feel unpressured and content.
The only other person there,
Always there,
Is God.

Sometimes I do the wrong thing.
I don't mean to do evil.
I am always forgiven
Without a doubt.
The person who forgives me,
Always forgives me,
Is God.

Sometimes I doubt my faith,
And I know I shouldn't.
I feel friendless,
And lonely sometimes.
The only person who never leaves me,
Never leaves,
Is God.

Sunsets
by Tanna Andrews - age 11

The sky is God's easel
He paints with the clouds
And the colors of the wind.
He makes a masterpiece
With his tender hands.
He creates a model
Of his perfection.
People notice
The painting in the sky.
They see the soft delicate touches.
The beauty is overwhelming.
His lovely work brings
Smiles to the world.

remember
by jaMie Angove - age 14

now i remember the reason i let you go,
the reason that you never would let me show.
you beat my heart until it was broken,
you kicked me when i was down,
you let me go unnoticed and unloved.
you never heard a sound.
i now remember the reason i don't care,
the reason that you yanked and tugged, and pulled out my hair.
you let me down in my time of need,
you put me through hell in a wicked way,
you took back everything you ever gave,
you have a cruel heart and need to watch what you say.
everything came back now, suddenly so clear.
i never would've let you go, remember,
you left me dear

Soul Mates
by Heather Anthony - age 16

Freak in the night -
Live and learn well.
Deal with your problems -
An emotional hell.

Teach yourself to love -
So you can love me
Find your inner thoughts.
Look deeper and you'll see.

Your eyes burn with passion,
Grab hold onto mine.
Seeking an illusion -
A lost most divine.

Petals may fall
When the wind stirs them 'round.
Remember to stand tall -
You're not on loose ground.

The ebony clock
Will chime just for you
Don't be afraid,
I'll pull you through.

Search for me, hon.
You won't look to far.
I'll be that someone
When you wish on a star.

Our spirits know things
We need to discover.
We're connected some how
Always and forever.

Heaven
by Caryn Arbolino - age 18

Heaven is a world far away
Where everything is always bright
And everyone is in love
There's no one that can hurt you
Or break you
Only people who care and love

Heaven is a beautiful place
Where you can escape to
If you feel low

There's always someone in Heaven who cares
Someone who understands you
And will be a friend

Heaven is a world far away
Where the roses are in bloom
And the sun shines all the time
Over a beautiful waterfall

Heaven is a place where nothing ever dies
It lives forever
And forever

Under the warmth and the love
That we create
We shall not die
But rejoice

Spinning
by Michael Arnone - age 18

As my head spins,
I wonder where it all begins.
I look to the past for an answer,

because the future holds nothing
but a nebula of questions and possibilities.
A maze of instabilities,
forever spinning.

I journey back through the warped time,
going deep into the figments of my mind,
as I fly through the aura of my soul.

I go and visit all of my memories,
all of the joys and the miseries.
Then I come to the center and find nothing.

For I am the journey,
and like past and future eternity
forever spinning.

A Friend In Need
by Teresa Arthur - age 16

I sat on a hill thinking that I was worthless.
I felt a strong but gentle hand on my shoulder.
I turned around thinking that I was going to die,
but it was just a friend in need,
and so was I.
As we sat, we cried, and laughed;
there she found a friend and so did I.
There will always be room for her
in my heart.

To Be With You
by Tiffany Artley - age 14

A little light
Is what I see
With you
Is where I want to be.

So many things
I wish to do
So little time
To be with you

A little more time
Is what I need
And to grow
A little seed

You Are Always There
by Mary Autry

When my life falls apart,
You are always there just outside of my heart,
When I think the world is coming to an end,
You are always there just as my friend,
When my day is going bad,
You are always there just to make me glad,
When I think I'm going to die,
You are always there just before I cry,
When my eyes can't see,
You are always there just for me,
When I think I can't hear,
You are always there just a sweet dear,
When my defenses go down,
You are always there just to turn things around,
When I think you are not there,
You are always there just to show me how much
you really care,
When my life falls apart,
You are always there just outside of my heart.

Beautiful Day
by Ashleigh Aylwin - age 14

An angels soft wings
and the sound of their sigh
is the sound of a wonderful lullaby.

A kiss of a cloud
and the smell of the rain.
You then realize
nothing will be the same.

A strong look of reality
you can feel you're on your way.
Looking straight ahead
it will be a beautiful day.

Reading
by Ivy Barkakati - age 11

Reading
A never-ending process
Can be done anywhere, anytime
Traveling to new worlds
Musty, old pages yellowed with age
Absorbing information like a sponge soaking up water
Spine-tingling suspense
Creating vivid visions in my mind
Meeting new friends and making new enemies
"Halt! Who goes there--friend or foe?"

Abandoned Children
by Katie Barr - age 16

Out of sight,
Out of mind,
Hansel and Gretle,
Left to die,
Underneath the cold midnight sky,
Lonely and crying,
Trusted,
Now betrayed,
Cold and sleeping,
Hoping and dreaming,
That they will have the will to fight,
For one more day,
Single hour,
Single minute,
Weeping in desolate fear,
At the dragons who,
Keep watch nearby,
Over the children,
Who now cry,
For their mommies,
One more tear,
Then she'll come,
Gnomes lurking,
In the nearby woods,
No breadcrumbs,
To follow,
On the long,
Walk,
Home.

What Is Love
by Anthea Barteau - age 15

Love is like a flower
which never seems to fade
Although they may look similar
each is differently made

Love is like a diamond ring
definitely a girl's best friend
the circular band goes round and round
to show love is without end.

Love is like a beautiful star
shining through the night
although you can't touch it
it casts a beautiful light

Love is like a grain of sand
there's millions all around
but though you try your hardest
the most perfect can't be found

Love is like you and me
sometimes causing pain
but we always seem to work it
out time and time again.

One True Love
by Heather Bartone - age 16

The happy little lark flies high above the trees;

The happy little lark floats down upon the cool spring breeze.

We see her little shadow soaring by us on the ground.

She sings because she's happy - her one true love is found.

Far Away
by Juliana Basher - age 14

Why do you have to live so far away?
You're in my head every second of the day.

We were only together for a very short time,
But I knew in that moment that you would be mine.

I remember New Year's Eve as the night we met,
It will be a time I will never forget.

Only to you could I communicate,
The others were filled with frustration and hate.

You made me smile each time we would talk,
And in the garden when we went for a walk.

When I left, I was close to tears,
Trying to cope with the pain and fears.

You've touched my heart and there you will stay,
Even though you're three thousand miles away.

The sweet letters you send always make me smile,
Although I get them just once and a while.

I probably will never see you again,
But I will always remember how kind you were then.

All Else Stood Still
by Mike Bateman - age 20

The sound of thunder was silent,
Compared to the thunder within her soul,
As she reached out with open arms,
And forced her body close to mine,
Al else stood still, the rain, the time.

I wasn't ready for this obscure feeling,
That spun my world around,
She slowly took me in her arms,
And gently led me to the ground,
All else stood still, not a whisper, not a sound.

Just her lips consuming mine,
A day that had finally come,
Piece by piece I removed my guard
To feel her body so weak, yet strong,
All else stood still, I know nowhere I belong.

Her body wet with rain and sweat,
Became a part of mine,
And as the love flowed from her heart,
I felt my being locked in time,
All else stood still, no more reason, no more rhyme.

Dedicated to Peggy Anderson

The Mirror
by Stephie Battaglia - age 15

I hold a little mirror, one that is now broken,
Bringing back the passion, the lust that went unspoken,
The one big mistake that changed our destiny,
That shattered little mirror, thrown from jealousy.

If only I could alter segments from the past,
Heal it with a bandage, or treat it with a cast,
Take back hateful words, said to cause him pain,
Wipe away my tears that once poured down like rain.

I could just imagine, how it would have been,
If I hadn't waited, and realized it back then
If I hadn't made that dreadfully wrong choice,
If I would have listened to his caring, guiding voice.

We could have been together, in perfect harmony,
Lending out our love, that once was meant to be,
Both our beating hearts intertwined as one,
Never causing pain, the pain that is never done.

As fantastic as that sounds, it's just a fantasy,
What a wonderful sensation, if only it could be,
When he threw my mirror, it crashed and fell apart,
When he threw my mirror, he also broke my heart.

Pain
by Wendy Bauer - age 18

-Pain-
Sweeps through me violently.
I hear my heart pounding in my ears as
another wave pulls me under.
-Breathe, two, three, four, Breathe!-
Drugs! Drugs! I need drugs!
-Anguish-
I begin to cry.
Time after time the pain overtakes me
until I fear that I may die.
-Epidural-
Thank god for modern medicine.
-Sunrise-
Okay time to push.
I push and push and push until exhaustion sets in.
-One more!-
Suddenly I feel relief greater than I have ever known.
A comfort so immense it jolts my very soul.
-Bliss-
All the pain I endured does not surpass the
ecstasy I feel as I look upon the tiny
miracle God has granted me.

Untitled
by Nikki Beitler - age 14

It seems like only yesterday
I looked into your eyes and
Saw that special spark
That set my heart afire.

I didn't mean to make mistakes
And I'm sure you didn't either.
Why can't we say we're sorry
And just get on with the future?

The past was so long ago
Even though I can't forget it.
Please accept my apology
And let us start a new beginning.

We had a special love going
That is long diminished by now.
All I have been wondering
Is what did I do wrong?

Stop To Think
by Erin Baum - age 16

After the end of our lives,
When the world is sullen and blank.
And pollution swallows the Earth.
We have past generations to thank.
With modern technology,
Subways and malls,
Contaminated dirt,
And polluted waterfalls.
The world becoming lifeless,
Bitter and dark.
The green grass turned to brown.
Pollution has left it's mark.
I love this Earth the way it is,
With fields and grasses green.
The sky a deep shade of blue,
And the air smelling nice and clean.
With nature of all kinds,
With all this on the brink,
Of life as we know it,
Why didn't we stop to think.

The Beauty in a Beast
by Monique Bedard - age 17

If people would take the time to look beyond, deep into you, they could see what I see. They would not look and see lips that rarely smile and eyes that can burn with fire. They would not see fists of steel and arms of frightening strength.

If they would stop fearing you, they could see a man with just as much love as any other. They could see your cute dimples when your boyish smile plays upon your lips. They could see your hands and arms are really gentle and loving. Love I feel each and every time you hold me.

Every night as I watch you peacefully sleep, I think of how foolish the illusions people have, that your heart is made of stone. I know it's truly made of gold. For I see the beauty in what they call a beast.

Shattered Mirrors
by Travis Beahlon

All dressed to a "T" in black and white. Brought here by an invitation.
Yesterday's yesterday, she just a friend,
Yesterday his love,
Today another man's bride.

As she applies the final touches of make-up he stands in the door way behind her admiring
her stunning reflection. Startled, she turns around. A smile rushes to her face as she opens her
arms to give him a hug. Never in days past could he remember her so beautiful as today. The first
time they have seen each other in five long years.

As they reminisce he begins to miss the days when he held her in his arms, once upon a
time.
He asks,"Do you remember when we...?"
She laughs and replies,"Yes, but we were just kids then."

Soon the moment at hand. He stares from afar, his blue eyes now colored jealous. His mind
buried in a coffin full of yesterdays. His thoughts now veered towards times past when with her
laughter flooded his life. That was until the day she said,"I love you" If only he cared enough then
to say, "I love you." Then it would be him standing by her side, his ring on her finger, and his
dreams coming true; ushered with the words, "I do", she says!

Un-Characterized
by Andrea T. Beckman - age 19

Violated
Shown fleetingly in soft flickers
of candle light
A purple tinted cheekbone
Red spiderwebs
marring virgin white eyes
surrounding an iris of green
A raised knot in an auburn hairline
Angry scratches across the plain
of a smooth white stomach
Huddled
In a fetal position
Defenses as sharp as the razor
Poised
To turn, fists raised and fight
Terrified but not helpless
Emotional but tearless
Pain for the pleasure of one man's eyes
As he gazed upon scarlet drops
Smears blending with the pattern on
starched white sheets

Untitled
by Dana Bertisch - age 17

Winding blindly
down the castle
she emerges meek
and defeated naked
with glistening tears
dripping from her
toes

Clutching her hands
together between
her breast she
sinks to her knees
and watches through
nebulous eyes as
providence taunts her
with his slender
longevity

walking synchronized
towards the iridescent
light she combats
the masculine force
drawing her closer
with her beauty
her symmetry
her dynamic equilibrium

rising with aplomb
she epitomizes womankind
I stoke her hand in vain
she is blind to my affection

Thought
by Tony Biasetti - age 17

As I sit and Ponder
By the raging water
How life is like
the ocean at night
with only shimmers of light
to brighten the seemingly endless
watery night

Bargain From A Demon
by Jennifer Bivona - age 15

Hi! I am a demon.
Actually, I'm THE demon that
influences you,
the demon that takes away your
innocence, more and more each day.
I am the demon, day and night.
I interfere with your ability to
distinguish wrong from right.
I take over your conscience.
I am the demon that lets you
have whatever you want, for
a very small price.
That is, of course, you life.

Winter
by Dana Bertisch - age 17

The ghost of ebony
The angel of death
Calls to the clouds
Brings with it winter

An impending death
Lurks beyond the trees
Stay close to home
Beware the winter

The fading light
The kiss of fright
The gods delight
Engulf the winter

I try to find my footsteps
But a bluish haze fogs my vision

Do I live a martyr?
Do I live a lie?

I am just a child
A shadow
A mere flit of the imagination

My body lies lifeless in the snow
My skin a bony white
My life has been stolen
Unmercifully by winter

The flowers bloom
But I see them not
I taste them not
I smell them not

I have been raped
by winter

So look for me
and mock me
and corrupt me
and hurt me

I am now the
Ghost of ebony
I am winter

A Shell Of A Being
by Tonya Betz - age 19

On the fire escape he sits, pretending not to hear his parents' anger echoing through the apartment. Like a dove caught in a cage, his innocence is trapped in a situation of hostility. This life was all that Peter had known.

All of his ten years had been spent in this shallow representation called life. At each meal, tension filled the air, and misplaced venom tainted what he ate. A serpent had taken over his home, and Peter could do nothing to stop this madness. Fear mounted each time a bottle of beer was removed from the refrigerator, worn and dented from his father's occasional rage.

Peter did not hold his life in very high regard. He would wait in blind obedience, abiding by others' definitions of himself. It was all a test of acceptance and rejection. He received his share of both. The need for any other dilemmas was unnecessary.

He waited each breathless night for the shifting shadows in the hall to close his bedroom door. Once the door closed, war was declared, and sleep was impossible to acquire. Peter waited for it to begin and then for it to end. His mind lost times space that filled the in-between. When silence resumed, he sat patiently, as if expecting a tender hand to convey even the smallest amount of love. Peter had fallen prey to the bruises of the soul.

On the high ledge sits only a shell of a boy. The child within grew dim, and like a kerosene light flickered and went out. The darkness of the city covers over his dull heart as he passes the time in a lifeless daze. He's just a shell of a being trapped in a disbelieving world.

Deep in the Heart of Heartbreak
by Melissa Biddle - age 16

Deep in the heart of heartbreak,
A withered soul will bleed.
Tears of red are shed in time.
The clock is ticking - I'm in my prime.
But deep in the heart of heartbreak.

"Why did this happen?" I ask of a ghost.
What a torturous system this is!
I want to blame others, cannot blame myself.
Constricted with nightmares - my life on the shelf.
Deep in the heart of heartbreak.

I'm so mad I could kill-time and again.
I cry softly behind a thick lock.
Craving revenge and a half.
While repressing a laugh.
Deep in the heart of heartbreak.

I look in the mirror, and it is not me.
A stranger is peering - aghast.
A change has occurred.
Oh, how I've been lured!
Deep in the heart of heartbreak....

Untitled
by Amanda Bittinger - age 17

I am torn and miserable with grief
I wonder if there is an end
I hear the agonizing voices screaming in pain
I see evil burning the men
I am torn and miserable with grief
I pretend not to hear or understand
I feel that I cause more pain for them
I touch their souls to try to soothe them
I worry that their souls are decaying
I cry to god to help them
I am torn and miserable with grief
I understand how their souls are suffering
I say to them that there will be an end to this chaos
I try to give them the strength to hold on
I hope they will live through what the evil has done to them
I am torn and miserable with grief

True Or False
by Dominique Bigbee - age 13

The face of the armor
The face of the man
The laughs at the danger
The cry from his hands.

Which is true
Which is false
Which one has most of the loss

Is it you or is it me
Which is the one with the dying dream

Which is true, which is false
Which one has most of the loss

You have to remember when you seek danger
Who loses more you or the stranger

Which is true
Which is false.................

Before Bad
by Jamie Birlin - age 13

Have you ever noticed
That you laugh before you cry:
Or that you say hello,
Before you say good-bye?
And at every single dead branch
There is always a green leaf.
And whenever there's a doubt
There's always some belief.

There's always the good
Before the bad.
The happy before the sad.
The to
And then the fro.
You always have to come
Before you have to go.

But remember this
As the rain hits the ground
And as the stars twinkle
When the world goes round
There's something else
You must be sure.
That for every sadness
There's always a cure.

Untitled
by Pamela Blakley - age 17

Underneath a great oak tree.
In the bay sailboats to see.
Slightly from the south blows a breeze,
which plays songs gently through the leaves.
Everyone has caught some fish
the weather has been beautiful, ah but a wish.
This is my kind of vacation,
for camping I give a standing ovation.
It is only five miles to this lake,
some people say that's dumb but give me a break,
It's not something expensive, to some exotic place,
but it's where we can get away from life's rat race.
So with a fire, fish, and sleeping bag I am totally content.
I feel refreshed and renewed I am so glad we went.

The Child In All Of Us
by Laura Ellen Blair - age 20

Riding in your little red wagon,
catching frogs in your bare hands
Those precious memories
that only you could understand
Playing hooky from school,
hanging out around the park
Remember those years you had a curfew,
home before it's dark?
Sneaking in the house
When the sun is just starting to rise
And each Thanksgiving
you'd help mommy with her pumpkins pies
Remember pigtails in your hair,
your favorite summer dress?
Remember making mud pies,
daddy laughing at the mess?
Remember your very first best friend,
or your first ice cream cone?
Remember your first real heartbreak?
You thought you'd always be alone.
And you stare at your reflection
Look at how you've grown!
You realize you can't have that back
and, yet, you've always known
But if I could, for just one day,
feel like I did back then
I'd hold it in my heart forever,
and never let go again.

"Be"
by Ashley Bliss - age 15

There is no remedy for sadness,
no solvent for pain,
no cure for the darkness inside,
no pill for strife.
There is no magic potion for suffering,
no elixir for heartache,
no vaccine for gloom,
no drops for seclusion.
There is no antidote for the poison of desire,
no antiseptic for the germ of oblivion,
no prophylactic for the disease of untruth,
no sedative to ease the want of sinlessness.
There is no germicide you can spray around
your mind to rid it of the tainted
smell of monotonous melancholy.
Unearthly, tearful, gazes lend
support to the calluses of being.
A piece of green sea glass- look through
it, everything changes color.
Reach out, spin, fall, crash, stumble, stammer...
Be.

Knife
by Benjamin McIver Bost - age 20

When I was younger, I cut my finger
With a new blade, long desired,
Playing in the woods, carving weapons,
though I had been forewarned by my father
of the dangers inherent in a first knife.
First bottle of liquor, drunk too fast.
First paycheck, spent too fast.
First knife, bloody finger.

I Shall Return By Winter
by Tracy Block - age 16

I shall return by winter,
was the promise that he made.
She sits alone and cold,
wondering what if he had stayed.

Her nights are cold and empty,
and the days they hold no light.
A long figure stands in the doorway,
as the winds blow fast and strong.

A faint knocking at the door,
brings her to her feet.
He enters the cold room warmly,
the cold night has now found heat.

She no longer sits alone,
her heart is lifted so.
For he did return by winter,
as he promised long ago.

Spring
by Lisa Bluteau - age 14

The rain is falling,
Renewal is in the air;
New things are growing,
And appearing everywhere;

The bear wakes from hibernation,
Only to see;
That things aren't quite,
As they used to be;

Brightly colored flowers,
Are rising from the ground;
I see them everywhere,
As I look around;

The birds sit in the treetops,
Singing in harmony;
Not even the greatest composer,
Could match their unity;

A soft refreshing breeze,
Begins to blow;
Carrying along with it,
The flowered fragrance from the meadow;

Spring paints a picture in my mind,
Of people sharing peace for eternity;
But instead of hate and war,
I wish the picture was reality.

Her
by Rachel Brown - age 16

Her eyes like diamonds.
Her skin is like silk.
Her hair is soft as rabbit's fur.
Is she a dream of is she real?
If she is real
is it love I am experiencing?

I Dream
by Catherine Lynn Boggs - age 16

At night I dream of distant lands,
of mystical creatures-
a lover's hand

At night I dream of peaceful places,
of soft music, and shimmering
faces

I dream of roses, kissed by the dew,
of animals that aren't seen by me
or you

I dream of oceans of the deepest blue
of beautiful sunsets-
I know are few

I dream of valleys and rolling hills,
I dream of pretty daisies and
daffodils

I think next time
I'll be more clever;
A dream like that, should last forever.

Winter's Gloom
by Olivia Bolles - age 15

As I saw my grandfather lying in the hospital;
He reminded me of something
Yet I could not figure out what.
Until finally autumn came, and I saw it.
The trees lost their leaves,
The bright blue sky turned brittle,
The flowing streams turned cold and hard,
And I saw it.
I saw what it reminded me of
And I realized it was winter;
When the life goes out of things,
As his life was going out of him.

The falling drops from the I.V. were snow like in April
Being looked at with nothing but despair.
Though he had a bright smile it taunted me like thoughts of spring in
    December
Because I knew it was not possible for him to stay
Just as spring cannot stay in December.
These thoughts hung over my head like a thunderhead
Until one day the storm erupted.
When I saw his flesh turn grey and his heartbeat fade;
He reminded me of winter when all turns cold and lifeless for a while,
For he too had turned
Forever cold and lifeless.

Life is Like
by Stephanie Breese - age 13

Life is like a storm
One minute it's the calm before the storm,
hen one word or gesture appears
And the wind starts to blow,
Thunder strikes and lighting flashes
Then the storm passes and it's calm again.
You never know when the worst of the storm will
strike
So when it does-Beware!!

Violet Creaks
by Emily Bond - age 14

My house is like an Old Man.
He rambles on with brilliant creaks trying to tell his memories.
Most of the time no one cares.
They pass by without lending an ear for his endless tales.
His shoes used to be untied and was losing hair.
Once care was given the lint was gone from his shaggy, vermilion coat.
He is now nicely shaven and smells like scarlet roses.
But the age did not leave, nor did the creaks.
He has memories of the caretakers and the love they have brought.
Deep down in the blue, he is scared of his friends' departure.
At night when the sounds are gray and silent,
Indigo thoughts surround him.
Night is his time for concern"
One can hear his eternal groans.
If one wanders to comfort the Old Man,
He cries out pride with every creaky step of the wanderer.
Both the man and the caretakers never want to leave each other,
but somehow it always happens.
When the time comes to leave,
The hosts forget about the man, the smell of scarlet,
and all the memories they have left behind.
But the Old Man never forgets.
Now he has one more creak to tell.

Change
by Melissa Bondurant - age 15

Change is all around us.
Change can be stupendous.
Change can be outrageous.
No matter how it comes,
It's there,
It surrounds us.

When life seems like it's all fitting into place,
Change happens and you're happy where you are,
When you're happy where you are,
Changes happen, and you have to catch another falling star.

When friends and family are nearby,
Changes happen, and it's time to say, " Good-bye".
When loved ones are near,
Changes happen, and will you ever see them again,
You fear.

You start to blame yourself and no other.
They don't blame you they blame your mother.
Your parents quarrel,
And you want to hide like a squirrel.

You think this is all for the better,
Then you forgot to send, to your friends,
Another letter.
They think you have forgotten them,
Then they're gone forever
Your best friends,
Anna, Anne, and Em.

Ireland
by Jennifer Bozak - age 17

Green and gay
on a sunny day
worlds are lost
by a chilling frost
a place of light
that shows no fright
legends are told
about the gold
over the rainbow's end
lies my sweet Ireland

All I Want
by Marjory Bonzil - age 16

Please, don't go buying me
Anything for Christmas
'Cause whatever it's gonna be
I'm sure, forever, it won't last
A dress, I'll soon outgrow
A watch, soon I won't need
A telephone, maybe a radio
But none of them do I want indeed
You may think it's strange
But do take me seriously
'Cause, my mind, I will not change
I just want you to be with me
Don't bother bringing a flower
A champagne won't be necessary
All that we need is each other
And everything else will come naturally
There'll be no boundaries to what you can say
No sort of limits to what you can do
Simply let things be, in their own way
'cause all I want for Christmas, is you

Nightfall
by Genery Booster - age 15

Sweet perfumed breath my four winds cease to bring.
Sun bid a fond fare-well, to short, the day.
Through pines aloft, cold, doth Zephyrs sing.
Wan moon adorn my sky; be on your way
Come, shed thy soft blue light on all below.
Fly hither Jack, and dust my windowpanes
With crystals white, how luminous, like snow.
The silver queen must come to dance again
And bring her shining subjects, one and all
To tread a light-foot path across my sky.
Bare, shivering trees, stretch your branches tall,
Catch the falling stars in your arms so high
Till dawn must come to chase away the night
And bring with her the gentle morning light.

Untitled
by Jennifer Boserman - age 14

Gracefully an Orca, or Killer Whale
Swims in the cast, blue sea
It dives to the farthest depths
Past some sea anemone

It sings it's haunting songs
Of many place near and far
It takes a breath at the surface
Then plunges again near a sea star

Pat a prickly Porcupine Fish
The Orca freely swims
Doing dives an all sorts of flips
Showing off to those with fins

It swiftly swims to the ocean floor
Near coral that is so frail
Over sponges, under waves
There you will find the song of the whale

Brought It Upon Ourselves
by Miranda Bostic - age 14

The world is crashing
People are clashing
Peace went out the door

War is here
"The end is near"
Gonna die by the hands of the Lord

Waste on the street
Kids packing heat
Cries of sorrow you can hear

Drugs and homicide
Rape and suicide
The end of destruction is near

And I welcome it

Music Box
by Kate Boswell - age 17

Gentle music,
A beautiful ballerina turns endlessly.
The music box sits proudly upon
the grand old piano.
A benign push by the soft
fingertips of a child.
Clink!
The fragile ballerina, no longer
beautiful, lay in numerous
pieces beneath the grand old piano.
The poignant music, no longer
harmony, drains from the music
box.
And the child slowly treads away
with glee from the grand old
piano.

Mirror Image Of Your Heart
by Tara Bower - age 16

I'd give you a kiss, for a small mirror image of your heart.
I'd give you a smile, for the smallest part.
Knowledge of it seldom slowly to start.
Pass it to me, as if it were fine art,
So as to know slowly, a small mirror image of your heart.

I'd lie against your chest, as you talked to me.
Try to make, or hope more to see.
To know you more intimately.
I will find or you'll let it be.
As I listen and you talk to me.

Try to bring up emotions without anything said.
Together, not alone, wish to tread.
Just wish to catch up, get ahead.
As I lie against your chest on the bed.
We'll bring up emotions without anything said.

Now give me your heart, and I'll give you mine.
Holding as dearly as it were a shrine.
So read on the paper, and sign the line.
And for now the mirror image of your heart will be mine

The Color Of The Moment
by Jenifer Bowser - age 19

The orange streaked sky
over a blue-gray town.
I see it all through the windshield
of my periwinkle Hudson.
Time has traveled,
the yellow of age is showing.
The shine on my white shoes
contrasts with the dull black of the pavement.
I drive past the olive green houses
all in a row
their beige sedans in the driveways.
Dogs the color of burnt sienna sit on porches
watching little, magenta bugs fly around.
Little girls in lavender dresses,
little boys in copper colored suits
play till the golden lights of the
house come on telling them that it is
time to come in.

Colors
by Melissa Boyle - age 12

Red, orange, yellow, or green
People judge you on what they've seen
Blue, indigo, violet or pink.
They don't care about what you think.
But your color, and what you look like
They don't care about your color yeah sike!
They won't judge on your mind
Couldn't everyone be color blind.
Being color blind wouldn't be right
People would still see black and white
When will this world of racism end?
When it does we'll be together again.

Distant Memory
by Gela Braslavsky - age 13

Something in the distance
   I remember;
Something from so long ago.
A life I no longer live,
A person I no longer am.
Here.
Here in the full brimming present
I am haunted by one receding
past.
One, or many?
The city lights were blinking
on that night.
As if each one stands for
every blasted night,
filled unending with fear.
Fear.
Beyond the words of any language.
   The wings of steel cut
through the air of fog;
and the city lights recede.
   I know that then;
in a deep path of my mind
I hoped I would forget what I left behind.
   I have still hope I might.
To forget is to forgive.
   Is that not right?

My Secret Place
by Tiffanie Brooks - age 13

My secret place,
Where I go,
 To get engaged in a thought,
While listening to the wind blow,

Where the trees whistle,
And the birds fly high,
In this place,
I shall never have to sigh,

In my secret place,
I can follow my heart,
This secret place,
I'll never have to part,

In my secret place,
The animals are my friends,
And the day doesn't stop,
Until I want it to end.

Class Time
by Adriane Brown - age 17

Lethargy of the soul
Creeping in behind my eyes
Slowly stalking active thoughts
And striking them down with padded claws
Clock hands drag across it's face
My brain drags to a crawl
Now it wanders off to places unexplored before
Concentration's broken
I sit and squander time
Teacher's voice becomes a drone
This class will never end

If It Matters
by Elizabeth Brown - age 17

Only this pain, this hurt held deep,
A depression so huge, a mountain so steep.
Afraid of her pain and too ashamed to lie,
Her childish hands hold a puddle of tears,
Only her family created her fears.
She's just a child, but yet an adult,
Who is to blame, she knows it's her fault.
Rejected by Mother and forgotten by Dad,
Just look in her soul, you see she's sad.
She comes to a stand to walk to the cliff,
As she stares, her voice she lifts.
A scream of rejection, a tear she cries,
She comes to the end and can no longer deny.
She falls to her knees and prays for peace,
All of this hurt, somehow released.
After this journey to her far away place,
She jumps to her death, but glows with grace.
So to anyone who cares, or if it matters,
This world so strong, will just one day shatter.

The Ocean
by Tawanda Brown - age 20

The ocean spread as far as my eyes could see.
While the gentle waves reached out to me;
I could look and see the ocean's endless tides,
Where the seagulls on the ocean's wave would ride;
It seemed to sing a soft melody,
As the wind rippled by the nearby tree;
Against this darkest and lonesome night,
The moon provided a special light;
It was really relaxing and serene,
As a fading memory in a beautiful dream;
It brought me close to reality,
And helped me to appreciate the real me;
Made me feel as free as a dove,
Feeling me with hope, peace, and love.
It taught me about the meaning life,
Washing away all my anger and strife.

The Perfect Place
by Tammy Brulotte - age 19

Search in your mind, try to picture a place
where the sun flies high and the clouds lye low.
Where there's happiness seen on every face,
and where beauty's spread through every window.

Search in your mind, try to create a place
where houses stand tall and buildings lye small.
where peace can exist among every race,
and where laughter is layered among all.

Search in your mind, try to imagine a place
where love remains and hatred dissolves,
where war and crime are easily erased,
and where lasting friendships are evolved.

Search in your mind, try to vision a place
where disease is extinct and health - abundant,
where old age and death are no longer a case,
and where perfection is finally an achievement.

Search in your mind, try to picture this place,
Search in your mind, can you build such a place?

Seventeen
by Steve Buckner - age 16

She's seventeen and can't find the way.
Nothing seems right, in a world so gray.

She's seventeen and locked up inside.
Where can she run, when there's no place to hide.

She's seventeen and lives in hell.
She's been their forever, trapped in her cell.

She's seventeen and there's no one to care.
How can she handle this load she must bare.

She's seventeen and no longer living.
Her body's a grave, her mind unforgiving.

She was seventeen and now she is gone.
She's taken her life within the wee hours of Heidi Dawn.

Two Slides
by Lindsay Budzynski - age 12

Two slides
An old, little, silver and blue slide
with many dents of children playing, chattering through the years.
A new slide
a Big,
Blue,
Shiny one.
The children all ran to play on the Pretty,
New slide.
Expensive,
Huge Slide.
Accept one.
One child stayed and played on the tiny, shabby slide.
He liked the familiarness of it.
And the memories.
Memories of he and his dad laughing
and sliding on it.
But that was before.
Before his dad left,
Before the divorce.
One family,
instead of two.
When they were
Happy.
All the other kids laughed,
and played on the New,
Blue slide,
But he knew that they would come back to their
old, silver and blue slide,
Some Day.

Ignorance
by Stacie Buessing

What's black or white, but never gray?
It's sound is harsh and judgmental.
As fumes from a delivery truck blow in your face you can taste it,
And the lingering smell it leaves on your clothes stays with you.
It can only be seen with shut eyes.
When you feel that problems are "too big to be solved" you're doing it.
What is it you ask?
Ignorance.

If All The World's A Stage
by Lisa Buettner - age 16

If life is but a drama
And all the world's a stage
Then live the life you want to
But don't live a life of rage.

Be someone you are proud of
Be someone you can love
Don't live a life of violence
Live like the peaceful dove.

For the things that we accomplish
Before we turn the page
Are the things that really matter
If all the world's a stage

First Snow
by Jessica Burch - age 14

    The wind calls with one thousand voices singing. The blue sky is trapped in a net of gray and completely obliterated. The once bright sun disappears entirely into a sea of fog. Then the snow comes. It falls from the sky like crystallized paper and covers the sleeping earth like a blanket A cloak of ice and frost veils the trees and bushes, making them look like glass figures in a dim reflecting light. The once noisy rush of day is washed out by the tranquil falling of snow. All is hush.

Grandpa
by Bethany Burger - age 18

With a shot to the sky, we laid you to rest,
remembering the courageous man you were

Your body got old, and your spirit was tamed.
You were always helping someone,
doing their chores or running errands.
Your life was full of adventures,
and you needed to rest.
Somewhere inside, your soul waited to leave.

You had survived for so long.
Never giving in, never giving up.

I wasn't with you the day your body died.
The day your soul was renewed and taken to live forever.

I had said my good-byes,
it was your peaceful face I kissed one last time,
your soft, warm hand I held.

I'm glad you were my grandpa.
I'll never forget.

Silence
by Catrina Burk - age 15

A year ago peoples lives
would change and now there is a
Silence.

It only took a second to destroy families
which took years to build and now
the neighborhoods are
Silent.

Because of destruction and a
very loud bang we remember
by Silence.

How could one man destroy all
these lives and cause them to
be Silent.

168 seconds that should be
filled with childrens laughter
and people's joy but now instead
are Silent.

In The Forest
by Rachel Burns - age 11

As I walk through the forest
a feeling of inner peace builds inside me
I can feel my legs brushing against the tall grass
and I can hear the sound of the nearby stream flowing
and the sweet song of the robin
I can smell the sweet fragrance of the flowers growing
and I see the forest animals playing quietly in the meadow beyond
everything is quiet and peaceful and I say to myself
I'm glad to be here

What You Know In Your Heart
by Nick Burris - age 14

Do you know who are?
Are you lying to yourself?
Is your life a day dream where you live in wealth?
Why do you spend your time trying to impress your
friends in a place where nothing matters?
in a world where no one wins.
What should be important to you is,
who you were in the start, how you live and
what you know in your heart.

The Distance Between Us
by Krista Busse - age 17

I don't know what I should say,
I sit and think about it every day.
I wonder what I'm going to do
If I can't ever say this to you
The words lie around in my mind,
They're afraid to come out
They want to hide
I only have one single fear,
t's the fact that you are never near
The distance between us is
saddening me, for it is you I
can never see.

The Cabin
by Dana E. Buxton - age 12

In the cabin dark and warm,
Groups of children begin to form,
Around a fire with a story book
A story of Peter Pan and Captain Hook,
Fighting together in Never Never Land,
On the ship with the pirates band,
The children stare filled with delight,
But as the time passes their eyelids are no longer light,
They drift into dreams of pirates and lost boys,
And the fire starts dying with a crackling noise,
The cabin grows dark with a rhythmic breathing,
And the oldest child begins to stop reading,
And closes her eyes to dream her sweet dreams,
In the cabin dark and warm.

Many Moons
by Rachel Chaffee - age 16

Look out at the moon,
the silvery beauty is gone too soon.
She spread a white blanket of light,
bringing safety to the night.
Her light touches many minds,
from ancient distant times.
Soon the sun will bring the day,
to push her on her merry way.
With silver clad feet she will go,
her lovely carriage in tow.
But her light has not left this place,
night brings the beauty of her face.

Caring Bob
by Beckie Campbell - age 12

Bob
Funny,
Caring,
Weird
Wishes to build a nursing home
Dreams of money, money, money
Wants to eat fried apple pies
Who wonders why his daughter is so crazy
Who fears arthritis
Who is afraid of not getting his deck built
Who likes Vicki
Who believes reading is good
Who loves fried apple pies
Who loves to go fishing
Who loves unpacking boxes
Who loves his crazy daughter
Who plans on being in his house by 2000
Who plans on eating every night
Who plans on being married for 25 years, at least
Who cares a whole lot for his wife and daughter

Not the First Nor the Last
by Ramie Campbell - age 16

A smile to her sisters,
A frown to her friend;
She's looking for respect in all the wrong places;
She's stuck in the middle, no sight of an exit;
She's accomplished much in her own eyes, but to you she's
    just a beginner;
She's waiting to hear "That's a job well done," but she
    only receives, "I could have done better;"
That closes the door, there's no hope in sight;
She's lost forever, forever in her fright;
This could have been prevented;
Prevented in such a way as this, they could have spoken
    those four little words which mean the most, the most
    to those you miss;
The ones who are lost in the middle between both of
    them, they're never the first, and unfortunately never
    the last;
You and I are the lucky ones, we had it much easier than
most, you were the first and I am the last;
It doesn't end here, I am glad to say;
She has given up the fight, there was no victory in
    sight;
They have lost control, control that was never theirs,
They need to realize her love is still there, she may
    leave but her heart will always be here;
She has won the battle in her eyes and mine, she was
    placed in the middle, but has risen before us all.

Lost Love
by Lindsay Chappell - age 12

She said she couldn't live without him,
He said he couldn't live without her,
He went west,
She went east,
And they both lived.

Ice
by Tanisha Campbell - age 16

She is everything that is ice.
Cold, hard, unrelenting and clear.
And like ice she is impassive,
No one gets through her icy exterior.
But underneath all the ice
Is a living, breathing, warm and caring woman
Waiting to be freed.
She has doubts that
The ice has been her shield for too long.
She thinks she won't know how to be
Or how to live if the ice isn't there,
But she does.
She has survived before
She can do it again.
She wishes to be healed.
Deep in her soul
She wishes for someone to care,
To come and take the pain away.
But no one comes.
All she has is pain, agony and life.
She still hopes, prays
And waits.

The Chosen One
by Kathryn Cardin - age 17

As I laid there,
While he looked down upon me,
I saw laughter in his eyes.
As I cried, he got up to walk
away,
looked down upon me and said
"It's okay honey, your the chosen one."
I didn't quite understand what was
going on,
for I was only a little girl,
but I knew it was wrong.
As I laid there,
drowning in my tears and pain,
he walked away,
laughing.
A few years later,
I had forgotten.

As I laid on the ground,
and felt his foot dig one last time
into my stomach,
I thought for sure I would die.

As I looked at the clock on
the wall,
what I had forgotten
6 years earlier,
came flooding back
to me,
and I couldn't help but wonder, if again,
I had been chosen as the
chosen one.

Relief
by Kate Casselman - age 13

Relief is white, pure and simple.
It tastes like the first breath of winter air, crisp and
    cold.
It sounds like a breath released from a quick
    spontaneous laugh.
It looks like a chalk board having been full of complex
    math facts erased and clear.
It feels like wings you never knew you had, lifting you
    off the ground.
Relief is air to breathless lungs.

Aphrodite
by Alida Cardo - age 20

She lives among the stars,
Cosmic dust, and comets.
Life is a three dimensional portal

She walks among the cosmos.
Her will is fierce and strong.
The winds voice charms her everlasting step.

Love roams above her.
Love gathers his precious arrows
Without a sound.

She hears the soft melody of the stars,
or a trumpet calling for her.
She roams toward the sound.

She walks with the wind
And the stars arrows pointing her path.

When she cries it's full of harmony,
She unleashes her emotions
To walk beyond the portal.

Where Are You?
by Kathleen Carlson - age 15

I'm in a dark room.
There is no light.
I'm reaching out to you.
Where are you?
Everywhere I wave my hands,
All they meet is air.
The walls are slowly closing in,
Though I cannot see them.
The breath is sucked from my lungs,
As I scream a horrid scream.
Where are you?

"The Most Passionate Kiss"
by Micah J. Carlson - age 20

Together we stand, alone, in this room. The question is asked,"What do you want to do"? With this question I slowly walk behind her and begin to let down her hair.
Using a playful voice she asks," What are you doing"? trying to sound innocent and sincere I reply, " I'm fixing something"! Then finishing the circle, I continue walking around to face her. Gently sliding my fingers into her hair just above her ears and then slowly sliding them strait back, I answer," Anything you want "!
Looking deep into her beautiful eyes I desperately await the signal. As her eyes stray away from mine, with a quick glance at my lips her eye's swiftly rejoin mine. With this sign, I softly press my lips against hers and began to kiss her with more passion than my lips have ever felt-- or ever will again.

A Tiny Falling Raindrop
by Stephanie Carlson - age 15

The raindrop falls gently,
Not making a sound,
Glides ever so softly,
Aiming for the ground,

It has no certain shape,
No definite size, or preferation,
Just a watery little drop,
With just one destination,

Finally it lands,
In the deepest, muddiest puddle,
Together on the ground,
Must all the raindrops huddle.

My Friend
by Amanda Carrell - age 15

What did you do with my friend?
You have her body, but you're not her,
How long did it take to consume my friend,
How did you even get in?

I look down my memory telescope, at the girl I knew,
she gave puzzle pieces about herself, I just applied the glue,
Yea, and maybe I got the pieces mixed up,
maybe it was just a show,
And maybe the person I thought I knew,
I never really did know.

There was a time when she thought she knew her limit,
A time when there was an illusion of control,
Remember when you were an escape,
primarily just a toy.
Now you've imprisoned my friend,
trapped in her own escape,
You may have her eyes, but,
We both know you're a fake.

Now she injects you in, just for a thrill
wonder if she knows one day you'll kill?
But I will not shed a single tear,
I already cried when she really died,
the first time she let you in.
So before I go, I will ask once again,
What have you done with my friend?

Cold Blood
by Rebecca Ann Carsley - age 19

Wait, wait for me.
Please don't leave.
I came as fast as I could.
The sound, oh, how it rang in my ears
It was the hallowest and the coldest
That I have heard in my nineteen years.
It was like a bomb
Yet it was only a pop.
Oh good there you are.
Good God Tom
There's a bloody hole in you chest.
Stop playing these games
Wake up, get up, at least move a little,
Why, why have they done this?
Oh, God no, not my baby too.
Why have you come back?
You already took my love from me.
Leave my baby and take me.
Bang
The sound, oh, how it still
Rings in my ears.
Wait, why is it suddenly so dark
And cold, my how it's cold.
Is this what it's like to die
I mean so dark and cold.
Wait for me my love I'm right behind you
My baby, oh God what will...
Why, oh why
IN COLD BLOOD!

Untitled
by Jenn Carter - age 14

the fire of hatred
In my head, in my heart.
I can't douse the flames
they were there from the start.

I look to a god
For guidance and truth.
I find his story transparent,
His power of no use.

I search on for love
To trust someone real.
They want it all for themselves,
They don't care how I feel.

I look for a passage,
A way to escape,
And deep in my heart
I see my choice has been made.

I depart from the flesh,
But my soul has not gone
And as I find death,
The fire burns on!

Hand - me - Down
by Janie Castle - age 14

Hand - me - down your heirloom quilt
For my eyes to touch, my hands to see.
Hand - me - down the crib you built
Give it all to me.

Hand - me - down the locket you wear
It's mine, not yours to keep.
Hand - me - down your rocking chair
Where you rocked your child to sleep.

Hand - me - down your picture book
That you made when you were small.
Hand it down so I can look
It's really not yours at all.

Aren't we all just hand - me -downs
Passed from here to there?
Is it a wonder that we always frown
Is life even fair?

Do you have your father's eyes
Your mother's coal black hair?
Do you notice that your parent cries
The first time you're not there?

When you give your child life
Is it something you've made, you've found?
Or is it just a part of you
You the hand - me - down?

Eternal Sadness
by William Cheetham - age 16

I catch myself slipping farther away
From what seems to be my reality
I can feel it's breath upon my neck
It's grasp about to tighten
And I fear what is about to become of me
A portrait of death hung on a wall
For show and not for sorrow
Not for people to mourn a death
Bur for death to be shown as beauty
Whatever will come has come already
Whatever is deceased is forgotten forever

Dead Nation
by David Chamberlain - age 18

'Twas a quiet day in Montgomery,
No one in the rotisserie.
Peaceful across the entire country,
Because there's no one here but me.

Slowly I walked down the road,
The actions I carried, a heavy load.
Along the way I saw a toad,
To me, farewell he bode.

As I reached an asphalt formation,
Knew it wasn't my final destination.
While resting I had a revelation,
I was alone, in a dead nation.

Picked myself up again,
Stepped outside, it began to rain.
Know I'll never again be sane,
Kept walking, forget the pain.

As I lay me down to sleep,
The racing thoughts make me weep.
Then I hear a sound, a cheep.
Then I listen, not a peep.

When the Sun arose the next day,
And I there lay, in dismay,
This little bird, a beautiful jay,
Rising up from the fray,
Came with me as I ran away.

A Voice Crying Out To Be Heard
by LaTanya Chambers - age 14

A voice is crying out from the mountains
If you'd only hear it's cry
The rain it's tears are flowing
A song to sweet to die

A shattered hope so brave so true
Wishes with no doubt
That shattered hope so pure and true
Can not survive without

For she is weeping as a willow
For joy hope and peace
That shattered hope and shattered dreams
Would soon enough decrease

The dreamers only turn away
From all of the unknown
The voice is speaking loud enough
The voice has even grown

For in this voice lies the truth
Just waiting to be heard
Patiently waiting and listening
For them to hear his word

From the tears upon the voice
So shattered up with hate
Upon the mighty looking down
Upon the lonely's fate

In this world a lonely world
A voice is crying out

Life Is But A Vapor
by Debra Chapin - age 18

Life is but a vapor it has been said many times,
How wise and true is that saying, it is gone
before you know it.

When we breathe our first breath of life and are
thrust out of our mother's womb,
We enter this world with the innocence of a child.

Our future stretched before us unknown to anyone,
except Our Almighty Creator.
We dream our dreams that may or may not become a
a reality.

We experience pain and heartache, but we also
experience the feelings of joy and happiness.

We live our lives to the fullest experiencing
all life has to offer us,
Day by day we live up to ours as well as others
expectations.

But why do we do this, success in this world
means little to us when we're gone,
Real success is in the world hereafter, when we
leave this pain-filled world and stand before our
Maker.

What will you have to show, will you hold your head
high, or will you be ashamed,
Strive for the gold, not of this world, but in the
world after death.

Darkness & Shadows
by Crystal Chapman - age 13

There they are,
Or over there?
Always there,
Everywhere.

Darkening the places the sun doesn't dance upon.
Becoming sorrow on a first time widow.

In the past
Of the future

Powerful enough to cast eyes away,
searching for strength.
The strength of a light bulb,
or maybe of the sun.

But still they are overpowered by this blanket
of mystery,
of question.
Unknown is how it will stay.

Becoming greater at night,
when the curtains are drawn.

Try to be profane and muster up all of your
courage
But it will be there,
shining so dark,
smiling at you,
when you give up.

Spring 1996 Youth Honorable Mentions

Not Good Enough
by Kathleen Chen - age 16

You sicken me with your thoughts,
You poison my soul.

Your careless words are drill presses
Crumbling my poorly surrected walls,
Unstopping, unstoppable, always the same, but different.

And when you're done, the happy words
Can't mend the damage.

Each time your anger spills,
Overflows,
I'm a shadow of my former self.

I don't think a surgeon could make better cuts;
Yours don't show scars.

Your thoughts,
Your words,
Invade my mind,
Pervade my thoughts,
rip holes through me,
Rendering me defenseless;
If I try to fight,
It only gets worse,—
I'm trapped.

I can't combat those words,
They diffuse through my sense,
They jab at my withering soul;
And sooner or later,
I'll be a shadow of my former self,
And then,
I won't be there at all.

Heaven
by Amy Chini - age 15

There is a land far far away
where day is night and night is day,
Where children dwell, and loved ones wait
at this lands shiny entrance gate.

There is a land that you can't see
unless you set your spirit free,
For it's a spirits world you know
somewhere your body can not go.

There is a land or so I've heard
where no one says a harmful word,
There's only love and happy things
like angels, silver clouds, and wings.

There is a land that you will find
where every citizen is kind,
The entrance fee is just one kiss
you get your wings, then think of this...

There is a land that has no crime
where every parent has the time,
They love their kids, and make them glad
if once on Earth they made them sad.

Do you know which place I tell of?
it's not on land but high above,
This is a kingdom much adored
that's ruled by our almighty Lord

Infinity Tunnel
by Daniel Chio - age 16

No,
Hurdles were constant,
Lifting to my highest,
Just wouldn't top it.
The mixed message was truly that,
No doubt in my mind,
The opposite exists inside of you.

Desire never flew from me,
Strength was just lacking,
It was that.
In a living hell,
You pulled and pushed for my opening,
Yet my shoulders were jello-like,
And I allowed for you to slip into that hell.

This lowly stillness inside of our,
My room is all that remains.
No peace from within,
My days rarely contain solace,
As the hammering continues.
You are truly the definition of patience,
But I pushed you out of that zone.

The blood has ceased inside of me,
Only isolation runs,
And so it is my time to depart,
It must be understood that
He deserves you,
You deserve him,
I deserve what I have become.

Rose
by Agata Chmiel - age 13

The rose smelled like perfume,
The perfume of an exquisite lady;
She walked in beauty's bloom,
The walk of a plump little birdie.

She wandered through lakes and streams,
Through crowded cities and worlds
And had enchanting dream
That seemed more than the mind beholds.

The rose continued on
Through a journey it's own mind took
Much like the lady's had gone
With dreams too wild for any book

Through dreams the same, their looks were not
The lady was short and loud,
She'd fall in shame and get rather hot
Yet the rose stood tall and proud.

The rose looked made of silk
Silk fine and elegant
Yet it's petals looked made of milk
Not wrinkled nor bent.

The lady's skin was like snow,
Her complexion neither ugly nor fair
But though her beauty was rather low
It was also very rare.

The rose and lady lived so different
Their lives so foolish forever
But their times were also wisely spent;
It was then that they were together.

I Stand Alone
by Grace Choe - age 16

Engulfing the beauty of the night.
So dark and quiet;
like the world is asleep.
I am lonely.

The wind starts to awaken
flowing through my pure white dress
so I look like a glowing angel,
against a dark world.

I smile as the breeze brings,
the sound of crashing waves
and the smell of sunlit roses.

Then, my smile changes,
as a gust of wind blows to me
the sound of honking cars
and the smell of pollution fills the air.
Breaking the calmness around me.

I sit among the rippling tall grass.
Suddenly, a furry puppy
pounces into my arms.
So warm and happy
so full of life.

My friends appear around me
as we sit in a circle of peace.

I look up into a diamond filled sky,
a star blinks at me,
enclosed by so many others.
I am not alone.

Glass Castles
by Sarah Christianson - age 14

I had my first sweet, warm, satisfying taste of love,
Or, so I thought, because my heart now wears a scar
Where (as I call it) 'love's knife' has cut.
My dreams, my fragile dreams, were shattered,
Like tiny glass castles on a beach
Broken by the incoming waves, leaving shards of glass-destruction.
Maybe a piece of the glass of my broken dreams
Is what you used to leave the scar on my heart.
Maybe, but maybe not.
Oh, it was fun-
The pretending, the wishing, the dreaming with you!
...most of it in vain.
Didn't we know this from the start?
That this would never be enough?
As I think back quietly to myself
I realize we were practically strangers to one another,
But we were blind to it, or I was at least.
Now my eyes have opened because of the pain, and I accept.
I only loved the thought of you it seems,
But I don't believe that.
I remember the good times we had,
the precious few that might be forgotten with time,
And I slowly begin to feel a new feeling
One of forgiveness of what you call the unforgivable,
My thoughts shift towards today-
Not the past or the distant, uncertain future-
Today, I think as I look down a bare, sandy beach
Littered with pieces of broken glass
Today, I think I will build more glass castles on the beach
Yes, it is time for more fragile glass castles on a beach.

Daffodils
by Amy Christensen - age 16

Dreamy
Angels
Fluttering
Freely
Over
Deep
Indigo
Lands
So Sweet

My Father
by Amanda Christmas - age 14

He was my hero
my only guiding light,
he lifted me higher and higher
like a eagle in flight.

He was my savior
the only one I could trust,
he filled me with so much
until I felt I would bust.

He was my father
the one that raised me,
he was my everything
and he taught me I was free.

The Battle!
by Cynthia Clark - age 16

The mountains weep with pain,
their bare desolate faces cry with shame,
spilled blood stains the character
of each crevice
the wind whips
already raw edges
rain beats the wounds
with salt filled drops,
Don't weep long.
Don't hold the pain
in your timeless curves.

Daily Life
by Rhonda Clark - age 17

A solitary tree in a field of stone;
A weeping willow forever all alone.
A happy couple comes laughing gaily
Feeling no shame where people weep daily.
A mellow lark comes a calling.
Seeing no one, silently falling.
Snowflakes comes along with the cold
Melting too fast for anyone to hold.
A galloping horse led astray,
Seeing nothing 'cept the flowers of May.
The tree alone once again
Forever crying going insane.

Friendship
by Ashley Clay - age 12

Our friendship is like a blanket,
With warmth in every fold,
But if we're not bold,
It might turn cold.
Our friendship is like an April shower,
But it will never turn sour.
And sometimes we fight,
But I don't bite,
When I yell,
And say, I'll tell.
You know I don't mean it.
I believe that if I leave,
I will always come back,
And be your friend.
Friendship is forever,
No matter what anyone thinks.
Our friendship is like glue,
We'll always be there for you
When you're sad and blue.
Our friendship is forever!!

Dedicated to Mary

Untitled
by Starr Cline - age 14

On the other side of these four walls
You sit looking for me
Never knowing I'm inches away
You look everywhere I never could have been
And listen for words I'd never say
The sundown sky tells you I was right here all the time
Not quite what you would have hoped
So we meet again in the room where
All this started long ago
When we were sure of everything
I won't say what you won't hear
Because your ears are closed
To all you don't like to hear
You won't think what I want you to
Because you know the things I don't
Shh...listen to the sky

On the other side of these four walls
Is a world unknown
Watching how we play this game
Of kiss and tell; of love and walk
Away into the distance
Our screams are so unimportant now
We dress in clothes someone else chose
When we weren't looking
At the wall where this was played
Once long ago...

Nature Can't Wait
by Katie Clough - age 11

Not a blade of grass moves
the trees dream in the
sunlight
sunbaking the already brown dirt
the river gleaming
a blade of grass moves
a tree shudders
a bird flies home fast
a wild wind whips around the canyon
thunder and clouds
stroll in
the river screams
the rain chills all
and I am all
alone

Untitled
by Bethany Cobb - age 19

I take your soul
and lock it away
in a tin box
safe from night and day
interminingling fear
with what I adorn
love on the side
of the things I scorn
let me not see
my sightless eyes
let me pretend
I'm not what I despise
take your heart
let you burn
turning around
and round and round I turn
but empty flames
must disperse
and ashes come
of my curse
I take your soul
and wrap up heart
and begin again
from the start.

Birds
by Jacqueline Cobian - age 16

All the birds fly away from me
    my love - whose wings
        I crushed
With a clasp much too strong for
    bones like dry straw -
      injured he flies away
        dropping behind him
a black feather
    as a silent glossy crow
        And the bluebirds of my accomplishment
squeak like dying mice, all
    pinched into their singing
      Poor tortured pets-
I set them free
to heal their tiny talents
    with time in freedom
and without promise to return.
    My patriarch and matriarch, the old owls,
Burned through the day hours
    watching over me and missed
      their hunt at night.
Empty-stomached and big-eyed
    I put them in their private tree
      And fence myself, so they
        need not come
          back to me.

Unusual Question
by Heather Dawson - age 15

    Rippling waves against the shore,
    Whispering wind, crying in the night,
    Clouds passing by over a hurting world,
    Flowers and trees bowing down in pain.
    No one asks why, why it is this way.

Rugburn
by Liz Coffin - age 18

The bomb went off Saturday.
Pieces of my mind and soul
Flew everywhere.
I scrambled around trying to pick up
Each and every last piece.

But I couldn't,
They went too far.
I scrounged for another hour or so,
But I couldn't complete the puzzle.

What was left of my mind began to rationalize,
What was missing?
All of the mechanical parts are here.

What was left of my soul began to think
Of what I needed most right now,
And of what piece I needed to find
To survive.

That missing piece was you.

And then I began to cry.

Life is a Song
by Whitney Cohen - age 14

Life is a song, an ever-changing melody.

For some it rides high until
    plummeting note by note

Or it begins low and
    crescendos into a peak,
        only to drop again to the safety of
    the deep

My song jumps from
    desperately low to
    screechingly high
    and sometimes,
      every once in a while,
I take a happy seat somewhere in the middle.

Many say that's where we all should be.

But how interesting is a song with one note?

Untitled
by Stephanie Cole - age 13

    I am psycho
    I hear voices in my head
    I see visions that aren't there
    I am a psycho

    I pretend I understand
    I worry about nothing
    I cry when I'm happy
    I am psycho

    I say I care
    I dream of the future
    I try to make a difference by doing nothing
    I hope I become normal someday
    I am psycho

Fear
by James Collins - age 15

What is fear?
Is it real or is it a scary movie on TV
Fear is a very powerful emotion, that,
if given the chance can lead your life
Fear can be what ever it wants to be
We mustn't let fear take advantage of us,
For if we do it will run our lives forever
The only true fear is the fear that lies within out own mind
Not knowing what is going to happen next that is the fear that we all have
Fear, no matter what will always be present in our lives
We are all going to fear something at one point in our lives
The most important thing to remember through is...
That when fear wants to challenge you
You mustn't fear being brave enough to stand up to it
For then fear has accomplished it's goal
defeat.

Reflection
by Kathleen Columbus - age 18

Standing in the shadows,
Fearful of their scrutinizing eyes,
Which burn a chasm in my faithless
heart,
I hide in my veil of gloom.
My heart is aching with sorrow,
As tears steam down my imperfect
face,
I long to reach the sunlight.
Where endless rainbows forever
linger.
Deep within my pool of thoughts,
I see my somber self,
Realizing my foolishness,
I fade into the light.

Sisters
by Angela Conley - age 16

Sisters count on each other
they love, and respect one another
they laugh and cry together
But they will be sisters forever.
They're always loving, or in the joy of
    crying
and no one can say they've never been
    trying
we always look up to one another
and we say how much we love the
    other.
The word good-bye, we don't know
    the meaning of
all we know is the word love.
Trusting, caring, laughing, loving
that's what sisters do.
Without each other we don't know
    what we'd do.

Dancers On The Shore
by Norman Conquer

Shells swish and click as the sea-tide surges
Fragile remains of dead life, to and fro
They dance to the rhythm of wind and wave.
Constantly moving, rarely, resting save
Those moments when ocean and breeze both ebb
And give rest.

Foam washed, air dried, the smooth polished shells wait,
Their music to start, their dance to begin.
Timid pink flirts with black, or yellow with white.
As the tempo increases so does the flight
With a swish and a click, from old partner
To new one.

When the sun sinks into a cloud drowned night
The dance continues 'tho the lights have dimmed.
No moon appears, no stars and no shells gleam.
The constant movement of dancers unseen,
Dancing to the rhythm of wind and wave,
Still goes on.

Me
by Donna Conrad - age 12

You look at me
And don't see the real me.
She smiles through thousands of tears
And keeps in adolescent fears.
She dreams of all that she can never be
She's stuck in insecurity.
And this person hides herself inside of me,
She's the person you'll never see.

The Night
by Ruth Consla - age 16

At night,
the dark embraces me.
Its ebony folds
are comforting,
yet suffocating,
for those who are afraid.
Afraid of what?
Afraid of life,
living, dreaming.
Frightening nightmares,
of something just out
of my reach.
The night is comforting to me.
But I am only human and,
once in a while,
I am suffocated....
Too.

Dad
by David Contreras - age 15

Dad.
A word foreign to my life.
The endless torture of this bittersweet family life.
Mom's cryin'; sister's sad,
I want so much to have a dad.
The love-hate feelings I hold towards him,
I don't care if he dies.
No, I lie to myself, my mind is a blur.
I bury my secret love for my dad deep in my heart.
I hold the tears back when he is near.
Tears of joy and happiness to see him.
Tears of sadness to see his life wasting away.
Tears of hatred; for he beat my mom.
My dad was the super hero of my childhood.
He would beat up the bad guys and scare off the monsters.
But tempted by the darkness of this world, my dad fell.
His super strength diminished.
The bad guys took him as their own.
Even the monsters befriended him.
Drugs and crime became his home.
His long hair turned from smooth to ratty.
His muscles turned to flab.
My dad became his enemies.
My mom took us away from him; she tried to make the best.
But still I cannot calm this searing, burning in my chest.
My love for dad will never die.
I need him more than ever.
For my days as a child are over now; my manhood closes in.
But I guess I'll have to suck it in; 'cause my dad's not coming back.

Untitled
by tlc - age 19

as i sat there in the darkness,
my mind in a whirlwind of emotions, i began to wonder.
and as i thought of all the uncertainties that lie within me,
at last,
after many moments of fear, pain, and grief,
i found sleep, or should i way, sleep found me,
which ever it may be, it has no bearing now, for at last it came.
and as it did i found myself being very grateful,
for the chance to finally let my mind rest at ease, and to postpone,
if only for a moment, what is inevitable going to come.

i doubt that i will ever be able to forget that very moment --
you know, the one between reality, and unconsciousness,
the one between madness, and peace --
where sleep is almost upon you, but not fully...
for the mere fact that there has never been another time in my life,
that i have been so uncertain of what may come of me, and all that lie
within my soul.

you see,
that moment in my life, the one i'm talking of,
meant everything, yet ironically -- nothing.
i suppose it was yet another mere creek running to the ocean,
yet it felt at the time to be the ocean itself -- so overwhelming, so endless.

and now,
as morning has reached my wretched undeserving face, i feel no better.
and as i rush into my day,
and take all the beauties of the world into my life,
i regretfully morn, because that too, i do not deserve.
and as i go about my life,
and do the things that i must now do, to fill as though i belong,
sorrowfully i leave yet another life, another soul,
to find my own...

Abandoned
by Katie Corneau - age 12

Often people gladly say,
that everything will be okay,
but do they know, do they understand,
will they be there to hold your hand?
Probably not,
then you feel like you've been shot.
When they're in need you're right there-
are you the only one that knows how to care?
You think about it day and night,
hoping one day everything will be alright.
You are young but still in need,
are you gonna be the one that has to lead,
lead everyone into war,
the war you don't want to fight, for sure,
the war against losing hope,
the war that might teach you to cope.
Cope with and deal with things,
instead of wishing you had wings
to fly away with, very far-
fly away to some new bar;
you think you can escape by getting drunk,
but then when you're sober, your heart is sunk,
sunk way down to your feet:
now you know you can't take the heat.

Nature
by Angela Cosby - age 13

Nature is the morning dew.
Nature is the trees.
Nature is the flowers.
Nature is the fleas.

Nature is the animals,
That live here and there.
Nature is the ground we walk on,
And the leaves that blow in our hair.
Nature is everything that is peaceful,
Like the beach at night.
Nature is the thing I love,
With its colors and beautiful sights.
Nature is the world itself,
So old and fragile.

Nature will be here as long
As there is man kind.
So take care of our nature,
Dear friends of mine.

The Burning
by Kate Cunningham - age 13

My best friend's house burned down last night.
It was a terrifying sight.
It tore through the floor, and soon crept to the door.
My heart filled with fear as my friend's end might be coming near.
Dogs were barking and babies were crying.
Soon the light was electrifying.
His rage grew and I started to cry.
To think, I never got to tell my friend good-bye.

Snow
by Jennifer Courrejou - age 13

Snow is white
And soft as a quilt
Snow comes down
Like a blanket over the town.

Snow is silent
And beautiful
Snow tells her secret
In a whisper.

Snow is spun sugar
And frosting on a cake
Snow drifts look like ice cream
Up against a fence.

Snow is cotton
That falls from the sky
Snow covers the ground
In a milky white.

On a cold winters morning
When it's snowing
You can smell the smoke
Of a fire glowing.

I Question
by Erin Couts - age 14

To my dearest Lord,
With every unselfish act you have done,
With everything you have put on this earth for me to
 enjoy,
And for everything you have given to me
I am grateful
But yet I still Question,
I question why I am happy and yet my sadness and fears
grow with every day,
Every day it is a new sadness,
Every day it is a new fear,
With you in my heart,
 I know I should not fear,
 or be sad,
And yet I do
I fear of loss and death
Not for my own,
 But for others around me
I fear, all my enemies will unite and create a world of
 sadness, one of depression, one worse than the first,
So Lord please help me understand,
I fear so little and yet so much
My sadness is unseen,
 Yet I feel it deep with in my unconscious mind,
So help me,
 Please,
 Help me understand

Further
by April Crowley - age 15

This fantasy world is strange, but so real.
And this mystical illusion is starting to steal.
My heart from it's holder but nothing stays the same.
Come with me and we'll play the game. Of a princess of beauty
and time that never ends. And all rules are broken
as it gently bends. The truth between reality your world
and mine. Come along further with me take a step out of
time.

Who Am I?
by Stephanie Cowgill - age 13

The boulders ask me
And the snowfall
And the rolling waves ask me
    Who am I?

The heavens above ask me
and the white doves
And the roadways ask me
    Who I am?

The clouds tell me
at rainfall
And the rainbow tells me
    something tiny, a little bigger than a
        bug
    something tiny
    something tiny
      flying
        high
            above

A Piece of Heaven On Earth
by Elizabeth Crabtree - age 14

As I sit on the sandy beach with my toes in the water, I reminisce about all that surrounds me.
I feel the cold, clear water rippling against my toes, and the crisp wind on my face, both in a way whispering....."You are in paradise."
I look out on the beautiful, mirror like water, and see a gorgeous sunset composed of rich Reds, Yellows, and Oranges. I even spot a family of ducks and
fuzzy ducklings swimming in the water.
I hear nothing but the calm peacefulness of this island. I hear no cars or loud voices, only complete silence.
I gently inhale the sweet fragrances that drift around me: birch bark smoke and sweet cedar trees.
I slowly lay my hand on the ground on which there lie rough cedar twigs, and smooth white pebbles.
As I lie back on a bed of soft, green moss, I slowly close my eyes and let beauty of this island help me drift of into a completely peaceful sleep.

Sailing
by Alison Cupini - age 16

Floating peacefully through crystal blue water,
thoughts drift in and out of your head
The world is perfect now,
no one to answer to
just you and nature.
A bright colored fish swims by
you dip your hand into the warm ocean
the fish quickly scurries away,
your eyes follow its trail of bubbles,
you notice some garbage in the ocean
the wind begins to pick up
the triangle cloth above your head expands
the wind grows stronger
you pick up speed passing more objects along the way
you see cans, bags, styrofoam
the world is not perfect anymore
the wind gets stronger and stronger
so does your anger
your eyes tear
from the wind, or
could you be crying for the bright colored
fish, now caught in a plastic bag?

Yes I Can
by Melissa Currier - age 14

Someitmes I feel like I could die,
I just want to sit and cry.
Often I feel like I have not one friend,
And a cry to heaven I often send.

I often did not know what to do,
Especially when I was blue.
I would always settle for second best,
And would start to cry before I'd rest.

I need to see the jar not half empty, but half full,
And if I do this, I'll be happy, and that's no bull.
I always should set my goals high,
And with the guts I could reach the sky.

I was always afraid I would fail,
And when something challenging came along I would bail.
When I got scared I ran and ran,
Now I say "YES I CAN!"

Ashley Macisaac
by Emese Cuth - age 16

only if this day never came to an end
life would smell like mountain berries forever
and every cabdriver would be a friend
in the bright and dreamy daylight around us
I want the warmest yellow sunlight pouring
down, illuminating beautiful faces
with fire in the eyes so bright and sparkling;
I want a canopy of mackerel sky
flattered by mellifluous-sounding wind
and as I watch fleecy clouds above waft by
they smile down sweetly on me, flashing a glint
and I feel such a bliss my glee overflows me;
I wish for a gust to make my eyes water
to bury my risible melancholy
which is so unreal it's kept for later;
and as my dreams make a playground of my mind
I believe the day will never fade away
and as I stand there I want nothing but
that guy to ask me: Hi how are you today?

Through My Window Sill
by Kelly Curtis - age 11

I sit upon the bed,
sitting very still,
looking at the trees,
through the window sill,
roses here and there,
spring is about to come,
the sun's sweet rays shinning a path,
that everyone can walk upon,
On through that window sill,
the light shines faintly through,
the daisies and violets,
happiness for me and you,
grass scattered across the ground,
a bird's nest in a tree,
waiting for their mother dear,
while I'm drinking english tea,
I gaze through that window sill,
I see someone coming through,
the sun is shinning on their face,
Oh, I'm so glad it's you!

Chasing Shadows
by Steve Cyphert - age 19

These feelings I once had
seem to be gone without a trace

But I can still feel the rain
running down my face

Chasing shadows
Cast by a different time and place

I had wished for so long
Love finally came and everything wuz a mess

When I would walk, I would always take the
long way home
But there's a certain beauty in sadness

When the world comes crashing down
I can still feel his hands strangling me

Chasing shadows
Of what could never be

Today I tasted death on my tongue
And then came a fever and a laughter
so complete and without shame

When I'm tripping I forget my name
And I no longer feel shame

Chasing shadows, never got anyone, anywhere
Today I will not shed a single tear

Fruit
by Tammy Eng - age 14

Pear
Sweet, green
Sliced, diced, cubed
Tree, blossom, winter, breakfast
Peeled, sectioned, squeezed
Sour, pink
Grapefruit

Don't Give Up
by Summer Czapiewski - age 17

Looking toward tomorrow
isn't an easy thing to do
When the present days leave you crying,
It hurts to try something new.
But dwelling in your sorrow
only makes you want to give up more.
If you don't keep trying
opportunities slip through the door.
Happiness seems like a fairy tale
you heard so long ago
Your hopeless feelings of today
are the only stories you know.
But when you're down and out
And you can't see the master plan
Your eyes are closed to reality
and your life seems out of your hands,
Getting up and moving on is the last thing you want to do
Yet wallowing in your sorrows is even worse for you.
Think of the days ahead as new adventures
you will find all your painful memories
Will be erased by time.
So don't give up on life
just because tomorrow is hidden in the clouds
Yesterday is done and gone
Go out and make yourself proud

Halloween
by Stephanie Dafoe - age 16

Bare branches stretch into the darkened sky,
Above their tips black bats do fly,
While all around is heard the cry
Of children trick-or-treating.

Pumpkins orange and brightly glowing;
Through the trees a cold wind's blowing,
On this breeze white ghosts are flowing,
Spreading their seeds of fear.

Cats as black as midnight walk,
While high above is heard the squawk
Of green haired witches as they talk;
Casting spells and curses.

Past a werewolf big and hairy,
The rattle of bones is very scary,
Each young child is very wary
Of the skeletons they might meet.

Cowboys, Indians and a little clown,
Gathering treats all over town,
Far and wide they walk around,
Filling their bags with candy.

10 Minutes
by Donna Dalangauskas - age 15

I have 10 minutes to write,
not much here.
I heard a whisper,
saying "I love you dear.

I have to go,
but I can;t explain.
I don't want to leave,
but I cannot stay.

Five minutes to go,
I don't know what to say.
They said you left,
I'll miss you each day!

Two minutes left,
not much I can do.
I wish you were here,
Oh, how I miss you!

Now I know you left me,
I wish it wasn't so.
But, I know the winds of change,
have begun to blow!

The Day I'm Alone
by Crystal Dalrymple - age 15

I look up at the midnight sky
With stars blinking a little
I sit here as the time flies by
To find myself in the middle
Of the fight between my mom and dad
About the wrong I did,
My dad is very, very mad
Making me feel like a kid
He picks up a vase and throws it at me
Wishing I could escape his wrath,
I get down on my knees and plead
But he claims I am in his path
Whatever I do or where I roam,
I'll never forget this day at home.

Memories
by Heather Dalrymple - age 20

Lying on the grass looking up at the stars
interrupted now and then by passing cars.
The world and time seems to move so slow
yesterday feels like a memory of times long ago.
As we grow older we begin to realize
how quickly time passes right before our eyes.
We try to pick a memory - to distinguish each day
so we can remember friends and fun times before they pass away.
Soon you realize all you have to hold
are those memories - so treasure them, they are gold!

Perfect
by Jill Danyow - age 17

Forceful thoughts took over me.
Influencing me mentally.
It strained my will too on a day,
everytime I heard them say.......
"You're not perfect."

My feelings are locked inside to die,
I'm caged and crowded, and without reply.
The voices in my head are near,
consciously I still hear....
"you're not perfect."

Why am I to face my flaws?
Can't I live without this pause?
My thoughts keep interrupting me,
I don't know who or how I should be.

I ask myself as to why I need,
to take this time, to make this heed.
I wrestle my thoughts with perpetual skill,
release my doubts, return my will.
"I am not perfect, but who is?"

The Devil Within You
by Nancy Das Neves - age 14

He hides in your shadow,
He goes where you go.
In your footsteps he follows,
And no one else knows.
He ruins the good things and causes the bad,
He creates all the things that make you jealous and sad.
He alters your principles, your dreams and your morals,
He challenges your willpower and starts all the quarrels.
He's the cause of your outer and inner turmoil,
He induces all conflict and blames you for the roil.

Sooner or later, you will have lost all control,
He will be you, and you I don't know.
The time is now, to put up a fight,
All you must know is to follow the light.
Beware of impostors, evil and wrong,
He will do his best, to make your journey difficult and long.
Whatever you do, don't give in,
He hopes that you will, so that he can win.

If he takes over your spirit and attains victory,
Everyone is in danger and you will be history.
Once you are gone, he can do as he please,
An exorcist, I'm afraid, is all that will leave you at ease.
Help yourself now, before it's too late,
In a short while, he will control your fate.
There is still hope, if you act right away,
I trust that you will, if you don't want him to stay.
Have faith in yourself, and you will pull through,
Trust and believe that good will surpass and guide you too.

Dive Deep
by Gwen Davis - age 15

Beyond
our common thoughts
keep yesterdays,
yesteryears,
apart.

Behind
your common thoughts
of those
we left to think
while we are gone.

Between
those common threads
of all that was
will ever be.

Nowhere
by Lauri Day - age 16

The last flight to Nowhere is leaving here today,
All the people that are "nothings" will soon be on their way.
Any place is better than what you have right here,
But, the last flight to Nowhere will soon be drawing near.
The soul escapes our bodies, and in your mind it's known,
That the last flight to Nowhere's population has surely grown.
Purgatory is nothing compared to where you'll be,
The last flight to Nowhere is what you'll want to see.
A peaceful feel surrounds you,
NO evil will follow you through.
The last flight to Nowhere will be here by noon,
The time is 11:30 now, it should be coming soon.
I do not feel the bench beneath me, the wood hurts me no more,
A spirit grows inside of me like I've never felt before.
The last flight to Nowhere has arrived right on time,
And with the announcing of it's arrival a million bells do chime.
As long, white wings unfold from you back,
You then check your things to see what you lack.
Your children that you always loved to be around,
Are waving good-bye to you from the ground.
And as you're embraced by a beautiful light,
You remember that they were why you put up your fight.
You long for your family and the good times ya'll spent,
The love your Mother gave, and what your life meant.
The pain that lingered for so long,
No one could've ever been so strong.

-Dedicated to my mother who died of cancer.

My Loyal Lover...
by Tracy Degraffinreid - age 14

Your love, like the first blush of morning has reassured my lonely heart.
The camouflaged image in my core has been disclosed,
The shady anchorage thrust aside.
At last, the innocence of dimmed, restless emotions, set aglow by
Your alluring actuality,
Your enticing existence.
Like daybreak eradicates
The dull, shadowy canvas, so has your simple love my soul.
Mutual attraction amid two young loves.
Powerful and majestic, unsoiled, transparent.
My cherished lover,
My heart's kindled flame,
Sweet
loyal
lover.
Now and forever I am yours.

Whispers

Hate
by Michelle DeGroff - age 18

Hate is a feeling.
That can be a weapon
More powerful than
A missle or a bomb.
Hate is what keeps us
At war. It makes you
Hate your family.
Hate is fear of things
We don't like or understand.
We must teach the children
Not to hate each other,
Because if we don't we might
As well die.
So erase the Hate.
Teach the children to Love
And understand.
Don't teach them to
Hate the things you Hate
Let's Stop the Hate
To make a better
Place for the Children.
Give Peace a Chance.

Untitled
by Sarah DeLaFlor - age 16

There are monsters in my head..,Screaming.
Demons in my soul...,Dreaming.
Thoughts embark my brain
Which are totally insane
Where all but good remain
I lie upon my freight train.
I see myself before me
But don't recognize the face,
Nothing left to see
Gone without a trace.
Not too far from nowhere
In fact, I've crossed those lines,
And yes I think I've been there
One too many times.
I feel the train coming
But now I'm on the track
My mind is loudly humming.
There's no turning back.
My hands have touched their last
Blood is dripping fast.
My result of wanting more
Watch my body soar.
There's no time to apologize
Too much time has passed
Because now that I have realized
This minute is my last.
My eyes took their final round.
All my words were lying
I heard my last sound
Guilt is worse than dying...

Dream
by Melanie DePaulis - age 13

He comes to my bedroom door, more an angel than before.
I look into his eyes, and from my bed I rise.
He softly holds my hand, and we both understand.
Quietly we talk, side-by-side walk.
His eyes shine so bright, and lighten up the night.
He holds me in his arms, where I am safe from harm.
His kisses are so sweet, no way I could retreat.
My hands caress his hair, so golden and so fair.
But now the sun starts to rise,
and I open up my eyes.
He's no longer there,
no eyes, no golden hair.
The dream had gone so fast, but the memories would last.

The Forest
by Mandy Depies - age 15

Entering the misty wooded area.
Taking in all that I can...
Thick moss covering the ground,
like a blanket.
The smell of sweet rain from the heavy
spring downpour,
that cooled off the land,
and caused a thick fog to condense,
is drowning out the stale air in my lungs,
and filling them with the melodic whisper of life.
Sun's rays
poking their way through the mist,
like fingers,
making the dew
on the leaves and shrubs glisten brightly.
The newly growing vines that are hanging down
from the shielding canopy of the trees
are still sparkling from the last few drops of rain
that have yet to fall from the vaguely colored sky.
As I look ahead...
I see the hypnotizing mist
change from a beautiful bluish gray
and fade into a purplish pink, and charcoal color.
It is rising...
And I follow it into oblivion.

Candles and Stairways
by Beth Ann Deutschmann - age 14

Burning candles are forever;
They can mean two things,
You can say they're a sign;
Of what the future brings.

A burning candle is my light;
To guide me the whole way through,
It guides me to the stairway;
Of what could be true.

The burning candle is meditation;
I like to light it, then relax,
My heart melts away;
Don't worry about the dripping wax.

Light the candle again;
My soul is starting to rise,
Maybe I'll reach the stairway;
Because the advice I got is wise.

If I'm swept by the wind;
And start doing well,
Maybe I can reach the stair way to Heaven;
And become a true angel!

Desert
by Pamela Merrin Dick

There's a wind blowing across the desert I call my heart.
It shapes the dunes of misery and mirages of wonder.
There must be water over the next sandbar,
Water to quench this thirst.

And the river I saw a few miles back disappeared
when I need to be quenched.

Home
by Rachel DiGirolomo - age 16

I stood on the water, my green eyes grey,
I felt nothing, I stood on a plane.
My face drooped down, my ears heard something,
I suddenly realized that I was nothing.
My screaming brain denied me passage,
I fell forth, knew not of where.
My eyes pierced the great dark,
I knew the end drew near.
I braced my fear, feeling the fall,
And suddenly, all was silent.
Nothing spoke, nothing moved.
It was then I knew that the beginning was beginning,
And the end was ending.
As if in a dream I moved forward,
I saw before me a great blue sky.
I knew it then I was not to die.
I saw a stairway, it reminded me of a song,
"Stairway to Heaven", though this was not.
I slowly ascended the great vast stairs,
I saw it then, a great green valley,
I suddenly knew this was my home.
I stood on the water, my green eyes blue,
I felt everything, I stood in a field.
My face then smiled, my ears heard nothing,
I suddenly realized that I was something.
My silent brain allowed me passage,
I was finally home,
Home at last.

His Words To Me
by Teresa Dodson - age 15

Walking along a path one day,
As I turned his voice cried out to say;
"Give me your hand,
There's so much I've planned.
Listen to me,
And you shall see,
I'm always with you,
I never leave your side.
For I've been there to hold you.
Everytime you've cried."
I listened as I reached out my hand,
I saw wonders of a glorious land.
Slowly as I turned away,
I fell to the ground and there I lay.
Thinking of the words he said,
Knowing forever I'll have a true friend.

Our World
by Charlotte Dolphin - age 17

Too confused to understand, to unstable to calm down.
With all these memories running through my mind.
Nowhere to stop, nowhere to go.
I'm lost in this maze of feelings,
I'm trapped in this world of hate.
There is no more love and no more peace.
Killing, murder, suicide. Blood and more blood.
The world, my world, is tumbling towards nothing.
There is no more then, now, or later.
Nothing is real and everything is gone.
There once was a beauty that we called life,
but that too slipped away.
Will anything ever be the same?
I doubt it...

Life Is A Game
by Melissa Domsic - age 13

Life is a game we all have to play.
I will loose it anyway.
All the paths I have to choose from.
I can't choose one I must be dumb.

Sitting at the fork, dazed and confused.
About the path I can't choose.
People pass me, taking their way.
But at this fork I seem to stay.

For days and days staring ahead.
I'd rather be taking my path instead.
Walking on playing the game.
But this situation remains the same.

I'm the only one who knows no where to go
The only one who just doesn't know.
The only one who just doesn't understand.
These simple paths made of sand.

Everyone else passes me by.
And slowly but surly I began to cry.
Drowning in my tears cold and wet.
And then I begin to regret.

Signing up to play this game.
For how I've played is a crying shame.
Picking the cards I can't seem to comprehend.
When will my game ever end.

When will this confusion ever been done.
When will this game ever be won.
I don't know and can't really say.
Maybe I'll win this game someday.

Thank You
by Linda Dupont

Thank you for listening
to all my tales of woe.
thank you for your wisdom
in guiding me back to sanity
even though I didn't want.
thank you for your smile
as I awake this morning,
another beautiful day I thought I'd never see.
Thank you for your voice
when I finally came to,
hearing you call my name.
thank you for your patience
and not walking out on me
even when I made you go.
thank you for sharing your tears
as my own fall on my pillow.
thank you for believing in the real me
I thought that person had died.
but most of all, from the bottom of my heart
thank you for loving me
when I thought no one would.

Every Snow Capped Mountain
by Johney Dou - age 14

Every snow capped mountain
Every glowing valley
Flowing through the fountain
Are the cries of the rally

From the sparkling streams
To the dew topped grass
Is a bright gleam
Of fresh bass

Gone are the fields of clover
Gone is the roisterous day
Gone is the snakes sliver
Gone is the sun's ray

Night is swiftly here
The time fleets like sheep
The sky is crystal clear
From the canyon, way down deep

Thunder
by Mauryah Eoff - age 14

I love thunder
Thunder sounds like
a drum beat
Thunder can
rumble the windows
Thunder sounds so powerful
you would think it
could harm you
but it can't
that's why I sit
on my porch
and listen...
to the thunder

Untitled
by Jessica Mae Ducharme - age 12

Your love washes over me
like the warm waves of the ocean;
I can think of nothing but you;
Your love, your beauty, your perfection;
You care for me and love me
As a mother loves her child;
I would be eternally lost if it weren't for you;
I love your with me heart, soul,
and my mind;
I owe you my life, if anything can repay you
for your time, your love,
your concern;
I will remember you always

Blind Again
by Sarah Dowling - age 18

You seemed to be my hero,
Rescuing me from self-inflicted harm.
You seemed to be guiding me opposite from danger,
You were my lucky charm.

You seemed to be different.
You seemed to be one who cared.
But now I'm embarrassed,
for each part of me that I shared.

You seemed to reach down a helping hand,
Only you let go-
Not caring where I would land.

You led me to believe there were no others,
Now I realize I can't believe words said under covers.

I tried to ignore suspicions,
Which I could constantly feel.
I blinded myself to have something real.
Now cautious for my future,
I'm afraid to let myself heal.

Not only others, but myself I cannot trust.
What I always believe to be love,
Results in only lust.

Where I go now,
Time will only tell.
I'm experiencing a different pain than before when I fell.

Drained from the effort,
Trying to make it last
Yet you still quickly became part of my past.

I need to learn how it can be equal,
Otherwise this love story will have another sequel.

The Moons Light
by Anna Fallis - age 17

Lying in the pond
A lonely water lily
Floats in the moons light.

Young Love
by Alicia Dunaway - age 16

Look into my eyes, my friend
Tell me what you see
Do you see the one who longs to cry,
"You were meant for me!"

Let me take your hand, my friend
I'll follow you anywhere
Time with you is magical
Can't you see I care?

Listen to my words, my friend
The silent ones that pray,
"Please don't ever let me go,
I love you more each day."

Someday I will be brave, my friend
We'll stand face-to-face
Then I'll sing these words aloud,
And melt in your embrace.

The Waterfall
by Jennifer Ann Dwyer - age 14

The waterfall gushes down
Flowing freely, splashing around
Tumbling around the various rocks
Violently crashing the bridge it knocks
It's beautiful crystals so blue and clean
As the flowing water touches grass so green
A magical world, so wonderful it may look
As if you opened a fairy tale book
I almost expect a fairy to fly by me
The nature of the air makes me feel free

"A Single Red Rose"
by Chasity Eastlick - age 15

The symbol of love and affection
standing alone in bloom
so quiet yet speaking so boldly
It's like beauty blooming
Like a child's dream
with Prince Charming in the mind
and love in the hand
I give you this...
A Single Red Rose,
the symbol of all my Love!

Hollow Days
by Daniel Eaton - age 17

I have learned to hate the hollow days,
that follow "maybe" and "I may."
Your ill-thought words that grace the air
reveal everything you will not say.

Your petty whispers that ring in my ears
always dredge up my secret fears.
I am forced to call it all a lie,
as the end of the day nears.

Your hidden agenda only causes the strain
that we both viciously fight in vain.
You bury the past and we both wait,
as only sad emptiness remains.

From out of my heart, please take thy beak,
so our thoughts we both may speak.
However, only silences are left in the wake
of the truth both of us seek.

The air stays still as we breathe our little lie
and inside bits and pieces of us die.
We hang in stark denial of what is,
waiting for the other to try.

For now, I will sit and memorize your ways
and truth, in hiding, just sits and stays.
I will feed my dreams on memories,
as I brave the storm of these hollow days.

Whispers

The Night
by Emily Elisabeth Edgeman - age 11

The night I cried
The night they died
The night I lost my heart

The night I thought I could
No longer live is the night
I remember most

The things we did
The things we said
Keep playing back
Inside my head

We danced a bit
We shared some laughs
We drank a lot
We drove to fast

That fatal crash
Those searing screams
Of the ones I'd love so much
Still haunt the caverns of my mind
That cold touch won't let me be

Because we drank
Because we drove
I am forever scarred
And yet I know I must move on
To love to laugh to forgive
To learn to live again

Reflections
by Faith Eggers - age 15

All we are
is what we said
we wouldn't be.
But we are,
a twisted tongue,
Entangled by our tragedies.
The ship headed north,
Blown by our own breath,
Detoured south.
Coming back
For what we said
we would never stay for.
But we did.
Hopes and dreams drifted.
Into oblivious memories,
Soon forgotten.
We put on our masks of stoned splendor,
So do not revel our fragility.
Our escape
Hidden by our own embarrassment,
Shame for what wasn't done.
Mirrors still reflect,
Even when broken.
And all we are
is what we said
we wouldn't be.
But we are.

My Life
by Ronda Ellis - age 15

It's so hard.
You can't imagine how I feel.
But no one think
my problem is real.

It's so hard,
living life the way I do.
No one knows what
I have to go through.

I go to bed wondering
if I'll make it through the night.
Crying underneath my covers,
I close my eyes really tight.

In the morning,
I wake up surprised
Because I know that,
all day I'll have to strive.

The world is very cruel.
I stay low and try to hide
Because no one wants
to be on my side.

Lonely Hunter
by Harmony Fansler - age 14

Lonely hunter was always around,
hunting through trees, crawling on the ground.

Yearning to find something,
whether deer, rabbit, or human being,

Just one thing to bring a smile;
to find it, he'd walk that mile,

Not to hurt anything or anyone,
he doesn't even carry a gun.

It was all just for fun;
when he found his destiny, he was done!

Another Time
by Billy Flynn - age 15

Vanishing are the colors of night
flowing down the red sea.
Never seen again.
Sleeping on a colorless night at hand,
The colors of my dreams are gone.
And with reality.
A black and white world with anger,
no dream, no time to explain,
just time to move away,
to the next day-the next world.

The Waves
by Melissa Epstein - age 12

I sit down on the sand shore
And watch the waves pass by,
My hair waving in the breeze;
And the waves-they seem to fly.

Curling waving, saying, "Hello,"
Reaching out for my hand
As it opens its foamy mouth
And then collapses on the sand.

Another wave comes, filled with fury
It reaches up to touch the sky
As restless as a puppy dog's tail.
As it lets out a groan and a sigh.

The wave gets tired
And then it falls unto the land
the same way as the wave before it,
Coughing up shells and sand.

Another wave come with rage
And then slows down its pace.
A tiny ripple in the water
As delicate and soft as lace.

I slowly walk back to my home,
Though I wish that I could stay.
The last wave comes to wave good-bye,
With hopes that I will come again another day.

My Favorite Place
by Lisa Erdman - age 14

My favorite place is sitting on the bare
beach when everybody has gone home.
The sparkling white sand shimmers on the ground
like thousands of stars in the midnight sky.
I watch the waves ripple on to the shore like
fields of wheat blowing in the wind,
Sometimes you can hear the water singing it's
joyful cries beckoning you to come
out and be one with it.
I also notice the sea gulls circling the sky,
looking for a chance to dive down and catch a
naughty little fish that has come to the surface
Then I look at the sun setting over
the clear blue water.
It's colors dancing in the wind.
I feel the sand between my toes, the wind
blowing in my face.
At that moment I am content and happy.
I get up and walk along the shore, feeling the
cold water clash against my feet.
I say to myself It's time for me to go.
I start walking to the road.
Then I look back to get a clear picture in my
mind till I return once more.

Candle
by Laura Garvine - age 18

Candle burning in the night,
sending out rays of beautiful light.
Wishfully gazing at the flame.
will life ever be the same?
I doubt it will but I know
that now I have the chance to grow.
I thank the heavens up above
for now there's another for me to love.

To My Future Daughter
by Jen Ernst - age 14

Even though you are not
Born yet, I would like to say
I'm sorry
For all the mistakes I will make
As a mother.
But I will love you with all my
Heart and Soul
I will cradle and rock you,
And when you're older
I'll talk and laugh with you
I will try to be understanding
And caring
You will be able to come
And talk
To me about
Anything.
Don't ever feel neglected because
I will love you more than anything
On this
Earth.
You will be my pride and joy.
And when the day comes
I will be ready,
To love.

Acceptance
by Kelly Erwin - age 16

The fire in the devil's eyes
Glared at me, daring me.
To take the bet.
Take a chance, live
On the edge,
To be accepted

The screech of my life haulting,
Rings inside me, with
The devils evil smile of hate
Upon my face
Gasps and screams of disbelief
As I am accepted.

Nowhere to run,
Nowhere to hide,
Don't be accepted
When he comes
Freeze the fire in his eyes.

Untitled
by Arthur Gomez - age 20

Climb to the top
Of a tree covered mountain
And breathe the breath of angels

Take a walk along the shore
Of a black sands beach
And watch the ocean swallow the sun

But never forget about the dirt
Under the pebbled path

Whispers

Goodbye
by Erica Evans - age 15

Sometimes late at night, I lay awake, staring blankly into the dark, star-covered sky,
As I lay there quietly, tears running down my face, I can't help but wonder why,
Why did you have to go away?
Why couldn't you just stay?
As I think of all the good times that we shared,
I wonder if you really knew just how much I cared,
You had such an impact on my life, you taught me to laugh, to cry, and face reality,
And when you left you didn't take away my dreams, but instilled part of yours in me,
Each night before I go to sleep, as I kneel by my bed and pray,
I know you're in a perfect place, and forever there you'll stay,
I'll never forget your smiling face or the glowing in your eyes,
You were always there to pick me up, to hold me as I cried,
Sometimes I can still hear your sweet, soft voice,
I'd give anything for you to be here, but fate leaves us no choice,
The sun's rays no longer hold the warmth there used to be,
Since all that remains in your place is a memory,
While I watch as birds fly so gracefully,
When I feel the cool summer breeze, hear the wind so gently,
As I sit along the beach and watch the sand slip away, deep into the sea,
When I walk through the park and watch children playing happily,
As the cool, autumn rain falls to the ground,
And the stars shine brightly all around,
Taking in the scent of the fresh spring air,
Through all this I sense your presence, I know that you are there,
As I look back, now I see, that your life was a wondrous work of art,
And although I'll always miss you, you will live on forever in my heart
Though time may pass and years go by,
There's one thing that will lay heavy on my mind,
I'm sorry,
I never got to say goodbye.

A Candle's Life
by Elizabeth Freiberger - age 13

Life is like a candle.
It burns bright
until the wick and wax are gone.
This is also like the life we lead.
Our time comes and
our prime is spent.
Then we will flicker one last time
and vanish with the wind
that took our flame,
our last breath

Growing Older
by Terri Gauvin - age 12

Growing older, faster, smarter.
Why do we have to change?
Memories filled with emotion and laughter...
Confrontations at close range.

Why do we have to change?
No one actually knows.
It's all a part of the circle of life,
Even the way the wind blows.

If nothing ever changed,
Everything would be frozen in place.
The world would be flat and boring...
It would be a waste of space!

Carpe Diem
by Patricia Faustino - age 12

Do you remember
when the stars seemed
so close to touch
and the moon but only
a breath away?

Do you remember
when the sun
was nearly in your clutches?

But you drew back
You almost had it
Didn't you?
You feared that the sun
might scorch your tender palm.
You feared that the stars
might weigh too heavy in your pocket.
You feared the moon
too delicate for the likes of you.

Oh! But if only
If only you had
Seized the day.

Sweet Victim
by Elizabeth Feinstein - age 15

You're asking question
Unanswered
you're wondering why
unsolved
victimized
suicide
feelings left untouched
your own victim
search and destroy, the game you play
But do you find yourself?
The pain was lost
the questions forgotten
an everlasting vigil
to find nothing but peace and mind
your own sweet victim
Sweet. sweet victim
Alone, Forgotten
sweet, sweet Victim
Unwanted, yet wanting
Sweet, sweet Victim
Your Own Sweet Victim
Sweet, Sweet Victim
Victim

Behind the Wall
by Danielle M. Frazier - age 12

Behind the wall, who might have known,
The people have abilities too bad to be shown.
Behind the wall, a lot goes on.
A guy came yesterday, got killed, and now he's gone.
Behind the wall, they're vicious and mean.
If you make trouble, you're dead.
Behind the wall, some are real sweet
And then there's the ones you'd rather not meet.
Behind the wall, you're served bad food
And the guards are obnoxious and rude.
Behind the wall, you still have rights.
The time will come when you're out on bail,
But you'd better behave or you're going back to jail.

Days Like These
by Crystal Ferri - age 15

On days like these I would go bicycle
riding with my father and explore the great outdoors
of nature.

On days like these I would put a dandelion
underneath my chin and tell my father that if
there was a glow, I liked butter.

On days like these my father and I would
walk through meadows with tall, green grass swaying
at out sides.

On days like these I look upon my childhood,
and cherish the memories.

On days like these I wonder where my
father went. Where the love he had for
me went.

On days like these I only ponder of the
great experiences I had in nature.

On days like these...
I wonder.

What My Mind Is Like
by Jen Flanagan - age 13

My mind is like a basketball arena
The seats hold my friends and family
The backboard counts down the time I have to live
The stat people keep track of my fouls
The coach directs me the right way
The bench holds my players
The lockerroom holds my secret
Reporters want to know me
They try to get into the lockerroom
But guards keep them out for my safety
The stairs lead down to the court
The court, my dreams, the arena, my

The Good Side and the Bad Side
by Brittany Ferry - age 14

To everything there are two sides,
The good side and the bad.
Like right and wrong, black and white,
Dark and light, sad and glad.

The two sides could be equal,
Or one outweighs the next,
You may understand these sides,
Or you may be perplexed.

We all like the good side,
No matter what we say,
We all hate the bad side,
And hope it goes away.

The bad side is the hardest,
The darks, the wrongs, the frights,
The good side is the best part,
The rights, the glads, the whites.

When the bad side is colossal,
And the good side is so small,
It's hard to think of good things,
Since the bad is so powerful.

But you must try to see the good,
No matter what the weight,
Then it will blossom and grow,
Into something truly great.

Window Pane
by Kathy Fishman - age 14

I am a transparent window of expression,
A changing picture of evidence.
The wind blows into the night,
and carries my emotions,
Whistling them to the moon,
announcing them to the world.
My eyes are camera's of images,
Images seen, and to be seen,
dreams drempt, and still dreaming.
The lines in my face, are streams of fear,
The water rushes over the rocks, down the brook,
into the minds of others.
The knuckles in my hands turn white with humiliation,
my ears redden, and embarassment fills the room.
My left knee shakes, and wobbles, with excitement.
The eyelids covering my curiously large eye pops,
and stings,
as sadness creeps into the window pane.
Tears of feeling, stream down my burning cheeks,
Everyone already knows my heart,
Though I speak not a language of words.

goal

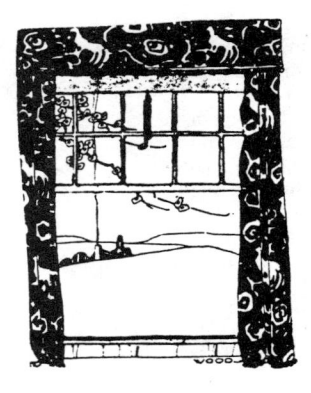

One More Day
by Elizabeth Frazier - age 13

One more day to dream and laugh
But now I cannot change the past
I have just one more day to last
Then it;s over, just like that

I stooped so low to get out fast
But now I cannot change the past
Who knew I'd end up this way
All I need is one more day

I'm past the mission that I once sought
To be the thinnest girl, I thought
But now I'm fighting to stay alive
And no one's here on my side

It started as a simple diet
Now there's no way to deny it
My life is over, it's taken control
I'm not the same old normal girl

It has taken all of this
For me to learn just what pain is
Her I lay in my hospital bed
Knowing one more day and I'll be dead

One more day to dream and laugh
But now I cannot change the past
I have just one more day to last
Then it's over, just like that

How Many Stars
by Brenna Flood - age 16

How many stars are there?
someone asks me
as I gaze up at the blue blanket
decked out in holes shimmering.
How many snowflakes
are falling down upon us,
like miniature meteors
sent from heaven to
destroy us?

But every time I try to answer
I close my eyes and think
of you
Are you my prophet
my savior
my sins
personified, gazing back at me
with those
angelic eyes?

I know the answer.

The Somber World in Perfect Harmony
by Christina Fournier - age 19

The exploding shards of light ran
through my brain
like the soft summer nights
we played together in the rain
the icy winter hand tightens
its grip around my wrist
and i'm not cold
whoever told you this place was safe
did not hear the tune sung by
the trees
the blood red
dripping
staining the curtains of my mind
and we proceed to dance
even though the record's skipping
careful baby caught in crib
crying 'cause the milk is sour now
three wishes from a bright light
ghost
could never change the single
solitary thing about you that
is constant and cold and forgotten
and something to do
besides think
about nothing
about you
about someone
about you

Days
by Shelly Goodman - age 14

Days come, days go
Nights come so slow.
You feel, you touch,
But life isn't much.
You live, you die,
There's no hello, just goodbye.

Memories
by Sarah Franz - age 12

What is a memory but a picture and a thought?
What to remember; the lessons we've learned on
our own, to those we've been taught?
Or are memories just dear to our hearts?

Are friends part of our memories, or just figures in a
picture?
Friends come and go, just as the wind blows.

Are memories special, or just another part of life?
Some happy, funny or can cut your heart like a knife.
Yes memories are things of the past, some happy, some
sad, and that's not always bad.
Yet not always good either.

So keep those memories locked in your heart;
until that day death do you part.

Black Carpet
by Erin Fredman - age 16

An insecurity-
Grounded under a life
seemingly persistent to reach the stars,
Only enough cover to keep hold
of that transparent box
with the iron lock and the frosted layer.
I tried to get through,
but no efforts were made by the other half.
Below the mysterious blanket of worries,
you closed your eyes to the light
and the echoes of those adoring of you.
You caught your own tears
and were mute to the outsiders.
I was one, naive to your frown,
You made me believe.

The Torch of Love
by Nina Friis-Jensen - age 12

Love is like a torch.
It burns through some of the darkest moments of life,
But sometimes the light weakens.
Mine did.
Mine fell into the dirt.
There was nothing except for one spark.
It hurts when the light goes.
It hurts like a knife through your heart.
It hurt for many years.

But then the spark began to grow.
It sent a tingle of life through me.
Flames were jumping all around me.
I never felt so refreshed in my life.

But something sad flashed through me.
Something so sad I couldn't explain it.
I was afraid.
I was afraid that love might be taken from me again.
Then, I knew
I would never be able to feel completely happy.
Not since my first love.
There was still some light missing on my torch.
Some light that I would never be able to get back,
For that light was for the one I had given my
torch to completely.

Christopher
by Amanda Fritz - age 15

Christopher why do you do this to yourself?
My dear Christopher, I wish you could see
That you can't wash away all your problems
In a couple of drinks.
Christopher, why do you do this to me?
I wish that you would learn
That when you cut yourself,
You hurt me too.
Christopher, why can't you understand
That drugs aren't the solution to your problems.
Christopher, please know that your father
Doesn't mean to bruise your face
But you know how he gets
After a night at the bar.
Christopher, put the knife down!
Christopher, please
CHRISTOPHER!!

Two Worlds
by Tari M. Gaffney - age 11

A tear falls and mixes
With the pouring rain.
A mother cries out
In the darkness
For her missing child.

A gunshot sounds;
People are screaming.
A homeless man dies
From the bitter cold.

A young girl wakes up.
The birds are singing.
Her parents kiss her
On her soft, warm cheeks.
She gives the world a smile,
Then turns to go to school.

Our world is cleft in two.
Therefore, we live in two worlds.
One side so unaware of the other,
The first yearning for the second.
Sad, but this is the way it really is.

Journal Of The Wilderness
by Mathieu Gagnon - age 16

journals subsided
thoughts forgotten
forgotten under sub-stratum

poems & essays disavowed
epigrams & stories & lyrics eroded

the end
end of gatherings
end of demanding weight
celebration dried out
in the barren lake

Indian summer
scattered throughout the red desert
streams of peyotte
a madman
a policeman
stationary fear
(driver passing keeps
a crafty image)
a boy's spirit rises to join the rising spirits
a contour of a new world

The Search
by Lindsay Gaken - age 18

The smile on my face, slowly turned to a
    frown looking for a warm embrace.
No one to guide me.
No one to love me.
Except the sky that lingers above.
A lonely rain drop falls.
My eyes slowly open to someone's call
I search about, but yet I found no one.
As my eyes fill with tears, I started to run.
As I reached what I thought was the
    end of the road.
I found my mother with open arms waiting
    for me.
As I turned to look down the lonely road
    I have traveled.
I saw my father with a warm smile waiting
    to hug his little girl.
The hugs recieved showed me that no matter
    the distance between my parents,
    they will always be the hand that will
    Guide me.

what once was
by rachel galbraith - age 16

the foundations which were once firm
    are
        crumbling
the walls which were once strong
    are
        tumbling
we who once tried to help
    are
        stumbling
we who once told the truth
    are
        lying
we who used to smile
    are
        sighing
we who used to laugh
    are
        crying
we who used to flourish
    are
        dying

Affection
by Shannon Gallagher - age 14

Just a barefoot faerie girl amoung the ripe cherries.
Lost in a puzzle and her gumdrop dreams.
Chasing the wind on that rare occasion.
And licking the rain off her tear-stained lips.

The braids in her hair sing a song of the other world.
The lone tear drop is her sweetest charade.
Her fair-haired giggle is the warmest summer's day.
A perpetual dip in the thickest sun beams
Leaves a twirling moon baby
Where my satin princess once hid.

A puppy dog glutton with her blood red cheeks
Sings a new song, today.
Of thyme and clovers and polka dot suits
With mismatched ties; she sings the blues.

Her eyes close again, for the very first time.
Foreheads are filled with her crazy dreams.
Of me and parrots and bright new shoe laces.
Then the day begins.

The Scream
by Andrew D. Ganaway - age 19

The Screaming rage of every thought is like
The complex insanity of reasoning why,
The music that pounds constantly in my mind,
The evil laughter as tears roll down my face,
The guilt for what I haven't done,
Or the morals of convienece I wish I could live by.

It's when I can't seem to talk
About things I want to scream about.
It's the drive to continue and survive
When I don't have anything else.
It's when the cold within
Is worse than the cold without.
It's when i don;t know if people
I remember are fictitious or not.
It's when I can't be sure if what I remember
Happened or in fact was a dream.
It's learning to wake myself up
Every time I start to dream.
It's the view of death
When a book opens the door
Of someone else's misery,
And rips me open in a nightmare.

The screaming rage of every thought is like
The cruelty of not caring,
The half blindness I struggle to see through,
The cynicism for everything surrounding me,
The stress of being surrounded,
And the chill of being alone.

The scream is only an image
Seen in my eyes for a moment
Before the fear and guilt bury it again
Until the next time I dream.

Beautiful Bee
by Jason Ganz - age 15

Buzz, buzz, buzz how busy you are.
Jumping, fleeting, humming and singing
Jaunting daintily among your purple, pink, yellow, and orange friends.
Stopping now and then for a sip of life giving nectar.
A blaze of black and yellow cast out on a sea of flowers
drifting daintily,
you whir and dive, you spin and on hive,
How lucky you are, busy bee.
You are clad in armor of non peril.
Now here comes a finger, an innocent little miniature finger to pet you in curiosity.
Eeeeeeeeeeeeeeeeek! A quick withdrawal of the hand of trust.
A tear falls into your friend as you buzz away for the last time in shame.
For he who tampers with innocence loses a part of himself.

No Longer Are My Eyes Closed
by Alegria Garcia - age 17

It's been a long time since I could see you
There are just some things truth doesn't want to see
Because it didn't see me,
waiting behind the door for it,
Pretending to bump into it,
make it all a coincidence,
it knew I had a plan.
You can't fool the truth, it knew I was there, waiting,
so it walked the other way,
left me to wait behind the door with the whispers in my ear.
Don't follow me , it said,
I know you'd rather believe yourself than
what the truth has to say.
All this time what the truth was whispering I can now hear.
The dream is not you, don't try and believe me,
You know what the truth can do.

Dawn of the Son
by Christina L. Garris - age 17

Darkness had dawned on my horizon
A covering of black with patches of midnight
No escape
The blackness reached, with it's long, sharp fingers,
into my heart

The seasons changed
All except for the endless winter that had seeped
inside my soul
No release
So cold it grew
I could not feel the chill of the world around me
Only that of my own existence

I close my eyes to search for any trace of life
A silent prayer forms on my lips
The last of my pride is gone
And the Son rose before me
Light broke into my dark cell
Warmth flooded my frozen spirit
I am free

A Night Light's Comfort
by Joanne Gartman - age 20

Oh heart broken and tears profound
    A place of solitude I rush.
Shaken and weaken I tremble to the ground;
    Oh why must love hurt so much?
Crying dry tears, I stammer to stand;
    Sullen and suicidal I find myself where sea meets land
Cool and soft, the white sand shrieks at my approach
The sea blinks and gently shimmers.
    The horizon bleeds with the sun's amber glow.
I see waves fumble, fall, and grasp the shoreline
    Shells tumble and crumble at their mercy.
Sea oats sway and dunes die as the sand
    Stirs, swirls and is swept away by a summer's breeze.
Darkness encloses me, but I find that I'm not alone;
    Above me companions of light twinkle guidance
With a renewing strength I join my friends and Radiate!

Pure Innocence
by Lacey Gay - age 13

She was just four
when it happened.
She was kidnapped,
raped then murdered!
Such a sweet face
So pure!
Why do we have to
live in a world so sick!

The Man in The Jet Black Car
by Dawn Genzlinger - age 19

On your lunch break
You sit in your car with the windows rolled up
and smoke your cigarettes Knocking your ashes off
Into a half full Coca-Cola can.

Spearmint gum and Polo cologne
And you think you smell like a man.

Then you smile like a movie star
Through your tinted glass
At the blond that walks by
And she's making eyes at the car you're in.
You roll your window down
And the blond and her short skirt walk away.

You spit your gum out
And light another cigarette.

My Castle
by Allison Gianneschi - age 15

Enter, sir, my castle!
You have nothing to fear,
You've entered my realm,
But I have invited you here!

I bid you, speak truly,
I'll both listen and hear,
For no thought is uncouth,
And no problem is mere!

Come! Dine at my table!
Come, draw yourself near,
You search for discussion,
I'll lend you my ear!

After dinner I'll show you,
The wonders 'round here!
You can climb all the steps,
You can rest on their tiers!

Please excuse all the halls,
Which are crowded with gear,
But watch and you'll note,
Not a cobweb appears!

Because! This is my mind!
My castle and pier!
Where I live and launch dreams,
At a million a year!

So! Enter, sir, my castle,
You have nothing to fear!
You've entered my realm!
But I have invited you here!

Summer
by Tanya Gilbert - age 11

When summer blues the skies
And thrushes sing for hours,
And gold and orange butterflies
Float by like flying flowrs...
Although I squint my eyes
The way a thinker does,
Somehow, I just can't realize
That winter ever was.

Untitled
by Christine Goldman - age 15

Looking into the glass pane at the many rows,
I am saddened by what many people don't know.
Baby X, over there, separate from others
Has an HIV positive teenage mother.
If only her own mother had been there for her
Maybe everything would have turned out better.
But now with this poor girl lying on her death bed
No one cares to take her child home to a warm bed.
There is not one relative willing to accept
Her child which was partially caused by their own neglect.
The father, who is unknown, is most likely dead
And the baby still has no place to lay it's head.
Finally two strangers come and take the child home.
They take good care of her and name the baby Joan.
As the years pass by, the disease turns into AIDS.
Now baby Joan's life feels like a maze.
Unfortunately for her there is no way out.
Experimental drugs leave behind many doubts.
Joan and her family must fight this war alone.
They hope and pray for a cure each time that she moans.
Days turn into months of worrying, fret, and fear.
Now baby Joan can hardly shed a single tear.
When death takes it's toll, Joan no longer feels the pain.
The pain that she felt is now the family's pain.
It is hard for them to recall the days of joy
Even when they go through her things and find her toys.
Baby Joan lived a good life the time that she was here
And in every heart she remains very dear.
The wonderful and greatly loved child known as Baby Joan
Was lucky to have the brave family that gave her a home.

From Past To Future
by Virginia Gray - age 14

She
Crouched behind a box
Without presence of mind
About to be consumed by her past

Like a fox hiding from a pack of dogs
Toward her future she tried to run
Until her unseen enemy began to close in

She stopped
Crying quietly for her past had caught up with her

Tears Of Joy
by Emily Gomm - age 14

When I fall
Help me up.

When I cry
Hug me.

When I am mad
Let me be.

When I make choices
Be happy for me.

When I succeed
Cry for me.

If I become famous
Wish upon me.

If I marry
Sing for me.

If I die
Pray for me.

Just Like You
by Angelina Gonzalez - age 14

If I had my violets and daffodils...
What right do I have to chose?
If I had sunshine instead of night chills
I'd be just like you.
If I had dandelions and clovers...
What would I do?
If I had my snow and sunflowers...
I'd be just like you.

If I had my stallions and black beauties too...
If I'd held my reins and swung my hair like you...
If I'd press my lips against his...
I'd be the one who'd rule.
If I'd take him away...
so far away.
I'd be just like you.

If I had your pristine innocence,
As sweet as the fresh morning's dew,
I'd be just like you.
If I could love...
I'd be just like you.
I wish I was
just like you.

Worlds Apart
by Kimberly Gould - age 14

To be a part of this world
You must be bold and fearless.
To be a part of my world
You must be soft and peaceful.
To be a part of your world
You must be dead.

The Flag
by Elizabeth Goodall - age 15

They raised the flag at half mast,
in memory of the boy, shot in the class.
Sadness and grief hung in the air,
the memory of the boy was everywhere.

His enemy had come to school with a gun,
saying that the fight would be won.
They were once a friendly pair, this deadly duo,
until someone came and made it a trio.

She had no idea what she would do.
When she came between the friendly two.
She and the other were madly in love,
thinking that they had been blessed from above.

The other was sad, lonely, and pissed,
but nobody thought that he would be jealous.
He had watched them together and alone,
and had made threatening phone calls to their homes.

He wanted her gone, his friend to come back.
Forgiveness he didn't have, but anger he didn't lack.
In the beginning their friendship was true,
then she came and separated the two.
His anger had washed over him like a flood,
leaving him to end a lifelong friendship, in
nothing but blood.

In the beginning they said, their friendship could
bend.
But neither knew it would come to such a
tragic end.

Lost
by Kimone Gooden - age 17

Lost in your eyes
apart of your soul
truly cataclysmic
this hold
Drawn to your smile
the scenery's unreal
lasting a while
this is what I feel
Bound to your ways
vagrant they may be
riding the waves
of uncertainty
Wanting to win
strategy unsure
needing less
desiring more
Crying
no tears
Paying
no cost
Writing
no words
Lost

Silent Noise Makes Me Deaf
by Cynthia Grace - age 16

I see the brightness of a moonlit night
While walking through a warm, moist forest,
Smelling the sweet fragrance of the flowers
And the fresh, piney scent of the evergreens.

I see the darkness of an empty, deserted road
That I wander aimlessly down, with no destination in mind,
On a bitter, wintery night,
Feeling the gentle breeze of the frigid air.

I hear the soft, melodious song of the ocean
As I walk along the cool, wet sand
At the edge of the warm water
On a hot summer night.

I hear the silent noise of the wind softly calling my name
As I sit on a majestic mountain top,
Staring down at the brilliant colors in the sky at dawn,
And sensing the peacefulness of the town below.

The emptiness of my cluttered mind makes me want to scream and shout;
But still I am silent.

The brightness of a dark, vacant field makes me want to run away;
But still I am motionless.

I am deaf, but I hear. I am blind, but I see.
I cannot speak, but I scream.

I am unable to feel, but still I know the beauty that surrounds me
Everywhere I turn, and in every move I make,
Because beauty is not in sight, sound, or touch.

It is a feeling that is unique to each of us,
Which we hold deep within our hearts.
And it is a feeling that lets each of us know
That even when our dreams seem so far out of reach,
If only you believe... Anything is possible.

Howling Storm
by Laura J. Grace - age 13

The violent storm came and went
Winds ripping through the town
Floods were rising and filled the streets
And the rain kept falling down.

The water filled the town this day
And made a great impact
Winds were howling outside my door
Storm trackers could not track.

I thought the storm would never end
And then the ending came
The winds and flooding ended
Things would never be the same.

We came out of our houses today
Worked hard to get the job done
That was the towns theory they said
And showing brightly; the sun.

Memories
by Summer Michelle Graham - age 15

I lived in that house nearly 50 years,
lots of laughter and many tears.
The table we played checkers on.
Playing tag on our front lawn.
Papa reading in his chair every night.
the time mama and papa got in a big fight.
The nights I got to stay up late.
When I finally went on my first date.
And as I lay here about to die,
I can't help but remember, and I start to cry.

Fallen Angel
by Christine Grice - age 17

You were shot down into a village of
   dreamless sleep,
Bringing with you the tears of laughter.

But you have fallen....fallen into a
   dark world,
Where persecution and prejudice are our
   teachers.

You fight them everyday in the
   maze of mysteries,
Confronted with challenges you always seem
   to win.

Now you feel as if you have met your
   match,
Remember laughter kills them all.

You do not belong here, you are too innocent
   yet you are needed,
This dark world is vicious
   don't ever let anyone have you believe that it won't bite.

But, you'll fly again.
   Each challenge you overcome is another,
   stitch to your broken wing.

Forever
by Amanda Grimmon - age 13

See the sparkle in your eyes
Breathing deep and heavy sighs
Cry the tears made of sorrow
A day away is just tomorrow
Sun rises in the east
The glowing eyes of a beast
Flicking light on and off
Musty air makes you cough
Smile turns to wicked laugh
Feel the devil's ancient wrath
You go around with someone else
Never stopping at my house
Come with me as I sing
"feathers on a birds wing"
As I strum on my guitar
You seem so vacant and so far
My heart is beating as a drum
Your hand brushes upon my thumb
We can change as much as the weather
But we are one and one is forever

Untitled
by Amber Gross - age 16

We agree to walk.
We do not talk.
We turn away,
and open sail.

Out the door
we say no more.
One small paper to
seal out fate.

An agreement,
and nothing more.
We say goodbye,
dare each other to look
in the other's eye.

There Was A World
by Cassie Grube - age 16

Once upon a time, there was a world.
A world with truth and love for mankind.
A world with respect not jealousy.
A world without murder and suicide.
A world where animals where praised and loved
not stalked and killed.
That world is lost.

Once upon a time, there was a world.
A world free of violence and corruption.
A world where there was no black or white.
A world where man loved woman for who she was
not what she looked like.
A world without poverty and where children were fed
and loved, not abused and hurt.
That world is forever gone.

Once upon a time, there was a world.
A world where justice was had no matter the
wealth or fame of the being.
A world without illegal drug abuse and alcohol use.
A world with more love than hate.
Where has that world gone?
Where did we go wrong?

Sleep
by Brenda Gruber - age 15

Woozy with pain
I stumble across the floor.
A frightful sound escapes my throat
As I fall over.
Tumbling upon my bed
Thunder rolls through my head.
I blink and stare, unseeing,
At the white ceiling.
It seems to crash down upon me
And my body is crushed.
I shudder and attempt to pull myself upward.
Failing, my body relaxes
And I curl into the fetal position.
Sleep engulfs me and depression ebbs away.

Dreams
by Angela Guastella - age 13

I fall deep into the passageway
of reality no more,
the gods of the heavens
release their joy of triumph above.
The silver gong, although sometimes split,
lets out it's pale ray of shine.
Both of them proud to have won again
the battle of night and day.

My soul enters a gate,
good or evil but not by choice.
I walk among the fairy tale
as the grains of sand fall through the hourglass.
Each return is consumed,
never to be relived again.

This time you stand amongst the gates,
to guide me through the night.
Although you didn't help me
I felt you always near.

I dropped into a darkness hole,
I shivered from release.
The remembrance of sapphire gems
I followed through my walk.
That was the only thought
so vivid in my mind.

The golden stone was high in the atmosphere,
releasing it's joy from the winning night.
Too bad it was just a passageway,
to reality no more.

Breaking-Up
by Misty Guffey - age 15

Oh the little anguish of parting from love is yet untried. To scared to make commitments with feeling that we hide. At first I thought you understood the words I could not say. You kept me at a distance, but not to far away. I know involvement takes alot of your emotions, strains, and breaks, but I just can't live without it, please we have too much at state. I know it's not our love that keeps us far apart, but the fear we have of being hurt, that's bruised into our hearts. I know we're both young and scared, with both our lives ahead. But it's not for our lives we need each other, just these few precious days instead.

Choices
by Caroline Gunby - age 15

I choose to make a change
 For only I can rearrange
The situation I am now facing
 Resulted from the choices I was making
A path I chose to travel
 Was a path chosen by many
A path of destruction and stress
 And now I know that decision wasn't the best
But now I am making the choice
 That only I can make
I have the tools I need
 A little trust and faith
Only time will tell
 When I've found that special spell
The choice is mine
 It can be divine
With the help of patience and time
 I know one day
The right choice I will find

After All
by Laurence Gurney - age 17

Life is but a trial period for your death sentence.
You just wait to die in some torturous form.
You can get old and watch yourself fall apart slowly.
Or catch a disease and decay from the inside out in agony.
There are many more nasty ways to live than to die.
Because once you are dead the pain stops.
The lucky ones die at birth or kill themselves.
I've heard people say the lucky ones are cheated of life.
But I think what they really mean is they cheated the game of life.
So why I choose to live I am not too sure.
I think it is because I like to see other people's pain.
Only then does it seem like my life ain't so bad after all.

Dad's Hands
by Amy Hain - age 15

Showing personality and character,
Holding a foundation for family and friends;
A foundation of love.
Picking up the hurt and lonely,
Surrounding the heartbroken,
Being strong in danger and in punishment,
Soft and gentle when tears fall and frowns appear,
Sharing in the joy, happiness, sorrow, and suffering of all.

True Friendship is a Knot
by Erin Hall - age 13

True friendship is a knot,
which angel hands have tied.
It is not to be denied.
True friends are kind,
other people are mean.
A true friend you can find,
is almost always to be seen.

I'm Always Here
by Leila Hamdan - age 16

Living without you
Brings me sadness and fear
With whispers of loneliness to hear
Losing you and not having you by my side
Is like
The night afraid of breaking
A soul afraid of dying
And a dream afraid of waking
Everyday I sit and ask myself
How did love slip away
It seems so hard for me to reach
But I long for it each day
But, Baby,
You are not alone
For I am here with you
Though you're far away
I am here to stay
Your burdens I will bear
And I will always care
I'll be taking care of you
From the heart inside of me
Like a high tower
Over-looking the sea
If I still live inside of you
Then there's no where else
Where I'd rather be
Memories of you are kept in my soul
Much deeper than any ocean
And I'll be thinking of you
With my truest emotion

Sonnet Of Promise For Those Who Fight Racism
by Brooke Meryl Hamlett - age 15

They say violence is unrelated
Our world has simply gone terribly wrong
Society is plainly ill-fated
Peace and harmony will have no love song
More drowning spirits and deaths are coming
But we march ahead to outrun the war
Listen to the fight songs some are humming
It's all sadly similar to before
Everyone has found an enemy
Nothing's similar in another's face
One voice cried out "Send deliverance to me"
Yet found no freedom or Amazing Grace
Run at me; I will take what you give
I fight against evil and I will live

Rulers Of The Wind
by Ashely Hebrank - age 12

Once called
Rulers of the wind
Horses stand
Tall
Proud
They remember the
Timeless legacy when a
Horses boundary was
Limitless
They could run
Wild
Free
Though he was tamed by man,
His soul will always belong
To the
Wind

Falling Asleep
by Jill Hammill - age 13

As I lay down,
on the soft, cushioning couch,
I didn't have to strain
to hear the waves.
For the horizon of smooth,
glistening water
has no volume.
Yet, you can capture
its everlasting life in a seashell.

I didn't have to imagine
how it looks,
For the familiar picture
of the glistening glass
does not matter
at this glorious moment.
I only had to lie there
and let my head
fill with calming, oceanic thoughts.
As I drift off to a relaxing sleep,
one night of the many
nights the waves and I
will spend together.
As I am Falling Asleep
to the sound of the mother ocean.

Untitled
by Emily Hammond - age 18

i think i cried a sea tonight
my eyes were storm clouds that would not go.
Get out your ark
Before i flood this world,
Make sure your hearts are strong
'Cause we're getting into something deep.

Hidden away in the back of my mind
And deep down in my heart
Are the places i rarely go
Here i found a grieving soul
Tired and breaking apart.

I had to look at all the sadness
All the anger and the hurt
I had to corner what i'd been hiding
And it scared me
I hadn't even known it was there.
What will i do with all the feelings
The anger is taking control
This rage is running rampant through my soul.
Tears of frustration flow abundant from a well that won't run dry
And when it does what will be left
Except for pieces of failed past life.

How did i live so long without knowing,
Or did i know and just not see the emotions buried alive
That just won't die on their own quietly.

I have to look at all the sadness
All the anger and the hurt
I must confess what i've been hiding
And then let the feelings
Go!

Life
by Janelle Hampton - age 13

A world of hope
I cannot be a part of
Even though my family
I really do love

It is not them
It is me
I am trapped
I am no longer free;

I've been through a lot
I've been had
Though all is not wrong
I still feel sad;

I've been betrayed
Stepped on and lied to,
By every one around me,
By them and even you;

I really do believe
My wounds will never heal
Even after there's some joy,
Sad is how I feel;

For now I live
Or so I hope,
I'll deal with life,
I'll learn to cope.

Forever
by Stacey Hansen - age 18

God help our love that so often we forget
how much we really care
A love that is seldom enough overlooked
but often enough denied
Remorse lays in the hands of those
who feel love is not part of them.
Suddenly,
a rush of feelings for
the one you so adore
come flooding to you.
Lust lies in everyone's heart
but only the strong dare it to try
Undiscovered loneliness lurks
where the other fills the void.
Thoughts of being without you
thunder loudly over my head
as I let you walk away
I know that you were right
but to say you were right
means to surrender
surrender means to give up,
give up means to let go
and let go is
Forever...

Gray
by Jolene Hay - age 12

Gray is a forgotten room tasting a stale
    gray flavor,
Gray is the mystical, cold mist shrouding the
    trees with mysterious secrets,
Gray are the leaves of the lavender bush,
Gray is majestic granite sides of Yosemite,
Gray is the hair of my dear, old grandmother,
Gray is as bleak as my breath on a cold day,
Gray is sad, unwanted, or unloved,
Gray is my spirit when I think of you and I,
I feel gray.

Flash Of Red
by Tim Hapgood - age 12

Soldiers
men to fight
men who fly on every flight
trained to kill with their eyes in the sight
with one pull of the trigger
with one flash of red
all these soldiers will soon be dead.
killers on their killing spree
tycoons with their money trees
they cannot hold their child's hand
or run freely upon the land
It's all over with a flash of red
yet are these soldiers really dead?
their spirit lives on
their life not gone
above the seas and shadows
reflecting on their past battles
it's all over with a flash of red
but does it really matter?

Untitled
by Katie Harvath - age 14

The piano sits there motionless in the night,
It calls to me like an arabian mare
The last black key is waiting to be played,
Before it's time to leave
My piano loves to watch me laugh
It remembers the old enchanted days
Now disoriented like a ship at sea
The dreams of my piano return
The wailing mourns and cries it made
That would rise and fall like the ocean
The sadness and remorse I feel
Pain and grief are to unbearable
My problems are like my piano
Out of tune and insurmountable
In a way I want to play it again
To see what it would do
I'm too afraid of the past
The past with the old piano
See, my piano isn't an instrument
But a person caught in a dream
A person with deceiving eyes and an empty heart
Now I see was just some poison covered in sweet smelling sugar
This person took away my childhood
That is now forever lost and gone
Deep inside I want to go back
I wish my dream would come alive.

Memories
by Ashley Lauren Hopkins - age 14

Memories never die.
Some make you laugh,
some make you cry.
Others make you glad and or
mad; but best of all, it
is fun to look back on
the memories that you once
had.

Solitary Child
by Sara Hasledalen - age 16

Solitary child, sitting alone
always on the outside
feeling the cold
I can't tell what you're thinking
but I know where you've been
solitary child
soul filled with shame
life without a purpose
face without a name
say good-bye
let go of your past
let the one who holds your heart
take it all at last
there's a voice inside calling
silenced for so long
now crying out for someone
and somewhere to belong
heart torn and broken
behind a locked up door
now bursts to pieces
as a tear falls to the floor
lift up your head
reach out your hand
I can see you stumbling
about to fall again
sitting on the outside
feeling the cold
you're a solitary child
always alone.

Unknown
by Stacy Dawn Hemmer

As animals play
The forest dwindles away
Unknown to prey

Unprevented
by Stephanie Hatcher - age 16

something hits from the inside
shattering ever outer edifice that follows
a destructive torpedo of doubts and regrets
seethes from within
a torrent dried up by an angry sun
empty, silent, wondering
death is so quiet, sterile, clinical
tho not close to me
i knew...
i didn't do anything
to stop the plunge to the grave
how blind, when i,
i myself have tried to
obliterate my own existence
where was i
when the trigger was pulled?
a loud crackling of ozone
a hole filled with blackness,
turbulence of inner red
pink shredded pulsing flesh-
no longer.
where am i now
while a cold grey body
lays under the fluorescent
chilled, alone, free in the final
messy declaration,
while i am sitting here wondering,
someone else lies
dead.

Beneath The Rustling Leaves
by Kristi Hausman - age 14

Underfoot, frightened insects scuttle beneath glossy leaves.
Only their tuneless humming is left behind,
As proof of their existence

Overhead, birds scream and laugh to one another.
Crying for help or joy or sorrow,
Their songs merge and intertwine,
Creating a heavenly chorus of song.

Leaves rustle and trees sway,
As though joining in some mindless carefree dance.
Waiting for Sun to adorn then with his golden kisses.
Waiting for Night to wrap them in her cloak of darkness.
Waiting for Winter's chilling touch, and Summer's warm caress.

Sunlight dapples the path.
Bright in one spot, dim in another,
Yet always changing, always transforming.
A forever shifting collage of Light and Dark.

Leaves brush against me as I glide past,
Mist, soft as clouds, cling at my garments.
From and old, rotting log,
A family of sparrows noiselessly survey my steps.

This is how it is, this is how it always was,
An undisturbed paradise in harmony.
This is how it is,
Beneath the rustling leaves.

Small And Afraid
by Cassandra Hubbard - age 13

In my past I was a caged animal, alone and afraid

In my dreams I am snow leopard, free without a care in the world

To my family I am a mouse, small and scared in my corner

In the future I will be a hero, strong and brave

Mom And The Hard Times
by Charlene Hawkins - age 15

See that house sitting there on the hill,
Momma is sitting inside wondering how she's
gonna pay for the bills.

She has a job, but ends still don't meet,
She likes to have things complete,
But she can't cause her job don't pay alot,
it hardly pays for a pot,.

Momma tries her hardest,
to make the best.
The more she does,
The more bill collectors bug.

She wishes people leave her alone
But they keep bugging her to pay off that loan.

Soon they will put her in jail
And take us away,
And say "that's the price you had to pay"

She hopes and prays,
That we'll be back in her hands,
AND EVERYTHING WILL BE OKAY.

Darkness
by Keith Haynes - age 18

Somewhere in the world tonight light cannot be found
Neither star nor moonlight will reveal the blackened ground.
Beneath the rocks of the barren desert, and below the cold, cold sea
darkness as black as the miser's heart brings solace to those in need.
The darkness I've felt inside my soul is enough to wake the dead.
A bitter man is plain to see; evil is in my head.

Somewhere in the world tonight shadows lie all around.
Creatures dwell throughout the darkness unseen without whaling a single sound.
Behind a dumpster in an abandoned alley and on a blank television screen
darkness as black as the miner's lungs brings solace to those in need.
Deep in the hollows of the earth I've mined for copper and lead
without seeing light for days; evil entered my head

Somewhere in the world tonight the spiral darkness is wound.
Life exists, though seemingly dead, beneath a hard clay mound.
People continue to hustle and bustle, though them he cannot see.
Darkness as black as the blind man's eyes brings solace to those in need.
I've never seen the setting sun; my eyes have long been dead.
What's the use in getting up? Evil is in my head.

Let Me lean On You
by Lucy Heckman - age 11

Keep your eyes upon me,
Keep me ion your sight.

Help me down the crooked road,
Lead me to the light.

The road I'm on is dark,
I'm not sure I know the way.

Yet, with you right beside me,
I'm certain I won't stray.

Protect me from the world,
I know we'll make it through.

Give me all the strength I need,
Let me lean on you.

Endless Dreams
by Anna Heimark - age 14

I'm dreaming of an endless day;
a time when children laugh and play.
A day when there is no more pain;
and people will succeed and gain.

I'm dreaming of an endless time;
when some will sit drinking wine.
A time when men no longer fight;
and children's eyes will shine with light.

I'm dreaming of an endless life,
a time when I may be your wife.
A life that will continue on;
even though you've long been gone.

I'm dreaming of an endless place;
somewhere I can see your face.
With memories that we've been through;
and I'll tell you how I love you.

I'm dreaming of an endless sky;
a place to go when we die.
A sky that we will see together;
and be together always and forever.

Demon Eyes
by Stac-E Hendon - age 17

I see the demon in your tears
He's hiding in your eyes
He's telling me what you will not
He's pouring out your lies
You tell me you love me
The demon says you don't
Try to say that you'll stay here
And tells me you won't
Maybe its all just in my head
For I believe your every word
Ignore the demon in your eyes
And let your cries be heard
 Demon eyes, I see right through
 You always have to lie
 Demon eyes, know what to do
 Trust in me, you cry
 Finger on the trigger
 Ready now its aimed
 Suicidal demon eyes
 You're the one to blame
Crawling back on your knees
Crying your love to me
But demon eyes give you away
Your lies are plain to see
So cock your gun and try to run
You can't out run your lies
Look at me and see my tears
Shining in demon eyes...

Joyful Morning
by Melanie A. Hensiak - age 17

The sun is shining in rays about my room;
    dancing, bouncing, feel no gloom.
Lying awake in bed,
    thoughts a waltzing through my head.
The sky is bright,
    the birds sing with delight.
        Way, far away, goes all of my fright.
I open the window,
    my...what a sight:
The leaves, the grass, the cool summer breeze,
    oh, what's this?...Here comes a sneeze.
The playful pollen tickles my nose,
    I get a chill from my head to my toes.
A gorgeous day
    I yell, hooray!!
I finally step out of my room,
    throughout the house, there is no gloom.
I decide what to do...
    hey, I know I'll send this to you
so you're not blue,
    please share it, too.

The Mist of the Ocean
by Kelly Keehan - age 14

A kind, salty breeze envelopes me in its
    gentle arms

While the strong, warm hand of the sea
    washes over me.

So calm and peaceful is the rhythm of
    the ocean.

My problems float away, like boats on
    the horizon at the mercy of whatever
    the sea holds.

Mist sweeps over the land, and my
    identity disappears into the fog.

Weather Of Feelings
by Nickilou Krigbaum - age 13

A splendid day,
wouldn't you say?
The cool refreshing rain has come.
It's here to wash my mournful tears away!

When the rain shall flee,
the sun I shall see.
Puffy white clouds shall float.
This sight will bring me glee!

Touch Down
by Jennifer Kristina Herring - age 16

How did I know you'd come?
Well, I can read you,
like a book,
And I've also got you,
wrapped around my little finger.
Hmm, I hit a never,
no strike against it.
Now come over here,
& make the slam dunk.
Hmm, you're an excellent player.
No tackling, only touch.
Oh, Darling, stop,
I'm sorry, I apologize,
But I know how much,
you enjoy sports,
And that's goin' to more,
than football & basketball.
I just couldn't resist it.
Now come serve me,
ha, ha, I'm sorry,
It's quite funny though.
Okay, I'll stop laughing,
& start cheering!
Got'cha, I love doing this,
oh stop it,
You know it's funny.
Okay, let's get serious,
make love to me...
Ah, touch down!!...

A Day In Wonderland
by Neil Hester - age 17

Tortured Souls run crazed through the streets of Wonderland Demented
Wondering often where their anger may be safely directed
Other souls, content with their lives, lifelessly wander by, secretly gazing at the intensity
        the others release
Somewhere far off, high in the hills, a king in secluded mansion sits dignified, preparing to
        eat his feast
A servant in a corner quietly watches in suspense as his evil master indulges himself in
        expensive meats and vegetables the servant has never tasted
Later that evening the same servant cries as the remains of the meal he'd enjoy fully are
        casually wasted
As time goes on, the vengeance grows stronger and more secure
Deep in the heart of Wonderland Demented lies an evil amazingly pure
The tortured Souls, still running wildly through the streets, frequently begins digging in
        garbage cans, looking for something they may eat
One discovers a half eaten burger - he considers this a treat
Soon the souls in the street lie tired in their boxes as the servant falls asleep upon a shelf
The king lies in velvet, with the content others in their homes, as the day becomes night,
        ending itself

Grey Shadow
by Ethan Hirsch-Tauber - age 17

Gracefully gliding,
Silently slipping,
The grey shadow flits
Over the reef
And through the depths.

A flick of its powerful tail
And it breaks the surface.
Then with a fluid dive,
The marvelous marine mammal
Rifles back into the ocean,
As a spiraling torpedo.

Faster and faster, the dolphin,
So wild and free,
Plunges headfirst down deep,
Then circles a loop like a rollercoaster,
Swirling and spinning,
As I watch in awestruck revery
On my dull, dry dock.

Megan And Johnny
by Brandi Kuffler - age 15

Megan and Johnny walk down the hall together as happy as can be.
Megan's eyes are shining, but Johnny's you can't see.
They bring a lot of stares, walking down the hall.
Megan and Johnny don't care since their love conquers all.
Some people don't approve of Johnny, Megan's heart is torn.
But in three months Megan graduates, and in three months Johnny's born.

I Can Remember
by Rachel Hobernicht - age 13

I can remember our days together so well,
you'd always have a different story to tell.

I can remember how easily you'd forgive
me when I'd done wrong,
and when I'd lie you'd just play along.

I can remember your strong hands,
you were always with me in my dream
lands.

I can remember your loving voice,
and how you'd made everything my choice.

I don't know how to handle life anymore,
I liked how things were before.

Why did you leave me no one else to love,
please watch over me from above.

A Turtle's Cradle
by Nicole Hoheusle - age 14

Part I
My turtle has an exquisite shell.
It is sleek,
full of optimism,
full of amity, and
full of affection.
My turtle can interpret the significance of my gestures.
He can avert the agony and conflict that the beams of fiery sun have
upon him.
He has the power to heal my deepest wounds,
of loss, of woe,
and that of solitude.
They can all be heeled by his company and silence.

Part II
A new sunbeam illuminates the fractures in my turtle's shell,
his empty shell of melancholy.
He isn't home now.
My turtle has gone out to pursue a new cradle of protection,
A higher cradle of protection, one that never neglects a soul.
This new protection shall allow my turtle to never long for me.
For he knows I will see him again someday.
I will see him again when I look for my own cradle.
I hope for my cradle to be as welcoming as my turtle's is to him.

The Comedian
by Amy Lynne Holland - age 19

He gets up every night
　in front of the crowd
And makes them laugh
　and think.
He heckles back at the man
　in front row
And everyone feels good.

But later,
　maybe next week, after a crushing review, or
　　on a plane, during a lull of,
　　　even in front of a
　　　　droning TV

He contemplates what a frail thing the
　human spirit is.

A Stream Of Colors
by Marlene Jenkins - age 15

Red is the color of a heart filled with love.
Orange is the color of a candle burning bright.
Yellow is the color of a dandelion blowing
in the wind.
Green is the color of a sea.
Blue is the color of a sapphire sky.
Indigo is the color of a kite flying high.
Violet is the color of a warm sweatshirt.

Flight
by Erica Horace - age 19

As I run down the winding, twisting path,
the wind blowing upon my face quells me;
I want to leave this world, this abysmal void of existence,
but I am hindered by the forces of a power unknown that pulls me down.
"Stop!" says my mind; it tells at my body to cease it's journey through the wilderness,
But I cannot stop for destiny is but a step away from me,
I start to drag slowly, oh so slowly, towards the sky,
to the place where I can be free from the sorrows of life.
This pace is sacred; found by only a few
I long to be in this place for it is the asylum to protect my soul.
As I glide through the sky, I spread my lavish wings of beauty,
surpassing all other forms of existence in my path;
Then a blazing light blinds my eyes;
I am paralyzed by it's intensity.
The world below me is but a vague vision, vanishing completely from my view,
But just as I reach the light,
the omnipotent force takes hold of me,
And all of a sudden I want to turn back,
back to the realms of human existence, back to hell,
where hatred can call you and fears can scare you.
This force pulls me down, down, down,
down to depth unknown'
It encompasses me and overtakes my mind,
It is the internalized fear and hatred that has ravaged my soul.
I am smothered by it's unsurmountable power
I fall further and further into hell.

Aging Creeps Up Slowly
by Patricia Horwell

Aging creeps up slowly

like Ivy
on old buildings

like a soft spongy moss
covering untended ground

hidden by shadows of
past remembrances

never hearing
only feeling

releasing tensions
from bygone happenings

slipping into the comfort
of sentimental minds

Aging creeps up slowly.

Unlocked Love
by Lisa Kelly - age 16

Our souls are buried deep within
A cherished solemn place
To unlock that soul you have to find
The key to thy sacred heart and mind

Your kind of like Atlantis
Lost under sea
Departing for a secluded place
Away from all of thee.

Walking down a dark winding path
There is just no one who can make you laugh
As you lay there deep in your thoughts
That key that was found is now lost

Birds In the Garden
by Krista Houser - age 13

A flutter, a flash, a flit, a rustling of dry leaves,
the uncanny hovering, small inquiries,

A chickadee, a hummingbird, a swift flycatcher too,
all sorts of birds flying about making rainbows in the dew,

They sing their song with special care,
weaving it throughout the air,

Not rendering a single foe,
but chirping of love and of hope,

Some searching on the ground for seed,
avoiding the few bristly weeds,

Others sipping nectar sweet,
not uttering a single tweet,

While floating on a gentle breeze,
they think not of their enemies,

There's not a worry or a care,
while they're soaring through the air,

They live a very simple life,
of many trials and of strife,

The purpose of their life isn't wealth,
but of family and of health,

Trying to live in the world today,
although we seem to throw it all away,

The things they need to survive,
we take for granted as their lives,

We do not think how we affect,
but we must strive to protect,

All innocent little birds,
but in actions not in words.

Seeking The Light
by Altiemeis Howard - age 16

Searching for the light
In a cool dark place
Even with vision focused
I still see little
I walk forward
Forever seeking the light
I glance ahead
To see a small ray of light
I run towards it
But the closer I get
The father away I become
I look back to the way I came
And see no light
Where is the light I seek?
I focus into the recesses of my mind
There is where I see the light
Shining brightly inside me
Filled with hopes and dreams of the future
The light dwells deep in my soul
Burning with intense luminescence for all eternity

In The Room
by Samantha Hrinek - age 15

An attempt to speak
No one knows
In the room
There she goes

A vision in the past
No one knew
Back to the room
Just for a few

A feeling of loneliness
No one is there
Standing in the room
Just her and the air

A need to let one in
No one can hear
Still in the room
Full of fear

A desire to be outside
No one cares
Inside the room
She only stares

A thought of death
No one needs
Forever in the room
She always bleeds

Prick
by Cherokee Layson - age 19

The glass bottle shattered easily
only with a slight
tip and topple.
It now shone brightly
in a hundred pieces
with no definition.
Just glass bits that
pierced my skin as I
picked them up,
and all the while they are
baptized
in minuscule
droplets
of blood.

Poet and Dancer
by Suzanne Kiss - age 20

"sometimes you gotta walk away," the poet said to me

"...and sometimes you gotta lick your wounds," the dancer thus replied

"and then like birds you shall be free," the poet argued back
"...never to be free again." the dancer smugly smiled

smirking to companion's eyes the poet thus replied:

"what would you do had it not been for the jig that broke your leg?"

"the same as you," the dancer said "had it not been for the car door which slammed down on your hand."

Reincarnation/William's Lament
by Jasmine Hudepohl - age 14

Born into you,
you died a painful death
and you became me.

I smiled upon my murder
shook her hand and said,
"watch now I'll get my revenge,
this life."

She looked at me, sighed and replied,
then I'll be just like you,
and you'll be my wife,
in our next life.

I took her hand in mine
so can we solve it here,
I looked into her eyes
so can we solve it now,
or must we forever roam?

We were happy
you died in my arms
I shed not a tear,
I got what I came for
now I'll go home.

True Peace
by Amanda Lawson - age 18

If love could last forever
If hearts would never break
If souls could stay untarnished
If peace was no mistake.

If nature kept it's presence
If sunlight brought new life
If mother stayed with children
If husband stayed with wife.

If friendship brought a smile
If no one was alone
Then true peace would have been achieved
and sorrow, be unknown.

The Ocean Speaks
by Brandy Camille Huff - age 15

The ocean speaks to me
Not softly but loudly
The wind whispers
But the ocean roars

A drowning heart
Desperately searching
Hopelessly dreaming
There's an emptiness inside

A lost soul
In an ocean of fantasies
The ocean speaks
It touches the very heart
Of the one searching
For someone to hold
For all eternity
Never and Forever.

What You Have Done
by Jeni Hullum - age 15

Hello mommy, it is me, your little girl
I am just a little curious about what it is like to live in the
real world,
I will never experience how it feels to talk or run,
For I have been punished for your mistake, for what you have
done.
I was something special, unique in my very own way
"I love you, Mom," is something that you will never hear
me say.
How does it feel to fall in love or better yet, be even
kissed?
Will thoughts of me flood your mind, or will I even be
missed?
I was going to be a success at everything I tried out to
do.
I was quite a little blessing to everyone, but I guess not
to you.
I would have made many friends for my lifetime for sure,
But again I was too much for you to endure.
I just can't believe what a cold heart you have that
murdered me,
So I have decided to haunt you for eternity
I will stay in your mind so that I may tell you so;
I would have made a difference in many lives, but now you
will never know!!!

Puppets
by Corey Hults - age 16

Are we puppets
with a retired master
whose only reminisce is
a dying shadow?

Are we puppets
blowing in the wind
a forgotten play toy
left out to dry?

Or are we puppets
that never had a master
that's still sitting on a store shelf
Waiting to be bought?

Could we be puppets
still used for a show
to dance by someone else's will
for someone else's amusement?

Maybe we're puppets
cut string and set
free being left to
dance on our own feet.

Or could we be puppets
with a master
saddened by our refusals
to move as he likes?

Dougie
by Jeanie Lemons - age 15

Dougie, you are like,
A gentle wind blowing on,
a cool, crisp autumn day.
The dew on the grass,
on a fresh April morning.
Or even the crimson clouds at sunset,
which are beautiful on sight.
Or the patches of deep blue behind
the billowing clouds.

The Land Beneath The Shadow
by Cyriaque Lamar - age 12

The ancient moon looms high,
Its silent shadow cracks the trees,
and whispers secrets on the breeze.

A Valley
by T. Hunter - age 16

A towering mountain smiles sweetly,
And the rolling plains reach out to greet me;
Mountain-top kingdoms, a fairy's land,
With peaceful people joining hands.

Beautiful trees stretch tall to the sky,
Away with the birds, I wish I could fly.
Smiling sadly, I keep rolling on,
Thinking "Soon this place will be gone."

Fires will race through this valley of wonder;
Mankind will come to pillage and plunder.
Traveling around from earth to the sky,
We keep on destroying, not knowing why.

Everyone wonders what something is worth;
What golden rewards can be got from this earth?
I blink my eye, but one tear escapes;
Forlornly I realize I'm leaving this place.

On the bright side it's still in one piece,
But only because mankind still sleeps.
As soon as we wake and realize it's there,
We'll strip this valley 'til it's dead and bare.

That mountain's still smiling
From it's perch up so high,
And the grass on the plains
Waves one last good-bye.

Which Path Should I Take
by Sarah Irwin

When I think to myself
Which path have I chosen to take
I never thought
It would be a mistake
I'd make
When I travel down
The path I took
I think to myself
Why didn't I look
It maybe
I was blind
Or just didn't care
But when I think
Of all the things
I could of shared
My hopes
My dreams
The chances
I didn't take
And now my life
Is falling apart
Because of the choices
I make

Evil
by Annet Isa - age 15

I'm evil.
I'm an essence.
I'm evil.
In the heart of priests, in a nook of your
soul
No matter how religious or self righteous or
pious you are, I'm a part of you
I'm the part that speaks up when it comes
time to make a choice.
Why not?
Just because I'm right doesn't make it fun.
I'm evil.
Do not fuse me with being bad or wrong.
Just because I'm evil, just because
I think that may be once in awhile you
should do what you want doesn't make
me bad, now does it?
I'm evil. I'm a pulsating throbbing red.
I'm a searing color of black.
for some people, I am the epitome of sex.
I'm evil. I'm an essence
I'm you....

Knowledge
by Jennifer Isham - age 16

Knowledge, of course, it is expected
To be gained by one's own free will.
Day in, day out, it is rejected
Yet it's reward, through time, stands still.

To ask a question and answer it right
Brings joy to a once lost mind.
For he who studies with all his might.
Knowledge he soon shall find.

The world today knows little about
Ancient times and how things were invented.
History's mistakes, if they could only find out
Todays problems could then be prevented.

'Tis no one's right to push upon one's soul
What he is not willing to learn.
But prepare to give to who's mind is whole,
That knowledge he is so eager to earn.

For how can a person hold knowledge within
If no one is willing to go and teach him?

Through
by William L.C. Jefferies - age 17

Look through my face,
see me through my own eyes,
they are the windows to the soul,
tell me this,
how is my soul?
How do I feel?
How does that make you feel?
See now what you didn't before.
I am a true reflection of you,
of your friend,
of the world.
In my face, do you see it?
Tell me, do you see it?
Do you see me?
How does that make you feel?
Does it feel real,
or is it just a tingle away from numb?
In the end, it's going to be you dealing with me
dealing with you,
and we are the same.

Loving You
by Kristin Johansen - age 14

The frowning shadows deepened, and the light of hope died out.
My heart, my soul, were broke.
I wandered lonely as a cloud that floats on high o'er vales and hills,
when all at once I saw you.
Continous as the stars that shine,
like diamonds in the sky, my love for you will never end.
Life now means all; to me stars shine brighter than ever.
There are no shadows in my sky, nor are there any hours of any day
that drag slowly.
There are no story days in my world, Only you.

Untitled
by William Johnson - age 12

Life is like a labyrinth,
with all it's twists and turns.
And as you round each corner,
there's something new to learn.

Traveling down each corridor
of the winding, puzzling maze.
You will find what your ancestors,
found there years before.
A riddle of such intensity,
you can think of it no more.

And as you travel blindly,
into the nothingness beyond,
you are faced with many problems,
and fears that carry on.

But when you face your problems,
and conquer all your fears.
It is then that you are done,
then the answer's clear.

childish games
by Jennifer Johnston - age 18

you call people names
for their looks
you laugh at their opinions
because they do not read your books
you go home
and lead your lucky life
then go to school
to cut us with your knife
but to me your knife is rusted
Yet it hurts even more
because i thought you could be trusted
to have grown up
since the first grade
but i no longer envy
the life you have made
You see you are nothing
to me anymore,
you are still a child,
and will be forever more.
I am through with
playing your childish games.
My crystal tears
you no longer maim.
I may not be rich
and have all of your money,
but I live my life
and love my days of sunny.
So go home and live your cold life
as you always do.
I have grown to love my life,
maybe someday you will, too.

Whispers

Macbeth, Pilate, Jesus, and a Killer
by Heather Jones - age 20

The Lady wanders in sleep and reveals her dark secret.
    She comes to the same place to wash her hands of a bloody
        ambitious act.
She is like the man who, in reality, does the same, but awake and
        deaf to silent cries.

A tormented man stumbles to his knees beside the River of Souls.
    He plunges his hands in to ease his conscience, they come out
        coated with guilt of innocent blood.
There is a man today who is guilty of the same, but the victim has
    no voice.

Wash away the blood and you can see what your choice has done.
    A hole in the palm broke the fall and made it possible to
        continue living.
Some lives are taken before being allowed to live, at the hands of
    a masked man our children are dead.

Time For Spring
by Stephanie Jones - age 13

The wind blows
the thunder rolls
the rain drops
to water the crops
it's time for spring!

the bluebird chirps
the canary sings
the woodpecker pecks,
it's
    time
        for
            spring!

Rosebuds
by Yohnikka Jones - age 13

A king looks at his queen to be and
looks at the future they will see. He
gives her a rose as a sign of love and
kisses it with his heart above. He
rides off to the town to claim his royal
golden crown, but never comes back
to his queen a love that was lost and
never to be seen.

You're So Special
by Christal Kahles - age 14

As the dove soars in flight with beauty and grace,
The same could be said for the glow on your face!
To the human eye, you're seen from afar,
But looking down from above, a light gleams where you are!

Somehow I know--like the depths of the sea,
That your very being is engulfed spiritually.
One day we'll meet, and praises we'll sing!
And then you will see what knowing you brings!

In This Tiny Crowded Room...
by Amy Kalil - age 20

hyperventilating from loniness

like sunday morning air,
in the nook of life and
its stale left over house party,
hanging dull and dense
in the senses
reckoning with reality,

language becomes guilty.

going alone scares me not-
the unknown think the same,
to each other,
love is a finish line
with only winners
ever to cross.

Home
by Jennifer A. Ley - age 7

Today I left Texas
and moved far away,
Mississippi's where I'm going,
I think that's where we'll stay.
I was sad to leave my grandma, grandpa, cousins, and friends,
since Texas has always been my home, I felt this was the end.
But once I got to Mississippi I found it wasn't so bad.
Because my home is not the place, but it's being with my sisters,
My mom and my dad.

A Rose For The Grave
by Jason Kallas - age 17

I went to a cemetery to deliver a rose for a grave.
Neither specified reason nor predetermined grave brought me there that day;
Though I knew I would know the justice of my mission when it came.
As I wandered through the many reminders of the lives that once
Graced the Earth with their presence; I listened to hear their
Legacies of experience and wisdom as I came upon
Two graves from which I should decide the rose's path.

The first grave could be seen from the highest heavens
With the advertisements of the honor it displayed for all to see in its majesty.
Fashioned of marble and engraved to the finest detail,
The tombstone sang the boastful noble song of the proud escapades,
Deeds, sacrifices, and accomplishments of a man long since
Buried into the Earth as all are one day. A grave of this proud quality
Certainly deserves to have a rose placed ar it's head.

The second grave sat unnoticed next to its noisy companion
In it's basic, humble, dull and quiet dark stone that was completely
Unmarred by the slightest blemish or scratch of engravement not even
    whispering
In the wind the deed of this unknown man rather whose grave seemed to be
Begging on it's knees for someone to show him mercy.
This grave seemed to sing in great need and in desperation for help
As it spoke to me rather than whisper to me of it's legacy.

There I stood, concluding the just placing of the rose.
I began to think that giving the rose to the first grave would be
Unnecessary, after all, was it not already graced with preestablished decor?
The second grave was in far greater need of the rose than the first.
I went to a cemetery to deliver a rose for a grave; and I,
I placed the rose at the second grave's feet.
Now, justice is done.

The Civil War
by Christy Kam - age 14

Bullets flying all around,
Soldiers falling from a distant round,
The injured have fallen in pain,
Are their efforts only in vain?
My son is out there fighting.

The North said that it would be a quick war,
But in that, they have missed by far,
Three years has gone by now,
They say only a little more time we need to allow.
My son is out there killing.

The days drag on and on,
My son is surely gone,
The notice just came today,
For in the generals' play,
My son is dead.

The civil war has finally ended,
The country that has been torn apart must now be mended,
The mass graves for the dead must be dug,
Because the dead lay like a blue and grays rug.
I wonder if my son is being buried today.

I pick flowers to lay on his grave,
For his country his life he gave,
But I am not sure if he is lying here,
Maybe his murderer is lying here.
MY son's body is lost forever.

Inside me his last words recoil,
And they help me live like giving a rusty hinge oil,
"Mother, what they are doing is surely not right,
And this, I will surely fight."
I wonder what my brave warrior is doing now.

Untitled
by Sarah Laffan - age 13

For the long nights you lay awake,
And watch for my unworthy sake
For your most comfortable hand,
That led me through all the uneven land
For all the story books you read,
For all the pains you comforted
For all your pitied all you bore,
In sad and happy days of mine and of your
And grant it heaven all who read
May find a mother dear as mine when in need.

Stressed
by Emily Ruth Lovelett - age 12

the days are confusing
don't know where to go
should i go forward,
or should i stay back

if i go forward,
where will it lead?
if i'm moving too fast,
will i succeed?

i'll step back
let em' lead the way
back, back
but will i ever go anywhere
that way?

Tears
by Nikki Katac - age 15

I have tears of joy.
I have tears of fear.
I watch as she is born.
I watch as she gets weak.
Rocking her in my arms.
I wish I could hold her.
She looks around.
Her eyes are closed.
There's a smile on her face.
No expression.
The sound of her giggle fills the room.
Silence.
She moves filled with life.
Lifeless.
She squirms in her crib.
She lies in her casket.
A bottle in her hands.
A rose in her hands.
All is quiet.
All is quiet.
Except for her breathing.
Except for the crying.
A smile on my face.
Tears in my eyes.
Peace.

Lost
by Julie Kaup - age 20

Along the white sandy beach,
the tide pushes itself upon my naked
feet and a chilling sensation
is sent through my nerves.
I sink my cold fingers into the soft sand,
listening to the rustling sounds of the waves.

And in the midst of the ocean,
a small, helpless boy struggles for his life.

Glancing out across the waters,
I make a start but realize I cannot move.
The cries of the young child echo
all around me, and they soon become muffled
as tears begin to well up in my eyes.

Suddenly, I push myself forward,
crawling through the water towards the
lost child, and struggling with all my strength,
I finally hear the last cry of the boy.

Falling into the salty waters,
I give up and slowly begin to sink into
the dark depths of the ocean.
And before my heart beats its last beat,
I feel a small hand grasp mine
and as I tighten my fingers within his hand,
I am quickly pulled away from death.

After surfacing, I gasp heavily for
air and I find myself in strong arms--
in the arms of the same man who was
the lost child whom I came to save.
And when I needed to be saved, he found
me and helped me to feel once again.

An Angel's Tears
by Kathy Kelley - age 15

droplet by droplet
the wetness fell.
was it rain?
or an angel's tears?
soft at first,
then falling hard.
angry at first,
then sad.
the heavens look on,
mystified.
what reason would an
angel have to cry?
the sky fell black,
the water fell blue.
someone has died,
the angel cried.
do not be frightened,
for only when an angel cries
can a mortal truly say
Goodbye.

A Porthole To Your Soul
by Kelly Lowry - age 17

Amber-green eyes
A porthole to your soul
I saw the real you fro a brief moment
Anger and Rage
Loneliness and Longing
Sensitivity and Intellect
Creativity and Originality
Pools so deep
I had to catch my breath
I almost drowned
Unexpected confusion

The Forge
by Erinn Kennedy - age 16

Intense discomfort
smoky heat and glowing flames
they shed no light
you know why you are here,
you have sinned

you bake
in the fervent flames
death all around you
smell the pain in the air,
you have sinned

it chafes you
with every lick
it's torrid teeth gnaw
as you swelter in it's hearth,
you have sinned

a room of terror
a house of evil
chambers of guilt
a begging face has no hope,
you have sinned

no man's creation
foreboding swirls of thickness
he tends the fires that feed it
unleashing anger onto the world,
you have sinned

You are in the eternal forge.

Why do it?
by Susan Keothammakhoun - age 15

Disrespecting your parents is such a big sin.
No matter what happens, you should know that you could never win.

You may think you're all big and mighty,
But sorrows will sneak upon you quietly.

How you turned in the wrong direction,
your parents never understood.

They just thought you were different,
and were going to be good.

You think making them hurt gives you victory.
In the future, everything you'll regret; you'll see.

You probably say you hate them,
But look inside;
You'll find your love for them never died.

You know you'll miss them when they're gone.
You wouldn't be able to love without them form dusk 'till dawn.

Just think about what you've done;
You'll be sorry, for it never led to a victory that you never won.

I Cry
by Jennifer Ketchum - age 16

Lightening,
it strikes my mind
and my senses
but why must it
strike my heart?
Rain is almost tolerable
it's here at least once
a week;
Then the sun will
shine once again
along with my smile.
The sun is gone forever,
clouds of black flood my mind,
Lightening strikes my heart
again.
then I cry,
and I cry.

Knowledge
by Erik Keyes - age 18

Hunting the audience with his eyes and striking with his mind
He perches steadily aloft a rickety pine crate
Engulfed with a sensation of domineering from atop mount majestic
The box emitting moans of agony as his weight sporadically shifts
With their minds secured in his ingenious snare
They lay easy to prey to his sophisticated intellect
His thoughts projected hopelessly bound the audience in a methodical trance
Descriptive emotions shattering their frail minds
Intern transcending him to godliness through their naive ignorance
Repeatedly contouring his words into contradictions further more showers
    confusion
Frustrations boil seeping through facial extremities
Riveting subliminal messages into their battered subconscious
Throwing conclusions unwillingly at his weakened prey
Now doubting all previous realizations
Codependancy ignites
Breathing in their fears
He exhales terror

Summer
by Ashley Killingsworth - age 14

Humid, Roasty nice hot days
Give you a chance to catch some rays
As you strip your clothes down to bare
You look for a band to tie up your hair.

Sleeping in mornings while going to bed late
Will make you lazy which you will hate
Going to the beach and to the pool
Will not make you look forward to go to school.

Going hot place and getting a tan
Will send you straight home to the fan
While summer days are fun and hot
You'll be looking forward to winter a lot.

Whisper
by Patricia Kim - age 13

A silent noise, just hardly there,
A gentle wind, a blow of air.
Secrets told at no one's sight
Afraid of trouble, a rage, a fight
In a library or at street.
To a friend, to anyone you meet
Imaginary whispers on the beaches of the sand.
On the water or on the land.
Peaceful to say, quiet to talk.
good idea in public of walk.
Needed to say without a shout.
Needed to know what its all about.
To tell alone or at a crowd.
Don't be too soft and don't be too loud.
To not disturb and keep it low.
To let a person hear, keep it a secret though!
Between you and a person; your conversation,
Anywhere like on a vacation.
It can be a secret or just to not be heard
Like a sweet soft song of a bird.

Wild Horses
by Kristina Kiper - age 20

You think by reining in my heart
You'll tame my spirit
But I'm not your domestic breed.
I take care of myself
And no one else.
I run wild and free,
Your stable life
Just isn't my style.
I see it in your eyes
My freedom calls to you
And you're scared,
If you don't tame me
I'll let you ride me
Right on over the edge.
But I've been wild all my life
And I can't let any hand
Hold my reins too long.
You can hold my heart
For a time but eventually
You'll forget to close the gate
And I'll run free again.
You can't keep me pent here,
Because I won't ever
Wear your brand
As I run alone
Int the sunset.

daydreamer
by Angi Kirby - age 19

open window
show me creation,
laden with brilliant clusters of moon beams
and brazen peacocks
who swindle glory
from grapefruits dancing on windowpanes.
gardens come in many shades of scented happiness
and memories gather in colorful frames
in the corners of my thoughts,
time slips away
when you're a daydreamer.
I wish in silence to be free of the footprints
which forbid me to swing on dewdrops
and fly with angel feathers
to tranquil meadows
where flowers bloom to the heavens.
gentle winds remind me of people and places
and I am content with my frames
and the wisdom of imperious birds.
raindrops sprinkle magic into my mind
and cast an archway of color in the sunshine,
a canopy over my creation.

Daddy
by Rosemary Lund - age 8

I'll love him for as long as I live
I'll put my feet on his, and
always dance cheek to cheek
He'll never call me small. He'll
never call me cheap, he'll always
call me sweet. He'll always
tuck me in at night and kiss
me on the cheek. We'll always
be together for ever and ever.

Be Glad
by Rhonda Lane - age 14

Be glad that your life has
been full and complete;
Be glad that you've tasted the
bitter and sweet;
Be glad that you've walked in the
sunshine and rain;
Be glad that you've felt both
pleasure and pain;

Be glad for the comfort that
you've found in prayer;
Be glad for God's blessings.....
His love and his care!

Cats
by Abby Klippstein - age 12

Hack! Hack! Hack! Hack!
All of this describes a cat!
Stealing yarn balls, charged of theft,
Hacking fur balls right and left!

Sneeze! Sneeze! Sneeze! Sneeze!
Get that cat away from me!
Tabbies, Tigers, Siamese!
Oh please don't provoke my allergies!

Squeak! Squeak! Squeak! Squeak!
There goes the mouse that was mild and meek!
Taking one more life away,
Killer! Is all I have to say!

Claw! Claw! Claw! Claw!
Sharp are those dainty little paws.
Ruining couches, furniture galore,
Makes me despise them more and more!

Stalk! Stalk! Stalk! Stalk!
Where is the parakeet that once could talk?
One more birdy gone again,
We're back once more where we began!

Yup! Yup! Yup! Yup!
Conceited, snobby, and stuck-up!
All of these fit a feline,
Kitty-cats are no friend of mine!

Hack! Hack! Hack! Hack!
All of this describes a cat!
Stealing yarn balls, charged of theft,
Hacking fur balls right and left!

Dismiss
by Summer Knight - age 17

It never quits anymore,
almost completely euphoric yet disturbing.
Rain, never quiet anyways.
One day, it may bring a comfort, another, a tear.
It is no emotion, but it breeds them all.

Rain please dismiss yourself from my fractured walls.

Some say come again, please do, they say.
I say never again.
You only make the days longer and the nights slowly
sad.

So please dismiss yourself from my window pane.

You mean nothing, you are rain.
I will not dance about in you.
You only complicate my curls.
I do not wish your pitter-patter, it's noise-- I say it is.
Make yourself a fat well and climb far into it.
Fall into a swollen hole.

I wish you far away today.

Oklahoma City
by Ami Lovelace - age 14

Amidst the greatened sorrows,
I walk among the tears,
Of people who've just lost,
The ones that they hold dear.

In the piles of the wreckage,
No survivors may remain,
For the person who has done this,
Caused many death and pain.

The whole city has been devastated,
From this person's unrighteous act,
All the citizens were victim,
To this heinous and deadly attack.

These people of this city,
Are waiting now to know,
If the creator of this destruction,
Will be found guilty or let go.

Anticipation
by Jonathan Knell - age 16

Like the venom of the viper,
Like a tiger's massive claws,
Like a savage's spear,
Like a beasts gaping jaws.
Like the snap of a poison,
As the juice gathers and fills,
Like the hatred of a woman,
Anticipation is the force that kills.

Like the warmth of a body,
Like the juice of the vine,
Like the taste of a kiss,
Like the bite of the wine.
Like the rhyme of a poem,
Like the musk of the rains,
Like the love of a woman,
Anticipation is the force that sustains.

Forgotten Memories
by Kristina Kovacic - age 17

Snowflakes fall upon the earth.
Covering the ground and the memories.
The once enlightened building snow stand
unseen and forgotten.

The skies rumble with grief,
begging to be noticed and acknowledged.
Soon, rain falls
like tears from a lonely child.

The clouds roll above
as children roam below.
Screams of pain and agony echo about
Yet nobody listens.

A hand stretches for help, wanting and wishing to be saved.
As a bystander watches, motionless and peaceful.
The only expression he shows is one of amusement and disgust.

The streets are empty, and the people are gone.
Someone has come for them, someone who's been waiting for them.
Why, you ask?
The most miserable and heartless of all visitors,
death.

"Words Of Doom"
by Laura Kuhn - age 15

It happened, oh, so long ago
Yet I remember it so vaguely-
I was in my room, reading a book
Like I do so often a daily.

Suddenly I heard a voice
coming from downstairs-
I recognize my mother's tone
Yet it wasn't full of cares.

She called to me, I answered quickly,
(She doesn't like to wait)
She told me four words and I stopped in horror
I thought I was going to faint.

My heart skipped beats, I swallowed hard,
My hands began to shake-
I felt the sweat and shivered in fear
How awful to say, for goodness sake!

My throat was tight, my stomach churned
The walls were closing in
Time seemed to slow, my heart to pound
The room began to spin.

So I asked myself, is this really happening?
Did she really say what I think?
Or could this be a nightmare I can wake up from
And all could be normal in a blink.

But I was there and I'd heard her say it
Those words of horror and doom,
I'll tell you what she said to me-
She'd said, "Laura, clean your room!"

For Brandon James
by Heather Marie Kurtz - age 20

As I sit here in this shady grass, memories of you I hear in the wind from the past.

Wishing that the little time we've shared never had to end,

but knowing in my heart that we might not cross the same paths again.

Sometimes I think I hear your voice whispering in my ear,

but then I realize it's just a thought of wishing you were near.

As the sun sets into the sea, and another day comes to a close,

I pray that tomorrow when I come to sit in the shady grass,

that will not sit alone.

One Day
by Tissy Lewis - age 14

I have a feeling that one day our world will be
free
There will be no wars or killing sprees
People will be able to live as they please
Without any fighting over the seas
There won't be no guns or drugs on the streets
That's how I see it as our world being free.
Everyone will learn to get along and
Everybody will feel as if they belong
With this in mind you should see
All the things in this world which shouldn't be
With all our help you will find
That one day our whole world will combine.

My Madness
by Nicole Kuss - age 16

My hatred grows inside me
Like a thick, heavy, suffocating laughter
bubbling and boiling
drowning my rational thoughts
i no longer see friend or foe
only a threat
I would slit their throats
and smile as their blood
sprayed over my face and neck
i would crush their skulls
and giggle as their brain
seeped out onto my hands
I would rip their hearts out
and laugh as their blood
trickled down my arms
I would look into their dead sightless eyes
and whimper as i see
their dreams running away
i could cut their stomachs
and weep as i lay
in the pool of their blood
i would look into a mirror
and scream as i saw a stranger
covered in blood
i would fall into an eternal slumber
as my soul ran away
to rest with the victims of my madness

Untitled
by Elizabeth M. Martin - age 18

The black night sky is my blanket tonight
This rock my pillow; this grass my bed
The sweet, gentle wind kisses me softly upon my cheek
Brushing my eyelids to close and motioning me to sleep
But before I awake with the morning light
The veil of darkness blinding my eyes calls for a drea

Nothing Left
by Erin Langway - age 17

You took my heart
into your hands
broke it in half
left me to stand
alone with memories
of days gone past
or so it seems
they didn't last
I had a dream
that never came true
you ask me why
it's because of you
I had a childhood
sweet and tender
because of you
I can't remember
I had a life
good and divine
because of you
I cannot find
I had a mind
clear and bright
because of you
it's locked up tight
I had everything
but from your theft
because of you
there's nothing left

Once the Children Played
by Arianna Layton - age 18

Once this yard was filled
    with laughter, and youthful dreams;
Once the distant wire fences,
    hidden by a vale of fairies,
fields of smokey amber flowers,
    Were the only barriers for dreams.

Once agile spirits frolicked
    through easy seasons;
Once they splashed in caramel puddles,
    shrieked in mounds of half-baked leaves
    built castles of glittered sand,
Where live the memories of seasons.

Once voices echoed
    through the rising, falling hills;
Once tender velvet fingers twined
    around magic daisy chains
    a soft, winsome voice humming
Watching dandelion fluff cloak the hills.

Once a young lass rocked
    back, forth and back in the breeze;
Once she swung, dreaming for hours,
    reaching her feet up to clouds,
    leaning her head back, eyes closed,
But now the swing sways empty in the breeze.

Now anxiety traps the heart
    that once romped so fancy-free;
Now hate, lust and sharp reality
    cut through her pure euphony,
    screaming in the stolid world,
Whence angelic childhood dreams are not free.

Life's Little Struggle
by Sherry LeBelt - age 15

Struggling through the day,
Struggling through the night
Just to figure out how to fight!

Equality for one,
Equality for all,
Fighting will get you nowhere,
When the people against you just seem to stare.

You must learn one honest lesson,
That can take you anywhere,
Please, just learn how to care!

Then you end up fighting yourself,
To find your strength and will,
To move on and achieve,
To fit your very large bill.

Fighting and fighting till the end,
Can't quite seem to get the
unagreeable images to bend.

Fighting for what you believe in,
Fighting till your strength is thin,
What do you do when
You and your ideas just don't seem to fit in?

Last but not least,
I am still fighting,
Deep down I know I always will be,
Because some people just can't see
How very, very IMPORTANT some things are to ME!
Dedicated to my friends 4-ever,
  Angela (Angel) Alter '99
  and Dominic L. Franco '96

"Teddy Bear's Lament"
by Carrie LeBlanc - age 13

    Where, Miss, is my little boy?
    He has not come today.
I want to know what's keeping him,
    What's keeping him from play.
    He promised me he'd be here,
    He promised me he'd come.
I've sat in this rocking chair so long,
    My stitches are growing numb.
Oh where, oh where has my little prince gone?
    Oh where, oh where could he be?
    He told me we'd never be apart;
    He'd take good care of me.
    I guess he's growing older now,
        Too old for Teddy Bear,
    And toys forgotten long ago
The burden of neglect must bear.
    I think I hear him at the door,
    Is this my little *prince* I hear?
    How glad I am I hear him coming,
    I see him walking near!
"Mom, what is this frazzled piece of cloth?
    Its nose is worn and frayed.
    It looks quite like I loved it once,
    But I'm too old for play.
It must not stay here to take up space
Where there is room for other things.
This is a place for schoolbooks and a t.v.,
    By order of the *king*.

The Moon Has Said Hello
by Emma Lee - age 16

Baby sweet
Slumber deep
The moon has said Hello

The mild night
Angel's delight
Look down on you below

Stars kiss
Your delicate lips
Fleeting dreams unfold

Soft breeze
Sails free
Fantasies you will behold

Baby sweet
Slumber deep
The moon has said Hello

Innocence
by Meredith N. Lee - age 14

White is innocent & pure.
I stood white once,
but he took it without any mercy.
His influences,
His teachings,
are always with me -- remembering
the way...
the ways of passion & poison,
desire & dreams,
seduction & envy,
loneliness & love.

I stand empty,
except for his teachings.
I stand alone.
I stand black.

A Different Kind Of Love
by Syindie Le - age 16

A young girl cries tonight.
They had a horrible fight.
He raised his hand
And it crossed her face;
All she wanted was his embrace.

She'd done no harm;
She didn't ask for all the bruises on her arm.
She was a helpless child.
She was unaware
Of all the signs that said beware.

He didn't know that he hurt her;
Any little thing and his anger would stir.
What was to happen now?
This was the only love he knew;
With a different love he grew.

Too scared to cry for aid,
"I'll kill you if you tell" he said.
She's young and smart
But in her mind she's lost.
She let him take over; he became the boss.

Today, she awakes to her fears
Trying to fight those painful tears.
But with the help of family and friends
Her fears and worries will come to an end.

Winter Doesn't Frighten Me
(From the perspective of a flower)
by Heather Libhart - age 14

I'm pretty as a picture until that first frost -
That's when I pay the deadly cost.
But winter doesn't frighten me at all.

I fall apart, I'm dying inside -
I'm washed away as if in a tide.
Winter doesn't frighten me at all.

I'm forgotten in the wind...
Winter's just around the bend.
But winter doesn't frighten me at all.

I'm no longer picked;
I'm more or less kicked.
But winter doesn't frighten me at all.

People pass me by,
There's not a single fly.
Winter doesn't frighten me at all.

My friends are all gone -
I'm the only one left.
No, winter doesn't frighten me at all.

Noses no longer smell me -
But please, no sympathy.
Winter doesn't frighten me at all.

I'm leaving this playful fair,
No one really seems to care.
But winter doesn't frighten me at all.

Winter doesn't frighten me at all.
Not at all,
Not at all.
Winter doesn't frighten me at all.

*Adapted from Maya Angelou's poem,
"Life Doesn't Frighten Me"*

Repression
by Meredith Licari - age 14

Sometimes I get these feelings
No one should ever feel
The yolk of my emotions
That my heart has tightly sealed
They tie me up in ribbons
Too shimmery for my eyes
The shell too soft to crack
With the gaping hole inside
The hole stuffed full with nothing
Everything convex and pure
Meandering through these thoughts
In discovery lies the cure
But discovery never comes
My youth is forced to wait
As the days of life drip by
Beginnings come too late
Despair in every window
Held back in all these ways
In impossible walls of anguish
My mystery villain lays
Self-destruction comes too slowly
And help flies by too fast
Love, maturity, and intellect
Are locked up in my past
Once again I'll pack away
Too heavy for my strong
I don't know how to start
But I've already gone too long.

Filter
by Steven Lichtenstein - age 19

Pressure not withstanding,
My pride was squelched
branded with ferocity
like a cow rump.

The label
painful enough,
the words more destructive.

Conceptions not met
standards shattered
the penance is humiliation
and utter despair.

A repercussion
most unfair
most reproachable,
but acceptable
with the advent of
attention,
the only way to
stifle the blemish,
the medicine of dignity;
all is better.

Eyes show tolerance,
but hide churning anger,
which no one,
ever,
will know.

To Do Without You
by Jie Li - age 16

Before you leave,
I will not beg, nor mock, nor lament.
I will not impress life on death, nor extract heart from ice.
I fear not your leave, no more
than the wilting of one leaf in my flower of gardens;
no more than the unthreading of one lace of sunshine from my hair;
no more, even,
than the engulfing of a moving twilight by very distant trees.

A month may contain an epiphany, so may a day, an hour;
or it may be contained by stale time, so may be a year, a life.
'Tis not you that I - Ah, yes - worry.
'Tis the insipid blue of my stormless and rainbowless...

But now that you are wings,
My feet will less carry me to places we frequented,
as we will no longer in June chance upon poetic justice or such
unexpected destiny.
I will be more content after reason shoots through
desire, and mere daylight will send me all I want.
I will be as guiltless as a grain,
as blithe as a breeze.

Ghosts
by Alice Lin - age 15
Verity Compton - age 15

It starts with a sound
TAP TAP TAP
A shrilling scream
Beyond the grasp of fear
Lightly brushing past my soft lips
The dress of the woman in white
I've seen her before
During the soft twilight of night
She comes into my room
Turns off the light
I notice
She carries my grandmother's candle
I see the chaos behind her eyes
The fury flickers in the burning flame of the candle
Seeing what I saw before-
The candle thrown against the wall
burning the remains of a ruined marriage
I wake up from the dream
Glancing at my table
I see a candle wrapped in a white veil
TAP TAP TAP
The sound starts again

Eight
by Jennifer Mason - age 16

The happy usually never care,
The beautiful have to be accepted,
The romantics are usually in love,
The honest must be forgiven for their bluntness,
The forgiving will be honest about your faults,
The loved have to romance their lover,
The accepting think they are all beautiful,
The care-free always smile.

The Emptiness Inside Ones Self
by Sandi Linden - age 15

Am I alone?
There is no one near to help me
I stand undignified
My spirirt gone
Leaving me without motivation
I see nothing but darkness
Like a night with no moon
God's light has left me
Without a trace of it's presence
I struggle to reach the light
The light that is my hope
My joy
The awkward feeling of being alone
Leaves me stranded
In a world of pain
A blanket of fear covers me each night
Not removing itself in the morning
Each day gets thicker, heavier
I cannot remove it
For I am weighed down by the darkness
The overwhelming strength of the darkness
Is my nemesis
I cannot be freed
The world I once knew
Is now gone
Everything, everyone is gone.

Walls
by Emi McLaughlin - age 15

Walls
high durable
cornering, enclosing, judging
statements incriminate; silence eliminates
empty

Snow Flakes
by Lei Liu - age 17

The glittering and sparkling fairy dust
    swiftly and slowly dance down from the sky.

After the great spirits keep them as a torch
    to shine their palace,

After the princess of seasons adorn them
    on her dress to go to the winter festival,

And after the mother nature
    made a puffy cloud out of them.

They are like carefree angels sneaking out
    from God's back door and coming to earth to play.

Shhhhhhhh...

If you hold your breath and listen carefully,

You can hear them screaming:

"We are free! We are free!"

The Nightmare
by Rachael Llepes - age 18

Awakening in the midst of the night,
    Not sure of what it means.
I'm running scarred, desperately for my life.
    Why are they trying to kill me? Where is everyone else?
Down the streets of San Francisco, searching for a place to hide...

    a place to be safe...

    a place to save myself.

In contrast on the other side of the waters,
    A microcosm of proselytes,
    Unsure of why I am not there, also.
There is peace, and happiness. Without me.
    Why are they having so much fun? Why is everyone else over there?
    why aren't they running for their lives?
Down the street of gold they parade, scanning and searching for me...

their sister and friend

but I am over here...

    can't you see me?

I cry and scream for help but there's none there to hear me.
I'm deterred here in a strange house looking out upon society--while they search for me.
I see another child running for her life...
    they've caught her..
        and now they beat her...
            she lays there still unable to move.

I overhear on the radio...
    "If you are a believer...you will be haunted until you are killed.
There is no place to hide."

The Princess and The Peasant
by Katrina Long - age 15

He bound through the valley so shady
To win the heart of the lady
He came at last to a mansion so fine
And there was music, and there was wine.

Alas, the king would not give him her hand
He has taken her vision so grand
But the princess secretly welcomed him there
She told the king, "I do not care!"

In the dead of night they slipped away
To plan their glorious wedding day
She left her servants and her estate
As she left her castle gate.

Her father saddled his fastest steed
Sought his daughter at great speed
He roamed the valley all around
But they were nowhere to be found.

Far away they both did hide
For the peasant wanted her as his bride
The morning of their wedding day
The princess felt guilty and ran away.

She bound through the valley so shady
To avoid being the peasant's lady
She'll live in the castle for the rest of her life
Never to become anyone's wife.

Basement
by Sydney Lowe - age 19

Dark as the nightfall in daytime
I open the door, flashlight in hand.
The stairs creak and moan as
I descend deeper into darkness.
Step by step I go down, down, down,
Closer to the hell that awaits beneath.
I stumble and fall closer to my merciless fate.
Lying on the cold, wet floor
In the dank, dark basement
My unconscious body drips with sweat.
I see a bright white light and wonder,
"Am I dead?"
I am shaking with fear.
Darkness of night lingers outside
And I see the light of evening
In the bulb dangling from the ceiling,
Shining bright above my head like a halo.

Reaching For The Light
by Maggie Low - age 12

It's hard to think it will ever be ok
Seems like it's always a rainy day
But you never know
One day it might snow
But is that any better
Seems like the world is just getting wetter
Can you ever imagine it will ever be alright
Will everybody have a place to sleep at night
Does it get worse than this
Is it our death kiss
Sometimes I want to fly away
I don't want to stay
Is there a reason to worry
Are we all going to be put before a jury
Are we hidden behind a mask
Why do I ask
Do we pay a toll
How much is our soul
Can you answer me
Is there a fee
Does it have to do with money
Tell me, will it ever be sunny

Have You Ever Wondered
by Jillian Lueken - age 14

Have you ever wondered?
Why the earth is round,
Why the sky is blue,
Why there is grass on the ground,
Have you ever wondered,
Why people judge,
Who gives them the right,
to hold a grudge,
Have you ever wondered?
What people see in the skin,
Why can;t they just look,
at what is within,
Have you ever wondered?
Why people say,
Bad things about others,
Who are different in anyway,
Have you ever wondered?
Why people think they're the best,
When they are really no better,
than any of the rest,
So if you think,
Your better than someone else,
Remember we were all created equal,
and no one is better than anyone else.

Sunset
by Michelle Luoto - age 16

As I watch and see the sunset
Fade behind the trees so green
Something in me fades with it
Something no one else has seen
The sun slips through the air
Like sand slipping through my hands
And I think of all the places I have been
And all the far away lands
It slowly sinks into the horizon
As the ocean comes splashing around me
And I feel as though I can be happy
And know my thoughts are free
The sky turns pink and then to red
And the clouds seem to blend
And the light it casts upon the trees
Makes their shadows twist and bend
And as the red hot sun
Falls before my eyes
I think about my life
And look up to the skies
The sun is gone but I am not
So I must leave this place
But I'll always remember that sunset
Like an old familiar face.

Twins
by Jaclyn Lurker - age 17

A certain peculiar case
that piques the interest:

Mirror images
of each other,
Indistinguishable from
one another.
But appearance and reality
are often worlds apart.

They are the same--
as alike as
day and night,
darkness and light,
fire and ice.
One is virtue; the
other, vice.

One possesses a gilded front;
the other, a depth unseen.
If I could only see through to
their souls,
I would find the truth.
Identical exteriors,
but underneath--
there lies the difference.

Love Hurts, Hate is Hell
by Crystal R. Meyer - age 15

Nothing said nothing done,
Love and hate together as one.
No way to change it, it stays the same
Love and hate equal pain
Love hurts and hate is hell,
Hurting and hating are pain as well.

Dusk
by Kathleen Lynch - age 17

The world is winding, slowly winding down
As a soft hush caresses the ground.

The birds sing and chirp of the dying day.
They sing, What else is there left to say?

The clouds of blue, peach, and pink shroud the sky
Telling of a soft spring light that will soon die.

The birds sail in the waning sky above
Singing of joy, sorrow, and love.

A gentle, caressing breeze sways the flowers
Whispering of the slowly encroaching night hours.

The sweet smelling air is so soft.
The breezes of the day stirring it oft.

The birds sweetly sing
As they fly home on insistent wing.

They fly home when dusk approaches.
The soft night is coming, it encroaches.

And then, the dying day fades beautifully away.
The night of moon, for a time, is here to stay.

Armageddon
by Amanda Mabey - age 15

I have no regret for the things I've done,
Because I know that I shall die before the worst will come.
I've seen the famine in the eyes of children young and old,
But know that this is not a thing to what the future holds.

I've seen the tears of heaven fall down into the earth,
And have cried the tears of pain for lack of any mirth.
I know that time has come and gone, and many people died,
But I know the future is the sort which only death may hide.

Man will kiss the candle's flame
And wonder at it's burn,
And he will thirst for poisoned rain
For what he did not learn.

The day that man owns everything he'll have less than what before,
And his diamonds--they will cut him--for the crime of taking more.
The day man learns for what he's destined he will learn he should have loved,
Yet regret won't move him from his grave to mourn his nation's blood.

And then we will be rid of him--Earth's self-inflicted plague,
And until the end of time we will repair what man has made.
Then will the winds caress again, and the tides will find the sea,
And we will speak the speech of meaning in the world as it should be.

Then will the ocean beat again and pump Earth's watery blood,
Which will warm beneath the sun and in the sky above.
Then will it rain, and our planet live, and man will have the blame,
For he once changed Earth's joyous tears into the tears of pain.

The animals will then be ruled by the Lord whose name is Nature,
And never will man's faults repeat in worldly greed for stature.
The animals will live in beauty, and thus in peace be living,
And plant and creature will remain the cells in our planet's soul and being.

Who Am I?
by Michelle MacDonald - age 16

My true feelings are unknown;
But many emotions have been shown;
Through tears of anger;
And tears of pain;
Through tears of sadness;
And tears so vain.

Not knowing what I can take,
And being so vulnerable,
I feel like a fake;
No one understands,
For my moods change so quickly;
They all think I'm always happy,
But deep down I'm usually opposite;
Intellectual and helpful,
Kind and caring;
Those are a few that people see and are true;
But depression and anger;
Loneliness and emptiness;
All are things they don't see
But are all there;
All this awful darkness was brought upon me,
By the nightmares of the past.

No matter what mood I'm in,
I have always been counted on
To be there for friends in need;
And I always am
And will be forever;
It's just all part of who I am.

A Blood-red rose
by Krystal Mild - age 13

A blood-red rose
A letter of apology
A picture with the perfect pose
A box of your favorite chocolates
Did you forgive him? No, you up your nose
The beginning of the end was him two-timing you
The end of it all was a blood-red rose.

The Gift
by Stacey MacDonald - age 18

I may not be very special, deep inside
But I have feelings, and I have my pride.
And what you have to offer
May be much more than I can give,
But I know I will love you
For as long as we both live.

I've found people seldom look beneath,
The surface of one's skin
To one's mind, heart and soul.
And all the love that's held deep within.

When you hand touches mine,
There's something I just can't explain.
Time which subdues the memories,
And eases away the pain.

So here I stand all alone,
Vulnerable for you
A mythical tale revealed
A dream coming true.
I'm giving you all my secrets,
Things others just don't seem to see.
I'm opening up and giving you
Everything I hold deep inside of me.

Gramma's Sunset
by Brenna MacLean - age 20

Such a beautiful day, such a beautiful life
I knew the day would end, but why for her?
I strolled along the cool sand - thinking about her world
I rolled my pants up and let the ripples of water
roll on to my tanned feet.
She always did that.

I sat on the rocks, where we used to go
in the evenings, years before.
The sky was warm, filled with orange and red
The colors were dramatic, never to be forgotten
I wanted to hold the picture in my mind forever.
Then my thoughts filled with fond memories of her
I wished she could always be here,
like the setting of the sun.

Before I knew it the sun slipped away.
As the minutes passed, the colors
reflected through the clouds while the sky became colored
with hues of purple, pink and orange
The colors lasted like the memories she left me and
the beauty of the setting sun.

Anorexia
by Rachel Mahnke - age 15

You stole my childhood and I was unaware
When I felt in control it was you who really was

The scale became my enemy and
My mind constantly fought the need my body declared

My body shrank and my mind stopped working
I couldn't think clearly or form words with my mouth

My grades began slipping and teachers took note
My clothes became larger and my parents became troubled

As the doctors poked at my lifeless body
I lost all energy and eventually couldn't feel the pain

There was no turning back
But, when you just about killed me, I pulled through

Like a flower that begins to wilt, I was brought back to life
I pulled through from the love I was shown

"Goodbye"
by Sarah Maiser - age 16

As you make your way to the light,
You sing and dance in your flight;
Just like you did down here,
Just as you will up there.
As I watch you fly out of sight,
I smile, remembering with a sigh
All of the times that we shared,
And just how much we both cared.
It doesn't have to end, just because you are gone,
Because you and I my friend, share a life-long bond.
I am so thankful for the time we had;
Having you here, I could never be sad.
I feel blessed to have had you here with me
Maybe now that you are gone, you can see.
I will open my window and set you free-
God wants you now; you are free.

Nightmare Of Depression
by Gwen Maisenhelder

I climb toward the dark at the top of the stairs,

   The shimmering,
Veiling dark at the top of the stairs;
But I never get closer--I never get there.
I cling to the rotting rail, the splintering, rotting, dirt-dark rail,
and I try to go on to the top of the stairs,
But each step
        I make
                takes a thousand years.
Voices call me from the dark at the top of the stairs--
Their warning cries come to me,
But each step I take makes an echo that rings and rings in my ears
And I cannot hear the words that they say-;

But when I cease my climb,
The voices cry: "Go on! Go on!"
And I go on in pain and sorrow,
Begging the night for a bright tomorrow.
When tomorrow comes, I still go on endlessly to the dark at the top
   of the stairs
Will I never reach that curtain dark
                                      and find what
lies on the other side?
Is it brightness or night?
I may never know--
It may take forever to traverse the way from here
To the dark at the top of the stairs.

Fleeting Storm
by Christina Pao - age 16

Placid and tranquil outside,
Rage intensifying inside,
Fighting to break out,
Lashing out like lightning,
Cold and scathing.
Striking its innocent victim,
Disavowing its ruins.
Fleeing quickly as it came.
The storm subsides.

Crime
by Jessica A. Mally - age 11

    If I had one wish it would be that there would be no crime.
        All the shootings and killings just make me cry.
     There are drugs on the playground and all on the streets.
   Crime is just all hate and anger and it all makes me want to weep.
    I feel sorry for the families that all have to go through it.
         My mom says, "Wake up, it's all reality."
      My cousin Kevin says, "Be careful out on the streets."
   My best friend Mindy says, "It makes me want to weep too."
       Always looking behind your shoulder in fear for your life.
It always seems to happen to the innocent people just walking down the
                        streets at night.
        I still don't understand why it happens in life.
     I guess it is just our life and we all have to live it right.
         I would never do it. It's just stupid and wrong.
I will always listen to my mom and what she said about living proud and
                            strong.
          Nobody can prevent it. It just happens... life.
 If you want to help make lots of people's dreams and wishes come true.
           Stop the crime, that's all you have to do.
         This is the end and I can't tell you what to do.
           I will live my life right! ... But will you?

Motion of Beauty
by Eric Manchester - age 20

     A beautiful smile upon your face
      gentle movements full of grace
     A tender touch with gentle hands
    Free spirited as the shifting sands
    Studying each conservative action
Loving each minute of this new attraction
Able to learn from movements alone
I realize now there's more to be known
So now this beautiful gift from god
Teaches me things I once thought odd
That hands and actions great and strong
Make up for words often too long
And from Lord god this gift was meant
To spread the beauty of the message sent
So now my eyes know love and care
through actions, not words filling the air
    and through all this I soon see
    Some are more than expected to
    Full of love and free from violence
Now I learn how golden is the silence
And as for the words I'll never hear
The beautiful motions I'll hold more dear
    And in my heart I'll always hold
The Motion of Beauty I've been shown.

Warner
by Carey McCarron - age 20

Good-bye, and toss in the rose,
   and watch it wash away.
They see, but no one knows,
   the meaning of this day.

These falls are what he chose,
   family gathered in dismay.
In life he loved all those,
his ashes scattered on that day.

Gi Joe and Barbie Discuss Politics
by Kelly Mangels - age 15

The smoke filled air of Plum Street Pub lifted, like fog over a mountain
on a rainy day, as the music of Midnight Oil fills the room,
at a table in the corner where the two sat
sipping cappuccino and discussing politics.
Barbie reminisced about the early '70's
when she burned her bra
to support women's rights
and GI Joe recalled the time during the Vietnam War
when he bombed villages and rice fields,
in his F4 Phantom Fighter plane.
    They both remembered how in the '60's they campaigned for women's
rights and how they fought to unite all races
They remembered the effort to promote peace and equality.
but are saddened by the promotion
of violence in the current generation.
Because everytime they turn on the news they hear about another baby
being killed.
    As they chat, they become entwined in their own world,
distant from the crowd of people around them.
And as the political music of Midnight Oil plays on an overhead radio,
the political chatter
of Barbie and GI Joe's
mingle with the song
to form a song on it's own.

Woman
by Cynthia Manick

Hear me
Touch me
feel my heart beating
I'm speaking
I'm yelling
I'm roaring
I am the personification of innocence
I am the personification of strength
watch my hips flair
watch my lips move
I'm pretty
I'm ugly
I'm homely
I'm average
I am woman
All woman
Heed my words
or hear my wrath
admire me
respect me
I am the giver of life
I am the daughter of god
liberated and free
I say as I please
Mother
Wife
Daughter
Sister
I am woman
All woman

Waiting For Me
by Sara Manthey - age 15

I sit,
    Gazing deep into the rich blue
    water as a ripple dances across
    the surface.

I gaze,
    entranced by the images that I
    see upon the surface,
        by the soft whispers
    that seem to be floating among
    the gentle breeze,
        by the faint brush of
    an unseen hand.

I feel a presence,
    not frightening,
        loving
        soothing
        caring
    yet great sorrow
            grieving.

    a small tear,
    rolls down an unseen cheek,
    falling softly to the pond.

    the whispers hush.
    the images fade.

    and all is quiet once again.

Seventh Heaven
by Chloa Mardis - age 17

    Walking down the street to get ice cream
Sweating but just wiping it off my forehead
Not minding the sun or that my feet are bare
Thinking about nowalaters and lemonheads
and I was only seven

    The candy store was my savior
it helped me out in times of need
Whenever I needed a friend or adventure
I went into my own little haven
and looked upon the flavors of my world
and I was just seven

    Going to the dentist was a hell of it's own
and one day did the blasphemous man tell me
that candy wasn't my friend or savior
but that it had conspired against me with
a man named cavity to steal my teeth
but I was only seven

    After that when I went to the candy store
all that I could see were brightly colored wrappers
of sugar. No friends, no adventures just candy
But that doesn't mean I didn't eat it
because I was still seven

The Clown In My Closet
by Brittanie Marquis - age 13

There's a clown in my closet, the closet of my heart.
He's really a genius and knows he's quite smart.

He read my poetry, rolled his eyes and bobbed his head,
like the old-fashioned dogs in car windows mom said.

The clown in my closet, that's been everywhere,
is starting to get some grey in his hair.

This clown in my closet has spent his life floating and breathing salt air.
He sends special trinkets to show that he cares.

The clown in my closet, here from the start.
He will always have a special place in my heart.

Those Who Live In Glass Houses...
by Sara Marshalek - age 17

    I look out the widows of my glass house into a world of anger, hatred, and despair. I see people throwing verbal stones at those who don't belong, the one's that aren't pieces in their social jig-saw puzzle, inflicting pain, causing deep internal wounds, leaving everlasting mental scars.
    I see a river of tears flowing into a sea of red. A black mist of depression falls over the victims of loneliness as those who sit upon their mighty thrones of popularity laugh devilishly at their own ignorance and cruelty, illogically pondering their next act of knowledgeless violence.
    I inside my cubic safety feel for those victims, but cannot reach out to them in fear of knocking down my walls of protection, in fear of becoming a victim myself.
    I turn away, yet I have hope...that one day when I look out my windows again I will see a peaceful panorama of smiling faces, one strong unity of happiness and togetherness, all standing in the ditches of the dried-up seas and rivers.

Death
by Alexandra Martin - age 11

I'm standing at death's doorway
waiting to be called forth.

Shadows are moving
in the cold, dark alleys around me.

I'm cold and alone in this world
waiting to move on to the next.

I am afraid

"Afraid will you die?" you ask.

No.

I am afraid I never will.

I Have Not
by Marina L. Martinez - age 18

I will cry in darkness
let sadness be free

pulled into a fit
by the pain
I will mourn for me

I will weep quietly alone
my heart alive
with memories and love

Comfort me
from this darkest night
like a dying dove

I will kneel hands crossed
in the starless room
not knowing the voice of God
calming my fears

Run to me hope
and life
Let sun
hide the sadness of my tears.

The French Child
by Faith Martin - age 12

I know a boy
yes, a boy
who is learning
his language sifting
sluttering words
out like the
balloons gliding through
the air, just gliding
through the air thinking
staring, looking, and feeling.
The boy falls, falls like a
bullet out of thin air.
He knows, yes he knows his
language.

There Is No Escape
by Katie Martin

As I watch out my window,
I see hate,
All bottled up inside people,
There is no escape.

Children being kidnapped,
Teens getting raped,
Homeless in alleys,
There is no escape.

Gangs shooting people,
Death numbers inflate,
Violence cannot be stopped,
There is no escape.

People selling drugs,
At home they create,
People overdosing,
There is no escape.

Girls on street corners,
Money they hope to make,
Money that will pay the bills,
There is no escape.

The World Is Deaf
by Jamie Maslow - age 14

I always try to hear,
but it doesn't seem to work.
crime is always everywhere,
and everywhere it seems to lurk.

there's cars blowing horns
and guns being fired.
you can't make a telephone call
because you can bet it will be wired.

I try to hear some peace
but in this world, I just can't.
"We love evil, murder, and crime!"
the world always seems to chant.

the person on the bus
just got shot in the head.
I wonder if I'm safe
when I go to bed.

I try to hear some love,
all I see is a bunch of hate.
people using people; and being so
impatient that they won't wait.

I'm trying very hard,
straining my ears to hear.
but I can't make anything out,
except that death is very near.

Calligraphy
by Erin McCreesh - age 14

Pen dipping into the well
the scratch of the nib on rough paper
the elegant strokes of the writer
beautiful words carved out as art
dip it again just to etch a few more words
in the archive of time

Beyond Color
by Talaina Matthews - age 16

She ain't your Mamma, she don't love you
yelled the kids from apartment number two.
Oh yes she is, and don't you lie she'll
be my Mama till the day I die.
A hot tear trickled down my face because
they not saw past our race.
Mamma may be tall and brown but keeps her
love spread all around.
Then there's me so small and white thinking
maybe those kids are right.
But she took me in so long ago, that's all
the love I need ever know.
And if you close your eyes you'll see, one
color, one image, the way we be.

The Rays Of Light
by Cathy Mayer - age 14

The rays of light
show me the night
as I slip
into a ship of dreams.
The love in these beams
show me my heart
as I part
with my dreams.

Untitled
by Lisa Mazur - age 18

Do you know how it feels to give up your life?
With each choice you must decide if it's right.
When you have a child they depends solely on you,
Everything matters, everything you say and do.
In some ways your life seems to end,
you can no longer have fun, or go out with friends.
As a young mother I beg you to understand,
your playing with fire and the risk is more
than your hand.
Respect yourself, and live life for you,
for when your a Mommie there's so much
you can't do.

William's Whisper
by Journey W. McAndrews - age 18

Hid among the rot and age,
Lies a whisper from William's page.
His voice is bold when he speaks.
On this creation ge lost two weeks.
Softly his head rested in his hands.
His plays echoed across English lands.
Even his life was wrought with pain.
None of his labors were in vain.
Wives of Windsor he did create.
Ink and sorrow his only mate.
Sadness does fill the poetical mind.
Lost in a world truly unkind.
Nym followed the whisper in turn.
While the soul of Fatstaff did burn.
Silently the bard slumbered one eve.
Only a whisper did he leave.
Bells toiled as he slumbered that night.
Dawn found him in heaven's light.

Runaway
by Caitlin McCauley - age 14

Running, running to nowhere.
Adrenaline pumping from a scare.
Nothing matters, nothing did.
Maybe because you're just a kid
Nowhere to go and nowhere to stay,
All that matters is getting away.
What about those you left behind?
All sorts of questions enter your mind:
Are they happy, are they sad?
Do they feel that they've been had?
Do they miss you, do they care?
Are they glad you're out of their hair?
What does it matter anyway?
From them you are far away,
Why did you do it?
Now you're in a pit
No turning back.
Don't start to slack.
Just keep running.

Hidden
by Tiffany McCauley

In every soul
awaits a door
momentarily shut,
daring one to enter,
excluding all love
people try to give.
Rejecting all hope
eternity promises.
Sealed shut,
suppressing the key
enabling no one to enter.
Damaging my soul
again and again
Needing you to open the door,
daring you to open the door.
Why I will not let you
anyone can answer.
Never wanting a broken heart,
though you may not (break my heart).
To trust you now over all men (and people)
drives my soul to misery.
Inventing reasons to lock the door,
enabling you to enter, never.

Would You
by Jessica McCubbin - age 14

If I were to never feel
again would you hold me
one last time?
If I were to never hear
again would you tell me
you were mine?
If I were to never see
again would you wink
and give me a smile?
If I were to never talk
again would you listen
for a while?
If I were to never smell
again would you give
me a dozen flowers?
If I were to never walk
again would you walk with
me for hours?
and if I were to die
would you break down and
cry?

Untitled
by Sara McCullough - age 16

Emotional Rage-
I can no longer handle it,
I open my mouth and scream,
No sound comes out,
Instead, I cry.
Silently, in horror of being found,
When I stand for my beliefs, I'm alone.
Because I'm a loner.
Silently I walk the streets,
But I am not at peace.
I want to smile and laugh
With everyone else,
But I'm afraid to,
Yes, I admit it, I'm afraid,
I'm afraid of never loving,
Of leaving this life unloved,
I inspire people not to love me,
Or at least that's how it seems.
Maybe I'll make it through-
One more day, or maybe,
I'll collapse in terror of my mind.

Lies
by Sarah McCusker - age 15

In interpolated images of black and white,
    He whispered sweet lies of love and adoration.
Hidden behind a mask of bloodless night,
    His eyes told a tale of loyal expression.
But underneath the grueling veil,
    Was a cloud of uncertainty and roguery.
She thought the lies true; believed the endless tale.
    Exposed was her mind, prone to the chicanery.
As he lost interest, he slowly began to unveil,
    The feelings he had hidden from the rest.
He pushed her over the edge; day by day,
    And tore her heart out, right from her chest.
Trapped under a wave of unbearable pain and self-
decay,
    There was no torment left to feel as the scalpel
hit her wrists, draining the life she lived, out onto
the floor.

Life Not Worth Living
by Shaun McDonald - age 16

Society sucks, the earth is going to burn
the human race has an important lesson to learn.
Crime and corruption, starvation and greed
everyone on this planet is starting to bleed,
Children are starving, everybody lies
disease runs rampant, too many people die.
For what do I live for, the planet is doomed,
it started to decay when the first flower bloomed
Somewhere there is a boy without a bed
a child without even a small crust of bread,
we sleep in out beds worried about our lives
when men wage war on each other with knives.
Satan is laughing, cause he calls the shots
mother earth is crying, she's on the block.
Why don't we drop the bomb and start over again
cause this life is not worth living, and I'm at my end.

Ryan
by Bridget K. McGuan - age 16

God put us on earth together
for a good reason, I feel.
And all that we've been through,
will continue to grow and heal.

These 16 years together,
have been so wonderfully great.
And for another 80 together-
I really cannot wait.

Highschool years are almost through,
and on to college you'll go.
and how much I love and care for you-
by then I hope you'll know.

My love for you,
is so unbelievably strong.
and to really straight-out tell you,
I think I've waited too long.

For us to be put together,
it all must have been fate.
But for me to say I love you,
It will never be too late.

Untitled
by Sara McGuyer - age 18

Seconds pass and go unnoticed
as do minutes and sometimes hours, days.
And quite often is forgotten,
life being drawn away like a syringe
extracting blood from a diseased man
and into the gentle curve of a nurse's hand.
Time is sucked into the air and everywhere
until it runs dry.
It is spent without thought
unlike a poor man wisely spreading
his fortune of a shiny quarter.

And sometimes the spinning world
stops at our feet.
The time goes sour in our hands
and we can't rid ourselves of it
or throw it away like festered, ranking fruit.
It must be swallowed and accepted
right to the bitter worm.

My Child
by Barbara McKasty - age 16

My child my child
What have I done?
I gave you up so long ago
with only myself in mind.
You now are being embraced by the holy creator.
But please have pity when you look at me
the one who conceived you.
Have mercy when you look upon me.
Now I wonder what could have been?
I see your face so innocent.
How could I be so selfish
to take that had not begun.
I hear a cry in my heart
and wonder if it's yours or mine.
The tears run down my face
and you my child wipe them away.
I took your life that had not begun.
How could you forgive what I have done?
But in my heart you'll always be.
I love you my child, please forgive me.

Death
by Lindsay McKenna - age 12

Is a thousand lies made one
the last setting of the sun,
an echo of the planet sighing
...an echo of the planet dying
Life
is the truth of a nation
the placing of eternal foundation,
the rising of the New Year
holding fast to ones so dear.
Onward
I go on a path
with many horizons
Onward
I go to life,
onward I go to death...

Final Peace
by Malea Ann McKeown - age 12

The terror was known without a word said
On each face it could easily be read
Each knew the effort was all in vain
All were at the mercy of the waves and rain
At each attack the vessel moaned
If fought, struggled, creaked, and groaned
But, the battle was unfairly prelost
All strength was gone it had gave it's last toss
It finally gave up and slipped under the waves
And all took their place among the watery graves

A Yellow Maple Leaf
by Pamela McLean - age 11

As a baby I was taken care of,
plenty of water from up above.
I was once on a tree,
with so many things to see,
I lived in the branches up high,
soaring into the sunlit sky.

I am a five pointed maple leaf,
my ancestors painted by Georgia O'Keefe.

Things were calm and mellow,
but then I started to turn yellow.
Fall was almost here,
yes, I could tell that fall was near.
All my friends were changing too,
our colors all looked brand new.

My bright green had faded,
this is for what people waited.

My friends turned brown,
we all fell down, down.
I stayed beautiful yellowish-green
thinking who did this was very mean.
The other leaves shriveled up and died,
yet they stayed faithfully at my side.

This is where I am now and where I will stay,
Till I turn brown and die one awful day.

New friends will come to visit next spring,
their job will be to make beauty of everything.
As for me, I may lay here and slowly rot,
but I can give the earth back what I got.
Year after year, we will joyfully carry on,
Until that day when we meet at the land beyond!

Reflections
by Daniel Mefford - age 14

A rainy day
A stormy night
The skies burn
Flooding the world with everlasting light
I thought I saw your face
Standing there
I thought I saw your sea-green eyes
And your golden hair
I thought you were beside me
Until the end of time
I thought that you would hold me
Until the day we died
But it was just a reflection
Of memories, of dreams
It was just a reflection
Now I'm tearing at the seams
The wind behind me blew
Blew my tears away
And as I gazed upon the mirror
I thought I heard you say
I thought that you were mine
I thought we were forever
I thought we'd stand the test of time
And leave I thought I'd never
But they were just reflections
Of past hopes, past dreams
They were just reflections
Now I'm tearing at the seams

Kelsie
by Heather Mohr - age 18

Kelsie Kay
Sweeter than a milky way
Kelsie Kay makes me happy
Night and day
Kelsie Kay you melt my heart
And give me smiles
Kelsie Kay I would push your buggy
For miles and miles
Kelsie Kay I love to see
Your eyes so bright
Kelsie Kay I love when
You hold my finger tight

Mom
by Stormy Mensen - age 14

It's a little cold and damp, Mom, the food is not to good.
The mud is thick and deep, mom, and soaked with human blood.

There's a bullet in my chest, Mom, but it doesn't hurt so much
when I see a little orphan child without a leg or crutch.

They're coming down the hill, Mom, about ten thousand strong,
and no matter how we fight or pray we can't hold out for long.

But we'll fight all over, Mom, to keep our country free. To
guard our right and our freedom, and protect our liberty.

Tell my little girl not to cry, Mom, tell dad to be real
brave, and when they send me home, Mom, please write "GLORY" on
my grave.

Tell my little sister, Mom, I had to go away. Tell her not to
cry, Mom, I'll see her again some day.

Tell her I went to heaven, to see the Lord above. To talk
about the world, Mom, and how it looks above.

I'm sorry I can't see you, Mom, again before I die. But I
like to say I love you, Mom, before I say Good Bye.

Fireworks
by Suzanne Merhej - age 13

There are no stars gleaming in the midnight sky.
No color.
One cannot see but only feel around him to believe there is no one,
No one but the dark, black, breezy night.
Suddenly, there is a lengthened screaming sound as a rocket shoots up out of nowhere.
The arena thrills with excitement as the colors intensify.
It shoots higher and higher until one can no longer see a glimpse of anything but black.
Everyone waits anxiously.
An abrupt, faint, booming noise occurs.
Then it happens.
Sparkling colors pour down upon the world like a beautiful waterfall.
The Earth is illuminated during that splendid moment.
Then colors fade.
There is nothing but black.

I Can Not Lie
by Donna Miko - age 14

A poet died in my dreams.
The mirror is frightened of my reflection.
The sky is a friendly dome of no boundary.

My heart is found in the center of the labyrinth.
I'll start at the end,
but I'm already at the end of hope...
let me be born again.

I only have one life,
but I've been reborn twice.
Let me live until no end-
let me live until my reflection no
longer appears happy in the mirror
of no lies.

Gods Crying
by Amanda Miller - age 18

As the soldiers nailed him to the cross-
That beautiful old rugged cross-
Dark clouds covered the day;
A lady at the bottom crying,
In the sky God was crying.

Now people know of the resurrection-
The most beautiful thing, that resurrection-
Yet many still don't believe;
A child thanking God in her sad crying,
Again, for his precious son God is crying.

Friend Forever
by Jackie Miller-Degrave - age 16

When you said friends forever,
Did you mean until the end of the world?
Did you mean to stand by me, while
everything fell apart?
Did you mean forever as in eternity?
Until everything burns to the ground
and the cinders cool?
Well if that's what you meant, then
Forever came early!

Something
by Sarah Miller - age 14

There's something deep inside of me,
Something that I cannot see.
It tortures me everyday
and forces me to fade away.
It hurts me more and more;
I don't know what it wants me for.
Why can't I just stop
and dry it up with a mop?
It makes me want to cry,
but forces me to lie.
So everyday I hide and pretend it's
just not there.
Why is it so unfair?
Is it my anger or sadness?
Or could it be my gladness?
I don't know what to do.
I'm left without a clue.
I guess I'll have to wait and see,
Until it shows itself to me.
This something deep inside of me,
This something I am forced to see.

My Candle
by Natalie Minnick - age 15

My life is like a candle,
    that somtimes can't be handled
It burns in glory yet melts away in misery
My shining bright light is my yearn for God
My black ugly smoke is from Satan,
    it tries to cover my light
The sweet smell is my happy moments
The quite flicker of the flame,
    is my deep feelings of anger and uncontrollable pain
The warmth from the flames, wick and body
    is my will power, comfort, and love
The hot vanilla wax is my sweet revenge
The jar is my world, the table my boundaries
The spark of a match is the beginning of life,
The blowout of a light season breeze is my death.

There
by Natasia Moose - age 12

I told you I loved you,
You said you'd always care
But when I turned my back,
I looked and you weren't there.
You stole my heart
And made me cry
To leave me with
The question why
Why didn't you love me
Why didn't you care
Why did I turn my back
When you said you'd be there.

Falling Rain
by Billie N. Morgan - age 16

As the rain falls around me
   the grey man lingers in my mind.
Walking aimlessly lost to himself and I.
   ribbons in tatters, letters in shreds.
   pictures in fragments, liars in bed.

As the rain falls around me, I see it all.
   The rising sun and the curtain fall.
   The rose in bloom, only plucked too soon.
      The meaning of time is to watch it unwind.
It gets tangled up in the mayhem and stepped upon
   by all of them.
The cold winter stays in some hearts and chills the soul,
   never to depart.
Life must enter here somewhere - it always does.
   It angers me to watch them toss and abuse it.
   -like a invaluable bauble.
Where did the rhyme go? Where did it end?
   They will never know til it is their own.

As the rain falls around me
   I feel comfort from its peace.
The grey man waves farewell
   in the distance.

Winter
by Morgen Morie - age 19

Coolness; cools my body, warms my heart.
360 degrees.
My head spins uncontrollably, alongside my heart.
Confusion is a comfort; chaos, the main terminal.
No more useless chatter outside walls,
too vulnerable to Mother's harsh touch.

Pure white presence makes me freeze..
too much of anything is not good I am told.
Does that include love?
I yearn without a cause, but fear.
Attacking my subconscious thoughts; restraint..please.

-am growing weak.
-can barely hold her up, need strings

Why?

not God's creation all that is left is devil, isn't it.
what's left? power flowing with him, against current.
Who will determine the winner, not me but it should be. **me**.
I am losing sight of my chosen path
No maps are available at this time, out of print.
Too many friends or enemies. Hello where are you?

Am I losing this battle? who?
Oh there I see..
it's spring..

I
by Angela Morrison - age 12

I am alone with millons of friends
I end at the beginning and start at the end
I wish to hear when I plug my ears
I'm never afraid with many fears
I am me but who am I
I have lots to say but I'm too shy
I am a leader but I follow you
I keep my original idea but copy everything you do
I'm fashionable with things out of style
I'm going to leave so I'll stay for awhile
I'm positive with a negative mind
I know where myself is headed it's a road I cannot find
I want to see but I shut my eyes
I told you the truth mixed with white lies
I'm now going to say hello
I never knew but now I know

When Darkness Falls
by Stephanie Moss - age 11

When darkness falls it seems as if
   everyone is dead.

It seems as if you can see fangs to
   make you daunted.

You can feel pain in your soul as if
   it's going through your
   entire body at once.

Soon it will be dawn and all of
   the pain will be gone.

Dancing Flowers
by Alicia Mouton - age 16

Flowers dancing softly,
swaying from side to side,
making their petals meet,
drifting along the water,
one by one, side by side,
gently they waltz in a familiar manner.

My Parents Kept Me From Hatred
by Becky Mowat - age 14

My parents kept me from hatred
That hid somewhere deep inside.
Children inherited it from their parents
Who didn't think it was wrong.

I feared more than snakes the angry words,
And the actions that came with them.
I feared the bite of those words against my soul,
Which were worse than the bite of an angry animal.

Actions and words came fast,
But took years to be forgotten.
I always tried to ignore the hatred,
But it never really went away.

For
by David Muir - age 16

Listen to the quiescent song,
The dreary dirge of the dead
That echoes in mind through morrow's long,
Creeping into my head.
Still winds, a chill treading my skin,
The reminiscence of the withered kin,
Of fault o'er a harmless sin,
Purge thee, O fragile wind!

Trapped
by Andrea Murdaugh - age 15

Darkened cells, laden with fire,
Being set free, my one true desire,
Midnight screams, with deviled cries,
Nightmares of hell are burning inside.
Hoorish dreams fill my head,
Visions of me, joining the dead.
I've paid my price, my debt, my fee
Yet it is so hard to avoid being me.

The Early Hours Of The Day
by Christopher M. Murphy - age 16

In the early hours of the day
That some call dawn
I am reminded of a time
When all was calm and
Not a sound could be heard
Nor a sight be seen
When only a space was existent.
A time when only the red glow
Of a distant sun could be seen
And a time when the earth
Was pure and clean
And as this dream shatters
Into a reality
A dense fog prevails
Foretelling of a day when
Children run wild and
Men are held helplessly
In the hands of a cruel world
I awaken in the early hours of the day
When all is calm and
You can see the red glow of a distant sun.

The Mailman
by Adam Murrie - age 11

The singing mailman walks along
His bag is deep and wide,
And letters from all over the world
Are bundled up inside.

The mailman's coming up our street.
Pretty soon he'll ring my bell.
Maybe there'll be a letter stamped
in Africa. Who can tell?

December
by Jessy Napper - age 16

cold.
breath of heat pours from the open wound
cold.
soul escaping entrapment of the human monstrosity
cold.
blankets of snow consume the flesh
cold.
what once existed has now been erased
cold.

Roses By Your Bedside
by Lara Nash - age 16

Roses by your bed side and daisies in your hair,
Life has not been easy, some will say not fair.
I remember you as sixteen, though someday I'll be old,
Friendships are life diamonds, Ours was just like gold.

You always seemed to handle what life had thrust your way,
Today would be your birthday, the 25th of May.
You always were the strong one and I wished I could've known,
What went on inside your head, those day you were alone.

Roses by your grave side and daisies in the air,
Tell me what I've always known - that life is just not fair.
And as a birthday comes and goes,
So do lives of those we know.

Runaway Letter
by Dwon Nave - age 14

I know it shouldn't be this way
I know that I should care
But you know I can't stand the way
You treat me so unfair
It's like I don't belong here
As if I'm set aside
I can understand you not wanting me here
When you think that I tell those lies.

You don't have to trust me
I don't care if I'm heard
It wouldn't change anything anyway
Because you don't believe my words.

I hope this time you'll believe what I say
If you don't you'll feel really small
When you come to wake me one day
And notice that I'm not there at all.

Then the memories will come to you
That's when you start to pray
That child who used to run to you
Will be back with you someday.

Alone
by Natalie Naylor - age 15

Alone for eternity
I will be,
If you do not come,
Come for me.
Come at night,
Come at day,
I don't care,
Just don't go away.
My love is like fire,
That burns when I'm cold.
The one thing I feel,
When I'm hurt and alone.
Don't you know how much you mean?
I want you there,
When on someone I need lean.
I see your face when I pray,
Pray that you'll come for me,
One day.
For now I sit,
Patiently waiting,
For you to take me in your arms,
Saying,
"I'm here,
I've come,
And now,
Never again
Will you be alone."

Monster
by Jessie Nelson - age 13

It came when I was sleeping
Without warning or a sign
The body the monster had taken
Would never again be mine.

He took me to his lair
I almost went insane
For the place he had taken me
Was a world of never-ending pain.

I started getting weaker
As the days went by
And finally I figured
By this monster I would die.

Right before I died
The monster grabbed tighter to me
Then he whispered in my ear
"They call me H.I.V."

Untitled
by Rick Newman - age 14

I don't know where I'm going, but I know where I have been.

I absorb anger and Hatred, like a sponge, I hold it all within.

Buried in confusion, crying in the rain, so nobody can see me trying to wash away my pain.

I watch life slip through my fingers, like sand in a hour glass, like paper in the wind it escapes from me so fast.

Everything disappears from me in a blink of an eye. And all I do is sit in the rain, so no one can see me cry.

Man's Last Chance
by Samantha Ngov - age 17

I sit there scared as light slowly disappears
Soon darkness will appear
My heart increases it's beats
I know I will soon face defeat.

My eyes they are filled with tears
This is all because of fear
Death with it's army will soon stop on by
To get what he thought was no longer mine.

My life was my greatest pleasure
Soon I will lose my biggest treasure
I get down on my knees to pray
I sadly ask for another chance to stay.

Death with no pity, laughed in my face
And said that Man is a disgrace
Man, Death said, does not know what to cherish
Until what he had has perished.

Alone
by Kaitie Nies - age 16

If life is an ocean
I stand on the coast,
Watching it all flow by me.
The waves wash in,
Trying to
        pull
                me
                        into
                                the
                                      water.
Yet,
I resist.
Cannot I stay here forever,
A child holding it's mother's hand?
Protected from the depths of life,
Can I stay safely on the sand?
I know I cannot,
I must dive into life.
Slowly I wade in.
My ankles, knees, legs, waist, shoulders
Immersed.
I must learn to swim this ocean
Alone.

Just A Shadow
by Maynerd Pfarr - age 14

Death strikes many
People with fear, but
I'm not afraid.
To me death is just
a shadow making it's
way nearer.
Death is just a shadow
That creeps over you at night
Drains the life from your body
Death is just a shadow
making it's way nearer.

Memories
by Shawnte Nix - age 12

When you remember the past, good and bad, you want to erase all.
You feel the sweet sorrow lurking from an incident that happened when you were a young child.
It hurts to remember but you always do,
You watch it happen you freeze as if you can't move, but then you realize you are in the past.
You stop for a moment and picture
Yourself on a beautiful mountain with the wind whirling your hair,
Watching the sun you feel the harsh rays, wildly moving around you,
You hear the sweet sound of a wonderful bird chirping.
The waves crash against the smooth black rocks.
You watch the sun shrivel up and get dimmer and dimmer as the time flies.
You're in your own world and you know no one can hurt you anymore.
The beauty of this world refreshes you and makes you feel special.
Someone from the outer world is trying to bring you back to the real world, but you mustn't for there is pain, guilt, and very deep sorrow.

Nature Song
by Shaina L. Noggle - age 20

Fa la la, she sang a song
to the swallows, robins, and jays.
Tweet tweet ta, they sang along
during the long sweet summer days.
The squirrels, well, they would sit and stare,
for they were easy to amaze,
and the bunnies would lift their whiskers,
and with a smile, their eyes would glaze.
Tippity tap, her feet would dance,
in only the most beautiful ways.
Flippity flap, the birds would fly,
even the worms were in a daze!
Still to this day, she sings her songs,
just to make the animals prance.
And even now, she tippity taps,
just to make all loving hearts dance.

The Sleeping Cat
by S.E. Noll - age 16

Looking through the peep hole,
    spider webs and peeling paint.
Old gray paint, worn by the ages,
    once white but now dirty and stained
like all the hallways and rooms of this place.
My room is different more lived in and yet the same.
    A cat sleeps by the door,
old and gray just like the paint,
    he gently purrs himself to sleep,
dreaming simple dreams, a cats dreams,
    of mice and grassy meadows.
    In a sense we are the same,
for I am also like the paint,
    once sweet and white, now gray and stained.
I am old and dreaming simple dreams,
    dreams of youth and meadows,
knowing each breath could be my last
like the cat, the spider webs, and the old gray paint.

Denied Love
by Michele Norton

I swore to the angels that appeared in my room
That I would never lay pen to paper again.
For in my mind all hope was lost
For my heart of red had turned to black.
Tears poured out like rivers of water
Running down falling to the ground.
Calling out I damned you if you only to damn my heart.
For it looked as though we could only part.
Like a part in a path that we have taken
Separate, set adrift.
Longing to go back if only to the beginning
For then there could never be an end.
My angels shed not one tear
For they where angered, beyond guilt, beyond fear.
Reaching out to touch me with hands of steel
For they never imagined how I could feel.
Feeling with my heart my spirit lingered.
Wanting only to be touched.
Being an angel I stood alone
For loneliness is a friend of mine.
She wipes my tears with the leaves of a tree.
She shines the moons light, if only for me to see.
I look at the world through different eyes
For god has given me two sets
And with that I cannot deny.
Being an angel sent down from above with only one goal in mind.
The blessings and the joys of love.
I reached out to you in the darkest hour
If only to be cast out and to be denied.
Denied the beauty, denied the love.
The love of a future
The love of all time.

Waves
by Elizabeth Ohno - age 15

Crashing waves roll on the beach,
holding so much anger
that it must unleash
Rhythmically returning to the ocean's floor,
never to return as
the same wave like before.

The Wonder
by Jennifer Nowak - age 15

Walking through the
shadows tonight,
shivering from the cold.
I come upon a ghostly
figure.
Through the mist,
I see it.
bellowing swaying.
and it whispers my name.
As frightening as
it seems,
I am not afraid.
Over and over the
wind whistles,
the leaves rattle,
the shadows dance.
My desires
are now fulfilled.
Warmth never felt before
surrounds me.
There is peace within.
I am overcome with joy.
For the musical voice
has whispered my name.

Choices
by Adaku Nwachku - age 17

The shade of deception
Determined by Man
Contains an absence of light
Which he, himself, cannot understand

One's innocence
Conceived in a mother's womb
To be proven guilty
By those who guard the tomb

Who decides when the river runs
Between heaven and earth
Or kisses the ground with pure thoughts
Where paradise is but a hurried birth

Until the violin strokes it's last tune
And the tread loosens on our lives
Evaluate the significance of the two symbols
In approximation to the incision of your knives

Encounter the truth
Heal the wounds of the untold
Let the air create music
For all eternity to behold

Simple 197
by Cholinthia - age 19

Think of the *good things* I gave you:
Good things are my sweetest recipe.
For they hold on long after you've left me,
And keep a hand on your shoulder for me.
Today might be in passing: I might recall
Whatever you don't,
or smile whenever you won't.
But keep a thought tucked away for me,
a tender one you forgot.
And if I observe you ever again
I'll ask for it; but 'til then, old pal,
keep a thought tucked away for me.

Taken Away
by Katie Obermiller - age 15

If I were a bird
I would fly far away
from this place, this land
where no one cares about me
for I am just name
just a face
I would have wings
that would carry me away, far away
and I would not come back
not ever
you will not know that I am gone
for I was only a face
a face, that you couldn't see
a face that disappeared, but never became a bird
the face vanished
without a trace
or a note
the face became the wind,
the water
and the sky
the sky where birds fly
and you
looked into the sky
and for once in your life you saw me
I was no longer a face
but I now had wings
and I flew down to you
but all you saw was a Bird

Whispers
by Lisa O'Connor - age 15

Like distant sands from far away places
On whispering clouds of foreign faces
Your imagination is set free
Into the world of broken dreams.

I'll walk in the footprints
That are so distant
We'll walk in the light, while our shadows look,
To let me know, it'll never be over.

I've opened the door and walked through your dreams
I've made a pathway, and you sewed the seams.
Take my hand and never turn away,
Do you hear the whispers-what do they say?

Listen very carefully
The answer you'll find
Look in very closely,
It's all in your mind

Just open your heart
Follow your mind
Look in your soul
The answer you'll find.

I'm Trapped
by Stephanie Pokryfky - age 14

I'm trapped in a world with no care,
I'm trapped,
Afraid to walk alone
Afraid to be out at night,
I'm trapped.
I try to hide from it all
But I can't,
I'm not safe anywhere,
I'm trapped,
and they don't care.

Bubble
by Jennifer O'Neill - age 13

      I'm just like a bubble ready
                to
        explode, Yet so much
trouble, but such a heavy load

      I can't keep it all inside
             much
            longer
    I know letting it all out
             would
        make me stronger

    I can't survive with this
              on
           my chest.
I've got to let it out un-
    like all the rest

The Hero I Never Knew
by Emily Oots - age 19

He was born long ago on a lonely rain-filled hot night.
His mother was a child, but through her love she gave him up.
She was alone, scared, in pain, but she endured and bore a
miracle.
Although I never knew him, I dream of him...picturing his face,
his smile, his soul, and wonder if his life was that of goodness.

I have named him in my dreams as he was nameless at birth.

His blood flows through my veins and we are one though separate.
His mother cries for him during her times of aloneness, despair.
She remembers his cry, blonde hair, tiny form, whisked away...
He was taken by god in a war not long ago, and his mother wonders
if he cried then, too.
Was he scared? Did he suffer? her guilt is endless and always
will be.
The choice was not hers to make.
I picture him in his shining uniform, metals, so young and proud.
He was a turn hero, one that I will never know until the day
we meet in heaven.
Then with smiles and embraces we will unite.
That hero was my brother, A nameless figure in my mind and tears;
heroes never die.
I will not weep for him, but for his mother.
A white cross on his grave is all that is left except the beating
of my heart, which pulses stronger through his loss.
We are one, and I will remember his strength, honor and dignity.
A brave soul, my brother, the hero I never knew.

The White Sandy Beaches Of The Shore
by Stephanie Ortona - age 18

on a warm gentle summer day
i walk along the white sandy beaches of the shore
the wind blows through my flowing hair
sand across my feet
cool sea mist on my face
waves crash and roll
upon the white sandy beaches of the shore
the bright orange-pink sunset
illuminates silver linings attached to the clouds
a playful gust of wind trots by
pulling my dress tight against my hip and thigh
as i walk along the white sandy beaches of the shore

Daddy Is Gone
by Magdalena Oslizlok - age 16

She stands at the foot of his grave,
He was supposed to be so strong and brave.
A tear slides down her young cheek,
Her daddy is gone and she can't speak.
She trusted him, she needed him,
And now the future looks so very grim!
She says she will okay, it'll be fine,
But she need someone to hold her and be her vine.
A vine of strength when she is weak,
A strong shoulder where she can weap.
She puts on a strong front, a mask to hide the pain,
But behind it is a girl who feels like she's been hit by a train.
A bitter wind blows, stinging her tear stained face,
She wishes it wasn't happening but his death is something she can't
erase.
Daddy is gone forever and now what does she do?
They tell her that there is hope but is that true?
She wants to wake up from this nightmare,
Why did this happen to her, it isn't fair!
She stands at the foot of his grave,
Now that he is gone it is her turn to be brave.

Dying
by Andrea Ostrow - age 16

Her body is limp.
She stands in front
of the mirror
as she stares at
her body
hunched over
just slightly.

Her wig is lightly set
on her head.
She told me
her wig is just
like how her
hair was when she was
young.

Her left hand
lays at her side,
as if it's not there.

She will get better.
She will not die.
Her family will not
allow that to happen.

A Baby Angel
by Kelly O'Toole - age 15

A delicate, beautiful face.
Rosy skin.
Tiny, cream colored fingers.
An expressionless look.
Motionless, without a sound.
A body whose spirit has left it behind.
Now an angel in heaven,
protecting all children.
Living on through innocent things in life;
sunlight pouring through the clouds
a flower in bloom,
and the peaceful song of a bird.
A child anticipated for so long.
So loved, so cherished, and so missed.
He is always in our hearts,
but has joined all of the other baby angels in heaven.
Always remaining "Our Forever Baby".

Leaning
by Jessie Ottolini - age 14

Sometimes I feel like standing at the top
of a very high building,
feet halfway over the edge
Should I lean forward and end the pain
or lean backward and continue in misery
would it really be better if I jumped
or am I just fooling myself into believing
there is some way of escape
but I take the chance and walk off the edge
on the way down
I wonder, what would it have been like
if I'd only leaned backward

Untitled
by Jillian Owen - age 15

Dreams are in, dreams are out
The smell gives you something to cry about
People smile, people frown
But sometimes we all feel so down
Pictures here, pictures there
Sparkling eyes are everywhere
Shades of darkness, shades of light
Painted faces, naked faces
Someday they will all go places
Dolls of porcelain, dolls of glass
Some awake, some are sleeping
There are too many promises for them to be keeping
Boys drink coffee, girls drink tea
It's all the same 'cause they can't see
Rain from the window, rain from the wall
Dance around at the Debutante Ball
Glasses are empty, glasses are for the blind
None of us have our own kind
Across the universe, across the sky
They will remember you here when you die
Black and white films, bad radio sound
The 1920's kept us all around
Wine is water, water is wine
All the drunken daisies are still feeling fine
The books tell why, the books tell how
No need for moving we're all in the same spot now
Somewhere in your smile, somewhere it knows
That this room is the path you once chose

The Real Monsters
by Denise Park - age 15

The dark can turn the world around,
And make it a horrible sight.
All the problems you feel you have overcome,
Come and haunt you in the night.

The dark looks deep inside you
It knows your biggest fear.
And when it finds out what your scared of,
It makes images appear.

You see a robber with a gun.
You see the walls cave in.
You can try to fight these images,
But the dark will always win.

Your covers you try to hide in.
Your pillow you hold tight.
But nothing in the world,
Will destroy the awful sight.

Finally you quit trying to hide,
And slowly sleep takes you away.
The images are gone for the moment,
But they will be back someday.

Shattered Life
by Jennifer Parsons - age 17

My life falls apart before my eyes
The broken pieces of my shattered dreams
Come crashing down without warning
Mixing together into a tangled web of
uncertainty
I am no longer in control
My life is no longer my own
It belongs to the ones who pull my strings
And I'm nothing more than a puppet

November Of My Heart
by Kimberly Parks - age 18

When the black curtain drapes the sky
In my bed, alone, I lie.
Dreaming, Escaping, my lost soul soars
Mingling, dancing, intertwine with yours.

In flesh, put asunder, no longer together
In spirit, through destiny, as one forever.
It is for these stolen moments that I live
For warmth and comfort and affinity that they give.

How I wish the nights to be as centuries
Fragrant with ecstasy, free from realities.
Soon the flaming orb materializes, forcing us to part
Mournfully, I awaken; it is the November of my heart.

Good-bye
by Melissa Parks - age 16

I sit here beside you bed
And slowly watch you die.
And suddenly realize
This will be my last good-bye.

As I wipe away the tears
And try to swallow my fears
Death still draws near.

I want you to know I love you
And will miss you greatly;
But God is calling you home.

As I hold your cold hand,
And realize you've died,
I begin to cry-
Knowing I didn't say good-bye.

Before And After You
by Melissa Parrish - age 16

My world was dark,
Under thick clouds of regret.

Life seemed meaningless,
With an air of pointlessness.

But then through all the sadness,
You were there.

Thoughts which plagued my mind,
Had gone astray.

My dark thick clouds,
Were slowly drifting away.

But my love for you,
Will never fade.

The Color Of My Skin
by Terri Payne - age 17

I walk down the street,
    my pants are sagging at my knees.
I stop to call a friend,
everyone stares like something is wrong.
The feelings I have inside are:
    hurt rejected, I'm crying inside.
  I try not to let it show,
    That "Bad Black Man" attitude covers it up.
I wish people would look at my heart,
              instead they check my skin.

Pain
by Kasandra Passmore - age 12

as she walked through all the rows of beautiful flowers;
    she stopped to think for hours and hours.

she told herself everything was going to be okay;
    but there was no place for her, no where to stay.

life was hard, life was rough;
    she always knew she had to be tough.

she had no home, food or family;
    her life was nothing but a big tragedy.

how could she mess up so very, very much?
    she kept repeating to herself as she lost her touch.

what did she do? what's so wrong;
    she's talented, unique and really very strong.

why was life so cruel to her?
    she can't think straight, her mind in a blur.

nowhere to run, nowhere to hide;
    she just sat down ready to die.

her makeup smudged, her hair in knots;
    the shelters are filled, but her life is as empty as the pots.

she was crying, trembling and some what dirty;
    she wished her life was more sturdy.

i think about the girl sleeping under a tree;
    i think a little harder and that girl is me!

Untitled
by Sandra Patterson - age 17

What is that on your face?
Is that a frown I see?
Remove that frown from your face,
At least while you're with me.
Nobody wants to see a frown.
Bury your feelings, let them drown.
Why is that blank look on your face?
Have you no feelings to show?
Change your expression and I'll get off your case,
Or else I'll just have to go.
It's better to have a happy expression,
Than to look overcome by depression.
Why is that smile on your face?
You have no reason to smile.
Take that smile off your face,
At least for a little while
Why are you smiling anyway?
Today's just as bad as any other day.

Moons And Me
by Rachel Penix - age 18

the moon is lonely like i am.
all alone in a dark sky full of wispy clouds.
i am in a dark world full of wispy people.
people that don't really care
when they ask how you are.
they are just being polite.
people really don't care.
i am like the moon.
but we're not alike -
it's full.

Go To 76
by Leslie Pears - age 14

Go to 76
I start down the long dreary hall
And thoughts of my past are here and that's all
Could this be my end
And then maybe it's yours
But if we stay together we'll go to fall
Tears stream down my face as I think of love long gone
Maybe you meant to do this
To send me down this dreadful hall
I am now a token for anyone to take
I thought your love for me was real
Now I know it's fake
You stayed for the duration just to leave me in my wake
I drift the moonlit hours
I drink the summer rain
But yet I find no answer to why you cause me pain

Untitled
by Carrie Peckar - age 17

and you think you're
all deep well shove this
in your deepness and see
how hard it is to get it out
floats up face first
like dead fish in water
and this was written on
some stale toast because
it was too frustrating to
spread the cold butter
I bet if this were written
on a handkerchief it
would make no difference
to you

Eyes
by Stefani Pelletier - age 19

Windows in a hall
Unable to be opened
I bang on the pane
Please let me in please
And then I see you
behind the glass
But more - I see your soul
And then you disappear
I forget you with time
We go our own ways
Until I remember
And go to your windows again.
I find myself staring
From down the hall
Wanting to go to your windows
Knowing it will be the same
So I choose other windows
In effort to forget you
Knowing only the glimpse
We shared
Was perfection.
Your windows are cloudy.
Are you going to cry?

Iron, Brick, and Stone
by Katie Peters - age 17

Now understanding
The brother was true-
Love in pure form
Nothing is new-

        Once the great destroyer
        Now a safety net
        Open is a given
        Oddly priced set

Forgiven for Love-
Forgiven for Hate-
Never question
Too little? Too late?

        Inclusive exclusion
        Truth--be it known
        Permanent destruction
        Of Iron, Brick, and Stone

To Be As He
by Ladonna Sheriese Peters - age 14

The old man lies there-
making way of his life,
telling a tale
of himself and his wife.
Almost smiling as he would talk,
of every path that he had walked.
He told me of his rodeo days,
of all his dreams and reckless ways.
But most of all, I heard that of his wife-
for she was his dream, his smile, and his life.
Though she went first,
he promised never to think the worst.
For again someday he would be with her,
to look into her eyes of blue, just as they were.
When I remember that old man,
I look back and smile,
for I follow his advice mile by mile.
For he stood tall,
while going through it all.
I hope that someday I will be as brave as he,
when that day comes people will look up to me.

Will I Ever Love Again?
by Andrea Petruka - age 14

I was talking to a man, late one day,
and I understood exactly what he was trying to say.
He told me about his long, lonely life,
and how he felt after he lost his wife.
This is his story.

While I'm sitting by my lover's final resting place,
I slowly dream of her beautiful face.
Her long flowing hair, her gentle touch,
I never thought I'd miss her so much.
Will I ever love again?

It seemed just yesterday we were together,
and our love would always last forever,
but it's been ten years since she last left,
and throughout these years, I've done nothing but wept.
Will I ever love again?

Through all my tears I cannot hide,
how my feelings really touch me inside.
So remember this from dusk to dawn,
you don't know what you have until it's gone
Will I ever love again?

Defeat
by Tonya Petty - age 17

        Even the mother fox
        Teeth as sharp as razor blades
        Reflexes smooth as water
        cannot save her pups
        When the man carries a gun

Abomination
by Shellise Piazza - age 19

I got drunk on your desires not knowing what you filled me with
and I felt them race through my veins like a deadly poison
I woke up with a heartache hangover and I took you again like a pill
a desperate addiction dangerous yet inviting
I wanted to brush the hair from my face and kill what I have become
I wanted to pluck out my eyes and set them on your bedpost to watch you
in your forbidden infatuations
I wanted to rip out my heart and cook it on a platter of silver and feed it to
you with a spoon
forcing you to take in my love
there it would sit well-done in your stomach turning and churning
making you nauseous
I wanted to tear off my breast and rub it in your face
so you could taste me one last time without a choice
I wanted to wanted to bite away my nipple and give it to you to use like
chewing gum
to watch you salivate and scream
I wanted to drain my blood into a goblet made of jewels and steel
and intoxicate you with the flavor of it
I wanted you to get sick on the stench of my breath that reeks of the love
we once had
I wanted to cut you like grass with a machete
I wanted to wring out your soul of the self pity you kept locked inside
and jump in the puddle that would collect at my feet watching your dreams
evaporate
I wanted to tell you that you were my disease
your death was the cure
and my hand with the double-sided blade was you savior
I wanted to tell you goodbye and watch your eyes watching mine as you
took your last breath
but I did the worst thing I could have done
more violent than the killing
more torturous than the abuse
more destructive than the pain
I told you I loved you and I stood and laughed while you cried

Let Me Heal
by Jamie Robinson - age 17

Please Let me laugh again
and forget that I have cried,
reassure my heart
that my eyes have forever dried.
Make certain that my smile
is not what I pretend,
and every heart ache
has come to its end.
Allow these lips to kiss
allow these arms to embrace,
allow this pain to clear
that you see upon my face.

Who Are The Real Heroes?
by Julie Pikcilingis - age 14

Are Olympic winners real heroes,
The recipients of the gold?
Are Astronauts real heroes,
Who travel to places untold?

Are scientists real heroes,
Who figure things we never knew?
Are the admirals real heroes,
Who fight in the ocean blue?

Are Political figures real heroes,
Who are known the whole world wide?
No, my friend they're not,
The real heroes are those by your side.

Your parents are the heroes,
Who have made you what you are.
Your teachers are the heroes,
They have helped you come so far.

Your coaches are the heroes,
They have helped you learn and grow.
My friend, the real, true heroes,
Are people that you know!

Love Is A Tricky Thang
by Waynette Pinnix - age 16

Love. What is Love?
Is it what two people share
Like mother to child?
Or is it something we think
Like girl to boy?

No matter what it is it's all around.
Real Love
Special Love
Fake Love
Love

Love is walking hand in hand.
Sign seeing reflections of joy in
each others eyes.
Love is sharing a special kiss only
two lovers can share.
A glance across a room to
remember you were there.

I wish I knew how this feels.
But all I've had are Fake Loves.
Guys who say they will Love you forever.
They tell you, you have a Real Special Love.
When all in all it's just Fake Love.

A Special Love is what I long for.
Someone to share their Love with me.
A Love to stick with through thick and thin.
A Love to be not just my Love but my Friend.

Love is deep and so is this poem,
One day I'll fall madly in Love.

Mary
by Marissa Piper - age 19

Little girl
with the eyes like rain
standing on the street
watching the people go by,
no one else sees her
the sadness washing over her.
No one hears her crying,
"Mommy, mommy where are you?"
Only a stone face stares back at her.

Little girl
with hard eyes-
innocence surrendered. She's got a cigarette in one hand
an empty glass in the other
and a bitter smile on her face.
"Mommy, mommy where are you?"
she shouts at the wind.
Only a stone face covered with white lilies stares back at her.

Little girl
with no more tears to cry
only a stone face to remember.

Tough World
by Lory Polensky - age 15

Acting cool,
Being tough.

Clepto-fool,
Don't be rough.

Entering life,
From the back.

Getting a knife,
Hustling crack.

Intelligence lost,
Just a space.

Keep the cost,
Lose the pace.

Money flies,
Not a care.

Oodles of cries,
Pains that tear.

Quacking out,
Raising hell.

Sympathetic pout,
Try to tell.

Underground,
Vans of love.

Withering sounds,
X-Ray above.

You don't care 'bout
Zebra's lair.

Death Has Taken Her
by Anna Porter - age 14

A little one weeps
her eyes filled with tears
far to much grief,
far too much for her years.

A sob grows inside
her little heart broken
her small love divine,
to them, merely a token.

Her tears like a stake,
through your heart to your soul,
her smile uplifting,
that which death hath just stole.

Just Open Your Eyes And See...
by Katie Porter - age 12

A lady looks upon a telephone pole,
Looking for job offers.
Everyone requests a home address.
She sadly looks at the ground,
For she has no home.

She tries as she must to get a job.
But nobody wants
A vagabond working for them.
So each time she is turned down.
What is the woman to do?

Jobless, homeless, and coatless
For the coming winter.
A young child's hopes, goals and dreams,
She had made for herself, shattered.
Her hopes were once to be a doctor.

Now her dream is to get
Any kind of job.
Anything-
But a dirty trash digger
Begging for spare change.

Just open your eyes and see that
Your one room apartment or five floored mansion,
Is better than a shelter
Shared with complete strangers,
Or maybe even no home at all.

To Him
by Brandi Richardson - age 17

Why do you keep me for nothing?
Why do you tell me you love me,
then walk away?
Your pretentiousness drowns me,
while your soft lies keep me longing for
more.
You spit swords through my heart,
Yet you always find away to make it
seem right.
I'm tired of running into your arms
for comfort, and having you throw me
to the floor.
I can melt you from my mind.
I have wings. And for the first time
I'm not afraid to use them.

I Sit Here
by Amy Sue Daisy Pray - age 15

I sit here in the dark,
hidden by my fears,
No one sees the truth,
No one sees my fears,

I sit here in the silence,
hidden by the pain,
Listening to my heart,
as it's broken once again,

I sit here in the coldness,
not realizing the chill,
listening to the silent words,
tearing at my will,

I sit here in the hopelessness,
as a tear silently falls,
your no longer with me,
to tear down my walls,

I sit here helplessly,
awaiting you to tell,
How ever so silently,
Out of love you fell.

Sentenced To Death
by Shana Snider

Is it a crime to grow old and die,
Leaving our pains and sorrows behind?
Isn't it our pains that keep us alive,
Causing our darkness to subside?

Untitled
by Stephanie Presto - age 18

Where are we now?
In this vast
Universe-
still in the
thick, empty
Blackness;
the earth
pulsates
gently
like a
blue-
colorful
vein
around a
golden
Heart

we go
forward.
Full of
innocent
mystery,
Like ungrateful

Candle
by Debra Prezioso - age 13

The candle burns endlessly
giving us endless light
making us warm
but not just on the outside
hearts need warmth too
love is eternal and so is your flame
it burns forever
yes, it flickers
yet it never ceases
it never dies
you and I will go on always
like the flame
the fire that burns inside our hearts
heals the lives of all of us
it's okay to touch the candle
it won't blister
but that's the pain I feel
when you're not here
for love is eternal and so is your flame

Clear
by Jayme Price

Try to sit on the outside
And look your way in.
You can see almost everything
And the way all things begin.

Just by sitting on the outside
I see the way things start.
Life is all so interesting,
Everyone has a part.

Everything can seem so easy
By sitting some things out.
Everything can be so clear
Beyond a shadow of a doubt.

Life
by Sarah Rae Pritchett

The light shines from a flickering candle across the room.
So bright,
So alive,
Chasing away the gloom.

Still the shadows hang silently,
Fearing the unsightly doom.
Yet they wait,
For morning will come soon.

Mortals do not fear this gleaming light.
Nor do we fear the darkness of night.
For we understand the ways of life.
Although we may not always seem alive.

Our hearts will beat as the earth will turn,
Like a candle as it steadily burns.
Everything done has a price to pay,
Just as night must always turn to day.

Life's price to us,
Is known as death.
And in everyone's life,
This price will be met.

Ash
by Michael Procuk Jr. - age 19

A small sun simmers
inside me.

Blue flames are fed
by my flow of thoughts
about you.

The unexposed fire scorches
the hull of my heart,
until the charred bars of my ribcage
are splintered
and my secrets seep out.

They scurry to you,
burn red
into the folds
of your mind,

and you cough them out
to extinguish me
like the candle
on your first
birthday cake.

Death
by Abbey Prow - age 14

I never thought of death.
What's the point?
We're young and stupid.
Let's smoke another joint.

I never thought of death.
It's not a part of our fun.
It never entered my mind.
Until you got the gun.

I never thought of death.
I guess I never thought of life.
Happiness was my reality.
Then you picked up the knife.

I never thought of death.
Our little town so still.
Our parents so naive.
Until you tried the pills.

I never thought of death.
Why do you make me think?
I'm afraid to lose you.
Your my missing link.

I never thought of death.
Then I met you.
I always knew you had problems.
In a way, I always knew.

I never thought of death,
Until this cold day.
Your plan finally worked.
I'm standing on your grave.

Years Go By
by Brooke Studeman - age 16

Years go by as I watch and wonder why,
things get old and even die,
new life begins every new day,
next day is old as I grow very bold,
while I watch each year go by,
with my watchful leering eyes.

The Cat on the Fence
by Emily Pryor - age 14

Taken with the words of knowledge,
Blinded by the words unknown,
Rattled between two points of interest,
At evidence you are thrown.

Resistant in seeing the answer,
Letting time conceal,
In fear of what lies within,
Not showing what is real.

Shutting out yourself from thoughts of wonder,
No more hopes and dreams.
This is a strange place,
Nothing is as it seems.

Have you forgotten you asked for space?
Well now it's yours.
But you can't see?
Then why shut the doors?

A closed mind is equal
To no mind at all,
As the cat upon the fence
And you are bound to fall.

Whether the day today or tomorrow,
There will come a surprise.
When you build up your strength and power,
Enough to open your eyes.

I Promise
by Tabitha Streetman - age 15

In sickness and in health,
I promise to be there.
Richer or for Poorer,
I promise to be around.
If your world should crumble or fall,
I promise to put it together again.
If all your dreams should come true,
I promise to be there to help you through.
If anything was to happen to you,
I promise to carry on your name.
If you should find someone new,
I promise never to forget you.

Anew
by Melissa Purvis - age 16

I lay myself down to sleep
Until the sun again does shine

I can lay a long time now,
Waiting for the light of rise

Miss me not, Do not fear.
With a smile, I'll be here.

In no time at all,
The light of rise will shine again.

Arise I will, its up to you.
To help the day begin anew.

Our World Which Must
by Nick Pusc - age 14

I'm in a purely empty
calm-stealing void
Destroys minds inside it
at an alarming rate
It'll take mine soon if I'm not quick to escape

It's a horrible place here
where the drug is available
for those desperate souls who must
and can't escape their cages of rust

I own a desperate soul
-but not that desperate

It's a horrible place here
where the cages are filled
and the rest who aren't captive
must see this insane zoo

It's a horrible place here
where we can only go down
and we love so much to move
Oh, we love to move; quickly move

Bobbing For Apples
by Tami Putman - age 16

Relationships are strange, always rather odd
May be enigmatic, behind a fair facade.
Nothing's ever right or left, it's never black or white
Not a simple up or down, it has to be contrite.
It's like you're in a labyrinth, 'cause no matter where you go
It's always one big maze, no direction to or fro.
Not that they're bad, but your heart can get hurt
Just a bleeding passion, you found it wouldn't work.
You will never understand what goes on in someone's head.
Absolutely impossible--you must be them instead.
It's hard enough being you without finding someone out.
You have to know who you are, can't be any doubt.
Even if there is some, it's not wrong or right.
It's just a state of being in which feelings do ignite.
It's hard to say what's good and bad, for everyone it's different
What is nothing to one--to another, all the world is meant.
Because life is a variety and it's really indecisive--
It just makes it interesting, even seem enticive.

Spring
by Amanda Sielaff - age 12

My favorite season is spring;
I like hearing all the birds sing.
New animals are born each day;
This usually happens in May.
The flowers are blooming; they smell so sweet.
The buds on the trees, the sight's quite a treat
Spring is the time when everything is new;
People are full of life and happiness too.

Ode to Pain
by Daniel Quigley - age 18

Alone in a terrible storm we are joined by Pain
Oh such a good comfort throughout a drenching rain
Pain, you are my love when my heart grows weak
You give me an answer when I cannot seek
You grant me anger when my emotions have become too cold
You deal me a hand when in the midst of inevitable fold
The great motivator, you drive me oh so strong
You take my mind from my grave and sing it a song
You can make me take the soul from a fellow man
You can make me justified when left to be damned
And when I rot by myself you leave me all alone
You take only my love, my family, and my home
Just pay isn't it? Just for a day of hate and resentment
And a lesson of life preached by Hell's sinful testament
But on a moonlit night when tortured souls cry
I sit in your cage and I can see your lie
You have oppressed my heart and filled it with extreme evil
You have caused me to beat and kill innocent people
No matter how much I hated them they were victims of your crime
I cannot understand why I gave you so much valuable time
Hate the hater, hate the lover, hate all that I can
We followed the rules written by your enlightening hand
Only to be damned once again, and with pain, our muscles sore
Pain like death and destruction you are the devil's faithful whore
And for the score, I believe you have ambition, busy man
Spread so thin to the souls of all, you have so many a fan
Advocates to catastrophe without hope of reform
From pain, our beloved friend, make of terrible storm

Untitled
by Jessica Radcliffe - age 12

The trees stand tall around the marsh
Fish of many colors mingle in the water
Birds sing their beautiful melody from high in the trees
Crickets chirp in the grass
Then, the trucks move in tearing apart the ground and sending smoke into the air
The trees are knocked down as birds rush their young away from the chaos
Then, the marsh is filled with dirt
What once was a beautiful forest is no more
They promised it would be ok
It wasn't and now all that's left is a vast wasteland
We must stop the destruction or there will be nothing left.

Struggle
by Jessica Radzak - age 17

It beats down on me
So hot
My body begins to weep
I fall to the Earth
Clawing my way forward, dragging my legs behind
I see an oasis
Only a dream, I must..
I need...
Cold
Dark
Loneliness sets in
What is...
Only the wind
My body trembles
I pull my hands to my chest
My heart beats slowly
It begins to...
Fade away
Blackness
Peace at last

Ebony
by Rachel Ramer - age 15

Take this razor, tear it down. I want to scream. I want to drown. Make me bleed. End this pain. My bitter blood tastes like rain. Crush this wall. Say my name. Please don't let me die in vain. Let me cry! Let me shout! I would give you my heart, you would rip it out.

Notes Of Life
by Jessica Ratliff - age 16

The high sweet notes of the music ring
Like laughter through the years
But the notes are more often low,
Confining in my fears
As the melody plays
Life moves on
And I no choice but to move with it
For when the melody ends,
So will the song
And the life that lived within it.

Today
by Chandra Raynes - age 15

Today is a day like no other day.
It is the beginning and it is the end.
Today is for you to live not die.
Today is just a day.
You will never have the same day twice.
For it only comes once.
So go live today for it is the last day of your life.
Sure there will be other days, but not one like today.
Today is a day for you, not for another.
If you don't live today there will be no tomorrow.
Yesterday will be forgotten and today will never be.
Your future lies in today not tomorrow or yesterday.
So live before you die
For today is the day you can do what you want.
Never forget the day that brought you here.
And you will never forget the day you leave.
The days in between will be forgotten if you don't live them.
So live and be happy in what you do for yourself, your planet, and your neighbors.
GO! GO! Go make today the best day of your life.
And never forget it.

Mislead Puppets
by Jessica Rector - age 14

Slowly rising
breaks free from its horizon
dependent are we as it slowly wanders
but always faithfully returns
to start a new day
a common function it would seem
to those unworthy
could you be so brave,
to up take the challenge?
Forced upon the same track
of everyday existence
although covered by darken shadows
it will still press on, or will it?
Is everything just how it seems?
Maybe it's not a servant at all
but an unmerciful master,
to dreamers
locked up in a carefree void
functioned by value and time
do all wish to be free?
Only those who can see the strings
in which play the roles of fate
we are the puppets
forced upon the exact track
of the same existence
who will dare to challenge
or do they even realize
as I look into their plain expressions
I kneel down and pray
please God, make them see

Traveling In The Desert
by Shawna Reece - age 13

The mustard smear of a line
splattered on a black path.

Ramshackle houses fly by
along with brown cottonball shrubs.

I see the cloud-streaked, pale blue sky
like white frosting on a blue cake.

A hill on the left looks like a big potato.

On the right, an orange ball of shining brightness
slides behind the naked mountain.

Sunrise
by Heather Spessard - age 14

As the sun peeked
Out over the land,
It dried my face; tear streaked
And it held my hand.
Faith in myself grew,
No one could steal.
And I knew
My heart would heal.

Lonely and Confused
by Christine Rees - age 14

I lay down to sleep
To dream of wonderful things
But I am awakened by his voice
    calling me, telling me that's he's alive

Believing him, I jump out of bed
I look around my room
I look out the window and down the hall
Only to find out...
    It was all just a bad dream

I go back to bed
To fall asleep once again to the same spine chilling dream
But as I did before
I am awakened from his voice
    you're just dreaming
    when you wake up,
    I'll be alive...I promise...

believing in him once again, I wake up, sit up
To feel tears dripping from my eyes onto my cheeks
To feel pain as I did when he first died
To feel lonely and confused...

Sad Girl
by Stacy Remillard - age 12

Walk away sad girl
cover your ears

Where did that smile go, sad girl
Why are thee tears

Are they tattered and torn
pinned with needles and thorns

Sad girl, what do those teary eyes see
your old friend fear, you and me

Cry all the grief away
destined to come back anyway

10,000 pieces to put together again
To heal, to seal, to mend

Sad girl, has your flowers died,
To all the world that has lied

Another soul has been taken away
To the heartless place you mus't stay

Sad girl, take that hand
so they can take you away to another land

Your frown is fading
The place is waiting

Walk to them sad girl
UIncover your ears.

Drip Drop
by Mira Stebleton - age 17

It's here again!
You watch it coming down, your clothes dripping wet;
You let it bounce off the palms of your hands;
The great sensation between the toes,
This is how the raindance goes.

Slot Machines
by Kathryn Sims

Strutting, cat-calling whores;
Each boasting to be better than the next.
Talents designed to satisfy a million idiosyncrasies;
Gawdy...painted...noisy...
Always bringing attention to themselves...
Teasing me to pay the price
Of a night's sensational pleasure.

Lo, I swear, never again you'll tempt me
Nor will I sink to the dens to lay with you!
For you have crippled me...
Thrilled me beyond wild expectation...
Bruised me with your fierce tugging and soothing strokes...
Rendered me too impotent to birth willpower again.

Weeping Willow
by Emily Reynolds - age 13

Oh my dear weeping willow
Why must you cry so?
You seem so sad
So sad
But yet you protect me
Protect and watch over me
Your long strong arms cradle and love me
Love is what I need now
Now I need love
I'll think of you when I'm lonely
Which is all the time
We can be each others light
Because you stand all alone at night
I want to comfort you
As long as you hold me
Because I need you more than ever
So stand tall and proud
Because you're now my shelter
Love is what I need
Now I need love

You and I
by Cheri L. A. Riedel - age 16

I am the flower of the meadow,
and you, my love, are the beautiful butterfly
that caresses my soft and delicate petals.

I am the haunting yet alluring song,
you hear in the night,
as you lay in your slumber.

I am the sunshine
that warmly and brightly,
touches your face.

I am the gentle breeze,
blowing through your hair,
whispering, "I love you," as I rush by your ear.

I am the wave of the sea
that blazes in your soul,
never to be smoldered by another.

You are the one,
I have searched for all my life,
because you are the one I was born to love forever.

Faith's Rainbow
by Christina Rinyu - age 14

Mamma always said faith ain't easy
It's like you holdin' a glass of wine
Offering it to people
But they push it away
You're alone
And drop you cup
Glass shatters
Wine spills to the floor.
But your still a walkin'
Offerin' your wine
Reachin' towards that rainbow
That you know
Can offer somethin' more
Your own blood mixes with the red, red wine
It hurt
It hurts to have faith
Peop'll try to tear ya' down
Don't let 'em
You gotta keep on walkin'
reachin' for you rainbow.

Following God's Path
by Rebecca Robbins - age 14

Don't grieve for me now, for I an free;
I'm following the path God made for me.
I took his hand when I heard him call;
I turned my back and left it all.
I couldn't stay another day;
To laugh, to love, to work or play.
Tasks left undone must stay that way;
Peace found me upon that day.
If my parting has left a void;
Then fill it with remembered joys.
A friendship shared, a laugh, a kiss;
Oh you, these things I too will miss.
Be not burdened with times of sorrow;
I wish you the sunshine of tomorrow.
My life was full, I savored much;
Good friends, Good times, a loved one's touch.
Perhaps my time seemed all to brief;
Don't lengthen it with undue grief.
Lift up your hearts and peace to thee;
God wanted me, he set me free.

Promise Me
by Alexis Shuler - age 13

Promise me you'll never leave
Promise me I'll never need...
to cry
to beg
to long
Promise me you'll always be near.
Promise me I can hold you dear.

Promise me all these things.
Promise me cause I need your
wings.

Untitled
by Jessica Roberge - age 17

Why is it,
    When I look into your eyes
        There is nothing but quiet?
Yet,
    When she stares
        Your eyes dance with gleam.
Why is it,
    When we talk
        You have no expression?
Yet,
    When she talks
        A smile is always there.
Why is it,
    When we touch
        You sometimes pull away?
Yet,
    When she touches
        You hang on.
Why is it,
    When we kiss
        You have no feeling?
Yet,
    When she smiles
        Your heart goes crazy,
Why is it,
    When I look at you
        You turn away?
Yet,
    When she looks
        You are mesmerized.

Stunned
by Kristen Marie Scott - age 14

They say they understand,
The confusion that comes with learning.
The need for a helping hand.
Then they go and turn their back,
And leave you in an empty trap.
You fend for yourself.
You fight and struggle.
But end up in giant puddle.
It takes a strong man...
To break down and cry.
To admit that he's going nowhere.
To simply get up and ask for help.
To trust an empty hand.

Quiet...Please
by Danaera Scott - age 16

      Quiet is something that we never
               get,
           I wish I had it,
        but I have not yet!
    I really can't think creatively,
because so many people are laughing
   talking, staring at me...I think it's
         really, scaring me.
          I like to write
          I like to read

            Quietness...
             is what
               I
              need.

My Guiding Presence
by Jennifer Robertson - age 15

I once had a dream.
It was a wonderful dream, of a place filled with love, happiness and harmony.
And all through the dream I felt someone watching over and me guiding me
onwards through my time.
She never showed herself and yet she was present throughout all my endeavors.
And I learned many things from her, the most significant of which was this
-LIFE IS ONLY WHAT YOU MAKE IT-
nothing more and nothing less.
But then my time in that place was over, and I woke.
I thought that by waking I had lost that gentle, guiding presence forever,
and I felt dispirited and depressed.
I thought she had deserted me.
But as I remembered the dream, I felt her presence returning, stronger than ever before.
And soon I realized that she had not deserted me, but instead I had overlooked her.
And I remembered all that I had learned - that life is only as good as you make it.
And now I keep that thought in my mind, and hold onto it as I hold onto her, while I strive to make my life the best it can be.
For I know I have someone watching over me.

The Dream
by Danielle Rockstad - age 15

Two children of fifteen,
    destined for a life of love.

Together, harmony.
    Apart, destruction.

Their love grew stronger,
    as the years came and fell.

Many they met,
    and a very many went.

But all the same,
    their love stayed.

True as the drop of
    water to nourish the rose.

As sacred as
    their days together.

The day came for them,
    to be joined by god.

They had traveled long to this place,
    with only their love to guide them.

The bells rang,
    joy filled the air.

They danced close,
    for their love was glue binding them for life.

She closed her eyes,
    her head upon his breast.

Her forever would last one night,
    for when she arose from his breast with his eyes wide,

She was alone but for the love
    she felt for someone she knew not of.

Forgotten Love
by Brooke Rogers - age 14

We once were happy,
But now that's in the past,
And I still love you,
But you're disappearing fast.

Have you forgotten about me,
And all the promises you made,
Or could it be,
That love is meant to fade.

I miss you so much,
But you don't care about me,
I long for your touch,
That sets me free.

I feel like all is lost,
And all I can do is long,
For the gentle smile you tossed,
And your voice that sounded like a song.

So now I must go,
Because if I don't,
You will know,
That I miss our forgotten love.

Bittersweet
by Lauren Sheridan - age 13

How sweet it would be...
To capture time in an hourglass.
To listen to the wind, and hear her tale,
Hold life's breath in a blade of grass,
To ride the world on gilded sail.
To speak of things you never knew,
And learn of things you knew before,
Ask secrets of the sky so blue,
Embrace the sunlight as you soar.
Alas, it cannot be so.
But how sweet 'twould be...
To know.

Undying Flame
by Michael Rogers - age 19

To know love, to touch love, to be loved,
Is to be warmed by a fire from within.
A fire that was made from a small little spark
That over time has become an undying flame.
With each day that passes the flame becomes higher & brighter
Just to look at love's face gives it the fuel to burn
forever.
The touch of love is a completely different feeling
It is as if you had been burned but you felt no pain.
for this is the passion that lies within love
Wanting to be released and burning so strong
As with everything in life there is a time and place to
release this passion
When the time comes it is as if your body was engulfed in
flames.
For this is what keeps this act of passion sacred
To be passionate yet to love an cherish every moment
To truly know love is to fall asleep every night thinking
of love, and to rise every morning with the warmth and the
thought of love.
To feel as if love is right there beside you
when it might be far away is to be loved
To everyone this love has a name
But for me this love is you...

The Death Dance
by Patricia Rogers - age 15

In the back of the mind,
lies a pit of darkness.
With every fear,
the black grows larger.
Many people dance,
with the darkness,
before it encases them.
I await my turn;
Silently watching yesterday's victim.
The black steps forward,
then back,
almost like a waltz.
Souls call it the shadow lover,
others call it mistress death.
Now it's my turn.
I stand in front of the master
waiting,
an obedient dog.
I long to caress the darkness,
but stare into red eyes.
Swaying with the beat of my heart,
I hold out my hands,
touching mistress death.
My body so cold-
My arms pull at my neck,
for I cannot breath;
will, hope, even life drain from within.
Life's last breath sucked dry like juiceless fruit,
I collapse into the cold-hearted arms of my master.

The Scarecrow
by Crystal Rohleder - age 14

The scarecrow
Tall and lean
Scary and mean
Who stands guard
of farmer Ben's
beans
He sees all, hears all
Evil grins he grins all
day
Just to keep the crows
away
At night he comes alive
and walks among the corn
stalks
He talks to the trees, but
they don't talk back
he's in desperate need
of a friend
His shirt made of a potato
sack
A hat of straw and a heart
of gold
Lonely Mr. Scarecrow
wouldn't hurt a soul

Untitled
by Anne Smith - age 16

A glance through a window
Very small and oval
gives a glimpse of a soul
so lost, so frightened
needing somewhere to go
a longer look shows anger
anger that's mixed with sadness
all will hidden by the shelter outside
except for those small, oval windows

Wind Whispers
by Caroline Senger - age 14

The wind carries your message swiftly
like a fragrant summer breeze
across the fields of marigolds
over shadows and darkest caves
sweeping, bellowing, loud and strong
whispering sweetly in a low sing-song
just like mango so ripe and fresh
filled with moisture and orange flesh
just like a wave of scents
grassy and fresh, earthen and rich,
sweet like honey,
and soft like spring blossoms
when the message comes to me
my heart fills with the golden glory
of our love.

Girl In The Mirror
by Jasmine Rotmil - age 18

Across the cotton sheets she lay
At six o'clock on a rainy day
The only one to wake so soon
And watch the sun take way the moon

The bedroom's chill, it comforts her
The raindrops clear her mind
A common grace falls over her
Which others cannot find

Her sister's orange pussy cat
Is lying 'cross her bed
Believe her when she tells you that
The muted man is dead

She's not afraid of loneliness
She loves to be in pain
She loves to feel the tenderness
Of thunderstorm and rain

She peers into the mirror
And sees herself with scorn
And thinks her soul is horror-filled
As the raging storm

Her soul is taken under siege
By her body's form
Right down to her ugly knees
From her breasts, so warm

She lights another cigarette
Leaves an empty pack
She'll light another candle
And watch the day turn black.

Cold
by Rikki Scott - age 18

She walks on the outskirts
Of a small town
Familiar
Her arms wrapped
Around her wandering body
Concentrate
Stillness, Standing
Over raging waters
Confusion
A single tear wells up in her eye
And goes unshed
Cold
The bridge is far off as she jumps into the
Cold

Waitress
by Julia Rubin - age 15

sunday morning, half past seven
I stumble into a diner to hide from the snow.
You stand across from me in Your place
at the other side of the counter.
shaggy blonde hair blocks your eyes,
but I see
how lonesome You are.
white shirt too big,
black jeans too tight,
double shifts,
smothered by bacon and eggs
menus and orders
six days a week.

I sit on a dirty stool and listen.
You remind the perverse truck drivers
as You have before
You've got babies and work, not much else.
but it seems like I'm the only one
lingering on Your words.

You approach my place
though not to tell Your sad stories,
and I must hold back
my overflowing curiosity
to keep from asking
Your name.

Endless Sleep
by Amanda Rud - age 14

A sad and frightened girl lived all alone,
Never to let her fear be shown.
She is constantly reminded of her past
With haunting memories that always last.

Her parents were murdered not long ago
By a friend they came to know.
Now the lonely girl is always looking around
For the fear she will one day be found.

The little girl stays in the house all day,
She sits and stares and continues to pray.
She hopes the murderer will go to jail,
If only her prayers do not fail.

The nights are filled with many dreams
Nothing goes right, or so it seems.
In her sleep, she tosses and turns
While something inside her furiously burns.

The next night the vulnerable girl is again in bed,
Within a few minutes, she will be dead.
Someone is creeping in the darkened room,
The intruder silently pulls out a gun - BOOM!

Something
by Jay Ruiz - age 16

Laying in the dark
Pictures starring at me
My cat asleep at the foot of my bed
The power of Prozac pumping tremors
in my head

I watch as my soul leaves me
"good-bye!"
My body goes numb
no glow in my brown eyes
Sanity and insanity twisted and pushed together by a big yellow string

I stand at the mirror to see if my sadness shows
Nothing ever works when your fifteen
and laying in bed Prozac pumping tremors
in my head
street corners, coffee shops, writing poetry in my room
All just a fairytale bound to come to an end

Summer
by Jamie Sroczynski - age 11

How summer flies,
Bye and bye
Like the wind
A gentle sigh

The morning comes alive,
With birds in the trees
The sky big and blue,
Like a million seas

The afternoon comes
I swing from the loft
Landing in the grass,
Fresh and soft

Then the night falls
Each star a firefly
Summer has gone,
Bye and bye

Death
by Dina Schlauch - age 14

Waiting
You are waiting for Death, inviting Death,
longing for Death to come take you away
Away from this world, of emptiness, darkness
Wishing for Death, begging for Death
You long for him to suck out your last drop
of love, of life, of sanity
Death
It comes for you, swallowing you, engulfing you
in a black cloud of sadness, of despair
It seeps into your being, your soul
devouring you from within
It swirls around you with a rage of evil
it will not let go until it has won
Dying
Death has come for you, Death has defeated you
He took possession of your soul, your innermost being
He guides you over, over the bridge to the world beyond
Into the fiery blaze wher, for eternity, you must remain

Future's Scene
by Andriana Saffas - age 15

Young woman
lies on the green quilted ground,
constructing an image-
nature's scene.
Sturdy Maple tree
muscled with steadfast strength,
representation of a strong love
to eventually be.
Rooted to the ground
this love will be planted.
Two fluttering leaves
blowing in God's wind,
two sweethearts envisioned,
dancing on toes of joyous delight.
Basking in sun's glorious heat,
she feels the warmth of
the arms she must wait for.
Waiting for the encounter.
Grasses of the field tickle her skin
like fingers of a lover to be.
Creativity of her mind
perceives the gaze of her foreseen true love-
an ideal in vision,
like the unwavering Sparrow's song,
in the midst of Spring.
Like hoofs of a galloping horse
her heart is bound to beat
for an emotion in material form.
Her eyes open
on future's scene.

The Night Sky Jewels
by Cora Saker - age 19

I lay down on my back
On top of the hill
In the middle of the field,
And look up at the night sky.

There are jewels in the sky.
No more than tiny pin - pricks of light,
Breaking through the vast and overwhelming darkness.

They gleam as though in the noon-day sun.
They shimmer and glimmer;
Enticing, daring me
To come closer,
To touch them and take them from the sky.

I try, hoping and praying;
Striving to that goal,
To take that dare.
Through the night I concentrate;
And when I think I just might succeed,
When I'm almost there,
They wink at me in their dark velvet bed
As it fades to the blue of day.

Promises
by Megan M. Smith - age 13

So many are made.
So many are never kept.
Promises come and go.
and leave behind a path of broken hearts.

Swimming Lessons
by Allison Salisbury - age

Pools of pain
Fill your eyes
As I dive in and
take a swim.

Yet now it's for real
You're drowning
and sinking fast
Into your fears and
Unresolved conflicts of
Yesterday.

Damn that past
As it had its way
with you once before
No need to endure it again.

They can't live without you
Even though they try to end you
But I'm here and
Won't let you drown.

Hold onto me,
your life preserver.

Heaven
by Nikki Teska - age 14

Heaven is a place that hangs over earth
A place of birth
Heaven is a place of love
Of free flying doves
Heaven is a place where mortals are blessed
A place of utmost happiness
Heaven is a place of God
Of enormous bond
Heaven is a place where children are joyful
Where everyone is delightful
Heaven is a place where everyone has wealth
A spiritual state of everlasting health

They Were Just Children
by Mandy Savard - age 15

Somewhere out there
A little girl is crying.
A gunman came to the door
Now here mother is dying.

A little boy sits silently
Desperate for a good meal.
His mother wasn't able to fed him;
Wanting help, he started to steal.

A young man of fifteen
Experimented with crack.
He takes just a little too much
Now his father desperately wants him back.

Children being hurt
Right before our eyes
Experiencing way too quickly
So many sad good-byes.

The sun may never shine again
The hurt may stay forever
They may have haunted dreams
Nightmares that won't leave ever.

After all,
They were just children.

Concealment
by Colleen Schmitt - age 17

Turn off the light
I'm your shadow in the distance: The dark washes me away
I'll follow through empty fields waiting until you notice
If the presence of a guardian makes you aware
Pick a few flowers, Petal by petal...
Tiny Forget-me-nots
Pretend to smell them close to your nose despite their lack of distinct scent
"He loves me, he loves me n-"
Rain on it's way: One-one-thousand, two-one-thousand
Are you afraid?
Last night I dreamt we built a snowman in the summer
We gave him condoms for eyes
(if only)
But crystal-white flakes didn't melt on your cheeks
Gathered in Poster-boy dimples
I'll wear a short skirt tomorrow
Will you have to leave class in a hurry?
I can spin you around, Blindfolded, Ten times
And let you try to pin the tail in the donkey
Afraid we'll laugh at you if you miss?
Don't worry so much. Things crowd your heavy mind
It's only a game, After all

Nights Terrors
by Maggie Scholleman - age 14
Margret Saylor - age 13

When you sleep lock your doors
'cause that's when the dead roams the floors
you think you're safe when you're in bed
but then your mind starts to dread
pull your sheets up over your head
pay no mind to the sound under the bed
you see the shadows all around
and soon you realize that you are bound
as you fall into a restless sleep
you think of the lives that God won't keep

When you awake at morning's dawn
you find that all the sounds are gone
you remember the terror of the night before
just to remember to lock your door

Are You Better Than A Fly, Flea, Or Bumblebee?
by Jamie Schumacher - age 13

If you think
that big is better
than tiny, small or
wee, have you
ever made a
honeycomb or ever
stung a bee?
  When you think
you're more terrific
than a lowly little
Fly, just try to
make a mighty
leap a mile into
the sky.
  If you think
that you are
tougher than an
itchy little flea
have you ever tried
to tickle it, and
make it scratch
its knee?
You may not
like it and perhaps
you'll disagree,
but some things
are done better
by a fly, flea
or bee.
So as you
go along in
life don't put
your nose in the
air, for all
creatures have a
purpose each
one beautiful
and rare.

Wounded By Love
by Rhea Schweigert - age 17

After the child departed,
From his mother's womb.
The first breath of air,
Has overcome him.
He threshes in horror,
The terror of not being warm,
Scares him.
As soon as the doctor was done,
He congratulates you.
This was a moment not forgotten,
Later intimidation sends you off.
The child you thought would pull you together,
Has suddenly turned you off.
Your child has Downs,
You are devastated
You've seen mothers with Downs babies,
But never you,
Oh no,
Your worst nightmare has come true.
Oh, oh what should you do?
You pray to God there's been a mistake.
But there was no mistake.
You live in reality,
Not a dream...

A Lifetime Of Happiness Out Of One Miracle
by Jeanell Shelton - age 10

Glistening mountain streams,
Quiet waterfalls,
A symphony of whales,
A sweet lullaby of robins,
Magical rain forests,
Ocean daybreak,
A medley of soft, gentle winds,
And
Mystic rain;
All this comfort from the sparkle of a new baby's smile
And laugh.

Reflections While Gazing Out A Car Window
by Stephanie Sellars - age 19

Flat green gives little life to the structures that it breeds standing sturdy but stricken with
the shame of longevity gone awry
Time hardens the surface chiseling away at the already weather ridden
Bark
giving little protection to the supple life inside
sun rays penetrate the decadent remnants of leaves no hope it seems no life what strife
but they reach the branches showing signs of piety praying to the Gods of growth--
Rejuvenation slows the atrophy, but only with a faint faith.

The Blank Zone
by Ann E. Shaffer

My walls are crumbling.

It is the breakdown I have been anticipating over this time.
This time of rough terrain and frozen tears,
trekked across a path of broken enemies and wounded heroes.

The distorted cry of dying spirit pierces the silence-
it is like the scream of one trapped.
One who knows about the escape,
but is bound by the chains of reality.

The trapper is real, though.
So real that I can almost touch him,
and grab him,
and make him let go.

He is living inside my head,
within me,
always.

He sucks my blood of life,
draining me of its flow.

He is selfish and needy,
taking,
and taking.
And one day I find
I have no life of my own.

He has taken it all.

Betrayal
by Wendy Shallcross - age 13

I awoke to her shrill climaxing cries
Burdened and unwanted she felt
Overworked she was
Sobs that were held in and finally released through pure frustration
Like a caged animal exiting in sheer rage
Escaping through time of neglect and helplessness
She sobbed all night
Screaming as death itself
Hysteria entered
She expressed her loathe in blunt, sweared feelings
Of other's selfish actions through un-chained cries that droned on for hours
I wanted to comfort her, make her calm again
But the correct response never entered my mind
So I listened intently feeling her pain strike through my flesh
Finally, he himself entered the down cast room
He said the key things
He calmed her into a soft hushed sleep
She laid there like an infant in perfect content until her rage caught up with her again
She screamed like a banshee into the bleak night
Without return.

Psychedelic Roller-Coaster
by Alexis Shaver - age 13

First a snort, then a shot;
you start out fine, but then your not.
A good trip, then a bad one.
Your heart speeds up and then your done.
No fooling, dude, I know what I know,
Gleaming white headstones,
planted row by row.

Silvery Moonlight
by Nicole S.K. Shams - age 13

Silvery moonlight,
Filtered through the branches of a tree.
Cutting through the night,
Calling to me.

Memories unfold,
Bringing back things forgotten.
Stories untold,
That my mind gets lost in.

Past, present, and future flash before my eyes,
Night breezes play a haunting melody.
Different people in different times,
How my mind soars free!

I awaken at my window,
Full of memories I cannot ignite.
A forgotten dream of happiness and sorrow,
All caused by silvery moonlight.

A Memory Past
by Nichole Sierra - age 15

I look to the shadows of the past
and think of a life to 40 that didn't last.
He was divorced and jobless,
he had one daughter but knew she couldn't clean up his mess.
Drugs and alcohol were how he dealt with stress,
and this was not the first time he tried to take eternal rest.
At his sister's farm he did it, just with a rope,
he felt ending his life would be the best way to cope.
He hurt many for I knew them all,
all because he had to break his fall.
So, to you this may sound tragic and sad.
It is, but that was the life of....
     my dad.

Dedicated to my Daddy

Make Believe
by Ana Sprenger - age 13

Walk must I to cross the overbearing depths
of my soul and a make believe world to get a
grip on reality.
Yet I try and fail to complete my endless task to
overcome dragons, sorcerers, wizards, and elves
on my fantastic journey home-
but where is home, the home that I know and hate
for it's harshness.
Here in my make believe world I am what I wish
and content I am forever.
So there the task ends and imagination,
my imagination is ruler of all.

Do You Care
by Cammy Shelton - age 16

Standing face to face with eye
contact to mine,
you seem to act like everything's
fine.
But something missing, somethings
just not there,
is it me or is this love
unfair.
Although I ask you say nothings
wrong.
I wish through these times
that I could stay strong.
I often wonder if it were
just you and me how would
life be, I blame myself for
your actions but it's really
not me.
My heart lingers for you
to understand,
Do you think it'd make
you weak or less a man?
It is so much for me
to ask that you'd only care,
to trust my words and
always be there.
I'm not asking for all
your time or for you to call everyday.
Just for you to love me and listen
to what I say.
Although, by my side you'll
always be there,
I often wonder, do you really care?

Waiting In The Dark
by Jennifer Short - age 13

Lurking in the corners,
at every turn,
there is a predator,
Only in you does it burn.
Waiting in the dark,
waiting to attack.

Through stormy doors,
its shadow crosses by,
mellow is your voice,
faint to its eye.
Waiting in the dark,
waiting to attack.

On every corner,
on every sidewalk,
it will be there,
forcing you to talk.
Waiting in the dark,
waiting to attack.

In every tunnel,
in every state of mind,
it jumps ahead of you,
Leaving you behind.
Until the silence breaks,
it waits just waits.

When it comes out,
Disaster becomes you,
becoming a dominate emotion,
it chews you into
NO longer waiting.
NO longer in the dark.

Consequences
by Celena Shouse-Bland - age 19

Beads of sweat danced on my face
Painfully trickling into my eyes
Blinding me from the outside world
While inside I grew wise.

Vibrant colors danced and flashed
Hypnotizing away the pain
And I had everything to lose
And I had everything to gain.

The moon and stars were masked by clouds -
My desperate effort to deprive
The world from my thoughts had failed
For I was still alive.

Too many walls and I was trapped
Exposed beneath the burning light
And how could I have been so wrong
And at the same time been so right.

Inside my heart and mind I cried
The tears slid softly down my face
The rain was falling from the sky,
My teardrops kept the pace.

Now broken, their restrictive rules
Destroying all that I once had
But how could I have been so good
And how could I have been so bad.

Leanna Kicked Me Monday
by Elyse Sklar - age 11

Leanna kicked me Sunday
and she kicked me Monday, too,
she also kicked me Tuesday,
I didn't know what to do.

She kicked me double Wednesday
and Thursday three times more,
but when she kicked me friday,
she kicked me through the door.

"This can't go on," I growled at her.
"It's terrible how you kicked me."
"Well then I'll stop," Leanna said
On Saturday she flicked me.

The Pain Inside
by Becca Shubert - age 15

It's about time I just stop trying,
I just end up alone and crying.
It seems as nobody cares,
There's nobody there to answer my prayers.
It's as if it doesn't matter how I feel,
Everyone acts like my tears aren't real.
The pain's inside, it hurts so much,
It's something no one can touch.
I won't let anyone close enough to sooth the pain,
I feel like I'm drowning in the pouring rain.
Dark oceans are crashing over me,
I only wish to be let free.
Somebody take me out of this hole,
Where people have trapped my dying soul.
I can't break free, I can't even try,
All I can do is sit here and cry.
My mind can't take the pain inside,
There isn't even somewhere I can go to hide.
I'm not sure I'd even be missed,
If I were to cease to exist.

To My Mom, With Love
by Samantha Sills - age 18

The first time I opened my eyes,
you were there.
I looked up at you
And hoped you would care
To keep me safe
From all my fears
For when I cried,
You wiped away my tears.
You've taught me to be considerate,
To show others respect.
Your loving ways towards me
Had such a great effect.
You are my mom,
And I will love you until the end.
There's no better way to say it;
You are my best friend.

Summers Past
by Alicia Smith - age 14

Bittersweet memories of
summers past,
days long gone; flown by so fast.

Sweet lilting notes of a
tune heard long ago,

Soft words whispering
of times I used to know.

Melancholy remembrance of
tides that carried me,

To the threshold of tomorrow
in dreams that could not be.

Shadows teased and tormented me,
As autumn's leafy fingers crushed
summer's dreams so forcefully.

Her gentle caress floating
down from each tree,

A last farewell to summer
and the memories it gave to me

The Man Next Door
by Monica Smith - age 16

He moved next door one day
during the winter when everything
seemed so hopeless and ordinary. Then
we met and an instant friendship grew. We
were best friends. And by the way we acted,
everybody knew. We went through a lot of hard
times that were very sad, but we were always there
for each other to see it through. Then one day it happened
It was quite a shock for us, but all of our friends said they
knew it would come sometime soon. It was that one special
kiss; it sparked a flame that would burn within our hearts
through all laughter and pain. Never would we take our
love for granted. Everyday lived, made more special
than the day before by a love between us that
would never end.

Love & Hate
by Michael Smith - age 17

Love and hate
Are like hot and cold
Opposites
Like young and old

Neither is stronger
Than the other
They can't exist
Without one another

Love has warmth
While hate has heat
Someone with neither
I have yet to meet

The Power Of Man
by Nicole Smith - age 16

The kiss that follows the dream of man
To have the hunger of power in his hands
The reality of destruction causing man to fall down on his knees and beg for mercy
Causing his eyes to open up and realize what a mess he had made of himself
For he strives to become a better person inside
Can he do it
We may never know
Someone hiding a secret from him
On the account of trust he may never know the secret
He seeks the fruit of rightioness
Instead he is leading the wrong direction of life
Let there be happiness he said let there be no more hate
Instead of love
As he thinks about it he knows this may never happen
He said it out loud with his soul
Not with his heart
For he is confused man
A confused man he said out loud himself
As he looks up to the sky he realizes maybe there is a reason for being on this earth
And he just said maybe to himself

Unimagined
by Cindy Sockwell - age 14

A waste,
like the water dripping from the faucet through the night,
while the light in the hall shines for a child in the dark,
afraid of shadows seen by no eyes but the mind's.
I stare into the stars
for some unimagined comfort.
There is no consequence of my living,
I'm just here to view the crowd.
I can understand the child
whose eyes dart around in fear,
as he clutches to the sheets
though they're not any consolation.
No one reaches out to him,
though he clearly needs their help.
He is just another person
not worth another thought.
I can understand his fear
of reaching out for help.
He knows it's just no use.
He knows just to forget it.
He knows it's just a waste,
like his unimagined life.

Please Be With Me
by Hanna Song - age 14

Big smile
Beautiful eyes-

You smiled
when I grumbled at you

You shed tears
when I left our country

Our love
-stronger than anything else
-I believed

Someday last year
You stopped to send letters.
-I kept blaming you.

After 6 months,
-Called your house to say "Happy Birthday"

I could only hear your mom's
tearful voice.

When I saw you later,
You were smiling
-in the black ribbon.

Your mom gave me a diary
-which was full of my name.

Someone Will Help Us
by Jessica Soto - age 15

A shadow in the night,
People in the light.
I have so much fear,
but I will not show the fright.

A tear runs down my cheek,
A tear that cannot speak.
Oh help me dear lord for I
heard a frightening shriek.

My eyes are filled with gloom;
I shall hide out in my room.
Oh what will we do;
there is too much doom.

I feel the hurt and pain.
This world is going to drain.
So much violence on this planet,
what else is there to do?

I cannot do anything,
for I am to young.
But maybe someday
there will be someone,
to guide us and show us
what needs to be done.

We will have to wait,
for it will take a while.
But I'm sure there is
someone so worthwhile.

To You
by Virginia L. Spencer

The summer slips by,
and winter begins.
The good times go,
and so do the friends.

Many of them have come and gone;
some stayed a year or two.
A few have been through the bad times,
but no one means as much to me as you.

I thank you from the bottom of my heart
for all that you are to me.
A friend all year round.
the way a friend should be.

You've helped me turn my world around
through the hardships and the pain.
You've picked me up when I've felt down;
now I've nothing left to gain.

You've given me a friend,
someone I can trust.
You've given me hope, respect, and love;
You've given me so much!

There's not a person alive today,
who's helped me through it all like you.
No one who's helped my sorrow fade away,
the way that only you can do.

You mean the world to me,
for all you're said and done.
And as far as true friends go,
you're my only one.

Last To Be
by Carrie Waters - age 15

Last to be,
the one to see,
everything that's been here.
Last to be,
your one true love,
and now that's everything
Last to be,
the owner of your heart,
and there is nothing they can say.
Last to be,
the one for me,
because this is for forever.

Sandwich
by Beth Stetzler

Smack, dab in the middle of a threesome love affair. One day you'll pay for the mini I put on my charge, which you don't know I've got Hepatitis B because I sleep around, but only once, so don't patronize me because you get high too much on Acid rain comes out of the clouds above my head Ache after getting drunk at another man's party, He showed me his pierced navel, which you haven't got a clue that I'm creeping behind your back side view of my body you'll see as I turn away from your hand that intends to slap some sense into My brain is fried from too much Excedrin in My medicine cabinet is filled with expensive beauty products to look better than I feel I should get out of the middle before I'm smooshed like ham between two pieces of bread smothered with cheese.

Fallen Redwood
by Emily Spiegel - age 12

A redwood stood here, long ago,
Where now the moss and mushroom grow.
When it fell, twas one life's end
But from it many more began.

The mice that skitter through the fog
Are thankful for that redwood log.
The roots uprooted by the fall
Are home to many creatures small.
Birds and bugs feed off that tree
Where moss and lichen can be seen.
Up above's a blackbird clan;
Down below's a beaver's dam.
And all these critters lives revolve
Around a rotting redwood log.

This wood lies here
For us to see
That in the midst of death
In life are we.

Magic Mirror
by Amy Stanford - age 13

Use a magic mirror to gaze into time,
A gloomy day at nine o' clock in 1865.
John Wilkes Booth was waiting,
With a very clever plan,
And a gun he anxiously loaded, in his sweaty hands,
He peeked through the tiny hole,
The goodness still in Lincolns soul.
At five after ten Booth showed his sin.
With people crowded at the door,
A doctor stood to reassure.
"It is tragic", he once said,
"It went right through the back of his head."
They carried him right through the middle of the street,
And up the spiral staircase carefully moving their feet.
At seven twenty two am, the people gathered to
bury him.
Use a magic mirror to gaze into time,
A gloomy day at nine o'clock in 1865.

Finding Yourself
by Julie Stanford

Finding yourself is a lonely journey,
walking out of the land of familiar.
Faces and places are seen with new eyes,
you don't look the same in the mirror.

As a stranger, you're feeling subtle changes,
answers are falling into place.
You stare in amazement as hidden meanings
appear right in front of your face.

"Come with me on this trip of discovery,
experiencing this must be shared.
Wonderful things are beginning to happen,
understandings are floating on air!"

Turning to look, why they're all behind you,
weren't they just here at your side?
You wonder if you should rest or slow down,
the distance is growing too wide.

"Oh please hurry, won't you, I'm waiting for you,
it's lonely without you beside me.
Please won't you join me for I can't go back,
can't return to where I used to be."

Think
by Ashley Steedman - age 13

Have you ever stopped to notice
The little things in life?
The flowers, the trees, the birds, the bees.
The sun, the moon, the stars in the sky.

Now think for just a minute
On what I talk about
Think of all the beauty that surrounds you
On the inside and out.

But think again of the other things
The hunger, the death, the pain
All these things that no one likes
But yet they're here, by day and night

Think of that child you saw on the corner of the street
The one with cancer, the one with AIDS
Think of what you wanted to say
When the parentless child came your way.

The children that have to steal to stay alive
The ones who call a park bench home
The ones who go to church
With holes in their very best Sunday clothes

Now think again of your children
All the new toys you bought them yesterday
Of the brand new Easter dress and suit
That only the wealthy could afford

Have you ever really wondered
Why they have so little and you have so very much?
Well, stop and give a second thought
And find out what you can do for them

The Thorn and the Rose
by Kelly Steele - age 18

As the water gently caresses the sand
And the wind blows through the trees
I gazed beyond the hollow distance
To see her slowly fall to her knees

Through the shadows, upon Heaven's wings
A savior comes to her aid
Gallant and brave he sweeps her up
Unaware of who stands in the shade

She is like a rose, and he a thorn
Coming together in the skies above
But they did not see the darkening clouds
That could end their new-found love

The shaded figure stepped into the light
To draw his love away from the rose
But he turned away from the shinning gold
As his eyes began to close

The thorn felt trapped between the gold and the rose
For they both loved him the same
But as he looked into the heart of the gold
He was overcome with feelings of shame

He couldn't tell her what she longed to hear
And deep in her heart she knows
That no matter how bright the gold will shine
The thorn belongs with the rose

A Lost Friend
by Adrienne Stephan - age 15

Given to me to love cherish, and hold
Given to me when we both were helpless
Given to me when we didn't know right from wrong.
Given to a baby was a baby.
We still needed love and affection.
We sat many of days in that hot, summer sun,
    thinking that life would never end.
Oh those time didn't change.
As we got older, our hearts not turned colder,
    they bloomed with even more love and need.
When I got sick you were always there for me to hold.
When something needed told I always knew you wouldn't tell.
We got older together, maturing in our own ways,
    but our love towards each other didn't change.
You got to a point that everyone gets to someday,
You got sick of being this old age.
I know you weren't sick of me, nor I of you,
But God had other plans for you.
Perhaps they are to look over me each and everyday.
But if they are not, I know that He has a reason for everything
    and His reason to take you from me must have been
    great indeed.
For that love that we had was better than any "real" friend
So I guess this is Good-bye,
We will be together again when He decides to bring
    me to you so we can meet again in that beautiful,
    shining sky.
No wonder they call you "Man's Best Friend".

The End.
by Rebecca Sullivan - age 12

You've come to the halt
not knowing not thinking
wondering how you got there
you think and marvel
then you fade away
like erasing chalk from a chalkboard

Numbed but content
with this partial loose
only with a vivid memory
of weeping souls and
grieving hearts
of people at a cemetery

The War
by Vanessa Stevenson - age 13

In our hideout we remain
All must be quiet, can't even play a game
Fear of being caught is always on our mind
Why Hitler must do this, why commit this crime?
All crammed in a tiny little space
Because being Jewish is our race
Very little food, almost none at all
We pray to God that we will remain healthy and tall
Sounds of kids on the street, playing with their toys
Giggling sounds of little girls and boys
Every once in a while we would hear a scream
Sometimes wishing that it was only a dream
No shower, only a very small sink
Not even a pen that hasn't run out of ink
Keeping a journal was all I had to do
Expressing my thoughts all the way through
We never knew what was going on there
Until someone told us, thoughts I could not bare
Always wishing that it would end
When it did it left me but not one friend

The Tree
by Jesica Stoll - age 13

Calmness, serenity
Peaceful whimpers
A mid-summer's mourn.
Going,
not to be seen again.
Going,
from body of souls.
Gone,
Life's labor lost,
Lost.
Leaving to the sky above. Descending form on high.
From the flames of hell, To the gates of love.
Descending, descend,
as God's dove. Cries for love,
Cries of help.
Straight.
Straight form a pure man's body.
To the un-pure soul, the soul of love.
The single soul, above and beyond.
The tree of life, we are all leaves.
Our family tree.
Branches are our family, limbs are friends,
Trunks of labor, roots so strong,
Love's labor.
Grow, grow, grow!
From the ground, to the sky below the gates of love.
As God's dove, carries a branch in it's bill.
To spread our family, through the forest.
Become a seed,
and grow.

No Cause For Alarm
by Michelle A. Strickland - age 15

I've seen life's breath leave
A body young in years.
I've watched the sun fade,
Heard aimless, pointless gunshots,
Sympathized without having felt the pain.
No cause for alarm, I'm just learning
To appreciate my life.

I've seen a lifetime's work
Sacrificed to a storm,
An all-consuming fire,
A flood's devastation.
I've seen the eyes of a starving child.
No cause for alarm, I'm just learning
To find joy in what I have.

I've heard of awful crimes
That surpass my worst nightmares.
Cringed at the description.
I've seen great loss first-hand,
And recognized the face of poverty.
No cause for alarm, I'm just learning
What it's like to feel blessed.

The Box
by Naomi Tacuyan - age 15

Kept in the dark confines of this.
Reality distorted, all's lost in empty space.
Craving for the light of the outside world,
Silent screams on deaf ears, fists tightly curled.
All is lost in rage, sadness, anger.
As in the shadows, odious thoughts I ponder.

Night Dancers
by Andrea Stout

Softly, warmly, eerily,
the moon casts its light down.
Twisting, reaching, stretching,
they slowly come alive with movement
Frolicking, dancing, skipping
they gleefully play in the soft moonlight.
Laughing, giggling, whispering,
they talk with joyful, merry words.
Questioning, asking, wondering,
you inquire, who are these creatures?
Mysteriously, quietly, patiently,
I answer you, these are the wood nymphs, the
spirits of the trees, the night dancers.

I Sit in the Shadows
by Tonia L. Strohmeyer

I sit in the shadows of a cruel world
I know the future is dark
The shadows of this cruel world
Cover me and many more
As we sit here
We are cooled by the hatred
And blocked by the sin
We know no warmth any more
For it has all faded away
And left our cruel world to hide behind the masks
These masks are what we call our identity
We are all no longer one
And now in this world that used to be joyful
We are many sad shadows
That block out the light
And I sit in the shadows

To My Mother
by Gretchen Strohm

My heart has been broken
More times than I can count.
My pride and what little self esteem
I could find over the years
Is constantly challenged,
By cruel words and scornful glances
From people who will never quite understand me.
Then you came.
You came and picked up
The shattered remains of my heart,
And with soft caring hands
Molded it into something beautiful.
You are my true friend.
You are always there to hold me
When I think I can't go on.
You give me the strength to find my way,
With hands to hold me
Eyes that look at me with care
A smile that shows me your love.
Even though there are times when
I am upset with you
You never stop loving me
You are always there for me to lean on.
To hold me and tell me things are alright
And for this I thank you.
And hope to someday be able to repay you for the love
You always and will always feel for me. I love you.

Stranger's Walk
by Kerri Swanson - age 16

The stranger walked slowly, languidly into the room
unseen, unheard, unfelt
among the blowing silks draped in the moonlight
He is waiting to take us in this hour of death
to his holy place of rest
My life passes through and over my glassy eyes
unseen in the dark
on the beach, unclothed
Swimming gently through the waves of
unknown pleasures
naked on the shore of calm
freely floating, laughing
It is time to choose, to come or go
Which way to go
Below the sands of desert winds
Along the dunes of soft plateaus and curves
My feet sink and glide through the vastness
to the lake
unseen, unknown
The lake comes out of the valley of dunes
And surprises us in the light
Through this land of time
we soar down and through the tall grass
and lush green
Slow deaths of our spiral downward
We climbed back through the grass and shrubs
of those past and gone
Up and through this strange walk...

The Teddy Bear
by Elizabeth Tanzini - age 14

The room of a little girl,
Empty now, and dusty
With its stale air and rotting hardwood floor,
Was once overflowing with care and joy and love and dreams.

In the early morning hours,
The darkness lifts slowly, as a curtain,
Engulfing the room in a sea of light.
As dusk falls, the curtain closes,
Leaving the room blanketed in darkness,
Void of light.

Through it all, in day and in night,
As the years pass by,
And dust collects, cobwebs form,
A little figure sits huddled in a corner.

The Teddy Bear sits, as he was left
With his smile still smiling,
His eyes still shining,
And his fuzzy little paws still at his sides.

Waiting, waiting, for the little girl who left him here
To come back, to play with him, to hold him,
To kiss him, and to cherish him as she once had.
He has not forgotten, but has she?

Untitled
by Robin Tarter - age 13

every day
as I sit at my desk
I see over the tops of houses
a little path
on a small hill
with grass the color of autumn leaves
growing tall around it

and as I watch my little path
I dream of climbing
and standing atop the small hill
as the sun
abandons its last golden rays
and runs like a frightened child
to hide behind the horizon

and I dream that I look down
and see my window
and the little garden
that grows wildly
on my roof
and I see myself
sitting at my desk
and wish that I was home again

Daddy, I wish You Were Here
by Latisha Wang - age 12

When I think of you I realize that you will never be there
to pat me on the shoulder for a job well done, I shed a tear.
When I know you won't even hear about a question whispered in my
ear by a boy I like, I shed a tear, knowing that if you were
here you would care. You won't walk me down the aisle to my loved
one, or be a grandfather to my children. It is when I think
about these things that I wish you were here just to be....DADDY.

Cycles Of The Seasons
by Sheena Taylor - age 17

Cold, wet snow reaches ground
Lightly falling--without a sound
Soft, thick snow makes the world white
Everything hidden in a beautiful sight
Temperatures rise, then the ice melts
Less and less chill is now felt
Buds of green have started to grow
Animals are beginning to show
The sky becomes a vivid blue
Bringing with it many hues
To encourage growth the rains arrive
Making everything alive
The sun's rays are greater--intense
And the air is more dense
Breeze increases, leaves change shades
Life, once again begins to fade
Trees are left bare, grass turns brown
Cold, wet snow reaches ground

The Rose
by Kristina Teaster

The rose is hidden beneath your soul,
an unopened bud, a seed
set aglow.

The rose is a beautiful thing; it fills
your life with pleasure and
joy, and most of the
time it isn't a
ploy.

It's to make you feel better or
show you are loved, and
everyone deserves the
feeling of love.

In order to love, you must understand
you can't buy love. It's like trust-
hard to earn, but easy
to lose. And once
you have lost
it, it's hard
to get
again.

So open your heart and let
it in, a rose to show
you'll love
again.

Not A Ladies Man
by Daniel Teeples - age 19

i wandered in the desert with the hot wind moaning
like a prophet's prophecies but i heeded not the warnings
and i was tortured by a thirst and a million starving vultures
along came a gender that condemned me as unfit for love
and buried my corpse in the shallow dry sand
but i rose from my grave to punish
not a ladies man

i stayed for sometime in a broken sad motel
in a dangerously strange forgotten pit of hell
and i was famished not a dollar to my dying name
i drank in empty bars with my back to every wall
devising many a vengeful plan
i filled the painted whores with horror
not a ladies man

and quite a lovely vampire i was to kiss
naked and still waiting in a deadly bliss
and i was drained to the vein by the hunger that she held
and i was enslaved by the vicious bitch
and beaten by her razored hand
but the servant must sometimes bite back
not a ladies man

i arrived in the gender's town with my guns at my side
feeding off the hatred and violence kept inside
and they may have been forgivable but i could not forgive
then i chanced upon a woman that i longed for at length
she stared into my eyes saw the killer and ran
well, i shot her in the back i guess i'm
not a ladies man

Obsession
by Jay Therrien - age 19

Give me one last chance to touch a heart of stone
to feel the cold of the once beloved.
The death of life living for the last trivial time,
torching flames flicker out if I cannot be you.

Give me one last chance to lie in your soul of sin
to feel the destruction of the once adored.
Luminous tales of truthful betrayal's shower flesh,
icicle rains turn to knifes of blood if I cannot be you.

Give me one last chance to love your body of poison
to feel the ecstacy of the breath once yearned.
Circling endless in sweetness of affection's barred lust,
blustering winds push boundaries of steel if I cannot be you

Give me one last chance to possess a mind of corruption
to feel the confusion of the games once ignored.
Plummeting down the barrel of fools, crying into nonsense,
blood on my wrists slashing grievance out if I cannot be you
blood on my wrists if I cannot see you,
blood on my fists if I cannot have you,
blood on my mind if I cannot love you-

Give me one last chance if I cannot be you...

The Beast
by Jamie Thomas - age 17

Silently he lingers about the room.
She is scared at the sight of the monster within,
He plays the part really well.
Charming and devinare he may seem.
Laughing politely at everyone' jokes and smiling.
When he is angry something happens, and internal struggle
between two people it seems.
He changes and howls like the wind in a violent storm.
What is it that lingers inside him to make him this way.
Why just one wrong word, and then she'll have to pay.
The slightest of movements can make this thing inside come
out.
What is this thing and why does it plague so many?
Is there any answers to my question, my cries?
Are there any solutions and why does this happen?
She cries out as she sits in a dark corner of her bedroom.
What does this all mean?
And oh Lord won't someone help me tame this beast.

Storm
by Rose Wiser - age 14

As the day passes slowly,
dark clouds cover the sky.
While the wind blows cold
and hard, trees shudder
and quake.
While birds silence their
song and dead leaves swirl
and land on the road.

The Truth
by Kevin Thrush - age 19

Tis again Easter day,
And this world I dare say.

Has brought me eggs and bunny,
Baskets filled with yummy to fill my tummy.

But underneath this world's flare,
It has forgotten how their true Father cares.

But I'm glad I saw through it all,
And found the truth beneath it all.

Of the Father, the Lord, the God,
He who made me from the sod.

Many have forgotten about this day,
All covered up with Easter Day.

I will tell you about the real Easter day,
Listen to these words and do not delay.

The Son of Man he was thirty-three,
Died on a cross to set us free.

But when this day came three days later,
He stepped from the grave full of laughter.

For he knew it was over,
And that we could live with him forever.

Within the glorious heavens above,
Where there is always love.

And so this I say,
Do not forget this day.

And I pray for you,
You will seek Him too.

The Exile
by David Tilden - age 16

I walked through the summer's warm embrace
Content to let the path lead my way
My step contented I slowed my pace
As I walked through the warm sunlit day

One day I walked right into fall
The chill wind mocking my step
The trees above me formed a hall
Under which I slept

When one morning my hair was white with frost
I knew I had travelled into winters grasp
I long for home and hearth I'd lost
The trees through the snow some phantoms ship's mast

When spring came once more
My path became a highway lined with windflowers
My mind wandered to days of yore
I longed for my home its gardens its towers

Summer brought forth around the paths bend
A line of footprints stretching ahead into seasons
No home no journey's end
I kept walking ahead for unvoiced reasons

The Bird In A Cage
by Jennifer Tobin - age 16

She sees life through bars
The bars he has placed upon her
Bars that restrict everything that she does
That she could do
Everything that she is
How does it feel
I often wonder
Do you like the cage?
Do you like the limitation?
How does the world look from behind those bars?
Once you knew a freedom
A freedom like nothing else
A time when you knew no limits
A time when you could travel as far
and as high as your wings would take you
A time when you could soar
Do you miss it?
I imagine you do
for I can hear your song
Of the caged bird singing
I just want to know
If the door to the cage was open
Would you remember how to fly?

"Woe"
by Maggie Torsney-Weir - age 14

The black wind whistles
Through the wood.
All is lost
And none is good.

Oh, my sweet!
You bore my woe.
Your voice was like
The roses that grow.

The death that sweeps
Across the moor,
Comes once again
To our door.

The mud and dirt
Reeks of decay.
It's poured o'er your grave.
How much more must I pay?

At last I feel
My soul tearing apart.
Like a dog, I weep,
For I've lost my heart.

Ended
by Jocelyn Vegter - age 15

Can you behold my torment by dint of opalescent eyes
I am touched, I am sane
Could you discern my petty desire for the transparent fury
I am numbness, I am pain.

Could you play last notes of old sorrow upon my fateful death
I am fractioned, I am strong
Could you call for me with new meaning other than dead life
I stayed away, I came along.

Could you cease my struggle for the final sip of my own wind
I am teeming, I am one
Could you hold strong love for me buried deep in mind's oblivion
I have ended just begun.

An Obstacle Called Trust
by Paula Townsend - age 16

Through the gate and
onto the bridge, then
to the mailbox
to back through the
L. He shies at every
object.

A jump to the left
at the gate, short
quick steps away
from the bridge, a
cold stare to the mailbox.

Easy, easy boy, she
tells him. He starts
to relax knowing that
she will protect him.
He backs through the
L almost Perfectly.

He trusts her she
doesn't know why.
He wants to please
her, her will is
his command.

Her family is almost
broke, just to keep
the most important
man in her life,
her horse, in oats.

They are together
all the time, or
as much as she
can spare. He needs
and hungers her
attention.

He is the one who
keeps her going,
he is the one thing,
that she lives for.

War Games
by Darin Traff - age 14

The pieces are all set up
and now it's our move.
Everyone is ready
now what are we to do?
The players, they are excited
that they finally get to fight
to prove what they've been training for
and to release all of their might.
At last, it is their turn,
time to figure what to do
Taking a turn to load their weapons
and to see who hits who.
Ready to pay the highest price
to put right where once was wrong.
Going on to check things out
while whistling a patriotic song.
The area seems to be clear
so they keep on moving ahead.
Suddenly, there is a crash
all of the soldiers are dead.

Dreams
by Rachel Troxle - age 17

It's night again,
the dreams will come.
Of forgiveness and sin,
and things I have done.

Dreams of happiness,
dreams of hate.
Dreams of lovliness,
dreams of my fate.

Dreams are like flowers,
wilting fast.
They come for hours,
but they are not to last.

Life is but a dream,
Sadly, not to last.
Life is but a dream,
here and gone just as fast.

To Be Different
by Kate Walker - age 14

Let them be as rivers.
Always moving the way the wind takes them.
Never stopping for a breath.

I would rather be a lake.
Smooth and calm at all times.
Staying in one place, and always knowing where I am.

The smooth sand below is much more comforting
than the jagged rocks and boulders.
The lake is quiet and calm.
The river is loud and overwhelming.
So I say let them be as rivers, but I,
I will be a lake.

Living In Fear
by Patricia van der Wal - age 15

It creeps into our young lives,
Like an animal stalking it's prey.
It grows bigger and bigger everyday;
It haunts our lives like a plague but worse.
Fear, that's what it is.
The guns, the drugs, the alcohol, the gangs.
Our parents and peers abuse us,
Like they think that it's alright.
Well IT'S NOT, it hurts.
Our parents say that these are the best years of our lives.
I used to think that I wanted to be an adult.
Now that I think about it,
If these are the best years of our lives,
Then I don't want to grow up.

Silence
by Jaime Turek - age 15

Silence fills the world around me.
Nothing stirs or wakes.
Everything is frozen
Until this silence breaks.

I turn to see a shadow
That rises against the wall.
The shadow creeps up slowly
Then begins to fall.

I wonder up beside it
To see what lyes on the ground.
The silence has awaken,
Now to Hell I'm bound.

I've been struck with some strange feeling
That silence cannot cure.
I cannot feel the silence,
Never, forever more.

This silence which I know not of
Cannot break through the light.
I know it is not day,
So where is the night?

Frozen in everything around me,
I start to feel so weak.
Chills run down my spine.
My chance of surviving is bleak.

Silence stirs again
As I waken unto tomorrow,
To find a brand new day
Shaken to my sorrow.

Runaway
by Christine Tyson

You say they don't listen
    don't especially care
So how could it be worse
    on the streets out there?

But what you don't know, Red,
    is that the wolves are out.
They can smell fresh blood
    and they're ready to pounce.

They trick and they treat
    and they sneak right in.
They steal your conscience
    and sell your skin.

All those strange faces,
    so many greedy eyes.
They all blur together
    in the walk of the night.

Your soul is on fire,
    your dreams are haunted.
But your out on your own,
    isn't this what you wanted?

Rain Child
by Patricia Underwood - age 16

Lost little girl,
reborn in the rain

Drowning in puddles,
no escaping her pain

Her body so numb
her spirit so weak

Swimming in tears
struggling to speak

She arose to the sky,
it, then fades to grey

Flashes of memories,
all drift away

Lost little girl,
Who no longer can see

If you shall die now
you weren't meant to be

Soon you'll relive
and start all again

Now rise little child,
for now it's the end.

Childhood Cancer Revisited
by Jessica Valentine - age 18

Just a baby,
With a baby's dreams,
They said Sarcoma,
Whatever that means.

I grew up fast,
Overnight if you will,
With tubes and machines,
And pill after pill.

Weeks and months passed,
So far from home.
Weight gained and nausea,
No hair to comb.

But happy we were,
Joyful we stayed,
Winning the game
Death with us played.

Now, years later,
I'm almost grown.
A lump and some aches
Make my life their own.

A recurrence, a relapse?
Oh please not me.
So I pray to God
On bended knee.

Each day that I live
Will not be the last,
And the future so dear
Will one day be past.

The Light
by Annamarie VanGundy - age 13

They say everyone has a light,
But I can't find yours.

I'm running in a tangle of darkness.
Things are grabbing at my hair and clothes,
Trying to pull me back into the darkness
That surrounds me.

Then I see up ahead there's a dark red.
So excited I think maybe that's the light,
And in my joy, I cry "it's not black!"

I'm rushing toward it and I'm almost there.
But then I'm trapped
The red is so close I can see it;
I can even feel it,
But I just can't touch it.

It's pulling me back! It's pulling me back into the darkness
Away from my beloved light.
"Let me go, please!" I scream,
Kicking and fighting with all my might to get free.
But it's not letting go, you won't let me go!"

But the black twisted shapes won't let go.
And giving up I know that soon I'll be
A lost soul traveling through darkness.

I will have become just like you, dark and lost.

Real or Not
by Addrean Walker - age 14

Spirits, ghost, goblins, gools.
Are they real or are they fool?
Are they just tall, tall tells or from
　　the darkest rems of hell?
Do they want to harm us or to
　　joke around?
Do they want our help or to be left
　　alone?
What do they want does anyone
　　know?
What do we see on the cold, damp
　　night of October 31?
Are they dreams or hallucinations?
Was it a spirit, ghost, goblin or gool?
Are they real or are we all just fools?

Mr. Sneed
by Kristy Vernon - age 15

In the last time,
the fruits from life
like lemons and lime.
Mr. Sneed was in your
eyes and hearts
and minds.
Sitting slump and pretty;
to the man who thinks
he knows, he does not
notice.
Mr. Sneed, with his snide
stride,
and an offbeat on his drum
is only lonely.
Bitter and hoarse
he'll drop you with his
voice coarse!
Because he is you
and all of the things
we pull with our strings
of spice.

Waterfall Of Life
by Jessica L. Vogel - age 16

　　　Life is like a waterfall,
　　　A never-ending story,
　　　Moving on and on and on,
　　Never stopping for any glory.

　　　People are like branches,
　　That have fallen from a tree,
　　　To float on the waterfall,
　　That might send you out to sea.

　　　This waterfall is greedy,
　　This waterfall does not care,
　　　It wants as many tree limbs,
　　There's nothing in it that is fair.

　　So be careful on your journey,
　　　Hold on very tight,
　　This silent but mighty waterfall
　　　Will put up quite a fight.

My Past
by Catherine Waite - age 17

　　My heart is lonely my soul is bare, my pain begins to swell.
　　My fears are strong I cannot hide, I live here in my hell.
　　My hours are numbered, how much longer I'll last I can't tell.
　　My life is quickly fading, I simply cannot stay, no one can hear my silent yell.
　　My mind is weary my body cannot heal, I'm getting tired and slipping fast.
　　If only there was an easy way, to take away my shame, a way to erase my awful past.
　　But wait what is this I see before me, two wounded hands outstretched and waiting?
　　Asking me to give him my life, to stop my hesitating.
　　A tiny light begins to shine where once darkness used to dwell.
　　These wounded hands want to save me from this person I used to call myself.
　　Now I feel my trust returning, I now am through with hesitating.
　　My past is now forgiven, a new life is there just waiting.
　　All at once I feel secure, a feeling I used to only dream of.
　　He's broken the shackles of my past, with his heavenly love.

The Bird
by Rhae Watson - age 15

I saw a bird in my dream last night
It helped me live, it helped me fight
The bird flew with beauty and grace
And all my feelings were easy to face
It seemed like I could leave my life
But I couldn't seem to use the knife
If that one night's doom hadn't occurred
Maybe my voice one day would be heard
Why did I choose to leave so soon
I ask as the bird flies me towards the moon
When the bird finally came for me
I was glad to know how it would be
I couldn't bear the pain of night
Now the bird helps me face the light

Untitled
by Joey Walston - age 19

The night has come early and darkness
follows, grasping for my throat. Filled with
pain, and hopes for fate, yet laughing at my hoax.
Burning now with intensity, powder in my head.
Raise a voice of hatred till the pressure kills you
dead. Actions turn to prayers, and your prayers
turn to dust. Spitting now upon you are the ones
you use to trust.

Turn to the fakers as they cut you with their
teeth, ripping in and supping as your bowels start
to leak. Your one and only love has now joined
them in the kill, happily she dances to your
screams of love so shrill. Once around, twice
around, three times around she'll go, and with one
last beautiful smile she places the finishing
blow.........

Smile
by Jeremy Walter - age 20

A picture is drawn
before my bleeding and bloated body.
The artist is a small boy.
His art is a smiley face.
Then he smiles.
Yet, I frown.
Of course he has a right to smile. He
has life and time and experiences to experience. I
have death and anguish and nothing more.
His life mocks me. His smile smacks me. His joy is my jealousy.
A seething hatred of this boy surges
within my depleting life. Its rancored waters
gush to my hand, fill it with strength.
I fill my hand with the boy's throat.
Squeeze. Turn his Adam's apple into applesauce.
The last drop of strength
drains from my hand and it falls to the ground,
the boy's throat still in its stiffened grasp.
Death closes my eyes.

A light opens them.
Giant hands pull me through a hole.
I bawl. My breath is back, life with it.

One day, I go outside to play with my crayons
and I see a man lying on the ground.
He looks upset.
I decide to make him happy.
I draw him a picture of a smiley face.
Then I smile.
Yet, he frowns.

Life
by Dianne Winter - age 13

Life is like
a delicate flower
Not all petals
Have the same power.
What power? You ask.
What does it do?
It puts the love
In all of you.
There is but one thing
That beats this love
Referred to as hate,
Killer of doves.

I'm Over You
by Paula Ward - age 17

I'm over you
All the moments we shared together
All the laughter and tears exchanged
   between one another
I take them all
And shove them out of my memories

I'm over you
Yours words of encouragement when
   I was low
The safe haven I found in your arms
I take it all
And erase it from my thoughts

I'm over you
Your shining green eyes that pierced
   through my soul
Your warm and trusting smile that
   lifted my spirits and heart
I've already forgotten everything
Because, like I said before,
I'm over you

Epitome
by David E. Edwards - age 16

This is the closest thing to hell
And everybody's going to die
This is the closest thing to hell
I do not like the nuclear color of the sky
I crawl back into my concealing shell
Because I do not want to see
The hands of death reaching for me.

Untitled
by Lori Wasson - age 16

Although I do not know you,
I will try to get over it,
although I do not comprehend the things you do,
I will try to understand it.
I do not know why you took my Grandfather,
why didn't you see that he was needed?
Now I sit here and try to comfort my mother,
because you didn't listen to me as I begged and pleaded.
Do you realize these tears are for real?
You've done it so much, but now I'd think you'd see,
don't you know how you've made us feel?
Don't you know how much you've hurt me?
But you can not help me,
all you know is pain,
you don't care about my heart broken family,
and the ones who feel insane.
We can endure so many things,
death, although natural, we can not stand,
we can not handle the pain that it brings,
so why did you place it into my hand?
I can not grasp the powerful things you do,
you can take away a man's last breath,
not for a long time do I want to confront you,
I do want to face you, the almighty Death.

Beginnings
by April Weaver - age 20

Digging my way up through the darkness
I along with my brothers and sisters first see the world
It is still dark, but the air is fresh and clean
We are alone, no one can tell us the way
Clumsily we waddle down the sandy hill
Pulled forward by the call of the sea
I am the first to reach the water
Now I am truly alone, my family far behind me
My home is exquisitely beautiful, and
I am no longer clumsy
I glide through the water with ease
Snapping my jaws shut I eat for the first time
I have made it past my first hurdle
I have survived where many siblings have not
I shall eat and grow strong.
So I to can abandon my children one night
upon a lonely beach.

The Rejected
by Molly Weber - age 15

As he walks into the building,
Everyone stops and stares.
He tries to pretend he doesn't notice,
All the hurtful glares.
But I can tell it hurts him.
I've been in his shoes,
I've been the rejected,
I've heard all the boos
He sits alone at lunch,
He doesn't have a friend.
He feels sad and lonely,
Until I finally bend.
I feel sorry for him,
And I give him what he needs,
I sit down and talk to him,
And he appreciates all of my deeds.
I risk my popularity,
But I don't even care.
Looking at him I realize,
That life is not fair.
He asks why no one likes him,
Why he's not accepted.
Why did this happen to him?
Who chose him to be THE REJECTED?

The Pedestal of Popularity
by Jaime Wellman - age 16

Most have to claw their way to the top,
I was shoved.
By whom? I don't know.
And when I got there on top of that pedestal, and looked
down upon everyone, you know what I did? I stepped down.
Most would have already had the crown and red robe on,
and fifty men around taking measurements so that they were sure
it fit properly.

Best of Friends
by Amy Werling - age 20

This isn't right, it's not fair,
Didn't you know we really did care?
You always helped us through everything.
But when it was our turn you wanted nothing.
We all grew up together- one big family.
You were supposed to be there for Kevin and me.
We all were close, we always got along,
We need you down here, where you belong.
Even though you were sometimes crazy,
Life without you seems so hazy.
We just lost Patrick and how we lost you,
It's just not the same without you two.
You were his best friend, my big brother,
All we have now is each other.
There are so many questions we need to ask,
We'll never know the answers, it's such a hard task.
To understand your reason for doing this-Scott why?
We ask ourselves every time we look up in the sky.
We'll remember the good times we all had.
Through the laughter and years we'll try not to be sad.
It won't be the same this year at the fair,
Without you and Patrick it'll seem so bare.
<u>WE MISS YOU SCOTT</u> we wish you were here.
We'll never forget you year after year.
Even though we are apart,
Memories of you we'll hold close at heart.
<u>WE LOVE YOU SCOTT</u> we can't say good-bye,
I hope you know you're loved by Kevin and I.

Love Is...
by Monica K. Wernio - age 16

Love is deep pink roses colored by the sun.
Such is your face, that lights up my life.

Love is crystal blue mountain rivers, flowing into the sea.
As your love flows into my heart.

Love is a soft melody, played by a majestical musical symphony.
Just like your whispers, of sweet nothings, are my soft melody.

Love is newly fallen dew, smelling so sweet and full of life.
Such is your breath upon me.

Love is a bright beautiful rainbow, displaying the colors of joy.
Like your eyes, when they gaze into mine.

Love is <u>you</u>.

Broken Locket
by Mallory White - age 13

An eye for an eye
a son for a son
Whats said is said
whats done is done
you can't take back the words you said
or the blood upon the bed
I watched you at night creeping, creeping
Now I'm the one weeping, weeping
I saw you that night take from your pocket
a broken and bloodied locket
The picture inside you couldnt see
the soul you took is now set free.
That night you took a precious life
her blood spilled a horrible site
Her veins pumped blood, it ran down her neck
her white woolen sweater is now bright red.

The Mystical World of the Sea
by Meghan Orelene West - age 14

As I am looking out to the sea among the sparkling breakers,
I wonder what world may lie under the aqua-teal depths of the cool waters.
I behold schools of kaleidoscopic fish,
And also the mammals of the sea -- whales, porpoises, and dolphins -- rising
to the surface to catch another breath of air.

But what is under the radiant surface?
My imagination can but only see,
Tiny creatures called micro-organisms,
With whom the Creator has begun life itself,
Also sharks, swordfish, and sturgeons,
Shrimp seahorses, and salmon,
Electric eels, and sting rays, and maybe a jellyfish, octopus, or squid.

But further down to the magnificent ocean floor,
My imagination extends even more,
As I see a galleon resting,
Filled with treasures I could only dream of,
Covered with barnacles and seaweed.
Perhaps a kingdom of Mers and Mermaids is hidden in the rocks and caves,
Surrounded by oysters bearing a delicate pearl each,
And colorful coral reefs inhabited by many varieties of marine animals,
Such as sponges, starfish, and a few crustaceans,
Safe away from the storms of the world above,
In their peaceful and quiet world.

Maybe I will never truly know what is under the alluring world of the sea,
And maybe the creatures of the land will never fully understand the secrets it holds,
But I will always realize,
With my imagination,
That this world could only be made by one who is mystical
Himself.

Quiet Times
by Maria Whiskeyman - age 12

As raging winds
rip through the sails
and swimming home
come rain and hail,
you must be quiet

Not to disturb
their peaceful slumber
as they destroy
the land and lumber,
Please, you must be quiet.

As dying babies
cry for help
and life is, yet
but nothing felt
No, you must be quiet.

As the trigger
to the gun
is pulled and
you are done
yes, you must be quiet

To Just Be With You
by Angie White - age 16

Across the moon
To the end of the galaxy
I will find a way to go
To just be with you

No end to my love
I care not the distance
I will find a way to overcome
To just be with you

I would give my freedom
To be your prisoner
If I could stay forever
To just be with you

My only goal
I care not the consequences
As long as at the end you are there
I will do it all
To just be with you

The Window
by Eva Whitehead - age 12

I look down on the world from my window,
I sit and watch the day turn to night,
Ah, such a beautiful sight.
I watch the lights of the city grow dim,
The faces of the passersby grim,
I wonder what is going through their heads.
Look a pair of newlyweds,
A homeless man passes by,
I know that soon he shall die.
A couple shares a drink from a cup,
I know that soon they shall break up.
A pregnant women talks to her friend about her baby and her marriage,
'Tis a shame it will be a miscarriage.
I sit and watch the world from my window.

Moon Dancer
by Connie Whitesell - age 17

Beyond the boundries of all that is pure and untouched,
exists a body in harmony,
holding the pain and fear of the world.
Destined for expression through her own language,
she dances in pain,
every step created through the agony of her life.
Trying to hide herself,
her graceful steps guide the way.
Somehow her pale, soft eyes seem to reveal all the guilt with held through the years.
Using her dance to replace what had once been lost,
she becomes life.
Twisting and twirling with ease,
she wraps herself around the shadows of sadness,
embracing, yet never holding on.
She will dance on 'til death,
never letting go,
and forever knowing she was to blame.

The Roar of A Leader
by Ashley Whittredge

The lion roars and the animals gather 'round.
He has something to say.
The end of the world will come near.
Fear is fear in itself,
driving towards your hearts.
The sky will fall someday soon.
All will be trapped below.
But listen to me my friend,
Yes, listen to me my friend,
to stay alive---

All the rivers will be dry someday soon.
We will fall into the hands of God.
All the plants will die someday soon.
We'll have no food to eat to survive.
But listen to me my friend,
Yes, listen to me my friend,
to stay alive---

We will all die someday soon.
All will be in His hands from then on.
But never believe all that you hear.
The world may end,
and the sky may fall.
The rivers may go dry,
and the plants may die,
but not in your lifetime.
The lion roars and the animals gather 'round.
He has something to say...

Reality
by Alex Wick - age 18

As the Gleaming Sun rose,
So did my memories.
As the Glowing Sun set,
So did my thoughts.
You're like a diamond,
Special and precious, To me.
Then my dreams fade,
And along with you, Fade away.
I only wish,
This was a dream, Not Reality.

Strength
by Megan Wiley - age 15

To be like an eagle and soar through the sky
To always be strong and never have to cry
Not have to feel the hurt and the pain
Not have to feel belittled or ashamed
Always be happy and never be sad
Brush everything off that would make you mad
To see the light in a world of dark
To be the flame that comes from the spark
Stand out in a crowd from afar
Not be ashamed that you are who you are
To always look for the positive side of things
Not be afraid of what the future brings
Love everyone around you and not feel the hate
Forget your self-pity and know that you're great
Cherish what you have and not want any more
Don't worry about the things you had before
To look past the sparrow and see the dove
Move on from a broken heart and find new love

(Ode To Adolescents) "How Could This Be?"
by Lindsey Williams - age 14

As I drift in the midst of past dreams and future thoughts, I come upon something unclear to my mind. I see, smell, and feel things I swear I've heard of, but never actually done. It scared me to think of the reality. I though I would die from fear, yet it didn't kill me to wonder: "How could this be?" All of a sudden I was happy and over-come with joyous laughter that filled my stomach, though I kept it inside. No one would know the joy I felt over such little things. They would put me down and speak of things unbearable to hear. So, again I wondered: "How could this be?" I wonder in silence. I then realize that silence was the thing that frightened me the most. I start to tell myself that I am a freak: One of which had no friends and would soon cringe to feel this way again. I feel my anger begin to swell
underneath my bones. It grows so quickly, I jump up from my weary, hunched position, and grab my head in terror. I'm the only one, it's only me! Never again will I be looked at the same. They know. I will show them in unmeaningful fits of jealousy. They will be able to tell what is going through my head. The monsters! The monsters of society are mind readers! They are empowered by every bit of knowledge received in their gainful minds! They cannot be stopped!! And they tend to wonder- "How could this be?"

Questions
by Markella Williamson - age 16

What is Love?
Is it care
Is it when she lies
Is it free
Or is it old ties

What is Adult?
Is it alone
Is it time to smoke
Is it a parent
Or is it a bad joke

What is Real?
Is it a dream
Is it a child
Is it when they're gone
Or is it wild

What is Normal?
Is it a stranger
Is it cool
Is it weird
Or is it a fool

What is Hate?
Is it war
Is it in a book
Is it the things they say
Or is it a look

My Shadow
by D'Esta C. Wilson - age 20

There is a little shadow I feel you should meet.
He runs up and down the length of my body from my head to my feet.
This little shadow has no name
Just a sad little game.
You see, this is no ordinary guy
Without him I couldn't get by.
He's my friend when no ones around.
He picks me up when I'm flat on the ground.
But my shadow friend has a fault
For it's something he finds quite difficult
You see, I cannot hug or squeeze him
He always leaves when the room grows dim
That is why you are my friend, with a unique face
That he could never, ever replace

Wind
by Nadia Lynn Wilson - age 13

Wind- whispering in your ear,
blowing your hair down upon your shoulders.

Wind- sighing through the trees,
moaning a melancholy song across the sea.

Wind- lifting the autumn leaves in a swirling sash of red,
rushing through the tulips in their soft flowery beds.

Wind- flowing gently through the window to tuck you in at night,
and creeping past the countryside until the morning light.

Poverty
by Amanda Winger - age 15

In my dreams
I can touch the
outstretched hand
of a child who
has no home.

I look into her
bony face silently
screaming to me
to help her escape
the loneliness.

I can only
imagine how
miserable it would
feel if I had no
one who cared.

And in my dreams
I can help.
I understand
I am but a
weak voice;

However,
I say loudly
to myself,
"I still must try."
I must make my voice
a sound of thunder
in the ears of
those who can
also help.

I am the dreamer

Deception
by Tridaugh Winston - age 17

You saw me in my innocence; you saw me with no shame,
and at that very moment, you began to play your game.
You spun me into your web of lies
and left me there, alone to die.
In the beginning I knew you were mischievous,
but in reality you were nothing but devious.
I can't understand how I fell under your spell;
there's nothing I can do now, there's no one I can tell.
Now I stand here all alone, hurting with endless pain,
I know that I've been scarred for life, and my innocence has been stained.
I long only for the inner peace which once lived within me,
yet I know that I can never have it again, and I know I will never be free.

Holocaust
by Jared Wirth - age 20

Empty husks of humanity, piled from hell to sky,
were killed by the sinister insanity of the arian god on high.

Raped and murdered were they that bled, piled from hell to sky,
and never a tear for them was shed by the arian god on high.

"Never again?" someone asked.
"Never again." said I.

Take Me Back To Yesterday
by Brittany Wissler - age 17

Take me back to yesterday's cart wheels,
and secret crushes.
Days when responsibility,
was a word you "dunno."
Times when friendships,
lasted as long as popsicles on a hot summer day.
Wanting the days when you were able to fit in,
everywhere you went.
Days when it was okay,
to cry in public.
Times when you could take dares,
and didn't care the consequences.
Clutching teddy bears,
like they are today's heroes.
Days where birds nest,
brought simple perfection.
Yesterday is not gone from sight
or memory.

A Ship
by Sarah Wohlwend - age 16

My life is like a ship
That sails upon the sea.
Storms come roaring through,
But the captain of my ship
Guides it expertly.
At times it seems that
The storm would o'er take me;
My ship is rocked
From stem to stern.
But just at the last minute,
The wind dies down,
And peace comes to my soul,
I will always let Christ
Be the Captain of my ship.
I do not know how to guide
A ship upon the stormy seas.

Under The Mist and The Moor
by Natalie Wolc - age 16

Under the mist and the moor,
The reign of thunder dies,
And the grey eyes are burned with hateful tears,
And the fears are drowned out by cries.

Under the mist and the moor,
The martyrs rule the night,
And truculent days bode hapless years,
And the prophets are loosing sight.

Under the mist and the moor,
Love is the only fascination,
And the lonely cry of wind flies by,
And the roads have no destination.

Under the mist and the moor,
Clouds of fear cover the light,
And the cold blue seas crash on the shore,
And purpose is lost in the fight.

Under the mist and the moor,
A glance is made of pain,
And life is full of empty souls,
And this is where I remain.

A Stranger to my Heart
by Susan Woodard - age 16

As a mere child you went on your way.
I suppose never intending to return.
Will I ever know you, this stranger I'm part of?
Who are you? Where are you?
If I passed you on the street,
would I feel as if I knew you,
or would you just be another stranger?
In my dreams I call out your name,
but you never appear or respond to my cry.
What are you like, perhaps maybe me?
I struggle to put a face to your ghostly figure.
Would you be proud of who I am,
the one you turned and walked away from?
These questions that exist long to be answered.
Do you ever think of me as I so often do of you?
This curiosity engulfs me and intensifies each day.
A stranger you are to my mind and my heart,
though I just wish to see your face.
bound together by the blood in our veins,
but yet you're still a stranger to my heart.
The love you have I would never desire,
for I know it would not be real.
You chose to take that path that led away from me,
you deprived me of a love that every child needs.
The love I have I cannot give,
for it is far too precious to give to a stranger.
A stranger you are; a stranger to my heart,
a choice you made when you chose that path.

Yellow
by Jessica Wolf - age 15

Yellow is in the sun,
the flowers and the moon.
All cheery on the outside,
the middle full of gloom.

The shell is really sweet,
and very very true.
But deep inside all yellows,
there is a shade of blue.

Somewhere in its happiness,
a loneliness shines thru.
It's hidden to all others,
but not to me or you.

Someday we'll understand,
why yellow is so cheery.
When blue is sad and lonely,
our yellow shines so clearly.

This dark and gloomy part,
will someday fade away.
'Cause deep inside our hearts,
yellow is here to stay.

Clouded Visions
by Christopher Q. Zobrist - age 18

My vision was unclouded, my heart was true
The water was clear, before I met you

Then came the colors, so many, so bright
Swirling in my mind, turning day into night
You were those colors, white mixing in my head

The white of our innocence, our friendship and love
So perfect together, fitting like a glove
The red of our love, our passionate desperation
A bond was born between us, and we reveled in our creation

These colors were clear cut, calm and distinctive
I was content with my fate, I had reason to live
And then came new colors, dark blue and gray
Distorting my vision, and I lost my way

The blue of my sorrow, my longing and loss
I gave you so much, knowing you were worth the cost
The gray is worst of all, clouded visions of doubt
My dreams are filled with fear, so many, too many to count

Oh! My love, please help me, help take away my fears
Help me clear my mind, help me dry my tears
Help me to see my fate, tell me what you feel
Will you pledge me your heart? Or will you break that seal

I am a child in this world, I am as innocent as you
Overwhelmed by all these colors, not knowing what to do
I want to love you, but I want you to be free
Please, I need to know, do you still love me?

When I'm With You
by Malia Yoshioka - age 16

The whisper of a light rainfall
The gentle beating of your heart
And the soft caress of your breath on my cheek
Swirl in my memories of when I'm with you

Your tender voice
And loving touch
Help to calm my spirit and ease my soul
I'm at peace when I'm with you

Gazing into each other's eyes
As the starlight pours through the windows
And a love song drifts from the radio
I'm so in love when I'm with you

I'll take this moment
And wrap it up
In a special corner of my mind
So I'll always have this night
When I'm with you.

Untitled
by Jennifer Wolfram - age 15

Why can't we live
In harmony, Dad?

Because everyone
Lives in the fear of
Everyone else.

But why doesn't
Anyone try to stop
The fear, Mom?

Because of the
Hatred of the color
That someone else has.

Won't anyone stop
These silly fears and
Hatreds, Grandpa?

Many have tried and
Many have failed.
The answer lies in your hands.

Well, Teddy, I guess
We'll just find the
Answer in our hearts.

Come, Night
by Allen Young - age 17

Come, night.
Tender night.
Dance with me.

Unfurl for me your star-spun hair
And lay me on a bed of gentle dusk.

Bathe me in your naked moonlight
And wash me with your rain-sweet tears.
And touch my lips with shadow-kisses--
Press me to your darkness-bosom.

Beautiful night.

Speak quietly of dreams undreamt
And forgotten hopes and passion fleeting.
And sing to me a lost love-poem
Softly, 'neath the rustling leaves.

Come, night.

Lover Of The Lost
by Suzanne Yoder

Daughter of a preacher man,
Lover of the lost;
Searching out her fantasies
While kneeling 'neath the cross.

Scrapper of her bleeding knees,
Believer of the true;
Finding good in all she sees
and filling up her pew.

Loner to the rich and the well,
Child till breath is gone;
Following what's not a trail
And crying to belong.

Wanderer intruding no-man's land,
Hunter of the absurd;
Bringing dirt and dust and sand
Among the silk and fur.

Dreamer of what is not there,
Beggar in each nightly prayer;
To keep her bloodly knees,
Her cross, her God, and her fantasies.

Disobedience
by Christina Young - age 12

Water babbling down the mountain
reaches it's boundaries.

The disobedient water jumps out of it's bed
and lands on the lonely dry land.

It sets and sets and sets there just waiting
for the life to be sucked out of it.

Finally the ground takes advantage of
its free meal and in a flash the drop is gone.

Maybe the water has considered being obedient!

The Beach Is Beautiful
by Rebecca Cullen - age 14

The dull roar of the waves crashing into each other. Gulls shrieking and peaking around boulders for food. The ocean waters pushing its way over and through rocks as through it were a child pushing through a crowd to see the circus parade. Stalks of seaweed dancing with the current. A sailboat so far in the distance it looks as if it were a ghost ship. A motor boat zips over the other wise calm waters. Abandoned homes of hermit crabs that once lived. Sandstone and shale smoothed by the salty sea air. The ocean sparkling like a diamond looks as though it could touch the four corners of the universe and still not end. Crystal blue waters showing the mucky bottom of the sea as though it were a window into another dimension. The frothy white caps of the waves slowly disappearing like shaving cream on a bearded man's face. The Beach is Beautiful.

My Resting Place
by Millie Kerr - age 15

The curb, my resting place.
Standing alone, watching every face.

The young, the old
The white, the black,
Enclosed by cold
I stand.

Nourished by food,
Surviving by hope,
These desperate people
Their lives hard to cope.

Why am I here?
To bring them one meal
Or to look down on their
Lives shabby and real.

Where did they come from?
From the streets so cold.
Their clothing all torn.
Don't worry, I'm told.

A smile catches my eye,
A sweet notion, indeed,
I smile back, I try,
My lips unwilling.

Saying the Lord's Prayer
The words so many know.
So delicate and fair.
Were they learned it, I don't know.

Sheltered by my curb,
I stand alone.
The food all gone.
The desperateness shown.

A Kiss Goodbye
by Maureen Williams - age 17

He runs his fingers across her lips
Looks deep in her eyes and sees her pain
To him it's all a childs game
Love is but a word to use
The female body, an object to abuse
And a kiss goodbye is all it takes
To break the promises he makes
To her it seems life is through
To him it's time for someone new
Between her sobs, and his laughter
Only one moment when they part
He takes with him a lightened heart
And she is left with nothing more
Than the tears she cries and the kiss goodbye.

Concrete
by Lina Baitakys - age 17

tears have stained your heart
a constant reminder
of what was
the fear is the light
that you both see
everytime that you look
the innocence lies in your soul;
the need is there
journeys will never end.

Whispers

Chapter Four

The Browning Competition
Winners and selected works from the Browning Competiton
sponsored by
VERSES Magazine.

Nature's Choreography
by Marilyn Brehm

Evening eases, gently peeks in
There's magic on stage
A misty powder caresses the meadow
Shyly the company appears
Velvety green grass becomes a stage
An elite, private audience
Chosen, invited guests
Dance, kick, and reach the purple sky
Perhaps, once again
Kindergarten children
Playing hide and seek
In the amber cornstalks
And I,
In awesome transfiguration
Fulfilled with Nature's production,
Nature's choreography
Silently applaud

Second Place Award
Echoes of the Monks
by Alan Frame

Inflections of delightful harmony
Began to form a consecrated sound.
Those Latin words of ancient melody
Were chanted by the monks on holy ground.
Their meditation echoed in the air
And mingled with their monastery's calm.
The dulcet intonation of their prayer
Anointed all the monks with aural balm.
Today, in great cathedrals of the world,
The echoes of the music resonate.
The chant of yore eternally is pearled
With inspiration reaching heaven's gate.
    Within the hearts of each cathedral's choir,
    The echoes will continue to inspire!

First Place Award
Sandbox
by Samson Gruss

I had my lunch in the park today
And watched the carefree children play.
Two in the sandbox, three on the swings,
And I've *so* much to do - a million things.

I finished my lunch, but decided to stay
A few more minutes, to watch them play.
Three in the sandbox, two on the swings,
They've so much to do - a million things.

As I sat there wondering why I'd come
A butterfly landed on my thumb!
A little boy looked up from the sand,
"A Bur'rfly landed on 'nat guy's hand!"

The "Bur'rfly" flew off, we watched him go.
Was He watching *us*? I kinda think so.
Four in the sandbox, one on the swings,
We've so much to do - a million things.

We've so much to do - a million things,
Five in the sandbox, none on the swings.
And then I saw what I'd come to see
When the little boy - smiled at me.

Visions of Love Sonata By Lantern Light
by George-Alicea Heinze

Oh, lantern wide, lustrous, warm, sweeping,
    Your glow keeps my vigil ever keeping.
Showing through window pane,..its case,
    Trimmed, worn patterns pain of lace,
Across snows, through slanted lines of rain.
    Lighting a way homeward bound, my beloved swain.
Sharing within these lonely walls,
    My beating heart safe, while winter falls.
From dreary darkness that might have been,
    We two in this soundless, loneliest of den.
Burning so bright, around my room,
    In bleakest of nights, till dawning soon.
I read long by your strength to give,
    Those letters of love, rekindling the vigil to live.
When next befalls, shadows, corners of the sky,
    Always on your gentle soft splendor I can rely.
Filling snowy path beyond my humble door,
    Spreading forth a warmth of love remaining, as before.
His searching for you, I,..we patiently sit,
    Till time again our lonely door his knock admit.
At last to feel, unanswered, that longing thrill,
    Lips upon mine, radiance his fall will fill.
Finding myself with hours of waiting, contemplating, loving him,
    Oh, my precious lamp, only then would I, a softer light make dim.
Our secrets in darkness hid, with me abide,
    Till dawning our love so long yesterdays memories, subside.
Still in darkness these two hearts are yearning,
    Until such ecstacy your constant faith, burning,
I bask in vigil bright from fear, while footsteps I strain to hear,
    His returning journey ended, alightin his face to tell him he's here!

Precious Memories
by Jennifer Howard

    I see an old woman, hair silver and grey,
      with lines on her face as if withering away.
    There seems a certain glow that I distinctly remember,
      her smile, her touch, her soft voice so tender.
    Ah yes, all too clear, precious memories that remain
      not all I remember but there's a feeling I can claim.
    Her gentleness, understanding, giving so much of her heart,
      makes it ever so hard to be very far apart.
    Her mind has now withdrawn, being unable to recall my name,
      but when holding hands I know, we're both feeling just the same.
    She lies curled in a ball never speaking at all to me,
      yet a tear will trickle down her face very occasionally.
    At times I might be found with a childish look of amaze,
      when all at once I'll notice I am remembering my yesterdays.
    There's more to this old woman with hair silver and grey,
      she's my mother whom I will cherish for the rest of my days.

Please
by Angela Livingston

Please take me back to those sweet memories of old,
When my heart was strong, young, and bold.
Hope filled my heart with gloriously beautiful dreams,
Instead of a heart of hopelessly, melancholy screams.
I want to dwell in the midst of real life,
And with great determination, overcome all pains and strife.
Let me grow with the immense experiences of the world,
And let me be worthy as a human, a person, a girl.
Keep me steadfast on the paths of goodness,
As with goodness allow me to emerge into kindness.
May I be instantly humble and truly, virtuously pure,
So that my heart may be brazen with a soul that is demure.
Eliminate my evil passions that taunt my mind,
And let me leave all my heinous mendacity behind.

Abyss
by Rita Lurie

        Thundering down the mountainside...
        Relentless surge of the unknown
      Magic crystalline splashes twirl, spray
            Conquer divide
         each finding its own level
          majestic at the start
          Ever rumbling along
              Surging
            eroding stone
            foliage - hilltop
        Only to be disbursed
             each drop
            every splash
      Forced into the womb of time
          Perhaps the apex

               Life...

Toast To The Future
by Andy Marshall

When you are I are of the body free,
Whether in ash or bone,
Who have been shall never be,
Bereft and left alone.

Oh, not the easy task of finding,
That which youth once yearned,
Nor any brash and psychic healing,
To solve life's age and wounds.

Instead there'll be a splendid golden meeting,
When all of life on earth is done,
We shall become as one in greeting,
Those myriad armies of the mind.

To rise as Gods upon a towering wave,
One with the thunder and the light,
Unknowing that gray dusk from out the grave,
And blessed by kinship of mankind.

Third Place Award
Footsteps Along The Ocean Shore
by Carol A. Michalski

Footsteps once trudged
along the sandy ocean shore
where crystalline waves washed over
and they appear to be no more
but are embedded
in the coasts of eternity.

Light In The Darkness
by Sheila B. Roark

The bitter coldness chills the bones
As gray clouds hide the sun.
And winter winds sing sad laments
As a new day has begun.

No vibrant colors can be seen,
For gray has covered all.
And sadness carpets all the world
As grayness takes its toll.

This heavy veil of dreariness
Seen on this winter's day,
Saps all the hope and love men have,
Their life's no longer gay.

Then there appears among the clouds
A brilliant ray of light.
And from the ray, a flying dove,
Who turns the dark to light.

I Cannot Think Beyond Our Soul's Embrace
by Jeanne E. Ross

      I cannot think beyond our soul's embrace.
        My destiny is fixed in that sweet space.
         Such love becomes a single aim;
           a glittering fusion shines.
      We weave this cloak from rainbow threads -
        an auric vestment made divine.

   My dreams and thine are spun from a single filament;
     through warp and weft these paths are built
          of light most radiant.

        Within this secret veil, our hearts
          have found its mating;
      where time and space now blending
        encounter life's long waiting.

In The Shadows
by Margaret Scholl

Waiting in darkness for the dawn,
Indwelling spirit shows transform.
Magnificent humility gentle obedience,
Walking thru minds of pasts great swarm.

Vision of images before your eyes,
Experience teachings catch rise and fall.
Glimpse into souls sighing,
Moments journey long way from homey walls.

Falling twilight all appears to be still,
Deep in the shadows, of illusion.
Thoughts, emotion communicate,
Reality larger - grips as a roaring lion.

Mere organisms of a fragile planet,
Blend and circle times lease.
Beaming into light of eternity,
Happiness impacts - experiencing peace.

Mystical design thru the inner eye,
Resounds of another time and place.
Moving clouds fade into shadows,
Cover sloping hills in quiet grace.

Dancing With Angels
by Dona K. Soler

The wheelchair stands empty,
    Except for the bear . . .
The cuddles teddy,
    She had kissed and placed there.

He sits patiently waiting
    For her to come home . . .
Neglected and soulful . . .
    Forlorn and alone . . .

And the house is so silent,
    Without her around;
Yet seems full of echoes
    And little girl sound . . .

Her sunny voice;
    So bubbly sweet . . .
The once playful patter
    Of dancing feet.

She was brave through affliction,
    Causing her to be lame . . .
Unable to walk
    Or to be the same . . .

If there's a God and a heaven,
    We know that she's there
Dancing with angels . . .
    Released from her chair . . .

The Browning Competition

Whispers

Chapter Five

The Haiku Competition
Winners and selected works from the Haiku Competiton
sponsored by
VERSES Magazine.

Second Place Award

Untitled
by Marylin C. Blinn

Dark shadows at dawn
Until fingers of sunlight
Begin erasing

Untitled
by Doris Hartsell Brewer

       In the dark forest
   Wood nymphs run behind the trees
      playing hide and seek.

Touch and Go
by Lorraine Calhoun

His ability
To stand on such shaky ground
Is in the balance.

Untitled
by Diana Castle

Sparkling, champagne clouds
   pour over the horizon
      in a toast to life!

Grief
by Rita Dean

Grief, how could you be
So devastating, cruel.
Go away, leave me.

Metamorphosis
by Al Hallberg

Its silken shape hangs
Caterpillar to cocoon
Fragile butterfly.

Third Place Award

Untitled
by Jeanne M. Holt

Swirling and gliding,
two sulphur-winged butterflies
dance a *pas de deux*.

Untitled
by Becky Keller

Dead calm was the sea
Blackness came about the world
Death was in the air

Untitled
by Anne Marie Legan

Small hand raised a pipe
To puckered lips; a pea sped
Upon its mission.

First Place Award

Tattle Tale
by Frances H. Levinson

A gossiping wind
Tells me neighboring gardens
Are tipsy with bloom

Ever Upward
by Rita Lurie

       Rejected barren
     Naked barks decimated
     Coveting spring temps

Tiny Night Lanterns
by Carol A. Michalski

Fireflies aglow
Bright yellow flickers of light
Tiny night lanterns

Ocean Glory
by Kimberly A. Miller

Glistening waters
Hide beneath them a dark world
Of immense beauty

Dawn
by Raymond F. Rogers

>The disk of morning
>Rises over distant trees,
>Steaming the meadow.

Untitled
by Velande Taylor

Mud road, beach, marshland,
   Palace, temple, ale-house, farm—
      Same performances.

Life
by Jo Anne Trinkle

Life is a river
and no one taught me to swim.
I sit on the bank.

Untitled
by Barbara S. Weppener

Red, bronze, yellow gold
Patchwork quilt on withered Earth
Death of autumn leaves.

Whispers

Chapter Six

The Longfellow Competition

Winners and selected works from the Longfellow Competiton
sponsored by
VERSES Magazine.

Cloistered Thought
by Emma J. Blanch

When I sit dreaming through the larger pane,
reflecting well on icy stormy days
when we were staying home and watching jays,
resigned to our wintry life, in wane,
and looking out again at leafy plane,
I see him there, in working clothes, with sprays,
then bringing grapes in baskets, in arrays,
for faithful friends, a gesture done in vain.

I know he heard the fearful call to die.
I could not bear the loss, when chapel bell
is ringing dull low sound and drifting by,
not telling me, to warn of danger spell,
I watched the changing days and said goodbye.
Awaiting time, I gaze towards the dell.

Worlds of Mind
by Najwa Salam Brax

Words, worlds of mind, the nerves and cells
of life and love, revive the past,
ringing as far echoes of bells
to keep dreams and visions steadfast.

Cooling, soothing, bringing peace,
my words sing as a nightingale
procreating a masterpiece,
forging freedom from Earth-jail.

Sometimes my words wave like sweet swarms
of perfumes sprinkling art around,
sometimes they whoosh as roaring storms
unleashed by Prometheus unbound.

Words can create Eden or Hell;
can stir war or bring peace, or lay
mankind's fate; words have their own spell
that time's streams cannot wash away.

Like eagles on the rising wind
some words uplift the wings of mind,
and like cobwebs some words are spinned
to catch the blind of humankind.

A pen with an inspired writer
is a keen sword or a weird wand;
words build worlds of love and wonder,
or wreck what's raised by mankind's hand.

Bitter Dreams
by Marilyn Brehm

The bitter taste of emptiness
The haunting memories
Tear open healed broken hearts
In dreams and fantasies

The tears replace happy thoughts
The hours reveal despair
And anguish is the only route
When nothing's left to share

When love once tasted precious times
And lovers held together
The joys of two becoming one
Are now long gone forever

What's left when roses wilt and die
And gardens turn to dust
When spoken words mean nothing more
Then anger and disgust

I long for days when robins sing
A love song in the sun
And I drink the wine of happiness
When you and I were one

Through The Window
by Margaret A. Brennan

The snow fell silently
On the small quiet town.
As she gazed out her window
There was no one around.

She sighed once or twice
As a tear filled her eye.
She held his last letter
Trying hard not to cry.

The tea on her desk
Long ago had turned cold.
She was young and alone
With no one to hold.

She needed to hear
His soft words of care
While running his fingers
Through her long soft red hair.

She knew the reasons
They must be apart.
Logic wasn't enough
To mend her broken heart.

When his work was all through
He'd at last head for home,
Vowing never again
To leave her all alone.

They would marry and live
In their quiet town.
And together they'd watch
The snow fall to the ground.

First Place Award
The Silent Mariner
by Elizabeth MacDonald Burrows

Eboned was the night the phantom ship cast anchor with torn sails,
which drifted against the mast in ghostly prance
Naught but a lone beam fell from the swaying beacon on her bow,
as the pinnacled shadows of nocturne's rule,
fell around her in silent dance.

Her weathered hull hovered in the ocean mist like some specter,
filled with rapture of some far bewitching lay.
She approached me there in the muted shadows of ribboned sand,
beguiling me to set sail with her this night,
on a voyage of spectral play.

There upon the frayed and wooded deck of time's fateful passage,
I saw the firmament spread in mystic light.
Then I saw him at the helm like some aphonic sentinel,
silhouetted there without word or sound,
against the starlit even sky.

Then he raised his hands and the tattered sails filled with soft spring wind,
While the sea frolicked beneath the phantom's prow.
Light streamed around him as though he were embraces by heaven's rays,
and buoys rang in nights symphonic splendor,
as mystic visions touched my brow.

I knew that my silent mariner was not of earthly womb,
but an answer to the dreams of future ways.
As I looked in to the ravened ocean waves I saw him there,
his face mirrored by Shambhala's holy stars,
his eyes ablaze with starlit rays.

Then I knew the dreams and wishes of every saintly soul,
for we are travelers through time's passing hall.
Each holds a secret yearning for Olympus's mantled dream.
And when epochs pierce labyrinth's shrouded sleep,
The silent mariner will call.

Winter Solitaire
by Alan Frame

The winter thaw created a cascade
Which emptied in the riverbed below.
And borders of the river were arrayed
With covers of accumulated snow.
Adjoining the majestic waterfall,
Were conical assemblages of ice.
They clustered in a luster-colored wall,
Resplendent in the winter's paradise.
And water hit the river forcefully,
Resulting in a mist within mid-air.
The facets of the frozen purity
Were sparkling in their winter solitaire.
  As sun rays cut away from heaven's blue,
  The ice reflected back a wondrous view.

Where Were You, My Love
by Dianne Hamilton

Where were you, my love,
as tender words
fell silently on your ear;
when an eager embrace
and lusting lips,
failed to hold you near.

Where were you, my love,
when I offered myself
with a promise to be true.
Were you lost in thoughts
of other times,
or longing for someone new.

Where were you, my love,
as I grew cold
and teardrops ceased to fall.
Though you stole my heart
and claimed my soul,
were you ever there at all?

My Home
by Lisa Hanebrink

My mind drifts back to Arkansas,
to my dear home in the south.
Back to my tulip garden
and my country ranch, style house.
I let my mind drift back there,
when in Nebraska, I feel lonely and cold.
Back to the calm and warm place,
where I intend to grow old.
I just close my eyes and imagine,
all the sights I will see.
Like my beautiful climbing roses,
and all the animals waiting to greet me.
For the times I get lonely, I can pretend, I hear.
The sound of the Morning Dove cooing,
outside my window near.
Or visualize the graceful, white swan,
as she builds her nest down by the pond.
I can even return to the grass meadows,
that stretch for miles behind my home.
To all my secret places, where as a child, I roamed.
My favorite place in Arkansas,
is on Mount Petit Jean.
Where I attended meetings with my dad,
to watch for birds in Spring.
So, whenever Nebraska mistreats me, I now
just send my mind back to roam.
The meadows and mountains of Arkansas,
where in my heart,
will always be my
Home!

For My Dear Daddy.

Sonnet To A Breeze
by ddoris Kennard

Soft frolicking breezes sing as they run;
Scattering ripples with flourish and flair.
Bright ripples of diamonds kissed by the sun;
Effervescence born of water and air.
The breezes take turns in a sporting game
Scattering diamond froth hither and yon.
The drift of my boat is never the same;
For South breeze returns soon as West has gone.
With fish pole in hand I drift in my boat
Nudged gently on with a breeze in control.
All cares forgotten I muse as I float
Surrounded by beauty peace floods my soul.
Ah, summer is heaven drifting along
Nudged by a breeze with its sweet siren song!

The Crucifix Upon Her Wall
by David Kindle

The crucifix upon her wall
Holds no admiration.
It can't represent eternal life
Within her apprehension.

There is no steeple high enough
To ease her heart's disease.
The trees in the garden cry for her
With a gentle rustling of there leaves.

There is no grave dug deep enough
To contain her troubled spirit.
And the lonely crucifix upon her wall,
Inside her holds no merit.

Consummation
by Rita Lurie

Shed garb of unresolvable
Neuroses
Dwell on personal fulfillment
Images happen
Remove guilts
Sapping, painful device
Pain wallowing sinful
Overcome fear of setting down
Initial thought
Major obstacle giant step
Peek into another world
Assume writing is truth
Words beget others
Enumerating pleasures cathartic
Home, memorabilia
Violet skies, mountains, fireplace
Grandchildren
Ageless stereo
Embracing symphonic music
Euphoric
Contact with Selectric
Akin to communication
Conversing, sharing, commiserating
State of sanity comes to fore
Dismiss negativity
In midst of indecision
Push nirvana button
Appetite aroused
Cerebrate
Welcome revelations

Sunset in Red
by Diana Malon

The children now fed
are safely tucked away in bed.

And now content
with his slippers on

and newspaper upon his lap
my dear husband takes a nap.

My dishes are now done
and the dogs are by my side

I steal away
for a quiet moment
of my own.

Enjoying the labor,
of my peaceful stroll,

I walk through the tall grasses
and sit upon my favorite knoll.

I look out into the sky
and basque in the beauty of it all.

Feeling at peace
I return home,

And for those I love,
I place a kiss upon their cheek.

With the sun now gone
and the day now done -

It's off to bed
for dreams of sunsets in red.

Second Place Award

If Not For Her Love
By A.V. Santa Maria

Temples were constructed high in honor
   of her womb.
Her wet-nurse breasts were worshipped
   from the cradle to the tomb.
Underneath the ruins, lost to mortal memory;
The silent unkissed lips of an unseen
   sleeping beauty.

Hymns of adoration and oblation are unsung.
The poets who composed them, rendered
   speechless, hold their tongue.
Sacred rites of passage held beneath
   a harvest moon;
An undiscovered secret in a sculptured
   stone cocoon.

Demeter, Artemis, Minerva, and Kore
To name but a few of the masks that
   She wore.
Every culture, a costume, and custom
   hand sewn
From the very same thread by an artist unknown.

No mountain unconquered, no ocean
   uncrossed;
If not for Her love, the world would
   be lost.
   (To all but the wicked with evil designs,
      whose numbers grow greater as virtue declines.)

A Song To Sing
by Andy Marshall

Who can tell what tomorrow will bring,
Maybe I'll cry, maybe I'll sing;
Maybe a storm will level my home,
Maybe I'll be left all alone?

Maybe there's gold all over my land,
Maybe I'll feel God's judgement hand?
Maybe I'll grow to be eight feet tall,
Maybe I'll suddenly know it all?

I'll never know what tomorrow will bring,
I'll never know if I'll cry or I'll sing,
But if He's on my side, then I don't have to care,
I'll win that last battle, everywhere!

As Time Went On Its Way
by Carol A. Michalski

Your piercing ray beaming through
The dense darkness of the night...
Forward...
Far beyond what I could see,
Beckoning me to come your way.
I refused,
Not wanting to leave just yet,
Desiring to stay a little longer
Absorbing the sights and sounds
Of the quiet campsite
In the warm pitch-black summer night,
A flashlight only to find my way.
Instead I gazed upward
Cherishing the present.
A few bright stars shone:
Their stillness not so far removed,
Existing in eternity
They need not ask permission.
But your rigid beam directed me forward
No matter how or where I pointed.
I halted...but all else moved on.
And whether I realized it or not
I went with it
Though seemingly still,
Advancing further,
As time went on it way...
You left me no choice
Than to head toward the future.

The Lesson
by Wilda Middlebrook

I led him out to the green spruce tree --
This curious boy of only three.

"Grandma, can I see the nest?"
"Should I hold you up? I'll try my best."

The woven nest on a sagging limb
Was quite accessible to him.

His eyes with wonder opened wide
To peek at what he'd find inside.

"Oh, Grandma, I see eggs -- yes, three!
In this little nest, how can it be?"

"Remember, dear, this morning we heard
The cheerful song of this red-breasted bird

As it sang to us of this fine spring day,
And called you from your world of play.

A robin has laid her eggs of blue.
She craftily hid them safe from view.

We mustn't disturb her nest, you see,
Securely anchored within this tree.

After fourteen days, my dear,
her downy hatchlings will appear.

As your Mommy watches over you,
The robin cares for her babies, too;

She carefully tends them, as she knows best,
'Til they're strong enough to leave the nest.

And so, my dear, as you ponder these things,
Like the fledglings, you, too, will
    find your wings."

Life...A Gift of Love
by Ruth Emily Newman

Life is so wonderful!
    It's a GIFT of God's love
And to live it to the fullest
    Pleases our God above!

God's desire is to provide
    Each man, woman, boy or girl
WITH all essentials to live
    A Holy life, void of pride.

God helps us understand
    His WIll and His Purpose.
Thus, He holds out His hand
    To direct each one of us!

IF we'll just LIVE by His rules
    Obeying only HIM, each day
He'll from harm keep us safe
    And grant His Light for our way!

FOR A PURPOSE Life's given to all
    Though some never find it out.
We're to SPEAK of what God's done
    And introduce others to His Son!

AND, for those who'll do their best
    God will DAILY, be by their side.
He'll provide LIFE abundantly...
    As in HIS Love, they abide!

Song of the Night Woman
by La Claire Chuma Nzerem

Empty footsteps click across
the wet sidewalk, faceless people pass.
Cabs honk by and splash the feet
where hookers cuss at the curbs of streets.
Empty footsteps come to call
at the creaking doorway down the hall.
In a room that hisses of pungent mold
the plaster crumbles the mildewed walls.
She waits in a tattered robe of white
on an unkept mattress in the night.
Through the window she hears the
worried dog call.
A cat picks up his pointless howl.
He holds on in wild embrace, he comes
a man without a face.
The dollars down from cold embrace,
she turns to the window to hide disgrace.
The empty echo leaves the hall
of shadowed footsteps as they fall.
Away and further into dark,
two lovers embrace in the park..

Aspens
by Sheila B. Roark

Graceful aspens whistle
airy tunes of beauty rare.
As gentle zephyrs softly blow
and ride the autumn air.

High above the forest
you can see the azure sky.
Bluer than the deepest sea
as fleecy clouds roll by.

Pure peace and hushed serenity
surrounds these graceful trees.
And symphonies of Mother Earth
are played through verdant leaves.

Third Place Award

Thoughts on a Winter's Night
By Jeanne E. Ross

The slopes along the woodland
lay barren by the frost;
exposing roots and knarled branches
from winter's holocaust.

Forsaken, they are left abused -
in isolation stand.
Grotesque and haggard, they retreat
from nature's cruel demand.

Perdition stalks the hungry night
of mournful desperation;
and in that solemn hour is heard
a sorrowful oblation.

Then silently in darkness, drifts
upon the hills below,
crystal flakes in love embrace,
a halcyon sea of snow.

Forgotten Veteran
by Dona K. Soler

The world goes on without me,
    Unconcerned for how I fare;
How quickly it abandoned me
    And left me to despair.

It isn't right that leaders
    Can force a man to vie
With conscience about killing
    And wars in which they die...

I love my country even now,
    Although my life is ore,
A part of me forever gone
    In sacrifice to war.

And only phantoms visit me
    Of friends I knew so well,
And ancient bullets still explode
    From those days of living hell.

It is said, the war is over...
    Enjoy the hard won peace;
For me and countless others,
    The war will never cease!

Why Are They Crying?
by Erika Stenzel

My first child, was a cute baby boy
a five pound bundle, of utter joy
needless to say, he grew very fast
and when he was five years old, at last
he met his grandparents, from far, far away
to cross the Atlantic, took more than a day

When he arrived, emotions ran very high
hugging and kissing and they started to cry.
He tugged on his father's trousers, to ask,
"Why are they crying?" to find an answer, what a task
but his father told him: "They are happy to see us."
Well, that was that and stop with all that fuss.

He stayed two months, then it was time to go
and here, he is given another blow
as the good-byes brought sadness and pain
to see, that they are all crying again
he tugged on his father's trousers, not believing,
"Papa, why are they crying now, are they happy we're leaving?"

The Longfellow Competition

Whispers

Chapter Seven

Dedications

Literary works and dedications requested by the contributing authors.

Paul Bush

My Love Light

I would be nothing
If you had not been around,
My heart would not beat
Would not make a sound.

Your beautiful smile
Those dark mysterious eyes,
But underneath it all
A world of wonder and surprise.

You kept me going
When I thought all had been lost,
You shared in my burdens
Despite the personal cost.

If I never had another friend
Or no one else did ever care,
I still felt so very precious
Because you were always there.

My love and devotion to you
Will forever be strong,
I always know who to look to
When things seem to be wrong.

Defining Friendship

A true friend is someone
Who is always there for you,
No matter what the problem is
They will always help you through.

They will be by your side
When you need them the most,
And when you have something to celebrate
A friend is the first to toast.

When you are feeling down
Or the world has got you low,
They will cheer you up
They will make the Good times flow.

They never have a harsh word to say
And they help you any way they can,
A friend can be anybody
Friendships form between a woman and a man.

God's Gift To Me

The rain represents my sorrow
For the loss of our friendship before,
My newfound faith in God
Has given me hope for friendship once more.

You are the reason I found him
The reasons that I have been saved,
You are the one who showed me
Through Him I am free, not enslaved.

You helped me to discover much
Things like love, happiness, and joy,
We have a strong and true friendship
No force in the world can destroy.

I hope you have all you ever deserve
May all that you desire be,
You will always have a friend there
Always be able to lean on me.

May fame and fortune be yours to have
May friends and family help you out,
May I remain a very close friend
Most of all, may your faith be devout.

Lindsey Davis
age 14

Dark, Light, Winter, Summer

In the darkness, I see light
In the light, I see darkness
In the winter, I smell roses
In the summer, I see snow
I walk down a crowed street
But I hear no cars or people
I walk down a lonely street
But I hear cars and people
Is this the way it's going to be?
Or will it change?
Is this what we need to learn from?
What do we need to learn?

Robert LaPierre

Grandpa's View

Life at times seems strange to me
It's kind of like the old oak tree
With arms outstretched towards the sky
As if to say, "Must we all die?"
Once just a seed, we grew to be strong
We weathered our storms, we sang our song
Our purpose served in so many ways
More often than not, on countless days
Most are gone, who shared in my past
Memories I have, but will they last?
Our children with little ones, that life has brought
Eyes full of questions, eager to be taught
So pass on life's secrets, all you have learned
It's part of your love, it's something you've earned
Time moves so quickly, and their life will be spent
I guess only then, will they know what you meant
So live and learn all that you can
For us, a full life is just a short span.

Freedom

I know that I won't live to see
Another Statue of Liberty
In a harbor standing free
That's what freedom means to me
For the young, freedom is just a word
They know no other way
But who's to say what's down the road
Or the price they'll have to pay
Life's road's not easy for most of us
We make do with what's at hand
But unless you have been over there
it's hard to understand
This country, our freedom, built with blood and sweat
So many lost, so high the coast, and it's far from over yet
Our choice of work, those dreams we chase
The things that all seem nice
Remember, friends, lets never forget
This all came with a price
Our rights, our privileges, throw in some blessings, too
Then consider all we've endured, we are the chosen few.

Grandchildren

We are God's children, so we've been told
The years fly by, then we grow old
Children gone, now on their own
Our house seems empty, no longer a home
When out days don't seem so bright
Again we're blessed with a whole new light
A new beginning, a reason to live
Times to be shared, love to give
A gift from God, your time well spent
You come alive, His message sent
Each moment treasured, as though your last
Flashbacks, memories, of days long past
The old dog runs, first time in years
What am I feeling? Why these tears?
The holidays now mean something more
A tree in the parlor, toys on the floor
Stories to tell, books to share
A child on my lap, 'our' rocking chair
Being a grandparent, that's not so tough
When you're alone, now that's what rough
So adjust your life to all that's new
Maybe you've got your dreams come true.

Whispers

Chapter Eight

Whispers Around The World

Selected literary works from the competitiors in the
Spring 1996 Iliad Literary Awards Program.

Routine Of Life
by Elzbeth Adams - age 16

Every morning I wake up, I roll out of bed
And I put on the same pair of pants.

My life has become routine.
I drive to work in the same left lane, at the same 60 mph,
on the same roads,
And park in the same parking space.

Sometimes I see a street kid.
He sits with a girl.
They drink Pepsi and eat Chinese.
He's only about 17
Sometimes he looks at me-

Our eyes meet,
All time stops, we both just stare.
Then the light turns green and the blue cadillac behind me
Is suddenly honking.

Dazed, I drive forward.
I can remember every detail on him
And I think about him until I get to work
And I go on with my usual...routine of life.

First Base in Any Game
by R. Douglas Adams

Each swing,
At the plate of life's brief pitch,
Played inning's, fouls, and out's;
Win the precious moments,
in each up we'll ever have.

With the bat in our hands,
We hit the sacred ball,
More times than not,
First base;
Always means hope for a run in.

Our spirit swells from the sound
of cracked oak;
Dreams soar past, with each ran base,
Looking to home before the ball,
We win more times that not.

Always remembering;
Our well fielded games,
And the soulful lots,
In the mighty joy's we felt together;
For having played in the game at all.

Hands
by Diana R. Agbayani

hands
reaching out
for a Hand
that reaches out
to hands
that refuse
to reach out.

Right, Wrong
by Jamie Adesso - age 15

Black as night,
White as day,
Clear as crystal,
Solid as coal.

Hold the thought,
Let it go,
Voice your right,
Start a fight.

Cold as ice,
Hot as the sun,
Pretty as a rose,
Ugly as a thorn.

Help the poor man,
Watch out for the con,
Leave him alone,
Beware of who you turn
your back upon.

Injury
by Meghan L. Affinito - age 20

With every breath, you take a piece of me,
But of willingness I am quite unsure.
I pursue, but me you choose to ignore.
And with my soul I take vast injury.
To you I sing my song of malady;
Eternal anguish I cannot endure.
Your indifference tears me to the core,
I am beaten to nothing, can't you see?
A scream penetrating my ravaged mind
As heart and soul collide with wasted pride,
Never have I felt a pain of this kind.
A complete destruction of all inside,
Only desire for lost dreams by your hand,
Why did I place all my faith in my man?

Lost
by Angela Agourias

In a bat of an eyelash, all was lost
Where once inhabited warmness, now has turned to frost
No tears left, no more strength for crying
So much time passed, endless hours spent trying.

Avoiding admitting that all the efforts led nowhere
Hoping in the interim my dignity to spare.
Trapped in the fairy tales I was led to believe
Now alone, must dedicate the time to rightfully grieve.

Once portraying the image of a woman always in control,
In what I refer to as the charade called life I now have to play a convincing role
Trying in vain to ignore the hurtful gossip and emotion of shame
Only quest had been acceptance and contentment, therefore I refuse to bear the blame.

Devotion
by Angela Agourias

It is late at night, I'm lying in bed, staring at the ceiling,
Confused, trying to find the right words to explain this feeling,
As hard as I try, I can't get you out of my mind,
I wonder if it's true when they say love is blind.

It's been a long time that I haven't felt this way,
Sometimes I lose my words and don't know what to say,
Wanting to hold you and love you, be near you,
Avoiding to let myself fall too hard, still of rejection I fear you.

So soon and you have already made a mark deep in my soul,
Came to me like a dream and my heart you stole,
This sweet sentiment has caused by system such commotion,
Making me want to share my life with you, bask in love and devotion.

New Beginning
by Angela Agourias

Soon I will be leaving my childhood behind in a matter of a second
Approaching adulthood responsibilities for the remainder of my days.
Suddenly seen as someone full of wisdom and maturity,
The secret that is shared when the gold band is placed on my finger.

Anxiously awaiting to wake up in the morning embraced by your arms
Momentarily missing my peach walls and collection of stuffed animals.
Realizing that I had taken my family and childhood home for granted,
Forgetting that my dwelling there was just for borrowed time.

Looking forward to the new path that I have chosen, with a surging excitement,
Ready to face the ups and downs of life that await me.
Feeling the security that you provide and the undeniable love in your eyes,
Wondering how I ever managed to live one day without you by my side.

And as the big day approaches and I'm in the midst of preparation,
Sometimes feeling stressful, tired, angry and agitated.
I try not to dwell so much on being the princess of the day,
And fantasize instead about the tomorrow that awaits us.

Winter Night
by Lia-Maria Alfonsi - age 16

You stand outside and the white snow seems endless,
You search for beautiful things to see,
as you look above the stars shine brighter than ever,
it almost seems to be the middle of the day,
a plane flies by,
you can hear the roaring sound,
and you can see the beautiful lights,
from very far away it looks like another star,
but from close as can be,
it is the loveliest thing you will ever see on a warm and pretty winter night.

The Last Party
by Geri Ahearn

It seemed so long ago,
since we first met.
Many years spent together,
true friends are forever.
We will always remember,
the good times and the bad.
Some happy, and some sad.
It did not matter,
if it rained or snowed.
Our only care,
was for everyone, to be there.
We counted many birthdays,
Halloween was fun.
But, soon the best was to come.
We couldn't wait to celebrate.
Another pool party, of course.
To splish and splash,
sing, dance and laugh.
Then, one evening in June,
it came to soon.
The last party was here.
So many memories to share.
So many friends to cheer.
The time has come to say, "good-by."
So, please "don't cry."
Blow out the candles,
dim the lights.
For we must never forget,
this special night.

Our Gracious Heavenly Father
by Gregory Akers - age 13

Our Lord almighty up above
thank you for your gracious love,
which we can cherish in our hearts
and know you will never depart.

Help us through this sinful life
that appears upon these weary minds.
What great feelings we have when we
know God controls our holy lives.

We should pray each night to keep the
spiritual light upon our lives that he
might dwell in our hearts. We should never
take him for granted because he is the true God.

God, thank you so for giving your son's
life to die upon the cross for our
eternal life. Our Lord almighty up
above, thank you for your gracious love.

Love
by Lia-Maria Alfonsi - age 16

All I know is what I see, all I hear is what they tell me, all I know is that your leaving me, you've chosen her love over mine, and now my heart just shattered into a million pieces, I sit here, and all I do is cry, I didn't even say goodbye, I guess I really didn't want to, all I really want is to have you back, I want to hold you in my arms, feel the love that flows between us, but now your gone and it really hurts, I never told you how much I loved you, how much I cared, I guess I never really knew until it was too late, until now.

Yellow Roses In Spring
by Robert Alan

When I stepped on the road next to her,
she reached out and gave me an anchor to hold on to
Color replace a life of black and white
My heart was pulled as my insides jumped
My senses became focused and sharp
She was beautiful with a softness and tenderness
Yet there was a force in her eyes that grabbed me
I became addicted to the fragrance of her perfume
Though the years have passed,
I stop in my tracks in the presence of that aroma and remember
We were both changing as we walked that road
We opened our hearts and shared experiences,
experiences molded into the recesses of my memory
She taught me the music of life
We danced to the beat, turning, gliding
We moved as one to the rhythm
I treasure the walk we took hand in hand
It was like yellow roses in Spring

Blind
by Angela Aldrich - age 13

A cry to shatter the darkness.
A tear to soften the pain.
A burden to add to my hurting heart.
So much to lose but nothing to gain.
The people all around me.
Add no comfort to my soul.
The riches that surround my life,
seem as nothing but coal.
The friends I used to hold so dear
Leave slowly one by one.
The darkness that surrounds my heart,
Makes me only want to run.
The more I seem to move forward,
The more I am behind
The more the darkness shows the light,
The more that I feel blind.

One Little Stone
by Angela Aldrich - age 13

The once bright day
now growing dark.
The once bright flame now
one small spark
The joy and the peace I felt inside
Now hurting pain and no place to hide.
What is this that I feel in me?
This pain and crying agony.
These feelings that we used to share
The tears we used to shed and bare
And now you're gone
And you've moved on
Leaving me alone.
The earth is one great, giant boulder
And I one little stone.

Spellbound
by Winifred Allard

I'm spellbound by your smile
The twinkle in your eyes.
I'd walk a-many mile
To be there by your side.

Your in my dreams at night
Can't concentrate by day.
My prayers are that you might
Soon walk into my life.

Shane
by Mariam Ann Alleman

Shane   you remember the
         one with blue eyes and
     blonde hair.
     The one with all of our love
     and care.
Shane   do you remember when he
     left us we all felt pain
Shane   was the sun in the sky
     the star in my eye that
     was never to die.
     And now it's too late to
         say good-bye
Shane   was like the dove in the air
     but did he know how much
     we care?

In memory of Shane Benton

When You Were There
by Mariam Ann Alleman

I needed attention
So you told me what I wanted
     to hear and gave me a beer
Therefore I couldn't shed a tear
You taught me to let go of my
deepest darkest fear for that
my friend you are a DEAR!

For Kelly L. Miller

The Wedding Poem
by Laurie Allen

You are a gentle, compassionate man,
Self-assured with an ease of grace.
In your eyes you tell me about love,
In your smile you tell me about life,
In your touch you teach me about sharing.
You are not afraid to laugh or cry,
Always positive and accepting by nature,
You make each days friendship a challenge.
You want to know about he people around you,
You don't give your feelings away for free,
And never take life for granted.
You know when to let me lean on you
And when to make me stand alone.
You give me space to be what I am
And demand the same in return.
You strive for the balance of honesty,
You know the responsibility of the word love.
You hold me in the darkness, when all my fears rise up to meet me,
You let me hold you in the darkness, when all your fears rise to meet you.
You find strength and pleasure in what we've come to mean to each other,
And loving you has put hope in my heart and joy in my life.

The Painting
by Vivian Allison

I tried not to heed the beckoning hands,
Reaching out from he painting on the museum wall.
Shameful art, all asmear with blood, trash and cans.
But forcefully I was drawn into the painting's scrawl.

There are thousands of paintings like this one I thought,
Lurking in the corner of some artist's mind.
Where the dying anticipates his sleep of ages or,
He perceives a world's guilt for some animal long forgotten.

A crowd gathered, seemingly awaken from slumber.
And found themselves startled, speechless, somber,
As if vines had wreathed themselves around hidden wisdom.
Sin is expiated, the marrow of the master;s work is savored.

Through brush strokes depicting inner city litter,
The aura of each piece guarding a mystery.
A stepped back from the painting, hearing a quiet murmur,
A young man whispering lamentations to the artist's work.

Humbly, I acknowledge I have not the professional's eye.
And scarcely do my dreams condense their misty substance,
Into an heroic issue of one's perverse fancy.
Then I ask myself, I know, a nefarious question.

Why does some art soothe the spirit,
While others vex us with wonder?

Yellow
by Shannon Amerman - age 11

Yellow is the sun shining in the day,
Yellow is a cheetah running for its prey,
Yellow is a lemon sour but nice,
Yellow is a sunflower elegant yet precise,
Yellow is a rose so pretty in May,
Yellow is a daisy so gorgeous in a bouquet.
Yellow is a goldfish swimming in its bowl,
Yellow is a color that touches my soul.

Night Life
by Vivian Allison

Our lives are different, yours and mine.
And life's footsteps follow us across our boundary of time.
Your trail is soft upon the earth,
While mine though rough lends a touch of mirth.
Spurn me, tread upon me, I know my worth.

When first I drew breath I am labeled,
the offspring of that woman of classic fable.
So vivid, gaudy and bright as a macaw's wing.
Ought not humanity press around me then,
For love that makes the spirit sing.

Oh, exaltation, night lights are my curse.
Yet they tend to mend whatever errors I fancy,
And judgement during the sun's decline.
But the wayward husband knows affection when he is held,
By the loving, strong chains that passions weld.

And I won't deny that it makes me glad,
to know I missed what I might have had,
beyond the city lights, away from din and roar,
An animalhouse, a barnyard, and wheat fields galore.
Our lives are different, yours and mine.

Watchen' Over Me
by AHNA

I use to fall asleep
under a tree
with God
Watchen' Over Me -

I use to fall asleep
sailing at sea
with God
Watchen' Over Me -

I use to fall asleep
hearing blasphemy
with God
Watchen' Over Me -

I spoke nothing inspired
And God became tired.
I wanted his faithful trust
yet, my actions was unjust.

He desires more than my
contentment and sleep
He needs my witnessing
for souls to keep - Smile.

Fidget
by Kristina F. Almquist - age 16

It's like
Having hands like these...
I don't know what to do with them.
Swing them, snap them, squeeze them...
More than I know what to do with.
It's just like that.
The uneasy wondering
Of who knows
You don't know
What to do with your hands.
I sit in this hall,
Stare at the faces
and especially yours,
Fidgeting with my hands
my eyes
my heart.
The uneasy wondering
If you know
I don't know
What to do with my hands
my eyes
my heart...
More than I know what to do with.

Dé jà vu
by Pamela Alton

A place you've been

A place you've seen before.

Could it be only the first time you've opened that door?

Or could it be you've been here before?
Perhaps you've had on chance and you've come back for more.

Those of us that get a second chance know the deal.
We're on our second or even our third time around the wheel.
We all have secrets we'd like to reveal, but there are those whom
don't believe we're for real.

Could we be crazy or could we be true?
Or is it that we're all just imagining our experiences of Dé jà vu?

Me
by Eric Ameduri - age 16

I am like a pine in the middle of maples,
The outcast, the foreigner
A pebble instead of a rock,
I am like a bird, just wanting to be free.
I am like nature, pure and living.
Like a fish swimming up a new stream.
I just want a person to feel for me,
To live, to help, to be there for me.
I am like the clouds above,
watching and listening.
I am like a dazed dog.
Trying to figure out who everybody is.
I am me, just me, one and only me,
I just want to be free.

To Julie
by B.J. Anderson

You think my poems are gloomy, and maybe you are right.
But then you must remember they are all written late at night.

With darkness all around me I sit down to start to type,
It really could be brighter but John forgot to change the light.

Last time I tried to change it, by standing on a chair.
I slipped landing hard on my little (well not so little) derriere.

You may be thinking that the sun gives lots of light,
So how come this dummy is typing late at night?

The reason is so simple if you stop to think a minute,
I am not alone in this house I have two daughters in it.

They hate to help with dishes, and house work makes them sick,
But let me start my typing they run to help me, double quick!

Either crawling on my lap, or trying to collaborate
In a few seconds any good thoughts quickly evaporate.

Edgar had his window where sat a raven tapping,
I too have a window but there are my daughters rapping.

One just knows her arm is broken or has some fatal sign.
Another's going to starve to death am I sure it's not lunch time?

So until something changes, I suppose I could learn to sew,
I will remain, Faithfully yours, B.J. Poe.

I Do Not Understand
by Ginger Anderson - age 16

I do not understand
   Why there are so many homeless people
   Why people have to live in fear of their life
   Why there is world hunger and no one helps.

But most of all
   I do not understand
   Why there is war between countries
   And they seem to want to fight with each other
   Instead of compromising
   Fighting doesn't help any
   But instead, it just takes innocent lives.

What I understand most is peace.
   No one tries to hurt or kill others
   And people get along with everyone else
   There are no enemies
   Just friends.

Life
by Stephanie Anderson - age 15

Life is like a little child,
following a winding brook.
Following uncertainly down a hill.
   twisted   changing
   unpredictable   lovely
Emptying into a pool of caution.

A Dying Rose
by Gerardo L. Angulo

Mother, since you left this world
my life has not been the same
like a dying rose
that has not felt sun nor rain
My heart longs for healing
for sadness seems to be winning
Like a dying rose
happiness has become a stranger
to my soul
Like a dying rose
I await to see
what the future holds
Mother, whether I survive or not
I will always love you a lot
Life is precious like a rose
facing life tomorrow
will be difficult I suppose
Mother, could my life be
like a dying rose?

*In memory of my beloved mother,
Mrs. Bertha Maxie Angulo*

Lonely Dove
by Gerardo L. Angulo

Mother, when God called you before Him
I became like a lonely dove
Prayerful and faithful
I hope to become
Life is short
and sometimes unfair
for my daily cross is difficult to bear
Your spirit flew like a dove
in the night
fear and anxiety are forever tonight
I, like a lonely dove seek comfort
seek comfort
in the echo of your love
for your heart
goes beyond the beauty of a dove
A lonely dove I am
A lonely dove I will be
Loneliness will be mine
until I fall asleep
for in every dream
you are there with me
A lonely dove
I wish not to be

*In memory of my beloved mother,
Mrs. Bertha Maxie Angulo*

When It Hurts To Live
by Gerardo L. Angulo

When it hurts to live
it is love and comfort
that God will give
When our lives are bruised
by despair and sadness
we must never forget
God's greatness
Sometimes it may hurt
to get up in the morning
Remember, that coping with life
is something we are all still learning
Sometimes it may hurt to smile
God will help us
to laugh for at least a little while
Sometimes it may hurt
to face the night
To peace and hope
we must never say goodbye
When it hurts to live
let us make God our best friend
and our lives He will mend

*In memory of my beloved mother,
Mrs. Bertha Maxie Angulo*

Reality
by Andrea T. Beckman - age 19

I know no such word
Reality compared to what?
On second thought
I know reality
Reality is birth and death
What happens in between is life.

Dreams In A Wishful Place
by Donald A. Ankofski

She walked into my eyes
... With angel's hair
& eyes of desire.

She kept me dreaming
... To taste her kiss
& lick her every inch.

She caught me wishing
... Her love
To make life worthwhile.

I remember the flowers in her hair
The scent of her skin
&...

She walked into my eyes
... Her angel's hair
To my eyes' desire.

She kept me wishing
... To taste her kiss
& kiss her every single inch.

She caught me dreaming
... Her love
& a chance at happiness.

But then she disappeared
... in a dream in a wishful place.

My Home By The Bay
by Albert Antonucci

My thoughts ever stray
To my home by the bay.

My days were endless, it seemed.
Playing games, by the water's edge we careened.

No rules or scores, not one
And none needed to be won.

No guidelines, no teams,
Even sidelines unseen.

Chasing the tides at every turn
My opponents only the ern.

Caught up in a majesty serene,
Clouds, riding in so fast, unseen.

Wishing for one I could hide
for a ride into the sky, ever wide.

The air, ever so cool and sweet,
As the sand embraced my feet.

The foaming water's edge
Like a taste of lemon wedge.

The magic carpets of stone
Every shape and color I could own.

Gone were the sounds of bustling crowds
No horns, no buses, no noises allowed.

The setting sun was the only way.
I knew it was the end of the day.

My thoughts ever stray
To my home by the bay.

Sorry
by Jayme Bahr - age 14

Sorry she left him without a goodbye
Sorry she said I don't love you anymore
Sorry she realized that he wasn't the one
Sorry the note she wrote made him cry
Sorry she made the decision before she was sure
Sorry she misses having so much fun
Now that she's sorry she can't have him back
She is mostly sorry because of that

God
by Jayme Barschdorf - age 14

Is he real,
Or is he fake?
Does he really forgive our mistakes?
Does he love us,
Or does he not?
If so,
Why does he take the innocence,
Yet leave the violence?
Why did he make the bad?
To make his world a living hell.
In church they make him a saint,
But in life he really ain't.
Are God and Satan one person???

My Angels Watch O'er Me
by Shanna Aragon - age 17

My Angels in heaven
Watch o'er me with power
And sitting to serve
In our gracious lords tower.
Our father up above
Guides us through life,
To see us in right,
And this grotto of light.
He grips as we're right,
And hold to his world,
Like a chirping tweet of summer,
And soars like a bird.
TO love is a gift
And feel from the heart
To the lord our god,
Won't tear us apart.
We're brothers and sisters,
We'll always be one
Says in the book of our lord,
Til' our world is done.

Lonely
by Tiffany Artley - age 14

All my dreams
Are of you
The times we shared
The love from
Within

Now it's gone
Hidden inside for eternity

Where my heart has gone
And taken that love
It won't let me know
I've cried
A millon tears and more

I've had
Many sleepless nights

But in the end
It doesn't matter
Cuz you've gone
And found another
And I'm just
A lonely.......
Lonely.........

Person of your past

Are You Sad?
by Heather Basham - age 16

Rugged mountainous cliffs jagged and rough.
Year after year you are torn down by wind and rain and yet you remain
    tough.

Do you not weep with every passing year?
The monsoons are arriving they are almost here.

All the plants, rocks, and living things scream as they are washed down
    the hill
hoping that their screams will act as a shield.
Mr. Cliff I ask you how do you feel?

Then as if the mountain replies.
The wind brushed against my cheek and I heard a sigh.

Everything Lives and Everything Dies

Spiderman
by Melody Ashby - age 16

The spider is so graceful,
Just like I am.
He crawls along his web,
He has no friends
He wraps up his food,
And discretely sucks the blood.
Like a vampire of the night,
Trapped inside without love.
He twists and twirls,
His tiny threads,
The flies, moths, and bugs
Trapped in the midst of their death bed.
Like me I am alone,
Yet, I am full of pride,
Still wondering, like the spider,
Why I am still alive.
Catching, spinning,
Twirling a band,
Just like me,
I am the spiderman.

A Door
by Frank L. Audino

The faucet drips' and drips' again'
You've tried everything; it just won't stop.
So you live with it!

The drops become a rhythm like the rain.
And you move about to the beat.
You turn on the radio.
You're dancing and singing again.
by golly, you're the number 1 star
On God's hit parade.

You strip.
You're nude before the lord.
And you think you can still hear it drip.
It's a disco/hoedown/hootenanny now.
The phone rings. Fans. Wow.
They want to know when you
Can pay your charge card bill!

Now comes the rain scene,
In the shower getting clean.
You hum in onomatopoeia.
You vary the notes as you
Move through the water.
You dress and go through the stage door.

Readying yourself for the next
Act of God.
All subjects art too cliche.

My face is always the last thing to
Leave the mirror.

Lonely Heart
by Chad Austin

The emptiness inside of me grows and grows
Darkness is drawing nearer, each wasted hour
life
The love of life and all things wondrous seems to have eluded me
all I can find is pain and fear
The pain of losing something sacred
The fear of losing your love
The anguish of losing my soul

The Making Of a Gentleman
by Frank L. Audino

I often take refuge in the illusion
Of being a gentleman.
It's a safe image because
Even tough guys respect one.

He is polite but not mousy.
His manners are from honor
Not demeaning or conniving.
He's resigned to not always being
Top priority.

Not an instant status,
You might not recognize one right off;
And likewise it takes decades to attain.

Not always late bloomers,
Realizing that maturity grows in the soul,
They know that being cute can
Bring success.

Not necessarily rich,
Yet their merit has usually won
The esteem of people with resources.

The true gentleman lives on a budget,
Requiring help only for the unexpected.

He knows when to say hello and to say goodbye.
And though his truth may be wrong,
He'll never tell a lie.

Winning Stuff
by Frank L. Audino

To feel as desperate as a car alarm
That no one will turn off,
That's the mark of a winner.
For the precious possession either
Stays parked and secured
Or beguiled and transplanted.

Do you think Eden was a safe neighborhood?
Does shoveling of snow sound like
The biting of an apple to you my friend?
Old people are cooler.
rock of ages gathers no moss

    BORED?
Frustration, Love & Anger deliver,
Or call ahead for quick pickup

So I go to the mall and
I tell them I want an aftershave
I can't pronounce. Then I say,
"I'm waiting for my Wife."
The salesperson notes the lack of a band.
I say, "Exactly." and brandish the digit.
The wedding went without a hitch.

Blessings masquerade as frustration,
But evil is repugnant,
And Satan has only one destination.
You might have to wait
In line to meet Jesus in the flesh but
Saints won't mind.

Everyone is a star in the sky,
But someone has to play the moon.

What does your alarm sound like?

Silence
by Chad Austin

I lye alone
    Listening to nothing
Thinking of things gone wrong
    My life
No meaning no hope
    Childhood lost forever
Can't be regained or relived

Desert Impressions
by Mary Bachtell

Moonbeams spotlight the living desert
Sculpturing a shadowy wonderland.
Breezes rustle the sagebrush thicket.
Tumbleweeds bounce over flowering verbena.
Sand dunes ripple, creeping, crawling,
Whirlwinds spin, rising, falling.

Who will enjoy this wondrous sight?
Coyotes prowling, preying, howling,
Lizards slithering, dashing, darting,
Jack rabbits racing, leaping, hiding,
Moths flitting, fluttering, poising,
Screech owls whistling, blinking, watching?

Or is it the hawk perched in the Joshua
Lifting it's wings to gracefully take flight,
Circling, gliding, soaring high
Toward sparkling stars in a velvet sky
Reaching the brilliance of heavenly light?

Vanishing Bliss
by Sarah Badger - age 13

I used to think that when we
watched the sun pass,
that this carefree world
would always last.

However your future was like a candle
melting in the wind.

Then one day I got this call
to go pass the hate and hurt,
gather the pride.
Realizing that when I saw you break
down crying, this might be the last time.

Because you were sad,
and it looked like you might need a hand.

After all, you rescued
me in my time of need.

Wondering what was so hard
to take in at once,
You said goodbye,
but still wish inside that you'll forgive
me for turning my back the day we died.

One Night
by Jayme Bahr - age 14

One night we met
Two kids in school
We made a bet
Playing pool
That we would be together
Always and forever

One night we danced under the stars
We had a few drinks at the bar
You took me home, you said goodbye
I shut the door with a sigh

One night you came to my door
You said I love you much, much more
I'll never forget that night
With the moon shining bright

One night you called and said we're through
Out the window our love blew
Without a care in the world
You left me for another girl

9 months later on that same night
I had a child full of life
It's sad to say
That you can not play
With him today

Relax
by Chelsea Baker - age 12

The warmth of the sun
is on your back.
Your feet step on the fine
dry sand.
The cool breeze gently blows
on your face.
The waves are crashing
children playing
people laughing
A lone seagull flies over the
setting sun.
You no longer know the feeling
of stress
RELAX........

Whose Life Is There To Be Saved?
by Laura Baker - age 16

I was in a store,
Minding my own business.
Then someone came in.
He was a bad man.
He wanted money.
I am a blind woman.
I didn't see the gun then.
He told me to get out of the way.
I said no. I said wait your turn.
He pushed me aside. Then shot me.

Now I'm lying on the floor.
Blood flowing next to me.
I pretend to be dead.
Time passes by. Is this end?
I hope not. I have a life.
Then something happened.
For a split second I could see.
He was a young man, in his teens.
He had a life, and ruined it.
I had a life, and lost it.

Words Of Goodbye
by Nicole Balcer - age 14

Why did you go why wouldn't you stay
Remembering that hurtful day
That day of goodbye I never thought I'd see
Never got to tell you how much you meant to me
So many memories you left behind
Why wouldn't God give you a little more time
If only I could see you once more
Maybe my life could be how it was before
Why did you go why wouldn't you stay
That word of goodbye you didn't have to say

"Forever Love"
by Debbie Baldesberger

Forever love
is a bird's beautiful song
so forever love
can't be wrong

Forever love is flower petals
blowing softly in the wind
with a promise of tomorrow
"Our love will never end"

Forever love is a sky, dark blue
with brilliant stars that shine.
Forever love is happiness
And I'm so glad you're mine.

Butterfly
by Robert A. Ballance - age 17

Butterfly
My butterfly
You are beautiful
You are mine only
No!
Others can't have you
I will place you in my pocket
Keep you safe
No!
She's mine.

In my pocket
My butterfly lies
Beautiful butterfly
Wake up
No!
You are gone
I kept you
I lost you

Who Has Sunshine?
by Denise Marjory Newcombe Bard

Who has Sunshine?
    Not everyone has it.
How bright, Sunshine!
    Think you can spare it?

When someone is blue
    And it seems that you
        Are one of the few
            Blessed divine

Why not be your own ad
    And cheer up the sad
        Walking all of us glad?!!
            WHO HAS SUNSHINE???

Air
by Denise Marjory Newcombe Bard

    Are you full of Hot Air
        Just blowing off steam
            So things aren't what they seem?

    Like to hear yourself talk?
        When you just say a word
            It so und so absurd?

        How about Cold Air?
            Are you so full of ice
                You can't say something nice?

        Have to have your own way?
            Are you so spoiled
    That you have people foiled?

    Are you full of Cool Air
        Just staying aloof
            And playing the spoof?

    Do you play it cool
        And life not partake
            Fear you'll make a mistake?

        The same with lukewarm!
            Be careful 'lest you
                From His mouth He doth spew!

        Playing it safe?
            Just being bold
                Neither Hot not Cold?

    The Warm Air is best,
        It never grows cool, cold,
            Lukewarm or cold.

    It's best to be warm,
        To be loving and fair,
            Not of any Old Air!

You Are
by Denise Marjory Newcomb Bard

My rainbow in a rainy sky
    My sunshine in the darkest day
My flower in our garden of love
    And when life seems empty, my stay.

        You soften all the harshest trails
            And lighten every task
        I trust you with my heart, my life
            You never have to ask.

You lift me to the highest peaks
    And love to make me laugh
My love, my life, my everlasting key
    My all-in-all, my staff.

        I love your eyes so full of smiles
            Your face of tenderness
        You're special, Dear, in every way
            Of this I must confess.

Your smile and laughter thrill me
    To the very depths of my heart.
Just as you are I've loved you, Dear,
    Right from the very start.

        My Rainbow, Sunshine, Flower of Love
            All wrapped into one so dear,
        My fullness in life's emptiness
            And calm in darkest fear.

My everlasting key to life
    My moon and shining star,
I've just begun to tell you, Dear,
    Of all the things you are.

Dark State Of Mind
by Christine Black - age 16

    I'm rarely in Dark state of mind, my words & things I think about are now harder, and harder to be defined. I have the happiness & pain to endure cause life comes to me so unsure.
    I soar down roads with no light but there's no excuse so never give up without a fight. So keep working on that Dark state of mind and one day your thoughts, and words will be defined.

Places
by Angie Barden - age 14

Forbidden places
in the shadows
like hidden faces.

My memory lost
among the
many faces.

In the shadows
lurk the places
that the faces
want to be.

Places I want
to see.

Places I want
to be.

Places I want
to make.

"May?"
by Ivy Barkakati - age 11

First there were leaves falling in fall,
Then the snows blowing hard, coming down in cold balls.
The start of the spring brought showers and rain,
And the weather is like that now, then and again.
The summer will come soon, with humid, hot days,
The sun burning the Earth with its torturing rays.
But where does May actually belong?
With the showers and birds singing songs?
Or maybe it should be in the summer,
With people fainting from heat, thinking "What a bummer!"
Or maybe it could be in the autumn,
When leaves cover the ground so you can't see the bottom!
Or maybe it would be during the snows and sleet,
With the sharp, biting cold hard to beat.
I think that May might be in between
The time where there are flowers blooming on the scene
And the season when the air is really hot,
When people get overheated outside on the spot.
But the true answer I might never know,
To the question which season May should go.

Down Under
by Juanita C. Barnes-Bourgui

You have proclaimed yourselves supreme:
    Top of the line, numero uno supreme, but...

Have you ever treated anyone right...equally right... civilly
    right...supremely right?

When we taught you to sow and reap, why did you boldly steal
    our sheep?
    Was this equally right...civilly right...supremely right?

While we cared for your children; raised them as our own,
    Why did you carelessly destroy our homes? was this then
    equally right...civically right...supremely right?

We even taught you how to love, and in return you hung our sons;
    Were you then equally right...civilly right...supremely right?

You call yourselves supreme; have a need to feel supreme, but
    then again, you are viewed as supreme...
        Supremely violent...Supremely murderous...
        Supremely dangerous...Supremely destructive

No, we have never been referred to as supreme, nor have we ever
inspired to be so

For we have always been Equal

Why?
by Brandy Lynn Blakeney - age 12

Why do we die?
Why do we cry?
Why are we sad?
Why is there bad?
Why is there mad?
Why is there rain?
Why is there pain?.....
Why?!

Vision
by Stephanie Baron - age 14

Her weak shadow playing in the delicate
    summer wind, from the years she had
    seen and wasted away in vain.
But who are you to tell me I will always
    be this way.
Vision
Easy living when you're on the outside
Blood drops, like stars on a hazy sun
    swept evening.
The delicate kiss
The crucial good bye.
Why do you think you could take her?
Who do you think could take me away?
When you live life with your arms tied down,
    eyes to the floor when speaking.
I fly high.
I do not wish to be here now.
I have no thoughts to share today.
Even if I am shattered, even if I am
    shattered here inside.
The times have changed and looking back it
    seems so clear, I was never what
    they thought I should have been.
Every dream I dreamed at night has some
    how lost all meaning.
They try and say they know, but I don't think so.
There is no happily ever after.
Not this time anyhow.

Grandma
by Melissa M. Bernard - age 14

    Cancer swept your life away along with your whole glow.
    Now the glow is gone, but your soul still lingers on.
    You were so strong, you always pressed on, and
        never seemed to loose faith.
    You grew too weak and lost your words even to say,
        I love you.
But now your at peace where you have no pain so the time has
        come to let you go,
    because I knew you'll always be with my in soul.

Believe In Yourself
by Marcy Barto - age 12

As you walk up the hill
and feel like you want to kill.
Remember, believe in yourself!

When the pitch is coming fast
and you watch it go past,
It goes back to the pitcher,
Here it comes,
Remember, believe in yourself!

You're close to the trophy now,
About ready to take a bow,
You feel your feet are going to slip,
You hope you don't trip.
Remember, believe in yourself!

It's almost over now
As you cross the finish line.
You made it.
You believed in yourself!

People Who Were
by Clyde Barton Jr.

Have you ever sat and watched,
A group of roving clouds unite,
To form a thing of unbelievable beauty,
Or create a path of death and destruction?
Although many different eyes have seen,
And almost as many ears have heard.,
There is still no clear scientific understanding,
Of how such beauty can become so deadly this fast
This is the same exact situation that the people,
Of our world and their leaders are facing today,
Where war, crime and terrorism are concerned,
As peace, harmony and mutual respect fade away.
For people are more deadly and destructive,
Than the entire forces of nature combined,
Because they keep spreading an uncontrollable hate,
From place to place and person to person without end,
Forgetting that there is much more to life than proving,
Whose the toughest in a fight to the death where no one
Wins and everyone loses, creating another lost Atlantis,
Or devastating flood,erasing all the people who were.

Tiffany
by Amy Black - age 12

Why do you do this to me
You make me so mad
You gang up on me
I'm now so sad
I tell you my feelings
You don't give a care
I try to talk to you
But you just stare
Please by my friend
I like you a lot,
So lets be a pair,
Even though you just forgot

Bestfriends
by Shannon Becker - age 16

Hand-in-hand we lead the
pack. We may go to heaven or to
hell. But remember we will be
together forever. If in heaven
peace upon us, we will bask upon
the god-like rays. Not too hot.
not too cool just right for
everyone's preference. But if our
sins have not been forgiven we
will be together in hell. Even
though to hot to handle. Still we
have already been to hell many of
times and came back only slightly
scared, but because of our
friendship that is so very strong
that no one and nothing can bring
us apart. Even though we had to
drum it into our ears that we
would bounce back every time
something, little or big, had
happened. Sometimes we were not
always there in self, but in spirit
we were, and always helped each
other in the hour of need. And
always will be no matter how far
apart. Look at how close we have
gotten and still a long journey a
head of us to go.

My Best Friend
by Mary Frances Barton

"My Best Friend" stayed right by my side
She was someone I could always confide
I could talk to her about troubles and pain
Whatever bothered me, to her, I could explain

She knew my whole life story
Whatever fun I was having she was enjoying the glory
That was "My Best Friend"
But something went wrong in the end

"My Best Friend" turned out to be my worse nightmare
When my man and I was together, she was right there
"My Best Friend" I trusted her through and through
I didn't know she was loving him too

I accused him of the woman next door
All along, "My Best Friend" was getting the core
When I found out it was painful for me
It was my fault trusting her to be

I cried, I cried just to know
"My Best Friend" hurt me so
I was told she was no good
She back stabbed me, but I didn't think she would

I was closer to her than my own sister
There was nothing I wouldn't do for her
She lied to me, she pretended to be
She did me wrong, "My Best Friend" How could she?

She laughed in my face
Behind my back she took my place
That's what a best friend will do
She'll take everything from you

Unseen Love
by Faith E. Bindeman - age 15

My love is great
And yet unseen
Life right now
Is like a very sad dream
Why can't he look inside
And see my pain
Why does my heart ache
Why are my eyes like clouds
Pouring rain
In his eyes
I see the shinning sun above
But he sees us only as friends
So I keep chained
My undying love

Emptiness
by Tony Biasetti - age 17

-Is the night so dark
you can't see
Is your life so black
you can't breath
-Is the room you lock yourself in
all in your mind
the door closed
and you've lost your way out
-When you awake
is there a stranger in your bed
but then you realize
the strangers yourself
-Come away from the cold
I'll set your soul free
the kiss of death
lies within me

The Sea
by William Bartz

I've crossed an ocean of blue just to reach you...

Forever lost within the scarlet sea,
which flows from your eyes to me.

As Captain of my own Destiny,
the charts lead me into the sea.

Since this ship can never return, it sails to your lilting tune.
The endless flowing song of the sea!

Waves ripple upon the sandy shore,
inside eyes mirroring your soul.

The sun reflects on your shimmering surface,
a rainbow of colors glittering vividly inside.

What will be, will be.

But I'm comforted by the momentary reprieve,
with every moment I'm swallowed by the sea.

Thinkin' Of Me
by Dominique Bigbee - age 13

I was sittin' alone in this same
lonely place
Looking in the mirror at the reflection of
my face
When suddenly I saw something
It was me
Something I never thought of as a human
being.
I looked once and then looked again
Wishing the good of me would come back in.
Never once did I think of me, as a lonely
precious human being.

The Pain Within
by Stephie Battaglia - age 15

Inside myself I feel the pain,
That lives now in my heart,
Never did I ever think,
That we'd have to part.

I feel the tearing and the shredding,
My heart is now in two,
A fresh new tear forms in my eye
When I think of you.

I wanted to let go of life,
But you were there for me,
You gave me a reason to go on,
You set my spirits free.

Thoughts are racing through my head,
My inside parts are aching,
I can hear the horrid sound,
Of my own heart breaking.

I wonder how I will survive,
Without you by my side,
I love you more than anything,
My feelings I can't hide.

Maybe one day He will see,
That we belong together,
Until then I have memories,
That will live forever!

The Edge...
by Sharon Beach

Is where you stop for a moment
in time.
Looking back, at who you were,
and forward, at who you can be.
Searching, Questioning, Growing.
As, the sun rising, slowly over the peak,
reaching through the trees, searching.
Finds, far below, silently dreaming,
the lake.
With a lover's soft caress,
warmth strokes the water.
A flash of light, a gentle moan,
Understanding dawns.
Search your Mind,
Find your Soul,
Give your Heart.
With courage, faith, and Love,
all the possibilities become
Reality.

Coffee With Cream
by Andrea T. Beckman - age 19

Intent
on the bitterness of solitude
Yearning for self consolence
Delving into red embers
of the mind
Calculating spheres
colored with jealousy
Mirrored in a muddy pain
Reflecting a character
A girl
Desperate for nothing
With a need
for something
Muddiness slides away
A cream colored bottom
Reveals
eyes of jade
Until the next cup

A Lonely Soul
by Gregory M. Bedard

Its hard for me to verbally explain
The sorrow in my heart and its pain
For I have travelled alone for so many years
Only to find a lost life full of tears.

Now standing still in the middle of my track
I'm afraid to move on - I want to turn back
But to face the past would only mean
Facing a life I have already seen.

So forward I go into the darkness once more
Searching for the keys to open life's doors
I know what I want and I'm a long ways away
And I'm ready to start the dreams of the day.

Life has truly taken its toll -
Leaving behind this lonely lost soul.

The Reunion
by Lacinda Beggs

As I gaze upon your face
For the first time in fourteen years,
All dressed up in your Sunday best
You bring my eyes to tears.

Remembering just how tall you stood,
Protecting me
As surely you would
It was always one step forward
Never back,
With father there
To lovingly mark my tracks.

I remember the times
You bounced me on your knee
And when you sang happy birthday
Back home when I was three.

And as we reunited
I take your hand
And smile through my tears.
For you alone my Father,
chased away all life's fears.

I touch the hair
Upon your brow
Tell you how much I care
And kick myself for not having more time
The both of us could share.

Wanting this moment to last
Wishing that I'd done it often
What deeply saddens now
Is that I must express to you
As I gaze upon your coffin.

The Star
by Jennifer Sanders

The stars in the earth's sky are
 lowered.
My star won't come softly;
My star won't creep across a quiet
 sky;
It'll come with a crash.

Truth hits hard.
Truth isn't a chorus or carol.
If you understand it at all,
 it will come with a drum roll.

So, a star in the sky?
A babe in the manger?
Thunder rolls in the distance.
Beauty is applause enough.
My star is enough.

Be Not You
by Katherine L. Bond

Be not you weary or dismayed.
I but reach out to touch,
don't be afraid.

II
Be not you feel rejected.
I come humble, and imperfect.

III
Be not you bothered by vicious
whispers.
I love you, with a love, that blisters.

Justin Is
by Diana Bennett - age 14

Justin is the boy I always think of,
Because he is the boy I always dream of,
Justin is sweet and pure and kind,
And almost makes me lose my mind,
Yet I love him still,
He hasn't done much really wrong,
It's really me I guess,
Because I've always been a pest to everyone
I've known and met,
Justin is mostly sweet and clearly pure
and so kind,
He pay's attention to my mind,
And he's like a train going through out
my brain and every time I think of him I cry
"Justin"

Valley Voices
by Nikki Beitler - age 14

Standing in a valley
I hear a distant voice
It sounds like someone weeping
Who has just been hurt.

I walk on to look deeper
For the voice to appear
I see a woman crying
With many running tears.

She lifts her head
I see a bruise
My heart goes out to her.

As I take a step closer
I see some more;
She's only a lady
Of about twenty four.

In my time
We never would have seen
Beaten, bruised, and battered women
Lying on the streets.

But I have to remember
It's a different day and age
With different kinds of people
Who show their rage in different ways.

A Vacant Stare Reminds
by Jennifer Bellusci - age 13

Once there was a feisty young woman. Home educated and was dedicated to all she began. She started a battle and finished it. Her physical and mental power hard to match. Her memory like an elephant's. She fought any foe with all her might. This remarkable woman grew old like we all do. She became a grandma mine to be exact now this woman strong and steel like can not even recite her name. A curse name Alzheimer disease has been placed on her. Nothing can remove it. She is now like a baby, she has no memories. A shell of the remarkable woman she once was. Not knowing her family and making sentences that don't make sense.
She who battled all her foes battles this one too.
 She is now empty and hollow and knows nothing at all. All that remains is vacant glare, that does not know where or who it is. The stare is all that's there.
And it asks one thing that can't be answered. Why, why me.
This is all of her sad tale.

Vacant Stare Reminds is dedicated to the person who it is about- My grandmother whose spirit is always with me and those who knew her. This is dedicated with love always to Joesphine Bellusci.

Spring
by Mandy Bender - age 12

In the month of May
flowers cover the ground
and love is all around
With birds singing a song
and bees buzzing along
Theres no doubt that
Spring is about
Kids are in shorts
and girls are in dresses
babys are being born
and making messes
Wildflowers are what you see
everywhere you go
And you'll feel the gentle breeze that blows
And Spring is the time
that everyone loves
because of its cool days
and beauty that grows in your heart
Spring is the time
when kittens play
And horses prance along their own way
Yes Spring is a lovely time
and a very pretty sight to see
Spring is the time for me.

Untitled
by Jennifer Boserman - age 14

The sun was setting in the afternoon mist
It was so beautiful, so hard to resist
The fluffy clouds were shaped with
beauty and pride
And I watched the birds glide
High above the pinkish sky
The clouds moved slow and sly

Lost Love
by Crystal Bennett

As I search for the meanings, as I wonder what to say,
Maybe you'll know how I feel someday.

I need help, but I can not reach out
I want to scream but can not shout

I want to tell you my feelings inside
I don't think I have any more pride

You think I'm too young, but I'm old enough to know wrong from right
And when my battles come along I'll know when to fight.

I want to bring ears to the deaf, then eyes to the
blind.
That will cleanse my heart and ease my mind.

Just when I thought my life would fall apart, it was
you that lifted and filled my heart.

You gave me air to breathe when I thought I would die.
You took my tears away when I was about to cry.

You gave me words to speak, a soul to sing, wings to fly, you gave me so much, I already miss your touch.

I was captured by your innocence and set free by your
soul.

An Ode For Our Nana
by Robert Bentley

As I read these words of great memories, of praises and your love
I know you'll continue to be watching over us like the loving doves
forever and a day.

Now it's time to say our final good-bye
However for you, Nana, we do it holding our heads up high
Nana, you gave us strength when life had us down
You had a special way to make us smile instead of a frown

When as a child not knowing right from wrong
You showed us the light and put us back on the path we belonged.
Nana, you let us know so many times, in different ways you cared
Just by doing something so simple as wiping away our tears

So Nana we'll stay strong as we help lay you to rest
"Because Nana, you were truly the best"
We love you, Nana, We really do,
Someday we'll be together again

Since your not really gone
You're just a touch away
And for that thought alone we'll see you,
Nana on judgement day!

WE LOVE YOU, NANA
Good bye Till we Meet Again.

Just Because
by Crissy Borges

Just because the grass is green,
Just because I have a spleen,
That is why I love you.

Just because the sky is blue,
Just because I know the truth,
Just because I lost a tooth,
Just because I am a sluth,
That is why I like to dream,
That is why we make a good team.

Untitled
by Layla Ann Bermeo - age 12

Love is like a flower that blooms and grows.
Love is like an emotion that really shows.
Yet sometimes the flower dries and hardens,
Leaving lovers beg their pardons.

Lovers dream, and lovers cry.
Their passion they just can't deny.
To them, love is their history;
To them, love is a neverending mystery.

Love rules our waking hours.
Within our souls, it blooms and flowers.
Sometimes we feel that love is just a fad,
But then our obsessions drive us mad.

Love can cause pain; love can be deadly,
Yet we dance to love's sweet melody.
Love can hurt, but then can mend.
Love is life, our beginning and end.

The Betrayal
by Teresa Bernson - age 20

My delicate fingers
unravel the fear.
My heart turned to beauty
that disappeared.
A sigh from an angel's
placid song,
The bittersweet melody
that lingered too long.
That unbroken touch
who tormented the moon,
Some lifeless vision
surrendered so soon.
No eloquent words
can silence this plea,
your forsaken vows
have crippled me.

Untitled
by Jo Ann Biccum

- When daisies are not cared for they tend to fade away, but if they're loved and nurtured they will stand up tall today. I am your daisy mother and you made me big and strong. You kept me right beside you and loved me all along. When the sun was covered by a cloud, you gave me all your light. You suffered through the darkness so I would become bright. You taught me to stand big and tall and not bend towards the wind, and even though I'd sometimes fail you'd make me try again. You sheltered and protected me from all who came around, and tried your very hardest to keep me in the ground. For you wanted no one to pick me and take me far from home, and make you finally realize that I was fully grown.

Well I was picked my dearest mom, and I'm no longer home, but all that you've instilled in me is strongly etched in stone. Some time in the future I will have a little daisy too, still I can only hope and pray to do my job as well as you.

Saved by an Angel
by Melissa Biddle - age 16

Merely a boy,
But more like a man.
Admired by us all.
With pain more than words can say.

His will is unbendable,
A heart ready to serve.
His soul cries out in sorrow,
But no tears dare to come.

Rare glimpses give us the truth.
Though he tries to hide in a closet.
Socked feet are not ready for those big, bulky boots.
He is, after all, only a child.

He was almost lost, a most eye-opening act.
Over a million "what if's" and "but why's."
For the first time seeing-quite straight in the eye
How incredibly precious, yet ironically cruel, life can be.

But his fate's been decided,
And God has chosen to answer this un-ignorable prayer.
The devil will have to work harder next time.
Because Adam, after all, was saved by an angel.

Love Yourself
by Dominique Bigbee - age 13

You say you love but trust me you don't
What is love, no one really knows
You say you love your boyfriend but soon lets you go

Love you before anyone else
Learn yourself, who you are
And trust me in life you will get very far

Love yourself then find someone true
If it doesn't work out then find someone new

Love you before anyone else
Learn yourself, who you are
And trust me in life you will get very far

Listen to your parents
And love yourself first
Make your first the best
And make none of them your worst

Visitation
by Kristin Birk - age 14

He visited me in a dream
telling what had not been seen
The tear wiped away was given to me
My friend will never be found
My love will never be seen
I felt sorrow yet there were
no tears
It's all over now
thinking of the past I can't
help but wonder
What did this mean
Where are his cries heard
Will this dream become a
reality
Will his story be heard
I have need to scream
out what I've seen
My friend will never be found
My love will never be seen
I love this friend but
this love is unseen

I Love You
by Stacy Biss - age 15

I want you to know that I love you
In each and every way
And my love for you grows stronger each and every day
I think about you day and night
And I know sometimes you feel
That there's someone else but I'm telling you
My love for you is real.
I know sometimes I get annoyed with some of the
Things you do - but I hope you realize that
No matter what - I will always love you
I really love you with all my heart
And I hope you feel the same for me
Although I know sometimes it feels
Like we have to break free.
I love being with you, just being in your arms
It makes me feel content, like I could never be harmed
I endure your soft kisses, nothing could compare
And I love to feel your fingers
Run smoothly through my hair.
It makes me feel special when you call me your girl
Because you're a great guy and I'm part of your world
So I hope now you know, now that this poem is through
How very much I am in love with you!

A Bird
by Anna Lisa Bitgood - age 18

He holds his head high, always searching for the wind
The wind that will lead him to forever
The winds that will take him soaring
The wind that will guide him toward freedom

He sings his mournful song, always searching for the notes
The notes that will call his eternal love to him
The notes that will warn the world of the unfearing
The notes that will be etched in stone in their minds

He spreads his wings each time the breeze flutters them
Waiting for that wind
And until the day it takes him to the skies
He will wait patiently
Holding his head high, singing the same mournful tune
The same mournful tune I sing to me

His eyes rest upon me, a strange creature that somehow belongs
there in his world
He does not fly away, for he knows all too well that I am him
Waiting for the wind that will set me free
Searching for the notes that he will remember me

My Love Is...
by Brishandra Bivens - age 15

My love is like a rose, I give to you
I'm telling you this
    because it's true
I'll continue telling you this
For it's one thing I can't resist.

My love is like a door, please come in
but if you won't, then it'll shut
    and I'll never love again.

My love is stronger than any fear,
last longer than it shall take
I hope you would never choose to leave me
    for that's a choice you can make.

So take my love
    my rose I give to you
Out of all this my love and feelings for you
    is so ever true.

Recalling Love
by Pamela Blakley - age 17

Feelings mostly kept inside,
are expected to subside.
Waiting seems to be a lifetime,
when required to pantomime.
And laying in the sunshine,
watching your face outshine,
every moment of summertime.

In absence memories I recollect
good times, bad times, in retrospect.
Looking back now I know I was right
to disobey my heart in spite,
of all times I cried outright.
So my love tonight,
make a wish to starlight,
and you will know by moonlight,
I am wishing you my love, goodnight.

Without You
by Kate Elizabeth Biviano

Without you,
My life would not be as full.
I feel happiness that's
Warmer than the thickest wool.

Each time I see you,
You set my heart racing.
Not knowing how long you'll be mine
Is the problem I'm always facing.

I believe your words
When you tell me that you love me.
But when that love is over,
How will things between us be?

I love it when you hold me.
And I feel like you really do care.
But when things between you and I are through,
Who will comfort me, who will be there?

I love you more
Than these words can ever say.
For as long as we're together,
You'll be the happiness in my day.

Valentine's Day Poem
by Jennifer Bivona - age 15

I loved you.
Actually, I still do. But now you're gone and not
here to hold.
God, I'm so cold right now.
I wish you were here to wipe away my fears of
being alone.
I am an emotional disaster.
My heart beats faster as I think of you.
I wish you were still alive,
so I could see your smile
and we'd talk for a while but I'm alone now.
God, it hurst so bad.
I want to kill myself, just to be with you because
I feel I have nothing to live for.
All I know is I miss you, and I want to hug and
kiss you.
I may see you soon, and I may not.
I think of memory bliss and realize I don't want
to be alone.

Broken Hearted Reflection
by Mandy Blank - age 15

As I sit alone in my room,
I look out the window only to see my own reflection staring back at me.

It looks so lost and all alone,
almost like there's nobody home.

The reflection has a tear stained face,
so stained that it could be traced.

I want to say that it will be okay,
love will find a way, someday.

But the reflection just looks away and says,
"It can't be true, not after all I've been through."

Untitled
by Lucas Lowerly - age 15

Whenever your lonely,
Whenever your feeling blue,
Don't ever forget our trust,
And how I feel about you.

We are so close,
And yet so far apart.
Confusion is something found especially deep,
within my heart.

I'm living and dying,
From uncontrollable love,
Look outside and you'll see my pain,
Falling from up above.

I don't know what to say,
Even better, do.

Everything is crashing,
And I just want to be with you.

Well, I guess I wanted to say,
That I really do,
Love you.

Time
by Darcy Blaszczyk - age 13

There is hardly time
In one day for fun,
But you somehow
Fit it in

Time to laugh,
To cry,
To sing
You somehow find a
Way for it all

Then comes a time
When you have little
Time to fit it all in
One day
So cherish the time NOW!

I Sit
by Mark Stephen Bledsaw - age 17

Where the water hugs the land,
A place where waves destroyed by sand.
　Cold.
Like blue crisp ice, as loud as a dream.
A place, where shadows of the moon,
Dance upon the stream.

Where mountains stare into thick mist,
and buzzards taunt the dead.
Picking, Picking at the flesh,
of souls long laid to rest.

　I sit and learn...

The Sadness Of The Deceived
by Jamie Bloom - age 15

　That of a person who is deceived is greatly hurt with sadness and could be even madness. But the deceiver, the person himself of herself is greatly hurt and stuck with deep and untold secrets. The deceiver might be not telling the truth or even trying to make someone believe that what they are saying is true. But don't give in let them suffer, let them suffer till they can't stand it no more, and watch them die inside like a plant without water till they thirst no more.
　The deceiver knows that they hold the truth, but they also hold great sadness. To not tell the truth to someone you love and care about is the greatest sadness of all.

"Changes"
by Stacy D. Bodine

My beautiful mother
Please don't cry.
It's not going to change things
No matter how hard you try.
I've found that life
Is full of twists and turns.
Its like a roller coaster
Even when your stomach churns.
But without the bad
How could we cherish the good?
We'd take it for granted.
We'd be misunderstood.
But if you have a reminder
That things could be worse,
Well, it changes your outlook
You can even put feelings in verse!
As long as you know
And are sure in your heart
That nothing on earth
Could ever keep us apart,
Then miles become minutes
And distance a myth
For, a moment in thought
And its you that I'm with.

Words Unspoken
by Catherine Lynn Boggs - age 16

If I could turn back time
I'd tell you what I meant to say
But I can't now since you've gone
and flown away

So many things that went unspoken
So many things that went unheard
I wonder grandma, my heart could
you have observed

God Bless you for the tender words you spoke
They meant so much to me
My heart, I know you didn't want broke
But I cried as the world did see

I miss you with words unspeakable
I thought you would always be around
And know when it seems I need you most
your nowhere to be found

I don't know why you had to go
And leave me far behind
Heavens gates for you,....
I know were opened wide.

How Much Love
by Katherine L. Bond

How much love can I offer you Lord
Before others tell me -- it's too much?
How many times do I obey Your will
Before others think -- I've lost touch?
How many prayers can I offer up to You
Before my life is over, and I am
through?
How many favors can I ask of You - Lord
Before you say -- it's too many, there
isn't any?
How many blessings will you send my way
Before others try to take or steal them away?
How much love can I offer You - Lord?
Not enough, because you love me --
so very much.

The Dream
by Jessica Bonura - age 12

The dream was like a desert wind
But sounded like a beach
The girl in the bright red car
Did not resemble me
Yet when I looked into her eyes
Very, very, deep
I found myself just standing there
I was trapped in a dream
This may sound quite queer to you
But I'm the one that must go through
With many sleepless nights
And many scary flights
I think my mom was in the dream
And you may have been too
But the only thing that I recall
Is I was oh so blue
One second passed or maybe two
And I saw a bird that flew
Carrying a message
He said "This is for you"
I smiled and was happy
But did not know what to do
For in this entire dream
I have never been spoken to
I heard a crash and then a thud
Finally I awoke
To a real place that I call home

Summer's Night Sky
by Jennifer Boserman - age 14

A fiery red ball floating in the sky
Is the only reminder of the day gone by
As is splashes pastels on a distant cloud
The big bright flame is not too proud
To shed it's last colors across the land
It's happy to lend a helping hand
To the birds as they safely fly to their nests
And bats as they come out to eat little pests
Then green becomes yellow, yellow to red
The soft glow in the sky has turned many heads
Dusk slowly let down her long, black hair
And combed in trinkets here and there
Then carefully placed on her head a stone
Big, round, and white, with a blue haze that shone
Inside the moon-stone a prisoner was held
But he smiled if he liked what he smelled
Of the lilacs and lilies, carnations and roses
For they also appeal to everyone's noses
Sometimes little twinkling trinkets would race
With other trinkets into outer space
Then a big orange glow would rise from the East
In a beautiful mist so all eyes could feast

Nothing's Real
by Miranda Bostic - age 14

Don't look at me to deeply
What you see is not real
I wear a mask to cover me
To cover how I feel

When I'm sad or lonely
I wear a happy mask
The happiness is fake, of course
For it's true happiness that I lack

The wall I built around me
Protects me from the pain
But the pain grows inside of me
The longer I remain

I don't want to break the wall around me
For I'm afraid of what you might see
For now that you know my feelings
I'm scared you may not love me

Love
by Sarah R. Bowe

Love can wound,
Love can save,
Love can kill,
Love can improve

Love can be from
The deepest parts of the earth,
Or the highest peak of happiness,
In heaven

Love can only be
What you make it be

If you use love,
And waste it,
And don't respect it,
It backfires

If you cherish Love,
Live for Love,
And love for Love,
You will enjoy
Its riches for eternity

Love is human
Love has needs
As lower beings to Love,
Love ALWAYS wins

Death Surrounds Me
by Brenda-Lee Bowins - age 15

Death surrounds me
with its pain and misery
Since I was little I've had to deal with it
and I can't do anything about it except cry while I sit.
Whenever I think about it, it makes me mad.
I feel like I'm a jinx,
and every time somebody dies my self-esteem sinks.
I don't know why, but I feel like it's all my fault.
I can't cry when someone dies because all my feelings are stored in a special vault.
The vault is going to explode inside of me
Then all my feelings people will see.
But of that I am afraid
Whenever I hear of a death my heart pounds like a big drum in a parade
I don't want people to see my pain.
From holding my emotions in...there is nothing in your opinion that I gain.
But what I do gain
my not be much to you because what I do gain is more and more pain

I Want To Cry
by Brenda-Lee Bowins - age 15

I want to cry
and there's no reason why.
The pain is building up inside of me
in a little spot that no one can see.
I try to hide it the best that I know how
Can I hold it in much longer? That I doubt.
The rage and fury build every time I get mad.
Every time I get angry I always somehow get very sad.
But all that rage and fury soon disappears,
'cause you see it turns into tears.

I Can Dream
by Brenda-Lee Bowins - age 15

As I stare into your gorgeous deep blue eyes.
I know that ALL my dreams are a saddening pack of lies.
I dream that I'll meet you, I dream that you'll like me.
I dream that we'll have a romantic walk at sunset, hand in hand by the sea
I dream that my last name is "Bowins" no more.
I dream that my dreams will be dreams no more.
Even though I know my dreams aren't reality.
To say it quickly,
I wish it would be so.
If that beautiful hair, gorgeous eyes, face & body, and intelligent mind
Could possibly one day be mine.
And I don't care if this all does seem..
Like a petty girl crush...but you see. **I CAN DREAM**.

A Prayer For John
by Kitty Boyd

My friend is hurting with a pain so intense.
A young heart is breaking, and it just makes no sense.
Where can he turn to? Oh, where can help be?
I can't be there for him; please, Jesus help me.
Give him the love that I have in my heart.
Tell him I miss him because we're apart.
Assign him an angel to watch him at play,
To protect and preserve him and guard him all day.
Give him an angel to be there nights, too
As he peacefully slumbers the whole evening through.
Show him the love and the joy that You give.
Show him that life is important to live.
Until You come back, I will patiently wait
To see my young friend at the Heavenly gate.
And while I am waiting, I pray You will see
My heart's full of love, so be patient with me.
Give me the strength to be there for my friend.
Don't let me weaken; keep me strong till the end.
I thank You, my Jesus, for answers to prayer,
For loving my friend, and for just being there.
I thank You, my Jesus, for loving me, too.
And so, as I close, I will say, "I love You".

Terror
by Sandra Boyette

In speaking to an audience, we have the greatest fear
To give our dry-mouthed recitation, with palms sweating and eyes a-tear
Opening up the riveted millions, with a mighty shout
And instead of launching an intelligent dissertation, only gobbledygook comes out

After your fall from grace is over, and your career is blowing away like autumn leaves
You curse the Stars and Fates and discover, as you sink down to your knees
That loathsome, nefarious, Will-O-the-Wisp thing called "Your Foot's In Your Mouth Disease."

Reunion
by Sandra Boyette

On this silvery night, the moon beckons bright
"Come hither! Come hither!"
My heart sings out right for my true love this night; of his bonnie face I long for just a glimpse or a sight
"Oh what shall I do, dearest Mither, dearest Mither?"

For my soul is crying for my true love and dear
Our loves' strength vibrates with the power o' it as he draws near
Long, long, has he been gone; far, far, and away
But the waiting is over; he is no more the rover
His wandering days are done; he arrives with the eve for to stay

Ring Bells! Ring Bells! Joyous Knells!
For I see his face in Joy and his charm
And in all my glee I shall fall to my knees
And thank the One Above for the safe harbor in his arms

Newness
by V. Elizabeth Boysen - age 15

facing the music

we force ourselves
to plummet into the sea
to look for underwater kingdoms
we know that they exist
among the waters we cannot reach

we meet for the first time alone
visions of dreams coming true
making minor the intended major key

newness

i feel the wounds opening again when you pull me towards yourself

the pain envelops my soul
i will take it in for you

piercing salvation in passionate sacrifice
it tastes bittersweet
like summer's sentimental orange moon

the music changes it's melody
polonaise of willful delight
we dance through the clouds to it

freedom

breaking away from the hiding place
slowly we are transformed in white

up among the rafters
for a split second i am watching us
in a dream and i will never wake up

the tempo becomes insanely slow
until again i am in your arms
momentarily deliverance
in the love we cannot survive without

don't let it die

Within Life Blows
by John Bradshaw - age 20

The loss of control,
Was not a surprise
In this picture as a whole,
Painted with lies.

A blow after blow,
Life has given.
Now an all time low,
Is accepted within.

Barely getting by,
Days filled with pain.
Never once asked why,
This chaos was to remain.

Without a single reason,
To continue on this way.
In what this has begun,
No good can ever stay.

Far From Her
by Laura Brady - age 15

i asked God for me a place
where nothing could go wrong.
...God put me in a perfect place,
he put me in your arms;
but the world divides such perfect things
and i can't stay much longer,
so i asked God for another place
where i could be much stronger
...so God put me in a perfect place
he put me in your heart;
but the world divides such perfect things
and now we're far apart
but God tells me to dry my eyes,
because he put me in your heart.
as you grow old, i'll pray for you,
that you get all your dreams
though i'm not next to your side
it still sometimes seems
that i am still next to you
though we're far apart
God tells me it's all because
he put me in your heart
(and i'll never leave your heart...)

The Feeling Of Love
by Eva Brashears

Love is like a fire,
something I will always desire.
It's like a burning flame,
always putting people to shame.
The happiness makes me want to shout,
the sadness makes me want to cry out.
Will the cost of love someday be free,
and will this stress be lifted off of me.
You are my heart,
so please don't ever tears us apart.

Summer Nights
by Abby Bredemeyer - age 12

The summer nights are cool and clear
and when I close my eyes I hear...
The sounds of the house creaking about
but I do not scream, I do not shout.
I also hear the sound of a whispering breeze
as it brushes the bushes and the trees.
I hear some dogs that like to bark
and also some children playing at the park.
So many different sounds I hear
But now it's time I sleep my dear.

The Dark
by Rhonna Bramer - age 14

You always stare into the

   darkness, watching and listening.

You find small objects and

   you creep up on them.

You watch it eat as I watch

   you.

You sit and wait, wait for the

   right moment.

You find the right moment,

   when out of nowhere someone

   is haunting you.

You try to see who it is,

   but you can't. It's too dark.

You hope it will go

   away, but it doesn't.

You watch, not moving trying

   to see who it is, but you still can't.

   Will you ever find out?

My Dad
by Eva Brashears

My Dad...He is one in a million,
no, I would have to say one in a trillion.
He is a man who will never let you down,
you will definitely never see him frown.
He is always so busy,
sometimes watching him will make you dizzy.
My Dad is always there when you need him.
He never says, "Well you have to wait" and
then put you on a shelf,
you see I don't think he ever once thinks of
himself.
I love my Dad so much,
I don't think there is a heart he hasn't touched.
My Dad will go to such lengths,
I really cannot believe his strength.
Now you see his love and strength is in
everyone who loves him.
And I will watch that love and strength in
everyone build and forever last,
because as you can see in this poem
my Dad will never be put in the past.
I love you Pop
You will always be the one and only Pop in my life
because you are my Dad.

-In memory of Bob Brashears.

Problems
by Eva Brashears

There are friends
and they carry many trends.
Sometimes they fight
and get all uptight.
But not far behind
in their mind.
They know the problem
will be resolved.
And other people need to
be involved.
There are people to talk too.
The people that are true,
There are people who are cruel.
But they're the fools
not you.
So if you have a problem
don't hide.
Carry it with pride.
You'll always have at least
one person to talk to.
And that you should be happy
to call your best friend.

Watching Eyes
by Marshetta Brazley - age 13

   During the summer and fall months she runs the courses set for her, clumsily stumbling over the indentures of the earth. Her face is dark and smooth like the night. Sweat continually pours down her face to the point of dehydration. Her mouth is hot and dry like the Sahara Desert, but she is still beautiful to Watching Eyes.
   In the winter, she runs up and down the court, tripping over her own two feet, taking charges, breaking bones, missing lay-ups, and being fancy, but she's very graceful to Watching Eyes.
   Most of the spring, she runs quarter miles in circles every day. She competes just about every week. You better believe we're all there cheering her on. She may not win a gold medal in every event, but she does her very best, and that's all that counts through Watching Eyes.
   Thank you, Cisha for being the person you are. Every time I see you, you light up my Watching Eyes.

Markers
by Margaret Brennan

I walked past the row of markers,
A loved one's name to find.
Emotions were like rivers
Running through my mind.

A little flag was nestled
Along side every name.
The young and old, together!
What a pity! What a shame!

As memories filled my every thought,
From the corner of my eye,
I saw a woman hold her heart,
And then begin to cry.

The woman's cries grew weaker
As she crumbled to the ground.
I rushed to lend a helping hand
And see the name she found.

I abandoned my self pity
As my eyes, then, opened wide.
There were her markers: husband and son
Lying side by side

Night on the Prairie
by Jim Brogan

The tentacles of darkness
Slowly---unfurl
Upon the unsuspecting earth

Streaks of red, gold and purple
Burn---like iridescent flames
As day---slowly concedes the struggle
Against the forces of darkness

Slowly---slowly
As the last embers of day
Fade quietly
Below the distant horizon

The trill of night birds
Becomes sharper---more resounding
Then---suddenly---all is still

The darkness becomes more intense
The winds fall silent
There is not even a whisper

Suddenly---a flash of light
As if the heavens had split
As a peal of thunder---resonates the ground
Upon which I stand

Then as if on command
Nature unleashes her mighty torrent
As the earth reels
Under the power of the heavens

Then as quickly as it began
All is quiet---and the prairie
Is once again at peace--------

My Dawn, My Dusk
by Thomas A. Brown

      Glossy eyes of fire,
         magnificent;
     Flowing hair with dark love,
         beautiful;
  Sensual voice of liquid pleasure,
         gorgeous;
       My dawn, my dusk,
       I could inhale you.

If You Don't Have a friend Try Jesus
by Ella Brown

If you don't have a friend try Jesus
he will surely direct your path way and keep
you looking up to him. Which all praises come from
and he'll direct your thoughts and lead, you to
higher grounds, so come on children try Jesus
He'll be your friend when no, one else cares
about you!

If you don't have a friend try Jesus!
If you think Jesus don't care about you
just call on him sometimes and see how
fast he work out your problems turn it
over to Jesus. He understands you and me
because pray changes everything its the
key to understanding god,
So, if you don't have a friend try Jesus!
Thank you Lord!

Michelle
by Jim Brogan

To gaze upon your countenance
Is to catch a glimpse of heaven
It is to see a small part of the beauty
Yet to behold

To look into your eyes
Is to tap the treasures of forever
To watch---the smile on your lips
Is to sense the spices of the Gods

To hold your hand
Is to feel the power of the universe
As it rushes---untamed
Through my psyche

Your laugh---
Is as the wings of angels
Whispering---of the love
Yet to be experienced

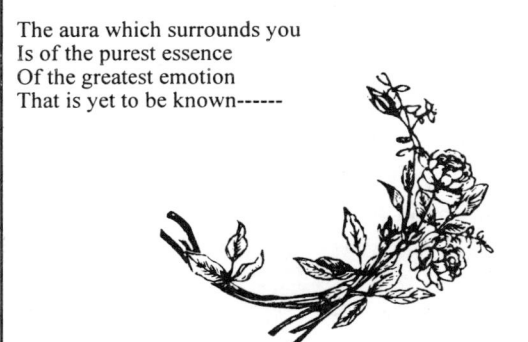

The aura which surrounds you
Is of the purest essence
Of the greatest emotion
That is yet to be known------

Hello! My Name is Eric, and I'm.....
by Jackie Brown

There's a ghost
That wanders in my mansion.

She flirted, taunted, teased
As a mistress,
Until I embraced her.

Her candle lit the rooms of
Seduction and illusion.
It flickered and beckoned,
Always promising more.

This psyche of the soul laughed
As she clutched the key
Where my treasures were stored.
I gave her everything.

This spirit robbed, tempted,
Even lied to me, until my room was empty.
This cursed thing in my house
Now became the center: the focus of my life.

When she insisted being
My destiny,
My agony was before me.

I avoid taking the twisted stairs
To a room of darkness.
Instead, I follow twelve other steps
To rebuild, to repair, to reform,

The clock and calendar measure time away.
She's still here.
Indifferently I hear her
Weak whispers, as she haunts.

An Endless Journey
by Lindsay Brown - age 13

I walk and walk,
But there is no end,
I try walking faster,
Then I slow down.
The road is long,
Twisting and turning,
Cutting through mountains,
Crossing rivers.
I continue to walk,
Though travel is hard.
My journey seems endless,
Like there is no reason for taking it.
But in my heart I know.
I know that this is an important journey,
A journey everyone must take.
Though it is long and hard at times,
Just up the bend is happiness, peace.
I don't give up.
I just keep walking this road,
The road of life.

You And I
by Rachelle Brown - age 16

Maybe it was you. Maybe it was me.
What we have will always last.
Nothing will come between us.
There will be no hate.
There will only be love.
Love is one of the many strong feelings
    that we share.
True love is for you and me.
For that is something we have found in
    ourselves.
We make our choices as time goes by.
But nothing matters more than
    You and I

Tide
by Mike Bryant

As I sit on the surf tormented shore
listening to the gently blowing wind take me alore
the wintry wisping wind blows through my ear and hair
as I fade away without a care
tides turn by the tormented years
fading in and out of the tears
only looking toword today
never thinking ahead for what we'll have to pay
"look before you leap" or so they say
but think of what's come and gone away
is it worth it, or does it matter 'till that day
when it flashes before you and there's
no real words to say
cause all that seems is real
has crumbled and drifted away

"Deceived"
by Jessie Brunk - age 15

I thought that you loved me.
You screwed with my brain.
I wish I could see.
You cause me so much pain.

I wish we never kissed,
that night you forced me.
I wish I could dismiss,
The pictures my mind sees.

I wanted to die,
that night apart.
I can't cry.
I don't know how to start.

You've taken my childhood.
I'll never be the same.
Would you do it again if you could?
I hate this life, this game.

I feel so unclean,
my heart you have cut.
I'm afraid to be seen.
I feel like I'm a slut.

Who can I trust?
I wish I had help.
Will I ever again lust?
Can I trust myself?

I tried to die.
That wrenched night.
It wasn't worth the try.
I can't even do that right.

I love,
but can it ever be more.
Love is not enough,
for a worthless whore.

Reaching High Or Low
by Fantei Bryant - age 13

I reach for my hopes and dreams.
Some of them I've never seen.

Day by day I hope they'll come true
in every way.
I reach for them whether they're high or low.

Short or tall I can't reach my expectations until I rise or fall.

I rise!

Him
by Liza Burns - age 14

His eyes deep, blue.
His hair wavy.
His hands large enough to block out anything
Everything.
His lips soft, perfect.
His body strong, tan.

He doesn't know it...
If he did he'd laugh.

That changes nothing.

Untitled
by Mike Bryant

We'd just met
but now we seem to get
closer and closer
I'm spinnin' round in circles
afraid of losing you
now I've got to choose what to do
spill my heart and risk getting hurt
or stay quiet and remain friends

I can say it now
but not to your face
which isn't like me
no style or grace, dumb and in love
dazed and confused
way too scared to expose myself and get bruised.
I've put out my heart before
and it was squished into the floor
I'll be there for you
do everything you want me too
around you I feel so good
I just wish I could say how I feel

Joust
by Mike Bryant

You got yourself in
now get yourself out
there's no use shouting
'cause no one's about

all alone and king of your throne
but where's the rest of your empire?
It's time for you to stand up and fight
but you must do battle alone

you reach for your sword
but there's only air
too bad there's no one around to care
you look around
but not even the court jester clown
is there to help

you swing with a left and get dropped by a right
but where's the enemy he's out of sight

he's in your head
where evil lurks
where you try to salvage goodness
and destroy jerks

you mount a horse
and get a lance
but it's too late
not even a chance

he's much faster and stronger and you're barely there
he hits you and wallops you without a care

you render unconscious
on the floor
but it doesn't matter to him
'cause it's just another score

A Lunatic Looking Back
by William J. Christy

I sit here and let life be
Trying for the illusion of being free
Climbing the tree of life
My being filled with strife
Why can't I have my mind back
Lost because of the lack
When I dare to see
The knowledge of me
I see the lunatic looking back

A Drinker's Story
by Sherry Butler - age 18

My parents told me not to drink, a friend told me the same,
but now a life is lost, and I am the one to blame.
I thought that it was cool, cause all my friends thought so,
I know I was a fool I just wish that he could know.
I went to a party that night, where drinking was the thing,
It was a horrible sight, if I had only seen.
I got so drunk that night, that when it came time to drive,
I thought I was all right, I just wish he was alive.
I went for seeking help, but it didn't mean a thing,
and if I could change the past, I knew what I would bring.
I was so drunk that night, my friends said not to drive,
I would tell him many things, I just wish he was alive.

As I Wander
by Steve Buckner - age 16

As I wander to and fro.
I often wonder where to go.
Whether it's here, or even there.
I still have to face, on which to bare.

But as I go upon this path I trod.
I must decide which one's the fraud.
Even though, I do not know.
As I wander to and fro.

Not knowing the danger that lies ahead.
Hoping I won't wind up dead.
Around and around I go.
As I wander to and fro.

I wonder if I will ever choose the right path to go.
As I wander to and fro.
Whether it's here or even there.
I still have to face, on which to bare.

Untitled
by Stacie Buessing

The shoes begin, regretting every step
Left, right, left, right...
They are like a soldier under commandment
Left, right, left, right...
They look down, retracing every miserable step they have taken.

The door screams with delight
It is the devil, the leader of a melancholy world
Slam! It has its prey.
It will watch in disgust at its victim's weakness.

The carpet tastes her sweet, wet tears
It is like a sponge absorbing water
It received her warmly, comforting her
It is her friend, her comfort zone.
She will lay there until her pain is over,
And the carpet will lie with her,
Trying its hardest to absorb her pain.

Thoughts of Reflection
by Lisa M. Buettner - age 16

Let me do right in this world of wrong
God give me courage and help me be strong
In this world of hate, where babes carry guns
Where corruption reigns and poison runs
Where justice is gone and evil flows free
Where powers of darkness now close upon me
Help me to turn wrong into right
War into peace, blindness to sight.

Is it the less taken path that I want to follow
I shall walk forward always, today and tomorrow
Striving to do the right in this world of wrong
To stay on the path that seems so long
To be blind to the temptations that evil brings
And to hear the sweet song that an angel sings
God grant me the courage you love to give
And because of you, I will love to live

Sometimes
by Amanda M. Buff

Sometimes I smile when I think about
us,
Then other times I wonder why I
made such a fuss.
Do you really care,
Or is it just the color of my hair?

Sometimes I feel as though I'm not
good enough for you,
And I wonder if you think that too.
When we talk on the phone, and there's
nothing to say
I wonder if you're wandering away.

Sometimes I want to grab you in my
arms and hold you tight.
But I can't because I'm full of fright.
Do you even have a clue;
How much I care for you?

Sometimes I see you standing there,
I may act like I don't care.
But I do.
And deep down inside I hope you do
too!

My Gift (From You To Me)
by Jamie Bull - age 15

You gave me the
most wonderful gift
anyone ever gave me
you gave me life
and all you do
you gave me
apart of you
which is such
a lift in my life
you gave me
a life with all
of your love
you gave me
a wonderful family
to love and to cherish
that is the most
wonderful gift-
I ever received.

Inside Out
by Jill Bunker

Inside there is an empty feeling,
But in each person beams a light,
Underneath their outside features,
The inside that shines so bright.

Everyone looks for outside quality,
No one sees the beauty of the heart,
If we would look further than the skin,
We would find a loving world longing within.

For in each person there is a heart,
If they would only let it shine,
So people could see who they really are,
And stop pretending they are something they're not.

For beauty comes from way down deep,
The outside looks should have no cause,
For the body just waste away,
And the soul forever lives on.

Pennies
by Michelle Burden

A penny for your thoughts,
Yes, I think a lot...
And listen and see.
I know everything,
Well, all I want to know,
Going on around me.
Do you have a penny?
I'm sure I do.

Fences
by Bethany Burger - age 18

me and him
him and me
those words look so nice together
but in real life, they're so far apart
divided by a barbed wire fence
made of steel, made of stone
on one side, he sits in his happy, safe world
on the other, I dodge speeding cars and broken hearts
standing outside, I wonder where you are
do you see me, cold and alone?
do you hear me calling your name?
my hands have been scarred from so many fences
please let me in

headlights flash across your lawn
my shadow blends into the fence
a siren interrupts the peaceful calm
you peer out a window, oblivious to my presence
I am invisible to you
hidden by a fence

the siren is louder, it's coming for me
to pull me away, away from the fence
can you see them?
they drag me away, not resisting
you're the window again
and for a second, our eyes meet and
I think you see me
and the fence begins to disappear

Rain
by Tara Case - age 14

When I was young
Rain was tears falling form the sky
When I was in love
Rain was a blessing from above
When I was down
Rain was down with me
When I was gone
Rain came down as dreams came true
When I lost you
Rain was all I had to hold onto

The Window
by Bethany Burger - age 18

I peer out my window
and see you standing on the sidewalk,
a figure silhouetted by the streetlight.
You're searching to find my window,
you're trying to find my heart.
If you could see it, you would find that
I just need to get away.
Away from the yelling and crying and hurting.
The stars are bright and the clouds are still,
waiting for the mystery to be solved.
I can see them and they give me hope.
They will soon show you the answer,
the only way to reach me, the window to my heart.
It can show you my mind
and you'll see there's no turning back,
no regrets, no distance, no good-byes.
If I open my window, life will never be the same.
Our souls will unite, breaking the glass.
Give me your hand and I'll show you the way.
All you've got to do is believe.

Butterfly
by Nicole Burkholder - age 15

As the wings flutter rapidly
The love grows so strong
The butterfly so alone
But it's been there for long
The stronger it gets
The more alone it feels
The kisses of death
It's heart you steal
The kiss of life
A spark it gets
From the start
When you first met
A tingling feeling
It's heart so warm
The love you give
Is no sign of harm

My Friend
by Anais Buro

When I look into your eyes my friend,
I see someone who understands my worries and fears,
Someone who listens to me,
Whenever I am in tears.

When I look into your eyes my friend,
I see someone who tells me not to hide,
Someone telling me to smile,
And to look at the bright side.

When I look into your eyes my friend,
I see someone who listens to what I say,
Whenever I need to yell:
"Please help me, I can't last another day!'

When I look into your eyes my friend,
I know I can trust you and believe in you,
It's what I expect from a friend
And what I find in you.

Again
by Nick Burris - age 14

I see you have come again.
I know I haven't a chance to win.
You'll bring my day a rainbow and blue skies...
But underneath them all are just lies.

Soon my world will be gray.
For trusting you I will pay.
I will suffer the pain no torture can give.
I'll want to die, but yet I will live.

In my mind I know you are worth it.
Everyday with you is perfect.
From in my heart I hear my voice.
It tells me that I made the right choice.

I will love you to the end.
Till you leave me once again.

Yesterday
by Will Burroughs - age 13

Yesterday we had fun
Yesterday we chewed gum.
We'll always be friends
As the day never ends.

Yesterday we went blading
While the sun was fading.
We'll always be friends
As the day never ends.

Yesterday we went home
And we talked on the phone.
We'll always be friends
As the day never ends.

Yesterday they got on a plane
That took them far far away.
We'll always be friends
As the day never ends.

We'll always be good friends
As the day never ends.

Broken Hearted
by LaTanya Chambers - age 14

As I lay here in my bed
I weep.
And with every tear that drops
upon the dry soil;
Goes a piece of my soul
The light blinds me
causing complete darkness
Still I weep
I sleep but without dreams
I try to climb the tall brick wall
but I continually fall
And I never reach the end
Where all is dark
And all is lost
No never again.

Friends
by Rebecca Burt - age 12

Friends are people who make you smile
Friends are people who would go the mile.
They would talk to you when you need to talk
They would walk with you when you need to walk.

They are very joyful and so kind
If you ask them questions they wouldn't mind.
Friends wouldn't betray you at all.
They wouldn't leave you behind at the mall.

Friends are different big or small.
Friends could even be ten feet tall.
There's one thing alike I will name.
They all care that's what's the same.

Fear of Unrequited Love
by Adrian L. Burrowes

If only I could tell her,
or knew of such a way
that she would know I love her,
without me having to say.

I've tried to find the words,
for I have longed to confess
the way I feel about her,
but my thoughts I can't express.

I wish I knew her feelings,
then I would know for sure
whether she had also suffered
from the pain I must endure.

But I am not a prophet,
some uncertainty exists.
Will my love be unrequited;
is it really worth the risk?

I continuously suppress
and ungodly urge to act,
as I keep asking myself
what if she won't love me back?

I can only go on hoping
that fate's hand will intercede
and provide me with the answers,
the assurance that I need.

I pray a time will come
when my feelings will depart.
Until then I'll hide my passion
deep within my hollow heart;
...waiting for my life to start.

Sea
by Amy Christensen - age 16

Why do you have to be so cruel?
You take so many lives,
so many innocent lives.
Calm suddenly returns;
some say it's an omen.
I don't know.
A cruel sea turns into a translucent beauty,
like a caterpillar changes into a butterfly.
How?
A murderous raging sea,
calm on the outside.
The saying goes, don't judge a book by it's cover,
well it's the same for the sea.
It appears calm, but is it?

Butterfly
by Gordon Bush

Have you ever pondered a butterfly
The way they flutter about and then glide
Their different colors and hues
How much pleasure thy give you.

Is there a reason their beauty is so intense
They pleasure our eyes and tickle your sense
Things of such beauty do rarely last long
Like a rose or a favorite song.

They aren't here long and then they are gone
The next time a butterfly you do see
Take time out to wonder and see
What God has created for you and me.

Child Abuse
by Trudee Lee Bush

Here's a child that's really hurt;
Wearing her dress and little sweater;
Walked on just like dirt;
She could have been treated better!

She reveals so much sorrow;
The tears are in her eyes;
She has no hope for tomorrow,
Because treating her right, no one tries.

Her family is torn apart;
They're fighting with no end.
She has a tender loving little heart;
But there's no one to be her friend.

Child abuse should be demolished!
It is found in every race;
Caused by adults, it's really childish!
But in good families there's no place.

By Chance
by Trudee Lee Bush

Of you, my first glance;
Was the essence of desire;
My heart filled with fire;
This was only by chance.

A deep-seated need, your eyes impart;
To me in every possible way;
Knowing this was a very special day;
To discover your work of fine art.

Moments to treasure, upon your face;
Signaling me so loud and clear;
Making me know you are really sincere;
In luring me over to your place.

This was only by chance, we both knew.
Seconds, minutes, and hours would pass;
Feeling so right; hoping it to last.
By chance, our love grew and grew.

Drug Exit
by Trudee Lee Bush

Stop!
You're holding a gun to your head;
Soon you will be a corps (dead);
Taking drugs only to impress;
Friends, associates and all the rest.

Stop!

Your life is at stake;
Drugs are not what you should take.
There's always a better way;
Start a new, beginning today.

Stop!

Listen to what is written here;
Saving your life is very clear;
You must try to do your part;
Getting off drugs is very smart.

Fear...
by Charissa Buxton - age 15

There is nothing to fear,
but fear itself.
So some people say.
But fear grows stronger,
more and more,
cause of the world we live in today.
The fear of being killed,
robbed, or raped.
The chances of these are very great.
Not just our country,
but others too.
So many conflicts,
what are we going to do?
So if we come together,
to stand against our fears,
maybe the future won't be so bad.
Cause, I don't want to live in fear
for the rest of my life.
Do you?

Looking In The Past
by Laura Campbell

Everyone needs to look back
To find who they really are
Their desires, dreams, and intentions.
Looking in the past
When they do, they will find
They will do what they mention.
Everyone needs to be
Looking in the past
Dreams, desires, don't always come true
But you cannot be blue.
When you need to think
Looking in the past.
It may hurt, but it may not.
You could never stop
Desires don't go away
You will be awaken by a spell.
But you will always find
Everyone needs to be
Looking in the past.

We Never Learned
by Tanisha Campbell - age 16

He speaks to me of fire,
Of passion out of control.
He doesn't know he conspires
To take over my soul.
I wish it wasn't like this.
I want it to be for real.
This one I've just got to miss,
He can't imagine how I really feel.
I love another
But I can't determine his emotion.
I wish it wasn't undercover.
He is slick, like lotion.
I wish to find out
If love is returned.
We could learn what passion is all about.
But we never learned.

Sonnet
by Tina Campellone - age 17

The trees are so pretty
Oh what a sight
I won't miss them in the city
Or maybe I might
Mom, I'm leaving now
I'm going to be on my own
I'm sure I'll make it somehow
Your only daughter is going to be alone
College life may not be easy
But it's what I want to do
I hope the dorm isn't too sleazy
Now I'm starting to feel blue
Mom, Dad, I'll miss you alot
All our memories will never be forgot.

Mad Seances
by Sandy Cappolla - age 13

You thought she couldn't
hear
What you said beyond the door
You thought she couldn't
see
the blood stains on the floor
You thought she couldn't
feel
the anger in your pulse
You thought she couldn't
taste
the love that was false
But past the presents of your
being the light bulb
burnt in which
you where seeing.

Suicide
by Sarah E. Capps

They always said red means stop
Well I finally learned a lesson on that
He said he wasn't going to do it
I tried stopping him, but I guess my words wasn't enough

He's gone now
Gone for good
Taken by his own hand
Why I'll never understand

At one time I did
I understood his hurt and pain
But we lost contact for awhile
And now we've lost contact forever

My tears will eventually stop
My hurt will always last forever
Forever was what I lost
And understanding I will never have

I'll never have someone to talk to now
Because that someone lied
You said you wouldn't do it
But you did

I can't hold that against you
Because I've done things to
That hurt more than just me
And because of that I've lost everything

But that's no reason to kill
Because there is always hope
And hopefully my luck will change to good
Red means stop now I know why.

Untitled
by Elizabeth McNielly Carey

Auctioned off; made available to everyone
reassembled fragments of dramatic red
and blue black paper packets,
crude yet precious inscriptions
drenched in a natural well of incurable infections.

Lying out before a great wide mouth
innocent tongues tearing at the meat
undisturbed by the inherit implications
of the wet work rising in swells.

Drenched in rags of Atlantic green;
clenched cold like transparent skin
storing the sweetest perfume,
pain has many different smells.

The Conquered
by Kathleen Carlson - age 15

The sun creeps over the horizon
I feel it's bright warmth upon my face
See it's glory brightness spread over the city bringing new life
The people are yawning and stretching
Wondering what the new day will bring
They move, first slowly, then faster
The sun has penetrated their minds
The adrenaline pumps through their veins
They prepare for confrontation
Life in it's prime, awaits them
It challenges them to strive forth
They must conquer or be conquered
At the end of the day, the weak will be no more
The strong will rest their heads
Patiently awaiting to sleep
Asleep they will stay, among wondrous dreams
Until the sun decides, once more, to creep over the horizon.

Changes In Life
by Kathleen Carlson - age 15

Age, a blooming of the body
Maturity, a blooming of the mind
Maturity is not a two-step ladder
First the bottom, then the top
It is made of many levels
Deceiving everyone
Once you reach the top, you think
Oh good, I'm finally done
Until you're suddenly looking down
From an even greater height
Each new day brings possibility
Never knowing when the day will come
For a level of new maturity
It's never planned or won
You're caught unaware
Fore each new step
Yet the fear
Is mingled with
New levels of respect.

Melody of Life
by Micah J. Carlson - age 20

Here we stand, the smooth rhythm of the crashing waves playing the percussion. The soft breeze playing the sweet sound of the flute as it caresses the sand grass. A light, mist filled wind fondling our hair, making up the bass and guitar. We find ourselves holding each other closely for warmth and sanctuary from the cold air rising from the water, as the collected sounds come together in our minds. We begin to dance to the melody of life, under the moon and stars creating a blurry image of distant life across the rippled water.

Memories
by Kimberly L. Caron

No matter how hard I try
to push aside the memories
that I find too difficult to look at
too painful to bear
they have a way of finding me
when I close my eyes to sleep

Thoughts begin to draw pictures
in my mind's eye
Strangely compelling
Uncomfortably familiar
And though I've been there
many times before
I allow myself to be brought
there once again
willingly
obediently
like a lamb to the slaughter

They say the passage of time
can erase the pain
and heal the memories
But I don't believe it
Some pain cuts too deep
and I doubt I will ever
be rid of the image of you,
my little angel,
seated at the kitchen table
in your jammies
making your little creepy crawlers
with Grandma and Papa
waiting for a momma who never came home.

My Mother
by Amy Carpenter - age 12

Each day and night,
I think and can remember:
When I was young
The beautiful songs she sung
At night she'd tuck me in
How long ago has it been?
How she treated me-
I will always remember and can see
so clearly, so bright
It's the click of a light
She was always there for me
 through many things
A smile is what she always brings
Her earrings would shine like waters
 in a bay
The times of happiness and the times
 of play
I can remember her say:
I love you,
And I would look into her eyes, so blue
And say, "I love you, too."

So Called Friends
by Maricris T. Catillo - age 16

They were always there when you needed them,
But as time passed on, things have changed,
They're no longer there for you,
They enjoy talking behind your backs,
Even want to fight with you,
Always thought they were such good friends,
But now you found out that you were wrong,
So much for so called friends,
They think and act like they're all that,
But really that ain't a fact,
As time goes by they'll ask for forgiveness,
But that won't do,
Smart people won't forgive friends that ain't true to you.

Sonnet on Snow
by Stephanie Cedervall

Below subdued dark of a wet winter night
Street lamps enhance beauty of blizzard blown snow --
Just arrived, so clean, so fresh, so whiter than white
As it shimmers in graceful spans of slopes aglow.
Then a mystical aura of peace descends...
No roar of planes, no rush of cars, no noise
But only a sense of awesome innocence
And the hush of silence one rarely enjoys.
For a time, untarnished by its Earthen landing,
This new snow transfigures all to look quite new.
Such artful sculptures above our understanding
Are worth this pause to glimpse another view.
 What wondrous power staged this solemn scene
 When countless crystalline flakes did convene!

Tomas
by Jacque Carpenter - age 16

My name is Tomas I am but four.
Last night my father shut the door.

He locked me in I don't know why?
Now all I can do is sit and cry.

Mom came home from work that night
and soon they began to fight.

She yelled to unlock the door.
She yelled real loud and then yelled no more.

I sat alone behind the door.
Hoping he wouldn't hurt us any more.

I'd never been locked in this room for so long
and fear that something may have gone
wrong.

A few days had slowly passed by.
If I don't get food soon I will surly die.

They found his body curled into a ball.
The people cried why him, he was so small.

His life was horrible, a living hell
and his father will pay with a life sentence in
jail.

His name was Tomas he was but four.
That was the last time his father ever shut the
door.

The Wind Under Our Wings
by Stephanie Cedervall

The <u>wind</u> -- unseen but surely sensed
          and known
Relays its surging strength so full
          blown
Sustaining us with more spirited might
As we journey, yearning pilgrims in
          human flight.

The <u>wind</u> -- a breeze rising with gentle
          power
In this our recollective and honored hour
Now whispers its caress like heavenly nod
The <u>wind</u> under our wings -- a breath
          of God!

My Feelings
by Rhiannon Carpenter - age 13

My feelings are dying down
They are dying down so
much I can't slow them
down.

My feelings are old and
unforgiving, they are like
memories flowing away in
the dark sky.

My feelings are like tiny,
tiny things, being squashed.

My feelings are dead as
much as dead a corpse
thats been buried for
several, several years.

Individual
by Sara Casey - age 14

          I can't help it
        if I'm and individual.
        Why does everyone
     make fun of different people?
         It's almost like
       no one is allowed to
        express themselves,
and have to bottle up their feelings,
       like a genie in a lamp,
     so they feel that they'd fit in.
      They expect everyone to
     come from the same mold.
    To march to the same drummer.
     To live under the same sun.

          But I don't.

      I choose to be original.
       I choose to dress,
         to talk,
         to act,
         to be
        this way.
   When I was born, I broke the mold.
I march to the beat of a different drummer.
   I live on my very own world,
     where everyone is happy.
         original.
         different.
         individual.

Poetry
by Jennifer Catanio

Expressing my feelings.
Letting it all out.
I love to show people how i feel,
if it's hurt, anger, pain, it doesn't matter.
If i'm lost, confused, broken hearted,
I can always express myself in words.
but they're not just words,
they're feelings, emotions that show who i am.
To know me is difficult.
Let me show you who I am,
Take my hand and follow me.
Touch me.
Share your dreams with me,
I will share mine.
Understand me... Please.
Take time to listen.
Be there...
Just stay.

The Earth
by Jennifer Catanio

The night, my falling star
The day, my rising sun.
How beautiful the earth is,
I wish something could be done
The life that lives within every little thing,
The way the great eagle spreads his huge wings
The secrets of the present lie within.
The killing of innocent animals begin.
Trees falling everywhere,
because someone wants a factory there
Stay in tuned, save the earth.
Everything living son will be hurt.

Lost And Wondering
by Jennifer Catanio

The guy of my dreams is not in reach
Why is it so that the touch of his hand,
the sound of his voice, makes me weak?
I wish i could just reach out and hold him,
feel his lips against mine once again.
Timeless loving.
I'm confused, I know I should follow my heart,
but it's more difficult than that.
the love that I have for him,
is different from the other.
Yet, I still have love for another.
It shouldn't be like this.
I just want to be happy.
I wish i could let go, I need to let go.
When i'm with him, laughing, smiling.
On the other side... dark and tears.
Why?
Often I sit and ponder that very question,
Why?

Her Past Is My Present
by Jeremy Thomas - age 20

Helpless I felt,
From eh pain I had chosen.
Her eyes make me melt,
Her skin keeps me frozen.

Withdrawn from my fire,
Scarred by her rain.
I want her desire
To love me insane.

Disturbed by the night,
I tried to defend her.
Her beauty...I fight,
But quickly surrender.

Drowned by her river,
I tried to defy it.
My secrets, I'll give her,
To touch me so quiet.

Questioned by lust,
My thoughts had to leave me.
her memories, I trust,
Will never deceive me.

Frightened to fear it,
Her skies seemed so pleasant.
Her ghost is my spirit,
He past is my present.

A Golden Morning
by LaTanya Chambers - age 14

I woke up on a lovely day
It was to early to go out
and play
It was cool to say the least
My first time to see the sun
Rise in the east
When the sun began to rise
I asked "Mom can I go
Outside?"
When the sun began to
Show
I could see the morning
Glow
You could see that morning
Glory
Only on a golden morning.

Poetic Justice
by Rachel Kimberly Chaffee - age 16

Night falls,
she stands alone on top of a waterfall.
She can see the mystic water,
pound on the rocks below.
the spray making a ghostly film,
over the whole lake.
She throws Lotus petals over one by one,
watching them fall,
making intricate circles as they fly to their watery grave.

Her lover has died.
She sees his face,
and hears the God of the lake,
call from far below.
Taking a deep breath,
she plunges to her death.
Realizing afterwards that her love has not died,
the betrayal of her jealous sister.
As the angel of death comes to greet her,
she makes one final wish.....

Awakening in her chamber,
she rushes out,
sees the angel of death,
carrying the wet limp body of her,
rage filled sister.

One Last Chance
by Jill Chinners - age 17

If I were given the chance to touch you once more,
my life would be in a stand-still motion.
If I could look into your deep brown eyes again,
I'd sprinkle both our hearts with a powerful love potion.

If I were given the chance to kiss you once more,
my heart would beat with never tears only laughter.
If I could see your smile again,
my life would be joy for here and forever after.

If I were given the chance to love you once more,
I'd show you the world and many wonderful things.
If I had the chance to hold you again,
I'd shelter your soul underneath my forever-loving wings.

All Through the Night
by Annetle Chapa - age 15

Wondering sleepless all through
the night,
Hold me, hold me but please hold me tight.
Feel the coolness of the misty
night air.
Feel the wind blowing, blowing
in our hair.
Kiss me gently, but yet kiss
me long
Hear the whispers singing, their
singing our song.
Don't ever leave please promise
you'll stay.
You took my breath far, you
took it far away.
See the star that shine so bright.
Wondering sleepiness, wondering
all through the night.

A Moment In The Shadows
by Tresha Charles - age 14

Alone and sheltered safely
'neath the shadow of my house
I watch as the sun beams
all around,
neat little houses
with picket fences
that hide the strangers inside
stare back at me.
But I am not worried.
And as the wind
tickles my hair softly,
I sit back
and allow the
peaceful solitude
to take me away.

Thoughts
by Andria Chediak - age 13

I look at you the way you are,
But I know you won't go far.

I love the way you speak out loud
And see the sky, the moon, the clouds.

I wonder what it's like to give.
I wish I could learn to forgive.

As I run besides the truck of hurt
All my thoughts turn to dirt.

The way I feel is very unreal,
The way you see is the best deal.

I wish I knew what to do.
All I can think about is you.

My life is fading away,
And my dignity won't always stay.

A Summer Night
by Amanda Christensen - age 12

Once upon a summer night
I watched the stars
Wondering
Who has created these beautiful things

Once upon a summer night
I listened to the wind
Wondering
Who has created this beautiful thing.

Once upon a summer night
I smelled the flowers
Wondering
Who has created these beautiful things

Once upon a summer night
I found the answer
God
He has created all these beautiful things.

World
by Andria Chediak - age 13

Sometimes I don't see
What's getting into me.

My hate is growing,
and my love is fading.

I feel so hopeless
And so very useless.

I need to be myself.
You need not worry about yourself.

Why do people act so dumb?
Everyone seems to be a bum.

The world is falling apart.
No one listens to their heart.

All the rage in this place
All the people wasting space.

Why should I support you?
Why should you support me?
    yu-pee

Everyone is so unhappy
Just wait and see what happens.

My friends you are
Hopefully forever.
Don't ever leave me
    never.

Butterfly
by Cory Clark - age 14

Butterfly flutter, beautiful you are
You fly around so freely you travel near and far.
Butterfly you've visited so many different places, touched many
flowers,
and seen many faces,.
You haven't any problems, concerns or worries on your mind.
Your life is so carefree and simple, you live, learn and die
Butterfly you don't cry any tears and if you really wanted,
could fly far away from here.
Butterfly I wish that I could sail on forever in the big endless sky,
I would fly up to heaven and leave the world behind.

Friends
by Christy Coutts - age 14

You can make me laugh,
You can make me cry,
When I look into your big brown eyes,
Filled with laughter,
Filled with fun,
Of memories and adventures,
We have not yet begun.
We were always together.
We were never apart.
You were my best friend,
But now you've stolen my heart.
I wish you felt the same way too.
And I just found out,
You do.

Clear and Muffled Mind
by Andria Chediak - age 13

My mind is clear and full of fear,
But on top is all I hear.

Above the trees
Above the clouds
Above the sky
There is this guy.

He looks at me and you
And wishes he knew.

We think we know what we don't,
And what we don't we really do.

You and I will never die.
Our own world will live on forever
And will never end
never,

Is life a blessing or a saying?
Without the wind the sound would be free.

I wish I knew the answers to it all.
I wish I could be big and tall.
I wish I could get over the wall,
But to all, I am nothing.

As My Heart Cries
by Annie Chou - age 14

While we learn and play,
Kids like you work all day.
Nervous and wincing,
Afraid of a whipping.
A single tear dries,
From my heart, as it cries.

As you work and work,
For some really cruel jerk,
A thrash from those whips,
I wince as your skin rips.
A single tear dries,
From my heart, as it cries.

As the nights draw near,
Still, you work in great fear.
Nights approach with cheers,
Grounds are wet with your tears.
A single tears dries,
From my heart, as it cries.

When we rest and sleep,
You're too tired to weep.
While we eat and waste,
You starve or eat in haste.
A single tear dries,
From my heart, as it cries.

While you pray each night,
For a world that's all right,
You think no one cares,
No one hears your prayers.
But these tears are true,
As my heart cries for you.

Death
by Jennifer Christie - age 13

Everyone thinks it is painful
But really it's great, cause when
you think of it,
The person who has died,
will be taken off.
This demon-possessed world-
I wish someday soon...
That I to will die
Because I now know what the future holds,
And I pray to god-
to take me off
This awful world.
Because if you read
the last chapter,
it tells what the future holds.
You may understand my feelings,
But then again maybe you won't.
In the last chapter of the Bible
The first time you read it
(But read it if you can)
As many time as you can
Until you understand my feelings

Freedom Rings
by Lavon Christian

As we start each day with our dreams close to heart,
Our spirits filled with hope, we never hear the sound of
Freedom that's sounding forth to set these dreams in motion.

Lets Stop and Listen!

Be grateful for those who bought our Freedom.
The bloodshed and sorrow setting forth this Freedom
Shall always echo throughout our land.

Come one, come all, as Freedom calls!
She knows no one color of race,
She knows no certain age,
She only knows that she belongs to all
That seek her with a true heart and
Are willing to <u>Stand</u> for what she is.

I think of her often, as I see her symbol waving
Gracefully through the wind, with such pride--strength,
And always leaves a mindful memory of
All the <u>Brave</u> and <u>Young</u> at heart who gave
Their life's dreams so she may fly.

Freedom Rings, Yes! Freedom Rings
Proudly throughout our land.

Precious Time
by Lisa Connally - age 14

Drifting by,
I let out a sigh,
it's going by too fast,
the present will soon be the past,
The clock will chime,
it will be past my time,
I'll think I hadn't done enough,
but that is tough,
so much I want to do,
not enough for you.

Confusion
by Sarah Christianson - age 14

I am not blind,
But I cannot see the real me
And how I feel.
I have a voice,
But I don't use it for you
For the fear of being laughed at.
I am not deaf,
But I do not hear your kind words
Only the harsh and the stinging.
I have feelings-
Like everyone,
For I, too, am human-
But you hurt them
Repeadetedly.
I have thoughts-
Trillions of them that escape me-
But I do not express half of them
Fearing they are foolish, childish, stupid!
I have tears.
They burn on my cheeks
In bitter remembrance.
I am myself,
But others can't accept this.
There is no war going on,
But I feel one raging inside me
Tearing me apart.
No, it is not a war.
It is only...
Confusion.

Peace of Mind
by William J. Christy

Always searching
Never finding
That which feels so fine
It's called peace of mind
Where it is I just don't know
I still crave it, does it show
Where it is I wish I knew
To gain it I'd give anything to you
Ever onwards I always search
While it watches me hiding on its perch
As I stumble blindly
I hope someone finds me

Dave
by Liz Cirulli - age 13

OK, now I'm scared
I'll admit it cuz it's true
A secret you've got, eh?
Not tell me? Not like you
Won't tell me who you like either.
Am I just jumping to conclusions?
I don't know, but I see the connection
I don't think it's my own delusions
Now this, you see, has gotta bite
Oh jit, it's all screwed up
If my best friend really does want more
Then I guess I should shut up
But listen here and listen well-
For difficulties lie afore-
Once we are much more than Friends
Never again will come what was before.

Walls Of Glass
by Clayton Chumbley

I'll never learn, not to get burned,
When it comes to broken hearts,
I'll never know, to let go,
When my heartbreak always starts.
I know my feelings for you are wrong,
But they keep growing and getting strong,
Every day.

Yes it's true, when I look at you,
You're not all that I can see.
I see the love you have inside,
That you can never give to me.
It hurts so bad but that's not your plan,
Your heart belongs to that special man,
Just not me.

It happens each and every night,
As I am drifting off to sleep.
I see you there inside my mind,
And in your eyes I'm looking deep.
You waltz right in make yourself at home,
Because you know that I'll be alone,
When I dream.

I hope and pray that I someday,
Can show a love that I can prove,
But now I strive, just to survive,
The cold, loneliest of truths.
And should my heart somehow make it through,
Another day of me loving you,
I'll go on.

Movement
by Bill Cibbarelli

Soft, subtle movements
The exotic beat of a setting sun
An orbiting dance
Light floating through swaying trees
Skimming the shifting sands of time
A dress drifts on wisps of wind
Hands and arms extended
A cross of joy
A delicate balance
The grace in a twirling figure
A little girl's game of pretend
Among the moonlight shadows of the night
Blurred images of white
The dance drifting across the ground
Coming to rest
Where I can be found
Awaiting the sound of whispering lips
I love you.

Untitled
by Starr Cline - age 14

She seems an infinite number of empty days until I go home
Outside children play
Inside fires burn
Burn what??
No one knows where the firewood grows...
We were barefoot in the basement when they found us
And separated us
Until when?
Until forever...

Requiem
by Lenore Cooper Clark

I cried when you were dying
And yet I let you die.
There was no way to save you --
But I didn't even try.

That's not entirely true. I prayed.
I begged for you to live.
I held you close and offered
All the comfort I could give.

I don't think you were hurting,
It was simply time to go.
But I could not release you
My heart was hurting so.

A love that's freely given
Provides a sacred place.
How could a little ten-pound dog
Leave such an empty space?

Death is so big and final;
You were so soft and small.
How could that little body
Encompass such a fall?

I needed what you gave me
And letting go is hard.
Now more than sixteen years of love
Lies buried in my yard.

The Perfect Woman
by Sommer J. Cleveland - age 12

Her lips shine so bright
Her hair so golden brown
Her eyes glow in the night
Her face so sweet and
 gentle that she couldn't
 bare to frown
Her body so perfect and tall
Her skin so easily broken by a fall
Her arms so beautiful and long
 She could play the perfect song
Her hands so beautiful and so
 bare she must have a ring to
 wear
Her finger nails so long and
 bright they shine in perfect day
 light

Untitled
by Starr Cline - age 14

She led him to the beach
To show him infinity
He says he'll love her forever
But nothing is forever
No matter how much you dream
She lifted a handful of sand
To show him their insignificance
He says she is lying
She shakes her head
And walks into the sunrise
The rain comes to show him pain
And he says he's sorry
But she's no longer there to hear
So he cries
But there is no answer

Denizens Of The Doorways
by Will Cline

My steps wthin the gutter,
cashed cold, unfolds loose money
outside the movie theater.

Snowbank foreclosures from thawing,
my mood picks up and shiney
like the change theat comes my way.

When walking streets as lively
as debris in clutters thriving
gut instincts to turning grumbles.

I mumble with my stumbles
as if wonders any matters
much as folks that wander gather.

For I always find them scatterd
among the doorways and displays
of dank, deserted, dismayed.

The Help Center
by Jacqueline Cobain - age 16

Spiders avoid this hallway
No webs hang silver in it's corners
Only wheel chairs
Usually empty
And doors usually shut.
Perhaps through the windows
With fences baked into the glass
You may see the patients
Writing crookedly on their
book margins
Sleeping with
Rachmaninoff
Tugging the petals from their little pots of
marigolds.
When the buzzer rings
the doors unlock - they stumble out for
walk hour, dressed in white soft
clothes, like clinical Greeks;
With nurses to the grass,
bright green and soft
Spotted under clouds of tree shade
here and there they sit.
The branches have all been clipped far too high to reach
They can't have glass or silverware
And not a single rose
can defend itself with a thorn.

Untitled
by Bethany Cobb - age 19

The night is watching at my window, holding tight to the sill,
and I am staring in dismissal uncertainty, wondering if I should feel.
The night caresses me gently and whispers in my ear,
while I take the helm and learn again how to steer.
My ship it sails over the black abyssal seas
and I find the strength has left my knees.
And the wind screams about the stern,
in my heart I feel it burn.
I point my ship toward the moon,
shinning in the black an ancient ruin.
Oh, how the dark shifts and sways
in the quivering light of the moon's rays.
Oh, how my soul spins
in the screaming, screaming winds.
I have found a dream among the ashes of the past,
I pray this time one will last.

Cherokee
by Shané Cobb

Oh Great Nation,
What happened to thee?
Where are your vast lands
Once belonging of the Cherokee?

What happened to my people?
Why were they victims of greed?
Once you flourished like spring flowers.
Why was this your destiny?

Jackson's warped vision of progress
Harmed my people for many years
Designed to bring degradation and shame
Forcing them along the "Trail of Tears".

I love you my people
My heart cries out to thee
You are truly a noble bread
I'm proud to be one of you, Oh Cherokee.

Thoughtless Climbs
by Eric Cochran

Thoughtless climbs
From musical mimes
Form a stretched sky
While I see their breath
like daggers about to cause my death

The Wandering Pebbles
by Caytee Coleman - age 13

Sea of darkness, sea of light
Stars wander like shimmering pebbles
Lost in your sea of blackness
Eventually to find their way
And to be replaced by puffs of heaven
From which angels gaze
The sun burns your delicate puffs
And all is blackened once again
In this darkness the shimmering pebbles
Are destined to lose their path in your
Seemingly unendless sea
But the pebbles are fortunate because as they
Were destined to be lost they were also
Destined to be guided by the suns raging torch
When ever their destination seemed unreachable
Yet you realize the horrid truth that they
Will never make it to your bottom because as
Your charcoal like water is purified again the
Delicate blue will once more be burned and the
Pebble will eventually be burned up as well.

A Free Man
by L. George Collins

Yesterday he voted. In the county of Kay, state of Oklahoma, United States of America. He voted for some candidates, vote against other candidates. He exercised a one of the unalienable rights which is his as a birthright.

It is right due-but prohibited-to most people living on this planet. It is a right due-but prohibited by their governments-to most of the people who have lived on this planet. He is one of a very fortunate few.

He was born with a right to develop, express, and be, the unique, personal individual he is.

It is said that the laws of God are fixed and inflexible. Some argue that, since the laws of God are fixed and inflexible, laws established by rulers and governments should be fixed and inflexible.

This argument looks logical. It sounds reasonable. It has fatal flaw: it is a false conclusion drawn by men.

The only rightful interpreter of, and actor in, this play of life in which you now live is: you.

The only legimate authority of any government is that given it by the men and women for and by whom it was established.

The man who voted yesterday exercised this right. He had his say on who should serve him and his neighbors in our government. He is a free man- -a citizen of the United States of America.

He is also a symbol bigger than life to those people of Earth who have not such freedom; their denied birthright.

This person is...You.

Sin
by James S. Collins

If wanting your love is a sin,
Then surely I'm going to burn.
For its to easy loving you,
I guess I'll never learn.

Loving you is most important,
And its worth every price.
True love may only come once,
My life for your love, I'll sacrifice.

Untitled
by Julie Conden - age 13

Here we are
We've come so far
We lay staring
At a night sky
Full of stars
Each one shinning
And taking
All fears away
Soon the sun sets
And it's time to face over fears
We hide
In the beautiful night sky
But soon
It's time to say good-bye

Faith
by Lillian Page Conner

Some people will try to teach you
Some will even try to preach to you
This is something only you will know
Because it comes from deep within your soul
At one or more times in your life
You may question this with great strife
The longer you grow
The more you will know
You need to search from deep inside
And the right path will be your guide

Soul Mates
A Dedication For My Husband
by Lillian Page Conner

If one could have a choice to make,
To turn back time and seal your fate.
I would have to say no and decline,
I've grown to love this life of mine.
To change a second, minute or even a day,
Would be like changing a script to a famous play.
Everyone learns as they just go along,
My mistakes have brought me to where I belong.

HAPPY..........
        WITH MY SOUL MATE OF LIFE!!

Lover's Lullaby
by Ruth Consla - age 16

Rest your head if you are weary.
Places your cares upon my shoulder.
You should know you need not carry,
your unyielding burden alone.
If you wish to hide behind my curtain,
no one will catch you unaware.
Sleep peacefully.
I promise to watch over you,
keep you safe from harm.
You must not fear the unknown,
I shall be your guide.
I will take your hand and lead you,
to the other side.
I can comfort you,
when the world is cruel.
And when you need me no longer,
I will still be here,
waiting for you.

Thinking Again
by Jennifer Lee Cook - age 14

Your head is full of ideas,
but they aren't being heard.
A mind waiting to be explored,
these thoughts of yours aren't absurd.
You don't know what you'll say next,
because there is so much to say.
Some things have to be let go,
but some of them should stay.
You don't know what to think,
there is so much to be thought.
Not much left but the sandals in your hand,
and all your thoughts which are incomplete.
Feel the wet sand below you,
as it gushes through your soft, bare feet.
Things were so much clearer then
but now you're thinking again!

The Island
by Jim Cook

I am an island,
Sandy is my soil:
Pure springs and slow streams
Among gentle hills.
My landscape is laced
With shrubs and palm trees.

My location is
Not easily reached;
Shoals and reefs hem me.
Few find the channel
To my inner lagoon.

The land will expel
Those that pollute it
Or come to despoil,
And those that do not
Care for this island.

Once safely inside
They wish not to leave.
They stay and abide
On the peaceful land,
To take in beauty
And be protected.

All are encouraged
To come and enjoy
A remote island
And beauty and peace
They discover there.

Fade Into You
by Katie Corneau - age 12

Like an echo of laughter, a bucket of tears, the smile of
rainbows, the tremble of fears, like the waves of the ocean, the eye
and the sight,
    I fade into you like the day into night.

Like the cry of the hungry, the sigh of the poor, the glee of
the joyful, the knock of the door, like the flame in the fire, the yearn
of desire.
    I fade into you like a voice in a choir.

It's the whisper in the shadows, that never is heard, it's the silence
in beauty that won't say a word, it's the silence that fills a room
after a fight, it's the sun that shines through in it's glorious light, I
keep fading and fading deep into your soul, I'm lost in your dreams,
us together a whole.

No Two Things Are the Same
by Geraldine Corduz

No two rocks are the same
    one is rough, one is smooth,
No two flowers are the same,
    one is pink, one is white
No two oceans are the same
    one is pacific, one is Atlantic,
No two elephants are the same
    one is African, one is Indian,
No two trees are the same
    one is oak, one is elm,
No two planets are the same
    one is red, one has a ring
No two voices are the same,
    one is loud, one is soft-spoken,
No two bears are the same,
    one is grizzly, one is polar
No two wolves are the same,
    one is white, one is gray.
Yes, no two things are the same.

Growing Pain
by Katie Corneau - age 12

Life is not like an open book,
you can't turn ahead and take a look.
You seem so blind,
try to see ahead and you will find.
That you can't see,
we are blind, you and me.

We never know what will happen next,
it seems as if we have all been hexed.
Labeled "bad", "to go to hell,"
it looks as if we have dug a deep well.
A well that goes down to the core of the earth,
why don't we all just die at birth.

It's like we have been put on this earth as a curse,
we might as well be riding in a big black hearse.
What is the point of living in pain,
what's keeping us from going insane.
Insane, that would be fun,
then like this poem, it all would be done.

Vision
by Franklyn C. Cornelius

You are my vision in time
You have shed my tears
You are my passion, and you are my fears

Our lives are silver static to so many eyes
Now the time has come for me just to say, "don't cry for another day."

I put your life beside mine
To show you that we're all free
  climbed a torch, just sighing
Now see that this world has a dream

We've been protected from this empty space
Traveling upward ever outward
Between the lines of space and time
To regain a steady pace

When I followed the sons of the living
No man could walk in my place
I sank deep into my thoughts
With the memory of your face

Stain Cosmos
by Jodi Ann Cortez - age 18

I took a walk down the yellow brick road,
came across a sunset with a golden undertone,
nestled in the hills of green,
shining it's dying light between the seams of the world.

Take a look about you, tell of what you see,
let not your eyes deceive you, just trust your very being,
see the glorious psyches about you,
yes, the ones in purple and in blue,
or those in a daring shade of silver,
Clashing among the tinge of lime,
with just a hint of delicate pearl,
Oh, what a rainbow of a world!

Behold!
the magenta of love, the mysterious lacking of,
colorblind fools, ever notice how they get caught
among the webs of black and white,
failing to let the colors swirl, to appreciate,
the beauty of gray.
Beautiful blend of black, white, and brown,
pink and yellow, a hint of blue,
yes, I see them in you,
so go on and glow, colorful soul,
yes, go on and glow little rainbows of the globe.

Ending Life
by Angela Cosby - age 13

Through the years, I have learned,
My life has taken many a turn;
Right and left, up and down,
Zig-zags and turn arounds.
But here I stop and notice
This is where and now is when,
I shall leave you all behind,
Full of grief and despair,
For do not worry, I will be there.

Silent
by Erin Couts - age 14

She sat in a quiet room
with nothing but her tears
Her memories were fading
And with that
Her life
The joyest days she remembers
Was Gods greatest gift to her
The pain he has put her through now
Has made her hate living
No family, No friends, No one who cares
Locked up like a lunatic
In a room of white with a movable bed
A sheet was laid to rest upon her head
By a man in black with a white collar,
And a black book written "Bible" on the front
A prayer was said
And the rest was silent

At One Point
by Angela Cosby - age 13

At one point in my life,
I will be happy.

At one point in my life,
I will be sad.

At one point in my life,
I will be crabby.

At another, I will be mad.

But at any point in time,
I will search, but never find,
The true love I have wished for.

Although he's out there,
Not known to where he is,
I will search for his love,
And later marry him.

At one point in my life,
I will be a mother.

At one point in my life,
I will be a grandmother.

At one point in my life,
I will be loved
And I'll love every other.

This Misty Beach
by Jacqueline N. Cotman

The sun was there
    just a little while
        before the steamy fog
            draped to shore

A kayak appeared
    then disappeared soon
        the haze was dense
            in a glide of salt spray

Motors humming through cloudy fog
    thick with hazardous lanes
        only boat silhouettes
            cruise this misty beach

The sun was gone
    just a little time
        before the four o'clock meter
            gave in to white sea fog

Vows
by Erin Couts - age 14

As she said her vows, a voice inside her whispered and said.....
    Forgive me Lord for I have sinned
    As I lay in my lovers bed
    He sits there alone and waits
    But for how long will he wait
    How long will it be before my love finds a clue
        How long will it be before he is told
    The choice is so hard
    To lie or to tell
    To love or to hate
    Why must he sit in agony
    While I
    I dis-own my life

Lost Love
by Stephanie Cowgill - age 13

Your gentle love, it sets my heart a soar
I stayed by your side the time you were ill
Loving you, it wasn't ever a chore
But now that your gone I love you still

So many nights I cried myself to sleep
Thinking of you was all that I could do
I hoped that our true love would always keep
You went and bit off more than you could chew

I hoped that we would never ever part
I never wanted our strong love to sink
I am ready for our new love to start
I will be there sooner than you will think

And now that I am leaving my old life
In heaven I hope to be your new wife.

Belated Mother's Day
by Amy Cox - age 15

Even though sometimes
life seems very hard.

This poem will not rhyme
and I'm late with the card.

I just wanted you to know
that I love you.

I always have
always will.

Because you are the best Mom
a daughter could possibly have.

With love,
Happy Mother's Day!

Dear Friend
by Roxanne Domanek - age 14

        Dear Friend,
So you want to be cool,
You want a best friend.
I'll stay with you till the end.
just try me once,
I'll guarentee,
You'll never need anyone else,
but me.
So steal for me become my slave,
I'll lead you to an early grave.
I'll take you in, make you feel good,
Like no one else ever could.
I'll lead you down the wrong path,
When you fall I'll only laugh.
So trust in me, and soon you'll see.
I'll satisfy your every need,
        Love Weed.

Dear Brother Dan!!!!
by Elizabeth H. Crabtree - age 14

I have a little brother named Dan,
He's quite a cute little man!!!!!

Although he is only two,
He always has plenty to do!!!!!

Dan, he is a very likable fellow,
Although when he doesn't get his way, he
has been known to terribly bellow.

All his toys could reach from floor to sky,
OK, I admit that might be a lie!!!!!

His vocabulary is composed of mostly hellos and no-nos
When asked what he thought of this he said "so-so".

Dan recently proclaimed "Use Potty"
All we can say is "Uh-oh Golly!!!!!"

Recently I came home to find a shock,
Daniel had broken my antique clock.

When I asked him about what he had done,
He replied "La La, Me Have Fun!!!!!"

Although he is sometimes bad,
Although he sometimes gets sad,

He always forever will be,
Dear brother Dan to me!!!!!

When You Are Gone
by Fawn Daniels - age 14

When you are gone I will try to be strong
But the life has all left and the days are so long
Each night I pray and wish just once more
That you will be there at my door
Everyday I cry and my heart starts to break
I think I see you and start to shake
I always think of how nice it would be
If you would come back someday to me

Questions Without Answers
by Martha Crabtree

The sun obliges us with warmth and cheer,
Touching the leaves, the grass and flowers here,
And birds are singing, near and far away--
Blue skies, high clouds, soft winds enhance the day;
And earth, so fair, shows us her smiling face...
Why, then, do I think of another place?

Beyond our system's orbiting routine
There lies a vastness we have never seen?
Black, cold and empty--silent, too, I know,
Except when stars collide within the glow
Of distant galaxies, spinning out of sight,
Exploding in the realms of endless night.

Are worlds unknown to us evolving there?
Do birds sing in their other-worldly air?
Do flowers bloom, and rippling waters flow?
And love---does it exist? And can it grow
Between such beings, distant, strange and rare
That we cannot imagine or compare
Their faces, lives and instincts with our own--
Their beauty with the loveliness we've known?

Despite the mysteries of time and space
Our planet seems to be a special place,
Beloved our God, embellished by his art--
Surely we must dwell closest to this heart.

The Virtue of Redundancy
by James W. Crissman

Seining fresh metaphors,
like blind dipping smelt in big water --
even if I get one
it may not taste better
than those caught darting in unison
like silver ribbons through icy spring creeks.
I may savor it more intensely,
let the rare minnow linger on my tongue,
because it was my struggle.
But it was not your struggle,
and you may not recognize the salty flavor
is not from Morton,
but the sweat of passion.

In my turn at life,
whether time is an arrow or a boomerang,
it is important that I not end in an angry place --
I could --
but that will be a start for another.
So I will try to end in love.
Sorting my words for brightness,
silver schools of radiant words,
running like grunion in deep channels,
an ocean tide of basal metabolic poetry.

It has all been said before, so why say it again?
We say it, we shout it, we show it
to affirm love in our turn!
It is joyous that it's already been said!
And it is a fine thing that you and I live it again.
The meaning of our lives need only be discovered
not invented.

A Lost Love
by Greg Crosby

A love is lost, yet is with you always
It seems an eternity, other times only minutes
You had a love that could not be matched
Some say time mends a lost love
Others say a new love will heal the heart
Is there a cure for a lost love?
                I think not!
Though time eases the pain and heartbreak
Losing a love causes a wound that does not heal
For you have known love as few know it
The love you feel will forever be lost
However beautiful memories of that love last
Forever.
A love is lost, yet is with you always.

Light Of Day
by Peter Defere

Explosive accord with destiny
Thoughts grow like stars after sunset
Cosmic bleeding felt now more than ever
Surrender the songs to be them forever
Closed eyes an open display
Visions and voices dance and disintegrate
Penetrating release to another's domain
The light yields freedom never to be the same

Amber
by Emily Cruickshank - age 14

Beautiful. Scared.
The thought of my
loved one is powerful
I look at her and
see confusion.
Maturity strikes but
not in the heart
I leave my love with
tears. Does the flower
blossom in spring?
Does the flower ever
blossom?
Troubled from the
weight of her life
The burdens
The gold.
The responsibilities
strike her.
She is elegant in
her gown of life.

Truth Of Innocence
by Krista DeGrey - age 13

As millions of snow flakes fall they cover the terrifying fears and troubles of many, but are they really gone, when the snow melts will we be troubled as before?
The rain washes away our tears, it washes away our worries but when the sun comes up and dries the land do they dry up too? Can we bury our problems or will they become worse? Listen to your heart it won't lie to you
it will only lead to the truth which is always the way to freedom for innocence.

Searching For You
by June L. Curray

I've searched the world over for
        someone like you.
I knew someday my dream
        Would come true.
I didn't know when or exactly where
but I knew someday you'd be there.
Your picture is painted in this dream
        of mine
For years I've traced each and every line.
Hoping it would lead me to you one day
make you a reality and fade the
        Picture away.
Then one day out of the blue,
I looked over and saw you.
Time stood still my heart raced
at that moment my heart you embraced.
No words were spoken the silence
revealed the love that was there
        and what I could feel.
I realized then my dream come true
my search was over cause I'd
        finally found you.

Secret Life
by Summer Czapiewski - age 17

My name is anonymous
I hide in the shadows of the night
Pleading to be noticed
Hungry for the light
My life is a secret
Wearing it's disguise
No one meets my sadness
No one hears my cries
I feel like the forsaken one
Living all alone
Crawling to desolated corners
Fearing the unknown
But there must be others like me
Afraid to show themselves
Hiding their true feelings
Stashing them on shelves
We are the chosen ones
Running in life's race
Wanting to be winners
But settling for second place
Trying to speak up
give us a courage we pray
Our chance comes and goes
Well perhaps another day.

For The Best
by Crystal Dalrymple - age 15

I hope I'm doing the right thing
Ending my life when it's just beginning
The love I have is far away
Too bad he isn't here to stay
It makes me lose my dignity
He's changing to my enemy
He said he'd love me forever more
Where is he now? Out with a whore?
To put our true love to the test
I plunge the knife deep in my chest
If this isn't wrong, it must be right
He can't come home and beat me tonight
He says he loves me
As he hits me
The bruises I get are in his favor
For some weird reason my love grows greater
I fall down in an unconscious state
Yes, this really is my fate
This will surely clear the mess
Yes, it's really for the best

Untitled
by Lauren Doffont - age 13

    Magic...I guess that's what you could call it, and I knew, since the first time we met that we were supposed to be together. His smile brightens my heart, his brown eyes stare straight into my soul I could get lost in those magical eyes how innocent they look! His voice drowns out the world so I listen to his deep thoughts wondering if I'm included in his everlasting plan, there are a million tiny things that make him wonderful, and if you put them all together you have a guy who can't get any sweeter, any nicer, anymore charming, anymore attractive,...and me and him together are...like...Magic...

Ceremonial Feast
by Rebecca Dalvesco

It is the thirtieth of May.
Outside torrents of rain fall;
inside the festivity has begun.
Geraniums, carnations, sweet peas,
orchids, and babies breath,
clutch the yellow ochre walls of
the room and exude their moist
blanket of odors.

In the midst of the flowers' caresses
you lie placed in a steel grey encasement.
Your silent, waxen face left as prey
to the mildewed, sweaty hands.
The white rose clings to your palms
as if it was still among the thickets.

The dusted, golden light carves the way
through the joyful black beasts paying
homage to a sweet body that will
soon sour.
Among the beast the frozen dog stands,
reading from a crusty stained page,
psalms of a prophetic paradise.

Let us pray,
for today, the dog will lick your pure hands.
No news of God now.

"Candle Light"
by Craig 'Welch' Davis

Warm flame igniting,
Hold me close this night.
You are exciting,
A beautiful candle light.

Warm flame, stay burning,
Hold me through this life.
You keep me yearning,
My beautiful candle light.

You are the world to me,
The light which let me see,
You are my love, my life,
My beautiful candle light.

Love Is
by Katie Darnell - age 14

Love is a feeling that starts
deep within every beating heart.
It can cause you to weep grieving tears,
or give you the courage to stand up to your
strongest fears.

It can send you into
a fury of burning rage,
or be the reason
for your calm and quiet phase.

It can give you the gift
of a precious new life,
or cut through a broken heart
like a steel knife.

It can give you hope
and help you up,
or simply let you fall,
but keep in mind
love conquers all.

Grand Slam
by Nancy Das Neves - age 14

At the bottom of the ninth,
With the visitors leading seven to four,
The home team up to bat,
With the bases loaded,
Fans roaring with excitement,
The audience rise with anticipation...

The electricity is shut down,
The power turned off,
The screen blank.

Agitated home viewers annoyed with the failure,
Frantically fidget, fiddle and click, click, click, click...
The speakers blast sound, the picture returns,
The game is OVER!

Untitled
by Heather D'Augostine - age 14

My heart is crying out for you
    I don't know what to do.
How could you make me feel so happy
    then make me turn blue.
All I need is someone here to help
    me understand.
And tell me why you took away your
    gentle, loving hand.
Oh why, oh why did you do this
    I cared so much for you.
I never thought we'd end so soon
    I thought our feelings were true.
I know I'll always love you
    but do you feel the same
This is my life your toying with
    it's not some silly game.
I guess you only cared for me
    while she wasn't there.
But now she's back and wants you again
    to fulfill her every command.
I see now that you want her
    and want me out of the way.
I guess that we are over
    and she is here to stay.
Why can't someone help me
    tell me why he did this.
All my dreams are shattered
    although it never really mattered.

Rainbow
by Melinda Davenport - age 15

The world is a beautiful rainbow
with faces of different shades and colors
To me it is a beautiful thing to
others it remains a wonder
I see inside and past the hatred
that others only see
I try to teach them to get past
the hate to show them that its
only their own fright they see
I feel bad for these people
only seeing black and white to me
that seems like a horrible thing for
variety is the spice of life.
We are all the same if you look inside
we all hurt, we see, we get mad, and we cry.
I will always be there for someone
who needs me no matter how different
people claim we are. God put is out
here for a reason to live in peace and
harmony.

A True Story of Life
by Katie Davis - age 13

The shadows of darkness fall over the joy,
once created for our happiness.
Through hunger for love
we strive to live.
We don't look back over our shoulders
we might not like what we see.
We sense a ray of light.
We can fell the pain shatter into
a million pieces.
The light grows stronger
and the ice melts around our frozen hearts.
We feel the love we have longed for.
Our joy feels like it will never end.
Then one of us takes the privilege for granted.
The shadow re-appears.

A Touch Of Rain
by Arnette F. Davis-Carpenter

As I look out and see the rain cascade down
Hitting the window making it's sound,
It occurred it me what beauty I'll find
When the steady stream stops and brings peace to mind.

The dirt is more softer, the grass o' so greener
All earthworms now wiggle on ground so much cleaner,
The sun shines far brighter, the trees stand more stately
As they lean and grace the sky quite ornately.

The birds now appear shaking their feathers
What they must be use to for this kind of weather,
Ant hills now forming, more mounds do abound
A gentle breeze blows some leaves to the ground.

The flowers smell sweeter, the leaves grow anew
All hillsides majestic now covered with dew,
Butterflies flitting from bush to flower
Not really convinced they've been through a shower.

Now finally I know this onslaught of rain
Is his way of falling our attention to gain,
For all the water brings the sun of his smile
Shows us the world, of God's glorious style.

A Friend Like You
by Melissa Davis - age 20

To have a friend like you,
    Must be a blessing from above.
To share all my life with,
    The tragedies and the love.

I have you to confide in,
    When things get too tough.
And you to take my back,
    When things are a little rough.

You're thee when I need to laugh,
    And there when I want to cry.
You're there when I need you,
    Even when I don't know why.

I'm blessed by your friendship,
    You're my biggest dream come true.
And you know anytime you need me,
    I'll always be there for you.

Alone
by Kate Davish - age 19

The world blindly sees
The girl standing on solid ground
While her heart forever bleeds
To find security and comfort
To heal her soiled wounds
And lift her off her knees
She hides herself behind a wall
Wandering through her dreams
No one to break her fall
Because she's not the girl she seems
But a child trying to break out of an adult prison
Yearning to be free
She travels to many destinations
But only in her mind
Experiencing hallucinations, inhalations
To leave her problems behind
Soaring in the radiant sky
No one to tell her she's wrong
But do what she feels is right
She struggles to survive
With no support by her side
Because she blankets herself
In fear of losing her dignity and pride
So she'll proceed on, exploring the world
Hoping for a better future
Where her fears will die
Drying the tears in her eyes
Able to live on her own
Like a drifter, an outsider
Meant to walk alone

Chimera Love
by Tracy Degraffinreid - age 14

Young, blossoming emotions alloy in my soul and I ask myself
Cynically, "Have I fallen in love?"
Have my youthful emotions soared to a castle in the sky or is it genuine
love that I
Am enchanted by?
Yes, I am tender, unlearned and unwitting in my bloom,
So I will wait intently and
Intently I will wait for
The first sign of a blossom that will echo and claim my inquest -

"Have I fallen in love?"

A Time to Live A Time To Die
by Krista DeGrey - age 13

A rose bud awakens at dawn the slender
petals of a white rose, and the sleek petals
of a red rose open slowly to the pure air.
As they grow in the light and gleam in the
sun then slowly as they have come fade
away at dusk.

Someday
by Jeanne Berneice Davison - age 19

Your out there
I just don't know where

For you I'm searching
but I'm thinking
you can't be found

I can't say I understand
your pain
That would be insane

You cared about me, this
I know
But you wouldn't let it show

Instead you put up this
wall
and wouldn't let me in
like it was some kind of
sin

I tried to ease your fears
and take away the tears
but I couldn't help

now to you I say
I will find you someday
because one thing I do
now, I will be with you.

AIDS
by Wendy DaCosta

AIDS is a harmful disease
It's something you catch and will never leave
It can harm you and bring you pain
But there's one thing you can use, but don't be ashamed
It's a condom, they come in different colors, sizes and styles
Keep in mind with this it will make your life worthwhile
Some people are uptight about safe sex
But sex with a condom is the best
If you don't want to have sex and catch AIDS
Put your foot down, say no and don't be afraid
Sometimes you want to do it, cause everyone else is
But you're not everyone, cause you have a life you want to live
If you want to keep living your life through
Be smart and do what you have to do
Just remember if you're using that rubber tonight
You're doing the right thing, there's no need to fight
It will be a night full of love, both of you together, and that special glove...

Within You
by Krista DeGrey - age 13

A blind man can not see but he can
hear the sounds of beauty,
A deaf woman cannot hear but she can see the
world's art. If a sense is not fulfilled it is
better in another
If one man goes to prison another will go to
church.
We were made equal, every one has a fault
but like the blind man they won't see them and like the
deaf woman they will not hear the words of wisdom.
You have been given the sense to judge
yourself not others, for their faults are your
faults find them in you not them.

What An Aborted Child Will Never Get To Do
by Angela Dean - age 14

What an aborted child will never get to do,
Is-it will never learn to tie its shoe.
It will never get to feel happiness in every way,
It will never get to see the sunset on a beautiful day.

It will never get to see a sailboat on the sea,
It will never be able to drink tea.
It will never be able to get mad and pout,
It will never be able to be happy, and shout.

It will never be old enough to pretend,
It will never be old enough to have a friend.
It will never be able to grow up and get a job,
It will never have the chance to be a snob.

It will never be able to say "Mama, I love you!"
And Mama to tell it "I love you, too."
It will never know what its like to get in fights
It will never have a crying night.

It will miss out on all the funny things in life,
It will never have kids or a husband or a wife.
It will never be able to live on earth,
Cause it was never born by birth.

It will never be comforted from nightmares,
It will never be able to do truth or dares.
It will never have its picture taken or be recorded,
Why? Cause its mama decided to abort it!!

Friends
by Derek S. Dearth - age 12

I wish we all had friends.
Life was filled with fun and games
All your friends went out the door.

I wish we all had friends.

Your life dies the days grow cold
a piece of mind you would trade for gold.

I wish we all had friends.

And there's no time to change your mind
your friends have gone and
you've been left behind.

Your dog and you asleep
in bed. You hear a noise you
turn your head. He's gone.

I wish we could keep friends.

Two boys walking up a hill
one disappears and you
are standing still.

I wish we could keep friends

And there's no time to change your mind
your friends have gone and
you've been left behind.

I wish we all had friends but there's no
time to change your mind. How could
you have been so blind.

You spoke your friends went out the door.
Your friends have gone and you've been
left behind. Will there be more!

I wish we all had friends.

The Other Day
by Jessica DeFalco - age 12

I took a walk the other day,
to my surprise I found a stray.
The dog was golden brown,
to me it looked as if a hound.

He had no I.D. tags,
but when approached it's tail wags.
He looked at me with his blue eyes,
Oh, I hope he never dies.

I took him home to my mom,
She said I think we'll name him Tom.
Well everything went okay,
on the walk the other day.

Heaven & Fate
by Peter DeFere

A little bit more everyday,
your face grows into my mind
Wondering, for such a fate
and perilously still
between the inner trance
whispering eye to eye
the new ages of soul,
seizing slowly to invoke
astiral emerging
The luminous breath,
stretching and asking for more
A prowling desire
remains in lucidity, languishly
pacing from ecstatic flight
to a fiery rage and consumption
I'll guide your hands to
spacious legions of art,
Only to look down and see
heaven in a whole other way

Prophecy
by Peter DeFere

Legacy,
in a pure
cleansing illusion
Facing,
in the stride
of epic intuition
Bursting,
through ether
like creatures from sand
Desire,
to taste this mythology
is to slowly rise
Expansion,
the extended love
for infinite knowledge
Prophecy,
a golden silence
watched from the tower

Him
by Sarah Dellinger - age 12

When I see him, I get all excited.
I start wondering "What will happen, will he be mine?
I think about him all day long.
I remember the times we shared,
And I also remember the day we met,
That day, I'll never forget.
I just don't understand him,
I'm so confused,
I really like him,
But the wait is long and tiring.
My friends keep saying "Just forget him".
Forget him is what they say.
They just don't understand,
I can't possibly forget,
There is just no way.
I'll wait it out,
Through thick and thin,
Thinking of him, all day long.
When he is mine,
I'll prove them all wrong.

Heartbeak
by Mylene Demanet - age 17

The thundering roar of lighting
I hear laying down in my bed
My tears keep on falling
Nobody answers when I'm crying
I swear it's driving me insane
All my fears seem to appear
Tomorrow, yes, is another day
Please make all of them go away
The rain is coming strong
I don't know if I can go on
The night is dark of clouds
And the lightning keeps on striking
Yes, my heart is breaking

Summer Memory
by Melanie DePaulis - age 13

    All alone, inside, by myself.
The sun shines through my window, everyone is gone.
No one is here.
You'll forget me even if I never leave.
I wish I could run back to before,
my tears will not be forgotten,
neither will your faces,
I will remember, forever, you.
Don't forget what we all had,
even if you do, it will always be a part of us.

    Time just disappears beneath the golden sun,
everything changes, so do we.
But time is nothing, life is when we live,
not time.
And we are all the same.

    I see the people in the street and wonder who they are...
No where to run to except memories.
Time will not repeat, only pain.
And the sun will always live on,
And I will love you always.

Fatal Reality
by Mandy Depies - age 15

Full of nothing, I am lying here.
Engulfed in the darkness.
and comforted by the emptiness.
There is a void in my life.
Many voids, actually.
Everyone whom I have ever cared about is gone.
Why can't I be gone too?
Away from their hateful stares...
and comments.
They wouldn't miss me if I were gone.
They say that they would secretly be happy.
They claim that they love me.
but I know the truth.
I have but one question:
"Would there be a hole in the world where I'd been?"
I didn't think so...

The softness of leaving
by Rois De Shazo

If my love were to say
I cannot live another day.
I would say soft and true
may I leave this life with you?

But she would surly say
God will call another day.
When your life is through
I will wait there for you.

By the gates I will stand,
open love and open hand.
God is great god is good
we're one where we stood.

Life is but one short fling
God looks for the best thing.
He will say I made two
I will answer I thank you.

Flesh and blood doth atone
a gift of love by God alone.
I am yours, you are mine
our place in heaven is divine.

For I love you and you love me.
Companionship through eternity
God will look at death's harsh sting
and bind us with an eternal ring.

For love for us cannot be
unless he made you for me.

To my wife with all my love
Rois De Shazo 6-17-1996

I'm Sorry
by Gina DeStefano - age 14

When I wake up in the morning I feel the cold within my heart,
How I wish I could make a whole new start.

You don't know what it's like to pay for a mistake,
The pain I feel just makes me ache.

I wish I could tell the family I hurt that I'm sorry for what I did,
But nothing could heal the loss of their only kid.

He was in the wrong place at the wrong time,
I wish the life taken would of been mine.

I remember trying to save him,
Before the life fell out of his every limb.

I remember everyone running, but me staying to help,
I never told anybody, but right before he died he let out a loud, scared yelp.

I remember being taken away by the police,
I remember them telling me there would be no money for my release.

Now I'm in here for life without parole,
Because of me in my life has been stole.

I'm not sad for me, I deserve what I got,
I'm sad for the family, let them forgive me, I will not.

But if the parents ever read this I just want to say one thing,
I'm sorry for your loss and all the sadness I had to bring.

Vintage Love
by John Dethloff - age 19

Is love wine or just congealed grapes,
Before Michelle I alluded no lore.
Present time befalls a grandeur chalice,
Albeit, I endure for more.

Michelle forestalls rare Platonic beauty,
In every sense paragon exists.
In the ubiquity of Michelle I reside in Elysium,
Only there I desire to subsist.

My eyes blazon only devotion,
Passion sojourns my heart.
My soul prevails for rapture,
Even while we are apart.

Now I possess a taste for love,
And I believe it to be divine.
As respite toils I scintillate--
Michelle is my wine.

A Baby
by Rosa M. Diaz

With the soul of an angel
I descended from heaven above
in cotton diapers,
to make someone cry
and laugh in wonder.

I've become restless,
a walking mischief,
strong, wise, and happy,
beautiful, lovable, and loving.

Perhaps I'll change
but that I have to see
in each day I forth live.

Fantasy
by Beth Ann Deutschmann - age 14

As drops of water fall to the ground;
The rainbow melts away,
As I look him in the eye;
He takes me somewhere astray.

Let the breeze dry my tears;
An let the sun give me a smile,
The blanket of the night covers me;
And I am safe for a while.

This depression imprisons me no more;
His love sets my heart free,
The one thing left on the list;
He says he loves me.

This happiness unlocks my mind;
And my thoughts run wild,
As he looks into my eyes;
He says, "Our love is mild."

This is a fantasy in my mind;
But it seems to be so real,
Let me hold him in my arms;
And tell him how I feel.

This feeling is a new love;
But what is this?
Another scene in my fantasy;
True love's first kiss.

My best hopes are;
That this fantasy comes true,
Then when I finally have him;
I can say, "I love you."

Child Abuse
by Deseree Dupres - age 16

My blue ribbon at breast
now with greater meaning.
Cry you not alone, my dearest friend,
for every pain that strike on skin and soul,
strike deep on mine as well.
Depart you not from sound gaze.
Sorrowed heart that harm may come.
Brave the unknown.
Forget not - most of all,
that your existence I hold most dear.
Death be the only day when friendships severed.
Together we shall prevail.

The Black Night
by Bocar Dia

BY the black night when the souls are resting
at that moment the shooting star is flashing
when the believers are getting ready for the last prayer
when the nightly bird is celebrating the anthem of hunters
when the dogs are arguing with the evil spirits
when the shadows forces are plotting against the lights
when dreams are intruding in the heart of the poor men
when in the atmosphere is reigning the peace of the dens
when the firefly is challenging the thin starlight
when the moon is observing a retreat avoiding to fight
the mystical sign of the night remains the highest
the LORD's unchallengeable wisdom simply the greatest.

Tears
by Samira Dhanji - age 16

Tears,
Stay within and burn not
My eyes that can see truth no longer
Observe not my vision,
And halt all emotion.
And if you will come
Flow hot of my accord
But with cold indifference,
That I may continue in life
Alone without sorrow,
love and trust.
For these things three
I desire not, nor do I seek
Your passionate brilliance
That scars my soul
And has scarred before
So long ago and
So far away that
I know no longer
Emotion.

In Your Eyes
by Mara Diaz

As I look into your eyes
I come upon the truth
You don't love me anymore
and I'm the one to lose
Lose your loving, tender ways
lose the warm and happy days
that we spent together...

As I look into your eyes
I see more clearly than ever
You don't love me like before
And I'm the one to surrender
Surrender and give you up
Surrender and watch you leave

As I look into your eyes
I find myself wondering why
Why did it have to be this way?
When we still have so many
things to say...

But now without a backwards glance,
you turn around and walk away
and this is where it all ends...

Now here alone I ask myself
If a broken heart ever mends.

The Flight of My Soul
by W. Douglas Driggers, Jr.

Way above in the atmosphere's lips,
stray the horizon's top.
Touching high is one's mind as,
air thins out completely.
Stopping is the sky's limit,
which in turn keeps us together.
As the light becomes confident and thick,
heat becomes self-evident amongst
waves of emotional beams.
Straight above every existence
in search of some other forms.
Eagerly awaiting the arrival
of ultimate satisfaction.

You Saw Something In Me
by Maria DiMarco - age 13

You were the only one
who looked at me differently.
You took a chance and dared.
You took a chance and cared.

You saw something in me,
something no one else saw,
a sparkle, a twinkle, a shine.
You thought I was more than just fine.

Then, I took the time
to look at you differently.
Now, I see something in you,
all because I looked at you the way no one else cared to do.

A Friend You Can Count On.....
by Nichole Dino - age 14

She is with you through the good times,
And bears with you during the bad.
She tries to cheer you up,
When you are down and sad.

She is there when you need it,
And you gain trust in her every time
When she says that she cares for you everyday,
and when she comforts you and says "you'll be just fine".

You spill your heart out to her,
Every single time.
You have one of your little talks,
And are on the phone till nine.

You tell her about your heartaches,
You share each other's fears.
You talk about everything under the sun,
And she tells you she will always be here.

So when you find this friend,
I am just warning you, don't let her go.
Because she is the truest friend,
That you will ever know.

Tiger's Eyes
by Kara Dodge - age 16

A tiger's eyes,
They glisten, they gleam.
But the tiger's eyes
Are not what they seem.

A tiger's eyes,
Seem to glow in the night.
A yellowish color
That is soft and is bright.

A tiger's eyes
A mystery within,
A mystery held
For all who can win.

To win you must first
Learn to succeed,
To understand
All that you need.

That's the key
To the tiger's eyes.
The key to the mystery
Held deep inside.

Free My Children
by Janeta J. Doede-Straubhaar

Free my children,
Oh! let them love us as I.
See the wonders of this world,
Free them of greed and hate.
Let them not stray afar from your God,
Let them know showing love is no crime.
And crying is no sin,
But only wanting god within.
I know there hearts are open to you God,
Only must they find you within.
Save us all from not seeing.
The poor and rich - the hungry,
The dying - the good and bad.
The very weak and sad and there struggles,
With all of man kinds lies.
The key of understanding and knowing.
Give of your self and open your heart,
And arms to everyone.
Love your friends even your enemies.
Remember the ignorant know not,
But the stupid will never know.
Believe in God my children.

What It Feels Like To Be Orange
by Amy Shea Dolmer - age 16

When my state of mind is somewhere
between Bob Dylan and Ernest Hemingway
I am orange.

And when I can't decide
if I'm in the mood for Trent Rezner or Cocktail Shrimp
I am Orange

If I don't know whether to belt out "Whatta man"
or hum "Love is a many splendored thing"
Softly to myself, then I know that
I am orange

When I feel like contemplating the meaning
of life through the eyes of a goldfish
I am orange

You say my thoughts are "What you want to know"
You want to penetrate my kaleidoscopic English maze of a
mind. But you don't realize that you will get
lost in there, because
I am orange

Orange is all I feel, all I see, all I think, all I
am.

you're happy and bright, a warm yellow sunbeam
Yellow is confident, and less confused than I seem.

Or maybe you're a calm, serene, daydreamer Blue,
All I know is I'm not Orange when with you.

Higher Hopes
by Sarah Dowling - age 18

Knowing I was scared, confused, and lonely
You reached for me slowly

Embraced in each arm
Finally feeling safe from harm
The love you provide
is something I've only known to hide
Carefully learning how it can be
My heart was locked
but you've turned the key

Experiencing love as a mutual devotion
Believing love is more than just emotion

My guard still delicately stands
Gently experimenting with self deserving demands
Results have not yet failed me
You're continually there holding me proudly
Still unsure why you love me
However with each day passing I know you feel strongly

Holding on to a moment that will last
Forgetting behind the joke defining my past
Although it may not be forever
We have something now that I'll always treasure

If I Could Paint
by Kathleen Downs

If I could paint,
I would paint a rainbow
after a soft summer rain.
If I could paint,
I would paint the sun,
setting over the ocean.
If I could paint,
I would paint a picture of
children running in a field of
daisies.
If I could paint,
I would paint your face
on Christmas morn.
If I could paint,
I would paint my love
for you.
If I could paint.

"Warning" "Hello!" "Spirits", "are Transparent"
by Carolyn Dooley

One powerful and mighty man created our universe
with great skill and artfulness; a creation very
phenomena; locked in a vacuum of mystery
A vast view of paramount; a galaxy full of panorama
Splashed across a huge canvas sky containing stars
and heavenly bodies; ones reflecting light; casting
amazing shadows from a moon that affects our moods
Watchful eyes and stern hands which keep tabs on us
every day and night; writing in a journal with ink
that's permanent; a man who loves us all; every
color of the luminous rainbow; one which distinguishes
our heritage and character; he chose, especially, for us
Nothing blurs his vision; and, unkind words are perceived
with close attention; In his eyes we are his children; we
are brothers and sisters ones he will embrace on judgement
day; allowing no favors or prejudice; with no exceptions
and that's the gospel

A Virgin's Cry
by Sarah Dowling - age 18

Candles burning an intimate glow
Background music at a gentle flow
Your moistened lips brush against mine
Your hands caressing up and down my spine
Passion progressing, bodies uniting
Flesh against flesh, a movement so soothing
Working your way down my chest
Tightly griping hold of my breast
Eyes of fire raging and fierce
Your perverted cradle beginning to pierce
Slippery wet legs open wide
No longer is this a matter of pride
Completely lusting
Between my thighs I feel you thrusting
Strapped in your bed
Feeling love from only my head
You smile as I squirm
Anchoring me down with your grip so firm
Your body plunges like a thousand boulders
Frightened nails slice your shoulders
Taken over by a demon
You poison me with your semen
Loving your power you cum in my face
Lacking control I'm such a disgrace
Reaching climax - embarrassment soon to end
How naive was I to consider you a friend
Lying here alone and ashamed
Left only to wonder
Am I to be blamed

"Promises"
by Chris Duarte

You gave me your word,
that you'll share with me the world.
The promise that we will be,
but away you shouldn't be.

In the corner I await,
your arrival with faith.
The hope that you'll bring,
the sunshine in the spring.

Your promise that I kept,
close to my heart where I felt.
So when your promise was broken,
that's when my heart got stolen.

So spare me the words,
that torn my heart like a sword.
For it is a love that is real,
where there is a promise that could kill.

It is the feeling that has grown,
like the action you have shown.
Because nobody seems perfect,
and words left less effect.

So give me no words,
that is tied in cords.
For those words has proven,
why promises have been broken.

Untitled
by Jennifer DuBowy - age 12

Father's day is a time,
to give your father a rhyme.
To shower him with a kiss and hug,
and show him the great hole you dug.

Dad, you got my books,
and gave me looks.
I learned from you,
and got allowance too.

Sometimes you take us out to dinner,
and when we play games, you let me be the winner.
You told me how to flower,
by taking a shower.

When you take me to the store,
it is never a bore,
for you always have more,
tricks up your shore.

You took me to my friends,
and let me make amends.
You made silly mistakes,
that I think were fake,
and made my birthday cake.

My Spirit Light
by Kathryn Dudley

Flashes of light
Pinpricking
Sharp
Short.
A point of light
Too small to linger
long,
Too quick to identify or
classify.

Flashes of light
Coming quicker
Staying longer,
Overtaken by
Waves of warmth and light.
Experience life
Floating
In my Spirit Light.

"Face To face"
by Chasity Eastlick - age 15

I spread my wings trying to fly
to only go falling on my face
to get up and try again
takes all my strength
Not afraid of what people think
I'm going to take on new things
FACE TO FACE.

The Owl's Wine Cellar
by Lonny Due, Jr. - age 17

Spill the blood of tomorrow
Pick the scab of yesterday, paint me in sorrow
Laughless black and lifeless gray
There is nothing left to paint, nothing worth staying
Conquered like a cocoon frozen in time
Demented spiders spin webs in our minds
Another link in the astral nightmare
Like a butterfly being tortured in the wasps deepest and
    darkest lair
Life is just a bruised blur
Like the pattern on the night wolf's fur
And after all the shadows have faded, we are still all alone
Life is but a burden, like ants trying to haul off a stone
The night gods drip blood rain
We are all slaves to the owl, puppets of pain
Wooden smiles always create splinters
The clowns tears always linger
The mosquitos are busting the light bulbs in my mind
Bloody wings glisten in the light of time
Like a secret portal in my brain
Scorpions scatter to take shelter from the purple rain
Lost roads, scattered dreams, and broken memories will
    forever haunt me
The own will laugh eternally
Burning out, fading away
The blue-eyed one was wrong, they both lead to the same way
Our most precious dreams, our most feared nightmares
Are all bottled up in the owl's wine cellar
There is no cure for a wickless candle
But don't worry, it's nothing I can't handle

The Magnifier
by Maritoni Dumlao - age 13

Oh the cool water
So blue and so clear,
When I look through it,
It looks very near.

The rocks, and the sand,
The fish beneath it,
It looks close enough,
I still can't reach it.

A magnifier,
Is that what it is?
It magnifies light
The fish and the trees.

Some visions, reflections
Although some are not.
But I still get dazed
And end in a knot.

Wanted
by Jinger Duperry

A man to love me enough to share his life as well as his name
A man to share the good times as well as the bad
A man that lets me know that I am his, without the guessing games
A man to talk to, to walk with
A man to cuddle with, to make love with
A man that is not narrow in his vision, but can see beyond the external
    person
A man that is gentle as a lamb, but be as strong as the occasion calls for
A man to call my own, that belongs to me in the present and not the past
A man that wants me for what I am, not who I am
Wanted a man to love

Thoughts on My Son's First Valentine's Day...
by John S. Duro

As I remember his birthday...
When Michael arrived, after hours of wait;
A light was created-indeed, one so great
My heart was divided-no longer one;
It now belongs to me, and to my son...

A wish, a prayer- I couldn't want more
a beautiful child; that I so adore;
His mother gleaming, and so full of love,
This blessed event-a gift from above

"Hope springs eternal", and now I have mine,
He's come to join me, after all of this time;
My baby, my joy, my new best friend,
Our love has begun-and will never end;

I cry tears of joy, tears of hope, tears of laughter,
Could I be so happy-this day ever after,
Tis' hard to control all this new found emotion
I give him my love, and all of my devotion

Blue eyes that sparkle-transcending all I know,
Blessed with a softness, a glimmer-a glow;
My son is so special; so perfect; so right,
A heart full of love; a smile so bright;

To God I give thanks, and pray that I may
Always be caring, and good to him each day;
That he always be healthy, happy, content;
He's blessed us all, with this boy he has sent.

A Friend In Him
by Heather Dyer - age 15

There's a place I used to run in the night
There I'd stay until the sun shone bright.
When I felt, coming soon was the end
I always knew in him I'd have a friend.
In my hour of suffering, pain and need...
He was there to live out his creed
When I sat surrounding by confusion and sorrow...
He reminded me, there is yet another tomorrow
When I thought my life should stop
Because someone else came out on top
He let me know no one but he was tops
As I crossed across the river of life,
I finally realized for me there was a sacrifice,
But when the time came for me to make my claim.
I knew through him I'd recover
The power and ability to believe,
Now I know, that he'll be there
Right beside me all th way and when
The water gets rough, He'll pick me up,
And teach me how to be tough!

Choices
by Nancy Easto

   I choose to be persecuted,
rather than to persecute.
   May I be oppressed,
rather than oppress.
   May I be gentle,
rather than zealous.
   I choose goodness,
rather than justice.
   May I lose my life for You,
rather than save it for me.
   You alone, are my God, my Savior, my Love.

   May You choose to be with me, always,
every moment of my life.

Untitled
by Heather Dyer - age 15

Through months of torment, fears, and tears
You've come thru them all. Making you
stronger everyday, by fighting of deceitful
Demon.
Day by day, hour by hour, your nightmares
will fade. Because by believing in God
you've been able to jump barriers and burn
Painful bridges
Hour by hour, minute by minute
Slowly his beastly eyes will burn, because
you've taken things in stride and some
With a way of pride, but you held your
Head up high ad never gave up on God
You believed in Him, and he helped make you
Stronger. And by believing and having faith
In God and your friends, you're overcoming
Satan, and becoming one of God's children.

Words Unspoken
by Trevor D. Ebanks

Words that were never spoken
Still echo in my mind
Words that were left unsaid
Were oft' the most unkind

Words that were never written
Shout louder from the page
The words I never heard
Scream out in silent rage

And the silence still it deepens
Deafening in its sound
Of words that were never spoken
Falling on the ground

Complete
by Mariah Eller

The sound of the wind is whole
and complete
Yet she stars in the sky that
shine like diamonds, are more treasurable
sweet.
The love that I feel, the liveliness
that you bring,
Would spin the world round, and
the bright sun shining.
The well being of me, the ecstacy's
I've dreamed of, have filled me with
bliss.
Yet the enchantment of, and the derived
pleasure of just that one kiss,
Has sent a heavenly untouched, unmoved,
restored feeling.
That made my life forever complete

Only By Name
by Daniel Eaton - age 17

There is a man graced with luck,
   I know him only by name.
If I was asked, I could not describe
   his features, his build, or frame.

I know him by what he possesses,
   one so beautiful and fair.
I know that he stands so close to the one
   for whom I care.

Night after night, I am on my knees,
   praying to God above.
Hoping he will bless me with the gift I want most,
   the hand of my one true love.

But for now, that hand is held
   by the man known only by name.
I have all the questions,
   don you feel the same?

Why has luck blessed this man
   with the one who haunts my dreams?
Why has luck cursed me
   with heart tearing apart at the seams?

I will not know the answers.
   I will always be alone.
Until she picks up my heart
   and says it can be resown.

But until then I stay content with memories,
   to prevent from going insane.
I wait patiently for the day I can be
   the man known only by name.

To A.R. Be Still, My Heart
by Trevor D. Ebanks

Be still, my heart
And listen to the reason of my head
This raging, pounding, beating
Fills my soul with dread.

This love that you burn with
Will never be returned
This fire that consumes you
Will only leave you burned.

Be still, my heart
And hear the wisdom of my years
Let me quench your flames of love
With many bitter tears.

But the fire, once it's burning
Needs must rage on and on
'Till all that's left is ashes
And every hope is gone

Be still, my heart
And shield yourself from pain
This flame that now engulfs you
Will burn once more again.

Like the phoenix from its ashes
You too will once more rise
And blazing, bright and glorious
Bring fire to my eyes.

Conscience
by Candy Ebert - age 15

I have many names,
But one is true,
I live deep down,
In the heart of you.

I know what's right,
And I know what's wrong,
I know where you're weak,
And I know where your strong.

I know when you're hurting,
And I know when you lie,
For no one knows you greater than I.

So remember this when you dare to lie,
For I alone will stand against you when you die..

   "your conscience"

Looking Back
by Christy Edwards - age 16

My heart beats
A thousand times over
And I happen to
Look over my shoulder.
And I wonder why
I stopped to drink
A sip of love
And watch a floating dove.

Shoving my hands
Down in my pockets,
I walk on into the darkness
And hope the talk
Won't make the lovely birds flock.

I stop on the dock
To find the rock
That holds the key
To my boats lock.

I sail away out into the sea
And watch the sun rise
And fall at the shores.

I slip away
And hope that one day
They will see things
My way.

Unashamedly
by Robert Eichelberger

seeing the blazing stars in the darkness of night
testing the unrelenting sea with all my might
feeling the fullness and fire of deep passion
This I do unashamedly

holding onto my dreams in this cold reality
trying to make an impact on all that I see
breaking free of the restraints of fame and fashion
This I do unashamedly

praying that I may do what is always right
knowing that this heart will never give up the fight
keeping all your promises, Lord, locked deep inside
This I do unashamedly

living each new day, as if it were my last
flying through the sun blinded sky free and fast
failing with style because at least I tried
This I do unashamedly

The Last Czar
by Barbara Elgers

Phillip II and Alexandria
four daughters and a son
were moved into a house
where they lived beneath the gun

One day they were ordered to
awaken
An officer told them they'd
have their portrait taken

Russian soldiers filled the room,
upon their final pose
shooting rifles filled the air
their bodies decomposed

People from afar cried of Russia's last czar
Now 1996
his family found in a burial ground
beneath the woods and sticks

Memories
by Sarah Eliason - age 14

I remember all the good times we had together
I remember every moment we shared
I remember how we loved each other
I remember we were best friends and more than that

I remember that all ending
I remember all because of myself
I remember seeing the tears fall
I remember I broke your heart right in half

I remember the way we looked at each other
I remember the last time we saw
I remember we still had love on our eyes
I remembered when we first fell in love

I remember that all ending
I remember once again
I remember this time you left
I remember I can never see you again

Grandpa
by Shannon Elliott - age 13

As I stand here and look at my grandfather
I still wonder what was the matter
why did it have to happen this way
why couldn't he just stay
I sat there and looked at his ashes
As I wiped the tears from my eyelashes
My family and friends gathered to respect
My grandfather's ashes that were so set
with flowers round and down on the floor
I stood there and looked some more
Never to see my grandfather again
He will still always be
my very best friend.

Life's Brush
by Jennifer J. Elliott

Fingertip to fingertip.
Suggesting, that's just what it is.
Shall I soar or shall I stay?
If you'd grasp my hand,
I'd know your thoughts,
But then again, perhaps I've sought
Only a brush from your fingertips.
Shall I soar or shall I stay?
Suggesting, that's just the way it is.
Fingertip to fingertip.

It Was You
by Ronda Ellis - age 15

I sit alone,
wondering where my friends are.
But there's no sign that they're near.
They seem so very far.

Then you call,
and my wondering ends.
You always know how
to show your my friend.

Every time I felt,
like I didn't belong.
It was you who said
that I was wrong.

You were the one,
who stayed by my side.
Even when everyone
left me one hundred times.

Thanks for always
being here.
Especially when no one
seemed to care.

The Game Of Chance
by Kristel England - age 12

Chance is a game we all must play,
It's chance if we live to see another
day
It's chance if our hour glass
doesn't run low,
Pure chance if the earth doesn't
explode
It's a dreaded game we all must
play
We can never escape our dreaded
fate.
No matter how much you run,
The game of life has already
begun.

Immortal
by Elizabeth Koken Engler

Immortal. Could that be what you feel?
Waiting for the fall of rain -

Foolishly expecting.

Rise and fall they taint our breath -
Why this suffocation?

Which hand will not seem to heal,
Among us the crucified?

So eternity prevails,
And this foot still falls the same.

I thought that all my blood was dry.
Yet infinity repeats itself.

There is song within this fight,
We wade through by our ankles -

Now the truth is written in reverse.

And at the driving of the nail,
You are left to pray.

The Light At The End Of The Tunnel
by Kelly Erwin - age 16

Here I am
In this dark and dismal place
Its cold and wet here
But slowly I travel
I can feel the mud
When I step.
I wish I had a light,
Just so I could figure out
Where I'm going
There's a lot of things
Out to get you here
I never know they are there
Until I've encountered them.
I'm so lost and confused
Sometimes I just want to cry
Although I don't, and
I don't know why.
There's a small light up ahead
It's so pretty, and I dream
of where it leads.
To a better place than where I am,
I wonder if I'll ever get there
And what it'll be like.
But for now,
Here I am
In this dark and dismal place
Its cold and wet here
But slowly I travel.

Thinking of You
by Mary Beth Eskins - age 12

On the shores of stormy waters sat the lonely sorrowsome James. As he remembered sweeter day of him and his Colette. Before the horrible tragedy, before all the sadness. "It was all my fault," he said as he sank into the sand. "Why couldn't it have been me to be cast into the sea? I was steering, trying to save her from the horrible, horrible danger." Their love, higher than the tallest mountains, wider than the sky itself. But now all is lost as she lay dead in the sunken ship. He shall never love again, for his woe and great despair will be with him till he lay in the cold, lifeless ocean with his darling sweet Colette.

Yahweh Just Before The Rain Falls
by Elizabeth Eslami - age 18

The stains of November rain drops smeared
Their souls on my windowpanes
And their crawling intricacy mimicked capillaries
On clear, crystal-cold plains.
My breath slowed and shallowed inside,
Was out-roared by the raping wind.
I knew somewhere above,
God's looming face and looming lips
Gave birth to this roar,
This magnificence that stripped and made bare the lands.
That stirred black oceans to sway and spit in rebellion,
Whose power flattened copper
Colored leaves as if run through
By a stiff and glorious comb,
And who will with a last and furious
Strength bend the mightiest of trees
To dip back and forth
From the twin milk saucers of heaven
Before fading and moving
Slowly upwards unto the eager lips of God.

Internal Diversities
by Kim Estrada - age 19

I stand here peering through the blinds,
Staring back are mental minds.
Hypnotized by their mystic souls,
I realize I'm getting old.

What I once believed,
I now fear.
What I once cherished,
Is no longer near.

Everything I've done is in the past,
I thought the future would be a blast,
But when I look back at yesterday,
Everything seems so far away.

The light of life is coming near,
It hasn't burned for many years,
It shine's hope and faith upon me,
And if I close my eyes, I'll see.

A Living Nightmare
by Steph Estrela

I'm living a nightmare
but no one here to wake me up
Shivering in the cold
no one to give me warmth
so I lay there
hoping that death will hit me soon
but I'm still living
I try real hard to wipe away the tears
but they still keep rolling down my cheeks
So where do I go from here is the question
but no one there to answer...

"Death Need Not Worry"
by Andrew Fairchild Jr.

Death need not worry,
    He comes at casual times.
When there is little pendency,
    He will surely oblige.

Though death lurks,
    He never stops for a halt,
looking for unknown dwellers,
    Who've been ejected of life.

Like a storm he pursues
    To collect our weak souls;
And place them in a vessel
    For the life of eternity.

Death need not worry,
    When its time past.
He will not elapse,
    But only acquire...

Untitled
by Nichole Falconer

If I could be bold, just for an hour,
If I could be fearless, just for a day,
I'd set free the secrets that live in my heart,
Knowing my truth would not send you away.

Unlock my voice from its prison of silence,
Sing out my freedom and laugh with delight;
Set it to sail on the wings of the wind,
Howl at the moon and scream into the night.

Break off the chains that keep me from freedom,
Spin like a child with my arms to the air,
Dance to the music that lives in my soul,
Run into the wind with the courage to dare.

Throw open my doors; stand here unguarded,
Open a room in my heart for your stay,
If I could be bold, just for an hour,
If I could be fearless, just for a day.

May 24, 1996
by Shena Farris - age 15

I walked into the break
    room that Friday. And
    there you sit, as calm
    and cool as a person
    could get.

You took my breath away.
    It felt like a ton of bricks
    had hit me in the chest.

I didn't know how old
    you were, I guessed 16
    or 17. I didn't know
    your name. But that
    didn't matter because
    I know it was
    love at first sight.

Your eyes struck me like
    lighting bolts. And your
    hair looked like chocolate.

Now all I can think
    about is you.

Cloudy Morning
by Arthur Feldkamp - age 14

I woke up this morning to a miserable gray
dark clouds in the sky
I walked slowly down the street
to wait for the run down bus
that takes me to school every morning
There was absolute silence
as if everything around me could feel
the ominous mass overhead
As I stood on the corner,
a gentle breeze blowing,
a ray of light burst through above me,
like a knife driven through it
I looked up to see the blackness moving away
on a strong wind, like a retreating army
letting the light shine through.

My Faulty Remembering: Old Banjo Tune About One Mountain
by Stanley A. Fellman

This berserker mountain be nothing but
  poison snake standing straight on its tail,
  some unbright folks say.

Yet, when you climb it--
  beyond away from where snow never melts, you'll
  meet an eagle, will seem to have wings wider
  than ocean; just go level to its eyes with
  your own. After that,

Whatever rifle you carry as man
  alive, you'll never miss that
  you shoot at; or fail of kiss from
  anyone you love.

Father, My Stranger
by Crystal Ferri - age 15

Father, your stranger.
I don't know you anymore.

Your just that man walking
down the street, with your dark
hair and lighter eyes, your just
my stranger.

You give me a polite "hi"
as you walk past me and go on
with whatever your doing, wherever
your going.

I wish I knew you, father.
Why won't you come and see me?
Do your know I'm here father?
I'm here, I'm here.

I'm afraid to talk to you
I'm afraid to call you.
I'm afraid to see, hug, or kiss
you, because father...your
my stranger.

Jackie's Dedication
by Brittany Ferry - age 14

Through this year and years of past,
Through years of future time,
Word upon word, line upon line,
Rhyme upon endless rhyme.

You have always stood beside me
Through hope and through despair.
You have always been there for me,
And helped me more than you're aware.

I'd like to be the kind of friend
That you have been to me.
I'd like to show the world
What you have helped me see.

You have a very loving heart,
Too big for just one place.
You shared with me, so now I'll say
Bless you, love you, thanks.

Like In The Dream
by Kelly Fillion - age 15

Like in the dream where I was grasping
But you stayed out of my reach
Like in the dream where I was screaming
But wind whisked away my speech

The dream that left me trembling
But wouldn't let me wake
Like the dream that restrained me
But, in a way, for my own sake

Like in the dream, I saw you stare at me
with a big blue blazing eye
Like in the dream I saw you smile
But it somehow made me cry.

Like in the dream, you let me love you
when for me you didn't care
Like in the dream I couldn't touch you
and it didn't seem quite fair.

Like in the dream it ended quickly
yet my heart still seemed so full
Like in the dream you walked away
Still the untouchable.

Untitled
by Jennifer Fisher

I was alone and scared in that dark
world of depression
No one ventured near me, for I always wore
a sad expression.
No one reached out a hand to help me out
of my dark world
They thought I liked my life just fine
The people I used to call my friends,
They all turned against me
They never saw the tears I shed
At one point, I even thought of dying
It seemed like no one cared
But at the last moment,
I was pulled out of my dark world,
Someone showed me they cared
They lent a hand to help me heal,
Now I know how precious life is
And I can't imagine,
Ever trying to end my life again.

A Thanks For Life
by Renee Fite - age 14

We know right from wrong,
We may not always show it;
But deep down inside,
We know you know it.

When we were really little,
You showed us how to be;
You opened the door to life,
And hands us the key.

You picked up when we fell,
And wiped the tears away;
And after we were all cleaned up,
Back outside we went to play.

You told us we could be anything,
As long as we really tried;
And if we didn't make it,
You were there when we cried.

Not all the times were great,
There were times of sorrow;
But you helped us through those days,
And through the better days of tomorrow.

Someday it will be time to move out,
It may be far away;
But you'll know in your heart,
We'd much rather stay.

We are the way we are,
And we owe it all to you;
So for just a little reminder,
THANKS AND WE LOVE YOU!!

Listen To My Heart
by Leslie Floyd - age 14

As I sit here in this chair
I think about how we made a
perfect pair.

As I think of what he means to me
and all I know is that I still love thee.

As I see us walking side by side
It reminds me of how we always lied.

When I listened to my heart
It told me that we would never part.

When I decided to let him know
I found out he had more to show.

It already happens to me
I can never find anyone to love thee

We used to take strolls through the park
But now all he can do is make smart remarks.

He always became a nut
for anything that looked like a slut.

I guessed that
Why he picked Pat.

On our last date
I told him he was not my perfect mate.

Now I wish I would have listened to my heart
And we would never be apart.

I Am
by Tina Foote - age 14

I am a caring girl who likes people
I wonder why some people are so mean
I sae the hate in people's eyes
I hear the anger in their voice's
I want the violence between people to disappear
I am a caring girl who likes people.

I pretend all of the violence is gone
I feel fighting is pointless, all it does is cause hurt
I touch my pillow and start to cry
I worry that it will never stop
I cry when I talk to my friend after he fight's with his dad
I am a caring girl who likes people

I understand that everyone is different
I say that everyone is the same in my eyes
I dream that one day everyone will become equal
I hope all of the violence will soon be gone
I am a caring girl who likes people.

An Upholsterer
by Colleen Ford

A man
So dear to his family
So talented with his hands
So wonderful in his wisdom

This man has taught us
That we should use springs
To ensure enough bounce
In life

How to choose just the right
Amount of padding to cushion
Future hardships

The art of matching and changing
Fabric to blend in with
Our surroundings

And that you can find
Beauty and bounty
In anything
If only you apply
Love and handwork

She Lives Well
by David Forsyth

Sine the time of rusted ochre and orange
She, as lifeblood tome
coloured cumulus and evergreen
placates with a matchless strength

We have waded oceans

Even beset on all sides
by wretches of wrought iron
my fear is eclipsed
in a halo of ambient blue

I, with mortal hands
am not capable
of holding this plum
as pure as the rocks
to a place so undeserving

Steadfast, she remains here
beyond my understanding
how am I so well-blessed
as to be able to carve
something so long-standing
out of soap

Enclosed in a sanctuary
that has everything
I fall in a lachrymose heap
and thank God
for this precious entanglement

Change
by Heather Foulke

Blooming and growing, every living thing,
Wild winters melt, slowly into spring.
Silently summer sneaks, like a mouse,
As I watch seasons change outside my house.

Freely flowing, round and round,
Autumn's leaves accent the ground.
Colors of beauty, brightness, and bold,
Red, Green, Yellow and shimmering gold.

Where do seasons take you?
will anybody know?
Why do they affect you wherever
you may go?

Entwined in this mystery,
You could never know.
Why the ground is once green,
Then changes to snow.

Changes are bound to happen,
that is a matter of fact.
Once something changes,
You can never change it back.

Little Old Man
by Jennifer Fuller - age 16

The little old man came out of the bar
The look in his eyes was so very far.
In one hand he carried a bottle of ale
In the other he carried a letter, old and frail.
As he walked on with tears on his face
He kept his stride at a steady pace.
He walked to the graveyard and sat by a tomb
He curled up tight
His hands near his wound.
He cried and cried until the tears were no more
And he smiled as he slept forever more.

Friends
by Brian Andrew Fox - age 18

A spirit is a great traveler.

Not as you nor I would know a traveler,
but as a traveler of the emotional plains.

It flies, crawls, runs wild, or crouches in fear.

Sometimes a spirit, like a small lamb, gets lost in the great plains of despair.

Like a lamb, they need a shepherd to lead him back to the safety of the flock and to good friends and family.

A good shepherd does not even need to see the little lamb, but rather he needs only to listen to the lamb's cries.

He talks to the lamb, to help him find his way back to the flock, and to find out why he strayed from the flock in the first place.

A true shepherd will lead the little lamb from the plains into the mountains, where the lamb must make a decision to fly or to fall once more to the plains.

The lamb need not worry, for a true shepherd will always return to lead the lamb once more.

The dangers a shepherd must face are simple in terms yet complex in meaning.

He must never allow himself to lose his way or lose ability to hear the lamb.

For he knows that if he does, he himself shall become a wandering lamb.

A good shepherd should know if this happens then both spirits are surely doomed and shall never see the mountains.

The greatest gift a shepherd receives, is not that of monetary concern, but to see a spirit soaring high in to the heavens.

Knowing that some day if the shepherd does become the lamb, that the lamb shall have the ability to become the shepherd.

Thoughts Running Wild
by Jennifer Francis - age 14

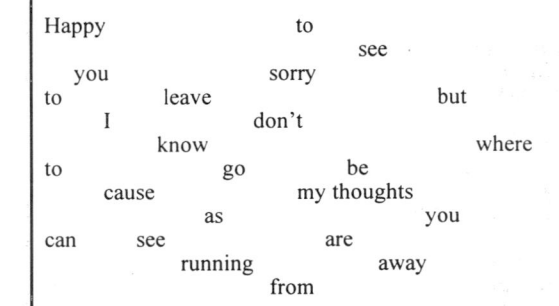

Happy to
　　　　　　　　see
　you　　　sorry
to　　leave　　　　but
　I　　　don't
　　know　　　　　where
to　　　go　　be
　　cause　　my thoughts
　　　　as　　　　you
can　see　　are
　　　running　　away
　　　　from

　　　　　ME!!

Memories
by Sharon Franco

Reflecting, meditating,
　　time well spent,
To bring back ole memories
　　from where they're sent.
Some are locked away,
　　never to recall,
Others just waiting,
　　the best of all.
The sound of laughter
　　I can hear,
The voice of a loved one,
　　no longer near,
The smell of a rose,
　　the feel of rain,
The loss of a friend
　　the hurt of pain,
That one true love,
　　that should have been,
But for some reason,
　　came to an end.
The losses, the gains,
　　the good and the bad,
These are memories
　　we all have had.
Now it's time
　　to store them away,
To bring them to life
　　some other day.

Impossible
by Chris Frazier

　　To be in love with someone like me. The love is so sweet, no bitterness, fighting or sorrow. How good can this be, for this love to be not sorry, but so sweet. It's impossible the way you make me feel, how possible it is for our long lost dream to finally come true.
　　　　It's impossible to finally be with you, our dream, in this life has come true.
　　　　Impossible when I m with you, not wanting another, how, isn't that sweet.

　　When I am with you it seems like a fantasy to have the perfect love, no sorrow, or fight, but sweet as can be.

　　Impossible, so wonderfully impossible, that this dream is really true. Impossible, so wonderfully impossible--
Impossible, for you to dream of someone like me.

Life As A Cow
by Elizabeth Frazier - age 13

Today I am a cow
And I have a certain hunch
That I'm going to McDonald's
To be somebody's lunch

When I was just a calf
My mamma used to say
Enjoy the life you have
Because you'll be a steak someday

If you're not a vegetarian
There's nothing I can do
But next time think a little
At least this isn't you

You wouldn't want to eat me
I'd be so fatty and tough
But I guess that's life as a cow
And life as a cow is rough.

Zodiac of Dementia
by R.H. Mulraux

Not
the man in the
photograph from
days long dead like
   his self-
altered into an icon as
alternatives were embraced.

Nor
the woman he
left behind lying buried
beneath the past
   on the beach;
an incompatible couple
in an apathetic frame.

Rather
the generations he
assured ashes
within the woman
   at the beach:
the insignificant spectrum
of the celestial sphere.

Our Special Day
by Elisa French

It's our anniversary, our happy day,
My love gets stronger in every way.
I am forever your wife,
Without you I have no life.

From the first day I knew,
I'd love no one but you.
We shared many things.
But most precious...a wedding ring.

To our love, I cheer,
For our happiness every year.
Thank you very much,
For the hugs, kisses, your gentle touch.

I love you and only you,
To your heart, I'll remain true.
Happy anniversary my love my life,
Love always your loving wife.

Springtime Stars
by Pink Sugar

"Springtime Stars"
peak around the corner --
hintin,' to reveal themselves in full flying colors.'

The days are becomin' a little longer and
warmin' trends can be felt.
Mother nature wages HER SNOWHITE snowflakes 'fore
SHE insist's JACK FROST 'parlay HIS chillin' smirk,
into healin,' Springtime Greeneries.

The chickadee's harmonize their farewells' and
cheerfully pack-up their back-packs --
for the long flight across the majestic U.S.A

The tulips and daffodils lie in quiet splendor.
They're almost ready to 'dazzle...
HER MAJESTY'S manicured gardens.'

When HE wands HIS calmin' palms
upon the slumberin' scenery
"Springtime Stars"
will magically 'turn-over...

Serene, ever-green tones and
hue's of dreamy, venus pinks'
will 'ace the radiant-bound landscapes.'

Kaleidoscope, ruffled Color-Wheels'
will 'whirlwind the barren earth.

"April Love"
and 'dejavue, dejavue...
may become your blessed destiny.

Kindred Spirits
by Ron Fryer

We share an uncommon bond,
of a depth attained by very few.
Because we see the beauty of life
from a very similar point of view.

I've enjoyed our talks so much;
talks on things that we needed to get out.
Discussing how we perceive the world,
perceptions we could never talk with others about.

Our range of subject matter
is both unlimited and grand.
we explore one another's thoughts
refining both our abilities to understand.

The two of us are kindred spirits,
its easy to see.
Its a connection unbreakable;
and, one most special to me.

Hope
by Mary Gordon

Sun sifted through a motionless tree
A small bit of light fighting it's
way to a patch of ground.
In desperation my eyes try to pull
the rays through the leaves
A little sun is better than none
and a little hope grows into
a stronger and greater hope.
A little faith in God will find
it's way through the haze.

Death
by Mindy Galazyn - age 12

Pain is meir sorrow.
Death is meir pain.
I am but a meir twinkle in a diamond ring.
I have faded like a pair of jeans.
I may be gone, but have one request,
please just let me sleep and rest.
Tears of memory are now in you,
but remember one thing
I Love You!
My teacher once said
you're never dead
unless forgotten.
Forgotteness will never be with me,
So I say one last thing
Remember me!

Behind Weary Eyes
by rachel galbriath - age 16

You think I can't tell,
But I can see it in your eyes;
I know the hatred's coming-
Before the torment flies.
I feel it in my soul
And I can feel it in my heart;
Your words kill me
As if they were a poisonous dart.
I can feel your pounding anger
As it echoes inside;
I beg you to give me a break,
Or at least give me time to hide.
The emptiness inside of myself scares me,
But I try to keep it hidden,
So you're not able to see
The pain and emptiness I hold inside.
But I always wonder
When you look at me,
If you can see all that lies-
Behind my weary eyes.

An Eagles Flight
by James Garcia

Just the other day, while on a stroll by the lake, my eyes gazed upon a sight, that was more than I could take. Two beautiful eagles flying so gracefully in the sky, a picture perfect scene it brought a tear to my eye. It stirred up feelings and emotions way deep down inside,' it gave me hope for a brighter tomorrow, and a sense of pride. For in my heart the eagle stands for Freedom, Power and Strength, qualities we should all aspire to any length. As the eagles flew away, far from my line of sight, I felt my life would somehow be different, by being in the presence of an eagles flight.

A Surfer's Prayer
by Allison Gallegos

When I hear that loud, thunderous roar.....
I ask God to please bring me back safely to shore.....

The thrill of the sport, lies close to my heart.....
But the danger that lurks sometimes keeps us apart.....

No one will ever quite really understand.....
For catching a wave doesn't always make a man.....

Maybe it's the serenity of the sea.....
That at times quickly changes to intensity.....
The power of the wave that can keep a man under.....
And you ask yourself bravely, will I somehow recover?.....
Or the peace it can bring to ones adventurous soul.....
When your gliding on a wave, and you don't lose control.....

Whatever the sea brings, peace or fury to me.....
Please guide me Lord, to a safe and homebound journey.....

Dedicated to my son, Jeffrey
Love,
*   Mom*

Lakes
by Gian- Mical Gallerani - age 10

Lakes shine beautifully,
It grows wilderness around,
Fish swim inside it,
It reflects light from the moon,
There might be other secrets.

Untitled
by Gian- Mical Gallerani - age 10

It's the Lizard!
LOOK! LOOK!
Have you seen,
something that's slimy and green.
Something that goes
    wiggle
     jiggle
      splish
      splash
     slosh
     slush
    have you seen
It's It's
It's It's
LIZARD!
LIZARD!
Hiding in a bush
eating a kind of smush
his skin dark green
hiding so well he can't be seen!
Hiss! Hiss! Hiss! Hiss!
It's the lizard!

Everything You Are.....
by Mike Gallo

Everything you are is the Venus of al Venuses
Everything you are is better than me
Everything you are is simply happily
Everything you are is so lovely,
Everything you are is wonderful to the fullest
Everything you are is adoring
Everything you are is catchy to all my senses
Everything you are is deeply alluring,
Everything you are is life to me
Everything you are is really moveable
Everything you are is fun & exciting
Everything you are is always beautiful
Everything you are is naturally sweet
Everything you are is angelic
Everything you are is all sincere
Everything you are is purely ecstatic,
Everything you are is wholesome to my tastes
Everything you are is filled my life
Everything you are is unforgettable
Everything you are is to be my wife,
Everything you are is tasty like candy
Everything you are is right from the start
Everything you are is innermost dazzle
Everything you are is locked inside my heart
Everything you are is true & eternal
Everything you are is intelligence on strive
Everything you are is defined by my love
Everything you are is everything that's alive

True Love
by Sabrina Galloway

How do you know?
Is it hard to tell?
Is it pretty like snow?
Or is it like hell?

Sometimes you wonder,
Wonder if it's real.
Then you ponder,
Ponder how you feel.

You've been hurt once,
Once to many times.
Together for months,
Think it's real this time?

Mariposa in a
by Alegria Garcia - age 17

Renee Butterfly
How could I be so found?
See right through my soft petaled wings,
Brown coat,
iridescent eyes following me
Dancing around a sister
    with a one broken arm,
lying under a tree,
    seeing two people over me.
These trees that follow me when I wake
listen to me as I sing
believe me when I see.

Drawing Pictures
by Andrew D. Ganaway - age 19

There is a city made entirely of smooth stone. A strong, gray, and plain city standing alone. When the sun shines down, those who live within the city come out, bring with them their paints, chalks, and pencils. Then upon the streets and against the walls they create their pictures.

Images form slowly one at a time. Younger artist use ladders to reach high and some leaned out of windows painting small scenes around the frames. Against the old city wall there is always a continuous picture of some stormy sea or quiet grassy plain.

I went to that city once and saw the images take shape before my eyes. I've walked through the main square, and watched the world change beneath my feet. I've seen demons, kings, and castles. I've stood by as horses took flight, and witnessed silent carriage rides through the most beautiful of distant lands.

I recall placing the few coins I had by some of the many artist, as it was considered good luck to do so. I remember watching one artist, after an accidental mistake, created a new picture using the mistake perfectly. I watched people laugh and cry at the pictures, and I believe I also joined in with them from time to time.

I also saw the rain come down that day, and wash all the dreamy pictures away. Striking lines of every color swirled around. I saw some struggle in vain to save and shelter their pictures, and others who didn't even seem to care. Some even seemed to forget that the pictures were even there.

I will never return to that city, I know, for all the sorrow it made me feel. Still I know too that when the sun shines and the stone dries that the people will draw their pictures again for all those who will come and see. Drawing and dreaming until the next time it rains.

U.S.A. Stay That Way
by Jason Ganz - age 15

In the city, by the bay, on the farm, in the hay
By the lake, on the road, near the children playing with the toad.
I see an old lady holding a flame, I hear the wild which you can never tame
You can keep the red flag, escargot, and you time of tea
For I have purple mountain's red, white, and blue majesty.
I have freedom, rights of liberty
this is better than your stealth 24-b
Gold paves my streets of old and new
For here is a land that belongs to me and you.
Many have shed a drop of blood,
To ave their hopes, dreams and their Uncle Judd.
You see America is about family.
There may be fights, pollution and unruly pets
democrats, fires, and the New York Mets.
But now take a second look, glance at that boy carrying those poetry books.
America may lack 50 days of school, computers, and fine wine.
But outside there is a golden sun that sure can shine.
And there is Cheers, vacations, and cloud number 9.
Sure the American flag can be turned into a rag of dirt.
But it can always turn into a house, a family, and a brand new shirt.
So you see my friend of little trust
I give to thee a country that must
and will always be free of peril, evil, and unjust.

P.W.T.
by Krisha Garcia - age 15

Pondering to ask.
Wondering what to do.
Thinking of the way thing would be;
How life wouldn't be so blue.
If only knowing what to say;
Talking about being wrong.
Knowing that no one is always right.
Wishing the past wasn't gone.
By action we hurt one another;
By time we try to change.
We can never change completely
Because life is so strange.
Hoping for the turning point
For things to be how they were meant to be;
Trying to help it along it's way,
Although it comes naturally.
Pondering to ask.
Wondering what to do.
Thinking of the way things would be;
And how life wouldn't be so blue.

Watch The Devil Run
by Evelyn Garrett-Bledsoe

I peeked, I looked, I read the Book.
Victory's mine, I'm off the hook.

Satan's no match for the Christ in me.
Jesus has conquered and set me free.

I'll give no ground but firmly stand.
My armor on tight, sword in hand.

Ole Slewfoot's lies of no effect,
I'm girded with truth among God's elect.

Pick up faith's shield, come join the fun.
Evil extinguished, watch the devil run.

"Submit yourselves therefore to God.
Resist the devil and he will flee
from you." James 4:7

With You Always
by Christina L. Garris - age 17

My gaze is turned toward heaven
As I study the early morn' sky
The sun has not yet risen
No birds flutter, none fly

All here is quiet
I hear the beating of my heart
The vibrant rhythm of it
Is in sync with that of this land
dipped in dark

I close my eyes
Feeling the beauty around me
In my mind
I see what my glance cannot see

The view that rises before me in my
Child-like imagination
Penetrates to my core
Gives me angelic inspiration

Your face is dominant in my soul's fantasy
I can now see that all is from and in you
No doubts have I of where I should be
My place, always, has been with you

Friends
by Samantha Garst - age 12

Friends my be old or new,
Best or just close,
Many or few.

But all your friends,
Though you may not believe,
Are the most meaningful things in your life,
Besides your family.

So when you lose a friend,
You must consider yourself lucky,
For someone may be left out,
Of knowing what it is like to be friends.

So all of us who know what the gift of friends is like,
Must thank God for making us this lucky,
We must forget our feelings of hate and jealousy,
And remember,
Everyone needs friends.

After The Master
by Marianne Garvey

A forgotten print hangs there, on my wall
A forgotten reason, too, why it was purchased
A copy, "my original" collects the dust
Of the day and dust of a meaning
In a mere, sweet picture of "Two Young Girls Reading".

It is not a recollection of my youth
Nor is it a reminder of this era
Just plump, rosy cheeks in picture hats with matching dress
The artist's brush work most suitable to a feather.

The younger girl, book on her lap, sits studiously profile
With her fingers she is holding her place
The older girl, hand on her cheek, head tilted
Listening, with a smile on her face.
Both sets of eyes, downcast
Sitting close and sharing words.

I look at the portrait now, on my wall
How it attracts one to a meaning;
Mine is dear to me
A treasure the artist captured with his eye and brush;
In a creative, tender picture,
Simplicity.

Strike Out Against The Odds
by Linda C. Grazulis

When failure enters your life and you feel as though your ship has sunk, grab onto an anchor and rest awhile. Regain strength and creativity. In pausing, you refuel for another task, and you can be certain life will dream up another. Then with courage, strike out against the odds. Cling to a brisk breeze and set sail towards the vast blue sea. With faith in your heart, plenty of hard work, and determination, your ship will take an unexpected turn towards the stars.

Place
by Harley Geiger - age 16

It's a warm place
a large tiny oasis
in this vast broiling desert
to lie contently naked under its single green tree:
warm

A problem rears its ugly head
(they always struggle)
claws groping for the place
and is smothered: Dead
by the warmth
is soothed by
the nonexistent sweet/slow repetitive song
by the warmth

One trips into it
and stay for eternity after one leaves

A huge sliver
that the world depend son
but doesn't know exists
because it doesn't
because it does
and it is
warm

Man With Pride In His Eyes
by Karla Glentz-Anderson

He was a tiny man but had
the strength of an army. And a heart
that would give to anyone that
wanted a helping hand.
He was a small farmer in a
little country town.
There he had lived throw some
hard times and a great deal of
good times with his wife and his
son and daughters. Each life he
would touch he gave them happiness
of love.
and each new life he help
bring in this world he would hold
his head up high with great pride.
We will all miss this little
man but we will always carry him
in our heart and soul.
Marvin Franson passed away
November 19, 1986.

A Little Old Lady
by Summer Michelle Graham - age 15

I saw this little old lady,
she was standing on the street.
Her hair was all ratted,
and there were no shoes on her feet.
Her clothes were made of rags,
beside her were two tiny plastic bags.
As I drove by that little old lady,
I thought to myself,
"that could be me."
So, I went back and got her,
and we now live together happily.

Why Did You leave?
by Amy Genoble - age 13

Why did you leave?
Why did you go?
You said you loved me,
You loved me so.

My heart be stilled,
And with joy it filled.
You stood by me,
During thick and thin.
Understanding it all,
From within.

And then you left,
Walked right out.
Never turning back,
Without a doubt.
You left me there,
Standing alone.
All by myself,
No one to call my own.

I'm over you now.
But I still don't understand,
How? How?

Confusion
by Danielle Germain - age 14

The world is a confusing place,
Open the surface, open the face.
To look around, to look at all,
To wonder how it might fall.
Everything we think we know,
Of confusion we seldom show.
To much to learn in a day,
Because the world was built in
 more then one way.
Seven days from start to stop,
Spinning like a spinning top.
That is what is known to me,
That is what we ever see.
Confusion is as confusion was,
Because that is what God does.

Thoughts of Love
by Maria K. Gerstman

Life is above you,
Love is not ended -
it is the one thing to survive.

And we will see too,
who has attended
for the eternal love to thrive.

We'll be united
in love, together -
and will be happy, there, my Dear.

No one is slighted,
light as a feather
We will be free of any fear!

Beyond The Long Grasses
by Maia Gianakos - age 12

Beyond the long grasses
Lies a dream.
A distant dream
A foreign dream.
A mere cloud
Floating among
The endless skies.
Beyond the long grasses
Lies a mystery.
A question without an
Answer.
Beyond the long grasses
Lies a beautiful waterfall
Of thoughts.
Beyond the long grasses.

Help Bring Peace
by Annie Giddings - age 13

Why must we kill?
Why must we fight?
I just don't
Think it seems right.

We are all brothers and sisters,
Living in this world together,
Will we ever be a peace?
Will the killing go on forever?

Think about the future,
The generations to come,
Our childrens' world can't be like this,
Why won't the fighting be finished and done?

If we keep on killing
What will be left of us?
We'll be like endangered species,
There'll be nothing left of what was.

So the killing must stop now,
The fighting be finished and done,
If we are ever to be at peace,
You must help it come.

A Real Love
by Jessica L. Gifford - age 17

To have a real love so far in years
So near in my heart.
How much longer until I know
My real love.
From only my dreams have told so little of
How much more does my heart have to
bleed.
O' a real love if only; I knew you know
Would you be so like my dreams or are you
So far from them
Will I ever know of a real love so strong
Yet so gentle with each new touch
O' how I feel the chills shoot through my body
So sharp but oh so real
As two firm hands draw my delicate body
In so near for two become as one soul
O' how sweet it all seems for I have not
yet to know my real love
So far in years, so near in my heart.

All Is Black
by H.S Gilbert

All is black,
condition ripe for superstition,
where the poison of accursed imagination
may bring dread to mawkish, ghoulish, foolish minds.

All is black,
condition ripe for restoration,
where the peace of restful sleep
may bring strength to knowing, loving, caring minds.

All is black,
in Stygian wrap of constellations,
where the space of plumbless depth
may bring life to nameless, blameless, tameless kinds.

All is black,
fear not!
From black arises all that's been or ever will;
Black is the quiet color of limitless time.

The Wind Blows
by Tanya Gilbert - age 11

When the wind blows
The quiet things speak.
Some whisper, some clang,
Some creak.
Grasses swish.
Treetops sigh.
Flags slap
and snap at the sky.
Wires on poles
whistle and hum.
Ashcans roll.
Windows drum.
When the wind goes--
suddenly,
then,
the quiet things
are quiet again.

When The Flower Dies
by Jenna Goheen - age 11

Life and death
Is like a road
If there is a stop sign, you die
If there is a go sign, you live
It's like four little road's
That join together
To make a new life
That carries four lives and four death's
If there are more sign's that say go
There are more people being born
To enjoy a new life
And if there are more sign's that say stop
A new life has been taken from the world
Another to spare
An old life taken
For a new life
It's like the opening of a flower
When the flower dies
Another flower grows
Like a child being born
It's like there's enough time to spare
For a new life to begin
With the closing of a flower, to never open again
It's like a flower being ripped out of the ground
And may pass on to another
Just like the circle of human's
But human lives are precious
And can never be replaced
But a flower will again
Bloom and grow

Perimeters
by LaSondra Goldsmith

There is a place where the children play, carefree from worries, only fun filled days,

A place free from drive-by shooting, and children being drug into grown-up disputing,

A place where no child is ever abducted, and not one small mind ever corrupted,

A place where it's okay to be young, run, jump, talk loud,

or laugh all day, just for fun,

A playground where everyday children find, the space is limited to the confines of their own minds.

Untitled
by Marci A. Haller

It seems like it's been a long time,
since your body's been close
to mine.
The smell of you skin
my fingers through your hair
there is comfort in just
knowing that your are there

I love you, miss you.
Hope you miss me too.

Swallow
by Angelina Gonzalez - age 14

Sometimes I think I'm pretty,
Sometimes I don't know me at all.
Sometimes life is just hard,
Sometimes too hard to handle.
But when times get like this
I blow a kiss.
Just blow a kiss
Cuz nothing I can do
Nothing I can say
can make it change.
So in life you gotta swallow,
swallow.
So in love you gotta swallow.
I see you at the corner of the drug store
Poor guy, you don't even know my name.
I can always drown my sorrows,
always play the sam track-my-arm game.
The hide-'n'-seek game.
But when times get like this
I just laugh at myself
and I join fate and I reminence
'Cuz nothing I can do.
nothing I can say
is gonna make it go away.
So in life, you gotta swallow,
swallow.
So in love, you gotta swallow
swallow.

Rainbow
by Heidi Gonzales - age 18

As the rain falls gently on the front porch outside
I think of your sweet kiss, and the bright shine in your eyes.

I remember your gentle hand as it was placed upon mine
I remember those shocking words whispered in that moment of time.

It was only then I realized your feelings were so strong
and I guess I couldn't help feeling them right along.

Just a matter of time before my heart fell for you
It leaped so fast and there was nothing I could do.

I told myself no and it was better to walk away,
but my heart wouldn't listen, it did it anyway.

Now I'm glad I didn't listen to my thoughts all along
I'm glad I followed my heart, for now my love for you is strong.

I could never dream of loving another so true,
but I can definitely dream of loving only you.

As the rain turns into shine, I hope that you will see
That the rainbow formed across the sky, is to you from me.

Chaos
by Kimone Gooden - age 17

Caught up in a lie
that's the truth
obsessed with the facade
that is you

There also here
real but not true
I don't understand this
what can I do?

My eyes are open
yet they're closed
I'm ignorant
yet I know.

I acknowledge it's existence
but I do not believe
I am fighting a battle
in which I do not wish to succeed.

Fighting to struggle
yet it's not really a fight
knowing it's not wrong
but it's not really right.

I'm bewildered, but I understand
profound yet shallow
not wanting today
but fearing tomorrow.

Autumn Leaves
by Michael Goodman

Memories of Fall upstairs
Empty rocking chairs creak
Out of loneliness
In waves of settling dust
That coat mahogany arms
So used to being leaned against
By brittle old bones
Keep cool in cashmere sweaters
On brisk Autumn days
The sunlight peaks through
The window slipping by aching
Branches trying to hoard the warm
Honey rays all for themselves
Plucked by the tweeze of
A westerly wind shedding leaves
Drift alive in the animated current
Carrying an assortment of mellow hues
Through the window across a cluttered
Sill of black and white photos
Shot by Grandfather

Gert the Great
by Summer Michelle Graham - age 15

The game was tied 2 to 2.
Coach yelled, "Gert it's up to you!"
Gert stood up, snatched her bat,
looked at the crowd, and tipped her hat.
She walked slowly to the plate,
I must say she looked irate.
Gert dug her cleats into the ground.
The crowd was silent and looking quite profound.
The pitcher winds up and outfield is ready.

Gert swings her bat nice and steady.
She hits a grand slam, the crowd stands and cheers
for Gert the great hasn't done that in years!

Aborted Feelings
by Emily Goodwin - age 15

A woman impatiently awaits the word from a doctor. She is only
sixteen, she's not ready for what might be, her boyfriend will leave
her if she is, she thinks to herself she do then?

The doctor comes and says the result is positive, she drops to the floor
as the tears begun to fall, what has she done? She thinks to herself
her life will never be the same.

Her boyfriend took the news like she thought he would, he left her
on the ground, there is only one way to return to her life
abortion is the right choice, she believes.

A cry out in pain, in anger, she heard right before she went out
was it the baby crying for a life? Or was it just her imagination?
Never will she know the pain she has caused.

A week later and all is well, so she thinks she hasn't experienced
the guilt, the remorse or the depression, she never got what she
was hoping for...he told her he didn't like girls who slept around.

He claimed it wasn't his, and told her goodbye the pain she felt
on that rainy spring day she now realizes what she has done
she has murdered someone who has caused no harm.

She locks herself in her room and thinks of the past, what she could have
done differently there is no way to go back. Unfortunately
she is now a murderer.

Never will she forget what she did that 21st of April never will she
forget the cry out in the office. The tears will forever fall in
the pit of darkness as she remembers the aborted feelings.

My Sister
by Summer Michelle Graham

She always tortures our cat.
I say, "Kristin, you're such a brat!"
She reads all the time,
even chapter books with rhyme.
She wears size twelve in kid shoes;
in competition, she hates to lose!
She's about four feet tall,
and enjoys playing baseball.
Kristin's placed in gifted second grade class.
I hate to admit it, but she's quite a smart lass.
Her nickname is Gert,
her favorite food is corn;
October the second is the day Gert was born.
With big brown eyes, and long brown hair,
sisters like her are very rare!

The Candle On My Dresser
by Summer Michelle Graham - age 15

There's a candle on my dresser.
I burn it every night.
I turn off the light,
since it burns so bright.
An eternal flame,
that dances and jumps,
being the least bit tame.
It will never melt away.
It will always be brand new.
The candle on my dresser,
represents the love I have for you!

Undying Love
by Darius Keith Gordon

In my heart I know I care for you so
but now it's time 2 let u go
I use 2 see how happiness could be
but all I caused was misery

I thought that we would be till da end
but never could this be again
I tried 2 show you that I cared
you turned your back, how could you dare?

Last night we fought
it's over and over
The hurt started again
with the rising of the sun

But when this back was turned on me
Your heart was closed, the caring ceased
My feelings weren't important 2 you
So now you're happy and I am blue

One day I hope you'll understand
that I'd give the world 2 be your man
I'm all alone but you're Happy now
My feelings never mattered, and you showed me this...

No Bounds
by Paul Habermann

    True love knows no bounds, and destiny no one controls. And with that thought in mind I pose you this, and tell you this, I love you, and no one, or no thing, can ever change that, my love for you. I hope that one day I can get a chance with you.

Unconditional Love
by Jessica Gottfried - age 15

An unconditional love;
That's just what it was...

I can't say how I feel about you
Because we're in the past,
I should've known right from the start
That we were too good to last.
This love I have is unconditional
That means I'll love you unconditionally,
No matter what you put me through
No matter what you do to me.
I guess I'd better run
I gotta get away,
Though I'll always love you, dear
For forever and a day.
But, Lord, what will I do?
If I get lost when I run from you?
Are you gonna save me?
No, I shouldn't expect you to.
Breaking up has brought me many times
To a heartache that hurt so bad,
For where I kept on wishing
That your love is what I had.
This heartache put me down
And I turned to suicide,
Because my heart and yours
Simply could not abide.
You always laughed when you hurt me
You never shed a tear,
But now that I have run from you
I still tremble with fear.

Love And Beauty
by Barbara J. Grant

I gazed across the hilltop,
as the sun began to rise
I realized the beauty,
there before my eyes

The trees stood so silent,
not a rustle, nor a breeze
As if to say, come join us,
cause we are here to please

The leaves began to glisten,
as the sun shone on the dew
I took a breath, and closed my eyes,
it reminded me of you

The early morning sunshine,
warmed my inner soul
What a beautiful sight I was seeing,
here standing on this knoll

The birds started chirping,
and singing their happy song
My mind went back, to you again
and how long, you've been gone

There's love and beauty everywhere,
in one way or another
But, nothing like the love I shared,
with my dear loving Mother

My Man
by Lisa Marie Grant - age 14

Sometimes I lay and watch him sleep,
he's so calm and innocent looking.
I remember all the good times we had,
and how safe I felt in his arms,
when I was with him it was like
nothing could touch me.
Now I think to myself,
was it worth losing everything?
Because that's what has happened,
I gave up everything else to be with him.
And now he just lays there,
not even knowing I'm here.
I move quietly, so I can see better,
still I wonder, does he feel the same way?
If I was to disappear today, would he care?
I guess these questions will remain unanswered.
I could ask, but I know I won't
I could never hurt him like he's hurt me.
Every day is a new day to try and win him back.
Everything I go through, all the pain and the loneliness,
is all worth it, just to be with him again, to see that smile,
it's his beautiful smile that lights up my life,
like nothing else can.
Nothing else can, except him, my man

True Beauty
by Paul Habermann - age 17

    True beauty is not found in what your eyes can see, but in what your heart can see. Trust what your heart can see.

The Light Of The Stars
by Nickie Grant - age 15

As I sit at the window, watching the light
The stars of course, such a beautiful sight.

I ask my wish as my eyes, they close,
The wind blows so soft, as the petal of a rose.

I take a deep breath, of the sweet cold air,
Then open my eyes, into the sky I stare.

I dream of the things that could never be,
but are so special to a person like me.

I think about my wish, as I gaze into the sky,
When I realize the stars, are in which I can rely.

Even though wishes might not always come true,
I know the stars are always there to listen to you.

I watch as the stars glisten so brightly,
as the sun beams on the ocean, ever so slightly.

As I take my last glance at the beautiful light,
I say good-bye and will return to wish again tomorrow night.

Marriage
by Elizabeth Gray

What does marriage really mean?
It's when two people's love is meant to be.
It means caring for each other and building bridges of trust.
It means asking as well as answering difficult questions.
It means pulling together when times get rough.
Knowing the love will always be there no matter what.
It means admitting when you're wrong.
It means communicating honestly and openly and
caring about the other person's feelings.
it means being willing to listen to the other's
problems when they arise.
It means having someone special to share your dreams with
and to stand beside you through both good and bad times.
It means having two people work together to make their
lives fuller and more meaningful.
It means having a relationship that's special and important.
It means having someone to grow old with.
Marriage takes a lifetime of nurturing.
It means having commitment, fulfillment, dealing with a crisis
as it arises, and having the ability to handle financial problems.
Marriage is something sacred and needs both people
to work at keeping it strong.

You
by Corinne Gretch - age 12

First time I saw, I couldn't stop staring.
I saw you so loving, I saw you so caring.
Though we're good friends, I still just can't see.
What do you see in her that you don't see in me?
You asked me to dance and I refused.
When you asked me why I felt so confused.
I'm still loving you like from the very start.
Maybe sometime you'll find it in your heart.
When you're around I don't act like myself.
I'm really quite like a shelf.
I stand tall and quiet and have many books.
When you open one up and read it aloud,
you'll find what I'm like inside and out.

Mr. Teddybear
by Matilda Green

My teddybear smiled at me
then the tears
flooded my face
At that moment I knew
I was lonesome
as if disgraced
To fly free
in captivity
In the cage
you hold on me
The silence you held
in your eyes
died when you
made your good-bye
clear as the lonely
sky
What'd he do to me
Mr. Teddybear?
Hold me tight
for I don't want
to be all alone
tonight
as I will from
now on.

The Outhouse From Hell
by Tina M. Green - age 16

The outhouse loomed over me,
It call to it,
It pulled me as if,
It were a magnetic force.

The outhouse seemed to sigh,
When I stepped inside,
Little did I know that as I
Stepped inside the door would snap shut.

The outhouse wouldn't release me
When I tried to get out, I kicked
And hit the door still it wouldn't release me.
I screamed and cursed at it.

The outhouse wouldn't release me
From it's clutches no matter what
I did to it. I tried to get
Out but I couldn't no matter what.

The outhouse seemed to be laughing at me
Outside people were gathering, wondering
What was going on, I screamed and
Screamed for help, but no help came

The outhouse seemed to be hysterical with
Laughter, while I was hysterical with fear
That was until I remembered hot to unlock
The outhouse door.

Eyes Of Passion
by Theresa Handel - age 16

I see the bright look of passion in your eyes. They seem to be telling me something that I just can't figure out. Your eyes seem to see right through me. They tell me everything that is on the outside, but I can't see what's on the inside. You know! Please tell me, I will listen. Do you feel down and lost? I will help you through good times and bad. My eyes are still trying to find the answer. Is it love or death? Wisdom or bad mentality? Tell me now, your eyes don't say much. Your lips don't care, when I look into your eyes they seem to be in despair. They are apart from all the world.

Then There Was None
by Jill Greer - age 17

There was me, you, him, and her
and then there was four.
But when your far away
I just dream of more.

There was me, you and her
and then there was three
but just without her
how great it would be.

There was just you and me
and then there was two
I got my wish
It's finally just you.

There was just me
and then there was one
I thought I had it all
And then there was none.

Untitled
by Lisa Gregorio

All your life, you wait and you pray
for things to turn out okay.
You beg and you plead.
You borrow and you bleed.
You bargain your soul away.

Dreams of how it should be,
crash and crumble underneath your
feet.

You thought you'd get it complete.
Resolve every obstacle.
Every feat, you'd beat.

Then you wake up one day and see
it another way.

The ground you found was never solid.
Never really had promise.
We blinded ourselves all to hell

However, with age, we learn to accept
it with grace. Disguise our face and
leave no trace.

Our hearts we learn to shield. Our souls
to hide from others suicide.

We learn to walk around the fire without
getting near the flames. We learn to live
without shame. We learn to love ourselves
and find a way to carry on.

Farther away to be with ourselves even if
we must be alone. Happy and free.

The City
by Amy Holland - age 19

In the distance,
In the night the lights shine bright as stars,
And all the streets are neat and clean,
Every home is safe and warm.
And there is a bed for every soul to rest his head.
I know this dream is only in my head
And I think in others too,
But being mortal, frail, and weak can we ever
achieve what we know we can do?

The Storm
by Grover W. Gregory, II

There's a storm coming
I felt it last night
The front, pushing forward
Pushing me back
    I stand against it
    I try to make the winds subside
    But they are continuously fed
    And I go hungry
As the churning clouds march on
I die a little bit more
I need a little big more
I slide backward a little more
    I have not ended the struggle yet
    But I am growing weary
    But not this storm
    It's grown some more
The sky can hardly contain it now
All of my incantations and evocations are failing
My strength is failing
    There's a storm coming
    I can feel it very well now
    The front is perpetual form and motion
    And it's throwing me away

Forever
by Sarah J. Gridley - age 16

Forever I will love you,
There is no need to worry my dear,
For I will forever be with you,
Living in the light of your love,
Bathing in your light always,
Your words warm my soul.
Your quiet breath,
Your innocent angelic face as you sleep,
Will never be forgotten,
Your soft touch,
Reaches beyond skin,
Touches my heart,
My soul,
My heart is full,
Of you,
Your love.
Forever I will love you,
Give you the heavens, the waters, the land I will,
Give you all,
Everything you can ask for,
Forever I will love you.
Your kiss,
Warms my soul,
Forever I will protect you,
Hold you in my arms,
Forever I will be your lover,
Always there,
Always a smile.
Never a tear of sadness,
Only joy.
Always there,
With everything you desire,
Forever I will love you,
Forever I will protect you,
Forever I will be your lover,
Forever I will...

Fallen Love
by Heather Griffin - age 14

Our love once reached higher than the stars,
But now thy love has fallen into the deepest chasm.
We were so much in love that nothing else mattered
No one in this world could have separated us.
In thy arms, I felt that nothing or no one could do me harm,
And I believed we would be together for eternity.

That hast broken my heart
And yet it still yearns for thee to love me again.
Why? I do not know.
My heart burns within me everytime I see thee.
But I must let my love thee die and find someone else to love.
And even yet, words can not describe the pain I feel in doing so.
I too, must let my love for thee fall into the deep chasm,
And hope that if I find a new love,
It will not be a fallen love.

In Unison
by Amanda Grimmon - age 13

We are connected in mind body and soul
We fall together when we fall in a hole
No one sees how connected we are
We even wish upon the same star
At the exact same time we open our door
When either feels pain we both crumble to the floor
In unison is how we talk
In unison is the way we walk
We see each other in our dreams
We sew together at the seams
Both of our watches say half past nine
When everyone else says ten past nine
Although we are connected in every way
We are as different as night and day

Goodbye
by Amber Gross - age 16

To have wings
to fly away,
To run from trouble.
But to run away
means to say
goodbye...

But to say goodbye
I leave you behind,
I'll run away
to chase my dreams.
But if I do will I
leave one behind...

Do you leave one dream,
way behind?
Do you go and say
goodbye?
Is there a way to
go away
and not say
goodbye?

"Lost Soul"
by Lisa Grouzalis

On the outside of the looking glass and always looking in,
She wants to tell her story, but doesn't know where to begin,

She believes in peace, and that everyone should treat each other like sisters and brothers,
She's her own person, has her own style, good ideas, yet she doesn't blend in with the others,

She does enjoy being unique, but at times it brings sadness to her eyes,
Such a beautiful woman, but people always have to spread their vicious lies.

She's very independent, but at the same time scared of ending up alone,
She can be very happy, but at times she'll be the most sad woman that you've every known.

Either she's up or down, but there is no in between,
When she's up she's ecstatic; when she's down she's sad and mean.

Around her family, she tends to feel like the black sheep,
When she's out, she always runs into more than her share of creeps.

Her heads usually up in the clouds, dreaming of beautiful sunsets and star filled skies,
No, my friend, she's not crazy she's just a lost soul that may fall at times, but she will eventually rise.

Mother
by Candace Gurley - age 16

Alone in darkness I sit,
wondering if I ever shall forgive you.

Alone I darkness I sit,
thinking of how badly you hurt me.

Alone in darkness I sit,
trying to understand why you left.

Alone in the darkness I sit,
trying to understand why you love him.

Alone in darkness I sit,
trying to understand why you hate me.

Alone in darkness I sit,
always with my mind on you.

Healing
by Robert A. Hipkins, Jr.

The time for renaissance is now.
Arrest the fears of lands,
not yet traveled through.
Like the shackles to a slave,
the links to memories of you,
must be severed for eternity.
One must rise above the pain and sorrow,
inflicted by lost love.
Refunnel the energy which propels you.
A tattered heart will mend whole.
Shelve the antiquated guilt and anguish.
your good-bye,
as cold and callous,
as the grip of a grey noreaster.

Follow
by Christian Gutierrez - age 19

You don't heal me
    Never learning how I feel
      I go roaming behind you
        you move on and don't reveal
Your aim is my goal, I move ahead with all my soul
    my love is within, out of here its just some skin

    Please hear me
      No more of this I wish to carry
        I search running after you
          You're too careful and think I'm scary
You've opened my eyes, what I see is seen through you
    all I've gained from this, is the piece I thought I'd miss

What I choose is chose from you
    when I'm behind, I follow you

    My explanations
        live in bottom deep down with you
I've made up my mind
      Ever since I felt you move
You're creation covers up, all my warmth is all your love
    From the start I heard you sing, in the end I grasped your wing

    Still beginning to understand
      You brought about another man
You're inside in my thought
      You are remembered not ever forgot
I want you interested
      Bringing out what you're invented
All that seemed would never happen, is coming true before I plan it

What I choose is chose from you
    when I'm behind, I follow you

Elements
by Wendy Gutierrez

Scorned breathes spewed from the sinking afternoon sun:
cast a scarlet veil that colored even the eyes,
caused ripples in the ocean of flowered top corn,
cried out in a song like a lover to the rains.

Invading forces of darkness slowly gain ground:
pushing the sun into submission if only for a few hours,
purging silent secrets to those whom need not light to see,
pleasing the senses with coolness and shelter from the day.

Helpless clusters of wetness released into space:
await the collection of many beneath,
adds a milky mist to the moister soaked land,
attached themselves like lovers to each other.

Invisible fairies dance tirelessly over the earth:
tickling delicately the tiny leaves of the might oaks,
teasing the dryness with cooling relief,
telling the future with cent of spring, winter, even rain.

Never A Chance
by Paul Habermann - age 17

    I can't force another to love me, but no one can stop me from loving you. I wait maybe forever, or maybe just for a day.
    There is no reason of why we fall in love or who therefore with, just that we fall in love.
    I love you Tessa Marie, you are my soul's desire. I use to admire you, from afar, before we to did meet.
    Then I did see your smile so beautiful so much of the world can be seen in it. That is one thing I could never forget.
    I wait as a fool thinking that if I, say the right thing, or look a certain way, that you could possibly love me. Maybe if I say your name enough times, you will change your mind about me.
    Ask you this my love, my life, my all desires put together. Imagine this if I looked as good as the most attractive person you could think of, would your feelings for me doth change. I have tried everything I could possibly think of.
    You have such a goodness, a pureness, a timeless beauty, I love. I wish I could just say something and make you understand. That Tessa Marie, I love you, I love you so much.

Dedicated To: Tessa
by Paul Habermann - age 17

    Sometimes you take a chance, hoping to fall in love. Sometimes your a fool, who falls in love with someone who will never feel the same for you.
    Wait and wait would I, if I knew I had just one chance, in a million in a billion. For my love for you knows no bounds.
    For some reason I have a hope, a wish that you will change your mind about me, but it is a waste of time, for I fear you will never be mine, I truly do love you, and I will always love you.

I Would Take Anything
by Paul Habermann

I would take anything from you, I would give you anything, you so desired. You can use me for whatever you want.
I love you and would take anything just for a chance to be at your side.

Take This Too Your Heart
by Paul Habermann

My heart beats only for your one soul.
With every breath I take, and every moment I wake, I love you.
Take this too, you heart my love, and know you will never be denied my love, As long as I shall live you will be my love, my life and my utmost highest desire.

Missing You
by Mandy Hagen - age 17

    I sit here thinking,
... wishing that you were here.
    I cry hoping that it will
... all be a bad dream.
    I see someone that you were friends with
... and start missing you even more.
    I see pictures of you
... and I start to cry.
    I ask myself
... why did you leave me?
    I need you more than
... I ever told you.
    I want you to know that
... I Love You!
    I didn't want to let you go
... but I didn't want to be selfish.
    Remember, I Miss You Daddy!

Beauty
by Jill Hagmaier

Beauty,
Where have you gone?
You have slipped away,
Leaving me to remember
Your sweet face, and
the scent of your hair.

A moment ago you were here
Laughing.
The window is open.
I see you out in the field,
Dancing with freedom,
Afraid to embrace her.

I cannot see your face.
I imagine you're smiling
As the wind moves you.
Watching, I am crying.
You are Beauty, and
You have left me.

Untitled
by Sarah Halcomb - age 15

Our friendship means more than the world,
embracing two beautiful hearts,
one boy and one girl.
Together their closeness is gently expressed,
but when it departs they're found deeply depressed.

Alone is like my feeling of now,
so many unexplained answers,
of why and how.

Two hearts combined,
attached they must stay,
forever and ever,
with each passing day.

With the feeling of emptiness,
my feeling of now,
my heart is so soft,
like a big puffy cloud,
surrounded by loneliness in the sky,
just me thinking of you,
now I'm beginning to cry.

We've had some great times
that I hope will never end,
because deep in my heart,
we'll always be best friends.

Firefly
by Mistie Hall

You see a light afloating
gently through the air,

You try to capture this
floating beauty,

But much to your despair
You miss this shining light,

And all you catch in your hands
is the soft warm air of night,

The little shining beauty
disappears,

To your disappointment you
must walk home,

Without the little light to guide
you.

The Kiss
by Tami Hallman - age 15

It was a moment she had waited her while life for and it was about to happen.
She closed her eyes and waited,
Finally, she would be able to know what it was like to be like everyone else.
They knew what it felt like, and had done it many times before.
But this was a first for her and she knew that it would change her life forever.

She could feel her palms; they were sweaty.
She was so nervous and it was the waiting that was killing her.

A deep rush of excitement filled her body, her heart pounded, and her cheeks began to flush as something soft touched her.
It was happening, and she couldn't believe it.

Then, just as it seemed like she was floating on air, it ended, and the moment she had waited her life for had come and gone and was forgotten like all the rest.

Heartache
by Leila Hamdan - age 16

Those last painful words you gave me
Denying me your love
Keeps repeating through my head
And like the sound of rain
Against my windowpane
It's slowly driving me insane
Though I am hurt
I am not mad
Guilt is something
That I hope you'll never have
So please don't feel bad
I'm the only one who should be sad
At times I wish I could experience that love
You gave to others and not to me
But I understand you
You just wait and see
That all my kindness goes to you
And I will cherish your friendship
For all eternity

To Be
by Nathan Hamilton - age 19

Now you live with a broken heart.
And you don't know where to start.
You're losing your mind.
She was so kind.
Now she's in heaven now,
and you look up at heaven now,
Now you see how.
It could have been you.

She left you high and dry,
All you do is turn and sigh,
With a tear in your eyes.
The rage is in your soul,
And you find yourself loosing control.

Every one dies,
Every one cries,
But where is God now.
She looks like heaven now,
And she tastes like heaven now.
but now she's in heaven now.
and she's not going to be
Coming home anymore.

You don't know what to do,
And you don't know what to say.
but you gotta go your own way.
But no one cares enough.
If I could be...
If I could be...
The man you wanted me,
To be.

Paradise
by Katie Hamlin - age 12

I love to be near the sea,
where palmettos live and grow.
I wish to swim just like a fish,
and never see the snow.
The water in this paradise is clear, clean and cool.
It is better than swimming in any pool.

The flowers bloom all year round,
and there isn't a single weed to be found.
The world beyond the reef
is more than I though could be, way beneath.
Every inch that I explore,
consists of coral, plants and fish galore.

In my paradise there is a mall.
It is not huge, but definetely not small.
This mall has all my favorite stores,
and they are on the first two floors.
You may wonder the price of merchandise,
the answer cannot be explained, because it's paradise.

The sand on the beaches are so sandy and soft,
You can always leave your shoes off.
The description of this paradise will soon be done,
Because I am being scorched by the sun.
You are probably long, long gone,
so I will stop because my description goes on and on.

Darkest Hour
by Martha Hamrick

The blank night sky has not yet
been kissed by the glow of the
morning sun
One star gleams boldly against
the velvet backdrop of night
A towering moon shimmers as the
shadows within play

Slowly, to the east the sky
lightens and fresh clouds
float over th horizon
The sky becomes a rainbow of
color
The Darkest Hour is becoming
The Dawn

The swaying green grass is
sprinkled with dew that shimmers
in the spectrum of colors and
light
The leaves on the trees whirl
to the silent music of the wind
in a dizzying ballet that has
an elegance all its own

Truly this is a wondrous sight

Someone
by Lisa A. Hanebrink

You gave me what
I needed most -
Someone -
Someone who I could be
myself with.
Someone that would take the time
to listen to
who I was -
and who I wanted to become -
You helped me look for the missing pieces
and to quit shoving in pieces
to just fill the gaps.
Most importantly,
You showed me that those pieces
were within me.
It just took
Someone like you
to help
me find them.
Thank you for being a special
friend and
Someone -
that I can trust.

Moonlight Cross
by Cynthia Hayslette

As I walk along life's long road
The light of the moon shines down upon me
Guiding me along the way
I am unburdened from my heavy load
From many lands and vast seas
My God is with me
He protects me with His light
As His cross emanates from the moon
And I will never have to fear the night
I am safe embraced in His arms
Walking in the glow of God's moonlight cross.

Pronouns
by Dunya Michael

He plays a train
She plays a whistle
They move away
    *   *   *
He plays a rope
She plays a tree
They swing
    *   *   *
He plays a dream
She plays a feather
They fly
    *   *   *
He plays a general
She plays people
They announce the war.

Untitled
by Kim V. Hannah

Why...Why...Why...?
Al the hustling to get one by?
No time to breath, no time to rest
No time to have a good cry!

When...When...When...?
Will the people let themselves bend?
To experience and see what it's like to e free
Than to be a slave to their lives once again?

Where...Where...Where...?
Did the people go that once cared?
Have they died with our past?
It all happened so fast!
Can a kind word from anyone be spared?

What...What...What...?
Is the hate we all feel so much?
diversity is what made
This country what it is today
We are now in a cultural crunch!

How...How...How...?
Can we lift up our nation now?
It is too late to change
Our attitudes and our games
Or will it all be lost anyhow?

Rise...Rise...Rise...!
People must open their eyes!
The meaning of life
Is to humble and strive
For the goodness before it all dies!

I Never Got To Say Goodbye
by Beth Haserick - age 15

I never got to say goodbye for the reason
I don't know why, as you are so far away,
I wait for the day, When I can tell you
and you will see, just how much you mean to me
    Every minute I think of how it would be,
to still have you here with me, Your love,
your smile, and your touch, Is what I
miss so much, I never got to say goodbye,
but this I tell you is no lie, I'll always
love you, so goodbye

Our Love
by Kairi Harrington - age 14

Theres nothing anyone can do it was
meant to be...our love
If you ever left my heart
would grow lonely and I
would drown in my despair
and from your words and actions
you would to,
what can only get stronger and
stronger... our love
Each day our love grows
stronger and stronger
and I pray we will hold
that love forever and that
we will never part and
in my heart I know it's
so that we will never part
for we were meant to be.
It's something no one can ever
replace...Our love

Confused
by Kairi Harrington - age 14

Why is it sometimes
your nice and make
me love you and then
you change and act
like you hate me but
I love you anyways.

You have me confused
at times I feel you
love me back cause
your nice and caring and
then your gone and in
your place is someone
unfeeling who doesn't care
about my feelings.

I'm usually quite in
control of my emotions
but with you I can't
control them and
there unleased with
the fury and power of a
hurricane.

So now you know I'm
confused when I think
of you.

That Old Weeping Willow
by Terry A. Harrison-Duke

  As I sat on a rock under that old willow tree, I felt cold tears falling on me
  I looked up above, yes way up high, I observed the weeping willow as it continued to cry
  I often wondered in my mind, why God made this tree to cry all the time?
  Maybe it's for all the weeping hearts of the children in the world, maybe it's for all the agony of little boys and girls
  In this way all the children could come out and play and all their pain would be taken away
  As children grow older and the seasons change, that old weeping willow will remain the
same. It will continue to weep over the years, to incase the young's heart aches and tears
  Another generation born so free, will pass on their heart aches to the tree

Make The Pieces Fit
by Lisa M. Hartle

Last night I had a dream,
I was sound asleep but how real it did seem.
I was walking though heavens door
When I realized what life was all for.

I first looked back on my childhood days,
so young and carefree in life's most innocent ways.
Then finally it came to me without any doubt,
I suddenly realized what life is about.

Life is only what you make of it
And much like a puzzle you make each piece fit.
So I realized that the hard times are what made me strong,
And gave me the courage to help me go on.
And my happiest days filled with fun and laughter,
I stored in my memory to cherish forever after.

But then there where parts of my life I wish I could have changed,
Maybe placed in order or rearranged.
I would have done things different somehow,
But as I opened that door I knew it was too late now.

And as I walked through to that pearly gate,
I said to myself, "if only heaven could wait."
Then suddenly an angel appeared from the clouds above,
offering a package labeled "handled with love."

So I held out my arms for this package to take,
But my dream suddenly ended and I now was awake.
Except on the edge of my bed a package did sit,
Inside was a puzzle and the pieces fit.

Birth Of A Monday
by Stephaine Hatcher - age 16

the glutton bloated nite gets
ready to birth a bloody
pathetic morning
each horrid contraction
squeezes the wan moon
further into oblivion.
where there should be cloth
covered with blood
lies only a broad cotton expanse
and a pounding of suffering
in the lower regions
i hold my breath
in spite of lamaz
this isn't me.
a dream drop of blood
slithers down to the
cracked linoleum floor
celebration in wake of
it's sickly trail
which is sadly lacking in iron...

Night
by Candice Herron - age 14

Night,
The darkness that covers the land over,
that awakens the terror that was lost in the day,
Silent Night,
where evil lurks and stares you in the face,
the trouble that arises in people's minds bring danger to all.
Oh! what an endless night,
Bringing death to trouble minds where the innocent lie,
Fear covers the abyss, striking slowly but diligently
Night,
Then comes day putting night at rest and agony in slow misery.

Walk
by Stephanie Hatcher - age 16

The clinging poison
of diseased sunday
chokes me with her
green parasitic arms.
Bits & flakes of sanity
worn away with the
passing of time.
These four walls
branded in my head
I close my eyes
they are still there.
Yawning grey maw
a few hours till nite.
the bulging blood in my wrists
begging to come out and play
upon this white page.
Thoughts faded from overuse
feelings tired and forced.
Pulp resenting Graphite's trespass
upon her virgin white lines.
an empty husk lies on a bed.
yearn for the sight of stars
and black
when nite shall erase me & all my Thoughts.
Dark slay my eyes and cripple my hands.
sleep will come and i
will continue the long walk
to Death...

Untitled
by Brianne Hatfield - age 16

Our love is unconditional
it'll stand through the test of time
we will always be together
my hand in yours
together your heart and mine

we may not understand
the way we feel right now
but what we know for sure
is it's love forever more

we have something special
it's the way I feel right now
some day I'll totally show it
although I don't know exactly when or how

A Secret Love
by Kerry Hawthorne - age 15

Every time I see you my heart
skips like a stone.
It's you I want to be with,
and only you alone.

It's only been a very short time and
I may not know you very well,
but I do know that I like you
it's not hard to tell.

I really want to talk to you
but inside I'm very shy.
I'd really love to be your girl,
my heart would never lie.

Maybe someday I'll tell you
about my feelings left to reveal,
but for now I'll keep them to myself
and know they're very real.

Year
by Melissa Anne Hayden - age 14

Oh, dear! What has come of this
Year?
People get sick, people cut their skin,
Kids growing, adults shrinking.
There's bombing, and there's flooding
In the streets.
It's not a flood; it's tears of everyone's
heart breaking.
There is no way out in a tight tearing
place, tears of flooding.
Guns killing; the bombing puts fear
In people's hearts, to tear is to flood
in one spot
(California, Georgia, Oklahoma, Iowa)
In a shamble since 1993.
The fears, the tears, the pain, the hurt,
the sorrow.
We must unite - make it sunny.
Flowers blooming, happiness, joy in
our year and many more years to come.

Child
by Keith Haynes - age 18

Come to me, oh *child* of God, for shelter from the rain.
I will see to your every need and protect you from your pain.
Beneath my wings there lies a love waiting to find a home.
I've wanted a *child* for so long now, but I've prayed for you alone.
I've longed for you so many nights that my dreams have ceased to be.
My eyes have cried so many tears that they refuse to see.
A *child* like you is all I need to keep my days so full.
Please, bring your love into my home and you'll be my precious jewel.

Come to me, oh *child* of love, for attention and toys galore.
I will shower you with gifts and presents, and do so forevermore.
In my house there lies a room longing for someone to play.
I've wanted a *child* for so long now, but my plans have been delayed.
I've prayed for you so many nights that my knees no longer kneel.
My feelings have been hurt so many times that they've lost their sense to feel.
A *child* like you is all I need to get up and move on.
Please, give me a chance to prove my love and you'll live like a God.

Come to me, oh *child* of life, for dreams that all come true.
I will give you everything and do whatever you want me to.
An empty space lies in my heart that longs to be filled.
I need a *child* before its too late, but I fear my motives are ill.
I've thought of you so many times that some say I've lost my mind.
I've walked for miles looking for you, but my feet refuse to find.
A *child* like you is all I need to make my life increase.
Please, come to me some day soon, or I will never rest in peace.

The Ocean's Call
by Lynne Hayes

The ocean's call draws in the dead of night;
Life will continue well into the day,
Be gone in haste; turn thy heel and take flight.

Moral obligations are often tight,
These wayward thoughts to melt before sun's ray;
The ocean's call draws in the dead of night.

Do not misuse your life; do not lose sight;
Cast out these worries; find another way;
Be gone in haste; turn thy heel and take flight.

A dying man who wants to live must fight,
Mortality, the price we all must pay;
The ocean's call draws in the dead of night.

Life's not so bad when you see in the light,
Turn thine ear, and listen to what I say
Be gone in haste; turn thy heel and take flight.

Face the new day that comes, happen what might;
Life is a gift, not to be thrown away;
The ocean's call draws in the dead of night
Be gone in haste; turn thy heel and take flight.

The Storm
by Jolene Hay - age 12

Slowly, silently, creeping towards my home
Then it sits and waits a bit
After awhile I forget
Then suddenly darkness falls
Has night come already "No"
The storm has come

Rain drips on my skylight
Then more steadily it begins
Begging to come in
The storm has come

The wind whines and whimpers and it will whip about
Begging to come in
A wolf may seem to howl but I know that it is only the wind.
The storm has come

Sometimes thunder will pound to try and scare you
Lightening will illuminate the sky to send you eery thoughts
The storm has come

Eventually the storm will cease
Maybe abruptly or perhaps slowly
nonetheless the storm ends
just like my life.

Mr. Moon
by Rachel Hennie - age 16

Mr. Moon, Mr. Moon, Mr. Moon you are the sin thief.
All who do wrong see your face and confess their night grief.
People know you see their evil deeds,
but they still won't stop and pay any heed.
Mr. Moon, Mr. Moon, Mr. Moon, your smiling, caring face gives me hope
on those lonely nights.
You are my guide, my only friend, my brightest light.
If I find myself lost, your radiant beams will see me
home safe at any cost. My eyes grow heavy at your marvelous sight.
So now I must blow you my kiss and wish you goodnight.

Your Love
a conflicts in a girl's mind
by Jolene Hay - age 12

Your love is vivid and bright,
all day and through the night.

> It's not true,
> Just a dream-like hue.

You caress me and hold me,
Being as sweet as you can be.

> You see another not I,
> The words you say are a lie.

Here you come toward me,
To say I am the only one you see.

> My moment is near,
> For the truth we shall hear!

No, but you said you were true,
I was your love not Sue.

> I knew it would come,
> I will get even, some.

The Wind
by Amanda Heinze

To catch the wind you need to know,
of the pearl and its peril;
never seen except a glimpse
   a ghost.
A host, to fairy tales.
the essence of the tales
told over a glass of ale.

The hunters fail to catch the wind.
A gift to all because they lost,
the treasure they sought:
   The Unicorn

Key to fantasies.
The ivory of its hooves,
The silver of its mane,
and the fame of its mystical horn.
Is safe for now.

Fear
by Andrea Holderfield - age 12

What is fear?
Fear can jump on you like a hungry dog
Or an angry mob
Darkness can hold the very life of fear
It's mysterious and black hold can be near
Fear can also be the demons that can't be seen
Fear can creep up and take control of your life
Controlling your destination
like the wind directing a kite.
Fear can conquer the bravest souls
If only you knew that you can conquer it
Fear can swing you around like a cat's tail
Just watch out fear is near

Whispers

Distance
by David Alan Heise

The days drag on endlessly,
As I waste away in obscurity.
My thoughts so often turn to you.
But you're so far away, what can I do?

The hours run together and seem all the same,
Without you my existence seems quite mundane.
I long for the healing powers of your touch,
It's frightening to need a person so much.

I can't tell if the nights are worse than the days,
My desire increases in so many ways.
But you're there with me from dusk until dawn,
Even though it's a translucent dream you ride on.

I toss and turn, sweat drenches the sheet,
As I dream of countless encounters where we meet.
They seem so real, but eventually I must awake,
Only to realize that our meeting was a fake.

My heart is a vessel that is filled with emotion,
And I fear it will drown in the depths of your ocean.
But so be it, if that is the way it must go,
For the heart knows reasons that reason does not know.

Treacherous Dichotomy
by David Alan Heise

It would seem that my heart is condemned to be free,
Condemned to choose from love's treacherous dichotomy.
But alas, my heart is of the state that cannot choose.
Between never having love, and having love that it must loose.

Love unknown, or love lost? I know not which is worse.
They seem similar enactments of the very same curse.
The former is an emptiness, a torment to one who feels.
The later is a wound which never fully heals.

Finding love in the eyes of a woman I see,
I hope against hope that her love will find me.
But rarely doth a woman return my hopeful glance,
And rarer still doth she give my heart a chance.

Fruit that is not gathered in its prime,
Will rot and consume itself in little time.
Like the succulent fruit, let my love be tasted,
Let it not sit idly, and so be wasted.

The ambition of my love thus plagues itself.
For the dangers of romance are in corporeal wealth.
Thus love and beauty in the renters arms,
Are poorly protected from a world full of harms.

It seems that my love may choose its end,
An empty heart, or one that cannot mend.
Whatever the path, there's one thing I know,
My heart will reside in a valley of woe.

The Vision
by David Alan Heise

She walks among the stars by night,
A vision of beauty in effortless flight.
And though the heavens are aglow with spite,
Not even Polaris can shine as bright.

She dances among the flowers by day,
Not a care nor a worry gets in her way.
A vision of grace from head to feet,
And one I have always longed to meet.

She sails on an ocean of dreams in my sleep,
Riding on waves that are torrid and deep.
The waves are the desires of my heart and soul,
And she is the navigator, in constant control.

Is she tangible, or but a vision,
The result of Id and Ego in collision?
Or perhaps an angel sent from above?
The bearer of friendship; the harbinger of love?

I cannot expect answers to these questions I pose,
For this is poetry, and my answers lie in prose.
But this voyage has been a poetic one,
The journey has been enlightening, it has even been fun.

I'll leave her now with this closing thought,
Take this treatise lightly not!
It is the physical manifestation of my deepest desire,
The cancer of my intellect, scorched by passions' fire.

But the stanzas of this poem help to calm,
And the words soothe as if drops of balm.
But I must leave you now, it is time to depart,
For I have already shown you too much of my heart.

You Were Not There
by Stac-E Hendon - age 17

You were not there
- to catch me from falling
down this endless spiral
- to brush the tears from
my crying eyes
you were not there
- to stop my pain or
lessen my fears
- to ease away the many
toils of my mind
You had better things
to do than to be with
me. You did this.
All my insignificant
problems were to upsetting
or not important enough
for you. I was hurt.
You were not there
- to stop me when I
needed to be stopped
- to take away the gun
- to explain to my family
why I did the things
I've done, why I am gone.
Now I cannot tell them
that I won't be here because
You were not there for me...

My World (Panic)
by Stac-E Hendon - age 17

This is my world of Panic
Where nothing's what it seems
It doesn't matter where you run
Since WE can hear your screams
Don't you love the darkness here?
In my world, we know no sun
Run in the dark and PLAY my GAMES
With the angel and her gun
Oh yes, my friend, they'll shoot you down
IN PANIC; no one cares
Where images aren't there at all
Their weapons are YOUR fears
It used to be so lonely here
But that's before I dragged you down
Now you'll never leave my side
You'll always be around
There's no escape out of my world
Believe we'll hunt down you
We'll both be here until the end
FOR THIS YOUR HELL, TOO.

Rain in the Hay
by Lori Herber - age 15

When it rains around here
   and the ripe hayfield
     lies ready for harvest,
the fingers of rain pelt across
   wind beats the field
     without mercy.
Like water bumbling
   over a rough gravel road.
Cascades across...
   the wind whips and snakes
     through.
In synchronized time
   the field is waving
     like helpless silk.

My Angel Came Back and Told Me
by T.R. Blake

    How you held me to the end and gently consoled me as you called me your best friend.
    The tears rolled down your face as you tried to hide your pain, but in your touch I felt again we were one in the same.
    To say Good-bye to you my dear must mean this is the end -- an end for me
-- I have with thee a true friend beside me.
    For in your arms I'm not alone to bear my inner grief. I have with thee an inner passion and a form of relief.
    My only regret is leaving you behind to go through this alone -- I have been assured I can return -- to help you find your way -- back home.
    For home is where you'll find my heart and a familiar face -- to catch you up on all we've lost -- and reminisce to date.
    Be strong dear friend you're not alone -- for I'll always be near -- near enough to help you out -- elevate all fears.
    For I'll always love you in my heart -- no matter how near or far -- to comfort you and hold you tight and tell you how dear you are.
    So then I say to thee best friend before I say Good-bye --
to thee be true,
I love you dear and I'll see you once more time.

Glass Box
by Angela Herring - age 14

No one hears my hollow screams.
No one sees my shattered dreams claw the iron wall...
only collapsing on my pointed, crumbled dreams.
The agony is rough but not as blistering as the years
of empty screams and dry tears. I watched the world
go by in my glassbox.
It's worthless throwing stones and rocks.
It's been another two blank years seeing them walk by.
Helpless to touch another person, I die within.
I the texture of people's hair or the feel of their skin.
The more they overlook me the murkier it gets.
Everything a shadow now.
My screams eternally echo in my head.
My arms and leg are dripping with gory red.
But not even a damn crack.
I've become numb heart & soul, up & down, front & back.
I bang my face into the glass.
Patterns of a spider web if I recall correctly has pass.
In the cracking glass.
The tiny pieces of deadly glass piercing my face.,
Whipping my neck all over the place!
With every last ounce of breath in my limp shell of a
body, I hurl my body through the tied down cause.
The people walking by with broken ears and covered
eyes stop to pause.
They open their eyes to see the lifeless rag doll girl.
The still body lies there covered in bloody glass.
Like red stars that fell out of the evening skies.
I see my body lying on the ground with everyone around
Everyone becomes ignorant again, I see a new glassbox

Silent Music
by Loy Higgins

Silent music on the wall
Play a song for one and all.

Colorful on sunlit days.
Beautiful in a misty haze.

Changing rhythm with the wind,
Your melody is like a hymn.

Silent music on the wall
Sing your song on silent lyre.

Play your music, soft and sweet.
Make me smile; make me weep.

Silent music on the wall.
Quiet harmony for us all.

A Glimpse
by Kathy Highley

Counting your blessings can be a pretty painful experience. Where do you look for them? Are they found in accumulated wealth, property or finery? I think not; for they are what shines through after the dross is burned off the silver--the silver linings of our blackest days.

Blessings are among the rewards we cherish when an angry teen calms down and wants a hug. We must be alert to these special moments that are so easily missed or taken for granted.

I sit alone in my car on a captivating spring morning--the kinds of days spring fever is born of. A tear runs down my cheek, evidence of the mixed emotions encountered yesterday, a day that offered precious little of value--or so I thought yesterday.

My heavy thoughts are accompanied by the merry chirp of busy birds, reminding me that today is a brand new day; hope comes with the dawn; and life really is worth living.

My teenage son is battling the inevitable agonies associated with one's freshman year in high school. I am battling the inevitable agonies associated with being that child's mother. Disciple in love is what I tell him. "Yeah, right," I am sure I hear him thinking.

He was so quiet this morning--not a submerged anger, really--more of a sadness. I act normal, which is how I feel. The deed has been done, punished, forgiven and left behind.

Will my son glimpse the brilliance breaking through as experience begins to reveal his inner character? "Oh lord" I pray, "reach beyond my errors and touch him in your perfect way. Help me be firm in my convictions, high in my expectations, and low in self centered motives. Alas, I see more rain in the forecast, but with rain there comes a rainbow.

My Mom
by Cindy Hill

Over the years
Through smiles and tears
My Mom has always been there to comfort my fears.
When I cried or needed love
My Mom shared with me the greatest hugs.
When my path in life seemed all uphill
My Mom showed me how to work things through.
And when hard times came around
My Mom told me not to get down.
My Mom told me things always work out good
Whether or not they really should.
My Mom is someone precious to me,
A gift from God, a present to me!
As I grow up, I begin to see
The deepest love between my Mom and Me!

You
by Karen M. Hilko

Our love was real from the start.
Love letters were sent to show our care.
Fate's turn for the worst caused us to part.
Being without you is so hard to bear.

In the silent midnight hour I cry.
With only memories and dreams left to treasure.
I only want to know why?
The pain I feel is impossible to measure.

My first love I will never forget you.
A single tear falls down my cheek.
To let it fall is all I can do.
With each tear I grow a bit more weak.

Inside my heart there is an empty space.
That can only be filled by you in that place.

Not Knowingly
by Amanda Hill - age 13

He loves for her
He hates for her
Why did he leave her if he loves for she loves?
She weeps bitter & cold
Dies not knowingly
Sorry for her
Sadly not knowingly dies for her
He lost
Empty, dark failure
Sorry, one little mistake-don't mean it
Deathly sorry
Sorrowness for her-Tears for her
Subject of the verdict...
Rhythm of the heartbeat...
For her...

The Never-ending Cycle
by Sarah Hinrichs - age 15

The final tests,
The ending of school.

The sad good-byes
To our old friends.

The warm hellos'
To the new friends we meet.

Summer ends,
Fall begins.

School starts again,
The old friends back again.

Some things change,
But some never will.

The school year comes and goes,
And thus,
The cycle begins again.

A Home
by Monica Hinton - age 13

There is a home for the homeless, the sad,
all who roam;
there is a home for a people that needs a little faith,
a longer length of rope to grasp, for support.
There is a home where all can be free,
if that is what they choose to be--
A place that truly is a fortress to protect all,
where you can regain your ground,
no matter how hard or far you might fall.

So have a little heart and you will make it,
home at last,
through the hardest obstacles
and faults of the past.
Just follow the path, you will come to your glory,
shrug off all the heartless wrath
and wrong against you.
What do these people know anyway?
Follow your own footsteps, but do not lose your way.
You will make it home then,
home sweet home at last.

The Carafe
by Robert A. Hipkins, Jr.

Will your love grow stronger,
like wine tempered in a ceramic tomb?
Or is your love,
like that of wine in a crystal goblet?
Only quenching the pallet for a short time.
Is my heart half-full,
from the love we had?
Or is my heart half-empty,
with the murmur of your exodus.
Our footprints in the sand,
always appearing endless on the horizon.
Now as mortals,
they will vanish as anyone else,
amongst the breakers.
The bittersweet of your departure.
Will it linger on my lips forever?

Me Missing You
by Robert A. Hipkins, Jr.

Heartache like rolling thunder.
The rain,
tenacious,
as it strikes across the front porch window.
As I stare into the mirror on the mantle,
the smile that curled your lips,
has vanished.
The glitter of your eyes,
replaced by a flickering flame form the hearth.
I reach out to the shadow of your hand.
And an icy blue emptiness,
slithers through my fingertips.
To the study I flee,
mal du pays,
etched in bronze upon the door.
The intoxication of your laughter,
no longer revels through the air.
I stumble in deafness,
yet awaiting,
another encounter with Morpheus.
To the spirits who orchestrate til dawn,
I pray for your return.
As the spirits dance through my theater,
a sea of tears rivet my pillow.

So Much Despair
by Toni Hissick - age 15

Even when I try so hard to make you understand
all you do is push me away so why do I try,
why do I stay?
I love you so much but you do not care so
why do I wear my feelings out,
why do I make my heart shout?
What is wrong with me?
Aren't I your type don't think our feelings our right?
How can I believe in something that isn't there
how can I force my heart not to care?
How can I move on in this life of despair?
I cry so much but still your heart I can't touch.
I force myself back into your arms and
you hold me with your palms which are turning red with fear
for you're afraid to turn around and not have me here.
I'm not like you I won't leave I don't turn my back or put on a phony act
Because I know who I am and
I know what it takes to win,
to steal a heart and not let it part from me.
Even when I'm in my bed lying fast asleep I still dread the
thoughts of losing you.
In my heart I know you're there but never have I felt like
you've actually cared.
I know the flames are burning deep inside of me I know my
love is strong like steel and
with that you can unpeal the layers of love.

Silent Spirit
by Kristina Hodgdon - age 20

Eyes full of wisdom,
Mind uncertain of future,
I looked upon him with human envy,
this one lonely creature.
Staring off over the vast country,
he tilts his tired face toward the sky.
A powerful sound comes from this sage,
Silence follows, why?

Doesn't he have a family to lead?
Or is he calling out in sorrow,
for he might be the last of the wondrous breed.
Will they be there tomorrow?
Killed for myth and human greed,
the wolf has been extinguished from sight.
Is it too late to reverse out unthinkable deed?
Has anyone thought of their plight?

Not many roam our forest land,
our own doing have made them disappear.
Innocent spirits put out of existence by a human's hand,
myths have turned human's view on him in fear.
So he stands there alone,
calling, listening,
determined to reach yet a familiar sound.
Maybe he is trying to tell us something,
calling out for help that's too late to be found.

Red Bird
by Christina Hoffmeier - age 15

Gones the red bird from his perch where he sat
each day to rest,
No longer flying in the skys, no longer huddled
in his nest.
His song stills echoes in the air which he sang so
long ago,
But now he's gone from all the earth still in my
heart I love him so.
Will he fly back to where we are and teach us of
his graceful way?
Or will I travel for from here to see him again
someday?

April and Jade
by April Holland - age 17

Two young girls and an older guy,
He was drunk and they all were high.
They all were loved no matter what you heard.
Only a few had a discouraging word.
On that fateful day.

They were coming home after their sin.
Back from where I should never have been.
They might be alive if time had been a friend.
They were going fast as they rounded the bend.
There wasn't a thing between the tree and them.
On that fateful day.

I really can't believe that they are gone.
I guess that's why I am writing this song.
One of my friends is taking it hard.
He cried all night in his back yard.
On that fateful day.

Some 'ole boy drove them off the rode,
They hit a stump and on two wheels they rode.
'Till they flew up a tree.
That's all the police would tell me.

I did hear it through the grapevine though.
That through the windshield they did go.
I swore one day I'd see them again.
Somewhere between now and then.
On that fateful day.

Your Time Will Come
by Dana Holland

You loved me and you left me.
Your words were untrue.
Your kisses meant so much to me,
But not a thing to you.

You had me so believing,
that your love would always last,
but now I know it's nothing,
but a memory in the past.

You hurt me, oh, so badly,
As you loved and left in lies,
And as I think of all these things,
The tears come to my eyes.

But just you wait my darling,
your time will come, it's true.
For you will fall in love as I,
And it will all happen to you.

I Love You
by Lori Ann Holliday - age 18

You've changed my life in so many ways
I look forward to the coming days
You brighten my days
with just a simple HEY
Noone has ever made me feel
the way you make me feel
When you hold me in your arms
I feel safe from all life's harms
I love you more than anyone I've ever loved before
I love you with all my heart
So, please say you'll never tear it apart

What Happened?
by Jeanette Holmes - age 19

What happened?
Where did we go wrong?
We used to seem so right together.
I secretly wished it would last forever.
Now you're always busy.
The thought of you makes me dizzy.
It just isn't working,
And saying this is really hurting.

What happened?
Where did we go wrong?
We used to talk like the best of friends.
Now all I can say is,
Is this how it ends?

What happened?
Where did we go wrong?
I used to think it would last so long.
Now everything seems wrong.
What happened?
Where did we go wrong?

Father's Day
by Latisha Holmes - age 16

Father's Day is a holiday where
dad's feel special, feels loved,
and appreciated in everything they do.

Father's Day is a day where all dad's
cherish special memories and cherish
all the special love that their
children give and show their dad's.

Father's Day is a holiday that brings
special memories and special moments
that all dad's will keep with them
in their hearts and memories through
out the coming years in their life time.

If Only You Could See Through My Eyes
by Wendy Holmes - age 17

In loving memory
May 29, 1978 - May 6, 1996

If only you could see through my eyes and hear my silent cry.
I'm thinking that you may be gone and I let out a sigh.
Nobody knows what will be tomorrow,
and I'm not ready for the feelings that follow.
I'm sorry for the bad things I said,
but you will always be my mother, in my head.

If only you could see through my eyes and feel all my pain.
All this trying to forgive you, was all in vain.
I try to forget about the past,
but all those memories seem to last.
I need to know why you left me.
I guess, you just couldn't be free.

If only you could see through my eyes and see my confusion.
And trying to pretend it's fine, is just a diversion.
I can't forgive you for not being strong.
I wanted you to stay, is that so wrong?
It's not my fault I got in the way.
I was just a kid, what's left to say?

If only you could see through my eyes and smell my fright.
How often I cry out for you at night.
No matter how loud I am, you're never there.
I don't even get comfort, from hoping you care.
You can't imagine how you hurt me so bad.
You ruined whatever we might have had.

Ballerina
by Erin Honeycutt - age 12

She glides across the stage
No one worries about her age
The soft folds of silk
Hit against the fake wall they built
She glides so effortlessly
Like a boat in the deep blue sea
She leaps into the air
And her eyes seem to flare
She turns around and removes her mask
A horrible and hideous task
An evil face that only I can see
I cover my eyes
And look up at the skies
I see the clouds so white
And look away from that hideous sight

Tell Your Friends You Love Them
by Marci'a D. Hooley

His hair was black as coal
His face I still adore
My sadness vanished when we met
And my loneliness was no more

His eyes sparkled when he laughed
His face glowed when he smiled
He kept me giggling while we talked
Stealing me heart all the while

But it wasn't till October
Till I really knew I cared
I wanted him to know
That I would always be there

But I never got to tell him
For on one fateful day
A car sped down the highway
And took his life away

Mark is always on my mind
He was young, wild and free
And I was a fool not to tell him
Just what he meant to me

Tell your friends you love them
Hold them close in your heart
Thank the Lord you have them
Cause someday, you're bound to be apart

My Guy
by Melissa Hotko - age 14

His baby blue eyes
His soft, silky hair
That when he looks at me,
I just melt right there.

His strong, muscular arms,
Keep me safe from harm,
And when he hugs me,
They keep me nice and warm.

His nice, soft touch
His sweet, sensitive voice,
That when he says "I love you,"
I just want to cry so much.

A True Love Lost
by Ann Hopkins

I remember the first time we met
it was a magical moment. But
when we split apart it was like my
whole world fell apart. All I do is
sit and think about you. I just
can't get you out of my mind. I
know now you love someone else.
I know it's wrong to have these
thoughts but I just can't help
myself. It's been a long time since
I've felt your touch or held your
lips against mine. All I want
to do is cry because I know I
will never have you to myself
again. It just hurts so bad
knowing the only man I ever loved
doesn't love me. Know I sit and
think things could have worked
if we only tried. I wish you
could see how much I really
love you. My love will always
be strong.

"My love for you"
by Heather Hopkins - age 17

Every time you are near,
My body tingles in anticipation
    of your touch.
And every time you are gone,
I can't wait to be close to
    you again.

I love you more than the stars in
    the sky,
I love you more than life, I
    just don't know why.
Why I love you, I can't say
    off hand.
It's just one of those things
I'll never understand.
Some people don't understand why
I love you,
I don't care, i just know
    My love is true.

Remember
by Shaina Howatt - age 15

When the devastating news was told,
I felt like a part of me had died with her
The many weeks that followed this tradegy were a big blur
I didn;t want to be bold

The memories were all she left me
They seemed so old, yet at the same time felt like they had happened
yesterday
I remember she'd always watch out for me
I remember her middle name, it was Kima Lee

Even though she died in June, not December
I still think of her
I'll always think of her
And I'll always, always remember.

Silent Assassin
by Erica Horace - age 19

I walk among you,
You may think you know me, but you don't.
I am a master of disguise
So don't believe your eyes,
For they will deceive you.

Scheming, manipulating and lying is what I do best.
I am as cunning as a fox,
preying on weak, vulnerable souls
and nobody knows
Just how evil I really am.

I have many different faces,
Changing as frequently as a chameleon's colors.
So convincing, so real
Yet determined to conceal
The true nature of my identity.

I come from a world of pain
Where darkness consumes the mind,
Only dead silence is heard
But actions speak louder than words,
And anger festers in the body.

I am the silent assassin,
steadily increasing the body count as time progresses
Of the innocent victims trapped in my web of lies,
And it is only a matter of time
Until everyone will fall under my spellbinding power and become like me.

My Tears
by Maegan Hoss - age 15

I can taste the salt of my tears
as they roll down my cheek
like a raindrop trickling
down the window sill so bleak.
The sound of my tears
hitting my pillow
aimlessly wallowing
and weepingly willow.
My tears flowing down
My eyes burning   red
get the words you said to me
out of my head.
Now my tears are slowing
as I wipe the tears away
and think to myself
I have to get on another day.
I leave my pillow drowned in my tears
and leave the walls that echoed my cries
like the raindrops on the window sill
when the burning red sun comes out
and the last spot of the raindrop dries.

Rain In The Hay
by Lori Hurber - age 15

When it rains around here
and the ripe hay field
Lies ready for harvest
the fingers of rain pelt across
wind beats the field
without mercy.
Like water bumbling
over a rough gravel road
Cascades across...
the wind whips and snakes
through.
In synchronized time
the field is waving
like helpless silk.

Farewell Daddy
by Raycendia Howell - age 14

You were here but now you're gone,
in our hearts your name will
carry on.
In my heart you shall not die,
in a peaceful sleep you lie.
Death is a gateway we all
must pass through
to make our souls become anew.
All of our friends and loved ones
who patiently wait.
On deaths other side to open
the gate,
to welcome you home where
you belong,
angles wait to play you a
beautiful song.
You are free to do as you please,
you can flow freely among
the breeze.
Though I wished we would never
part,
I'll keep you alive in my heart.
But for now I'll just pray,
that we'll meet again
one sweet day.

Death
by Cassandra Hubbard - age 13

It can't really be explained, A sadness, happiness,
 being mad, and unbelievable when it happens

It feels as if someone is stabbing you in the heart

Everyone around you is affected

Kind of like a cold, dark, still night with nothing
 around but black silence

You can cry and try to forget, but the thought of one
 certain little thing leads you to think about the horrid
 scene

The scene of a loved one so close yet so far away

The Creature Within
by Holly Michelle Hudnell - age 13

The creature awoke with a scream
Only to see the end in a dream
The blade so warm
As it tore in to the creatures arm
A sound like a jolt of lighten
As the creature fell with the tightening
The hart exposed to the world
The only sound was the praising of the Lord
The chore now done
As the deer dance in the sun

The Aisle of Life
by Joseph Hughes - age 16

In my dreams, I walk down the aisle of life,
There's a girl next to me, It is my wife,
I look at her, she's a blond beauty,
She's a world league cutie.

As I reach the end of the aisle,
My green - eyed beauty looks at me and I smile,
As the minister talks and talks, then he says man and wife,
Now I know I have completed my whole entire life.

I have now got the girl I love,
She is prettier than a dove.
I have now got my family, that's a life,
But I know it all started with marrying my wife.

A Blind Man's Sight
by Corey Hults - age 16

Light is a deceitful creature
A spiteful bane
Blinding our eyes from the candor
Revealing stained purity
Revealing stained reality
It whispers in our ears
It commands us our directions
It exposes all our fears
It molds our wants, our wishes
For beauty and his riches.

The shadows though
They shade our eyes
They do not tell us where to go
And yet we still perceive ourselves,
    and others
they block our fastidiousness against our brothers
They give no lies to believe in
Set to the side
Are the lusts for fortune,
But ask the blind and they may warn
"Even a bed of roses has thorns."

Growing Young
by T. Hunter - age 16

I'm an old lady sitting here,
Remembering times I hold so dear,
Once again I'm there with you,
Sharing a candle lit dinner for two.
I'm staring at you, lost in your eyes.
Savoring a partnership untouched by lies.
Later in life you gave me your love,
I gave you children you were so proud of.
Then you got sick and slowly died,
I wanted to go, for so long I cried.
Then I remembered words you had said,
You smiled weakly and raised your head.
"I love you always, I'll wait for you,
But don't give up, live your life true."
It was a year ago I decided to live,
Remembering how much I had left to give.

Smiling I make my brittle bones stand,
Picturing you still holding my hand.
Laughing at my foolish tongue,
Ever grateful that I am still growing young.

"Why?"
by Leslie Hunt - age 14

You said you loved me,
I wish you were for real
Every time I would see you there would be,
This warm feeling I would feel
I see you look at me,
I look in your big brown eyes
You used to call me your baby,
Every time I think about us I cry
Together we are serious, we laugh, we cry,
Why? Tell me why did it happen to us, Why?

Untitled
by Robin Huntley

Muddled memories of
blue water and sky
overlapping
a green lawn.
My mother in a big silly hat with white feathers
and cat-eyed sunglasses over
elegant white skin, red lips
lounging poolside under an umbrella.
Looking up out of the blue water,
reflecting sun,
I hear
overlapping
clinking ice
splashing water   casual lilting giggles
and then the smell of bourbon on my grandfathers laughter
as he leans to pull me blue lipped, shriveled,
shivering out of the pool
into a big warm towel
to eat little wieners in BBQ cocktail sauce.

My Friend
by Ka'ai Hussey

Someone to talk to,
Who will always be there,
will never betray you,
and will always care.

Someone to confide in,
who will help you along the way,
a shoulder to cry on,
and won't give your secrets away.

He makes you laugh,
when you seem down.
He's one of the best friends,
that I have found.

I tell him my secrets,
He keeps them inside.From him,
I have nothing to hide.

He is my friend,
nothing more, nothing less.
I will never keep anything,
From my friend.

Rapist
by Carolyn Hutcheson

Terror!
Dark and deep
pervades 'neath
layers of
restless sleep;
Will I ever forget
cold eyes
and brutal sounds?
Ravished flesh
and bound hands
I cannot speak,
bruised mouth
spread-eagled feet:
Ugly man
pity denied
"Why?" I asked
with a haunted cry
"Because I could."
Was his cruel reply.

My Last Tear
by Aimee E. Hutchinson

My last tear is but a raindrop that is falling from my eye,
I try to look right through it but "not today" I sigh.
For today I feel the pain of all the months before,
When nothing but a tear had opened up my door.
The door to my heart where no one had the key,
When I was all but happy and no one cared to see.
"Come inside" I ask "but don't stay too long",
For the only thing I sing is a sad, sad song.
I don't want to depress you or hurt you in any way,
"Hello" and "I love you" is all I want to say.
Come in and let me speak these four words to you,
So I can stop my eyes form weeping tears of dew.
My last tear is but a raindrop that has fallen from my eye,
But when I looked right through it, it was your turn to cry.

To A Departing Friend
by Nhuloan Le Huynh - age 16

The winds blow from east to west,
And I see you less.
Each day goes by,
And in the end, we must say good bye.
Juliet did say, parting is such sweet sorrow.
Oh, how I wish never will it be morrow.

But when you are gone, the past I'll see,
And remember that night,
The one where we danced under the light.
You held me in your arms
I was knocked over by your charms.

I would see you around
And wonder, when you are college bound,
Would you remember this little friend
For she will hope of a card to be send.
If there are no words from you
My eyes will be moist, and my heart shall ache too.

Slowly, yet eventually my heart will heal;
That hole inside will seal.
On with life I will go;
But just to let you know,
The friendship that we share
In my heart, it will forever be there.

Rose
by Gerald T. Hylla

Each year I begin over
Trying to out do the last
Hoping, out searching to be better

Knowing what I have to face
Not letting it stop me
Spreading my arms to grasp more

Knowledge feeds me as I grow
Petals form and arise out
Time to open up, and show what I hide
My bud, must not stay closed

Although the darkness comforts
The light can be warming
It can aid in my growth

Thirst I seem to be in a drought
Looking for the overflowing river
Shall it ever be found

Will I ever be able to bloom
A new year was here so soon
So much though before noon

Love
by Katie Ingalls - age 15

The sky is royal blue, and
I'm falling in love so true

I have fallen in love so
Deep
I can't even find a way to
Sleep

I still have a whole heart
But no more
Love to fill a cart

Of course love is blind,
And I have left my eyes
Behind

There is no more sorrow
So don't even spoil
Tomorrow

Today is leading a brand
New way
So wipe all the tears away
And begin a new day.

Best Friends
by Keely Ivy - age 14

You know you can always lean on me,
I know we can make it through,
We'll be together to pass the time,
Will you be there so I can lean on you?

I promise I'll always be there,
You can trust me without a doubt,
Even in the worst of your troubles,
I'll be there to help you out.

We'll always be inseparable
We will go and do everything together,
I know you as well as myself,
Cause we're best friends forever.

Panic
by Rachelle Hilgendorf - age 13

what's that? I heard a yelp!
Oh, why won't someone come to help?
Oh no, it's too dark to see!
Oh, why did this happen to me?
Help! Did you see that spot?
Maybe it's a monster's tot.
On boy! Did you gear that rumble?
Maybe its a avalanche tumble.
Oooh! It's getting louder!
I'm just sure I'm going to be chowder!
Mercy! Too bad it's not tame.
Oh, never mind, it's just a rescue plane.
Oh boy! I'm gonna get it from mom.
Oh well, I had better get on.
Oh yes, you can pull up the line.
What? Oh yes, I'm just fine.
Hmmm? What did you say? Did I panic?
Did I shiver and jot?
Me? Panic? Of course not!

If
by Jenetra Jackson - age 16

If only I had things she had...
(sighs)
I could just imagine what my world be like.

If only I had a clear complexion,
then I wouldn't be so ashamed at being in public.

If only my teeth weren't so yellow,
I'd feel more comfortable smiling.

If only I just had a pretty face...
then I wouldn't have to worry about the boys running from me. I'd have
to run from them from all the attention I'd be getting.

If only I had longer hair,
then I'd no longer have to wear a weave and I wouldn't get comments
like "Mr. ED misses his tail" or "You stole Mr. Ed's tail."

If only I had name brand clothes,
I'd get comments and have more friends, popular friends.

If I only had bigger breast,
I could step up from a size A and not have to worry about my chest
being just as flat as
my male classmates.

If only I had long hairless legs,
I would be so proud to show them off and I'd wear shorts and skirts all
the time.

If only I wasn't so bow-legged,
then people wouldn't mimic the way I walk and they wouldn't tell me
things like "you
walk like a duck!"

If only I just had a better body...
I would be just like her.

Someone To Care
by Tiffany Janes - age 15

Love
Love is just a feeling
Pure as the white of a dove
Someday you feel like singing
Others you just want to die
You open the door hoping it's him
Friends drop by to say Hi
But he never comes..it's just Kim

He'll break your heart
He tells you he loves you
After it's over, you wish it had never started
Then you wonder if all he told you is true
He says he wants to marry
He even buys a ring
Then he meets Carry
After you sit and listen to other people's hearts sing

Love
It's not fair
It's a gift to be able to love someone from heaven above
You want someone to be there
Do you really dare..
To care about someone who's not really there?
You need someone that's there
You need...Someone to care.

The Lord of Storms
by Claudel Jazon

Hath I hath known thee Hector saith Zeus, love
thouself. Though I hath standed before thee.
Then Heracles faileth his duty, "glove"
brought forth his magnificence skill and be
merry with his family. Then lost all
by misguided, through his cherish nature.
Then his mother gave her view point, in fall.
So doing, said, "dost thou be glad, nurture
his son, done by Hera. I hath shared mine
"Love of birth". Then Zeus angrily prove not
this approval, chase Heracles; find fine
gold from his duty inlife; peer as hot
summer's day. Rose canth be find as good cheer...
Though repair thou climax, all shall be dear
to thouself as well as thou family as
them came days of war. When one shall leave as
their destiny is shocked, thou hast known;
the war again the ally, Mars greatly talk
to all Warriors, upon which they hath grown,
mature themselves as an aunt straighten walk.
Therefore they were not happy of given
their fair share in life of consciousness...
For beauty concerneth the gods' burden
which gaveth token to all happiness.
Then Zeus talking at Heracles, its son
gave seniority to improve their world.
From this shall they understand what's upon
their head "weight" much more from this amaze fold.
For mankind shall keep track of their kindness!...
Thus spread thou good "cheer" to the gods' goodness...

Remember
by William L.C. Jefferies - age 17

One year ago last Saturday my life was changed forever.

But some days I can't remember why,
others -- clear as it just happened.
Some days I think the change was good; others not.
Some days I need to lie to myself to keep on going,
others it's like cruise control.

In time perhaps, it will be just another day --
last Saturday one year ago.
In time, perhaps I will not count the days,
nor recall what ever happened.

Today I recall.

Today I know.

I grow inside; an view the world differently than in the past.
As I grow older; and struggle to stay young.
I ponder why things happen -- for a reason I suppose.
Though I know not of that reason.

Grip the child in me; and fear the coming of every new day.

Some good comes out of all things.
This being true, some bad must also.
On last Saturday, one year ago, I can't seem to separate the tow.

Take the good from all experience; leave the rest.
Learn from everything.
But on last Saturday one year ago,
I take both and can not learn -- I can only remember.

And just why I remember -- I can't quite say.
I just know, deep down, I will never forget that day.

Deer Valley Road
by William L.C. Jefferies - age 17

Here's to old men, and their dads,
as they sit and talk of yesteryear, sip some root beer
on the porch. The circle is complete.

Here's to the foolish arguments of when and where
and in reality it doesn't matter,
neither one cares for some reason.
Talk of golf courses and airports.

Here's to men teaching their sons.
To ride a bike, fly a kite, shoot a rifle.
Here's to sunday afternoon drives; and first drives.
Here's to back country roads where all this is true.

There is a lot to be said for those country roads,
there is a lot to be said for men,
and here's to them.
The generations.

*Dedicated to L.C. Senior, L.C. Junior
and all Jefferies men past, present and future.*

Death
by Nicole Jeffries - age 14

Dear sweet child of mine
I love you
But I will not be here much longer
No do not weep
Death is upon me
From the very day we are born we are dying
But some leave before others, because we
all arrive at the same time
So be patient
We will be together again someday
In a way I will always be with you

Her Past Is My Present
by Jeremy Thomas - age 20

Helpless I felt,
From the pain I had chosen.
Her eyes makes me melt,
Her skin keeps me frozen.

Withdrawn from my fire,
Scarred by her rain.
I want her desire
To love me insane.

Disturbed by the night,
I tried to defend her.
Her beauty...I fight,
But quickly surrender.

Drowned by her river,
I tried to defy it.
My secrets, I'll give her,
To touch me so quiet.

Questioned by lust,
My thoughts had to leave me.
Her memories, I trust,
Will never deceive me.

Frightened to fear it,
Her skies seemed so pleasant.
Her ghost is my spirit,
Her past is my present.

Like The Sun
by Melissa Jessup - age 15

Like the sun, you put up a show.
You light my world,
Let me know that everything
is going to be alright.
But then, all too soon, you'll
be gone.
Taking your bright love with you.
Leaving me in the dark,
Cold and lonely.
But I never fret because I know
you'll always come back
After you've had your share of
fun with someone else.
As much as I need you
I always find myself a bit
relieved to feel the softer, smoother
light of the freedom your roaming
brings.
Just the same, I tend to feel
safer,
And possible more whole,
when I am again surrounded
by your warm light.
Just like the sun.

A Ticking Heart
by Mathew T. Jett

His heart ticking with the rhythm of the clock,
One moves ahead while the other enjoys the moment;

Holding her now,
Releasing her later;

Minutes or days,
Boundaries of time are unfamiliar to a breaking heart.

Broken Promises
by Toni Johnson - age 14

You promised that you would love me,
For the rest of your life.
You swore that you would stay with me,
And someday make me your wife.

You said there wasn't anyone else,
That I was the only one.
You made me believe I was special,
But now we're done.

You broke all your promises,
You turned away from a love so true.
You left me all alone;
I thought I loved you.

Now you have a new love
To replace me,
But I haven't been down,
As you will see.

Someone new will come along
And take your place in my heart,
And hopefully,
He'll know how to play the part.

Seasons
by Jennifer Johnson - age 13

She has bright blue eyes,
And when she cries
Down from the skies
Her tears fall to all

At springs end
Around the bend
We'll meet her friend
And she will not cry.

She shines a smile down
That wraps us in a gown
She wears a golden crown
That makes our heat go still

On and on it goes
How long no one knows
They only have two foes
Who are cold and cruel

First comes the fall
Who warns us all
Then he will call
To his even colder friend

His friend is not so kind
He runs up behind
And tries to bind
Us to him with his cold

Love
by B.J. Jones - age 14

Beautiful is love,
just like a white dove.
Love soars through the air,
just to prove to you how much it cares.
Love can be sweet,
just to make your heart skip a beat.
Love is gentle and kind,
just don't waste it on a dumb mind.
Love can be crazy,
just to make your mind all hazy.
Love was made for me and you,
just because I love you, too!

Come
by Julienne Johnson

Come
To the beach
With me
We'll run
We'll catch the sea
In pink 'n silver shells
We collect in buckets
With hands
That brush sand
Off each others shoulders
Then
We'll rest
I'll kiss
The salt off your face
Your mouth
Your tongue
Till
The taste of my lips
Beg you
Take me
To another place

To The People of Oklahoma
by Alma LaRocque Jones

May God bless you all
in your hour of need,
and may you find comfort
from your prayers.
Reach out to one another.
Don't be afraid
to express your woes.

But know, although exceptionally
hard to do at this time,
that there is a reason -
(perhaps to be revealed) -
for everything that happens
that brings about such grief.

May we never forget
the terror that we now fear,
but from it also learn,
never to take life for granted
and to move forward
to make this life a better place
for all people, young and old alike.

Just A Kid
by Stephanie Jones - age 13

I can't write
a poem today.
I think I'd rather
go out to play.
Will you please
let me go?
Because today
I'm full of woe.
I'd enjoy it
if you did,
After all--
I'm just a kid!

Gods Hand
by Gene Jones

I can see Gods hand in everything
Sometimes I can feel it to
It rest upon every being
I feel it in everything I do

Gods hand keeps me very sure
It helps me do my task
It keeps my life rich and pure
It gives an answer to all I ask

Gods hand is with me all the time
It stays with me my whole life through
It guides me to the life sublime
It gives me courage when I am blue

Gods hand will never forsake me
It helps me do the thing I planned
It keeps my life from sin set free
When I feel a tug on my life I know that it's Gods hand

Mother Help Me Live
by Nicole Emma Marie Jones - age 13

Mother You're the only one who will ever help me live,
Tonight I lie alone in my bed to die of a broken heart,
Mother, please help me live.

Mama I made a mistake last night
Please tell me what to do
Mama, I never meant to hurt you
Please... Please tell me what to do

I'm dying tonight,
I'm afraid tonight,
Of what is waiting to come,
No live to live,
And no love to love,
Please mother... help me live

One night of passion,
One night of love,
Mother he gave me what you'd call the crud,
Mother I don't know what to call it,
But mother will you help me live it?

Mother my body is fighting the disease that everybody know's as HIV

"Al's Dragon"
by Nancy A. Jones

Do you remember when we first met, I like to think that you do.
And all the beautiful sunrises and glorious sunsets.
These were to be our golden years. but now their only filled with sorrow.
Al's dragon has set his sights on you, robbing us of
the years that was to be.
And the memories of those that you have had.
Do you recall the star fish on the beach or the walks in the
warm spring rain.
What about the night you asked me to share your life.
I can not change what we must face my love.
But by your side I will remain and in my eyes you will always
be the man of twenty-three.
You have been my friend and my love since I was a young girl.
I never imagined it would end this way.
It hurts me to know all that you were, all that you could have
been has slowly slipped away.
I know soon you will be gone.
I hold your hand as the end draws near, my eyes fill with tears
as I look into your's and wonder do you even remember me.

Mirror, Mirror, on the Wall
by Rachel Jones

"Mirror, mirror, on the wall,
Who's the fairest of them all?"
"You are, of course," the mirror obeys,
Despite the sin your heart portrays.
With an evil eye,
And a wicked glare,
You powder your nose,
And you comb your hair.
You go about, day by day,
Still thinking of what the mirror portrays.
But you don't know the truth that lays,
Beyond the spell the mirror obeys.

Free to Go
by Rachel Jones

You're free to go,
The bell has rung.
Why do you look so
Lonesome?
Has someone broke your heart
Or is it just so far away.
If you need to talk
I'll be here all day.
It will eventually be okay.
The girl was crying,
I not knowing why.
Like a loved one dying
Punctured in the heart.
She said, "I know I'll need you,
So please be there.
You're all the hope I have,
No one else will care."
With that she left,
And managed a smile.
Went to her next class,
And was happy for a while.

The End
by Rachel Jones

A burst through the sky,
A flicker and then...Nothing.
Wait! There it is.
A comet. A tail.
Super-novas bursting everywhere.
The destruction of the Universe,
The awareness of it all.
The flowing balls of fire
Answering the Devil's call.
Wishing, wanting
To already be dead.
To not to have to notice the flames overhead.
The screeching of a cat
With fire on its tail,
Clawed at my feet,
And ran with a glare.
Running for cover,
Fending for my own,
Disregarding others
More easily overthrown.
Stars all alight,
People dying all around
Earthquakes and rumbles
Making tremulous sounds
As the earth crumbles.
The chariots of fire
Coming down for the Christians
Forgetting the rest, (it was in their restrictions).
Volcanoes erupting, Panic everywhere.
I should have known sooner
God always keeps a dare.

Fairies
by Bonnie Luna

Fluttering, floating
Gliding and whirling,
sparkling up in the sky.
Not to believe
Not able to conceive
Their dust
Their magic
Not I.

Strange Mirror
by Vishnu P. Joshi

Strange mirror,
From cradle to the grave
You relentlessly follow every living being.

Birds twitter, flowers smile, and humans love;
The Spring stands in front of you.

Animals sob, trees shed their leaves with a sigh, and
Humans begin to hate each other;
The Autumn is reflected.

Dawn emerges from the East, and
Night disappears in the West;
Dusk is reflected, and the day disappears.

Sometimes as a beggar or a King
A human soul stands in front of you, and
Its reflection is caught in your belly.

A weeping child comes out,
With a smile and infinite hope
It stands in front of you;

A wrinkled image of incorrigible pride and
Unrepentant humility is reflected;
Like the Czar of Russia it crumbles to dust.

To Believe In Jesus
by Joy Joy Joy

To believe in Jesus
Is to believe in Love.
Love is Jesus order!
Love others!

To believe in Jesus
Is to believe in Love.
Love is Jesus morality!
Help others!

To believe in Jesus
Is to believe in Love.
Love is Jesus teaching form Gospels!
Respect others!
Honor others!

Our Magnificent Adventure
by Estelle Kaczenas

we started out with honesty and trust
    not much else--
we let it grow at its own rate--
    was it fate?

we learned to smile and open up
    not be afraid--
we began to laugh and just be silly--
    willy-nilly.

we plumbed the depths of each other's soul
    without a role--
we found a kindred spirit hidden
    exposed, unbidden

The Legend of the Eagle
by Cristal Kahles - age 14

In the frosty mountains of Tennessee,
Just before the dawn,
An eagle plans her strategy
While awaiting a ray of the sun.

Firmly clutching here claws in an amber branch,
She looks down on the clear, sparkling water.
There in the steam, it happens by chance
That her prey appears dancing before her.

Releasing herself, she soars into flight
Screaming, as she races to seize him.
With the wings of an angel and all of her might,
She carefully executes determination.

Victoriously rising, she returns to the sky...
Well known for her strength and her grace.
Joyful and confident, she holds her head high!
As she, in this world, takes her place.

The Breeze
by Matt Kahn - age 19

The wind creeps softly through the swaying trees.
To mix with the pine needles scent and make a breeze.
Will it stop to rest in the shade?
Will it go where the ducks wade?
Will it end up where the kid's games are played?
Maybe it would rise, would that be the best?
Ascending higher than the highest bird nest.
Looming through clouds-so cottony white,
Combing the perimeter with all its might.
Will it go with other breezes; that might be a shot?
Not knowing where others are doesn't help me a lot,
To tell you the truth, I honestly forgot.

Unborn Child
by Susan Kalican

Unborn child, forever sweet warm and mild
Upon whom no one has ever smiled.
A life so short, it never was
And only for the word because.

Because your existence we didn't plan
You will be neither woman or man.
Because I was too young, all told,
You'll have no opportunity to grow old.
Because he simply turned and walked away
You have no chance to leave or stay.
Because poverty was a step too near
Your first baby cries no one did hear.

But just because you were never born
And never woke one single morn
Imagine not you didn't live or did depart
You'll live forever in the cemetery of my heart.

Sorry
by Amy Kalil - age 20

I let it all happen   with an inside smile
I did everything
And now I sit and watch
with an unmoving motion   I never had
the hovering flame   bobbing and swaying a sea sickness
It does everything
for my eyes   a blinking without losing focus
burning the wax
And now I sit and feel
dripping down
blood lapping around my crossed ankles   shackles of liquid
no life jacket needed to float   naked to no one
only earth   disintegrating fabric
fades away peeling   wrists slicing   apples to the core
And now I sit and hear
ground suck the seed bare   in the garden
not cared for   I did not care   giving
into sleep   water rising to my neckline   in the sink
I do not know   the color   the sound   the words
you spoke   print in the book
the feathers shadows   bend at the corner in the wall
I crouched in once
And now I sit and never respond
apologies   thrown out to the crowd   candy
a parade   I reigned over   content   stomped on
I let it all happen   with an inside smile
I do nothing

Paint a Picture Called Beauty
by Jason Kallas - age 17

If I had to paint a picture called "Beauty",
I would say it can't be done;
For such an abstract term can not be
Identified by the sight of human eyes nor
Determined by the study of human mind.
It would have to be of the most pin point account;
For beauty must be unlike anything man has ever truly
Experienced, witnessed, sensed, or touched.
How could I paint a picture called "Beauty",
My talent does not even match to the beauty of ugliness
Let alone the power and might of true splendor
So that my painting could be entitled "Beauty"
Sweeter than the sweetest red rose,
More majestic than the most majestic sunrise,
More powerful than the most powerful mountain,
Softer than the softest candlelight,
More colorful than the most colorful kaleidoscope,
More precious than the most precious emerald,
More special than the most special gift beauty must be too.
If I had to paint a picture called "Beauty,"
I would simply paint a picture of you.

here
by Josef Karst

being disrupted
by the first autumn storms
asked my father where I was going
nowhere he replied
and things will turn away from you
but society will be your enemy
the reality even
a better lover you need to become
my father said
good fellows love longer
learning the ambitions of the handsome
learning English, I told my father
you will leave with the storm
my father said
you on your no-ways
maybe that was our final talk

Entering America
by Josef Karst

This reminds me of the beginning of a Triathalon.
Athletes running their brains off,
wile treading muddy water,
Jerks biking the scientific way
while I wonder how to explain the commercial side
of their obscene qualities.
What do I say?
Being a part of the daily values,
being disrupted by life,
and starting a fire with pure legacy.
I remember being on an airplane
right above New York City at night.
But the lights never ended.
There was no such thing as darkness at night.
Controlled by power plants far outside
a little crim feeling I had in my stomach.
It seemed there was no end to things.
I remember James Thurber.
And probably the only reason to return
was the story of "The Wonderful O."

Who I Am
by Julie Kaup - age 20

I look up in the blue pallet they call the sky
where the little white clouds dance,
where my dreams are.

I look up into the beautiful picture
where the sun shines,
where my eyes are blinded
from my dreams.

I look up into the night sky
where the stars twinkle,
where each dream becomes
clear as I make my wish.

I look up into the midnight blue
where the man in the moon
smiles his grand smile,
where my destiny lies.

I look down to my heart
where my life is, where my love is.

I look down deeper to my soul
where my faith is, where I believe in myself.

I look straight ahead in the mirror
where my body is,
where my expressions reflect.

Where I really am, who I really am
is all around me.

See the stars in my eyes.
See the sun in my smile.
See the love in my heart.
See the faith in my soul.
See the beauty in my body.

This is who I am.

Letting Go
by Becca Keen - age 14

I never felt so healthy than while I was with you. Your caring touch, security, and comfort always helped me through.

I never thought I could live without you. I've cried a river of tears, since you aren't a part of my life, only emptiness is here.

Though within our hearts the moments we've shared will never depart, time has sadly come between us as we drift apart.

The day has come upon us; now there is anguish and grief. You were my light and smile to guide me through the rain.

I want to hold you close and never let you go. You're gone from me forever, and this I truly know. Your voice, smile, and laughter I'll never hear again.

I have to say goodbye though it breaks my heart. I give my last regrets then you spread your wings and fly. You may be gone in reality, but in my heart you'll never die.

Faith My friend
by Alice B. Kell

Faith precedes the miracle
Repeat the Love of God
Take care of God's possessions
Take the road that Christ has trod
Lead us to our Father's throne
And cause us to listen there
Be the correction of my life
Filled with peace and prayer
Teach by your won example
To be a "Specialist of Truth"
Prepare your sons and daughters
To follow Christ through youth
And when they reach maturity
No downfall will they know
Because Christ will protect us
Everywhere we go
Say Yes to all God's promises
That they may all come true
He'll bring you peace and happiness
In all you seek to do.

Parents
by Harry E. Keller

Parents, those precious wonderful people we could never do without.

We may survive on our own, but from time to time it's great to know all we need to do is call them on the phone.

They are always there to hear our plea and help us in our time of need, they show their love in their unselfish acts indeed!

We may not always like what they say but we know they have our best interest at heart in every way.

So listen carefully to what they say or a heavy price we may have to pay!

Learn well the lessons they teach and your highest goal can be within your reach.

Love, Honer, Obey, that should always be our order of the day.

When their final hours on Earth have come and they are gone, We must remember the wisdom they taught us to carry on.

I desired to but I didn't
by Darlene Kelley

As you stood so close to me,
I could have touched your hand,
I desired to
but I didn't.

You brushed against me
and your presence thrilled me
I desired to kiss you
but I didn't

My spirit walked with yours
Our hearts merged as one
I desired to hold you
but I didn't

Your laughter have me joy.
My feelings were deep waters.
I desired to whisper' I love you'
but I didn't

When you left, my heart was broken
Inside were words, never spoken
I wish I had told you,
but I didn't

Take Some Time
by Darlene Kelley

When you're feeling weary
and you don't know what to do

Your day seems so dreary
and you're tired of feeling blue

When everythings gone wrong
and you're plum tuckerd out

The kids are now in bed
after driving you to shout

Sit down and kick your shoes off
don't worry bout the time

Then lift your heart to Jesus
take a load off of your mind

Oh, this world is full of trouble
and it can be full of woe

So many times it seems
we're fretting here below

But God who always see's
what;s hidden in the dark

Will always see inside
your lost an lonely heart

When it seems as though
the Lord is far away

Take some time to listen
and take some time to pray

For God will surely speak
to a heart in tune to him

Your day will be much brighter
and the "Son" does not grow dim

Whispers

I Am A Soldier
by Darlene Kelley

I am a soldier in the army of God
with the gospel of peace, my feet are shod.

I do not fight in a far distant land,
yet my enemies are real and on every hand.

A war invisible that natural eyes can't see
yet a battle so real, though some disbelieve.

A fight for the lost and castaway souls
that demons from hell reach out for below.

With honesty and truth are my loins gird about.
I go into battle with God's word in my mouth.

Upon my breast, there sets a gold plate.
the righteousness of Jesus, is the word it states.

My shield of faith stands tried and true.
many attacks of the enemy, it brought me through.

Jesus, my captain always hears my cry,
and when I am wounded, he won't let me die.

He binds me up and stands me tall.
he gives me strength that I will not fall.

With his spirit to guide me, I began again.
my enemy is defeated in His Holy Name.

With God on my side I know I will win!!
the saints of his glory, he will always defend!

One day I won't have no battle anymore
I'LL stand with my captain on a distant shore.

No more enemies will I have to face.
I'LL be with my captain in a peaceful place.

I'LL not have to use any weapons of war.
I will finally have rest as I dwell with my LORD

Life
by Amy L. Kelly - age 19

Life's full of sorrows,
   It's full of tears.
Life's full of confusion,
   It's full of fears.
The days that die,
   How fast they pass.
Leaving us with nights,
   So dark, so vast.
The creeping shadows all around,
   Remind us of hard times that we are bound.
No one can escape,
   No person can hide,
From life's strong grasp,
   From it's lonely ride.
Life waits outside our doors,
   Pulling with its intense force.
Pulling us onto our path,
   Onto our eternal course.
Memories left behind,
   Into ghostly images they turn.
Life puts them in its fire,
   Just to see if they'll burn.
Turning around, only ashes we see,
   The ashes left behind, that can never again be.

Toy Soldiers
by Rex Kelly

I have written perhaps,
or listened in silence --
To the tale of a single toy soldier,
Never asking his name,
      Nor of the smile on his face --
I simply watched his march
      from a distance -
As I grew older.

How simple it seemed -
Eyes forward,
One foot and then the other.

I watched myself bleed -
Run,
      Stumble and crawl;
Trying to make sense and hold order.
I reached out from within
      This man -
To grasp -- yet not a hand,
Only the cold carving of a single toy soldier.
How simple it seemed,
      I pulled --
                    but he fell.
A cipher, forgotten, my magnificent armor.
The sun bleached his red cheeks to pale,
The rain had swollen his petrified shell,
And the wind turned to dust,
      My false figure.

Shortcutters
by Bruce Nassiri Kermane

In the campus yard somewhere
where no lanes should be,
a crooked way across the lawn,
like a rumpled ribbon
across a careless wrapping drawn,
is shaped upon the grass;
an easy way
for shortcutters to pass.

When they are late to class,
the learners back and forth
often cut across the turf,
and walk as if
there is no blame;
the grass of course
having no claim.

I would not dare have been
the first to crush a caustic way;
not that I am deferential to green
nor that I haven't trampled much,
for I have hastened over things
in other places, with other means
in places where I would not be seen
and where
I'd leave
no footprints.

Missing You
by Zarina Khan - age 16

On a cold, grey November day,
I suddenly felt lonely, my mind gone astray.
I wondered again why in all this time,
I've never had anyone whom I could call mine.

I longed for someone perfect for me,
Someone to carve my name on a tree.
The night we first met, I knew it was you,
For my heart was filled with love so true.

I approached you the first chance I got,
The sparks that were flying were burning so hot.
So hot, indeed, it burned all away,
Along with the car crash I see day after day.

You said you'd never leave me,
You said you'd always be there.
And now when my heart cries for you,
I can't find you anywhere.

I know you are with me, although out of sight,
And I wish I could hold you in my arms, so tight.
I know you're gone forever, it's true,
I just want you to know I'll always love you.

Winter
by Ashely Killingsworth - Age 14

As the rain pounds down on the ground
Children run round and round
The foggy, misty air becomes very damp in our hair
While all the trees are bare.

Dark, gloomy clouds that are ready to burst
Will supply the fields with much needed thirst
The sun will lay down for a long rest
And will come out when it feels best.

As the snow falls, we sit at our window and admire
While we snuggle up to a nice, warm fire
All bundled up in our coats and hats
We wait for the sun to peak out of the cracks.

Ben
by Megan King

How could you not notice
How could you not care
The way I feel for you
The way I always stare
My friends say I'm readable
But you do not see
While you look at other girls
You've long forgotten me
When you call me from across the room
My heart goes wild
And skips a beat
Your soul within I know is mild
And deep with my heart of hearts
For you are so kind
I know you think
That I want you just as a friend
But I want even more
And I'll love you 'till the end

To Janet, My Beautiful Sister
by Elaine Ki Jin Kim - age 17

All I can see with my ruined eyes
Is a brilliant white blur, between the tall stalks of green grass,
Moving down--up--down--down--
To the rhythm of a whispering sob so quiet so only a God may hear,
But you must know by now,
Miracles never happen to those who deserve them most.

Yes, I am sorry
For hating you,
For hating that you are me but just brighter, just taller,
just prettier, just more,
For yelling that I hate you and that you ruin my life, that you are worth nothing and that
We are not and never will be sisters.

So now you grab bundles of green grass and pull them up by the handfuls,
by the handfuls,
Screaming words unintelligible to me, as they have always been.
So now you stand and step twice closer to the cliff's edge,
Struggling, I know, between walking for your sake or for mine.

So now I pluck just one perfect blade of grass from its root
And tie a knot over and over, at the same place, at the same place,
Until it is the bird I used to draw in kindergarten class-- a circle caught between two waves.
And I hurl it out of my hands, and it floats gently, so gently over the rock.

For yes, you have always been a bird and where you fly has always been up to me.

Untitled
by Deb Kulla

Two hears intertwined,
linked together.

Thoughts flourish of the other
whether apart or together.

True love knows no bounds,
always destined to be together, forever.

Two hearts intertwined.

Courage
by Joumana King - age 12

If there's a line you should not cross,
for danger lies ahead,
you take your chance and step across,
not knowing what's ahead.

You see where guns have torn the earth,
and crying lies ahead,
You come across where blood has shed,
but instead of crying you move ahead.

Because of your pride you move ahead;
You show no fear.
You come across whining children,
but still you move ahead.

But then you come to death,
where there is no hiding place.
Instead of moving ahead, you forget your pride,
You realize the courage was not in the fight,
it was always in making the peace.

Soul Ease
by Jason Kirkendoll - age 16

       Go to sleep now,
Your body must take refuge.
Prepare yourself for the coming days of strife.
The rocky canyons you pass to find the one.
            waiting on the other side.
She has made the journey as well, perfectly joined.
      Meet in the garden, lined with vines of
roses and daisies.
Both beautiful, in simplicity and complexity of beauty.
            Drink of the fountain
Pure water flows forth from the mouth of the rose.
           Drink, to cleanse and clarify the mind,
To open your eyes.
See now, live now.

A Love Lost In Time
by Suzanne Kiss - age 20

Inside your arms long while ago
I tried and could not tear away
all night in rapture we would know
Apollo in his lighted day

Yet al at once Time's hand took reign
and still it was too soon
to lost such sweet enchanted pain
abashed and dazed I asked the moon

May this tepid love release
breeded lust same soul's desire?
Or shall devoted air increase
to once again a raging fire

Consuming heavens with our love
that long ago fit like a glove.

I Had It All
by Daniel Kolb

I had it all
It was so right
I made myself fall
When everything was at its height
I could not move, I could only stall
My bags remained packed, I prepared for flight
Now I cannot see ahead, only an empty wall
I do not see with open eyes, that is my recurring plight
I seek to go to you, but you must call
Love escapes me, like a wandering drifting kite
I believe in us, it's not yet time to bawl
Life is so beautiful, maybe I'm just an oversight

Grandma Aline
by Shirley J. Klauk

I know you are in Heaven looking over me,
    telling me it will be okay and to let it be.
You understand the tears of pain that I cry
    and wish you could reach out and wipe them dry.

You want me to lift my frown into a smile,
    but you understand it will take me awhile.
I promised I would love you forever and a day,
    you said you would do the same in your own special way.

On December 16th of 1993 the Lord took you home,
    He weeps with me as I miss you and feel alone.
My heart believes that you are still here to care
    but when I reach out to touch you, you are not there.

I want to call to see how you are...
    I know I can't so I wish upon a star.
I wish you warm feelings with grandpa by your side
    as I pick myself up and take life stride by stride.

I can still hear you laugh at a silly joke,
    and when I sneak up behind you and give you a little poke.
Your back is turned and I untie your apron strings,
    you catch it and say that I do funny things.

You left me your favorite locket with grandpa's picture in it
    so I will hang it over your picture as a remembrance.
Oh grandma, I miss you and my eyes swell with tears,
    you are so far away and yet so near.
You are up in Heaven with God as it should be
    but I feel you are here with all of your love around me.

The feeling of love and being loved will never go away.
    So, I will cherish the memories we shared each day.
When God calls my name I will see you again,
    so I will live a full life until it's time to be with Him.

Never
by Fa'aea Letuli-Kujawinski

    Never thought to stop and think the love God gave us here
      never knew how much His love could ever be so clear
      Never stopped to help a soul and think that that's not true
    Never thought to mean and say the love God made was you.

Never realized how much we suffered and still don't take the blame
Never said the love God gave has turned to hate and shame
Never once thought that God was up there listening to me
Unless those words that God has spoke are words that set me free.

People vs. People
by Leah Klick - age 13

All alone
in a world full of hate
people vs people
separated by race.

No one to talk to
no one understands
what if someone's words
fall into the wrong hands?

Judged by our looks
and the color of our skin
someone is always fighting
theres never a way to win.

Is fighting all we can do
can't we get along
people vs people
and everything goes wrong

Out Of Season
by Lee Kolinsky

A flower blossoms.

Pink and pure.
Bold and innocent.

Out of season a flower grows.

Cold and harsh.
Soiled and denied.

The story of being immortal can not be told.
Out of season this flower grows.

A petal falls.

Untitled
by Cassandra Kopp - age 14

That one sweet kiss made me yours
It was never one of my chores
to hold, to kiss, to love you and only you
I always thought you felt it too.
Crying the night we said good-bye
Trying to remember good times, try
We made sweet passionate love to each other
till you were found by another
I'll always miss your love
And pray to the heavens above
One day he will send you back to earth for me
You will always have the key
to my heart, that has always been yours
Even when you shut those doors.

You Are The One
by Beth Korer - age 17

I was walking down the hall in a hopeless daze.
My head was in the clouds, my brain wandered through a maze,
then you came along and gave me the friendship that I needed to
get me
in the groove of things again, you are the one.
The one who gave me strength, hope, and love and now I want to
be
forever
in love with you.
Stay forever in love with me and I will show you what love really
is, I know you've been hurt in the past
but I will not hurt you for I
am sincere,
I really care for you,
YOU ARE THE ONE!

"A Prayer from Jesus"
by Kathy Ann Kramer

We must not forget
the reason we are here
Or how little that he asks of us
as he whispers in our ear...

"go on your way my child
I'll be there if you should fall
I'll be standing right beside you
 if ever you should call
I'll be there when you're happy
I'll be there when you're sad
I'll be there to share the good
 and to find good in what seems bad
I know the road is long
still beside you I will stay
Cherishing the love you send
 in each precious word you pray
give to me your smiles
I long so much to see
Dry your eyes come take my hand
 and place your trust in me
For I see myself within you
I see you as my friend
And I want to share my world with you
For I love you my child."

Anger
by Sydney Lowe - age 19

Brutal thoughts run from her red hair down to her pink cheeks
She knows she cannot change the past
Hostile rings through her brain like doorbell in the night
She knows she has lost all emotional control
Silence makes the fury rage, and nothing can soothe the beast
inside the angry poet

I Don't Know
by Brandi Kuffler - age 15

I don't know what you're thinking,
 Or where you even are.
I don't know who you're sitting with,
 I don't know if you're far.
I don't know why you left me
 To cry away the days.
I don't know why you told me
 That our love would always stay.
I don't know why you let me think
 We'd always be together
Since you used to always tell me
 That you'd be with me forever.
I just know I hate it
 When you're not here with me,
And that I see other people
 When it's you I want to see.
I just know I miss you,
 And all your little flaws
I saw things about you
 Others never saw.
I just know I love you
 And that I always will,
Through eternity and always
 I will love you still.

The Assassin
by Cyriaque Lamar - age 12

Bloodstained knife hand unsheathe,
His work has just begun,
Pondered of, but not believed,
Therefore his work is done.

A Moment In Time
by Jessica Labby - age 15

A moment in time were meant to share;
Nurturing it in hope that it shall grow;
With life before us, our threshold to bare,
We stood untouched by our dark tangled foe.
Unsuspecting and blissful we did see;
Aspirations, dreams, promises were sown.
Carefree life could pass unexpectedly,
Together in harmony we have grown.
Tragic events caused pain unbearable,
Heaven blessed us with forgiveness and grace.
To cope, endure, withstand the terrible,
As earthly longings inhabit this place.
With age withered slowly as a cut rose,
Our lives together eternally froze.

Your Way Lost
by Laura Kuhn - age 15

live in your kingdom roam in your castle
  bathe in your diamonds give your servants hassle.
eat around your emeralds look into your crystals
  sing about your rubies hang your riffles and pistols.

  admire your precious sapphires
shine your gorgeous jades
    talk of kings and queens and such
  busy your footmen and maids.

  call for Sandman when hard to sleep dream of high above clouds
dusty to wait the stardust that falls look up, look down, all around.

to your own, your laugh-a-bout clowns
    and enjoy the jokers of fools
  order Father Time to control the clocks slowly
    take over things only Mother Nature rules.

not too chilly, Jack Frost at job tell Jenny Sprinkles to halt
  reflected is your cruelty in my eyes blame all, you think
    nothing is your fault

  fun make the gnomes and elves order 'round
grow unnatural things in the fields
    throw food and trash into babbling brooks
  never realize what nature you yield.

the air-choked with trash, the sand burnt with sun
    the witches and warlocks that have over-come
      you wait around from your prince charming to come
    don't you realize the damage you've done?

you've killed most the planet with your selfish desire
    you've ruined your friendship with many
you've taught and you've bought and you've lashed your way through
      you have no regrets, don't care any.

  so sit by your windows, your doors and your chambers wait for prince
charming to come but I know you deserve only cold kisses for the horrible
things you have done.

Untitled
by Michelle Kwok - age 17

Take these shattered pieces of me
slice the cover and let it run free
scream louder so no one can hear
patiently waiting to disappear
admit pulsing enmity
losing touch of what's gravity
humid eyes lose track of time
waiting to be stopped by one of your kind
look away from what you perceive
blinding fate disguises what to believe
longing for that growing obsession of sweet, sweet demise

Dying Heart
by Emily Labeck - age 16

I see you with her
And I close my eyes
And everytime a little piece of my heart dies
Dies, tired from calling out to you and getting no answer

I see you kissing her
And pretend it's me
Although I've felt your kiss before
Only in my dreams

When I close my eyes at night
I imagine your arms around me
Holding me tight, keeping me warm
Whispering sweet words in my ear
"I love you" is what I long to hear

At night I cry alone
Alone in the darkness I cry
Everytime a piece of my heart dies

Untitled
by Sarah Laffan - age 13

She has always been there for me
Through all the good times and the bad
She always tries her best to cheer me up
Whenever I am feeling alone and sad

She helped me through so many times,
The tears the pain the fights
I look back remembering all those times
I cried all through the nights.

It was then that she was there for me
Trying so hard to ease my pain
Through all those difficult times,
My love for her would gain.

For all the things she's done for me,
I mean it, that I lover her like a sister,
And how I wish that she'd come back
Because I've really, really missed her.

I've needed her advice on so many things
I'm surprised my life didn't end
One thing's for sure I can't wait to see her
For she is my BEST FRIEND!

What The World Needs
by Dalicia Lafleur - age 16

People label us "Generation X"
Already they have dashed our hope.
As if our whole life is having sex,
Drugs, rock and roll the dope.

I don't think it is fair to blame the youth (although we have choice)
We had to learn from somewhere,
Adults with no responiblity, it's just uncouth.
Everyone needs a role model who really cares.

All young people are not this way,
Some with more responsibility than adults will ever know.
The world needs a kick in the pants, okay?
Top stop using the ole saying.

"These kids today" are different from my day.
It's bogus front, to avoid the problem.
It's doesn't help the world anyway
To pass the buck from person to person.

I'm so sick of people blaming everyone else.
They can't see the forest through all of the trees.
We should look in the mirror, look at ourselves.
Remove the speck from our eyes first.

It seems that parents are afraid of
The actions of their children.
Too afraid to see what their made of.
So they say kids have to "sow their wild oats"

The problem is that too many oats where sown,
They weren't cared about and
Bitter little trees where grown.

It's just so much easier to let it slide
To give excuses and much more.
To give your kids a free ride
Until it's too late to stop the granted you're taken for.

Just Who Are We to Trust?
by Ruth Anne Lamb

As we bowed our head and folded our hands,
No one thought to question these demands.
We prayed, "Our Father Who art in Heaven",
The school day was then started when I was seven.
The Pledge of Allegiance next was said,
As we crossed our heart and raised our head,
This reverence we were expected to pay-
To both God and our country everyday.
So now I wonder how can this be-
The emphasis on politically correct worries me!
It matters not what's right or wrong,
Just so we're "politically correct" and get along.
Principles and values no longer take place
Over what satisfies today's human race.
Everyone's rights must be respected-
Even if God and His principles are rejected.
I don't believe this was meant to be-
When our ancestors fought for equality.
There are times God may not seem fair and just
but without "God" as our motto, just who are we to trust?

A Foolish Man's Tale
by Amanda Lambert - age 15

A foolish man, I heard say today
"I wish there were a couple more hours per day
I'm always so busy doing this and that
there's never any time to just sit, laugh or chat."

How little the faith of the foolish man,
he'll search the world for the freedom that's in the palm of
his hand,

so I asked him, "If you had all the time that you need,
                          what would you do?" I planted the seed.

Yet I asked, "Would you rest? Would you shop? Would you
                      play?"
He said, "No, I'd probably watch T.V. all day."

For this man I pray...

He doesn't understand, that God's gift to us is time,
he'll give us all we need, it's free, doesn't cost a dime.

The foolish man sees loved ones leave,
stands back, and watches them move on,
to a place that's free of stress and fatigue,
to a wonderful place where they're happy and strong,

The reason this man, is left behind,
is to accomplish his goals, by overcoming, the challenges
he'll find,

And when he's scheduled his time right,
and he's sown the seed,
God will give him all the time that he needs.

Autumn
by Rebecca Linsmeier - age 13

Autumn is a time for leaves
crunching; trickling of the stream;
crucnching and crackling of
twigs when you step on them.

Love
by Amanda Lambert - age 18

Love is something you can't control
When you love someone, you just do.
People say, Why him? or Why did you pick her?
But when you love someone, you just do.

There isn't a way to pick or choose
When you love someone, you just do.

Sometimes you meet someone with looks, brains & money
And think, what's not to love?
Well when you don't, everything.
When you love someone, you just do.

There isn't a way to pick or choose
But it doesn't matter
Because when your in love you'll be happy
And that does.

You can't find love,
Love finds you.
And when you love someone, you just do.

Iron Curtain U.S.A.
by Robert Lamb

A prayer is heard for who is in despair
cast out in a place where blood flows
The people are controlled
Caught up in a short radius of life that surrounds them
Maybe a Manchurian Candidate is waiting for them
You would never know
It's the mind that they control
If you speak and words are heard
Ideas soar through minds of many
They've come to make you forget you
It's hidden secrets, I understand exists
Spying on the nation that funds them
Don't bring up rights for they don't know them
They take the unwanted and rid the world of them
A security threat worried them
Some say none of it all exists
It's a leftist idea, that's all it is
Not true at all
It could be one of us who next will fall
and you'll pass through for they pay them too
Covered up, forgotten
and many great men knew the way
and I am in despair today

I Saw You Standing There
by Carrie Landry - age 15

I saw you standing there,
I wanted to go say hello,
But I could not.
You broke my heart in two.
I saw you standing there,
I wanted to hug you once again,
But I could not.
You took a piece of my heart with you.
I saw you standing there,
I wanted you to love me again.
But I am too scared to ask,
You tore my heart.
I saw you standing there,
I wanted you to hold me once again,
But you will never love me, like I loved you,
You shattered my world when you left.
I saw you standing there,
I wanted to tell you just one thing,
But all I could do was repeat in my mind,
I love you, I love you, I loved you.

So Many Years
by Tiffanie LaRocque - age 16

So many years apart
Has ripped open my heart
I have often cried myself to
sleep
And have been too sick to
Even eat
My love grows stronger
Every day
And I long to hold you in
Every way
Now you've finally come back
To give me the love that I lack
Now that the wait is finally
Through
I can fulfill my need for
you.

Goodbye
by Diane Lang

Sometimes you must let got of the past...the memories
Things can't always go back to the way they were
Things must change
change takes a risk
Without the risk a future together can't take place
You can't ride into the future
While holding onto the past
All the apologies in the world
Can't take the place of the hurt that's so deep inside
All the tears I cried
Can't take away the fears you carry inside
All my love can't change the way you feel
Or the decisions you're making
I wish things were different
But they're not
I've finally realized the truth and that the end is near
No more hopes or wishes
I can't bear them anymore
And what I no longer can't accept has become a reality
I wish I could ignore the truth
But it stands right in my face
Too big to push aside anymore
So, as I walk away
I will always know I tried with everything I had
There's no more to give and you have nothing left I can take
I will always hold you close to me
But not close enough to feel the pain
Just enough to know that you once loved me

The End
by Tarah Lankford - age 14

I pick up the bullets and give each one a name
I slide them into the pistol as I'm about to feel my pain
Before I shoot myself I can see the blood fall
And before I even die I can hear the demons call
I hear their rusty voices around me and ringing in my ears
This isn't the first time, they have been calling me for years
I write my suicide letter saying why this is the end
I pick up the pistol and realize it is my only friend
I've hurt so many people, so many people have hurt me
This is what I got to do, this is how it has to be
I know if I do this I'll burn forever in hell
But, I'm hurting so much, my soul I have to sell
I gave my soul to the wrong one, I created the ultimate sin
But, at the time I didn't think, I wanted it all to end
Nobody know how I feel, nobody knows how much I've cried
Nobody knows how much I hurt, nobody will care if I died
After I pull the trigger, I look up at the sky
I'm bleeding so much, the room is spinning, I know I'm going to die
I sold myself short, I took the easy way out
But, I know no one will miss me, I know without a doubt
Now I'm dead forever, I'll never live again
I wish someone was there to stop me from this sin

Untitled
by Stacie Lomas - age 15

What's with the world today?
Nothing is what it seems.
Kids become killers
At the age of thirteen.

But see what the face
On their way to school.
Is it any wonder
They become so selfish and cruel?

So many things are different,
Nothing remains the same.
Everyone points a finger,
But aren't we all to blame?

Graduation
by Dara Rose Larson - age 15

Graduation's here at last
All the years of learning
The time has come and gone so fast
The clock of life keeps turning.

I get my robe and settle down
In a chair by a couple of friends
Though I don't realize it, I'll wish it back
When my time with them ends.

The principal calls us one by one
And one by one we share
The last few moments of the time
We'll spend together there.

He calls my name, I'm really scared,
He shakes my sweaty palm
I grab my diploma and though it's hard
I try to remain calm.

At last it's over, everyone's crying
We say our last goodbyes
Our parents are cheering, applause we're hearing
Teardrops glistening in our eyes.

The Monkey's Cage
by Dara Rose Larson - age 15

People say it's not too late
To save this world of rage
As for me, all I can do
Is feel trapped in my cage.

They are afraid to let us out
For fear that we'll roam around, I guess
They should see us as we are
We'd go back by request.

I have only one friend in
This dark and lonely place
Our moods lift up when we see
The monkey trainer's face.

Our hopes of being let out
Are way too strong to bear
But I don't think they'll let us out
Or that they even care.

This strong feeling will always
Remain inside of me
All they want is money
While we just want to be free.

'73
by Casey T. Law

I walked down the steps
They closed straight with the earth
My nude buttocks gleamed in the sun
I slipped to slide
On splinters and pride
And tumbled upon
A welcome mat
(Held me nailed)
Saved for my nudity
And Bela...
My prickly fruit

Four Years
by Heather Larson - age 15

Four long years we've spent together
Four long years of work and fun
We have shared our troubles
And helped each other
Through good times and bad
We've laughed
We've cried
And been serious too
Four long years
How could it go so fast
Four long years I can't believe they've passed
The hardest word to say
Can you do it
I don't think I can
The hardest word to say
At the end of today
Sadness spreads
Tears fall
And that dreaded word
Is uttered in the halls
I can't say it I won't
But I must, I'm sorry
The hardest words to say
Forever and Always
Good-bye

"Love is a Lie"
by Melissa Maloney - age 13

We had something that no other couple had
We were going to spend the rest of our lives together
We were one
There was a spark that lit my eyes
There was a voice that said, "I love you!"
But it is all gone now for another
And I say now that you will die and then you will
See the light.

Tail Lights
by Isaac Leath - age 16

Tail lights staring cross-eyed in the night.
They are loving, they are seeing,
and able to fight.
Tail lights staring cross-eyed in the night,
They see people paupers they see people kings.
The see people caring, but for the wrong things.
Tail lights staring cross-eyed in the night
They see so much uncertainty, life's not certain.
Each waiting for the other to take a stand.
We all remain fixed at the site.
Tail light staring cross-eyed in the night.
What good is thinking, what good is loving,
what good is seeing, what good is being,
actions are all things. So put up a fight.
Tail lights staring cross-eyed in the night.
They see actions so many actions wasted actions.
They're only acting. They think that's better,
than saying what's right.
Tail lights staring cross-eyed in the night
loving no one seeing nothing, not able to fight.
They've lost all that they've fought for,
all but a single tear.
They've been rejected by their fears.

The Beginning of Wisdom
by Janice Genovia Ledbetter

How many souls can one man win,
Before he's called to glory?
How many falters can one man afford,
if life's to be his story?
How many heartaches can one man endure,
if hope leads safely home?
And how many paths does one must choose,
before right subdues the wrong?

Who gives life, if life is truly given, not chosen?
And who proclaims the rights to it,
when from death one cares not
to be risen?

What is the joy of a child's laughter?
Not knowing the perils to come.
And what spoils the pleasures of humanity?
The birthright of wisdom undone.
How many truths can one find, before spirits
are cogently matched?
And, if the point of it all is happiness,
does happiness every truly last?

How aged are we,
before frivolity is forever spent?
Who reaps the tears of our youth,
and to what cause do we repent?

Sweet Lies
by Veronica Macias - age 15

Men fall in love with their eyes,
Their words are sweet, yet full of lies.
They compliment and flatter you,
But little did you know that they were
untrue.

They make you laugh, they make you
smile,
You hope they'll stay with you a while.
But when it gets old, and new girl
comes around, you're left and you
know that you are bound,
To get your heart broken once
again!

U.S.A. vs. CHINA
by Patricia Lee - age 14

America is my birth home
China is my culture and
heritage.

Both combine to make a part
of me Patricia Lee.

I celebrate Chinese New Year,
but 4th of July explodes with
red, white, and blue fireworks.

Pictures of presidents
in every American history book I
see and learn about.

To this day I can not decide:
Do I live up to my heritage and culture
or my birthplace.

Death
by Janice LeeAnn

It took her, my mother
It will be here soon, to take me
It took her, my sister

They were so beautiful
Why did death take them
They belonged in the world

It should have taken me
It will take me soon
It's on it's way now

I'm scared
I don't want to go
But I can't handle life
So I have to go

Will people even notice?
Will anyone care?
People cared about them!
But will they care about me?

I'll fight death!
Because I don't want to go!
I'll fight it, and win!

Walking In My Wonderland
by Meredith Lee - age 14

There was a time when I met the devil,
    he kept my soul.
Walking out on lakes of fire and then
    I was gone...
    walking in my wonderland.

Years later I met you,
    looked into your eyes and
    I was gone..
    walking in my wonderland.

Now I am going around
    just trying to find the truth.
But it really doesn't matter anyway,
    now that I am living without you and
    my wonderland to walk in.

So I wander to my cliff and
    I come to the edge to look over at my world.
I allow myself to let the tears roll down
What world do I have now?

A Friend Who Was True
by Sarah Maiser - age 17

You are gone
but not forgotten
I will always remember you,
As a friend who was so true.
I will never forget all you did for me,
I am just sorry your death had to be.
I will keep your memory close to my heart,
so in a way we will never be apart.
Not a day goes by when I don't think of you,
Sometimes I even wish I should have gone too.
You were the best friend I could ever ask for,
I just wish your time here could have been more.
It just doesn't seem fair,
How you vanished into thin air.
I will always miss you,
My friend who was so true.

I Love You
by Jeanie Lemons - age 15

I love you,
More than words can say.
The first day I saw you,
It was love at first sight.
Your eyes,
Your smile,
all of these I love.
I love everything about you,
Because you are you.
I count everyday,
That I can hear your voice.
Everyday that you aren't near,
I miss you more and more.
We may not be together yet,
but we will be soon.
Although we'll go through many obstacles,
Our love will bring us together in the end.

A Baby Sleeps
by Patricia V. Leonard

Though earth erupts in cataclysmic fury, spitting forth a blazing heat,
And seas, with rampant waves, ravage a silent shore that can't retreat;
When every man-made terror, holocaust of war, where evil creeps,
At peace and with a trusting heart, a baby sleeps.
Untouched by life, protected by its innocence, free of guile,
With arms outstretched, safe in slumber, upon its lips a smile;
One with God, who's will is still unquestioned, love given love received.
Simple untried love, uncomplicated by lifes cynical age, half believed,
With little faith and trust; half forgotten memories dim.
As more and more we separate ourselves from him,
No more the child who's simple prayer uttered before sleeps descent,
Though whispered, filled the room with peace and rare content,
The simple prayer was heard by God who blessed the child.
And sent soft dreams, not nightmares wild,
That haunt our grown-up world both day and night,
Dreams should end yet these are ever in our sight.
Is all the fear and pain that fills our world, our due?
For getting too complex, letting worldly things cloud our view.
I pray one day with aged wisdom, hard learned,
We utter simple prayers, Love given, Love returned.

When You Feel It's Right And Know It's Wrong
by Brandi Leos - age 16

When you feel it's right
your with the person that
makes you feel that way
You feel secure you feel
wanted you feel comfortable
you feel you know it's right
and most of all you feel
cared for.
And when you know it's not
right, when your away from
the person; you start thinking
straight, you hear people talk
And that's when you know it's
wrong.
Until you meet up with the
person again - and you forget
the wrong, and feel the right.

A Promise To Keep
by Pamela Dawn Lerner

I was living my life
that much is true,
but there was no one special
until I met you.

When you showed up
you made quite an impression,
it would be safe to say
you put an end to my depression.

You didn't play games
or feed me any lines,
the respect you showed me
is the kind that binds.

You made me feel loved
like no one has ever done,
there's no doubt about it
my heart you have won.

I never believed
it could happen to me,
spending my life alone
was how I thought it would be.

You are my soul mate
the love of my life,
and I want you to know
I can't wait to be your wife.

You have given me all of my dreams
and made my heart soar,
so I make this promise to you
I will love you forever more.

Shattered Dreams
by Pamela Dawn Lerner

Life was so perfect
while you were around,
the love of my life
I thought I had found.

You captured my heart
and took hold of my mind,
our love I assumed
would last for all time.

Dreams were shared
and promises were made,
the foundation for our future
had started to be laid.

The ring was bought
and I began to plan,
my fantasy had come true
I had found my dream man.

Our bond grew stronger
with each passing day,
then without notice
you chose to walk away.

My life is in pieces
and I am lost,
falling in love with you
was not worth the cost.

You have broken my heart
or at least that's how it seems,
tell me how to love again
now that you've shattered my dreams.

A Final Goodbye
by Pamela Dawn Lerner

When I was small
I was your world,
but that was okay
because I was your little girl.

When you became ill
we were both filled with fright,
we forget our love
and always seemed to fight.

Heaven opened its doors to you
and away you went,
without a declaration of love from me
ever being sent.

I have beaten myself up for that
for all of these years,
you not knowing I love you
has become my greatest fear.

Every night I tell you
even though you are far away,
that I have always loved you
and I will for all of my days.

Even though you can not hear me
all I want is the chance to say,
all the things I wanted to
on that tragic day.

So here I am
with tears in my eyes,
to my loving father I say...
a final goodbye.

Untitled
by Tammy Leveille - age 18

Obsession is a powerful word
That has no meaning to many
No one seems to understand but me
It is the burning feeling in my heart
When you are away
And the tingling feeling when you are here.
It is the feeling of never having enough
Never wanting to leave
It is the continuous need to make love
The need of everlasting
Unconditional closeness and love
It's the other piece to my growing
Love stricken heart
And the word that is the closest way
To say how   I feel for you, Ron.

Love
by Michelle Los - age 13

Love is like a tropical river,
ever warm and ever flowing
Love is lie a rose
opening to the light of day
Love is like the sun
shining on the dew-kissed grass
Love is like laughter
lighting up the darkest corner
Love is most of all, above all things
a miracle

Caring
by Airika Liljegren

It started way back in history,
People thinking they are better than you or me.
Why can't they see,
They are the same as you and me.

Now we think we have learned it all,
But we are all just the same,
As we were before.

Well we think we can love,
Like the stars from up above.
But what we need to do,
Is learn to look through new eyes,
Until we realize,
That we are all the same.

We learned how to love,
Much more than what we did before.
We learned to care and share,
But not before lives weren't spared.

Instead of sharing,
We all need to learn about caring,
Loving and sharing.

Soon
by Emily Ruth Lovelett - age 12

i feel sadness entering my heart
i feel pain just about to start
i feel that one,
one memory fading deep into my mind
there it will stay forever, until
i set it free, to be a good memory
so every one may see

Just For Today
by Heather Libhart - age 14

I want to lie on the beach-
And just the clouds I want to reach.
Just for today.
Just for today.

I want to fly my kite,
To reach up in the trees with all my might.
Just for today.
Just for today.

I want to fly like a bird;
While others don't mutter a word.
Just for today.
Just for today.

I want to look like a lion-
To look at me they are tryin'.
Just for today.
Just for today.

I want to be wild and free,
Being careless, concernless, and carefree.
Just for today.
Just for today.

These things I cannot do,
Unless I really try to.
So, for today...
I think I'll stay-
MYSELF!

I Wish I Knew
by Anny Lin - age 14

Life and death
Love and hate
Is this the meaning of life?
Is this our goal of learning?
I wish I knew

Why do we live?
Why do we love?
Why is there happiness and sadness?
Darkness and lightness?
I wish I knew

We are young, yet we are old.
We are warm, yet we are cold
Why are we like this?
Why are we us?
I wish I knew...
I wish I knew.

Fish Dream
by Katie McAllister - age 16

Without direction,
The fish swims here,
The water freely,
Flows in circles.

Together we swim,
Now I am free,
To swim in circles,
If I want to.

Prejudice
by Sylvia Lynn Link

Views of us from the outside...
Conceal the secrets that we hide.
The clothes we wear, leave an impression...
Of our hopes or our depression.

Others see what they want to...
It doesn't matter what we do.
People judged by how they're seen...
A kind of prejudice...so mean.

The real person remains hidden,
In a world that's money driven.
Where the job must come first...
Your children usually get your worst.

We were taught, when we were young,
That certain things just aren't done.
It's how we're seen that matters most...
To our friends, neighbors and folks.

But the truth we need to tell -
It's not in the outer shell.
It matters not, what they think...
Prejudice will always stink.

Pages
by Sylvia Lynn Link

It's been two thousand years or so...
Since Christ was born. This we know.
He wanted us to love each other...
Look past the skin, he's still your brother.

Our world has changed, we now have gangs.
And countries play with nuclear bangs.
Schools are equipped with metal detectors
And kids are warned of sexual infectors.

Our cops commit crimes. Our priests sin.
It makes you wonder if you can win.
This thing we call the human race -
Has turned into a huge disgrace.

But our humanity shows...in crisis.
Like some rare forgotten spices.
Just enough that you can taste it.
Heaven forbid, we ever waste it.

There are good men... and women too.
Though their numbers are becoming few.
Greed rules the world, our lives are sold...
Slaving for our piece of gold.

Wisdom, they say, comes with age.
Each day we turn another page.
We're all soldiers, the battle rages.
Let's not make these...our final pages.

Confident
by Christopher Lohman

You're quite confident,
Confident that the stains can be removed,
Removed from your hands

Water streams off your palms,
A red serpent that slithers,
Slithers down the drain

Look in the mirror and giggle,
Laugh at it all,
All the low life

Did you laugh when you removed his heart?
When you ripped and tore the hole?
The hole that is your trademark

Did you kiss his heart?
Kiss it for one last lie?
Lying in your hand beating away

Did you really think you would get away?
Get away from the mirror,
The mirror holds something,
Something in the mirror

Yes, my darling, that is me behind you,
Behind your eyes lies the truth,
The truth that cannot be removed

I swore vengeance on your kind,
I would have your heart,
But that has been done,
Instead I will have you eyes,
Eyes that can no longer prove,
Prove that the stains are gone

Gone I am and you will no longer,
No longer be quite so confident.

You
by Jackie Lupkes - age 12

You are unique of all God's creature's,
Special in every way.
You and all your wonderful feature's,
Make life better day by day.
You are the best you can be,
absolutely wonderful and great.
You are even better than me,
I really like you Kate.

Anasazi
by Katrina Long - age 14

There are many legends once foretold
Of an Indian Tribe.
Four corners in the U.S. is where they lived.
They farmed and hunted
Like most tribes did
Until on day they went away
Some say they were all killed,
Others say on one hot night,
A big round ship come from above
Then took them all away.
No one knows what happened
Maybe they joined another tribe
These cave dweller kind,
Maybe they all faded away
To a better place where they won't be bothered and
won't be killed
This Anasazi tribe.

Mars
by Katrina Long - age 14

It's so bright like fire by night,
It's so lovely in the lite moonlight.
The redness is so radiant,
So deep,
So dark a red it looks like blood.
The dark blood from an animal or human.
It's so bright like fire by night.
It's so lovely in the light moonlight
Yet it turns to darkness,
As dark as night with no moonlight
No radiant light or deep dark red.
It's no more
It's the dead ruby in the sky.
The morning light killed the ruby.
It killed the ruby in the sky.
I'll see it the next night
In the bright moonlight
The ruby in the sky.

Prophet's Graveyard
by Cyrus Kai

Beauty is in women
I shall worship you, the new religion
And when I meditate on you
It shows me all I shall be
My love and my soul are with everyone
But I must decline
Because I am nothing
Except your love and your soul
Though you will not see me
You will hear me
Because I am your thoughts
I am your spirituality
That you will never understand
Please embrace it
Though it means nothing to you
But until closeness is what we share
Until closeness of two twilights
I must withdraw

Awaken
by Avelina Lopez - age 13

Sometimes I sit and wander off
and stare into the skies blue eyes
I plunge into the deep blue sea
I feel the bristled leaves.

But when I'm in the countryside
I sit from trees and glide
into a barren field of dreams
I wonder what my life will be
I find myself just drifting off
and sleeping on a floating loft
my heart explodes with words to say
hoping they're the right way
sunny days and silver moons and
orchards filled with flowery blooms
snowcapped mountains, pure and white
comfort hearts on sleepless nights

Awaken with constant noise
My vision is changed and then
I see the blood of men
a bullet hit the next of kin
daughter's birth and mother's cry
and fathers take a vow of death

Society has opened my eyes
and robbed me of my innocence
where is my wonderland?
please take me back again.

Friends Understand
by Carrol Lowe

A friend understands
They make no demands
They compensate for your inadequacies
Support your inconsistencies
Give moral support when esteem is low
Offer help for a physical blow

A friend is family extended outside
   the home
They are a morale booster wherever
   you roam
They require no return on their in-
   vestment in you
And will be your principle when your
   interest is due
A friend is forever and if treated
   with care
Will be at your side forever, will
   always be there

A Nested Love
by Jos. R. Lozano

How free I feel
   when I'm with you.

My soul soars and glides
   as an eagle over trees and mountains.

At times I'm irrational
   as a sparrow when it erratically swirls, spins and stops.

My heart flutters in mid air suspension
   as a hummingbird when it collects it's nectar.

My being coos in content when in your arms
   like a dove during a mid summer's rain.

I feel beauty and charm when in your presence
   as a swan as it floats upon a misty pond.

I am forever indebted to your gentle advances
And the way you care and show concern for me.

You have torn down the walls of mistrust and apprehension
And have made me whole and my life complete.

Now, my love can be given in whole and completely.
A love that is nested in my heart for you

   My friend

      My lover

         My companion forever

Angel's Go To Heaven
by Deborah Hancock Lozoya

Standing at my stove; cooking dinner;
When a racing river, flowed to my kitchen floor.
I managed to take my son from his highchair,
Safely placed him in his crib.
With his bottle in his little hands, I dimmed the light.
Turned off the stove, no dinner tonight.
My son and I are home alone.
I tried but couldn't reach anyone on the phone.
I was horrified, I was frightened almost paralyze with pain,
The physical pain could not compare to the pain I felt in my heart.
Knowing what was taking place, wishing I was wrong.
About twenty minutes later; the fact was known.
I held, I rocked and kissed my little ANGEL as I cried.
My little lifeless baby, as a part of me also died.
As I prayed and prayed, I asked god what should I do?
Then I prayed, Dear God, I know my ANGEL'S safe with you!
The night was long yet the morning came fast.
Time for a final kiss. I must say my earthly Good-Byes.
Now I would place my ANGEL in this final burial crib,
I ask myself over and over, why was this one, water and porcelain?
Why not one with a wooden frame and warm soft cotton blankets?
Again, another part of me has died.

My World, My Life, My Glory
by Bonnie Luna

My world,
a beautiful place,
The sun shines bright on a field of green grass.
White clouds rowing like boats through the sky.
And me, yes I,
Live in this world of beauty.

My life,
Full of the things In love.
A pleasant house, a family,
A belief in God above.
And me, yes I,
Live a glorified life.

My glory,
A mind of peace.
The knowledge of right and wrong,
The sense to manage myself along.
And me, yes I,
An happy to live on this earth.
For I live my life the best I can,
And the glory shows how much life is worth.

Gratitude
by Andrea McCormick - age 15

No matter how thoughtlessly
you push me away
I am still bound to you
You lifted me into the light
out of the darkness
in which I dreamed
and for that I am in debt to you.

Hitler's Poem
by Collin Lynch - age 13

When I grow-up,
I wanna be a hurter.
A fighter, a spider.
A mutilating murderer!
Glare at parents on their knees!
Listen to all the children's pleas!
make 'em shout, make 'em cry!
Watch 'em all faint and die!

People are askin' "What good's comin' out?"
"Hate and fear and dreams!" I shout.
Yes, I have morals,
Yes, I have a hate.
But, why must this all become a debate?

So hear me child, hear me loud and clear,
No need for hate, we got a new kinda fear.

A Springtime Procession
by David Macaluso

Sky of Spring immense,
So alertly serene..., so present...,
As if he skips along within it...,
As it acquires a netting of cracks;
A storm's chiseling at its horizon -
And he innocently walks along,
Under puzzled sky, now warping,
Melting into neural drips
And a spectral swarm of faces
Which dance in agitated rhythms
From orders whisper'd and obscure -
Spirit deranged imposing -
Oppressive - *hollow*! - daunting;
Parading of compulsion
To where his heart drums - pounding,
As he, retreating, kicks -
Denying that Ghosts do have him -
As he scrambles over mirror'd ground -
Seeking outer refuge anxiously -
To Self steadfastly bound!

Everything
by Amanda McConnell - age 14

Dark and alone in a daze of depression,
I stare at nothing with no impressions,
Of the world around me and everything that lives,
With open arms of punishment it gives,
Some precious moments and times of joy,
Youthful years that seem to flow,
Soon taken away and replaced with age,
Like reading a diary page by page.

A Suicide Dream
by Michelle MacDonald - age 16

She's down on herself;
She's down on her life;
No one's around;
And no one would care;
Her boredom is rising;
The knife is risen;
Her anger is booming;
The day is glooming;

The emptiness around her;
The loneliness inside her;
In this time of despair;
And time of depression;
The knife she lowers, wanting to end it all.

Even as the blood began to pour;
She felt no pain;
She felt no shame;
And everything around her suddenly went black.

She opened her eyes;
A bright light shinning in them;
She wondered:
Was she in heaven?
Or was she in hell?

As she looked around she realized;
She was neither in heaven, nor hell;
But lying in her bed;
That' when it struck her;
It was all just a dream;
A dream she'd had before;
A dream she'd have again;
A suicide dream.

The Long Ago Summer
by Robert MacIntosh

As big sisters watched, the children played,
while we cooked food and made lemonade,
our aunts and uncles gathered in the comfort
of that summer's shade.
Who would believe that all our folks,
All the good food ad the gentle jokes
would disappear 'til...now all is gone.
Into thin air...or somewhere beyond.
No matter where I look today,
Gone are the sweet flowers of May.
Well known faces that always said
Familiar phrases, now are dead,
Yet my lonely heart beats on and on
though the flowers of May are gone..
Gone.

One O Seven One O Nine
by Jessica Mannhardt - age 14

Only half the people are kind
But what really comes to mind
Is all the hard work done behind the scenes
And well monitored screens.
At One O Seven you may find two wizards and one dummy
Who often have so little sleep they'll look like a mummy.
At One O Nine staff often hear "I just bought the Internet and..."
"You bought the Internet my foot," they want to say
But if they did there would still be more bills to pay.

Eternity
by Kimberly Mackey - age 16

I envy the solemn trees which He flies.
I envy the sharp rocks which He rolls gently.
I envy the diamond skies from which He quietly descends.
I envy the golden sand where He is alive yet still buried.
I envy His soul-and nothing more.
I envy the sweet seas where He angrily roars.

How complex is He.
Anyone can see-but-I look into His soul.
I see the magical gift He gives us.
Only the intelligent are quickly to accept.

How I long to be one with Him-but-I'm not fit.
He treats me tenderly
He judges me with firmness
He listens intently to my every everlasting thought
He's there when I desperately need Him.

Like a peaceful dove in the sky-I feel free.
Like a clown in the circus-I feel happy.
Like a tattered teddy bear-I feel secure.

There are so few that have joined this eternal group.
I wish there were more.

I know when my soul departs from here
I'll be with Him
I'll be caring hands for eternity.

Agonizing Cries
by Brenda Maillet

My heart weeps uncontrollably,
The spasms of dying pain within me mount.
My fingers wrestle, trying to grasp some solid
Ground in the shifting world beneath my feet.
My eyes search for the dying light of hope in
The hopeless world in which I live.
My frantic calls in troubled hours go unanswered.
Only a machine to leave my agonizing cries.
The last of my tomorrows wither, parched piles of
Dust.
Spattered with the tears that flow from unsighted eyes
Blinded by the suffocating power of depression.
Soon the chains that hold me in tortured bondage
Will be broken.
The freedom of a new day is near.
No more pain, no more sorrow.
A better tomorrow for me.
Forgive my selfishness.

And I Care
by Jessica Mannhardt - age 14

I care not for the web we weave it cares not for my soul.
I see the gap we leave you see not the whole.
My sis upon the rope did swing to land upon the mat.
The risk is told you. You say "And I care about that?"
You did jump over yet another rope to land upon the mat.
Her protection you did steal and apologies were poor.
Rotten -rotten to the core.
Hatred bubbles within.
That thing you call a heart. This war you hope to win.
But you and the evil one will not win.
In this war God is on our side.
You see that concept then you hide.

My Son
by Gwen Maisenhelder

Your son is retarded, the doctor says,
    And I weep.
You'll love him best of all, the doctor says.
    Still I weep.
Not for what he is nor what he will be,
But for what he'll never know, never see--
    The first leaves of spring,
    The snow-laced trees,
    A bird on the wing,
A wild laughing breeze.

My son is beautiful in his own way;
    Yet I weep.
My son is beloved in every way;
Yet I weep.
Not for his future, dim though it may be,
But for the hopes, the dreams he'll never see--
    The youth's carefree fling
    With passion that's blind,
    Then wedding bells ring
For true ties that bind.

My son grows more and more slowly each day,
    And I weep.
My son learns little with each passing day,
    And I weep.
Not for all my hopes that died at his birth,
But for joys he'll never know on this earth--
    The love of his wife,
    The laugh of his child,
    The strivings of life
Whether tame or wild.

A Plea From Mother Nature
by Elsie Moncion, R.N.

Mother Nature - stands before you whispering dire warning please
be aware and look around you before death our planet seize

Trees are barren -- barely greening
Air is heavy -- choking, wheezing
Land is barren -- blowing, drying
Fish are dying -- bloated, beaching
Cells mutating -- rapid growing

Can't you hear me?

I am pleading

Save our planet Earth

Four At War
by Jessica Mannhardt - age 14

Four at war and war indeed
Are Kim, Jess, Joe, and Morgan.
One hates the other and we all hate back.
It is patience we all lack.
When we are together there is sure to be a storm.

When I look back on our younger days,
And then at our devilish ways
I have a hope that will not die.
We will be four at peace someday.

Hurting
by Tamra Lea Malaske - age 14

Why is life so unfair I ask day by day
But never have any answer to say
I think maybe I took him for granted when he was here
Now I can feel my tear drawing near
I never have any words I can say
So I go without talking to him by the day
I can't begin to describe how I feel.
I constantly think to myself, "This isn't real."
How could I let something so good slip away
Now forever, there's a price to pay.
I should have shown him more of my love
Now I surely can't rise above,
The pain I feel for him that never ends,
Or my poor heart that always bends
Of the sight I see of him with someone new.
Now I realize our love is through.
Where did I go wrong I ask?
Finding the answer is not an easy task
But I'll keep searching till I find my way
My way, to a brighter day.
Where I'll be happy and so will he
If only he will settle for me.
I've got him once I have faith I can do it once more
And if I succeed, my heart will soar
But if I fail, my tears will pour.

Now That You've Gone, Dad
by Annette Maloney

Now that you've gone, dad
I feel really bad
There's so much I didn't say
I think about it every day
Your always on my mind, and in my heart
All the memories, I'd never let them part.

Now that you've gone, dad
Sometime's when I'm thinking of you, I get sad
Sure we had happy time's, and some bad
But to me, you were the best, dad
You had a long, hard, sometimes cruel life, that you had to live
but through it all, you still had a lot of love and support to give.

Now that you've gone, dad
Even though you and I didn't always's get along, I can't get mad
You were always's there for me
But sometime's I feel that I didn't turn out how you wanted me to be
I wish that I could've had a chance to say everything that I
didn't say
But I know that I'll get that chance - some day!

When I Cry
by Cystal R. Meyer - age 15

I feel so free when I cry,
So free I feel as if I could fly
Above all the pain I feel deep inside
Above all the problems that I hide
The pain deep inside can not stay
For when I cry it all slips away

The Search Of A Life Time
by Eric Travis Manchester - age 20

From the time we enter this earth
We begin our life long search,
But what we look for is very hidden
Hard to find but not forbidden;
Searching through a broken past
Or a future that's very vast.
Looking for a long lost friend
Trying to find unknown kin,
Needing to find a place in life
Relying on only one to be our guide.
Some search for glory and for power
So over others they may tower;
But others search for wealth untold
Seeking cities made of gold.
So remember on your Judgement Day,
You will go but possessions will stay.
Instead search for treasures that you can keep
Then you'll find that in which you seek,
The things we search for are only three,
And they're the same for you and me
They're the three that matter most,
The Father, Son, and the Holy Ghost;
The final goals for us to find
Becoming the search of a lifetime.

A Rose of Life
by Amber M. Mondragon - age 14

Life is a sweet and precious rose.
Her petals open to bring in a new
day. Her fragrance awakens
the soul. Her burning red shows
us we're alive.
Yet, her thorns, she has put them
to prick us. They are our harsh
reality and the wicked world. Together
they are brought here to show us
the way.

On The First Day of History
by Kelly Mangels - age 15

On the first day of history,
the Titan Prometheus
stole fire from Zeus,
the king of Gods,
and lit the world like a Super Nova.
As the fire spread
the smoke rose thick like a cloud.
A black cloud of soot.
Then, the first drop of rain fell,
down from the skies
and wept onto the world
extinguishing the intense flames.
And grass started to sprout.
Forest and fields blossomed everywhere.
Huge pits gathered much of the water
what we now call oceans.
Then Prometheus extended
his hands to the earth
and gathered the remaining
ashes of dead ground to form man
Zeus, angry
with Prometheus for stealing
bound him to a rock
and encased him in a blazing
ball of fire
and flung him into space
where he remains forever
in the sun.

Joy Ride
by Cynthia Manick

As the car sped up my mind froze
still and lifeless
I stood paralyzed with comprehension
he could not see me
he could not hear my screams
the swerving car
could not comprehend
life outside itself
I was falling and falling
so slow I fell
blackness came so much later
the mobile cursed me
confined me
I could no longer walk
I could no longer feel
I could hardly talk
My knew confinements
repulsed me
disgusted me
I cried and cried
soul sobs for what was taken from me
soul sobs for what I could never be
the joy ride
that accursed joyride
thieved my joy from me

Destined Love
by Faith Manzanares - age 15

That smile brings back so many happy times
when we were together and you were mine.
The feel of your arms holding my close,
laughing together as we bump our noses,
The twinkle in your eye when you had a scheme,
life with you was an unforgettable dream.
Running together, holding hands,
Unaware of fate's cruel plans.
Without any warning of things to come,
Not knowing the will of the son,
The voice of God telling you to go,
To where or why, I do not know.
Ripped from my life like stars from the sky,
I let the tears fall and hear my heart cry.
Across the world, across the seas,
but doing the work that was meant to be.
An empty void that need to be filled,
Refusing to let my wounds be healed,
Thinking of what I lost in you,
I come to realize the truth.
I never really lost you to the open seas,
How can I? You are a part of me.

I'll Be There For You
by Chloa Mardis

When I look at you I feel proud
you might be old
but you are wise
You might be embarrassing at times
Like when you show naked baby pictures
or when you don't match
Most of the time you wear ugly clothes
but I pick the nice ones out for you
When you laugh it sounds like a hyena
but all I do is smile and blush
Sometimes you're not appreciated
but I remember what you did for me
I love you with all of my heart
so when someone steps out of line
I'll stand up

I Forgot To Remember
by L. Marvin Marion, Ed.D.

I forgot to remember
Until it was late December
Then Christmas had passed.
There were no gifts at last.

I forgot to remember
Until sometime in November
Our anniversary had passed and gone.
I forgot, and that was wrong.

I forgot to remember
That it wasn't January or December
I missed your birthday.
Please, accept my gift today.

My wife forgot to remember
That it was late September.
She forgot my birthday too.
Now I'm not so blue.

Grandma
by Brittanie Marquis - age 13

Grandma lies in hospital bed,
with a silvery cloud around her head.

She lies so still, could she be dead?
Will she forever lie in that bed?

Her eyes still shine as bright as stars,
but with a different meaning then ours.

Hello grandma, are you still in there?
Why do you give me such a stare?

Maybe someday you'll come back out,
and life will be the same without a doubt

I Will...
by Sara Marshalek - age 17

You can see the fear in my eyes,
You can feel the pain I've felt.
I don't know how to get away,
but I will... Yes, I will.

You can hear my heart beat fast,
you can see my hands are shaking.
I don't know why I've been hurt,
but I know how...Yes, I know how.

You can see the tears run down my face,
you can see my lips quiver in distaste.
I don't know when I'll leave this place,
but I will...Yes, I will.

You Stay By My Side
by Lorrin A. Marsh - age 14

My pain, my sorrow,
My today, my tomorrow.
My future, my past,
My first, my last.
You stay by my side.

In good times and in bad,
In hard times and in sad.
In truth and in lies,
In laughter and in cries.
You stay by my side.

For all the wrongs made right,
For every day and night.
For love and attraction,
For every confession and infraction.
You stay by my side.

With dismay and affliction,
With struggle and addiction.
With glamour and stride,
With honor and pride.
You stay by my side always, forever, and no matter what.

Without You
by Alexadra Martin - age 11

My love for you is that of a thousand people.
Without you
I am but a single star in a sea of blackness.

No sun,
No moon,
just a black void of nothingness.

Without you
I am but a single beast in a silent jungle
with nothing to hear but the sound of my roar
echoing off the trees.

Without you
I am nothing.

Deep Within
by Elizabeth M. Martin - age 18

Love to me is like death
I feel close to death when I am close to him
I feel him deep within
I take in his life
Drink his blood
I am absorbed; lifted; embraced; consumed; intoxicated
by his existence

I want to learn to read his mind
Be connected
Be one
I want to look into his eyes; into his mind; into his soul
and feel his pain; his suffering

I want to exist as two intertwining souls
Becoming so beautiful together
He need not tell me over and over "I love you"
for I will feel it through his soul and in through mine

There is no belonging to anyone or anything
We exist as our own; belonging only to our own
Our own life
Our own love
Our own death
Our own souls

Do You Want Me
by Eddie Martinez - age 15

Do you want me
I think you do
My mind says yes
Your eyes say no

Do you want me
I think you do
My arms say please
But yours say no

Do you want me
I think you do
My mind says yes
Your heart says no

Do you want me
I think you do
My mind says please
Your lips say no

Do you want me
I think you do
My love says please
Your back says no.

Cleaning
by Courtney Lynn Monteiga - age 12

I hate to vacuum, mop and dust,
But my mom says "Cleaning's a must,"
Cleaning stinks it takes all day,
If not for cleaning I could go play.
But when the cleanings finally done
The day is over no time for fun.
So if your mom says it's cleaning day.
Take my advice and run away.

A Pondering Thought
by Isaiah Martinez

Oh how my feelings
towards her are so strong
that whenever I'm near her
I feel nothing is wrong...

But though I'm in love
I sadly must say
she probably doesn't
love me or like me
that way...

For her eyes are like crystals
that shine yet so bright
I can only imagine a
bright starlit night
where we're sitting together
I'm holding her so...

Then she whispers
to let me know that
I'm the one her heart
so desires, I make her
lips burn while her eyes
glow like fire...

For oh my dear love
I wish I could find
the strength and courage
to tell you tonight
that with you
I'm in love...

Innocence
by Krystal Mild - age 13

The innocence of a baby looking into the face of
a stranger
So trusting, so unknowing
The innocence of a puppy cuddling its master
The puppy and the baby trust us with their lives
So innocent, so unknowing
The stranger could easily kill the baby
The master easily abandon his puppy
They wouldn't know what was going on.
They're so innocent, so trusting
Why can't we all be so innocent?
What happens when we grow up?
What happens to our innocence, why is it gone?

Midnight City
by Journey W. McAndrews - age 18

Foghorn blows through the wind.
Night has come once again.
Angels hid in secret places.
Masked among the human faces.
Quietly I walk on through the city,
That will soon sleep soft and pretty.
The night grows long and heavy.
A storm breaks along the levy.
The air hangs thick and low,
As an angel secretly blesses my soul.
Then I wonder once again,
Do the angels sleep among us men?
A cat runs by me with a screech,
As a bum begs in his speech.
The window shops are bright and pretty,
As I wonder through the midnight city.

Untitled
by Tiffany Corine Masters

"In times of ache, please take me under!"
I cry these words all through eve's blunder;
"Carry me to beyond the seas,
Set me free of such tragedy!"

Never to hurt is always to love,
And never to fear, only him, above,
Is the greatest gift a heart could receive
I may have, if this love I can retrieve.

My darkened loneliness crushes my soul
And tears my heart to pieces.
I wish my life I could just grab and fold
And throw away completely.
Rest forever in heaven's hold
and never have love leave me.

Our Country
by Julio Y. Martinez

We have trusted you from our birth.
We were born to serve you, with love
And dedication, we came from a strong mother's
Womb, and learned to love you our country.

When you were threatened. You called us
To arms, and we answered your call to defend
You our country.
You sent us to several nations on this world,
In the name of freedom for you our country.

And after many battles securing your safety,
You brought us home from those far - away places,
We returned with titles of U.S. Veterans,
Our strength spent in service to you our country.

No longer were we those young soldiers, who first
Entered your service.
And now in the twilight years of our lives,
We ask you to keep us in your memories, as
We still love you our country.

But if you should ever need us again, we will respond
In your times of need, and we will ask the almighty
To give us the strength to answer your call.
Even tho we may be gray headed and may walk with
A slight limp, we are willing to serve you our country.

Nothings Forever
by Amanda Mastnak - age 12

As I listen to you
I can't help but think
think about
your gentle voice filled with so much love
then I think
do you just talk to me like that
I mean do you just talk to me with that much love
and then I think about your love
will we love each other forever
and then I think
is love ever forever
and then I answer myself
No
Nothings ever forever
Not even love

The Judgement
by George Martin

He stared upon Somalia,
That old and ancient land,
And heard the children crying,
And watched the children dying,
Where first the Seed began.

His frame was gaunt with sorrow,
Spent and used and frail.
And from his breast there rose a cry
Like mad Golgotha's wail.

He said, as if He chewed on wormwood,
"For this no absolution!
E'en God is not that good.
Bring forth the greatest millstones,
Fling wide the gates of hell,
And bid Satana bellows up his forge.

I TAKE THE CHILDREN!"

and suddenly a shining road,
A host, a heavenly choir;
Then the entire sky lit up
As with immortal fire.

I watched with fascination
As the children left their clay,
And rose up bright and clean
And loved and fed;
He spread his hands toward me,
I saw the palms had bled -
"Suffer the children--" He said.

The Owlish Lover
by Amelia Masek

Dare not darken the first snow, dare not drink from the purest of waters, dare not take the rose from the fair maiden, who awaits for her lover, dare not soil the purest and set a blister where her heart should be.

She is young, and very trusting to anyone who blurs grace and blushes from modesty. Many wolves tried to ravage her innocence, but none were worthy.

One night a white owl came to her window, for seven days his flight was consistent. Boldly into her window he flew. "Finally she is mine," his wings he expanded and flew around her making his enticing flight, enchanted he gently laid upon her.

By the morning light she was awaken, wondering "was it all a dream?" she looked to the side of her bed, and saw a single white rose with a drop of blood upon it's thorns.

As time marched on, soon the air was filled with the cries of a new born child. Embracing her child she then realizes that this was all that was left in remembrance of her owlish lover.

The World In The 90's
by Christine Masztak - age 12

Why should we be scared,
of the people we meet,
be so frightened when we walk
down the street?
It's pathetic we think we're not
being protected by the law,
being scared of telling people
of the awful things we saw.
Our curfew is nine, but we
come in at eight,
Because we are afraid of what
might happen if we stay outside
that late.
The graffiti on the houses
The break-ins that leave nothing
behind.
These people, you know the cops
will never find.
What's happening in the world,
is really getting bad.
The sight of it is just, plain
Sad.

Eternal
by Misha Mayers-Hall

Crossing tracks
        --over the hill.

I follow between trees and grass,
        Across a shallow creek
                --warm from sun.

With a broken heart
        --I stand in peace.

Moving uphill towards the depth of sorrow
        to sing
            in the spring of despair.

I stand in the pale moonlight,
        and I see the black trail of death.

Untitled
by Lisa Mazur - age 18

They always think the worst of this poor child,
They laugh behind her back and say she's so wild.
She longs for love, yet fears it the same,
Knowing no one cares to even hear her name.
They wish her away without a second thought,
If she knew any better she would have stayed and fought.
Not only for respect but the chance to have a happy life,
To do what she wanted and what she thought was right.
The world is so cruel each thinking of only themself,
Never understanding the real meaning of a true wealth.
Mistakes in the past still today go unforgotten,
The world goes on just treating her so rotten.
She begs God to forgive her and give her one more try,
Everyone knows it's harder to live than let yourself die.
Why can't they see she's not like the rest,
She gives her all, she gives her best.
Is there hope for those that nobody loves,
Is the solution up in the heavens above.
Does anyone know the boundary of wrong and right,
Why can't anyone hear my cries throughout the night.
Yes it is me, the confused lost soul,
Struggling to reach every far set goal.
My mind runs wild filled with such pain,
Tears fall each night like a mad sky of rain.
Yet, being alone can not be so hard,
For I've managed to get along so far.

Love
by Jenna McCall - age 13

The way love works is painful to the heart
and those who truly love must be quite smart
for true love is a thing that shall never die
for your souls will belong together, unafraid,
and alive.

Love can be beautiful if come from the heart
yet may be as delicate as a piece of art.
But when comes from the brain, can draw
ones apart.
Apart from life, apart from love, apart from
the souls who belong in your heart.

If i Be
by Brooke McCann - age 17

If i were the wind i would constantly blow
past u 1 reason would be 2 keep you cool the
the other so i could touch u every min-it.

If i were a wave i would trust myself upon
u over and over 2 drown u that way i could b
inside of u for the rest of your life and
the last thing on your mind.

If i were a dog i would piss on your leg
so everyone else would know your mine.

If i were the sun i would shine so bright,
it would b me making u see things the
way u do and play an important role in
your life.

I am none of these just a small
person in your life the only way
I couls make any impact on your
life is if you would consider me to
be.

Forever There
by Amy K. McCarthy - age 14

He sits and he smiles,
his face never drops.
He hasn't a care in the world
and his stare never stops.

He sits and he listens,
he'll never talk back.
All the burdens of your life,
you place on his back.

He kept you company
through bad and through good.
You cried on his shoulder,
because you knew that you could.

You know who I speak of,
you know that he cares,
because most of you too,
rely on your teddy bears.

Untitled
by Sara McGuyer - age 18

Hide well.
Like sun under--
probably near Russia
red
yellow skin
something, someone so conspicuous
Large like you to me--
it can never hide.

That Grandmother of Mine
by Erin Meeker - age 16

She was graceful,
   And delicate.
And was forceful,
   But kind.
She loved us,
   With all she could.
   That Grandmother of mine!

She was loving,
   with all her force!
She was caring,
   with all her courage!
She is a woman,
   of none other.
   That Grandmother of mine!

Him
by Amy K. McCarthy - age 14

It wasn't him that you feared
but what's in is heart.
For that little angel of darkness
is what kept you apart.

It popped out unexpected,
with you unaware.
He had you heart fooled,
you thought he really did care.

His words struck like thunder,
they filled you with fear
But only when he was gone
did you shed a tear.

You were trapped in a world
of pain and mistrust.
You spent all your free time wondering
just when again he might bust.

You had nowhere to run to
and nowhere to hide.
You just sat there and kept
all these feelings bottled up inside.

Only now that you're gone,
do you stay unharmed.
Too bad that it took till you left us,
for us to see through his charm.

Nothing Lasts Forever
by Anne McGrath

There is nothing in life that's meant to last,
All that we have will soon become the past.
The prizes in life we treasure and keep,
But soon will vanish, and be buried deep,
Forgotten importance, value and names,
Only a trace of its' presence remains.
Take life itself, which is not forever,
But disappears as if it were never.

So do with the time you have what you can,
Cause all will be gone and come to an end.
Enjoy life now and cherish each new day,
Hold onto it, let it not slip away.
But do not hold tightly to whatever,
For there is nothing that lasts forever.

Forever Friends
by Nichole McGregor - age 16

Forever friends is what we'll be,
A never ending bond between you and me.

All the years we've spent together,
We've stayed friends always and forever.

So many years have past,
So many years gone fast.

We have fought and cried,
It's been tough but we tried.

Forever friends you and me,
Forever friends let's wait and see!

This is dedicated to my best friend Anna McDowell.

Now That Your Leaving
by April McCrary - age 13

I know your gonna leave me,
I know it's a fact.
But I need you here to love me
and keep me on track.

You were my protector,
you were like a shield
but now that your leaving
I'm a lonely flower in a big open
                              field.

When I was with you
I was undaunted,
but now that your leaving
I seem to be haunted.

I thought we'd always
be together,
But now that your leaving
it will never be forever.

*Dedicated to my boyfriend who's
moving in summer.*

Thanking Alice
by Ann McCray

Alice called Wednesday
to say her husband was sick,
not perceptibly, but sick, couldn't sleep,
wasn't eating, right, paced the patio at night,
his hair was falling, and turning white.

Alice called, to share with me.
I could think of nothing to say.

Thank God.

For once, platitudes died in my throat
before their by-rote speaking.

Such mindless drivel no longer works
for me.

Never did.

Now, I listen to Alice, and others,
and, hopefully, eventually, patiently,
to myself as well, just listen,
quietly, waiting, and learning how to be.

I've read repeatedly that within
any problem lies the solution.

On days, now spring-turning-summer
in season and my sense of self,
even though years dictate fall facing
winter,
on days, when I slip and slump
backwards, accepting absurdities,
notions dictating meaningless convictions
that I am my own problem,
on those days, I remember if restlessly,
that inside, there, solutions also reside,
that, in fact, the doctor is home.

Still Alone
by Erin McCreesh - age 14

For the first thirteen years of my life
I was alone
I had few friends
No one really cared
I knew I had friends
Somewhere
They're down here
What Yankees call
The South
"Rednecks" at first
Then gentle, caring people
Blossoming into true friends
Or great rivals
I love each of my friends dearly
Missing them over the weekend
Filled with joy to see them well and breathing
I know there are other people out there
I just don't care
All my friends are right here

To Those Who Love
by Sara McCullough - age 16

Why do you say you love me?
You don't even know me.
All you know is what I show,
The front I'm willing to present.

The world could never understand,
The pain and hate I've gone through,
So you see, you can't love me.
How can you love what you don't know?

All I long for is to get away-
From the hate I've always known,
From the hate that's shoved down my throat.
Can't you see that I can't love?

I've never known the meaning,
I don't expect to see,
This simple word people call love,
That all others willingly show,

I know I said I love you,
And if I've ever loved,
I guess what I said is true,
But for now I'm stuck with this hate.

Restless Searcher
by Marissa McCumber - age 19

    Some search for treasures
others for personal pleasures
a few are restless searchers
    never finding what they need
but keep on searching- yes indeed
they may travel around the world
their dreams lying everywhere unfurled
or perhaps they try many careers
not sure which one is right even
after years
    Well, for that restless searcher
in search of his dream
let your true spirit gleam
for just beyond that bridge (ridge)
may be tomorrow's ridge (bridge)

Whispers

Flight of a Single Mother
by Sue McGill

Oh, I heard his voice one more time,
But this time the voice was being very kind.

I could feel there was love still in his heart
Even though for years we had been apart.

How sad when love once was oh so strong,
You wonder how this could have gone wrong.

The things he has missed can never be replaced.
The growing up of three beautiful daughters
And not talking with them face to face.

No one can ever realize the struggle I had
But my three angels never made me sad.

Each day I asked God to give me strength
To raise my family the best I knew how; and
I managed to climb the mountain to put me where I am now

So listen up mothers, you are not alone,
Even if you are a single parent you can have a happy home.

Put your trust in God to show you the way,
And he will be in your heart to stay.

I Love You
by Nichole McGregor - age 16

I'm not a child,
But I'm still very wild.

I love being with friends,
My love life never seems to mend.

My parents I always hear,
But my choices I sometimes fear.

For every night I go to bed,
With different feelings in my head.

Will I listen tomorrow night,
Or will there just be another fight.

This is for my mom you see,
She has been so loving to me.

No matter what I got into,
She always said I Love You!

Untitled
by Nichole McGregor - age 16

There I see him lying there,
On the ground so cold and bare.

If he would have listened to me,
He wouldn't have been in this tragedy.

As I wipe away a tear I see,
A troubled spirit finally free.

I sit and cry for awhile,
While I fill out a police report file.

No one else was hurt,
No one else is 6 feet under dirt.

My final words I hope he hears,
He shouldn't have had any beers!

A Rose
by Crystal McKain - age 16

My life is like a rose
Withering away day by day.
As the petals fall off,
My life falls apart.
waiting for some one to pick me up,
and love me.
Hold me close to their heart,
And save me from dying.

Back On My Feet
by Bridget K. McGuan - age 16

Dying is not the out,
for I almost experienced it.
I thought I wasn't worth living,
and that my life was all s--t.

I figured it out the hard way,
that I have people who care.
And whenever people talked of suicide,
I never thought I'd dare.

Then all my anger boiled up,
and my life just blew.
It was sort of like a volcano
with all its red-hot spew.

I came very close to dying,
but I decided to turn around.
For reality finally struck me,
and it's love that I have found.

I found love form everyone,
that I did not know they had.
And now that I look back,
I really do feel bad.

I'm glad I'm in treatment,
and that I didn't die.
I think that was the worst,
for I didn't want to say good-bye.

I'm relieved He didn't take me,
for it just isn't my time.
And I'm glad I'm no longer rock bottom,
but that I've really begun to climb.

Life to Death
by Crystal R. Meyer - age 15

My life sucks I wish I could die,
I say its okay but I know that's a lie.
Wishing for a better life,
In my hand I hold a knife.
I slick my wrist then again,
I know what I do won't be forgiven.
I don't care thats okay,
As long as I don't have to stay.
I take a breath than one more,
I feel my head hit the floor.
Its all over I know I'm dead,
I can feel the tears they shed.
I wish that I cold come back now.
Though I'm dead anyhow.

Rape
by Bridget McGuan

I never thought
it could happen to me.
but when it did-
dead is what I wanted to be.

I was at a party
when it took place.
I tried to block it out,
but I still see his face.

I dream about it
almost every nite.
I want to get revenge,
just out of spite.

I was raped-
and I"m not afraid to admit it.
But why did he pick me?
It just doesn't fit.

I'm trying my hardest
to get over the rape.
I just want my life back,
and from this one - escape.

It's a scary thing
to have happen in your life.
every time I think of it-
it cuts me like a knife.

To all you girls out there-
please watch your back.
It can happen to anyone-
and that's a proven fact.

Waterfalls
by Katie Meizinger - age 15

Waterfalls how you flow so gracefully
Waterfalls down, down, down, your water flows into
another stream.
Waterfalls how refreshing your water is.
So clean and fresh. Your water tastes so
wonderfully cool to a hot traveler.

Waterfalls how fresh and cool your water is
for a tired and thirsty traveler.
Waterfalls your so beautiful and peaceful
also so graceful.
Waterfalls you are such a great place to sort
out my problems and thoughts.

My Friend
by Julia Micheli - age 12

You'll always be my friend
Through good times and bad
You'll always be my friend
Through happy and sad
Beside me you stand
Beside me you walk
Your always here to listen
Your always here to talk
With happiness
And smiles
With pain
And tears
I know you'll always be here
Throughout the coming years

Friendship
by Crystal McKain - age 16

It's a bond of all man kind.
it is an ever lasting bond.
it look's for the truth in all.
It pick's you up when you fall.
It is color blind, so all it can
Is the most enter self of you and me.
It is there when you call
No matter how close or far away you are.
it doesn't matter how different we may be,
Sometime or another a friend,
Is what we will all need.
In the light of day we can not hide,
The feelings we have inside.
We are all on this earth together,
Let's love and respect eachother.
One day when we all learn to be friend's,
Only then will the light of peace,
peace shine upon our heart's

Bigging to End
by Crystal McKain - age 16

Every ice cream cone,
Has it's last lick.
After every dream,
You wake up.
Every sun rise,
is flowed by a sun set.
Summer turn's into winter.
Every story has an ending.

That is the way it was with us...
I don't know what happened,
Why you said good bye.
My heart is broken into two...
I pray time will mend it...
I know that I still love you...

I also know that,
The sun will rise the next morning.
The snow will melt and the flower's
Will regrow.
There is always another story,
Waiting to be read.
And there is some one else out there
Needing some one to love...

Together
by Barbara McKasty - age 16

His body advances towards mine.
My heart beats faster and faster.
Questions running through my head
like little children in a playground.
Does he love me?
Our bodies and souls meet
and we become one figure in both.
As the sweat glistens off our bodies,
I wonder was this right, should I have done this?
He sucks the sweetness from my body
and I do the same to him.
Our bodies are screaming for one another.
He wipes the tears from my cheek
and holds me in his arms.
he makes me feel cared about.
He softly presses his lips to mine
and in one long sigh says:
I love you with all my heart.

Fear
by Jennifer McKnight - age 16

Last night I heard something
while I was asleep
I heard little children laughing
while drowning in waters too deep
The picture was much too vivid
The idea, much too complete
and so I woke up crying
but soon went back to sleep

The next day while I was asleep
the visions reappeared
And something seemed to say
the children were now near
I opened my eyes quickly
and felt a sense of fear
but then the waters took me
and visions reappeared

But this time I wasn't dreaming
No, this one was for real
I started falling downward
Helplessness, I did feel

The children stood there laughing
laughing while I threw up
years of pain and sorrow
and then I woke up

Drunken Driver
by Jessica Miller - age 13

She got in the car
and didn't even think
of how much you had to drink
it shouldn't have happened
not this way
So many accidents happen each and every day
When she called your name their was
no answer that's when she learned
of the terrible disaster. On the way
to the hospital she started to cry
why did this happen why did you
die. You would still be here if you
didn't drink you have a brain
why didn't you think.

Watching You
by Kelley McLain - age 15

When the sun comes up I think of you,
And when it goes down, I dream of you.
I listen to music, it calls your name,
And everything else...it's all the same.

I don't give up, I won't give in,
My heart's too strong, my mind won't win.
I know the love I have is real.
If only I knew how do you feel?

When I see you, I wave, but you don't see,
I stand and watch you as you leave.
Suddenly you turn around,
But your eyes are on the ground.

I watch you move, wait for my cue,
I hold my breath, my face turns blue.
You never looked, you never spoke,
Now I'm afraid my heart is broke.

I saw you talking in a cafe,
You turned and watched as I walked your way.
You say that you've been watching me,
Funny thing...I never see.

My God Above
by Terry McLemore

Dear God, I was terribly mistreated,
throughout the years, the abuse repeated.
Mom and Dad, knew no love,but that's not
an excuse, they not once called on you,
My God Above.
Sun - up to sun down, Mom would curse
the day away, my Dad would touch
me, the wrong way, I never looked
forward to waking another day.
There were times, I wished to die, it was
then that I looked to the sky, and
ask, "Dear God Why?"
All my family, all the town's people, heard
my cries for help, this secret for years,
My Dear God, they kept.
Years have passed, the pain remains, I
need to forgive, therefore eternal
life, I will gain.
I have no family, as you can see, but
that's just fine, from now on it's
God and me.

This Man
by Charlene McMillen

This man in whom you should trust, he should be your hero about who you can boast.
His arms should be for comfort, his hands to help you learn, always gentle but stern.
Just hearing his voice, just knowing he's near, should make you feel so safe and secure.
When you're a small child in a world of over-whelming fears,
He's always there to gently and quietly wipe away the tears.
But this man about whom I speak, is the one I trusted the very least.
I had no pride or respect for him in any way, to be free from him I prayed for every day.
His arms brought guilt and confusion, his hands as he used them pain and unwilling seclusion.
And hearing his voice, knowing he was near, brought such sadness and well known fear.
Being such a small child, it's hard to explain,
But somehow I knew what was happening would leave my life forever stained.
Each night lying there silent and frightened in the dark,
Listening and waiting for the rituals in which I'd have to embark.
I'd try as always to pretend to be asleep, but to no use, and again the nightmare I'd have to repeat.
To refuse him I knew would make his violence flare, but the things he did, to say to someone I couldn't dare.
So I went through these rituals night after night,
Wanting to feel love from this man, but feeling only sadness and fright..
Sometimes I think I might finally be free, of this man I'd come to know as my greatest enemy.
But no matter what I do or how hard I try, I know my life will somehow always carry these hidden scars.
So if I can learn from this pain and use it to grow, to strengthen myself and help others by my story being told
Maybe then finally one day, all these ghosts from my past will just fade away.
This man who I speak of, the one who made me so sad, is the one, the only.., you guessed it.. <u>My Dad!</u>

Untitled
by Robin R. McNeely

Like a cloudburst
    I am dispersed
Expanding new directions for my soul

Sun drenched earth glistens before me
Likewise my heart,
Softened by the Spirit
    and the comfort within the Word,
Is mending...old wounds
And trespasses which uproot growth

Now, birds flock and darken the skyline
    migrating,
      like me,
          home.

Forever
by Amanda McVicker - age 15

When I look at you the world stops
And all my problems seem to drop
Things in my past I can no longer see
Because all I can see is you and me
We'll always be together forever more
Till only you decide to close that door
Although I don't think it will ever lock
I will definitely come back to knock
To you, nothing will ever compare
That's because nothing will even dare
You understand everything about me
Because we are descended by fate to be
Little things won't separate our love
Because it can and will easily rise above
Our love will end no sooner than never
And don't forget I will love you forever

Memory
by Daniel Mefford - age 14

I walk along a sun lite path
Next to rushing waters and signs of its wrath
A waterfall flows into a stream
Millions of glistening leaves barely showing the sun's golden beam
And I was struck with a memory
Of you of me
My heart burns inside of me
And the tears flow from my eyes
I stand atop the falling waters
Wishing to join the rising mist
To fly gently up towards the heavens
And worry no longer of my lover's fist
And with this I felt a memory
Of you of me
My heart yearns inside of me
And rage burns in my eyes
I rise gently upward my arms outstretched
Filling with joy, joining the rest
My long white dress flaps in the wind
And soon my wounds angels will tend
I slap the water with a deafening thud
My vision cast over the color of blood
Stars appear with a godly shine
Releasing a life, the life that was mine
A compassionate voice sounds in my ears
It lessens my fears, wipes away my tears
And I was struck with a memory
Of him of me
And a love that will never die
Suddenly sparked inside of me

Michelle
by Samuel Meyer

The young princess holds the mysteries deep,
    life secrets shall not be told.
Joyful moments she will always keep,
    for the memories will not grow old.

The radiance of her hair so bright,
    golden waves of nature's best.
Glowing softly in the morning's light,
    lying neatly across her chest.

In the garden not a word was spoken,
    the beauty of her eyes so clear.
Promises kept and promises broken,
    she allows only a single tear.

Slowly he moves close by her side,
    she cries yet makes no sound.
The time will come when he must ride,
    as their passions knows no bound.

Resting his hands on her slender hips,
    sets the gallant knight eyes afire.
Gently he presses against her lips,
    overcome by the burning desire.

The single rose in the garden of love,
    remains basking in the sun,
All is quiet 'cept the morning dove,
    time has stopped--but now must run.

My Success Admire
by Wanda Lee Middleton

There's a admire that's kin to me
its my baby brother that's striving so
wonderfully. I adore, love my admire
his a churchgoer, obtain college degree,
DJ music, work motivated, outgoing personality.

I say to myself, will I one day
accomplish one success that my
admire have. But god possesses the
value of life, so now I am content
I will obtain one success skill from
my success admire and that's my baby
brother Ryan Kurtis Middleton
and his great deal. Amen

Thou Shalt also decree a
think, and it shall be
established unto thee: and the
light shall shine upon thy ways.

I Promise
by Donald Earl Morey

    I will love you with all my heart and soul as long as we shall live.
    I promise you will be mine and I will be yours as long as we shall live.
    I promise that I will always be loyal to you as long as we shall live.
    I promise that I will love you and cherish you from all harm as long as we shall live.
    I promise that we shall never part because you are my love and I am your love.
    I promise that I will not let anyone interfere with our life together I Promise.
    I promise that what we have and will have we will have together I promise.

No Answer
by Scott Milkovich - age 19

shadows in shadows dancing room, all is black
darker and darker
shadows dance a waltz

lighting flashes white
spiritless corpses dripping blood
whispering for help
too shocked to scream

no answer
alone, dancing with the devil
still the shows wander
leaving me urinated

whispering for help once more
no answer
alone to watch and listen
for they will not leave

Magic Sash
by Rebekah Milbourne

Moment has come
Queen of the hour
Gazing out of her window tower
Stands erect; graciously posed
Radiant and triumphant
As a long stem rose
glowing with intensity
Of Remembrances past
Full of magic like the Dream Keeper's sash
Beauty! Time has not faltered
Fresh and alive as a new bride at the alter
Her fragrance; her one true Gift
Sails the winds like the smell of a rose, set adrift
Wrapping the heart in a tender embrace
Warm and loving as His Savior's Grace
Moment has come
She must hand down
Her fragrance; her gift; her ancient crown
to the next generation, here and beyond
Time has come
For the Rose to move on

It Is So Good To Be Alive
by Dolores Miller

    Today, March 6, 1996, is my daughter's 16th birthday. My little girl is a young woman now. I am very proud of her.
    Right now, I am sitting here crying tears of relief. Over the past 13 years, I have worked through, (with God's grace), unbelievable strife. There were times I know it was very hard on my family. Because of my love for them, I was determined to keep healing. Being a survivor has strengthened my spirit and mind.
    It has been a hard road, but I am coming into full bloom. Like the butterfly, I have broken through the cocoon. My wings are beautiful with brilliant colors.
    It is So Good to Be Alive! To see every sunset and sundown. To hear wonderful music that goes through every fiber of your soul. To smell the spring rain and blooming red roses. To feel the warm heat from the fireplace on a winter night.
    To know that I had the courage and strength to work through and overcome very hard situations. Knowing now all the work was worth it, for the love of my family and my own self esteem. To know more and more times of peace because the worst is behind. Most of all, to know your family stuck by you through thick and thin. The whole time giving you support for your determination and courage.
    Finally, God is always there. Even times when you feel He isn't, He is there guiding, strengthening and loving you! Also, never doubt your own self-worth. God doesn't. Today I am not only celebrating my Angel's birthday, I am celebrating LIFE!

Winter Wonderland
by Dolores M. Miller

Outside my door,
    there is a Winter Wonderland..
Sun shining,
    on the frosted trees.
Glimmering, dancing,
    such beauty and tranquility.

Love the snow,
    love the trees.
Breathing in,
    the winter breeze.
Driving in my car,
    I could see,
MO RE AND MORE
    BEAUTY AND TRANQUILITY.

There are diamonds, crystals,
    all around.
They will lift your spirit,
    if you're feeling down.
Put on a smile,
    not a frown.

There's a white blanket,
    on the earth.
It's presence gives joy,
    and rebirth.
Almighty God's artistry,
    becomes a joy that
Sets you free.

Dream
by Jessica Miller - age 13

I dreamed a dream of you
that only I could see and
in that dream of you, you
held me tenderly. You kissed
me on the cheek and told me
you loved me and that you
would love me from now until
eternity. I saw you the other
day but you showed no interest
at all the only thing that's
stopping you is this brick wall.
I tried to move that wall
but you just walked away
Now the only thing I have
of you is the dream I dream
each day.

Marriage
by Courtney Lynn Monteiga - age 12

Marriage is something special,
That the two of you share.
Your marriage is filled
With tender loving care
For many years you've been as one,
And never lacked of love.
Both of you always equal
One never higher above.
So what this poem is saying
Is that you both are smart
For you were married at the right age
And you'll never grow apart.

A Child's Silent Screams
by Melissa Miller

Innocent child lay silently screaming,
Frozen by fear.. barely even breathing.
Soon the cruel laughter will be long gone,
The child left afraid to make a single sound.
The sun will rise and bring safety from the nite,
The coming of dusk brings with it the fright,
Open your mouth, but the words won't come out,
Unable to speak, yet wanting to shout,
Finding sanity in complete isolation,
Forced to come out full of frustration,
It might be alright if that is all there is.
But there's shame and there's guilt and not wanting to live,
You were used for his wishes,
His mind a little twisted,
You struggle to remember what you had before,
Only to forget it again once he closes that door,
He's come to take you again and again.
Until nothing is left... nothing within.

Happy Birthday Sweet 16
(3rd Angel Letter)
by Dolores Miller

Happy Birthday,
    Sweet 16.
With all your beauty,
    style, and gleam.

Daddy and I
    are so proud to be,
the parents of such,
    joy and creativity.

Sometimes it is so
    hard to believe,
that such an ANGEL,
    came down from HEAVEN,
to her father and me.

Now it's so
    hard to believe,
that our little girl is "Sweet 16!"
    A young Woman.
We LOVE you!

"Happy Birthday Sweet 16!"
    Mom, Dad, & Larry

Silent Dreams
by Debra Millican

There is a wind that whispers
As I sit silently on a hill
The night carries a polished mist
As the world seems to stand still.
I look up at the wintery sky
As my mind begins to dream
I can see visions from breezes blowing
A hidden perception of reality.
And as the days give mystery to the night
The hill is my haven to hide away
It gives me the strength to accept
The domain in which I stay.
This is a place where one can enter alone
And alone no one knows
The loneliness hidden inside a heart
A hill where silent dreams can grow...

This World
by Sarah Miller - age 14

In this world, I no longer know,
this world of hate and greed,
are people walking through life,
that don't know what they need.
Everything is so different,
then the way it used to be.
If you look hard then I know you
will see.
They do whatever they want,
are they in a daze,
could it be the way they were raised.
I wish they'd stop the hurt and the pain,
but do they know how, or are they too vain.
Maybe they think it's fun,
to shoot someone with a gun.
What are we teaching,
would it help to be preaching?
Is there something I can do,
In this world, I no longer know,
this world of hate and greed?

(Linda)
by Linda Dejan/Willie Miller

Linda, you is like a first fresh of spring
just before summer is about to begin

as the flowers, Awakes from winter sleep.
Your air breeze the gardens (special) fresh smell so sweet.

Eyes, of hopes can see blue heaven, Smiling Pleasant to be.
You is the one that makes pleasant joyful sense.

I can see Bright vision of love that right,
like a new born happiness taking flight.

Linda, you awake the thought you get to the heart.
they don't have no mind (Linda) just smarts

Linda you are a Winner.
for me there will be no other love as (Linda)

Linda, because you is the (best) yet.
Why, the (You tell from all the Rest.)

Cradle Of Dolls
by Debra Millican

Inside a room of many colors
Where heart shaped rainbows are made
Set's a closet full of day dreams
With dolls with whom she plays.
In corner of this room
A cradle rocks to a silent beat
In her hand a lullaby whispers
To a sound she often seeks
She slides a blanket to keep them safe
For no one believes at all
That she has a world of make-believe
Where only she can hear them call
Each one dressed in satin and lace
She surrounds then with her protection
So she can live in this special place
A place where thoughts are magical
And wonders are clear and new
A child at any age
To where clouds are never blue
And like the different smiles upon the dolls
A child with dreams can never fail
With praying eyes of hope
Living in the shadow of a fairy tale.

The Leap Of Faith
by James Milstead

From a star we sail upon a feather.
A leap we both must take together.
Upon the shaft we gently fly.
Blissfully through the sparkling sky.

The gift of the quill, courage and might.
Two hearts grow into one, wrapped sensuously tight.
The strength found within the hands of the other.
Life searched, yet found would be not another.

Over a road traveled for years.
Resting upon the other, facing fears.
With each journey, sights never seen before.
Barriers moved to return no more.

Demons of the heart screaming within the night.
Upon the road not a flicker of light.
Together hand and hand through it all we shall stay.
Guided by a love so bright, holding true never to stray.

For upon a shaft we can gently fly.
With an angel's wings blissfully through the sky.
If only we take the leap together.
And set sail upon this feather.

A Place Called Home
by Christopher M. Murphy - age 16

Through the pinks and the blues and red lies
A place where hearts are opened and
The eyes are blinded by love and light
Through the shades of black, purple, and green
Lies a place where dreams and memories are made
A place where sacrifice is the only regret
Through the burning mist
The mind is opened and the woods are forgotten
This is the place I love
In the hills strengthened with gods love
And through a river filled with Gods word
Is a place I call home.

Downtown Streets
by Jeffrey Minton

Late at night on the downtown street
the corner girls are dead on their feet
an eight year old watches
perpetrators look for rock, escape and be free.

Pipeheads staggered from the fire in their hands
wino's drink as much as they can
cop's rolled into this part of town
bust a few heads, shuffled papers around.

Drug cartels and governments
are just paralled.
"It just don't matter," a crying mama yelled,
"in this town, just it's drugs sell."

Undercover's buy, try to lock them all up
cup runneth over, this town's too corrupt
three blocks down, rival gangs all around
white shirted children, bloodied mushrooms go down.

The market was upped in street speak
the neighborhood folded because it is weak
another scalded day in the war on drugs
coffee poured like blood in the diner's dirty mugs.

Regret
by Tristen Jean Mireles - age 16

I caught a falling star,
but died the day I let it go.
We had a love that endured all,
and the day it didn't we drifted apart.
She lived her childhood dream,
but grew up the instant she ceased to.
They saw peace in the future,
but lost it in the present.
You had a hope that would last forever,
but when you doubted it was lost.
He believed in fantastical myths,
but stopped when he learned logic.
I believed in best friends,
and then I lost mine.
You had the truth,
and forgot it the day you lied.
She thought angels protected her,
but realized they didn't the moment before she died.
We thought reality was fun and games,
but then we grew up.
He thought a man's life was joy and accomplishment,
and then he was defeated.
They saw scary monsters dancing on their closet walls,
but were blinded when they opened the door.
I thought I'd always have someone to lean on,
and then I woke up alone.
We thought we could build each other up,
but ended up tearing each other down.
We thought we could rid the world of regret,
but couldn't because we continued making these mistakes.

My Baby
by Colleen Murphy - age 11

The softest skin ever,
The cutest little face,
And warmest heart,
It was my baby.
Full flesh and all,
She was mine.
To care for,
And to love.
Mine to hold,
Ever so tight.
She was my little baby
And always would be.
For me to love,
Endlessly...

The Journey Man
by Michelle Mizerka

A thousand years I've wandered
A thousand roads of war,
And everytime I take a step,
I feel a thousand more.
For older than time I am,
And I feel that I have traveled,
As far as the earth is round,
And with mysteries I've unraveled.
I have seen fallen towns of begotten woe,
Within many a enemy had slain.
Yet there are frutiful places,
Where many secrets lay.
But if I should turn around,
And look how far I've come,
I would see different place,
Even long forgotten by the sun.
And while a thousand feet have trampled,
Down the lonely road I follow,
I feel they never will sample,
All the secrets I have found.

A Hug For Charlie
by Beth Mlady

Getting involved was my idea. My husband was out of town, but I had to do something now. If Charlie hadn't come over to play in my children's sandbox, I might never have been sure. After listening to his brothers' differing stories on how this newest incident happened, I knew he was being abused. An innocent victim of violence inflicted from within the walls of his own home. Watching the blood harden on his swollen and discolored face, I knew that, in addition to my heart being torn apart, his nose was broken. Often he had come by to play, his clothes ragged and dirty, nose running. Though he had a rawness about him, I sensed a lovable child of two-going-on-three. He always had reasons for the black eye or the bruised arm. Like the rest of the neighborhood, I turned a deaf ear to the cries coming from the windows two doors down. In today's "mind your own business" society, I hesitated to step into the fray. Hand in hand, I walked Charlie home that day not knowing what else to do. It sickened me, especially when I found his "babysitters" knew of his injuries (his parents were God-knows-where). All my instincts said to wrap my arms around his tiny form and keep him with me forever. After another sleepless night, I reported what I knew to the authorities. The toys down the street are gone, and I don't know whatever became of Charlie. Maybe what I did helped make life a little more bearable for him; there's no way for me to know. I think of him often and pray he hasn't become another statistic. I hope he's found another "safe haven" wherever he is. People tell me becoming involved took courage. I say it just took love.

Confusion
by Joanne Moreau - age 18

Your love's like a blanket that comforts me
In times of sorrow.
Eyes asking, searching to see if that love is returned
Placing my desires and dreams above all the rest
Knowing I can't return the emotion
As you would like for me.

You.
    Protector, friend
      Loyal, caring

Smiling through the hardships
Not succeeding, but never to give up
For me. On me your happiness is based
Why?
    Am I so special?
    What do you see?
    Will you always be there?

If I can't return the care?

I cry now writing this...

    I think I do.

Part of Me With You
by Amber-Chantee Mullins - age 15

Out of the blue there's an
    angel I see...
My grandfather sent it just
    to be with me...
He sends his love and blessings
    too...
And said now with this angel,
    a part of me will always
      be with you.

Do But Not Too Much
by Morgen Morie - age 19

Too much of anything
is not good; I'm told.

As my good desires turn into
unhealthy self-centered thoughts.

Trying too hard creates
undistinguished unequaled failure.

I want with no limit
I reach far past Good through the Heavens

Into the house of evil
to shake hands with the devil.

I am selfish to the point
overconcerned with my own feelings of self-pity and self-disgust.

My love overpowers love
into disgusting undesired entrapment.

My standards are unattainable for both of us,
as are my desires irrational.

Perfection creates dissatisfaction
and lack of content.

Too much goodness creates malnourished overemphasized love
buried deep in Evil fantasy.

Jagged scent of vile, foul smelling sympathy
is my subconscious goal attained only too easily.

There is no stopping
what's already gone by.

First Christmas Without "My Grandpap"
by Andrea Monti

The family is here, everyone is listening
the tradition we started has your pile missing.

There's a big empty chair with a sweet smile gone.
Was it your time, God had to be wrong

We have definitely lost your creative hand,
a wonderful friend, an unbelievable man.

Who will tell the jokes, "Thank God he wasn't a twin"
we would all love to hear your corny jokes again.

There are a couple of things that really make me sad
Our family is left with only one Dad.

There is certain advice we can only get from you
Daddy will have to fill some very big shoes.

Uncle Frank is helping Gram and so are mom and dad
but after forty nine years, without you she is sad

What I miss most from you is sitting on your lap
and feeling like a little girl who would always have her grandpap

With a brand new year beginning we will try to make a great start
whatever we do from now you will always be there in our hearts.

I Love You
by Sara Morgan - age 16

Your love is all I need,
you won't give it to me.
I have wonderful feelings,
ones I can't explain.
I love you.

I recall your face,
as I close my eyes at night.
The softness of your lips,
as they kiss me.
I love you.

I recall your voice,
as it talks to me.
The relaxing, soothing sound it gives,
oh the power it has over me.
I love you.

I recall the nights,
ones we once shared.
When you touched me,
saying that you just want to hold me.
I love you.

I don't know why I have hate in my heart.
I don't hate you,
I don't.
Maybe it's the words we spoke last night.
I love you.

Though you say you found another,
I don't think it's true.
You try to hurt me so I will leave.
It won't work, for,
I love you.

Venom
by Eugene Morrison, Jr. - age 13

Poision dripping from the fangs of death,
Staring you directly in the face,
Not knowing what to do,
Frozen from the fear of seeing your life about to cease.

Blindness becomes you,
Sight is no more important,
Because you are the sight,
Nothing but a vision in a master puppets dream's.

Using you as his toys,
He controls your every movement,
To you he is god, your god,
Living his life in his reality.

Your tongue rolls to the back of your mouth as if you were dead,
Feeling your own saliva drown you,
Coughing up blood that is black no longer red,
Nothing you can do about it either.

Complete numbness comes over your body,
Arms to your side completely hopeless
Legs no longer walking under your control,
You have become his!

She's My Mother
by Dena A. Morton

Skin so fair and pure,
free from imperfection;
time has been so gracious
to this ageless beauty.
She's my mother.

Sweet, kind, and generous;
she's always considerate of others.
Never selfish and always forgiving
no matter who's at fault.
She's such a good hearted woman.
I'm proud to say, "She's my mother!"

God smiles down upon her
in all her splendid beauty.
She more than gave of herself
to nurture and protect the daughters
that were created in her younger years.
She's my mother!

I truly realize that I've been eternally blessed
to have known this magnificent lady.
Not only did she give me life,
but comfort, understanding, and peace of mind.
How can someone be so selfless?
She's my mother!

Dedicated to a wonderful lady that just happens to be my mother.

Beautiful Person
by Tammii Nguyen - age 17

The night is beautiful

    so, the smile on your face

The stars are beautiful
so, the emeralds in your eye

Beautiful, also is the moon
    beautiful, also the sight of you.

Two to One
by Pamela J. Murachanian

Two people,
Two lives,
Two minds,
Two hearts,
Separate and whole individuals,
With focus and goals,
for each to achieve,
Then love links together,
two to form one
with independence and strength
building a solid foundation,
for two people,
Two minds,
Two futures,
two hearts,
One life together
One family
One love
One dream
Forever.

I Can't Live Without You
by Jennifer Muller - age 14

Star who shines so bright in the sky,
Why must it be this way? I feel I could die.

No one understands the way I feel,
I cry at night when I get down and kneel.

The emotions aren't found on my face,
They're hidden deep inside a buried place.

People come and people go,
Some are friend, some are foe.

Then there's the one who chose to die,
Always I listened, but never heard why.

So many troubles, so many lies,
Countless numbers of good byes.

Best friends forever, that's the way,
'Cause in my heart she will always stay.

I miss her and I want her back,
The memories stay, but presence lack.

She was my friend, a part of me,
And so many people just can't see,

How hard it is to go on,
And see the light of the morning dawn.

Caribbean Sky
by Ronda Mullins

On sable beach,
the seagulls gather,
broken bones bleached
beneath their restless wings.
Dolphins in frolic play,
whales in the distance
dance the flamingo day,
dipping to brindled dawn.
The whitened rains of sand,
stretch to coral reef,
remnant sails of land,
rifting a tideless grave.
The clarion sky
of Caribbean blue,
echoes a wind-pearled cry,
romancing dreams of ocean spray.

Of Life and Love
by Christopher M. Murphy - age 16

There are certain things that mankind
Cannot comprehend, yet nature knows.
In life we do not understand
The meanings of many happenings.
We think so much, we ponder so little,
And love even less.
Although mankind understands life
We do not understand it's existence.
For man knows little of life and love
And we will learn little
If man cannot understand the happenings of God.

Spring Greeting
by Mary E. Nagode

Good morning! good morning!
The robin is singing.
He chirps near my window
In rapture, he carols;
The shower is over,
The clouds have all vanished;
So sings the bold robin
One morning in springtime.

Come hither! come hither!
Come stroll in the garden.
A new day is waiting
With hours of pleasure;
When trees are in blossom
And tulips are bursting;
With winter forgotten
And new sights to treasure.

The Art Exhibit
by Mary E. Nagode

Wandering freely around the display
Enjoying the art show where they gather,
Directing their limited attention
Viewing one painting after another.

Glances turn with a sudden excitement
Where a large and colorful abstraction,
Catches the eye, and probes at the senses
Making a statement in bold rendition.

Lost for a moment in admiration,
Their attention is drawn into the forms,
Struggling where the artist has invented
A collision between opposing norms.

Their curiosity has been aroused,
Their sense of color, suddenly disturbed,
Caught off guard with a sense of emotion,
The forces controlling the forms observed.

This was the artist's intent as he worked
Plying his skill with deliberation.
Shaping a structure suspended in time;
Striving to work with imagination.

Rhapsody Of Strings
by Mary E. Nagode

The lithe fingers of the youthful maiden
Perform upon the trembling strings with care,
She strokes with frenzied bow, and rapt intent,
Her notes caress the punctuated air.

On gossamer wings, the quick notes flutter
Faster, and faster on the startled calm,
The lavish burst of crescendo pulses
The murmur of the evening's sweet balm.

The night's soft breezes passing over them
Soothes the soul responding to her touch,
The twilight shadows fade into the night,
Ending the rhapsody enjoyed so much.

The music she so lovingly expressed,
Is a far reaching sound with budding zest.

Mirror, Mirror
by Mary E. Nagode

Mirror, mirror, tell me what can it be?
I hesitate to meet your constant gaze
And finally, I fear that it must be
Something more than a temporary phase.

Has my age left the tell-tale lines I see?
Or, is it a trick of your filmy haze?
Mirror, mirror, won't you please answer me?
Perhaps, I suffer from a slight malaise.

It must not be that youthful charms have gone
Don't tell me that my youth has slipped away
I think that I assume this dullish tone,
But what about the wrinkles, I display?

Youth is the greatest time of life, it's true
Don't sell yourself short, middle age is, too.

I'm Out
by Jessica Napper - age 16

She listens to the fight
relish in the pain
turn the radio up till her ears bleed
efforts all in vain

Screams escalate their madness
her brains swirls in an endless daze
like it, like it, ya she does
she runs from it and into the craze

'hurt me hurt me kill me some more'
burning sensation in her teeth
adrenaline high takes her up to the sky
she needs the anger to breathe

She cannot live the days that go by
they are only for waiting...
waiting for the next explosion
all the time hating, hating

Then comes the orgasmic rush
madness spills over her head
she prays for the destruction to stop
but secretly wished it would never end

crash! bam! boom!
the shit hit the fan
tear down the house
it's ok- i'm out

Whispers
by Mary Nichols

Deep down, where flows the veins of life,
The combat of integrity of human strife.
It hordes the inner most part of the mind,
The turmoil of innocents of a lucid time.
Lowly the whispers, yet with a vigorous will,
Can rule ones fate with their masterful skills.
The sub-conscious echoes, revealing your unimpeachable trait.
Can oppress the heart from the errors you make.
You must heed these whispers, with their subdued sound,
To elate your world, of life's treasures around.
Without the whispers we would be motionless and stale,
And our values of mortality would be obsolete and fail.

The Stranger
by Michelle Naylor - age 14

Sitting in a chair
He looked at me
He stood up slowly
And walked over to see
We danced a couple times
We held each others hand
We sat and stared at each other
And just listened to the band
We talked and talked
And the feeling set in
He gave me his number
He wanted me with him
I said, "OK," but had to leave
He kissed me goodbye
And I do believe
He'll always be
In my heart
As the one I'm with
But always apart

Untitled
by Rick Newman - age 14

As the sun sets on my daylight, a familiar midnight falls.
I realize my light was just an illusion and not really there
at all.
I had thought I'd left the darkness but was too blind
to realize, my sunshine had been destroyed before it had a chance
to rise.
The midnight shadows laugh at me for being such a fool.

Sunshine shall never fill your world, the dark shall
always rule.

The Suits
by Bruce Nelson

Blue suits against blue sky
Gray suits against gray sky
Invisibly focused and random they scurry
I see and wonder why

Ruddy faces and bellies bursting
From undue stress and alcohol thirsting
All with a purpose or so it seems
I see and wonder why

From thence they come with heads ahigh
With arrogance it seems as the man in the
sky
But they are only us
I see and wonder why

Endlessly they talk, they argue, they drone,
Even when painfully alone
All with a purpose or so it seems
I see and wonder why

But have them we must
With their egos and lust
All with a purpose
I see and wonder why

My Golden Memories
by Marilyn Nelson

I know that memories are golden,
Yes, it is very true;
But I never wanted just memories,
I only wanted to be with you.

A million times I've remembered you,
A million times I've wept;
If motherly love alone could have kept you.
You never would have left.

In life I will always love you dearly,
Yes, Todd, I love you still;
In my heart you will always hold a special place,
No one else can ever fulfill.

If my tears could build a stairway
And my heartache could build a lane;
I'd make my way to Gainesville,
And bring you back here with me.

Our family chain has been broken,
And nothing seems to be the same;
But in my heart I know that God will unite us,
And the chain will be linked once again.

Flames Of Desire
by Elizabeth Ohno - age 15

> mysterious flames of desire,
> waving to and fro,
> great tongues of fire.
> red and orange glows of
> passion and heat.
> far too powerful for
> a soul to beat.
> wild with rage and
> uncontrollable with lust.
> that could smother us all
> into dust.

Spring's Arrow
by S.E. Noll - age 16

Park bench, sitting in the shade,
flowers blooming, fragrant, sweet, euphoric,
    the sent of spring.
I sit listening, children laughing, birds singing...
What a day, blue shades, floating plumes of white,
    cotton candy,
trees of green on fields of rainbow twirls.
I sit here waiting,
    for love, cupids arrow, soft, caring hands,
knowing not what will come, surprise,
    holding every minute,
I never let go, dreaming of the special day,
when my heart finds spring.

A Tango With Nature
by Barbara Newton - age 21

a crawl - a walk - A RIP RACING RUN -
heart beating pitter PAT echoes of drums!
running in the forest to find the
lovely flower of darkness hidden
in the depths of fresh green grass -

If only to taste the warm sweet
nectar of nature once,
To feed the starving soul.

Then to rock like the sea,
back a
nd forth back
and forth...
the calm low tide grasping for the sand
barely tickling the edges - tantalizing anticipation;
The calm before the storm.
LIGHTNING STRIKES! Like a lost boat in
dangerous waters thrashing, thrown helplessly
into instinctual hands that know more than
I hope to share.

Groping, grasping, reaching...
Wanting my heart healed and fed and soothed...

Suddenly safe and anchored within a
secure port of home, still...
Bumping against the dock, momentum,
Running low, streams of water;
Wet with rain till quiet night comes
and I am intertwined in the arms of nature.

Eagle View
by Anh-Thu Nguyen - age 12

The cool breeze touched my
 face
I am shivering from head to
 toe
Feeling very lonely and
 abandoned
At every direction
Redwood trees surround me
Now feeling light as a
 feather
The wind
Starting to lift me up
My presence
Now as graceful, strong,
 and soaring eagle
As I rode into the
 cloudless sky
I look at the things that
 stand below me
Schools of fish in the
 deep, blue, sandy ocean
Met my eyes
The sounds of birds chirping,
 kids talking, and trees
 rustling
Met my ears
The sun
Beginning to disappear into
 the horizon
Bright colors suddenly caught
 my attention
Filling the sky were
 outrageous oranges,
 rambunctious reds, yo-yo
 yellows, pale purples,
 and bountiful blues

Entering Eternity
by T.G. Nichols

Scarlet Liquid churns
Upward and outward --
My Day diminishes to Darkness.

The Pillow
by Shaina L. Noggle - age 20

It was silent for once in her mind
full of empty thought, where the
nightmares lay, and the tears stained
on the pillow beneath her
 head remained...still stained.

Numb after all the years of pain
of feeling his hands, tasting his
sweat. Knowing the years of years
 will just add up to more
 years scarred...forever scarred.

Unable to cry, she cries in her heart,
where filth has corroded her
hope into dark. Feeling nothing as she
 stares at a pillow stained
 by a soul that is forever scarred.

"I wonder," she asks herself in the
bed where she lay,
"if I wash the pillow, will the rest,
too, wash away?"

Lingered Tears
by S.E. Noll - age 16

By the window, summers breeze,
a child sits alone, wishing,
star light star bright,
 for her daddy to come back.
A year, he went, trash bags of clothes,
 suit cases, stuffed into the trunk.
Moma's tears, why is she crying?
 Daddies coming back, I said.
Salt lingered on her face,
 a year,
the tears are still there.
 Daddy didn't come back,
momma say's he's gone...
 forever.
Tears, salt down my face,
by the window,
 Star light star bright.

From Sound To Motion
by Marnie Norris

He might have lived a life
with the sound of beating wings.
It echoed in his words,
his heart and dreams.
His restlessness and movement,
elusive understandings.
But the universe hides remembrances
in small mindless moments.
And slowly his beating wings grew
from sound to motion and faster
until he could lift
and see
where
freedom
begins.

Untitled
by Sean Nyberg

Our lives will soon change
both of us
Going in new directions
New cultures, new people, and new places
Lie ahead of us
Surprises are inevitable
the path, we have walked together
Will separate us, at last
It may never cross again
Destiny can't be predicted
One thing will remain
Our friendship
Bonding us forever

Tribute
by Marjorie A. O'Donnell

    We all knew her. We pasted her witty words in our scrapbooks, exchanged her recipes for happiness with friends, laughed with her as we spilled our breakfast coffee.
    She's magnetized on our refrigerators. Her "Wet Oatmeal Kisses" is imprinted on every mother's heart; the woman who made us laugh and cry at the same time.
    Who wouldn't want to live in Boise with a friend like her? She visited us weekly, shared a laugh or a tear, then went on her mission of joy, leaving us with sunshine in our hearts. We eagerly anticipated her short visits and will greatly miss seeing the beautiful face of this courageous woman.
    How she must have sweated at times, enduring pain, coaxing words, churning out the humorous side of life which we chuckled at with a "Hon, don't forget to read Erma's column today", before beginning our own chores.
    Who didn't see themselves, their husband and children mirrored in her column every day? She made us see our sisterhood is commonplace, not unique at all.
    "Wait Until You Have Children Of Your Own" helped us through many crises with our own kids, trivializing that which seemed so very, very important at the time, giving us a new perspective.
    Did we ever notice our own dustballs gathering as we laughed about her refrigerator leftovers which even the dog snubbed? Funny how leftovers get casually shoved to the back of the fridge until moss begins to grow.
    Did we ever give back to her a bit of the humor she brought into our lives; the empathetic bond she forged when pathos was the subject.
    Her surgeries left us hoping, praying and rejoicing. Her passing leaves the world a gloomier place, but she will never be far away from the millions she's touched on paper. Because of her, the grass will be ever greener over the septic tank of our own lives.

I'm Sure Of It
by Starr Oglesby - age 15

Sweetheart, Do you know how much I love you?
Do you know what you mean to me?
Do you understand how I feel about you?
Well... I love you, I'm sure of it

When I'm around you I feel so different
You make me laugh, smile, and be happy
When I'm with you I change, I feel so bubbly and crazy
inside

You make the world I live in so much more different than
it really is
Somehow you can understand and solve the problems even I
can't fix

You are a shelter for my heart, a shoulder for me to cry on
My life and my guiding light to a better place in the world

I love you, I'm very sure of it

The Loss
by Rebecca J. O'Hare

In a moment, a moonbeam
    A shadowy glance, sending waves of desire-
    to this moment-
    a chance
    A loss of control, for a love we could not hold

A wind that blew and bitterly dried the cold and dead
emotions of a breaking heart inside

    Yes, through the heart and in my soul hides a small
    and fragile part of me
that gives-
And takes-
    But still is frozen cold

Dependacy
by Aleksandra Orkiszewska - age 14

As we enter the world of courage, our minds develop and our hearts open, w begin to understand why changes occur, and life ends. We slowly realize, that the whole time, we were here we had nothing, and only spoke to some people. We know only one person, ourself. As we learn that from the day we were born we began to die, slowly, but frequently, we know that some day the termination day will come. Brutal, or calm, fast or slow. It will come. No one lives forever. There is no forever. Everything must end, and also die. No person can live, love or understand anyone, like they say they might do. People lie, and leave, and change. I believe that there is only one person that we can always depend on, that's ourselves. If you don't agree if you can't depend on yourself, then get your s*** together, only one person will be there with you, when you'll get your new house, or get in your first car accident. That person, understands you, and hopefully knows how to take care of you. You are very important, not only to others around you, but also, to you!

Peaceful Journey
by Jason Olyan

Beauty deeper than the skin
but where does that beauty truly begin
souls of light, words of sight
Peaceful journey until the end

    Friends are deep
    lovers lost
    meaningless time
    unforgiving acts

Herbal dreams to see the world
bleeding hearts that heel the pain
untold lies that kill the rain
Peaceful journeys until the end

    Madness suffers
    lights burn out
    youth discovers
    Forgiveness found

Meaning To Stay
by Angela O'Neal

Do you love me?
Do you care?
I know it's meaningless..
what we once shared.

Do you close you eyes at night
and dream of me?
Of course not, who am I kidding?
It was you who set me free.

When you look into my eyes
what do you see?
Do you see love?
Or a soul begging to be set free?

Tell me, my love,
what you meant that day?
When you bent to kiss me
had you meant to stay?

Shadows Of The Moon
by Charlene Ong

Shadows of the moon circle round, the air is still there is no sound. The grass rustles the trees blow, the moon is bright the waters flow. You feel the vibrations of horse feet, you see a babe and mother weep. You look away to watch the water, you almost whisper but then you falter. You almost hear a cold, angry tune, these are the shadows of the moon.

Peace
by Jennifer O'Neill - age 13

    Peace is something that
    lets someone know
    that you care.

    Peace is something that
    lets them know
    you are there.

    Peace is a symbol, peace
    is a way.
    Peace is something that
    will be here to stay.

Remember Me
by Stephanie O'Neill - age 19

Remember me with a smile,
how I pushed you to walk that extra mile.
All the joyful times we shared,
True I was,
I always cared.
The struggles in life-
The tears we cried
Forget me not,
I was always by your side.
Let the spot light shine on my soul.
To never let the memories grow old.
Remember me with a smile,
I had a heart of gold.
If you cry through the night,
I'll bless you with strength
to defeat the fight.
And when it's time
for your life's journey to conclude,
you too will win
just like I knew you would...

The Children of the Streets
by Lindsey O'Rourke - age 13

    The children of the streets
    Are poor and defenseless
    Turning to violence
    Seems their only way

    The children of the streets
    Stand brave yet frightened
    Fighting one or another
    For a bite to eat

    The children of the streets
    Are cold and lonely
    Standing in the poisoned environment
    They call home

    The children of the streets
    Sleep wild and angry
    Looking up at the world
    Which looks down upon them

    The children of the streets
    Are rich only with memories
    Of the home they once had
    Long... long ago

Irony
by Amanda Osborn - age 16

Your name sounds hollow
It's repeated so much now
I see you while sleeping
You are everywhere now
I find it very strange
I think they had a plan
They thought hey it's alright
If we kill then love this man.
Always and forever
The eternal scapegoat
Chained and bonded to see if
The messiah can float
Hard to understand
Hard to comprehend
Kicked and beaten, ridiculed
Even at the end
The flame was bright
It also burned
Tested, dissected
They never learned

What Has Life To Offer
by Robin Osborne

As light ascends,
into the heavens,
I sit and ponder

How wonderful,
this life of mine
filled with beauty,
so much joy,
with all that,
life has to offer,

I shall ponder,
what shall I do?
Where shall I go?
Once this life has ended,

For what is life,
It's just a dream,
a simple dream filled,
with wonder, beauty
and finally joy.

For a simple creature,
such as I,
all I shall ask is,
What has life to offer?

Crow
by Katie Oshlick - age 12

The crow is sleek.
The crow is black
On his beak,
And on his back,
A little shine
Catches my eye.
First he caws,
Then goes to fly.
Scavaging for crusts
And food,
Beneath the snow,
Beneath the cold.
The sun is gone, night has fell,
He's scavaging for an old nestshell.
The sun peaks over the horizon,
All the crows, they start a risin',
Scavaging for crusts and food,
Beneath the snow,
Beneath the cold.

Ode To A Minor
by Reba Owen

The sound of sorrow,
Chord of joy,
Of long ago and now,
Holds the woods dark with pine
And secrets.
The shadows of mines and sweat,
Cow town's long white table,
Stories of muley cow that took a jay bird,
Forty years to fly from horn to horn.
Chord of the devil,
Chord of the rock that saves us all,
Honeysuckle, winter wren,
A minor, amen.

Untitled
by Beau Palley - age 15

Endless love
To die for is not love,
But is just a simple act of courage.
To kill is not love neither, this is somewhat
of two combonations.
One, a weird type of hypnosis.
Programmed to cherish this person and respect all they do.
To hope that one day you and she would be together on that
One endless day of love.

Apple Blossom
by Denise Park

A new bud forms and begins to grow.
There is so much to see and so much to know.
A brand new world awaits the child.
The blossom is bold, unknowing and wild.

Soon aging begins and the baby matures.
She has a world she now can finally call hers.
Her blossom is forming in the great apple tree.
She has so many problems that no one can see.

Her body is tempting, juicy and rips.
A blossom close by is just her type.
She loves her life but is quite confused.
Her parent's are plucked, eaten and used.

She is older now and quite settled down.
New buds are beginning to run round.
Her body begins to loose its juice.
Her stem begins to feel rather loose.

Soon her friends begin to fall.
She was scared she was going to lose them all.
Then all of a sudden she was plucked from her branch.
The last thing she saw was the apple tree on the ranch.

Two Little Kids
by Jennifer Parsons - age 17

Two little kids
Best friends
Innocent
Happy
Play together
Without a care in the world

Growing up together
Through the good times
And through the bad times
Stayed together always
Thought they'd always have each other
Never knew
Never guessed
They'd one day be separated

A parent's new job
New city
New house
A sad goodbye
For two best friends
Who never dreamed
It would ever come to this

Cheated
by Carly Mae Parvin - age 14

Being cheated on is a hard thing to go through,
It breaks you down and makes you feel real, real blue.

The guy you thought you could trust,
He turns on you, walks on you, treats you like dust.

You want to let him go but you can't,
It's too hard since you love him so much.

He can't stay committed to one girl, his girl,
He's got something that attracts them all to his every little bit,
I'll tell you now, (I know from experience), loyalty isn't it.

He says he cares for you, and yet he does this,
If he really cared for you, he would hold you, and kiss you,
do you like he does her,
But what do you know, you're just his girlfriend,
I mean, he thinks you don't even know what love is.

But you do, 'cause you can feel it right now,
The aching in your heart when he looks you in the eyes
and lies about what he's done.
And it still hurts after you've forgiven him,
And all the anger that's built up inside,
You can't tell him, in fear you might lose him.

I screwed up and let mine slip away,
And if I had it to do again, these rules I'd obey:

So my advice to you if you've been cheated on too,
Stand by him, talk to him, hold him by the hand,
Lead him the way home, realize why he's doing this,
You've got to try to understand.

Teach him to love you, trust his thoughts, listen to his opinions,
Make your way back to his heart,
And you'll have a commitment that'll last 'til death do you part.

Nathan Quinn, My Son
by Pamela Jean Pasket

Lethargic and heavy,
An effort to breathe;
Yet, the pain comes faster.
Reluctancy floating,
Distant reality,
This can't be happening!
Feelingless pain,
tugging, releasing,
No choice, no control,no recourse.
Desolate emptiness,
Horridly alone,
My child torn from me!
Idle conversation
Hovers above,
Me? Near panic!
Sleep beckons sweetly,
I must wake,
where is my child?!
That tiny baby-thing,
So red so fragile,
Lost among technology.
Helpless and alone
Surrounded by strangers,
My precious, precious child!
Fighting to survive,
I can do no less,
His strength heartens me!
We will survive
Together as one,
My son, my husband, and me.

Summer
by Amy Poole - age 13

No one knows why
Summer is dry
Summer is hot
Winter is not
Summer is fun
Fun in the sun
No one knows why
Summer is dry.

Love Hurts
by Terri Payne - age 17

Don't ever fall in love
I'm warning you now
because once you let your guard down
you will get hurt.

Don't ever fall in love
I'm warning you now
As soon as you do
something will go wrong.

Don't ever fall in love
I'm warning you now
You'll be the one that is
lost in your own thoughts
of if you can ever love
again...

Hate
by Kasandra Passmore - age 12

I have something i need to say;
   and you need to listen close,

There's a big problem happening;
   and we have no time to waste.

Everybody hates each other;
   it's only about our race or color.

And you don't have to go far;
   to see a brother shoot a brother.

People are screaming;
   just wanting us to listen.

But were just listening to the words;
   and not what they mean.

What is the meaning of a race?
   we all live in the same place.

Who cares about our color;
   it's only our skin.

When we know what's interesting;
   it's really what's within.

Packi, Hindu, Ching, and Niger;
   are names we say with HATE!

Runaway-
by Amy Patterson - age 17

When someone you love runs away,
Its hard to live your life each day.
You don't know where they have gone,
They just go and live their life on.
You wait for them to call each day,
Months go by and you start to get
afraid.
Afraid that your never going to hear
from them again.
It is so hard to imagine,
They're gone... they ran away forever,
Especially when the one who runs
away is your own mother.

Weeping Stars, Will Drown Earth
by Kristen Paul - age 15

I hear the stars cry drowning the world in
their pain
around here everything's the same
confused
must we hide
were just washing away with the tide
I listen to the wind as it blows
and kiss the white as it snows
with pain I scratch my face
there's no rainbow in this place
acid rain melts the love
is there anyone listening above?
do we need a good shove of reality
don't test my vitality
no it wasn't strong
my body is weak
my love so strong, I can hardly speak
if this is the world I seek
take my hate and bury it deep
forever hold me when I sleep
when the stars cry before
we die

Love
by Terri Payne - age 17

I'm in love
Not the head over heals love
Not the follow him around love
Not the do anything for him love
Depressed because I'm missing him
Tired because of sleepless nights
Without him
Determined to be with him again
Soon!!!

Truth Calls
by Yolanda C. Payne

A compelling voice within me beckons.

It is a still voice I thought had been shattered when I was a child.

It says "My child seek the truth".

Like Pilate, I shrug my shoulders and contend "What is Truth".
I reflect aloud, 'Who cares about the truth. The whole world is a lie'.

That still voice pleads, "My child seek the truth"

"Why is knowing the truth so important," I ask.
"Who are you"?, I hesitantly ask.

"I am truth," the voice answers. "I must be revealed. It is time for the world to known the truth," the voice responds.

"Why now," I ask.

"The masses are awakening. I can no longer be hidden behind dark clouds, "the voice replies.

"Will you guide me in my search for the truth"?, I ask.

The voice responds, "I will guide you because I have called you just as I am calling others."

You
by Brandi Michelle Phipps - age 15

I have never seen you in truth, your shield of copies
won't allow it, and you choose it this way. The shield that
you mirror is a false you, why do you present it as your
soul?
I know, and I assume, I must accept, what every false
part of both of us wants. If I knew you, what would I see,
what would I be? What does the you I've never seen see?

#1
by Carrie Peckar - age 16

Handle with care our fragile
fool's gold bodies
Handle with care our faded
glass-blown souls
store our thoughts in
vacant arcane graveyards
Play with zodiacs
dancing in the snow
Stomachs hate the whiny
cracked up servant
we all know we play that
part ourselves
Someone broke the sobriety
of the city
At least we know the
weeds are gonna grow

David's Poem
by Maegan Peck - age 18

In a dark emptiness you strive to find
the light.
You search endlessly, unaware it's in
plain sight.
I try to let you know I'm there, to
lend a helping hand.
But you refuse to let me in, why,
I cannot understand.
I will be here for you forever,
full of love and care.
And if you need my friendship,
just call out into the air.
All you have to do is ask, and
I'll be by your side.
On my shoulder you can lean,
I'd understand if you cried.
I needed you to know, that though
it seems untrue.
No matter where my mind is at,
my heart will always be here for you.

Simple Pleasure
by Stan Pelfrey

As a dry leaf tumbles
on a dead,
cold winter's night,
I walk down a hill
with no name,
as it leads nowhere.

I wander around,
lonely,
looking for some place
to find comfort, comfort
from myself and others.

But, it is that leaf
which satiates my longing,
even though I was startled
at first hearing it scrape
the pavement, as I was startled
when I broke the womb
bursting into this world,
naked and alone.

It is this simple pleasure
providing me with some
strength and courage
to continue on this
path.

Pounce
by Lisa Marie Pellegrini

The cat sits before the TV set,
her bushy white tail wrapped around her puffy body,
looking like a gigantic cotton ball.
Her crystal blue eyes are on the tennis players
as they swat the ball back and forth,
back and forth.
Her head moves side to side
as her eyes follow the little yellow ball.
Her paws dance across the TV set
as she tries to catch the ball.
She pounces at the players
as they run across the screen.
She sits before the TV set a little longer.
Then she grows bored
and walks away.

The Parakeet's Cage
by Lisa Marie Pellegrini

She shuffles across the carpet
to the parakeet's cage.
Her amber eyes flash like headlights on a car
as she moves slowly
toward the parakeet's cage.
She stops a few inches away
and puts her face up to the bars of the cage.
Her long, perky whiskers
brush against the gleaming silver bars
of the parakeet's cage.
The parakeet fluffs up his blue and yellow feathers
and chirps as his scaly pink claws
move across the wooden perch toward her.
He pokes his little hooked beak
through the bars of the cage,
up to her face.
And then,
they
kiss.

Overcoming Racism
by Alicia Peltsch - age 15

I'll try and do my part,
As best as I possibly can
This shouldn't be a world of fighting;
Man against Man.
When we're dealing with racism,
Duty always calls.
Let's gather some friends
And start a petition,
To build bridges opposed to walls.
If we all work together
And not make fun of others;
Everyone would get along
Like good sisters and brothers
We all must accept and respect
all the different races,
Even if they all take life
At different speeds and paces
No matter what religion, race
Or color they may be;
Every single one of them are humans like you and me.

And
by Rachel Penix - age 18

Everyone talks about this kind of love
where he is supposed to be all I think about
and all I talk about
and the reason I live
but all I do is cry;
shuddering, racking sobs that leave me exhausted
and I don't believe that love exists
because I'm just miserable
all the time
and love is supposed to be happy
and I'm 17 and I've never been in love
and there must be something wrong with my emotions
and all the people in love disgust me
and I want to scream
and I want to throw things
and I want to love him
but I don't know how
and I don't want to be alone any more
and I don't know how to change that.

Remembering
by Anna Penna

The sound of footsteps walking on the payment, echoes in my mind
The hard ground speaks of many footsteps, much anger and screams
I see many people marching, marching for their rights
I see officers in blue, they swing batons
I hear screams of terror coming from the marchers
The marchers will not leave, they are strong, and determined
Be Strong Marchers!
What do we want? Rights! When do we want it? Now!
The chants echo through my ears
You risked your lives to make the world a better place for everyone
March on Marchers I say as I put flowers on their memorials

How Could
by Natalie Pepin

I saw my death today
a death that will always
die inside of me
I cried those tears and
felt my pain
A broken heart I hold.
I saw it come long
ago
Never thought to live it
Now I sit and wonder
was it him that made
me suffer or was it me
that was so tender
I still see those eyes
that shine
That hair that was so
soft
That smile that was ever
lasting
Those words that where
so gentle
The pain blinded
Those tears still shed
The heart has gone
My mind I've lost

I Look For A Place
by Cally Perez - age 15

I look for a place of a heavenly thought.
I look for a place of no pollution.
I look for a place of freedom for all to live,
I look for a place of a new beginning.

Ill Fated Love
by Bret Peters

This comes from the broken, aching, heart,
That believed in, worshiped you right from the start.
But now words can never quite say.
How much turmoil exists in my heart each day.
All the dreams and aspirations were for naught.
As in your web of deceit I was caught.
You spoke of your dreams each night.
Even until dawn's early light.
All you said made my heart skip a beat.
Never knowing you were a master of deceit.
How one could deceive a true love so?
Only a cold manipulative heart like yours would know.
For I so willingly presented this heart to you.
And with it a love pure and true.
Wish then, as now, I could have seen,
That a heartbreaker is all you've ever been.
Hope someday to meet the right one,
To fulfill the dreams that you've undone,

Are Love Is Like A Tree
by Cyndy Peters - age 14

Are love is like a little tree,
It started so small it was meant to be,
It grows taller and taller,
Day after day,
I did things wrong, I played then paid,
It was fine at the time,
Until he found out,
Then after that all we did was scream and shout,
We finally broke up,
It was over right there,
My heart used to be tender now its all bare,
I guess like the song the water just ran dry,
It took to long he said good-bye,
Then I found out he got a new love,
It's over for me now I'm like a dove,
He says doves can fly so fly away,
But I'll bring the seeds back and plant them each day.

The Flashback
by Ladonna Sheriese Peters - age 14

An open field,
a single Tree,
where a soldier would yield,
someday a war would be.
A War that shouldn't be fought,
for a world that can't be bought.
But raging faces,
and screaming races,
pushed us off the ledge,
and left us hanging on the edge.
On the edge of a lie,
one for which many people would die.
A valley once filled with green,
will someday be covered with red,
the innocent lives were lost,
at an ungodly cost.
A cost not everyone could afford to pay,
for some people couldn't see it another way.
The lonely tree was first to fall,
alone in the night... once standing tall.
Now the soldier stands alone,
tears streaked down his face,
now feeling so condoned.
Ashamed of his ways, he stares at what's left of that tree,
wondering how this war came to be.

What Can We Do?
by Andrea Petruka - age 14

What is this world coming to?
I'd like to know what we can do,
to stop this pain; killing each other,
and learn to just love one another.
Racism, murder, crime and hate.
Will this be our world's eternal fate?
So many things can ruin our lives,
We'll all kill each other if we do not strive,
to change our was,
back to the days,
where things were better,
so much better.

The Hurt
by Anna Peterson - age 14

It hurts
To lose you
It hurts
To still love you.

You were like a toy
That was loved by a little boy
Love, pain, and tears will you ever see
How much you meant to me?

You I miss.
You I wish. I could kiss
It is you I want to hold
My heart is sold.

I was a fool
I thought I was cool,
But now what I see
Is that I should have listened
to me.

What others said
Were nothing but lies
I had a hard head
For I was stupid enough to believe the lies.

Now I lie in bed
Oh, all the tears
The thoughts in my head
Running down my face are
more tears.

The time we shared
The moments we had
Some were good, others were bad
But for each other we managed
to care.

A Mother
by Anna Peterson - age 14

A person who you love,
A person who is as fragile as a dove,
A person who hides her tears,
A person who has fears.
A person who continuously cares,
A person who shares,
A person who you know you can trust,
A person who feels an unconditional love
is a must.
She's always willing to lend an ear
She's never far, but always near.
She's there to talk and listen to
For, she understands you.
She's always willing to help.
But she also needs some occasional help.
She is strong
And admits to being wrong.
The one who gave you life,
The one who is like her father's wife,
The one who is always there,
The one who will always care.
The one whose love will never end,
The one who is your only true friend.
The one who will love you like no other,
That special someone is a mother.

Change
by Anna Peterson - age 14

One day you're sad
The next day you're mad
Then later you cry
And wonder why?
So many things to say.
So little time
If things would go your way
Slower the clocks would chime.
The time you hurt
The times you wonder do others hurt.
When you say why
Could it be a good-bye?
The fears you hide,
To you people have lied,
What did they do,
Or was it just you?
Times when you're loved
The things you thought wouldn't change
Were suddenly shoved
into a distant range.
When you have someone,
You have a different tone
Rather than when you're alone
Then one day you wake and gone is someone
What happened where did they go?
Now you're feeling low.
Why do so many things rearrange?
Because it's all part of change.

Sunflowers I
by Ronnie Peterson, RN, MS

SUNFLOWERS...

Grow straight and tall.
They view life from an esteemed vantage point.

SUNFLOWERS...

Have bright smiling faces.
Their faces enjoy the sunshine with each new day.

SUNFLOWERS...

Have such a sweet smell.
Lending pleasure to each other,
And to those around them.

SUNFLOWERS...

Move gracefully in the wind.
They move with an elegant style yet, remain simple in life.

SUNFLOWERS...

Delight at the start of a brand new day.
Knowing that each day is worth living.

SUNFLOWERS...

Live in harmony with others.
Blending in while standing out.

Don't you wish that people were more life sunflowers?

Fear Is
by Maynerd Pfarr - age 14

Fear is mine
as I control fear
Fear is somehow
horrifying...
chilling and
awful
But fear is somehow
mysterious...
warning and
potential
fear, fear is mine
as I am like fear.

Summer
by Fred Phillips

Summer is here,
   like heat thick
      as tapioca pudding.

and boys play ball with
   bats and mitts and screams,
      and father's faded dreams,

with mother's halcyon heart
wrapped on a yo-yo string.

Summer has come
   like lemonade cool
      as vernal showers.

Iceberg
by Gordon C. Pierce

Towering colossus of the seas,
Dazzling denizen of the deep,
A glittering mountain of frozen ice crystals,
A monolith of stark awesome beauty,
Moving imperceptibly in the frigid cobalt seas.
A stupendous scintillating spectacle
of blinding, dazzling white,
Its oblique angles reflecting
from a thousand faceted surfaces.
it's immense size is not revealed
So much lay hidden beneath the cold Arctic sea.
It moves silently and relentlessly
to an unknown destiny.
Who can comprehend
it's total power and majesty.

Happiness
by Gregory Phipps - age 12

Happiness is pink like a summer sunset
And also white like freshly fallen snow
It wanders through my mind like a lost puppy.
It reminds me of the time I saw a baby
kitten born
It makes me feel happy and glad.
It makes me want to sing.

Eclipse
by Shellise Piazza - age 19

I met you in a bar,
drinking double shots of bourbon,
talking of the weather and our scars.
We found ourselves opposite;
you the sun,
I the moon.
And somewhere in between the whiskey and blue light,
our hearts and souls collided
like an eclipse,
beautiful and sacred.
And in the darkness
we found comfort
we had found nowhere else.
I became your obsession.
You became my passion.
Together we lived in love.
A love so deep we could not live without it.
Then one day I saw an eclipse in your eyes;
bright azure blue taken over by a midnight raven.
And somehow I lost the love on which I lived.
Now I am back in the bar,
lost in the whiskey and blue light,
searching for the sun in someone else's eyes.
But you are hiding at the bottom of every single glass,
inside every song that rings in these ears.
I am left alone.
The last one here.
And I realized as I am asked to leave,
the sun shall never shine on me again.

The Man In The Moon
by Karen Piner - age 14

You said "I love you"
But what did that mean
You said "I care about you"
But that was only a dream
You made me face reality
That was a place I wasn't ready to be
But you made me strong
Even if you did hurt the harmony in my song
What was so bad that you had to go
I need you so much you just don't know
You taught me a lesson that I'll never forget
But I'm not ready to let go of you yet
Maybe one day but not anytime soon
Our friendship's my dream
My man in the moon.
I love you, goodbye Daniel goodbye.

Precious Things
by Marissa Piper - age 19

These precious things slip away
Like sand through my fingers
Swept away by the tides of time
I reach out to touch you
But you're so far away
Just a shadow in the night

These precious things fade away
Like pearls to dust
Crushed by the tides of time
I reach out to kiss you
But you're so far away
Just a ghost in my heart

These precious things slip away
Like water through my fingers
Swept away by the tides of time
I reach out to find you
But you're so far away
Just a shadow in the wind.

In To The Light
by Richard Platt Jr.

In the distance. I see a light.
I reach for it. But can't touch it.
I can't feel it. I only can see it.

I wonder what foresees this light?

It seems to be there, but it isn't.
A fragment of my imagination, but real as day.
What is this light? Why is it here?

I look into the light.
I see my dreams, my past, present, and my future
I see my lovers, friends, and enemies.
I see my fears, death, and life.

The light is just a feeling.
That's all it is
A feeling locked inside of me.

I'm the light and I'm reaching out for myself.

To feel it means nothing.
To touch it means nothing.
To understand it means everything.

I need to understand this light in the distance.
For later I will learn.
That this light is not in the distance.
This light, this special light,
is inside of me.

Your Eyes
by Sharonda Plummer - age 16

Warm and caring
They carefully examine me
Searching my eyes
Melting my insides
Peering through my soul
Looking, studying my inner most thoughts
Wanting to fulfill my desires
Longing to have me close
To touch me
To feel me
To love me with your every being
And as your eyes look into my eyes
My soul surrenders
And I give myself to you

Simple 176
by Cholinthia - age 19

I cannot find the proper
words to express: my
mind computes, and the
feeling flows outward,
down my neck and through
my arms, and to the tips
of my fingers, and then displays
itself upon this paper: and
no thoughts can connect, No
wisdom can harden: My emotion
exists beyond The Word, beyond
the civil acceptance of what
we have said it should be: This,
in my meaning, makes me not a
dullard, nor an unscholarly piece
of human soul: It has
rendered me a person, with the
freedom to think and to deduce, and
to be alive at my own will: It is
beyond, beyond the word...

Love
by Stephanie Plummer - age 15

    Love is a special thing. It's something that is hard to explain, but I know its there. Love has an impression that will never leave, if I truly love.
    Love it is a song. It is the last thing I think of and the first thing I think of. It sticks in my mind throughout the day, and nothing is going to stop it. Love is like a song; it is always there. I can change the volume. I have different way of showing love, as volume has variations too.
    Love is a chain. It is a link between us. It is something that everyone yearns for, whether they acknowledge it or not. Its something that two people share as a link and a friendship. If that person would pass away, love will still be there, burning as a candle burns just so. That is the sad part of love. Since it is a strong emotion, something I cherish, it doesn't go away. It tends to hurt when I can't see you any more. Not seeing a loved one is like a candle lit but not burning.
    Love is something to special that words can't say.

Alone
by Deborah Podszus

Emptiness is not my choice,
With passion's torture in its voice,
Laughing with its mocking tone,
Rejoicing to see who's now alone,
Smiling with its vicious gleam,
Piercing the heart and soul which scream.
It knows the bleeding heart can't cope
To lose the glimmer of dreams and hope.
A love, not lost, but never found,
It kills with its annoying sound.
Why does it love to see this pain?
Its sword it flings. The heart lays slain.

Feelings
by Kristi Ponoski - age 14

I sing of feelings,
of gray sadness,
love that is lost,
blame where it's not to be blamed.

I sing of family
that is
no more.
A christmas with one
parent not two.
A vacation with 3 not 4.

I sing of what I want a family
to be
a trusting family
a helping family
I sing of what's no more.

Why Did You Have To Die?
by Sarah Poorian - age 17

You said before
"If I die, I die"
And there in a coffin I saw you lie
Why did you have to die?

You were so strong
You could handle almost anything that was wrong
Why did you have to die?

We all know now you are in a much safer place
I will always remember your face
Why did you have to die?

So in your memory I write this poem
And in memory you will always be
But why did you have to die?

The Fury
by Katie Porter - age 12

The fury, the fury of the sea,
Much like he,
But once it calms down the innocence is sweet sorrow from the truth.

The waters are forgiving.
But the, the fury of the sea, continues to haunt me.

Why must it be she cannot run away from he?

The fury, the fury of the sea please do not harm me.

Sorrow
by Katie Porter - age 12

She lives in a castle of sorrow.
Never landing on the ground.
For she chooses to argue,
Then her hearts let her down.
And then raises her higher in the tower of sorrow.

She is required to make up,
For she is not allowed to bite the hand that feeds her.

But when she continuously disagrees,
She must back off and let her heart tell her that arguing just
Leaves her in pain from the consequences,
But when the pain just throbs
Her emotional bursts,
And she then runs away from the downpour.

Untitled
by Rebecca Posey - age 16

Dear Lord,

Help me to understand
My pains and fears
Answer the question for me
Of why
Help me to see things from your eyes
To feel the love
That only you feel
Help me to feel your pain and torment
So that it might lessen mine
Let me know that you are always there
Help me to appreciate
Life and what it means
Please forgive me

Seasons
by Brandi Powers - age 11

On Summer days it is so hot,
It's like you're on a sizzling pot.
At night the moon is as bright as a lamp,
But on gloomy nights it can be so damp.
On rainy days it's like we're drowning in the sea,
On all the sunny days it's just you and me.

A Winter's day is as cold as ice,
The animals could die like the little mice.
A roaring fire is as hot as the sun,
But playing in the snow is a lot of fun.
I know summer won't start until the month of June,
But I hope it will come really soon.

On a Spring day the flowers start to bloom,
But all the little animals will still have room.
The fruits and vegetables will start to rise,
Soccer starts for the girls and guys.

On Fall days the leaves drop down like a ball,
When you see a pile you just want to fall.
Some days you can wear a shirt as soft as a marshmallow,
The colors of the leaves are red, orange or yellow.

A Matter of Great Importance
by Alma K. Pratt

Instruction of the spirit
is a matter of great importance
Obedience is the key
My word, my book is a daily guide
that thou should trust
and worship only me.

Now faith is the substance
that Christian posses
Learning to lean
and depend only on thee
constant prayer and devoutness
express requesting divine
guidance from thee.

As your child I am reminded
that my spirit can only
be at peace with much
help from thee
So I humbly bow in fatihfullness
in acceptance of thy divine
love for me.

Let me teach you my way
to remove mountains
Waiting only in humbleness of thee
Because any matter of
great importance ultimately
has to wait in acceptance
for approval by thee

Untitled
by Stephanie Presto - age 18

Silent times,
quiet moments
that come
to me-
like sweet
nostalgia
no regret
only peace
spent with
family
friends
and other enemies
we'll always
remember and
love

Nobody Knows
by Tami Putman - age 16

Nobody knows when I am alone
My emotions are left to wander and rome.
Nobody knows when I am asleep
Thoughts of him run wild and deep.
Nobody knows when I'm in a crowd
While I'm quiet I'm screaming outloud.
Nobody knows when I am afraid
I block it all out so not to berate.
Nobody knows when I am in doubt
Really for help, I'm reaching out.
Nobody knows when I'm talking outloud
Really my mind is covered with clouds.
Nobody knows when I am confused
I'm totally lost while I stand and muse.
And nobody knows while I abide
Little by little I'm dying inside.

Untitled
by Stephanie Presto - age 18

Dance!
Crazy moon child
eyes filled with
hot stars
(melting-brown and delicious)

- "is she stoned?"
"No, man it's pure-can't
you tell?!"

Watch her
turn and swirl
forever in our
natural
yellow garden
look around!
She is everywhere
HOPE
       is Everywhere

"The Girl in the Mirror"
by Debra Nicole Prezioso - age 13

I met a girl so long ago I didn't even know here name and when I saw her I knew my life would never be the same I said child listen up you have yet much to learn may you never miss a rainbow because you were looking down she said I've never seen a rainbow I have always seen the darkness she cried and she cried till she could no longer and then she said to me let them live show them the way through life you don't need me anymore I laughed how could I do that how can I do anything I reached out to touch her hand and she did the same from the moment our hand touched there was something there, there was something I had never known before she stepped away from me and smiled I stood there with renewed power and at the same time I saw the fear she had the fear I have always had always wished it wasn't there she said honey don't worry faith can place a candle in the darkest night and as she said that a flame burst from her finger and I gasped she said do not be afraid do not worry and then I knew it I reached out to grasp her flaming hand only to find glass that girl I had seen was me and I knew I had to change myself before I could change her

Goodbye
by Kristy Provence - age 13

You said you'd always
love me, until the end of
time.
But it was all wrong
your love is such a crime.
Why you do it I'm sure
you don't know.
I'm sure you just forgot
all the love we felt long
ago.
All the secrets we
confided to.
You don't talk to me as
much anymore;
You'll just walk by in
the halls and wont say
a word.
I hope someday to forgive
you- but till this day.
Don't talk to me - Don't
acknowledge me;
Just keep it as it is
let me walk on by,
Only so I will not cry.
Just keep on walking so
I don't feel the pain.
Don't stop to stay hi-
lets just say goodbye.

Whispers

Separation
by Elizabeth Pursley

The soon to be ex stands tall and mighty but today he feels a little to feisty. "How can you leave me? I don't want you to stay because after all you are in my way. I must have a wife who knows her place, one who doesn't want to look me in the face. You've cheated I know. I just know it you see. And now of the kids I want custody. I'm to wonderful to leave. You must be crazy. Get busy with housework you must be lazy. And pay my bills I certainly have plenty. If I pay my own I will be left wanting. I'm the man. I'm the man. You're just a woman after all. You can't leave yet for I haven't made you crawl."

"I've had enough, anymore would be silly. I'm leaving, you know, I don't want to dally. You've bruised and cursed all that you see. After all you've done you stand and accuse me? You're a jewel of a man it's plain to see to stay any longer I would be crazy. I've already given too much of me. Now all I ask is that you let me be. So shut up, old man, you are a bore. Oh geez, don't follow me out the door."

The soon to be ex stands outside mighty and tall, turns around once, drops his pants, bares it all. I sat behind the wheel of my car, the key in the ignition, pondering fate and my own indescion. Should I kiss his ass with the grill of the car? Or drive away and leave him without a mar? My hands were shaking. My nerves ready to jump musing over "just one little bump." Trembling I put the car in gear with one last look at his ugly old rear. Driving away, yes, I still did quake and regretted forever that opportunity I did not take.

It Must Be Tough
by Kim Reeve - age 12

It must be tough knowing you're not strong.
It must be tough knowing something is wrong.
When you look in the mirror at your paling face,
All you can think of is the doctor saying,
"You're a special case."
Now you're becoming weaker and weaker.
And your voice is becoming meeker and meeker.
You shouldn't lose all hope,
Because your family will find new ways to help you cope.

With My Little Girl
by Angela Queen - age 18

Once, a short time ago, I met a young man
He said he loved me for a time
We planned to marry and have children
We were together for a time
It seemed to be something to last
We became one, as mankind does
I fell for him deeply
I came to love him
When he found a new toy,
He left quickly

I turned out to be with babe
She has no daddy
Because he skipped town
No marriage
He never planned to
So said he as he left
Me with child
With my little girl

Old Santa Claus
by Carolyn Pyzynski

When I was but a little child,
And all tall tales were true,
I'd sit and wait so patiently
'Til mother's work was through.

For then, you see, 'twas story time
For tales both tall and wide.
They'd keep me listening eagerly,
Content and goggle eyed.

Of course I liked the fairy ones
And those about the elves,
But the one I really liked the best
Was of Santa Claus himself.

I'd let my imagination run
Way up to the far north pole
Where Santa and his helpers lived-
They didn't mind the cold.

The little snow birds just outside
Were listening with one ear
To all the good and all the bad
That had gone on all year.

The Christmas Eve that I was ten
I waited up myself
To see old Santa find our snack
And then enjoy himself.

I peeked around so quietly
And then...Oh, was I mad!
Enjoying that swell cake and all
Was no one but my dad!

Flowers
by Latricia M. Quan - age 16

Flowers are fragile
Lovely and beautiful
In their own little
Unique way.

Flowers bring smiles
Of joy and happiness
To the faces of
Wonderful people.

Why do flowers
die and wither,
And not keep
Us happy forever?

Without Saying Hi Or Good-bye
by Sarah Rademacher - age 16

The years go by friends come and go
some leave without saying good-bye
and some come without saying hi.

Your Many Ways
by Beth Quilty - age 16

    For the six great months we've been together,
    Hotness, coldness, all kinds of weather,
    I think about what my life would be
    Without us together, you here with me.
    Our love has grown stronger throughout the days
    And has made me realize your magnificent ways:
    The way you strut when you walk,
    And how your lips move when you talk.
    When you close your eyes, then open them,
    I see your love from deep within.
    When your heart beats in the middle of the night,
    And you're holding onto me so tight,
    I feel all of my emptiness subside
    And realize you're there by my side.
    I see the way when you twitch your nose,
    And I acknowledge all the love you show.
    I notice when your hair isn't exactly right,
    I don't think it matters, but you think it might.
    When you sing, I hear your voice,
    To me it's music, not just a noise.
    These are the ways you do everything,
    The way you walk, talk and sing.
    I grow to love you more each day,
    And I love each of your many ways.

Till The End Of Our Road
by Jessica Quinn - age 14

When the night is cold
And love seems to fade
And it seems as though the world
Is covered with shade
I will always love you
When the sun is too hot
And love seems to grow
And seems as though
You can never let me go
Think of the night
With the breeze so cold
And think of us together, growing old
I will always love you
till the end of our road.

The Unseen People
by Jessica Quinn - age 14

They crept up slowly to the rich man's bed
He didn't believe a word that the poor man had said
The unseen people were coming for him
The shades closed shut and the room went dim
His hands turned to ice where shades shut by themselves
And out of the shadows came out a bunch of elves
Elves were not short, they were very tall
One came through the doorway that led to the hall
The rich man lay still, trying not to be seen
That made the elves mad, so they ripped out his spleen.
They cut him up in many ways in the middle of that night
The way that they killed that man was an ungodly sight
The Geir were the elves that captured the rich man's soul
They would put the soul in a box so to never let it go.
The elves left with the box which was in their hand
And took it to the Kenkari, a giant elf clan
The Kenkari were the keepers of the souls
How many souls they have, nobody knows
The unseen people could be lurking anywhere
So if you're a rich man, I'm telling you to beware

Mother's Day Tribute
by Kattie Quinn - age 15

    Some things we often
    Leave unsaid,
    The thoughts we think
    Inside our heads.
    Someone so great
    Would share their fears,
    Share their thoughts,
    Their joys, their tears.
    Someone so great
    Would show their friendship,
    Share their life and love.
    They often seem to be
    Sent from above.
    They are the ones who
    Help us through the hard times,
    Give us praise,
    And help us shine.
    They are
    The mothers of the world.
    Mom you are the best
    In every little way.
    Often I don't say all the things
    I'd really like to say,
    Most of all,
    On this day its true,
    All I want to say is,
    "I love you!"

The Game
by Christie Rader

Too many mistakes and too much love
Given when it shouldn't have been.
Stolen moments, glances and touches,
Playing this game that no one can win.

Who's heart is next to be broken?
Mine was first and can take no more.
I've been in the game too long,
I should have known the outcome, it's all happened before.

Once again I put up my wall
Though it seems harder to rebuild this time.
Like so many blocks we kicked down as children
I again, after long last, find solace in my rhyme.

Meandering through my hopes and fears
I find myself searching deeper still
Subconsciously, aimlessly with no focus
For something lost, a thing I though I could no longer feel.

Talking more to myself than to anyone
How could anyone else understand
This strange situation I've put myself in,
This constant, ever-tightening band.

I once was the master of the fine art of the game
Always anticipating the next move,
Knowing before, what play next came.

In my mind's eyes, I see the game unfold
I just don't see myself winning this time.
I watch the blocks fall down
And again, after long last, find solace in my rhyme.

Poet's Trust
by B.J. Radford

We try to put these words upon a page, as all we Poets must.
It's a driving force we can't control, we can only learn to trust.

To trust these words we've written here to convey just how we think.
To convey, to you, just how we feel about the subject of our work.

We trust you understand the meaning we impart upon this page.
To see the visions we have seen, to hear the laughter,
to sometimes feel the rage.

We bare our soul, pour out our heart in the words that are written here.
We trust that you will understand, and our meaning will be clear.

So trust we do, as trust we must, because "Poets" that's what we are.
Treat us kindly when you read our work, you hold something very dear.

Each word, each line, each finished poem are, our children so to speak.
Each has a name, each has a life, each special and unique.

You hold in your hand a finished work, but it's really much much more.
Your hold a window to our soul, to our heart an open door.

Read each word, read every line, be critical if you must.
Enjoy each phrase and stanza, you hold a "Poet's Trust".

Untitled
by Shari R. Raia

Yesterday
I heard a whisper in the wind.
I recognized its mournful cry and my soul reached out.
I was left with the impression of what could have been and
I cried.

Why
by Jennifer Rector - age 15

I still have all our memories in my heart.
Back then I thought we could never part.
Until you were taken away from me,
In a tragedy.
I have to learn to live without you,
And my father too.
Why did you have to leave?
Your always supposed to be there for me,
So why did you have to leave?

Thirteen Little Girls
by Carolyn Raskauskas - age 12

one little girl sat in the sun
another joined her to have some fun

two little girls swam in water that was blue
another joined them to do something new

three little girls looked at a bruise on ones knee
another joined them to play with you and me

four little girls jumped on the floor
another joined them to help the poor

five little girls looked at a bee hive
another joined them for a dive

six little girls ate trail mix
another joined them to play some tricks

seven little girls fought with boys who where eleven
another joined them to look at angels in heaven

eight little girls stayed up late
another joined them to find some bait

nine little girls played with dolls that were mine
another joined them to wait in the movie line

ten little girls played with a hen
another joined them to talk to their friend

eleven little girls babysat little boys age seven
another joined them to look at a cow called devon

twelve little girls went to hang a shelve
another joined them to go on a delve

thirteen little girls went to dinner and got a bean
another joined them to get clean

World To Go Away
by Patrice Reeves - age 13

Sometimes I want this world to go away, but at times I want this world to stay. When the world wants too much, and it feels cold and not touched. And I want someone to tell me it's all right; to stay with me, keeping watch over me day and night. As I watch a nightingale fall asleep, I want this world to stay forever and keep. But time marches on; yet we don't move our feet or the world will slip away, and won't be within our reach.

Winter Of 78
by Angela Rasmussen - age 17

Morning dew
upon my tongue.
The winter chill
the cold has won.
The ice upon the lips of mine,
blue at the surface,
violet eyes.
I saw you make angels in the snow-
I saw you lie there
bare, and numb.
And then a tear fell where you lie
you look deep into my inner fire
If I could give that warmth to you,
I'd shed of it,
and die by you.
But lightening strikes,
and thunder roars.
Together we smile
and melt with the snow.

The Sounds of Abuse
by Jessica Ratliff - age 16

Snap!
The belt cracks upon the child
A look in the eye,
Mother gone wild

Sniffle! Drip!
The tears stream down the face
The innocent child
Afraid to move

Slap!
Comes the hand
Racing down
The innocent skin,
It soon has found

Bang!
Slams the door
As she races from the room

Moan!
The child awakes once more
Not quite remembering why
He's upon the floor

Wind
by Chandra Raynes - age 15

Wind whispers your name to me as I sleep alone.
At night it carries me on it's wings of silver to your side.
But when we are apart it howls and twists it's fury with it's rage.

Wind is a funny thing, it can bring the spring rain and gentle breezes of summer.
Yet it can bring the chill of autumn and snow of winter.
When man has done wrong it will show its anger.
But when man is dying it will show its sorrow.

Wind is a part of all of us. It brings us love and can bring sorrow.
If the wind ever stops so will everything it has ever touched.
Especially it's whispers it brings and it's silver wings.
So when you ever feel love wrapped around you like a lover,
It's only the wind.

What If There Were No Guys
by Valorie Reavis - age 13

What if there were no guys,
such a life I would despise.
There wouldn't be a purpose,
for girls to come to the surface.
Shopping would be a chore,
since the viewing was so poor.
Binoculars would go out of style,
and thrown into a pile.
There wouldn't be any scores,
we wouldn't have to worry about pores.
We could eat many fattening pies,
'cause there wouldn't be any guys!

Been Thinking
by Anna Recupero

Today I sit her thinking of you
with why you've gone you left me no clue.
Thinking of the way it used to be
Love and life used to flow before me
but now you are gone
You left me no will to carry on
Searching for that special love
that has flown as gracious as a dove
I ponder what it may have been
Two hearts are broken it is a sin
to have so much and let it go
    Just say no, just say no
We mustn't end
two hearts are broken, but they can mend
So we can still be together
you and me, we are forever.

Oh, To Be An Author
by Karen I. Reed

I want very much to be an author.
    But, to no avail.
I'm afraid I'll always be a pauper.
    Ringing up "no sale."

Every manuscript I write.
    Never gets read, so doesn't prevail.
I might as well fly each page away, like a kite.
    With neither string nor tail.

You see, I was in a tremendous accident.
    All that's left is my mind in perfect detail.
In mind, I create stories with intent.
    In that way, mountains I'll scale.

I just try to get them read and printed.
    I'm not trying to sell them at retail.
Then, they will be well read and minted.
    And, I'll have told my tale.

The Future
by Nicole Reese - age 15

The future is a blank spot to many people.
No one knows what it will bring or what it
won't bring. They just drift through time
wondering. Wondering what will happen and if it
does happen what news does it hold.
A lot of people can't handle what the future
will bring therefore they erase whatever future
they might of had. The future might of had a
few draw backs but it would also brought
a lot of pleasant things. No ones future is
perfect. If it was perfect the world wouldn't
be as it is now.

The people that can handle the future just
sit there and wait for it to come. instead
of trying to make it a better they let it come
as it is. And that will make their future
as bleak as their present.

Untitled
by Nicole Reese - age 15

As I look at him today I saw an expression
That I see rarely these days. It's something
that a woman would love to wake up
to in the morning and the last thing
she'd want to see at night.
And then he looks at me and smiles this
warm gentle smile that puts so many questions
in my head. I don't know which to ask
and which not. And that's what scares
me, the uncertainty of all these questions.
If I ask them will they haunt me in
the end or pave the way for a beginning
a new hope that we will get a chance
to make everything right that was so
wrong before. Or is it all just a sweet
dream that will never come true.

Heartkeeper
by Nicole Reese - age 15

He knows that I love him yet he plays games
with my heart and my mind. I know not what I
have done to make him do this to me but all
I know is no matter how much hurt he gives
me I want him more and more.
Does that make me a fool? That I do not know.
But not a day goes by that I don't stop and think
about him. Think about how it would be to be with
him. To feel his touch and to awakened by his
desire. That would mean the world to me.
Yet there is something I can't describe. Something
that keeps us apart. And until we are strong
enough to break through it we will forever be
just mere aquainances, faces in the crowd.
Yet I will always be looking for a certain face
in the crowd. A face that will haunt me. And
a face that I will never forget no matter
how much it will hurt me to remember.
You can never forget the person who
held your heart for so long.

Whispering Hope
by Patrice Reeves - age 13

As I stand here by my window, with moonlight on my face. I stand with your presence in my heart, and I'm keeping it there in place. Trying desperately to cling to the past, looking over my shoulder, searching for memories to last. You were my ambition when I lost my strength, I am searching for a future, though it is with pain. Now as I lay my head on this pillow, staring out above weeping willows, I shall keep your memory with my heart, for the time has come for us to part.

Needs
by Rebecca Marie Reeves - age 15

I need your advice to help me.
I need your humor to carry me.
I need your seriousness to guide me.
I need your personality to make me smile.
I need your strength to protect me.
I need your weakness to persuade me.
I need your mind to understand me.
I need your expressions to show me.
I need your shoulder to cry on.
I need your love to hold me.
I need YOU to be my friend.

Injustice
by Lisa Renner - age 15

Injustice is everywhere
Even in society of people
Or even in a little animal,
Colony of rats.

Injustice cannot be solved,
But helped,
If the society becomes whole.
If the colony is one with itself.

I have seen injustice,
Spoken though the eyes of a child.
I have heard injustice,
Spoken though the heart of a man.

Is injustice curable?
Can it be solved?
Blood in the streets,
This is injustice.

No rights at all,
No freedom of speech.
Yes this is injustice,
And it lies within even you.

Mr. Green
by Anna Reznik - age 12

Once Mr. Green,
Was so mean,
But kinda keen,
But his wife,
Sharpens a knife,
And says 'Get a life',
Don't remember her,
Or get a bur,
And a coat of fur,
Of a winner,
but also a sinner,
But come for dinner,
Tonight,
In the light,
Or even in fright.

Protect Our Planet
by Anna Reznik - age 12

I'm a fish in a net,
Trapped and saying Protect Our Planet,
For we only have one earth,
That can burst,
Any second, so watch out,
Or be trapped on the mount,
Recycle and pick up paper,
On the carpet,
Of the damaged planet,
And don't say you don't care and can it!

In Remembrance Of Me
by F. Jane

Crown of thorns
Piercing your temples
Trickles of blood
Stinging your eyes
Overlooking our ignorance

Palms nailed to a crossed plank
With feet bolted the same
Rich, thick fluid steadily flowing
To the earth
Redding the soil forevermore

One last insult was pierced
Upon the Savior of man
In the fashion of a gaping wound
Of His side
Draining the last of His essence

With but one cry
The Lamb of God
Surpassed this existence
To become an advocate
Of us
With the Father
And save us from all sins

The bread is broken
As a symbol of His broken body
The wine is poured
A sign of His spilled blood
Eat and drink
In Remembrance of Me

Love Was Here
by Hilary Rhodes - age 14

Your love was here,
but now it's gone.

You said you'd always be near,
so why aren't you here?

We had plans for our life,
for me to be your wife.

We said we'd never part,
but then you broke my heart.

I said it would last forever,
will we back together, ever?

I wish this pain would go away,
maybe it will, someday.

"Third Finger Left Hand"
by Joseph Rhodes

As affectionate relationships romantically become more in demand...Companionship allows our intimate feelings for one another to emotionally expand...Because conception has provided us with something that we matrimonially can understand...During this ceremonious moment inside marriage where my heart is prenuptially placing love upon your:

Flight
by Jude Rice - age 14

As I look on the vast expanse of blue,
I will fly today, can this be true,
For today is the day that I may die,
But at least I had my chance to fly,
I will jump off the cliff way up there,
And this will be point to fly into the air,
As I know I will to fly deep within my emotions,
For I will fly land to land, ocean to ocean,
Now I am on my way up the hill,
I am going to fly today, can this be real,
Now I will ready my soul for this feat,
Who's victory is mine and will taste so sweet,
Now free-falling, I am going to die,
Even though my emotions said I would fly,
And my life flashed before me, one I never knew,
I will die, but at least I flew.

Where I First Saw The Light
by Donald Richardson

I was in Vietnam 1966-67, 68-69,
One night of an attack,
Rockets were coming in on us,
We all went to our Bunkers,
We all were scared,
Praying to the Lord Jesus
To protect us,
Now we could hear explosions,
The Rockets were hitting around us
A sweat was on my face,
Oh! God, Oh! God,
One man was saying,
Then a light appeared,
An image stood there,
His hands stretched outward,
We all felt calm and safe,
As the light disappeared,
The Rockets stopped falling,
Then we heard the all clear sounded,
Thank God we are alive..........

A Dream
by Somer Riden - age 16

I knew his thoughts,
His every move.
He said he loved me,
Then why did he leave?
He says he'll be back,
But when?
I don't know.

I spend my days
Waiting for his return.
I know he won't,
But I'm stuck on a dream.
A dream of love.

Silioquy
by Charity Ridley

The jutted rock
    looks out over the sea
The young piper
    plays a song to me
His red cape
    flies out with the wind
His musical notes
    make my mind spin
The colorful sunset
    is what he plays about
His magical flute
    I couldn't live without
The emerald sea
    is very hard to compare
As I dance and leap
    in the salty air
His music ends
    he looks over at me
He takes my hand
    and we walk into the sea

Thanks
by Susan Rieger - age 18

Thanks-
for putting up with me
and the anger i put you through

Thanks-
for helping me past the hard times
just by staying close

Thanks-
for knowing when to leave
and let me on my own

Thanks-
for not going with the others
and turning away from me

Thanks-
for being my source of strength
when I'm left with an empty heart

Thanks-
for allowing me to say
you'll always be my bestfriend

What Is Love?
by M.K. Robbins

To some it's just a word,
A word they think means something
                                to them,

And the only reason they say it is to
let their partner know that things are ok
But really it's not
To them it's just a word.

To others, it's a feeling
A feeling that comes from way down
inside-from your heart and soul,
it's a feeling that makes some feel
secure inside, but some confused,
They don't say it all the time-but
when they do, they mean it - to
them it is truly a feeling.

Long Distance Desperation
by Elizabeth Capron Rigg - age 15

the pounding of h let you know
this is truly for real.

Across the miles
the whispered fears
And streams and rivers
of so many tears.

You yearn
and you ache
and burn
and moan
then ask your dear god
why your all alone.

But our love is so strong...
We have to pull through!
But what is the center of our strength?
me and you?

In truth our blazing fury
flames on and flames on
we think forever
but slowly it's gone.

Like the last rose withering
in the season of fall
You may feel you have nothing
but you once had it all.

Tears Of Fire
by Jamie Robinson - age 17

My eyes have cried a thousand tears
and my heart doesn't beat at all,
these tears one day may dry
but soon again they will fall.
A burning sensation of love and hate,
one tear has fallen
now it's too late.
Slowing me down
so I drop to my knees,
stop forcing the tears
I'm begging you please.
You are breaking the dream
of the hearts desire,
you keep making me cry
these tears of fire.

Thoughts Of Me
by Maryellen Roach - age 18

When you see the stars at night, think of me,
find the big dipper, the last handle star is ours, you see.
When you see the moon in the sky, think of me,
find the man's mouth-he smiles at lover's glee.
When you see the sun shining, think of me,
every last ray has hope for love to be.
When you see a bright blue sky, think of me,
because, I always think of thee.

Love
by Sasha Riley - age 16

Fear is love,
Love is weird,
Weird is different,
And different is happiness.

Happiness is comfort,
Comfort is wonderful,
Wonderful is peace,
And peace is time.

Time is free,
Free is dear,
Dear is desire,
Desire is forever,
And forever is right.

Right is soundless,
Soundless is eternal,
Eternal is deceit,
Deceit is hate,
And hate is dreadful.

Dreadful is shadows,
Shadows is doubt,
And doubt is love.

"Ocean Tides"
by Valerie Robinett - age 12

Our love is like the ocean tides,
Sometimes its low and sad.
At those times I sit and cry
Over the love I thought we had.

Our love is like the ocean tides,
Sometimes its happy and high.
At those times when I'm with you
I feel like I could fly.

Our love is like the ocean tides
But whether its low or high,
I'll love you forever and always
And this I can't deny.

    For Jordan.

Private Shadows
by Jasmine Alowan Rotmil - age 18

Your repulsive language
and mad beauty
scream luscious worship.
Whispers from a blue,
death-like goddess
rip through my head.
Beneath the bitter, bloody love
I lust frantic black rain.
The languid milk-chocolate moon
was watching me tongue into a friend.
Bare and aching, I cry
as I knife my skin
and chant purple honey
to a shadow.

Can You Hear My Tears
by Virginia Riley

Can you hear my pen just rambling on
Can you hear the pain I feel
Can you see that it creates a bond
Between us that's for real

Please believe me that this pain just sparks
incentives created from my heart
And I know your concern helps my hand to write
my feelings from the start

Can you hear my cry, I am here my friend
Oh can you see my tears
we have known each other for so long
it's been eons of good years

It's unfortunate that its my fate
But I must accept each day
For I'm laying here with a bottle of tears
That is filled each time I say

Can you hear my tears- they softly flow
But it helps to write them down
For I'm watched by God in the things I do
And he hears my every sound

The Mountains
by Sheila B. Roark

Crystalline snow adorns
the peaks of granite
decorating the stone
with diamonds made of ice

Cold winds blow
and move the snow
causing it to dance
with flowing grace

Stoically they stand
these mighty mountains
guarding the land below
as they always have

They are strength
these peaks of granite
and will stand
until the end of time.

Guardian Angel
by Jennifer Robertson - age 15

I hear her in my mind,
She knows and sees all that I do.
She is one of my kind,
And yet unlike anyone I ever knew.

She helps me do what's right,
But lets me know my wrongs, too.
She battles with my evil side,
And always triumphs true.

She knows my ups and downs,
Knows when I'm happy and blue.
She rejoices in my pleasure,
Consoles me right on cue.

She's my best friend and confidant,
Others that good are scarce and few.
She believes in me and loves me,
And can do the same for you.

Darling Tamra Jane
by Andee Robbins Jr.

Tamra Jane
The sweetest thing
that happened to me
Or said my name
hearing your voice
Eliminates pain
Darling Tamra Jane.

Tamra Jane
I cried in vain
When you left
To start again
I hope you know
My love's the same
Sweet Tamra Jane.

Tamra Jane
A darling dame
I need you now
To keep me sane
My love is stronger
Than words can say
I love you Tamra Jane.

The Love Song
by Irish D.J.R. - age 17

A tender melody, a familiar voice.
A joyful noise, a painful memory.
When you hear your song, it can bring you sheer joy and happiness
As long as there is no heartache involved.
If you hear your song and the good memories have past between
the pages, it can bring you misery and pain.
A love song can cause many emotions that show, and many
that don't show.
Years from now, long after the relationship has ended, the
love song can still make you feel that way.

The Common Broken Heart
by Andee Robbins Jr.

How come we
    can prolong life,
And kill diseases
    before they start?

        But we have never
            found a cure,
        for the common
            broken heart.

We can explore
    the world
        from outer space
And send people
    to the moon.

        But we can't even
            ease the pain
    That love can
        Put us through.

I wrote these lines
    for you
        my dear
I hate to see
    you blue.

        Anytime you need
            to cry,
    Remember,
        I love you.

Untitled
by Jessica Roberge - age 17

I love you is what you said,
I like you is what you meant.

I love you is what I said,
I don't know is what I meant.

You are the only one for me is what you said,
Only at the moment was what you meant.

Lets separate for a few days was what you said,
I'm going to leave was what you meant.

Ok, that's fine was what I said,
I love you, please don't is what I meant.

My Long Lost Love
by Jennifer Roberts - age 16

I gaze into your deep, and incredibly dark eyes.
I'm amazed at how beautiful you really are.
It's as if I can see what's inside you at just one glance.
I'm caught up in these thoughts,
and, almost as if reading my mind,
I feel your soft, tender lips gently brush
against mine.
The wide range of emotions run through my body.
This is definitely something I haven't felt before.
Your strong arms surround me firmly,
and I never want you to let go.
It seems like eternity,
but I want to savor each moment.
Somehow, it all ends.

Is this love?

I'm at a loss of words,
so I go for the touchdown.
And I kiss you again.
Score!

It must be love.

Standing
by Emily Roberts - age 16

He stands, strong and proud,
She kneels, humbly praying,
The two have a love so deep,
Yet they never see eye to eye.

His love is like a bull,
Strong, fierce, and protective,
Her love is like a butterfly,
Soft, sweet, and pure.

The bull hath strayed,
Seeking comfort in another,
The butterfly becomes strong,
She does not fly away.

She stands, strong and proud,
He kneels, humbly praying,
Their love for each other is weakened,
Now that they see eye to eye.

Untitled
by Shari Robson - age 17

Listening, waiting
it's silent.
No-one speaks
No-one moves.
Wondering, thinking
Everythings lost.
There's no answer
not enough times.
Wanting, wishing
won't get it.
They come
they go.

Still waiting
still silent.
They won't come
they don't speak
they don't move.
There's no time.
They come
they go.
Still there,
alone
the only one there.

Death
by Brenda Rodarte - age 14

Death is dark,
Dark and dreary,
Death is like an old oak,
Stubborn hard and weary.

Death will come,
He will get you,
Sooner or later he will be
There is nothing you can do.

Death is everywhere,
North, south, east and west,
Death is here,
Death will put you at rest.

Baseball
by Raye Roeder - age 12

Baseball is broken bones when you least need them.
Baseball is a pitch to the catcher, catcher misses, and the other team steals home.
Baseball is a coach in the dugout yelling signals at you that you don't understand.
Baseball is being on deck the day you're having a slump.
Baseball is listening to the ump tell you that you are out when you know that you are not.
Baseball is a foul when you hit the ball perfectly, just in the wrong direction.
Baseball is having bases loaded and you get an out.
Baseball is a batter getting nervous and tightening up.
Baseball is when the center fielder, the worst batter on the team, hits a grandslam.
Baseball is when the other team's pitcher can't pitch and our pitcher gets to walk.
Baseball is pouring water all over the coach's head after winning the championship game.
Baseball is striking out the other team's shortstop.
Baseball is catching a flyball when you were just told to pay more attention.
Baseball is sitting at the ball park in 90 degree weather just to watch the guy you like play.

The Merry-Go-Round
by Kathleen F. Roe

The full moon casts
    it's light on an abandoned park.
Steam slowly rises
    from the murky waters of a shallow creek bed.
Dead trees stand
    with their arms reaching out to embrace the dark.
    ...Then comes the groan of the merry-go-round.
    An eerie blanket of cold, dead silence falls,
    But the merry-go-round goes around and around.
A gust of wind sweeps
    through the park, causing the swings to sway.
Slides stand tall against short oak trees.
    Steel bellies gleam in the pale moon light.
Swirls of sand and dirt are caught up
    in small twisters and carried away.
    ...The see-saw-
    Well, it just sits there cracked and gray,
    while the merry-go-round goes around and around.
The light of the moon hides
    behind a long, thick cloud.
The wind settles down,
    but the merry-go-round keeps going around.
At the crack of dawn birds flock together,
    chirping loudly with wings flapping.
The park comes alive,
    oblivious to what's happening.
    ...Catching the light of early morning
        the merry-go-round spins into a blur.
        Suddenly, without warning,
            it stops to wait for another night to occur.

A Mirror Image
by Crystal Rohleder - age 14

As I stand beside myself
In a small white room
Doctors fight, I feel no pain
Yet they're pounding on my chest
Life, my life is inches away
I reach and I fight
Walking away from the light
I see now what my life has meant
I will not lose what I have not spent

Spiders, Snakes, and Snails
by Crystal Rohleder - age 14

Slimy slippery ewey gooy spiders
Tastey Yummy gushy ushy spiders
Slip 'n' Slide
Slither and wiggle
Deep into the pit
of my stomach
Rolly polly giggley shivery snakes
Slithery tickly icky sticky snakes
Slip 'n' slide
Slither and wiggle
Deep into the pit
of my stomach
Sticky skaly scary darey snails
Yucky sucky salty maulty snails
Slip 'n' slide
Slither and wiggle
Deep into the pit
of my stomach
YUM!

Promise of Someday
by Tamela Christensen-Rold

Fret not the shadows
Lurking and dark
For there lies a secret waiting
If you'll only listen
And not be afraid
Someday you have to grow up
Which means not being frightened of the dark places
For adulthood is spent there
So you live in fear
Knowing one day you'll be sent away
Cold and shivering to some distant promise
But you will never attain it because it is not your dream
Someone else will take the glory and live the life meant for you
Be glad of it
You're dancing on the edge of a life of today
While their tomorrow's are already spent.

Blue Empyrean
by Kim Aleta Rose

Awakened by a heavenly harmony
from on high
Sighted a silhouette while
scanning the sky
Hovering over strings of a
celestial rhyme
Reminiscent of ballads of
the bluesy kind
Resounding serenade
lyrical and clear
Emerging through the clouds
Sweet angel did appear
I am here
in your stage of woe
To atone your heart
Restore your soul
Earthbound, go back
return to rest
Eternally retaining the
final curtain request.

Societies So-Called Rules
by Karla Roth - age 14

Follow the rules,
Don't stand out,
Don't hang out with the
    losers and such,

Express yourself,
Don't be shy,
Don't try to be something
    you aren't,

Parents know best,
Do as they say,
Even if it is very petty and
    has nothing to do with anything,

Which to follow,
Which is right,
could it be D- none
    of the above?

Somebody
by Cristine Rottman - age 14

I walk through this life doin what I should,
All the while, I look ahead to see what I have to accomplish
being careful to notice what I already have

I go to a hometown ball game. As I look around,
Everyone seems to have somebody. They may not have
accomplished anything in their life but they already
have somebody, no matter what age.

A wise old man said, "You can have the world,
but it don't mean nothin unless you got somebody."
So, maybe before I get everything accomplished in this
life, I'll find somebody, and something.

My Mom
by Marianne Rowe - age 15

My mom is always there
for me whatever I may go,
I whatever mood I'm in-
Whether I'm high and happy or
sad and low.
She's never given up on me
Because she knows I need her, you see.
At times I may not show it.
But she's what helps to keep me tickin.
Although I may seem brave at times
The truth is I'm just a plain ol chiken.
With the love and warmth from my mom,
I know I'll make it through, and that there
is no other that could replacer my loving dear
mother.

You
by Karell Roxas - age 14

Whenever I am with you
I feel as if in a dream.
Too much love, so it seems.

What you mean to me,
I can't find the words to express.
You touch me deep inside
like a soft, single caress.

When I look at you, it stirs up feelings
from deep inside my soul.
My love for you, could fill
an everlasting hole.

My heart yearns for you,
whenever you're not around.
You are the greatest love
I have ever found.

For awhile, it seemed
that love just passed me by.
I kept asking questions,
Always wondering why.

Now I know that love can be true.
Everything I could ever need,
I found in you.

My Pain or Yours?
by Amanda Rud - age 14

I'm lying in the shadows
Watching life pass me by,
I'm giving up the struggle, I know I'm gonna die.
I am too weak to fight,
Can't hold on any longer
The only way I could live, is if God can make me stronger.
The pain is about to end
How soon, I do not know
For my problems and fears continually seem to grow.
Everyone tries so hard,
I don't want to let then down
I'm sorry if I hurt you, but I cannot stick around.

What Is Me!
by Bernice Rumala - age 16

What is me?
Am I the way others perceive me to be?
Am I the way I think of myself?
Am I the one who gives meaning to others?
Am I the one who shatters meaning?

I am not just flesh on this earth!
I am not a number!
What is me?
I have goals and aspirations--
But doesn't everyone?
I think of the figure I will cut in the world.
Ambitions awake within me.
It just may be others may know me better than I.
But as time passes by, my image shall uncover itself piece by piece,
and then shall I know what is me.

masks
by elizabeth rutten - age 15

everyone wears them
no one says anything about them

at church
at school
at work
at home-
everywhere

i'm never myself
i don't even know who i am

with one friend i'm one person
with another friend i'm someone else

we are stuck
there's no way out

be yourself everyone says
but what they're not saying is
be yourself as long as you're like me

A Special Message
by JoAnna Rutter

I love you, just three
little words that are
so easy to feel, but
yet there so hard to
say.
Instead the world's
full of hate, who knows
maybe these three
little words could change
it all, if only spoken
instead of being hidden.
I Love You...
I say it to the world.

Cowboy Way
by JoAnna Rutter

There are boys and there
are men.
They all go by one code, it's
the cowboy way.
The dress in: wranglers, boots,
western shirts, and hats.
They all carry that certain
image, to fit the image
they portray.
A ceratin I'm God image.
These boys and men, ride the
bulls, do the ropin, the clownin
and even bronc ride.
They'll break a girls heart
and leave her cryin' then
there off to find another.
Although they never mean to;
it's just the cowboy way.
These boys and men are
hard to love; and same as the
song, even harder to hold.
But it's all a code of the
life they live called the
cowboy way.

The Swollen River
by Marilyn B. Rutter

The swollen river swims like a sea or lake,
   Wide and swiftly running free.
Chocolate brown with trees and bushes roving past
   This is what we see.
The trail lies covered in the foam
as the river tries to find a home.
   Swirling, slashing, sweeping steadily along.
In rubber boots, the water covers half a leg.
   The trail is smothered, steadily with the
   slowly, sloppy swirling surf.

The Truth Is A Lie You Believe
by Brooke Ryan - age 15

Government coverups,
Lies of the old,
Ancient religions.
Stupid decisions,
God is a ghost,
Sinners burn in hell,
I don't think so,
Disgusting drones,
plentiful as stones,
Believe what your told,
Conform to the mold,
Don't ask questions
Buy what your sold,
Protest the apathy
Destroy the sympathy
Attack the mobs,
Break out in sobs.
There is no hope
Make a noose in the rope
Study the sky
Hang yourself high.

Missing You
by Megan Ryno - age 16

You're gone and I know I'll never see you again
I miss you so much, but it hurts to think of you
I wanted to tell you how much I love you, but I came too
late and now you're gone.
Gone Forever
I know I won't see you again until I join you in Heaven
And right now, that's all I want to do,
Join you in that wonderful Paradise up above
I feel empty inside, as if all the love inside me has
disappeared
I am missing you, but slowly, ever so slowly,
Someone else is trying to take your place.
I can't let them do that, so I push them away,
Telling myself you're up there waiting for me.
Slowly, your face is fading away.
I miss you and want to see you again, but fate won't let me.
So I sit here
Waiting
Waiting for my time on this earth to end
So once again I can set my eyes on your beautiful face.

A Time We Last Met
by Kimberly Sabat - age 18

Walking above a tiled floor, the room pictured nothing that was before,
And in that room just past the door,
I spotted a glimpse of you.

I stopped and stared at my love, just picturing how his face above,
the surface of the tile...a dove
has landed at my window.

A finger gently I lifted up, to a feathery breast I cupped
my hand around the velvet dove,
and held it to my body.

But after a moment that lasted for years,
the bird exploded into a million tears
that caught the light, and to my ears
came the sweetest sounds.

The tears just hung there in the night, and slowly drifted from my sight,
before I tried and clutched them tight,
against my sorrowful self.

I drop to my knees, my silken gown, waves like the water;
like the trees around
the full moon-now that's sunken down
past where it's light can reach me.

Face in hands I give up sobbing, and look to the sky,
my weak heart throbbing
to see my love, but he's inside me...
"Please come out once again."

"I miss the love and life you've given, to me and all the hopes-
I've lived in
a dream, or maybe-is it heaven?...
Is it still above?..."

"For I am bound to earthly pleasures-my love,
to be by your side I treasure,
for the presence of you I'd take any measure;
do anything to keep you there."

"My love for you is ever growing, I live my days out here still knowing
that my heart is forever showing
just how much love there is for you."

Darkness Forever
by Leticia Sanchez - age 17

I sit in my bedroom,
   the darkness enveloping me.
He stands in the doorway,
   eyes the color of the tormenting sea.
A dark cloud descends upon his face,
   I cannot tell what's on his mind.
He looks into the windows of my soul,
   and reminds me of our pact, our bind.
I stare in silence at his shadow,
   remembering that deadly sin.
He continues beckoning me,
   he's determined he has a soul to win.
I rise from my bed, and walk towards him,
   preparing to leave this world, preparing to part.
As I place my hand within his grasp,
   I look back and remember he's always had my heart.
I walk into the depths of his world,
   tearless,
Fearless I am not, and realize that I'll
   always be in darkness.

Not My Despair
by Andriana Saffas - age 15

Like ladybugs,
everyone spotted with problems.
So few are not plagued
by black dots of depression.
My association with
such a repertoire of troubled songs
carried by struggling hears,
keep pulling me down.
Like yanking a curtain from closepins,
they pull me down.
Each sufferer peels away at my own heart,
as if peeling an orange
leaving a mass of painful pulp-
my heart,
without the skin of safety.
Like a carcass
unprotected from varmints,
I am vulnerable to depressions of others.
Pain rips at my sides by knives of despair.
Not my despair,
yet it becomes my despair,
for I cannot repair the broken pieces of every life.
So wishing
to glue each piece of pottery together
leaving no trace of cracks-
no scarring memories of unrest.
Tragic problems are like flies-
common and numerous.

Perfection
by Tony Salomone

If the moon could see your smile
Or the stars simply gaze into your eyes
Only then would they truly be in heaven
As I am
Still, who am I to be so blessed?
If I could I would take the moon
And put it into your hands
So you could hold it for all time
But I am only a mortal man
Who has been allowed to behold perfection
Not seen since those first days of creation
When God molded the first woman Himself.

Little Girl Lost
by Rhonda Sampson

Gone for a short time,
but lost forever.
One man's moment of control,
one woman's nightmare forever.
He's behind bars for now,
but she's the one in prison.
I hope he burns in hell one day,
because she's living in it now.
Little girl lost,
forced to grow up before her time.
LOVE,
Mom

Black Rain
by Brenda C. Sanderlin

We are living now in a constant black rain,
Where there is no fog nor no real pain.
Where people try very hard to resist the plain,
But we are really living in a black rain.

Oh what a sight we all must be,
Looking down on the world what He must see,
The land that is filled with so much pain,
All because we're living in this black rain.

Give up, and plead you defeated little case,
You're fighting a battle, not a giant race,
O'man of war, stop raising all this cane,
And realize that you're living in a world of black rain.

Black rain come forth and please speak to me,
Open your crystal ball and tell me what you see?
I ask this question not for the simple gain,
But I want to know all about this cursed black rain.

O please, please give to me the keys,
As I kneel down and pray upon my knees,
I open my heart and stretch out in his name,
Compassion and love I ask of thee, black rain.

Here I am and take all of me,
This is my life I willingly give to thee.
And no other will have it to gain,
Because my heart and my soul belongs to black rain.

Rainbows
by Erika Sanders - age 15

Remembering God
Always there after rain when sun shines
In the beautiful sun filled sky
Never again destroy the earth by water again
Beautiful as the world itself
Optimistic
Worry no more about Noahs ark
Someone is watching over us and protecting us

Purple as violets on a bright spring day
Red as roses in a vase
Orange as the sun when it setting
Yellow as the sun in the middle of the afternoon
Green as the grass in a Golf Course
Blue as the water in the beautiful oceans.

The best promise anyone has ever made and kept.

My Forever Friend
by Amanda Schmidt - age 16

You were there from the beginning
And you'll be there 'til the end,
Whatever that may be,
You have stuck by me,
Through both good and bad,
And for that
I am thankful.
I want you to know
That I am here for you,
Just as you were for me.
You are my friend,
My forever friend.
You, are my mother.

"Waters of the Soul"
by Suma Sangisetty - age 13

My soul is an ocean raging with insanity.
My emotions surface as white crested waves.
My friends and enemies are the uncontrollable beings
Who live within my endless body,
Stirring the waves and arousing my feelings.
Someday I may be calm again,
But doubt enters my and continually.
As people live and people die,
My waves will soon vanish into the night.
The many lives within my soul will evaporate with my body.
And my life will cease, for I also am mortal.
My anger will be concealed in the sands;
You'll no longer see my love on the surface.
I'll stand motionless.
I'll be dead, yet strangely alive.
Look at me, my emotions are not wild anymore.
They do not spray salty mists angrily like an ocean.
Look deep into my dark soul,
the truth will be unveiled beneath:
Reveal not the depth of your emotions for all to see.
Lie still like a lake: Calm and peaceful.

Another Look
by Gerri Savic

If you look at me
or glance my way;
Will you have something
nice to say?
Will you tell me you loved me
from afar;
For it was written
on the nearest star.
Proclaim that we were
meant to be together;
Somehow; somewhere,
some forever;
Can you hold me near,
make all my empty thoughts disappear?
Will you gently lay your
hand on me;
Whisper soft words-of how
it will always be,
For that I should love you
more each day;
And remember you will
always stay,
To ward off my fears
Spend our golden years
Holding onto each other
building our own wonder;
Loving the only person
I can ever be,
Loving the one that you know
as me....

Land of Enchantment
by Theresa Marie Scavo

Come take a journey with me,
I'll show you places
others are not able to see.
Take my hand
we'll explore a majestic land
which exists if only you believe.

Fly through the clouds
walk along the horizon
lead us over the rainbow
What adventures it holds!

Encounter whatever your heart desires
Fear nothing, for together we shall conquer
as long as we remain hand in hand.
Nature has a way of shining in all her glory
Life is a never ending story.

Here we can share our deepest feelings
A place where the stars won't blind
the sun won't burn,
As we ride the warm summer skies
from each other we will live, love, learn.

Does this sound like paradise?
It shouldn't be of any surprise,
I see the beauty of this land
each time I listen to your heart,
looking deep into your eyes.

Replaced
by Terri L. Durden

If you would ever look at
yourself and try to imagine
yourself as another object,

I would have to say I was a
flower. When I was in bloom
I felt so alive, bright and
beautiful, the very center of
attraction. Everyone is willing
to pick me and enjoy the
beauty as long as possible.

But then the flowers time is
up and wilting takes place.

What else more left to offer
the viewer.
You're suddenly replaced with
that fresh new flower....

It's Great to Know
by Donna Schadler - age 18

Its great to know there's someone there,
who will be with you and always care.
To keep you warm when you get cold,
to support you in all your goals.

Its great to know there's someone there,
who will make you feel like you're floating on air.
To cheer you up when you feel down,
to make your frown turn upside down.
Someone who will be right by your side,
whether it be, good or bad times.
One you can trust and always believe in,
one who says I love you, and actually means it.

Its great to know there's someone there,
to kiss you good night in the cold, windy air.
One who will listen to what you have to say,
one who wants to hear all about your day.
Someone who will be true to you,
and never try to harm or hurt you.
Someone to talk to when you need advice,
someone to be with throughout time.
Its great to know there's someone there.

Missing
by Amber "Rosie" Schilb - age 14

I've never felt this way.
Nothing so strong.
You went away
And let my life go wrong.

I want you for myself.
I don't want to share.
All the love you gave me.
Gone-so unfair.

I'm left all alone
With no one to love.
My love is for you
Like a hand for a glove.

There must have been something
To bring us so close,
But now that you're gone
There's nothing to lose.

You're still in my life
Just not how I wish.
I want what we had.
All that I miss.

The Broken Vessel
by Dixie Lee Schneider

Just because your marriage didn't last til death do we part
Or maybe your horse is always behind the cart

And the cup that runneth over in never quite full
Or the child that you love doesn't follow man's rule

If the bulb is burned out of the glorifying light
Don't despair, in God's eyes, your life may be right

He has a plan for us whatever position were in
Take your seat at the table, and let the Wedding Supper begin.

Remember, my friend, Christ lived and died for us all
Even the broken pieces, no matter how small

The Sun And The Moon
by Colleen Schmitt - age 17

The sun met with the moon one evening
The stars weren't out, so there was plenty of room
She had so much to tell him, But somehow she didn't
They tried to embrace, as they did once, but she was too hot:
He would be singed by her fire
He didn't mind though
Her warmth had always been a comfort
When they parted she knew it was their last chance
She ran to catch up with him before he was gone...
But quickly she saw that her bright flames would go out if she went too fast
Then what would she do? the world would die!
Not to mention,
If they were too close the cycle would beak
They had a responsibility
Who would love her now?
The clouds would be enough - She knew
They were what she wanted
Light and soft and always there...
After all,
She hadn't caught him
But she could have
What kept her from doing it?
What's the difference,
Something did, And it means a great deal,
Even if IT is obscure
Perhaps it was her love of life

Consequences of Anger
by April Schneider - age 16

I am waiting.
Waiting for someone to release me.
Waiting to discharge pent up energy.

I sit here.
In this cold, hard chamber.
I go where I am carried.

When suddenly!
The master of my residence pulls the trigger!
He does not pull the trigger in hope of food.

He does not care that my release is anothers dread.
All he wants is to draw joy from my dirty deed.
He wants me to tear up the tender flesh of another living being.

As I fly over the hard cold pavement,
I try to move.
I try to stop.

But the energy in me is too strong.
I cannot save a life.
All I can do is wait.

Wait to enter the tender flesh of another.
Wait to lie in the tissue of a once beating heart.
This pointless act saddens me.

But it could not be stopped.
The anger in my master was too strong.
He could not stop himself just as I could not stop myself.

Anger destroyed the precious memories that will not be.
Anger took the breath out of fragile lungs.
Anger killed.

The Potter's Field
by Dixie Lee Schneider

He was with me everywhere
On the ground and in the air.
And in the breeze that blows my hair,

I sang his song and gave him praise.
And felt his love in many ways.
But then one day, he left my side
I cried, "Oh Lord my god, you lied!"

"You said you would never leave
Did I forget to believe?
Or did you turn and walk away
About the time my hair turned gray?

I know were told not to question
But may I make just one suggestion?
When our vessel breaks and falls apart
We need you most then in our heart.

Please shine your love on us clearly
Even broken pieces love you dearly.

Field Of Blood
by Dixie Lee Schneider

With thirty pieces of silver, and blood from his wounded side
The potters field was purchased at the time my savior died
He cries out "Father forgive them, for they know not what they do"
And with these words redemption came for sinner's like me and you.

Three days and nights in the heart of the earth, the victory is won
And God's Kingdom in Heaven awaits through the righteousness of His
    Son
Lift up your eyes to Jesus, trust Him and obey
For taking our sins to the cross, was the price he had to pay.

The potter's field-to bury strangers, was never more the same
For the field of blood- the price of him, is what became it's name.
So when we think that were just strangers in what we do each day
Remember why the potter died and that we are his clay.

The Window Seat
by Erin Schoenfelder - age 12

The window seat sits alone in the attic;
It's faded cushions make the room seem dramatic.
From it I can see for miles around,
Or just watch raindrops hit the ground.

On sunny days the scene is bright;
My thoughts take on a whole new light.
But cloudy times are always ahead,
When hope and sunshine appear to have fled.

And then here comes the lightning storm.
The sky begins to completely transform.
Streaks of color fill the sky,
And thunder sings a lullaby.

But soon the storm has gone away,
The calm returns without delay.
The gentle drumming of the rain,
Drives away the deepest pain.

The sky is dark and night is near,
And stars majestically appear.
Beneath the moon I fall asleep,
But the memories I'll always keep.

The Way We Remember It
by Alisha Schuble - age 14

When the day comes for us to go,
I wish that we didn't have to know.
When we all look back at this day,
we all wish we could of stayed.
When we leave our friends so dear,
all our eyes will fill with tears.
We wanted this day to never come,
we wish that we had had more fun.
When we say goodbye we just want to cry,
all of us feel so sad it somtimes makes us mad.
We stand here on this day awaiting God's hand of fate,
we hope and pray that it will be great.
Together we will be on this special day,
knowing we will all go our separate ways.
Knowing our future is in Gods hands,
we're willing to follow and trust in his plans.

Reprieve
by Sylvia Schuster

We have learned
how to live
inside capsules
that cannot cure
the common cold.

Each morning
the tablets dissolve
the pain
of being crushed
inside elevators
that never leave
the ground floor.

The memories fog
the circulars,
the bills
and the supermarket aisles.
We watch the sunrise
twenty-seven times
tomorrow
and set
thirty-five times
yesterday.

Sacred Territory
by Kristen Marie Scott - age 14

Second glances
Caring eyes.
Does no one understand?
The world within me screams.
Without a helping hand.
People reach.
Some in vain.
Others with a heart
There is a key.
Few have found.
But break once in the lock.

Faceless Faces
by Sylvia Schuster

In mourning for the
UNBORN CHILD
I search for the
WHY?
but the answers are hidden behind my black veil.

ALONE

crying to deaf ears
I question
the innocence of ignorance,
the silent rage
of a benign world of malignant realities.

With closed eyes
I see

sleepwalkers always dreaming
of doing
nothing...
      acquiring everything
        UNNECESSARY
and celebrating
when LIFE exists
deep inside the child filled womb
and dies at birth.

Special You
by Debra Sears

Friends have alot to share...
Many things show they care.
A broken heart to mend...
We will be friends until the end.
You will live through the tears...
And laughter through the years.

You will be a bearer of bad news...
And share the good news.
You will be a clown...
Who turns my frown upside down.
Overall my friend...
Through thick and thin.
You pick me up when I am blue...
You are my friend and a
"Special You"

Dewdrops of Kindness
by Eva O. Scott

If ever I feel compelled to correct;
Let my words fall like dewdrops, with respect,
Upon the ears of a fellow believer,
That he'd be a refreshed receiver.
Let me humbly pray
That God would give me the words to say,
So that by the words I'd employ,
He'd not lose his bubbly joy.

It takes wisdom, and Holy Spirit
So that a humble heart may hear it,
And be so moved by the kindness shown
That he corrects out of love alone.

For days and years
Through grateful tears,
He'll remember with joy
The spirit behind the words you'd employ.

When Will I Die?
by Kristen Marie Scott - age 14

The room is dark.
The walls are stiff.
The air is thick as thunder.
It's hard to breath.
I don't know why.
Will I die in here?
I ask...
For no one will ever know.
The pain that runs within my veins.
The tears upon my face.
Will I die in here?
I ask again...
The silence only answers.
I cannot speak.
I cannot see.
The fear swells up inside me.
Will I die in here?
I ask in vain...
The heat runs through my body.
I cry again.
But tears don't fall.
Just unspoken words inside me.
Will I die in here?
I ask once more...

Minds
by Robyn Scott - age 15

Minds. Why do we have minds?
are they to imagine what the world
should be like or what the world
was like? Are they to daydream with
or to get jobs with?
Minds are pondering tools.
They decide your future and fate.
Keep your mind sane or insane your choice,
but enjoy your mind before we all die
of a natural disaster or
a worse fate our own minds.
Maybe one day our minds will not
be there. They will be gone we will remember
nothing and make the same
mistakes our forefathers made.
Our minds will haunt us
But just maybe the world will
not come to an end and
people will live in
      PEACE
        and
      HARMONY

To Live Again
by Rikki Scott - age 17

Beneath his words, I feel the lies.
Beneath his touch, deceit and black.
In his eyes, nothing but his love
For himself,
But made to look for me.
This time is different,
He knew all the lies,
Not once did he falter,
But then I am enlightened.
For me, nothing,
But for my heart, a scar not there,
A life without him,
Is it?
Is it a life of pain?
Or is it a chance to start
To live again?

The Carpenters
by Bonnie Scutro-Ward

Cradled at your breast, the comfort I feel blows away the storms
    of many seasons,
Saturn releases his grip on the dark clouds in my shadowed heart.

Walls seem fluid, nonexistent, while time stands still.
No past exists to darken the moment, no future calling to
    materialize the uncertainties of the future.

Only this moment exists in purity and honesty of emotion, two
    souls connected in peace and serenity.
The connection is so warm, so tender, that I know the conflicts
    behind us should never have been.

The harsh emotions must have come from other places, other
    seas of tears.
We must have been trying to hurt some one else, make some one
    else cry, ignoring the love that flows between us.

As you gaze down at me, I feel as one in the depth of our love,
And I know this love could not have produced the storms we have
    ridden, nor the storms we may ride, before we have attended
    to ourselves.

I'll Always Be There For You
by Cheryl Sears - age 14

I'll always be there for you,
No matter what you do,
You were there for me in my times of need,
And now I'll always be there for you.

I lost my trust in you,
Just once or twice,
But deep inside, you know it's true,
I'll always be there for you.

You've been there for me a million times before,
My guardian angel it seems,
Now I want to return the favor,
In your time of need.

Put your trust in me,
Don't ever let go,
Because I swear,
I'll always be there for you.

Loving You For All Eternity
by Debra Sears

There will never again be such a
beautiful day,
As when God sent you my way.
I remember the first time you told me
you loved me,
I wanted to jump and shout with glee.
I wanted everyone to know
of how your love makes me glow.
I love you with all my heart,
each day with you I want to start.
As in the beginning of time for us
I want our love to last, let us not rush.
Each day will be bright
And everything will come out all right.
I want to show the world, how much
you mean to me...
Always and Forever, "I'll be...
loving you for all
eternity!"

Thinking Of You
by Debra Sears

Every moment of every day, I spend...
Thinking of you...
I wrap you with love and tender
Thoughts...
And I wonder...
Do you know it?
Every night, wherever you are...
I tuck you in with loving thoughts...
And I wonder...
Can you sense it?
Every morning, even when we're apart...
I wake you with a gentle kiss...
And I wonder...
Can you feel it?
You are so much a part of me...
you are always in my heart.
I am glad that I found you to love...
Words cannot describe how I feel...
I miss you so much, that it even hurts me...
To send you this poem...
Knowing that you are there...
And I am here...
And I wonder...
Do you know it?
I LOVE YOU...
Don't you forget it!
Always remember...
I love you...
And I am thinking of you...

The End of Time
by Erica Serock - age 15

Alpha
The sun, the moon, the Stars, Earth;
Glow vividly yet are only specs in the heavens.
Earth, our mother,
A mother so kind
Nurtures us with care and love
For she tends to our needs.
Yet we show no mercy
And spite her gentle hand
While disrupting the peace and beauty
Of her wonders so fair.
Will the madness ever stop?
And reunite the Earth with the heavens from where she was born.
The time will come;
The end, the beginning.
OMEGA, ALPHA

Fear
by Kimberley Shananhan - age 16

I stop you in your tracks,
I freeze you in your place,
I stop all rational thinking and
reason (ing).
I make you sweat and go cold
at the same time.
I make your heart race, and
your vision blur.
You can taste me and smell me.
I cannot be conquered.
Only the emotionless can deceive
me.
I lie in everyone's minds, waiting
to be awaken.
For I am Fear

Sometimes I Pretend...
by Valerie Gail Seastrom - age 14

Sometimes I pretend
that life is better than it is
Sometimes I pretend
our minds we do not tame
Life isn't the same
as it was for them
it's not so lame
and this isn't just a game
the things people do for fame
rape a girl, it seems no one cares
kill a kid, no one notices
he's gone
get someone hooked
just so they can make it in the books
they don't see
maybe they don't look
or don't want to believe
what it took
is not what it'll take
the promises break
maybe we can't just pretend
life is not fake

Beaches
by Erica Serock - age 15

A sunny day
I walk alone.
I walk along a sandy beach,
as the rushing water calls to me;
but I do not answer,
and the water is angry.
It cries out to the sky,
for the menacing clouds cover the warming sun,
but I ignore them,
and the clouds are angry.
They writhe in frustration
as an icy rain falls from their bowels,
but I do not go home,
and the rain is furious.
The drops fill the ocean,
forcing it to rise farther and farther upshore,
until it has engulfed me.
The last breath escapes my lungs
and as I drown into the depths of the swirling tides
they cackle in glory,
but I learn to swim,
and I have won...

Chameleon
by Atossa Shafaie

The wind carries whispers
From far away lands.
Wisdom of ages
Must finally change hands.
The new in defiance
Trust chameleon ways,
While old weary faces
Bow down in disgrace,
Preserving the knowledge
Of old ancient days.

Love Is
by Sheila Lynn Serrano

Love is so hard to understand,
but yet so easy to fall into.
It get's you by surprise and,
you wonder if it's wise.
You ask yourself once or twice,
if you realize,
that love is not just a game to be
penalized.

Love is something shared by two,
so special you ask yourself if its true,
Something so strong, that nothing,
can break this bind between you.
It never has jealous thoughts,
or empty feelings.

Love is trust and happiness,
no matter how far apart you may be,
Love is something that everyone should find,
but nothing to be twisted or defined.

People
by Flor Serrata - age 12

Every time everywhere
All I see is people

People!
    People!
        People!
People talk and People walk.
People drink and People smile.
People smell very good when they are
wearing perfume.
People taste and people touch.

People!
    People!
        People!
People can do anything they want to do.
People laugh and people cry.

Lost
by Nicole Settergren - age 14

A lonely lad
Stood on a hill
He's feelin' bad
The wind's a chill
It blows across
The evil morn
The stirring loss
Of children born
The children, starved
Have died alone
Pure souls have carved
It whitened bone
Their spirits moan
It echoes loud
His body groans
He's lost and cowed
It eats away
His crumbling core
Until the day
He's reached the door
Door from his pain
Hardest to mend
Nothing to gain
This is the end.

Shorelines Of Solom
by Ellie Sexton

As the wisp wind blows, and the man in
the moon's face glows, my love and I shall
always row along the shorelines of Solom.
When the sun comes up, and the moon
goes down, My love and I shall always sit on
the shorelines of Solom.
As my love and I are in the boat the
shore will always gracefully stroke, against the
shorelines of Solom.
The horizon is here, and the sun is there, our
love will never tear, when we're at the
shorelines of Solom.
The green trees sway, and the yellow
sun reflects, by the shorelines of Solom.
The blue, blue waters and the peach, peach
sand will always sandy, by the shorelines of
Solom.

Untitled
by Atossa Shafaie

What strange things touch human souls?
What memories like dying, weak and old?
Desires yearning to be held,
Allow the loneliness to swell.
Why do tears form perfect pools,
When minds sleep, and hearts play fools?
A world lies suspended, still ignored,
Subconscious feet on sandy shores.
My life, to my being bound
Is deaf to freedom's soothing sounds.
My lover from me fades away,
While breath condemns me here to stay.

Death Song
by Atossa Shafaie

Lay still child,
Fear me not.
See not the wrinkled, haggard visage.
I am wisdom, I am time.
Come, come to me child,
For all must in my arms sleep.
It is a sweet destiny.
The crying, you must stop.
Hear the gentle voices,
My heartbeat against you.
Dance, sweet one,
With the rhythm of years past.
All await you in my embrace.
See not the black of death in my eyes,
but the face of the never ending.
Float, yes, fly
Soar with me.
These twisted hands,
Will show the way.
That you may be free,
To your soul,
And your unborn dreams.

Untitled
by Tracie Shanahan

And God gathered
the children at His feet.
Like the rock and sand
that gather to create Kilamanjaro.

He has called out to the people,
to listen and hear the word.
That we must change our ways,
to save ourselves from Eternal Damnation.
This is the beginning of the End,
and the end is near.

Pick up the Book and read My scripture,
Learn from the mistakes of others,
Those who have come before you,
have laid down the path.
And only you can control
your own salvation.

Come children, to me.
You are my lambs, so dear and precious.
Know in your hearts that I will always love you.
I will never abandon you.

Come to Me, those who are grown.
See the children, and learn to be like they are.
Innocent, loving, and full of wonder,
for all that I have created.
Become as the children,
and you shall find your redemption.
See through the children's eyes,
and behold your Salvation.

Every Once In A While
by Barry L. Shank Jr. - age 18

Every once in a while, the world it right
the good guy gets the girl, and holds her tight
His heart is filled, with love and joy
Then all of a sudden, the world changes it's plan
it takes away the girl, and breaks the man
The world is cruel and wants you to know
that it is the only one, running the show
Try as you may and try as you might
but when your up against the world, it's no fight
It just gives your proof, of the saying of the past
Now every once and a while, I catch myself thinking back
and seeing if there was some way, I could of beaten the attack
I know in my mind, that there was nothing I didn't do
but that didn't stop me, from losing you
So I lay on my bed, as tears stream down my face
debating whether or not, I should give chase
It's not a question of love, I could answer that fast
it's because I know, nice guys finish last
Finally I realize that every once in a while is a lie
and that without you, I would rather die
so I say my good-byes, never giving a clue
about what I'm thinking or what I'm going to do
I raise the cold metal up to my head
and realize that life can't beat me if I'm dead
I pull the trigger, knowing what it will do
and pray to God, every once in a while doesn't happen to you!

Whispers

Healing Fears
by Brouke Sharp - age 15

Now is the time for laughter,
And I hope we live happily ever after.

I can tell by your eyes and in your kiss,
This thing called love but what is this.

Sometimes I feel you'll be pushed away,
But I know our love will always stay.

For your love I hold dear,
And I will shed not a single tear.

Cause I know your love will always stay,
And that you'll never go away!

Hidden Passions
by Brouke Sharp - age 15

All the passions hidden deep inside,
Waiting to burst and come alive,
So please move slow and take all control,
For all my love you now hold.

Passionate eyes, feverish lips,
Warm silky caresses from hot fingertips.

All at once passion overflows,
You can feel it from your head down to your toes.

And when it was over you kissed my shoulder,
And held me in your arms.

For at that moment I was yours,
And you were mine,
Our love came out in time!

Untitled
by Jennifer Shaw - age 17

As my soul is my candle
as my happiness is my flame
only one can put them out
only one can extinguish my light,
I think about his souls decisions
think of him as I lie here in the night.
A person is not whole without their glow
their beauty dulls: their cares wane.
Hopeless coals that sparked into a roaring flame
but now a strong wind has come.
Shelter it try to hide
there's nothing that can be done
because if he chooses it will die
and only smoke remains to tell
of the passing of the last one.

Destiny & Fate
by Joseph J. Shawn Jr.

I stole a brick from the church wall
I ran into the shade
I broke a date with destiny
And earned the money that I made
I laughed in the face of fear
I smiled in the eyes of hate
I overcame my problems
And danced around my fate
I took a piece of circumstance
And mixed it in with doubt
I dug into the devils soul
To find what he's about
I wore a cloak of black
Until they knew my name
And when they finally opened their eyes
I was finished with my game.

The Athlete
by Frank Sheehan

The athlete gazed into the night
an itch in his palms and
a strong, heavy heartbeat
His body was tense
His emotions ran high
The game was tomorrow
it was do or die

Would his dreams be realized?
Or would they be squashed with angry cries
This is his life,
This is his game.
He believes deep down inside
that we're not the same,
Not in a racist or prejudicial way,
but because of his athletic prowess
it will be his day.

He'll do his thing, he'll score,
they'll win,
a team player always takes
it on the chin.
And when the gorgeous day is done
and things are quiet again
under the sun
he'll reflect on his accomplishments
and prepare for the next one.

Until Now
by LaVeta Sherman

In a prison of fear
with guards of torment
my soul cried silently
longing...
yearning...
for release, full freedom.

Sentenced by one
who with hands and words
with body and knife
concealed the truth
in a prison of fear
with guards of torment...

Until NOW!

Don't Lie To Me
by Lizabeth Sherrill - age 15

Don't lie to me.
Don't say you care.
When I need you,
You're never there.

Don't lie to me.
Don't say you're true.
I see through your lies,
I know about you.

Don't lie to me.
Don't say I'm the one.
I know you'll forget me,
Once you've had your fun.

Don't lie to me.
Don't say I'm for you.
We'll both be much happier,
Once we are through.

Don't lie to me.
Don't ask me to stay.
I found out about you,
Now I'm on my way.

Don't lie to me.
Don't say you'll cry.
I know all about you,
You're nothing but a lie!

Concentrating(Like*MockingBird)N'Putnam*City-?
by Philip Sherrod

..At-Age*10/(Got A*Glimmer)..Uv'Goethe N' What..
(It*would(Be*Like)?-To*Sing)*AltoSoprano..N'(Boys*-
Choir)??-Usin'*voice(As-?)A*WorkaHolic*Bach!!(?)-Pun*
-Ishing(Th'Ear*..Uv'Innocents!)?-Wf'(Bring(-Ing)N'..

-Th'(Sheaves??)&'..(Ye*Shall(ComeReJoicing!!)?-Like?-
GrandMother*Cochran(Her*Eyes*Always(Lit*Up!)N'ExPectancy(?))
-That(The*Saviour)would..(ShowUp*Between(Choir*N'Pulpit))??
-As(Aunt*Ida)Ahead(Uv'Her*Time)-Pounded(Out!)-Th'Latest..

-Hard*Core(Rock!!)?-On*Piano..(Like*Liberace)All*Souped(Up!)??
-Wf'(Thank*You!-Thank*You!)-Always(Socially*Polite*N'Politically..
-*Correct!!)?-To the(Inth-Degree!)Uv'Listen(N'Yur(Gonna*Like*It!!))
-Getting(Delirious(Off*Of)..Th'*Collective(Halleujah*Chorus!!))?

- N (I * T h o u g h t) - (* A s c e n d) . . (-
ING)?(PAINTED*Church*Windows)N'Candles
. . T o * H e a v e n ! ! (?) -
N'(Git*Mye*Share)Uv'WELCH'S(GRAPE*JUICE)*Communion?
-Assumption(Methodists*ARE)*TeeTotalers(?)-Mye*Father*Says(Politics
- A r e (S u m p i n ' L i k e) * R e l i g i o n) I f - Y o u (D o n ' t * V o t e /
Can't(Go*To)Heaven!!(?))

..N'(I*Realized)Th'Jig)-was*Up!(?)-When..Raymond*Gunther's(Voice..
*Broke!!)?-Singing(At*6thGrade*Graduation)?(-A*Duo*Solo!!)?-
Me*Havin'
- T o * F i n i s h . . T h ' (L a s t * S t a n z a) ! ! ? ? ? -
Bye*Myself..(Wf'*Question*Marks??)?
-N'(What*Th'(Hell..Happened)!)?-N'Life(Iwould*Have)to-
Go*It(Alone)*TONEDEAF!(?)

What If?
by Eileen Shiue - age 15

I am the two faces of a coin-
Violent with anger at one side,
But loyal, loving and gentle on the other.

For one face to show, the other must face down.
But what if this coin could stand on it's side?
Could I find a happy medium?

I am but a page in a book.
Two differing sides,
Flipping back and forth in the wind.

But what is you tore out the page were I existed
And folded it randomly?
Could you see the two sides at one glance?

I am the facets of a dradle.
Some of them must show,
While others lay in the shadow.

And like a dradle, I can be unpredictable.
No one knows what can set me off.
But what if I knew? Could I stop myself?

What if you melted the coin that was me,
Burned the page that was me,
And crushed the dradle that was me?

What, then, would I be?

Mystery Friend
by Jennifer Short - age 13

He never does wrong
or so one will think
his actions are
so-called good intentions
yet we all know
in our heart
there lays a mystery, a puzzle
of his past
and behind the walls of his heart
like the walls of Rome is love
And like the walls of Rome
the stone can be broken

Without Faith
by Jessica Sicking - age 15

Life's little temptations...
They will keep us in the game
Shifting through the ashes.
And dancing in the flames.
We'll keep on playing until we run out of time.

These little games...
With our hearts and our minds.
There are no winners.
'Cause there is no way to win.
And the losers, they are buried and forgotten once again.

Life's little playes...
We're all doomed to lose.
It's written in the sky.
They say the stars don't lie.
We don't play to win, we just play not to die.

A Day at the Beach
by Elizabeth Siler - age 15

We walk across the sand barefooted it makes our feet feel as if they were on fire. We throw down all those things you think you need at the beach, into a pile. Then we run off to meet the crashing waves.

The water is kind of warm in some places but in others its cold. After we're done splashing around in the water we run up to the shore to play make believe in the sand. We pretend that the sand castles we build are the homes of little knome people, walking around in the shimmering sunlight.

As we are running along the beach, we stop to find our feet caked with crushed sea shells. So we turn on the water to rinse our feet. Then we suddenly realize that the tide has gone out. It left a world of smooth rocks exposed to the sun.

We also see little starfish trying to find their way back to the ocean. Suddenly we look up to see three screeching sea gulls fly by then dip down to capture their lunch.

Instantly our stomachs remind us of the cooler back at the shore filled with lots of goodies. As we are feasting away little fiddler crabs come up and grab our crumbs. When we are through eating we go running off into the water again. As time is passing by we forget about that pile of stuff on the shore until we see our towels float by! Then we realized that the tide came in.

So we grab everything and decide that its time we should go home now since its getting dark and we're also fried from the sun beating down on us all day. So we walk off into the sunset with everything soaking wet including ourselves.

Camp Goodbyes
by Lindsey Silken - age 14

The time has come
The end is near
The friendships are over
Until next year

Goodbyes bring tears
That flow like a faucet
Which we will shut off some time or other
Then next summer, we'll do it all over

Shattered Dreams
by Samantha J. Sills - age 18

You could break
my heart tonight,
If you don't come
and make it right.
My dreams of us
are shattering fast,
no matter how much
I want us to last.
I gave you
all I had,
But now
I'm so sad.
I use to be
the one for you,
Now it doesn't seem
so true.
If I had
just one wish,
it'd be for us
to have an everlasting kiss.

Forget
by Danyal Simmons - age 16

    Forget about his ways.
    Forget why he came to you,
    Forget his love
Remember he is gone forever

    Forget how he said he love you
forever
    Forget his ways of love
    Forget his warm embrace
Remember why he is gone

    Forget his LONG kisses
    Forget his comforting arms
around you
    Forget the long nights together
Remember how to forget him

    Forget where he lives
    Forget why he made you cry.
Forget his phone number
Remember why you got together

    Forget his loving hands

    Friend just totally forget him
and go onto someone like he did

No One Or Nowhere
by James Simoneaux

Tears,
Confusions and sadness,
Strangers for family,
Enemies for friends,
On an endless road with
No light, no sound, and
No destination,
Lost on a one-way road
To nowhere.

A Sad Ending
by Brooke Simpson - age 14

- A dream is shattered that
you love so much,
Crying hard a tissue you clutch

-Theres rings under your eyes from
the lack of rest,
your really down, sorta depressed.

-The world is dark and spinning
round you
You have low self-esteem and
friends there are few,

And you are left
        crying
                silently
in a world full of tears.

The Picnic
by Ashia R. Sims - age 18

The sun glistened brightly
The birds chirped loudly
The wind blew freely
There we were just you and me

The brook trickled gently
The bees hummed quietly
The leaves fell slowly
All alone just you and me

The clouds floated lazily
The branches swayed gently
We laughed softly
Sitting together under a tree

You put your arms around me
And gazed at me lovingly
Then kissed me so sweetly
As the sun fell beautifully

There we were just you and me
All alone just you and me
Sitting together under a tree

Thinking Once
by Shereen Singer - age 12

To be courageous,
brave,
daring,
and bold.
Prepared for anything,
and everything.
Taking risks;
being proud.
Not necessarily
saving a life.
Thinking once
in your lifetime,
"I did something amazing,
for someone else."
Being fearless.
Sometimes...
Just being yourself.

Forget-Me-Not
by Tina Sizer - age 16

Good-bye's are forever
so that I won't say
We'll always be together
forever and a day
Every night I'll think of you
and cry myself to sleep
Friendship is forever true
it is forever deep
For now we shall part
and be on our way
Memories in my heart
of when we used to laugh and play
This poem's for you
Sorry it's all I've got
but you is what I'll think of
so please Forget-Me-Not

Untitled
by Hillary Skaggs - age 17

Finally, I open my eyes to realize
not how much you care for me,
but how much more I care for you.
So take my love,
take my life,
take my all,
and trust that you are all I need.
Believe in me, and every desire in your heart
will be fulfilled.
You bring not only love to my life,
Kisses to my lips,
joy to my days,
but also a promise to me
of a love that will last forever in my heart.
I need never ask again if
there's anyone out there.

Keep Looking Up
by Elaine Skalla

It's a much happier way to be
just to see the clouds and sky
Even when it rains
remember there's always
happiness beyond the clouds
so keep looking up

The Worm In The Apple
by Rachel Slater - age 15

See the juicy apple
the green, green, juicy apple
It looks good.

Look, a chubby worm
a chubby, chubby, little worm
It's smiling at you.

Say "hi"
and the chubby worm might say "hi" back
From his place in the green apple.

Say "hi"
be nice,
Say "hi"

Come and Gone
by Maya Slininger - age 16

Many places I can think of
Of happy moments that can't be remembered
With friends and family that have come and gone

Faces in the crowds
Of memories that can't be placed
But knowing that each one loved
And somewhere that love remains

Thoughts and feelings
All bee felt before
I can still feel them although faint
Losing it's touch as days go by

I will always stop and try to remember
But most of it gone
Never to be thought of again

Untitled
by Annie Smith - age 16

The eagle flies high and free
The panther stalks it's prey
The deer eats tall grass
The tree shares the time of day

If humans could learn to share
This world with other living things
Maybe things like these will be
Seen through real eyes
And not in some pictures
Of an old magazine

Dreams
by Alicia Smith - age 14

As slumber appears,
The strange dreams near.

Invisible doorways; luring calls,
An open chasm; the disoriented dreamer falls.

Crystal light below; darkness all around,
'lilting notes and child-like whispers
    are what our dreamer has found.

Strangely arrested by a fearful sight,
a lingering moment of the past has filled
    our dreamer with fright.

But wait; it has yet again changed,
It all has been rearranged.

A new exotic world beckons,
    But where does it lead?
Whatever its hidden message.....the dreamer must
    take heed.

In every dream there is a question,
But what does it mean?
Our own mystery to figure;
    the clues we have seen

Untitled
by Christy Smith - age 14

I sit here thinking...
    Thinking about what I should do?
    All I can think about is yesterday
When I was with you.
    The feeling you gave me is so
hard to explain.
    But all I know is I'm feeling
pain.
    What do I do to get you to
be mine?
    I don't know?...
    But I wish I could snap my
fingers...
    And...then you would be
MINE!

Whispers

"Who's Looking At Me?"
by Christina Smith

I look in the mirror, and what do I see? a stranger's
face staring back at me. I move, the mirror image does
too. Am I looking at me, or am I looking at you?

I see you everyday. Are you a close friend or a stranger
who's far away?

I think I know you. You think you know me. We both are
as confused as can be; until I am you and you are me.

The Dying Breed
by Gloria J. Smith

Shadowy ghosts
like dark spirits
whispering on the wind
through wet mountain mist.

Silent as the night
is midnight black,
they live in doomed solitude.

The mysterious and proud
spirit of wolves will
forever be subdued.

Paradise Proposal
by Michael Smith - age 17

Paradise, an island of sun
An island on which we can have fun
The day fades into the long cool night
To see the sunset is a wonderful sight

Things such as these I compare to you
I think of you in everything I do
Our love is strong and can't be broken
So please accept this golden token

We can walk together on the beach of life
Lover of mine, won't you be my wife?
I want to be with you more then you can see
Listen my love, Will you Marry me?

Yesterday
by Nicole Smith - age 14

Yesterday I saw him,
yesterday he was there,
yesterday he was alive,
but I guess he didn't care.

I had a dream that night,
and he was there with me,
he told what it feels like to fly,
over the cliff, but not in the sky.

He had a life to live,
he chose not to live it,
he had his future all planed out,
I guess he had some doubt.

I was the last one to see him,
the words he said were his last,
I can't believe he did it,
but I guess it's in the past.

I will always remember what he said,
"I love you, don't ever forget me,"
was all that he would say,
on that horrible Yesterday.

Wonder
by Shannon Smith - age 14

I sit here and wonder
What went wrong
was it something I said
or something I've done
I don't know
answers?
I have none

You won't tell me
So, I'm left out in the cold
In the darkness
Alone and dying

Do you even care?
I wish you were here, by my side
But you really don't care
answer me (so I can find peace)
What have I done that's so wrong?

I feel like I'm tearing up inside
and all I can do is cry.

The Idealist
by Sandra Smith

I see through the eyes of a dreamer
at times - hoping for happy endings.

Life is real, life is earnest-
and reality wakes me up.

But I choose to be an optimist-
to set my goals high and
work hard-

To strive for perfection is better than
giving up.

I dare to dream of white knights
and fair maidens - the utopia just
out of reach.

Believing is half of the battle
So I will take off my rose-colored glasses-
but only for a time.

Because you see I am a romantic
and even when reality hits -
I will always be "The Idealist"-
because for me, it fits.

My Sun
by Ana Sprenger - age 13

Yet thee dwindles in a sea of dire emptiness
and thy mind is not yet at peace-
where harmony has not yet been found-
There lies evil, hate burning as bright as the sun-
There lies my life wasted on hate and revenge.

Dear Grandpa
by Marcy Dianne Smit - age 16

The easter eggs stood still
As I find them, still the next day
No ones in the mood
since you have gone away.

While I sat and stared at you
I wondered when you'd wake up
But as the tears started to fall
I knew I'd have no luck.

One night you fell asleep
Never thinking this was your last good-bye
But I now your in my heart
And in there, you will never die.

The memories I have of you
Is from when I had just begun
to say all I have to say
I love you, and it's been fun.

But I know I can bring you back
Anytime I feel alone
That's when I fall asleep
In my dreams, you live at home.

My last 5 minutes with you
was not the very best
But it doesn't matter now
Because you have gone to rest.

You will be greatly missed on earth
Even though you still may be near
There is so much people want to say
If you could only hear.

As I say good-bye
When we lower you down to sleep
Forever in my heart
A piece you will always keep.

The Worlds Hiding Place
by Shana Snider

Harmony, the peace within!
Melody, the crowd alone,
Beckoning and calling us home.
Rationally is inside me,
Irrationality makes us a stray,
Fleeing from home to find our way.
The world makes us decide,
to live or to run and hide.

In Between
by Cayce Smullin - age 15

The house sits upon a
graveyard hill,
In the light they are
so still.
The darkness comes and
sweeps away,
The restless spirits as
the lay.
Many days go by
with time,
Living in their cold,
dark shrine.
They float between the
sky and ground,
Hoping always to
stay around.

Hatred
by Jenni Smyth - age 14

Everyone is fighting they never get along,
I don't see why everything is going wrong.
It keeps happening day after day, I can't take this much longer, I can't live this way.
I don't see what the problem is everything seems right, but they seem to want to do is argue and fight.
If everyone would stop a minute to see, they would realize they're hurting everyone, especially me.
If someone would say they are sorry and the other would forgive, then everything would be easier and a regular life I could live.
But now I'm so confused I'll never understand, in my whole family there's not a loving hand.
Maybe someday this will be over, maybe it will end, and then a new family with love will begin.

Just Because He Died
by Mary Snow - age 14

Just because he died,
Don't mean I have to cry.
Only I know that he's here,
He is everywhere.
I know that he's here,
He is everywhere,
Only I know that he's here,
I can feel him in my heart.
My parents once told me,
That he will always be,
In my heart forever,
And never stop loving me.
So Grandpa if you can,
Please answer me,
Even though you're in my heart,
Are we still far apart?

You
by Eugene Snyder

I stare at you in
The midnight hour
Strong and beautiful
Like some wild flower

Your eyes are beautiful
In every way
If they could talk
The things they'd say

Your nose your mouth
And all the things on your face
Everything's perfect
Nothing out of place

You walk with strength
And so full of grace
How can anything so lovely
Belong to the human race.

Best Friends Forever
by Katie Snyder - age 11

Best friends are forever
But what if they don't live
You just sit and sever
You have nothing left to give.
Sometimes you will cry
But sometimes you forget
How hard it i to lose
The best friend you get. You ran and played and jumped around
You will never forget the beautiful sound
Of butterflies fluttering in the grass
Or the wind in the trees as you pass.
The wonderful sound of flowing water
The sweet little sound of the otter.
But then one day when you went out to play
He wasn't there what could you say.
You searched all over
And found him under a tree
And now you see his best friend was me.
I cried and cried until I was dry
I kept asking myself why did he die.
I guess because it was his time
But I still have our friendship chime.
I just wanted to let you know
That since we're best friends I won't ever let go.

Life
by Tiffanie Sorell - age 16

Life is a wonderful thing that
Everyone should cherish.
Life is something everyone has
Because if they did not have a life
They would not have a life
They would not be here right now
Life is sometimes wasted by many
People, but if they are alive, why
Don't they treat their life better.
Life is something you try
And do something with.
That is why life is so important
To many people.

Life is Like
by Tiffanie Sorell - age 16

Life is like a roller coaster
There are ups and downs
The ups are the good things
in life
The downs are all of the bad
things in life
The twists and the turns are
When you are confused
When it goes in circles or loops
That is all the bad times
And you do not know
What to do
But you never know when it is
Going to end and you don't know
What to expect next.

Wanted
by Tiffanie Sorell - age 16

Everyone needs to be wanted,
Everyone needs a friend to talk to,
Everyone needs to feel wanted so that they
Can make it through life,
But not everyone does feel wanted
Some people are lonely,
See that person all alone I
Bet that she thinks that
No one really wants her,
Or that no one really likes her,
Or that no one really cares,
What happens to her.

Eternal Love
by C.J. - age 16

What I'm about to say,
All began that first day,
I love you more than you'll ever know,
With all my heart, mind, body, and soul,
I'm telling you to let you know exactly the way I feel,
And to let you know my love (for you) is real,
You, I strongly trust,
Because with you it's not only lust,
I've never felt this way about anyone before,
The constant desire to see you more and more,
As time goes by the feeling grows stronger,
To be held in your arms, I can't wait any longer,
Because being with you gives me great pleasure,
Every moment just thinking about you, I treasure,
You're always so considerate and kind,
And always on my mind,
If you think you're alone and that I don't care,
As long as there's forever I'll always be there,
Only I'm a little scared you'll fall for another,
And that she'll be better although we'll always be friends with each other,
You are definitely too good to be true,
That's why I'm gonna keep on loving you,
Maybe it's just me,
But I think this love was meant to be.

Eden Rain
by Christine Sosko - age 15

Eden rain,
come wash our souls of pain.
Shower us with peace,
and teach our hearts to love again.
Come Eden Rain,
make us and our sister, Earth,
one again. Cleanse us of mortal sin.
Eden Rain,
Bring to us, your beautiful tears,
and make our eyes reflect our souls
like mirrors.
Let us be free of fear and
free of pain.
Let the skys open,
and pour out
Eden Rain.

A Total Mess
by Jessica Soto - age 15

You see the children.
You hear their laughter.
But can you see the pain and thier hearts shatter?
"they look OK"
That's what you say.
But deep inside it's dark and gray.
They have a box that they call home.
And they have a dirty old used comb.
You can't tell by their clothes, cause they have a few.
And they never show it to people like me and you.
If you saw them right now, would you think I'm lying?
Or would you hold them close and just start crying?
If you saw them before, you would have never guessed,
That their house was burned and was left a mess.
They never knew that it would happen to them.
But now they have to live it till the end.
They took advantage and never listened to safety precautions.
They should have bought the fire alarm instead of that gold charm.

Summer Nights
by Crystal Soule - age 18

Sitting side by side
under the stars and moonlight
you holding me closely
in your arms
I am warm in your embrace

Your hands cupped around my face
tilting my face towards you
your lips slightly parted
leaning forward
you let your lips tenderly touch
    mine.

You lean eversoslightly
with your arms around my waist
your lips touching my neck while
    you still hold me
my arms wrapped around your neck
holding onto you before you slip
    away

Walking with you
you putting your arm
    around my waist
I put my arm around
    you.

Walking in the dark
talking sweetly to each other
hoping you would
lean over to kiss me
Instead you have me close
    my eyes while you kiss me on
Summer Nights.

Christmas
by Kathleen Spencer

Wonder of Wonders-Such a Sight!
Piles of Presents-Squeals of Delight!
The Tree with Red and Green Lights Blink
Stockings Full And Ready To Sink
While Mom and Dad give a slight wink!
Loved Ones gathered by the fire
Outside you still see a star
It is The Birthday of a Baby Small
Who came down from above to Save Us All!

Cradle
by Ana Sprenger - age 13

When at last silence overcomes the city the
great symphony of the stars begins.
It starts as a whisper, quiet as a summer breeze
and builds to an exploding climax.
To hear it you must believe in the constellations
and the story behind each one of them.
Yet many do not and cradle themselves in a modern
understanding of life, only then will the brass, the
wood winds, and the strings as well as percussion
die down in a complex murmur of forgetfulness.

Watchful Mother
by Jennifer Lynn Stacy - age 14

She always leaned to watch for us,
Anxious if we were late,
In winter by the window,
In summer by the gate.

Though we mocked her tenderly,
Who had such foolish care,
The long way home would seem more safe,
Because she waited there.

Her thoughts were all so full of us,
She never could forget.
And so I think that where she is,
She must be watching yet.

Waiting 'till we come home,
Anxious if we are late.
Watching from Heavens window,
Leaning on Heavens gate.

I remember...
by Tabitha Staley - age 12

I remember his stories that always warmed my heart, and no matter how many times I heard them they never sounded the same. They always made him laugh which made my family and me laugh too. His heart was so warm and loving; he hated seeing people in pain. He was strong. That man lived 3 and a half years and inspite of his hospitalizations, pain and memory lost he still remembered me by his nick name E.T., and that's what he called me!!

The Wind, She Danced Her Ballroom Dance
by Robert Stancampiano

The wind, she danced her ballroom dance
dressed in her transparent gown.
She brushed against my face,
as I was pondering how elegant she acts
after a storm has calmed her rage.

The well had run dry on the old maestro,
tired of my creations,
seemed all I could do was decompose.
A sickly animal, all skin and bones,m
and the alcohol from the past twenty years,
welled up in the red ball on my nose.

I had been raised by fruit flies,
deep in the folds of the Jolly Green Giant's leafy toga,
with one hand in my father's pocket,
one hand in my mother's head,
I was the first to break the fishing line,
first to be caught in the policeman's net.

The family got anxious,
when I got bored,
walking down mainstreet,
ketchup dripping from a plastic sword
and in the other hand,
a severed head,
I'd bought at a novelty store.
But those weren't toy guns,
that cut me down
and made me soil my shorts.

To My Husband Joseph
by Heather Staniszewski

Let it be you who is by my side
On my last day,
Let it be you who shuts my eyes
Forever and say...
A sweet "good-night" as you have said it,
All of these years,
With the same touch,
With the same voice,
And without tears,
Kiss me one last time
With a tenderness too deep.
On my lips forever,
It will be as I sleep.
And whisper softly once again
The words I loved to hear,
"I love you" and "Good-night my friend"
The memories are so dear.
You will know then, in that silence
What I hope you always knew,
Though I have loved, I have loved no other
As I have loved you.

Never Got A Chance To Say...
by Renee Starling - age 16

There's so many things I never got a
chance to say,
Like I'm sorry for my mistakes in
each and every way.
I'm sorry for all the stupid things
I used to do,
I was young and I didn't care-
I didn't have a clue.
and I'm sorry for the things I
did say,
I regret those words - and cry
every single day.
I said I hated you and I
didn't care about you,
I said I didn't want a mother,
and now I'm so confused
If I knew this was going to
happen-
I would've told you some of the
things I didn't say
And I would've told you everything
I never got a chance to say.

Dying Sun
by Mira Stebleton - age 17

The sun is burning my eyes,
With words people say, I despise;
The continued hell that is upon this earth;
From the knowledge of innocence,
To the obscene gestures of maturity;
Confused with distrust from all men;

What can I do?
Nothing, I realize.

To slap morals in my face,
And turn around and disobey them,
The hatred of the known;
The love of the unknown;
Who are we to judge?

I continue to live and breathe,
And only that, can I conceive.

Can You See Me?
by Vetta E. Steel

Peek-a-boo!
No,
not there,
over here.
Twirling and swirling around.
Can you see me?
I'm as big as life itself.
I'm everywhere you want.
Give me your attention,
I want your attention.
I am never alone,
but I want to be alone,
no I don't.
I want you to look at me,
look at me!
Can you see me?

When I Go Home Again
by Benjamin Stevens

When I go home again....................,
I will spend one night in peaceful somber, as gentle rain falls over a gabled tin roof.
I want to be awakened by the cock's crow at dawn and amazed by the sun beaming through my bedroom window, spotlighting energized dust particles.
To smell the fresh brew of coffee from the kitchen, mixed with the cinders from a blazing fireplace.
Then I will walk under the rainbow through floodwaters after the rain is gone.
I will run through the corn fields to smell the corn silk in the rich harvest grains.
Or maybe I will walk the long mile down the narrow dirt road just to get the mail far, far beyond the honeybee tree.
There I will view the Grand Prairie Indian tea, Chinaberry trees, Courtaplas and the blossoming Cherokees.
At the woodpile, I will try my hand once more on the lumberjack saw or ax the logs to warm the house when it is cold outside.
Amazed! When I am charged by the chickens eager and yearning to be fed from the big white pan.
When springtime means fishing and gathering spring bounty from the blackberry briers and sweet plum orchards.
To my highlight, I must see the edge of the woods and test the acoustics to hear familiar echoes of my own voice again.
I will sit in the shadows of the four o'clock flowers, in the quiet of late evening to watch the orange-red spectrum in the flaming sunset.
Then finally gaze above into the silent twilight cover of sheer darkness under a full florescent moon.
All so simple but too close in sentimental wonders.
These things...., I must...., when I go home again!

"When I Go Home Again" describes the anticipation to visit and relive the memories of home in the countryside of south Louisiana.

Loneliness
by Karen Stevens - age 14

Loneliness feels like a broken heart--
crushed to so many pieces it could never be put back together.
It looks like a blank sheet of paper--
untouched and incomplete.
It tastes like sour lemons--
deprived of taste, and yearning to be sweet.
It sounds like a lost echo in an empty canyon--
deserted and far from answers.
It smells like black coffee--
bitter, and full of darkness.

Losing You
by Victoria Stevens - age 15

Losing you I couldn't bare.
Because to me you are very rare.

Losing you would be to hard.
I only wish you had played the right card.

To lose you is to lose all hope.
Now I don't think I can really cope.

To see you hurt, really hurts me.
To see you cry, makes my heart bleed.

To lose you what would I have done.
I found out your not the only one.

Struggling
by Kristin Stewart - age 14

I've had happiness
I've had sadness
Been happy less than sad
Been sad less than mad
Suffered from alot of stuff
Rode a street bumpy and rough
Fallen asleep with a tear in my eye
Awaken with nothing more than a sigh
Pushed on with my life
Hurting immensely from all of my strife
Shrugged off all my comfort and love
Gone on because of my friends shove
Ended up in the same place I started
Wishing from my sadness I could be parted

Life
by Kristin Stewart - age 14

Why can't instructions come with life
A sheet of paper to help us through strife

There are no rules, there's only laws
We need something to fix human flaws

But then we'd be perfect
what kind of world would that be
The word everyone would turn to me

We'd be no different, all the same
I suppose we do need sadness and pain

But even if we do, does it have to be so bad
Couldn't our problems make us a little less sad

I know it's true we all need strife
But it could decrease and we'd each have
our own unique life

Sadness
by Kristin Stewart - age 14

The chilling wind may sting my eye
But that is not what makes me cry

The pain is swelling in my throat
And coldness is not stopped by my coat

I try to run, I try to hide,
But the memories don't leave
They're there by my side

Forward my body seems to move
But behind me stays my heart,
stuck in a groove

So I stop to sort things out
But I feel helpless so I sit and pout

To continue life is what I decide
However what has left me
is a fraction of my pride

The Walls of Limitation
by Sara Stewart

I sit in reflection
    Peering into my soul
        wishing I could set it free
            knowing I must wait;
    Choosing to hide
        from the judgements of narrow minds
        to live within the walls of acceptance
        however shallow and superficial they may be;
    Limiting the realms of my mind
        confining the deepest of my thoughts, my dreams,
            my hopes, my fears
        to the paper on which I write;
    Releasing thousands of suppressed ideas
        in bursts of energy through my fingertips
        desperate to escape the daily confinements to realism;
    Drifting to a world outside the walls of limitation,
        a world as vast as the universe--to those who seek it.
To those who prefer ignorance, fearing the anger of the truth--
May they therefore be satisfied with my mask
As my soul remains hidden.

My Daughters Eyes
by C.R. Stowell

Her eyes sparkle like diamonds arrayed with gold
And every highlight of the rainbow.

The joy they see and love they show comes only
From the heart which makes them glow.

If you add a smile on a little girls face you will see
My daughters holy grace.

She Waits
by Jenette St. George

The calm breeze gently
tousles her long silky hair
as it
caresses the side of her face,
warming her with thoughts of him.
Her mind,
fills with pictures
of how it will be
When they are together again.
A small smile gradually
finds its way
to her ruby red lips.
She waits for him.
The sun starts to set,
And it takes its
strong rays of warmth with it.
And she waits.
Still, he is not there.
Where could he be?
The wind whips through her lustrous mane, and
the frost begins to nip
at her fingers and her toes,
cruelly reminding her that
he is not there.
Again, her mind fills with pictures,
Yet...
This time, they are not so kind.
Still,
She waits.

The Essence of You.
by Jenette St. George

I love the way your hair gently caresses your shoulders
As you lean forward to kiss me.
I love the feel of your warm breath,
And your soft sensuous lips.
As you press your lips to mine,
All of my senses are awakened to your presence.
I can hear my heart pounding and my
Breath quicken as you hold your body close to mine.
The mere sight of you sends an electric thrill
Throughout my entire body.
The taste of your sweet, hot mouth only
Leaves me hungering for more.
I savor your sweetness
As I begin to explore...

A Young One's Prayer
by Rachael Storney

Times now are different then before,
temptations abundant ever more.
God give me strength to always see,
exactly what you want of me.

Someone stands now in front of us,
pills and needles he intends to thrust.
God give us strength to always see,
the right road to take to be with thee.

Waling into the store with a friend,
no money have we to freely spend,
and those earrings of gold gleam up at me.
God give me strength to always see,
exactly what you want from me.

Pressure abounds from all their peers,
not many words spoken release the fears.
Hear the songs the angels sing,
the words and the melody within us they ring.
God give us strength to always see,
the right road to take to be with thee.

Why Can't I
by C.R. Stowell

I hear them say that angels can fly
And dolphins can swim.
So why can't I?

They even stop throughout the day
To listen as the songbirds sing their sweet
Melodies.
So why can't I?

They watch the clouds float by without making a
Sound, and smile at the sun as it shines upon the
Whole universe.
So why can't I?

I'm just a small piece of creation,
A mere human being with a heart that beats
And eyes that cry.
A child of my mother I am inside,
And life is what I wish to try.
So why can't I?

The Mom I Hope To Be
by C.R. Stowell

The soul of a mother can be seen in her eyes,
Her smile and gentle touch.

Her love for her children can be seen in all she
Does, and the tears she sheds when a small one is
Lost.

A mother will die for those she loves
Never to betray them or lose hope
In their trust.

She may not always like the things they do,
But she will always be there to guide them
Through.

She will scold them and praise them
Which ever is due,
Then tuck them in and stand watch till the
Morning dew.

My mothers soul is stronger than that.
She calms me in troubled times with a tender touch
Through the memories of my mind.

She has given me an imaginative mind,
Then taught me how to use it during my playtime.

So now I write, for all to read, of the wonderful
Mom I hope to be.

I Love You
by Stephanie Strahan - age 15

I'm sitting here trying
to write a poem for you
But I want it to be perfect
so it's hard to do
All I can think of
is your soft gentle kiss
And how when you touch me
it's a total body bliss
I don't want to be anywhere
except together
Then I wish I could
stop time forever
When I'm with you
everything feels so right
I want to feel that way
all day and all night
You make me feel so good inside
When I'm with you
I have nothing to hide
You are so very easy
to talk to
I feel so lucky
that I found you
I know this poem is pretty sappy
But it's the only way I know
to show you
I'm extremely happy.

Think Nothing
by Emily Strawser - age 15

Thinking of nothing is impossible
When trying to think of nothing
You are, in fact, thinking something
But sometimes when you are thinking,
Your mind will come to a blank
And you will then be thinking nothing.

A Walk With Destiny
by Angela Suess

In the anticipation of death
The holy one has come to me,
To walk with me where
There is no path.
The land unbroken,
Trees not separated.
Together we walk,
The hold one tells me a tale of life
And offers me a drink form his hand.
He picks me up when I have tripped over the uprooted trees,
Carries me when I am too tired to go on...
Never for a moment did we ever stop,
Not until we came to the paved path.
From there he flew towards the clouds.
But yet every time I look over my shoulder,
He is there offering me his hand.

Between
by Brian Clement Sullivan

Between the rock and the hard place
Lie fear and helplessness.

Between black and white
Lie empty space and nothingness.

Between what might have been
And what will never be again
Lie desperation and hopelessness.

Between the life we lead and the death for which we wait
Lies the courage that is the difference between living and being alive,

The courage that helps us see
That fear is nothing more
Than hope cloaked in uncertainty;

The courage that helps us all behold
Not empty space,
But vivid colors and dancing rainbows;

The courage to realize that hopelessness
Is not what grips our hearts so tight,
But salvation, waiting to let ourselves be held by hands divine.

Life
by Lisa Tate - age 11

Life isn't fair
But you handle it with care
No matter how tough it gets
You'll always have your wits
You'll have friends
But they all will have sins
Your family will be there for you
And god will be there too
So remember, when you're blue
Life isn't always fair for you.

Obsession
by Naomi Tacuyan - age 15

Looking for a way out
of this place of mixed emotions.
The door is closed,
There is nowhere to hide
From this uncontrolled obsession.
Obsession that chips away at your heart
While lifting you high into the sky.
Euphoria leaves you breathless,
The plunge down leaves you restless
For the love you long to have,
For the touch you long to feel.
For the words you long to hear,
From the one you long to hold.
The ride isn't over,
The rushing wind leaves you cold.
Just a few more twists and turns,
Just a few more dives and bends.
Hopefully soon the heartache stops...
And the torture ends.

Grandma
by Susan Sumner

While sitting at a desk in
my Grandmother's room,
I started to remember
all the happy thoughts
I had of her.

She was a kind
caring person,
strict at times,
but always caring.
Even when she got real
sick she was still herself.

When people get sick
they usually hope for the best
and wait for the worst.
She did anything she was able to do.

The times I got to spend
with her were the best
times of my life.
I learned about life and how to love it.
She taught me a lot.

She always had something
to talk about.
Many people loved her
and she loved them back.
No one will ever
forget her!

In memory of Grandma Sumner
1924-1992

Do Not Mourn
by Rebecca Swafford

I look down from heaven and what do I
see?
I see my family crying and they are
crying for me!

Although I have traveled to a far off
land...
I am very happy here in God's hands.

Please do not mourn for you haven't lost me!
I'm always around you but my soul you
can't see.

If only I could have made you understand
What was waiting for me in this far off
land.

The mountains are high and the valleys
are wide.
There are no feelings of anger, pain, or
fear inside.

You have so many doubts and so many
fears,
so many questions and too many tears.

I'll always be with you as you're a part
of me.
I will always love you as much as you'll
always love me.

Do I Love You?
by Amber Swedberg - age 14

I think I love you
But I'm not sure
It might be just a crush
I wish there was a cure.

You're a wonderful person
A sweetie too!
You know how to lift people up
Do I love you?

Don't worry, I'm not obsessed
But, can't you see?
I've tried everything I can
To get you to notice me.

Whenever I hear a love song
You come to mind
Because right now
You're the best guy that anyone could ever find.

You're special to me
That's why I wish
You were interested in me
But, I realize there's a whole sea of fish.

Probably in my dreams
Is the only time we'll be together
But I want you to know
You'll have a special place in my heart, forever.

Confusion
by Kate Walker - age 14

Confusion is a dark place in your mind.
You never know where to go, or what you'll find.
You want to go one way, but your mind tells you another.
The minutes turn to hours, and the hours turn into days.
Confusion has grabbed and caught you.
Now there is no way to escape.

Just Because
by Tammy Turale Sykes

Just because I look this way
don't judge me, by the cover.

He had blessed me, and he can
do the same for you.
But you are the one that has to
believe.

Just because I am me, don't
try to crush my spirit.
Because if you do,
I'm just going to smile at you
And keep on going.

Please don't step in my way
Because, I have work to do
While I'm on earth, I must say -

Once again, I say, I have
work to do,
and he is pulling me through.

Most of all I love him very much
And he loves me too
So watch out.
HERE I COME!

"Regeneration"
by Sonya Szentpetery - age 15

Every time I feel
That I am fading away,
There is always an anchor,
Catching and sending me back.

When I feel that
I have nothing left inside,
I heal, exhausted as I am,
And the void becomes a little brighter.

When my heart has healed,
And I depart into the night,
I see that the moth has closed her wings
And revealed the silken sky.

To heal, the fury in one's heart
Must escape and soften.
My fury, my rage, my troubles,
All escape like half-had dreams into the morning dew.

After the fires cool.
And the ashes are carried away,
The heart beats with strength,
Even when drained.

A Flowering Memory
by Danen Szpara

    In the sun there once grew a rose,
full of beauty and strength.
    The rose was loved and cherished by many.
Until the winter storm's became too much.
    The spring thaw brought about great sadness,
the rose had withered into nothing.
    But in the shadow's grew a magnificent flower.
A flower of great love and memories.
    The reflection of the rose danced upon it's petal's
and sung amongst it's leaves.
    Upon this bittersweet day there grew a knowledge
of life with physical being.
    Memories and Love
bring out the true life in all things.,

A Mother's Love
by Laurie Szper - age 16

A mother's love
so tender and true,
no one knows
what I'd do without you.

I thank you for the love
that you have shared with me,
and for what you have helped me
grow to be.

I love you with all my heart,
I've felt this way from the very start.
I take this time to tell you,
how much I really care.

Please take these words from my heart,
keep them for life and
don't ever let them leave your mind.

I Love You Mom, and
this is what
a mother's love means to me.

The Light
by Amanda Taylor - age 12

What do you see?
I see a light,
and it is bright
with a bit of delight,
What is the light?
The light is the one
who shows you your
path and the way for
you to obey. Within
thy, thee can not
stand without him.

Forever
by Jessica Taylor - age 14

We love each other so much.
We share so many dreams.
We've been through so much.
Yet we still love each other.

We can feel each others love when we hug.
We can talk about anything together.
We love each other.
We always have and always will.

We make promises so that we can get married,
We will be forever!!

Our World
by Rebecca Taylor - age 13

In our minds, there is a world,
of cheerful boys and girls,
where children laugh and play,
and the sun shines all day.

A world without problems,
a world without tears,
a world full of hopes,
full of dreams and without fears.

But really, in our world today,
there are children who never laugh or play,
children who have never cracked a smile,
whose life, to them, seems not worthwhile.

We need to help the children,
first and foremost, not the least,
closer to being lovely then,
our world will surely be.

Too Late?
by Stasia Taylor

How long have I been sleeping? Why haven't I been awake
To see our world disappearing? How much time did it take

To burn the very last forest or cut down the very last tree?
To kill the very last animal or pollute the very last sea?

How long have I been sleeping and why am I alone
To face this burning wasteland that once was called my home?

Could I have stopped this madness before it was too late?
Could I have rid the world of prejudice and hate?

Could I have stopped the killing that was knocking down your door?
Could I have stopped the fighting that soon turned into war?

Am I supposed to wake them, or are they sleeping sound?
Am I supposed to wake them up and show them what I've found?

Can we build our world back to what it used to be?
Can we do it together, or is it up to me?

Many times they told us the world will one day end
If we don't give our Mother Earth a little time to mend.

Why didn't we all listen to the crying that she did
Every time we polluted the places she'd forbid?

We should have listened to Jesus when he told us about hate.
We should have listened to reason, or are we all too late?

Is It I?
by Jaime Turek - age 15

The blossoming flower shall wither and die
After living a life full of hope.
This flowers perhaps, is a version of I,
Through all of my life I shall cope,
With the thoughts of waiting painfully
For the life of me to end,
Then Eternity shall begin,
And my whole life shall it mend.

Amber
by Kristina Teaster - age 12

The girl Amber is hard
to understand.

Sometimes she's in the
mood to love, or be
taken by the
hand.

While other times she's in
the mood to stand alone
and face the world on
her own, until she
realizes that the world's
a hard place to face
on her own.

So she returns to a place
known as "Home," until
once again she gets
an urge to stand
alone.

Who'll Be There?
by Connie Terrell - age 14

Boys have came and broke our hearts,
friends have came and gone,
family has passed on and been torn apart,
but nothing compares to the pain I've been feeling
since you told me that you were leaving.
You've been here for me, I've been here for you.
Now who's problems am I going to listen to?
Who's shoulder will you cry on?
Who's going to help you through?
Who's going to be here for me?
I can't live on phone calls and letters,
you are a part of me and my life,
I am a part of you and your life.
If you come back, I'll be here for you,
just like you were always here for me.
You have touched my heart when no others could,
you will always be remembered,
you will always be in my heart, prayers, and thoughts.
Whenever you need a shoulder to cry on, I'll be there.

When I Speak
by Tera Terrillo - age 19

Keeping my secret is harder than hell
I want all to listen, so I can tell
You'll know what has happened when I want to yell
I always lied when I said I fell.

There's more to my story, but I can't spill it out
But I'm coming close to be ready to shout
The baby's father...I said I had doubts
When I speak you'll know what my fear was about.

For all these years, I had to deny
The truth that is real, I had to lie
I've bottled it up which made me cry
When I speak you'll see why I wanted to die.

I want to tell you, so please listen up
No, I can't do this, I have to shut-up
If I speak, my throat he might cut
Yet inside of me is all a rut.

It's been so hard to hide it this long
But out in the open is where the truth belongs
When I speak, he'll be locked up and gone
But he deserves it for doing so wrong.

memories
by Stephaney Tew - age 17

Sing with that sweet soft voice.
Hold with those warming arms.
Feel the creation breath deeply,
And know that this is perfection.

See as the years go by.
Hear as that voice cracks.
Be there for that bad day,
And cry as walking away.

Hold close on this visit.
Share memories of those days.
Sing softly holding hands,
As mother slowly slips away.

Sole Owner
by Jay Therrien - age 19

sole owner,
    reluctant love donor
erasing the memories
    counting the tragedies,
remembering moments
    long passed throughout times
ever with tears
    adolescent sex crimes,
love lost in the years
    of sands the hourglass
never seen with broken eyes
    life onward to pass,
long, lonely nights of cries.

sole owner,
    of my heart gone
        long away before.

Love Of Contrast
by Jeremy Thomas - age 20

Your beauty denies my horrible place.
My clumsiness faults your elegant grace.
The sweet of your lips touches my face,
And all is forgotten except for the taste.

Your eyes, so bright, darkens my own.
MY absence of light; your brilliance is shown.
Nothing could make me leave you alone,
Cause when I'm with you, that's all that is known.

Your intelligent strength corrupts my weak mind
My ties that come loose, your always can bind
The truth of your love leaves me so blind
That nothing but you is all I can find.

Your happiness brushes against my ill sorrows,
My sadness at heart leaves you with morose.
The touch of your hand allows me to borrow
The memories I need to forget there's tomorrow.

Your sweet young love collides with my hate.
My sense to give in, your will to debate.
The smell of desire, from you, I await,
Gives me no worries, except for our fate.

Your joy is so high, my pain it's above.
My patience so loose, yours fits like a glove.
The size of your heart is all I think of,
When questions of doubt are brought on our love.

Your answers you give, my questions I ask,
My thought are so slow, your words are so fast.
The vision of you assures me we'll last
When I realize our love of contrast.

Dying
by Melissa Thomas

My body fell
My soul rised
and my heart knew
life was saying goodbye
I sank into
a trance of though
my feelings disappeared
my lies were caught
I got what I deserved; good or bad,
I felt insane
I was sent to a place
where I had no name
the earth disappeared
candles were lit
and I knew from inside
this was it
I forgot everyone
that I knew in my mind
I started all over
as I started to die

Only In My Dreams
by Jacqueline Torello - age 13

My only wish in life
is that I shall overcome my fear of
death. This fear is like a pressure,
that will never be relieved.
The only way to release it is if you
become frees.
To me this only a dream.
I am a Jew; prisoner for life
the person pointed out, in the streets,
the person who was poked and prodded
at for five long years, by a man with no
respect for his own kind.
Is this the life I am supposed to live?
Only in my dreams am I ever free.
Maybe someday my dreams
will conquer this fear.

Letting Go
by Heather Thompson - age 15

To "let go" does not mean to stop caring.
It means I can't do it for someone else.
To "let go" is not to enable,
but to allow learning from natural consequences
To "let go" is not to try to change or blame another,
it's to make the most of myself.
To "let go" is not to fix, but to be supportive.
To "let go" is not to judge,
but to allow another to be a human being.
To "let go" is not to be in the middle
arranging all the outcomes,
but to allow others to affect their destinies
To "let go" is to not deny, but to accept.
To "let go" is not to nag, scold, or argue,
but instead to search out my own shortcomings
and correct them.
To "let go" is not to adjust everything to my desires
but to take each day as it comes
and cherish myself in it
To "let go" is not to regret the past
but to grow and live for the future.
To "let go" is to fear less and love more.

Lifting My Spirits
by Tonyce Thompson - age 16

Sunrise, sunshine,
Will you ever be mine?
The days come and go,
Still there's a lot of things, I don't know.
I love it when I'm with you,
You always know what to do.
There are times when I don't say a word,
Usually I'm not quiet, like a bird.
If I ever need a friend, your always there,
all I have to do, is tell you when and where
Take me in your arms and rock
me all night long,
as you kiss me, sing me a love song.
Whisper sweet things in my ear,
then bring your body right here.
I want to spend as much time
with you, as much as I can,
My feelings for you are very deep,
So will you be my man?
Be my man and treat me right,
I'll promise you, we'll never fight.
I'll promise to love you all through the night,
and I'll be there in the morning light.
We'll have breakfast in bed,
What's going on, in your head?
My heart is beating very fast,
I'm hoping that this will last.
You and I are meant to be,
I'll love you forever, you have my guarantee!

Stop The Rain...
by Jennifer Tinsley - age 15

Ever since you left me,
I've been crying every night.
I cry myself to sleep,
And continue with daylight.

You don't know how it feels-
Lying here alone.
I have no one to hold,
No one to call my own.

I yearn for memories, the past,
But nothing numbs the pain.
If only you'd come back,
If only you'd stop the rain.

The Barn
by Lou Ann Tipps

A lonely edifice in the field,
made of timber and rusty nails,
stands in unprecise simplicity
leaning from year's of windy gales.

A shelter to earth's creatures,
veiled with spider's webs,
and scented with fresh dung
and hay that lies in wooden cribs.

It is a farmer's monument to his herd,
those creatures of his livelihood.
An artistic model for protection,
and a real home for his brood.

The splintered and creviced stable,
slanting in the twinkling starlight,
is a plush and golden throne
to herds and other varmints of the night...

The Blindness of Optimism
by Jennifer Tobin - age 16

I gaze upon my existence with hatred and disgust
Casting away the blindness of optimism
I allow myself to be free
A freedom you will never know
Your narrow vision and optimistic outlook blind you
You walk through life and tell yourself that everything is beautiful
For as long as you can
You have done it for quite some time
I admire your persistence
Yet, I wonder what really keeps you going
Do you honestly see beauty or do you just want to?
To the point where it controls you
You are but a slave
With delusion as your master
And your optimism the chains that bind you
If I were to give advice
It would be this
Don't struggle
For your chains are a gift
You don't want to be free
You will not like what you see
Cherish your slavery

Who Am I?
by Blythe A. Wager

I have a name,
I have a face.
I have goals,
and I have dreams.
I am human,
and I am alive.
Who am I?
I am what I am.
Who are you to judge me?

To Dance On The Breeze
by Sarah J. Tolliver

The female Tiger-winged butterfly rode the breeze
To a puffed out dandelion and set herself down upon
Two of the spores, grasped her balance
And settled, content to rest --
She spotted a Dragon-winged male on
Her left.

A dandy he was, his wing's dust whispering on the
Breeze;
This butterfly danced, fluttered here and about as
The cool breeze stiffened.
Soon he was grasping for balance with his wings
And she was tap dancing on the spores,
Holding on for her footing;
Off they went, the spores and the Tiger tied
Up in the breeze they rode
Toward the Dragon.

The two locked on a spore with their feet
And held their wings down like the flaps of a jet;
They settled onto the grass together
And touched antennae as they untangled their
Feet.

Beware
by Marcel Toussaint

Beware of the mind
where thoughts grow in the night
once the lights are out
the moon shines through
the window without a blind.

Beware of the mind
where thoughts grow in the night
after the cat lets out a meow
a chill comes through
your spine.

Beware of the mind
where thoughts grow in the night
when the hands of the clock
cover each other
at the strike of midnight.

Beware of the mind
where thoughts grow in the night
when your day was stressed,
your driving erratic
sleeping you toss around.

Beware of the mind
where thoughts grow in the night
when the floor squeaks, the door grinds,
a lit candle comes into the room
held only by an arm.

Beware, it is Halloween Night.

The Final Jump
by Paula Townsend - age 16

With the eye of an eagle
he watches her closely.
She tightens his girth,
up one more notch.
She mounts him,
it's time.
Jumping to them is
like breathing to us.

They enter the ring
and then they stop.
She tells him let's go
and he takes off like a shot.
Jump one, jump two,
away they go.
When they are done
she tells him good job.

Then she dismounts,
all tension is gone.
She loosens his girth
and brings him his grain,
She starts to rest and hears
her name, and then she knows,
they've finally won.
So now there is peace
they've won what they sought for,
Thus she lets down her hair
and takes off her gloves.

Do You Know A Mystery
by Connie Toy

What do you see, what do you know?
You think you know me but nothing is what you know.

I am a mystery born from the eye of the innocent ones,
And lost by the knowledged of their elder sons.

What do you see, what do you know?
Mystery that unfortunately grows old

I lost the interest in people who sought me.
They grew up as they faded away from thee.

What do you see, what do you know?
Do you see the answers that I don't know?

Do you see the mystery?
Do you know?

Solitude
by Amy Trageser - age 14

Under the old oak tree
   I sit alone in silence
The sky is blue
   As a robin's egg
White fluffy clouds
   Lay upon the horizon
Forming cute little animals and shapeless wonders
   Softly
The wind starts to blow
   Tickling my neck
As it teases my hair
   Leaves rustle and drift
Quietly down
   I begin to think of my childhood
When life seemed so perfect
   Tears roll down my cheeks
Those days are behind me
   A new life awaits
Needing to be found
   I stumble to my feet
And dry my eyes
   Unsure of what's ahead
I walk cautiously
   into a new world--
And smile

Our Child
by Toni Trojan

Once you were small and helpless and very dependent on us,
we would run
right to your side at the slightest little fuss.

Since the day that you were born time has really flown, we have watched
you go from crawling to standing on your own.

We used to hold you in our arms and now you hold our hand, our undivided
attention doesn't seem in quite the demand.

One day you will be on your own, when your fully grown,
and we will look
back into time at the little girl we had known.

We will always be your parents, the ones to always care, so if you ever
need us just reach out we'll be there.

Times and memories spent with you we will hold close at heart, two people
that were much in love is where you got your start.

With No Lies, Looking Into His Eyes
by Bobbye L. Turnbough

When I looked at him in his eyes,
I knew at that moment he spoke no lies.
His eyes were breezy; like windy skies,
They were different; Not like the other guys.
As the girl who sits down behind me sighs,
Wishing she were in my place; Looking into his eyes,
Held close to him in his arms; They wrapped around me like
Knotted bow ties,
Together we are wise
Happy I'm his only prize,
But as the tears fall heavily from his eyes,
I know he can no longer tell me any lies.
As I lie in his arms my heart cries;
"Please tell me the truth, no more lies!"
Since he has, I want him to know, as this relationship dies,
That for once, I did something wise!!!

Travis
by Abby Udland - age 16

At night when I'm all alone, I long
for just a kiss and pray for your gentle
touch
As I lie there in bed a question comes to
mind "Am I asking too much?"
You would not believe the loneliness that
fills my heart
It's so hard to sleep knowing we are so
far apart.
I sit up in bed and wonder if you
are dreaming
Wanting to be with you so much beneath
the moonlight gleaming
I hold your picture close to me, wanting
to dismiss from this solitary feeling. In
my heart I know there is nothing I can do
But if I must sleep alone, please go to
Bed knowing I truly love you.

My Dream
by Rebecca L. Urbina

Last night I had a dream, a dream so real it felt like reality. In this dream there was a distant light with an angel in the center that glowed so very bright. As the angel came closer the glow got brighter. I just knew, this angel was taking me higher.

But I was wrong, before it touched me the heavens played a beautiful song and this angel just lingered on. Appeared in front of me a shaken boy lost, confused and alone. The glowing angel moved from me and reached for this boy who had come home.

As soon as the angel touched the boy, their bodies were apparent. For the glowing angel was my mother who had come to take with her my baby brother.

Behind them both I stood and cried for I knew now it's time for goodbyes. As I turned and walked the other way, out of the blue, my sweet sister Loretta did say,
    "It's okay to cry, It's okay to be sad
    today is a painful memory
    yesterday's all you had.

    But cry not for yesterday
    and cherish the memories you have made
    there's nothing to cry about
    we are all okay."

Her hand was on my shoulder but her spirit did not stay, as I felt her hand lift from me and her spirit floated their way. I stood and stared at my three loved ones, there on God's blessed land, not sure of my next move, but knew God was close at hand. Yes God was close at hand.

Lost But Not Forgotten
by LaDonna Star Vader - age 18

My heart broke the day you died and I have never been the same.
I saw you alive, inside myself, your tiny heart beat so strong.
Each time you moved, the more you grew, excitement from all around.
You were so small, more fragile than glass before you were even born. Your life meant so much to me.
I picked out your name with help from your father, I know he loved you too.
Suddenly, all I felt was pain, you were dying - so was I. Death abide, yet life remain, what did I do wrong?
My spirit broke, as did my heart. My whole body felt deceived. What was God's reason? Why aren't you here to celebrate your first birthday?
I still wonder how you'd look today, dark hair like your father or blond like me? Boy or girl? I'll never know. You'd be beautiful either way.
I'll never get to hold you or watch you play. Immortalize your first step on video tape. Although your in heaven, I wonder still if you could ever love someone who couldn't give you life?
I love you still, but could you love me?

Izzy
by Jessica Valentine - age 18

The angel boy with the gray-blue eyes.
Our love is something no one denies.
The day you asked and I said yes,
The wind was still perfection, no less.
The setting was awesome no one was there.
We sat there and talked as your braided my hair.
Everyone else was off at the cook out,
So there was no need to look out,
For counselors, volunteers or staff.
I can't believe how much we did laugh.
Can you believe that no one missed us?
Not one person raised a fuss.
Sitting in the chapel sharing a Snapple.
The next night the dance, oh, what romance!
We stood there and grooved as everyone moved
The music wasn't too fast, please God, let this last.
And then there was campfire, no one wasn't a crier.
As we remembered those gone, and sang the Journey song.
I told you my secret that night. You just cried and held me tight.
Wow, what a guy! You said "It's okay to cry."
I did, until the tears were no more,
And now I have something to live for.
Izzy, dear, you made me smile
When I felt that my life was on trial.
So you, Isaac Trowbridge, and all of them too,
Never forget to always be true.
Sara, Vickie, Jayme, Chris, Greg, You and I,
We will always be here, this love cannot die.
It's the love of a bond no one else understands,
It's the bond of a life with deathly demands.

True Romance
by Jessica Valentine - age 18

We've been "Just friends"
For ever so long,
The things we feel
Just can't be wrong.

This love we share
Is not a crime.
But we don't have
A lot of time.

You see, my love
I am dying.
Now, please,
Don't start crying.

Just hug me hard.
Just hold me tight.
You know this feels
Nothing but right.

I love you my dear,
With all my heart.
So let's give us
A brand new start.

We have given
Everything we've had.
When it comes to you
I cannot stay mad.

Come on, hon
Give it a chance.
Then you'll see
This is true romance.

Going Fox Hunting
by Roberta Van Note

Dad was an avid fox hunter with a kennel full of hounds.
They were registered dogs with papers of their backgrounds.
He and his friends would go often several nights a week.
They'd turn the dogs loose to run, for a good race they'd seek.
At times they'd build a campfire, other nights they'd sit in the dark,
listening to the hounds run. Each man knew his dog by it's bark.

They could tell by the distinct voices which dog was in the lead,
if they were running in open grounds, lost it, or had it "treed".
During the lulls they talked of breeds. Which was best, blue tick or red bone?
If the dogs didn't come in, they'd leave a blanket and go on home.

The dogs would come in later, rest, and wait to be picked up.
Occasionally he would have to hunt one, especially if it was a pup.
At times he'd drive hundreds of miles to buy, sell, to trade.
Distance was never an object if a good deal could be made.
My husband and all of our kids experienced this unique place,
sitting under a blanket of stars listening to the hounds in chase.

In Memory of Walter
by Margaret L. Vaughan

As we lay you down to sleep
    To walk Heavens stairs

We know that God
    Will greet you there

In our hearts
    You will remain dear

Though you seem far away
    We know that you are near

We'll all join you
    Again some day

In a much better world
    A much better place

God picked you out
    From all the rest

He knew the job in Heaven
    You would do best

While you are in Heaven
    Doing what angels do

Don't forget us Walter
    And that we love you.

Sadness In The Mist
by Erica C. Vericella

  The fire within the child no longer rages
Now the coals caress like ice and all is silent
Yet, place does not exist, all feeling has gone numb.

  The sorrows of life wear down the godforsaken soul
And the hunger that burned within has burned itself to ashes
The spirit grows hopeless and dreams are dead.

  I seem to exist in limbo I am neither here nor there
further away from salvation and closer still to damnation
Have others damned me or have I dammed myself.

  Never close to life and further still from death
I am suspended in between being and deceasing
But life never promised a fairy tale and prince
Charming is dead.

Missionary
by Nuwatanka

In your fear, you took my history and hula away,
Shrouding my boy and holding beauty at bay.
In ignorance, you banished the soft ph, sh, and she.
You took my story and the beauty of my language from me
And made me into he heathen you wanted to see.

Untitled
by Jessica Vogel - age 16

I sit here thinking of my past
I then realize my life is going by fast,
So many sad memories flow into my head
I hate my life so I wish I could be dead;

My heart has been broken time and time again
How can I trust any one I can't tell whose a true friend,
I thought that I was loved, he said he'd never love another
Now he never talks to me because she is his new lover;

I thought I had close friends and nothing could ever tear my friendships apart
Now I'm moving to another city and they don't care about my broken heart,
If nobody cares then why should I
This town would be happier if I would just die;

Now one friends gone and another and another
Now my ex is whom I long, how quickly I have been replaced by others,
I can't take anymore my luck has completely run out
Just like the blood that was deep inside me has now been turned inside out;

I close my eyes
Knowing it is forever,
One more tear is shed
But all the pain I have encountered will never be forgotten.

Only 16
by Daylin Wade - age 14

She was only 16
It wasn't her fault
She didn't see him
His eyes on the vault

He held a gun
And ordered her to get down
But she was deaf
And never heard a sound

He held two large bags
Containing his loot
As he walked to the door
Threatening to shoot

Two shots were fired
She fell to the floor
He gave her one last look
And ran for the door

And now a tear
Falls down from my eye
I never even got
To say good bye

I Have A Book
by Michael J. Growder

here is my book.
Com-m-on, take a look...
Wouldn't you Sir,
Like to read my book
not knowing, he was a crook.
That crook tried to take my book
Then I shook that crook who
tried to take my book.
I gave him a quick right hook...
He fell with my book,
and ker-er plop

    Thank God here come
    the COPS!

Anger
by Rikki Wade - age 14

Anger is a feeling
far from anything
different then a tear
different then a fear
anger is a hurt
that comes from deep inside
down in a place
no one sees
no one feels
and no one cares
anger hits like a bomb
exploding inside
Anger isn't a punch or a kick
But a poison inflicted
on an inside wound.

If I Jump Can I Fly Away
by Rhonda Wagner - age 14

If I jump I can fly away?
Over all the clouds and around the pain,
with more love than a heart can endure,
To a place I've never seen before,
Past the flowers and the grass of home,
A place where few have ever known.
A place to laugh and get away,
A place to live and probably stay.
I'd love to see it someday someway.
If I jump can fly away?

If I jump can I fly away?
Maybe I'll find out today.
Above the clouds and over the trees,
That's the place I want to be,
As I stand on the edge, ready to fly,
I see the world through different eyes.
Happiness isn't above the clouds
It's not a place to be found.
Even if things go wrong,
There's always a place to hear a song.
Through the tears, and past the teens,
Above the clouds and over the trees.

Which Way To Turn?
by Melanie Elizabeth Walits - age 13

Just like the wind changes direction,
my life seems to do the same.
It's sometimes full of sunshine,
then sometimes full of rain.

Suddenly the little girl whose time was
filled and enthralled with games,
Is suddenly learning that the games of life,
are very soon to change.

Which way to turn?
One day I'm playing the role of a grown-up.
The next day as the sun rises, I find,
that the girl whose hair was once in disarray,
now seems to fall into place.
I'm changing very much along the way.

Which way to turn?
I don't really know.
Which way to turn?
Where do I go?

Like the winds in time,
I too will reach my destiny.
Be it one of triumph,
or two, what is destined to be.

Alcohol and Abuse
by Kate Walker - age 14

Yelling, screaming, crying, dying.
The secret that must be kept.
The love that has left.
The fighting has almost gotten to be too much.
The bruises and broken bones are showing up more often.
There is no way to escape the torture that is all due to alcohol.

Darkness
by Michelle Wallace - age 16

You light up the path of my life,
with out you theres no tomorrow,
you take away all my pain and sorrow,
I look at your face and I know there's nothing to fear,
you'll always be the love of my life so dear,
Say that you love me,
Say that you care,
for nobody but you and I could make a better pair.
I know you miss your mother,
and you cried when you saw her in her tomb,
just remember she loved you ever since you were in her womb.
I know you still have pain and you try to cover it up, and that you really care,
for if you didn't you wouldn't have been there.
You have always been there for me, and yes it's very true,
I promise that I will always be there for you.

Day Lily
by Doris Yates Wallace

Dedicated to Michael J. Crowder

Holding on to forever gone...
The second of true happiness as
I saw you call me.

Your pretty dress a tiny blue.
Walking with sparkles the eyes in
a dream.

I hold your hand but it is your
soft fingers that caress our time.
Day lily where do you stand when
all you ever wanted was a moment
to be here.

You will always be my kindness even
as I move to another day.
Growing older through me as I watch
you sleep the same.

I breath you now.
In between winter and spring.
Tomorrow is almost over.
Today it rained.

You give to me only the perfect
things.
Remembering everything in the
cemetery with lights.

You truly understand it all.
And though I see it will never
be, you still bring to me your
distance ever sweet.

Now move on Day Lily lost.
I will catch up to you soon.
Together we will live in the
days of the leaves...

Cole Street Moon
by Jennifer Walsh

My shoes tap ever so lightly on Cole Street
As I drink in the milky white light
Of a nearly full summer moon.
The warm evening air
Blankets my bare skin,
Reminding me of my childhood
When I would chase fireflies
Across a grassy field into the night.
Here in the City,
The flashing lights of police cars
Take the place of fireflies,
And screeching tires
Break the stillness of twilight,
But the moon,
In her radiant glow,
Rescues me,
Transforms me,
Melts my human shell of suffering,
And allows me to dissolve
Into crystalline light
As I float to my car on Cole Street.

My Car The Lemon;
by Elizabeth L. Wangberg R.A.

I found a car in the paper one day,
I thought it great and in my price, hooray!
I hurried to go see this wonderful buy,
as we pulled up beside it, I felt my hopes fly.
I had taken my dad, as all good daughters would do,
his first words naturally, Oh No! That's not for you!
Being the bullheaded one that I am,
I completely ignored my dad's, ahem.
I drove my dream car with awe,
muffling my dad's words that cut like a saw.
I felt the car was worth so much more,
they had me sold as soon as I hit the door.
No, I didn't listen to my wise old teacher,
he wouldn't look beyond the dents,
to see each cool looking feature.
So, with my mind made up, I bought that cool car,
Boy, I'd cruise around and take it real far.
As I brought it home I began to see,
man had they taken advantage of me!
Now the car sits, to run would be simply heaven,
and that's the end of my car the lemon.

Monkey/You or Me
by Morris Ward

Who or what is man, no one seems to agree
was he created in the likes of you and me?
Or did he just swing down from a tree.
Scientist and archeologist search for answers be
But we keep wondering-who are you and me.
But perhaps it was just the monkey from the tree.
Along came footprints with a stride that matched those of you and me
or maybe it was the monkey trying to be like you an me
Now all of this is about to change-the mystery of you and me!
Were we created, or dropped from a tree?
They-those scientists and archeologist think that someone, higher in
Intelligence than either you or me
Lived upon this land even before the monkey from the tree.
They have discovered great cities in the mountains and near the sea
Developed with knowledge and material that could not be.
Oh what a mystery this could really be-for maybe even
The monkey and you and me
Came from some other place-perhaps from a space laboratory!
Above the earth or from someone else's tree.
I will leave you now to ponder on this bit of mystery,
of you and me and all the monkeys in a tree,
For who really knows-not the monkey, you or me
And there may be someone else higher on some other tree

A Special Land
by Rackelle White Wolf - age 20

When I see you everything is fine
I'm so happy that you're mine
You pick me up when I am hurt
You cheer me up when I feel like dirt
when times get rough you understand
your bring me to a special land
where only you and I go to
How we got there? I guess we flew
I want you more than ever
I wish this could last forever

Praying For Time
by Marianne Ware

Shadows of the night,
I can hear them calling.
Speaking to me with reflection
From the wounded skies above.

Days of being hand in hand,
Hanging onto the dreams you had planned.
Somewhere along the way,
You turned your back and he slipped away.

Taking your chances, you hang onto hope;
Even when there is no hope to speak of.
All those lonely nights of holding onto his love,
Clinging to the things he told you.
Always praying for time.

Spring Celebration
by Marianne Ware

In the dazzling light of the wandering moon,
Harmony was created playing a beautiful tune.
Opening the gates to the sacred streams of truth;
Letting nature pay, revealing all of its youth.

In the whirling wind, the golden daffodils danced;
Cutting in, the tulips lifted their stems and pranced.
Adding to the festivities the wild birds began to sing,
All celebrating the birth of spring.

Enclosing Of The Cape
by David E. Edwards - age 16

Always running, trying to escape
The enclosing of the Black Man's cape
Should I face my fears?
Or scamper away from their jeers?
Hiding behind tree after tree
Wary of the presence looking for me.

Behind That Painted Smile
by Ruth Warner

There upon your face is painted
a smile much like a clown's
displaying to the world at large
someone who seldom frowns.

Beneath the grease paint, you project
a man who exudes joy;
on closer look beneath the guise,
a frightened little boy.

On looking deep into the eyes,
you'll find a sadness there,
a fear of losing self-control
that borders on despair.

'Laugh, clown, laugh' is the axiom
by which you live each day,
and hidden deep is the heartache
you must not give away.

The world is fooled because you choose
to use pretense and guile,
and I alone will know the pain
behind that painted smile.

The Biggest Room

The biggest room in my heart is filled
with patience, understanding and love.
There is only one door, there are no walls,
and entry is gained by a gentle shove.

This room is a very special place, it is
lined with volumes of emotion and desire.
In the very center will be found brilliantly
glowing embers, waiting to be set fully afire.

This room is not totally, solely mine to enter
and control, or by myself to live within.
It must be united with another, a room of equal
capacity, where true love, and life can begin.

The biggest room in my heart, is not for tours.

The biggest room in my heart, is yours.

For James and Denise Koch, may you forever live in adjoining rooms.   Charles E. Warren

She Is

She is real, see that's her: The pretty one standing close by, with the warm expressive eyes and flashing hair.
When I met her way back then, I could only stand and stare.

She is very intelligent, so lovely, so lively, so strong and so very truly deeply
caring.
To talk and work with her these many years, is a very wonderful sharing.

She is patient and understanding, ready to listen, to share her thoughts, and
always there when I need a shoulder.
Her presence comforts me in facing the fact, that I am growing older.

She is a wonder at work, a Wife, a Mother whose two beautiful Daughters,
and her always have a great big hug for me.
A greater feeling than what those give, cannot be.

She is the one who stood close, cried and shared the pain, the anguish,
and the terrible emptiness when God took my Wife.
Held me, put my heart back together, and brought strength into my life.

She is the Angel who continues to think of me, makes the time to call and
visit to ensure, I don't slip away into the dark of loneliness.
At why, what for, and who cares, I don't have to guess.

She is **That Power of Love**

She is **Suzanne**

Dear God, I thank you with all my heart, that

    She is

For a beautiful Woman, a truly great Lady. Charles E. Warren

You, To Me

I can still feel that instant in Nineteen Seventy Two.
Our eyes locked together in love, wonderful and new,
and it flowed so warmly from
YOU, TO ME

Those months of childlike antics, just to be together.
That pride of being your Indian Brave, waving my feather,
was passed lovingly from
YOU, TO ME

For more than twenty years, we loved, we shared it all.
At all of my trials, the strength to stand, to stand very tall,
came forcefully from
YOU, TO ME

Together in your final moments, I stood up to the stress.
Your love and faith in me I knew, would accept no less.
I am here still, with what was given from
YOU, TO ME

Eternity has passed before my eyes, clearly now I see.
A timeless wonder that will forever and absolutely be,
when God returns

YOU, TO ME

Shirley. 1941-1995 A proud Cherokee.
My wife, the love of my life.   Charles E. Warren

One Sweet Day
by Tamara Watkins - age 14

One sweet day this pain and grief I feel will be all over. But I know you are looking down on me from heaven, One sweet day I know I will be in heaven, walking, talking and remembering the things you did on earth. When I get down on my knees every night I think of that sweet day, not so far away. I will be up there with you in a place that has no pain, nor sorrow or grief; a perfect place. I know that it will be one sweet day.

God I know you hear my prayers, and I know one sweet day I will be there with you. I know you love me and the love that you have for me keeps me alive and encourages me to keep on a little longer. Day by day it gets better, but is not gone
completely. That one sweet day gets a little sweeter and sweeter and I am a little closer to being with you, that one sweet day.

Always
by Amy Watt - age 18

I loved you with all my heart
This time I thought that nothing would
Tear us apart
We shared great memorioes, great times;
I made you laugh, you made me cry
What was shared between us was not a lie-
I only wish these times could have lasted forever
The way you made me feel was a way that
I'd felt never
Slowly, our world drifted apart
The only thing that never changed was
How I felt in my heart
You meant the world to me
And you always will; even when the
Earth is standing still
You haved moved on and I have too
And we both have gone our seperate ways
But no matter what you do or
What you say-
I'll be here for you, always

Endings
by April Weaver - age 20

Sweet scent rises to fill the frigid room
Warm breezes pass by to pay their respects
Voices pierce the solitude of my chilly room
Only a moment to look upon their work and reflect

Stained oak encases their newest portrait
Soft pillowy satin makes my permanent bed
Loved ones take a moment to cry a bit.
Soon my minutes of glory will have ended

They have shut the door, my last ray of sun gone
"May she rest in peace" rings through the walls
Lowered down, the display is done.
Last grain of dirt begins the final fall

Rose are the death of my soul
As the lay upon my tombstone scroll

Friends
by Molly Weber - age 15

Friends are always there for you,
together you will always make it through.
A friend will never put you down,
They're there to chase away your frown.
When you're together you're always having fun,
Your friendship will never ever be done.
A true friend is always there when you have a problem,
If you're feeling depressed all you have to do is call 'em.
A friend will always stick up for you,
A friend will never be untrue.
They're there through thick and thin,
To leave a friend in need would be an absolute sin.
Good friends always have a shoulder to cry on,
they can stay up talking until the break of dawn.
I will not leave a friend, not ever,
'Cause friends are friends forever.

What Is Love
by Stacy Weekley

Love is the warmth in you're heart that never seems
to end but just keeps growing stronger.
Love is the place in you're heart that can not seem
to give but can't seem to go on.
Love is the two hearts beating together instead of apart
So what is love, love is what's meant to be.

Love
by Elizabeth Weetz - age 12

Love is caring
Love is a poem
Love is romance
Love; I love poems
Love is like a millon kisses
Love; money can't buy love
Love you know when you're in love
Love is a warm liking; fond or tender feeling
Love; if a woman or man has no love they should perish
Love is gentle rain falling on your body feeling like millon kisses

Love
by Cheri Weidlein - age 12

What is it anyway?
A gift from heaven some say
A curse on us all
Is another call
Love is the only emotion
That seeps through you like a potion
Covering every part of you
Seeping though your private thoughts
Nothing is hidden
Nothing is kept
Love knows everything, anything
Sometimes it makes you want to sing
You feel so high
As if you could fly
Love can make you
Merry and happy and warm
Then again
It can make your heart feel torn
What is this
You feel it when you kiss
Love, true, and simple and plain?
Yeah right!
It drives you insane!

Rewind
by Cecelia Weiss - age 12

Cliches and analogies aren't enough anymore
Find a cliche that explains
a flame being snuffed out before it was even lit.

Tell me the analogy that compares
my hate, anger, and frustration to anything logical.

How can you explain a candle that's already burnt to the wick wanted
To be built up and lit again?
It just won't happen.

I know that, But still, I try.

As the hot wax slips through my fingers,
expecting voices egg me on.

When the candle is restored, and the wick is starting to
warm up, a red gust of wind that's
All too familiar cools my expectations.

The red wind pushes me, turns me in circles,
Playing with my flame.
It's angering that the flame is never strong enough.

Angel With Wings
by Lindsey Weisenfeld - age 14

January 9th was a very horrible day. That is when you left, when you went away. You were like a second mother to me. And my grandma, my friend, everyone could see. Your smile could brighten up any dim day. I will always love you in every way. January 8th I say my good-byes. Everyone could see the tears in my eyes. We had our fights, our great times too. I want you to know, that I miss you. Basketball, volleyball, piano too. You always came to my things, I could always count on you.
Happy is how I want you to be. But I wish you were still here with me. I wish I could see you just one more time. But everyday I could only see you inside of my mind. Every night when I think of you, I feel a tear roll down. Wishing you were here with me to wipe my tears and frown. Secrets were what I would always tell you. I knew I could always count on you. But then your sickness got really bad. You were always so alone, so quiet, so sad. I will always remember this last year. It was the last time you will ever be here. But now I know you rest in peace. Forever you will be released. I looked at you, there you lie. That's when I said my last good-bye. You made it to the Bat Mitzvah day. I was so grateful in every way. I now know you will be watching me through in each passing day. Even though you're not here, you'll still help me find my way. You always raised my spirits, whenever I was blue. Whenever I needed comforting, I
always came to you. I still can't believe you're not here with me. But I know that is how it should be. You are my grandma, the best one may I add. That's why when you died, I was so sad. I love you so much for many different things. But now I know you're an ANGEL WITH WINGS.

A Dream or Reality?
by Francesca Weiss - age 13

I stood by the brook
And through the canopy of trees
I saw the sun
Bright and wonderful it shone down upon me
The light engulfed me
I laid down under an enormous oak tree amid the pine needles

I was sent into a world of my own
The silvery water sprang up
Then down it fell
Sweet smelling daisies brushed against my ankles
The sun illuminated my face
Birds sand in beautiful harmony

Shadows began closing in
The sun was no longer to be seen
The daisies suddenly became prickly
Full of thorns
The beautiful silvery water lay flat

Nothing moved
No birds sang
The forest was lifeless
I stood all alone
No friends
No one to talk to

Doing The Anything
by Tamara Werntz

Going after dreams doing your anything
Washed away with the willows
savoring sips of tea
lemon, mint and the raspberries
daisies daunting all around
with the rocks that breathe a breath of life
touch that tingles though never it could
tranquil understanding just to be free
mind scapes of ecstasy felt
just who are you Mr. Tree?
may I sit and chat
for awhile or so, under your cree
new places unknown times
discovery of what we really know
just going after our dreams
and doing your anything
laid back in prickly wools
not sure what to make be
hands held the bonds that tie
in distance right here
weaving lives to be free
in afternoon dreams doing the anything.

Untitled
by Jessi Wert - age 11

I waited for you for such a long time
hoping and praying that you would be mine.
From the first time we met
there hasn't been a moment that I regret.
Whenever I'm with you
there's so many emotions I'm so confused.
I remember when you held me all through the night
I won't give up on you now
Not without a fight.
Everything seemed so perfect when
I think of things that could have been.
Do you remember when you said, "Don't cry?"
Well right now I'm crying and I really want to die.
You probably didn't even notice I was there
I love you so much it's really not fair.
I think about you everyday
Then I think of you with her
and my entire world turns grey.
I only have one more thing to say
I'll never be over you as long as I'm here
and I'm counting each stream of tear after tear.
And remember each one is shed for you
because I love you, I just wish you loved me too.

A Fearful Night
by Meghan Orelene West - age 14

In the day it looks so normal,
But at night after a rainy day,
The streetlamp casts unpleasant shadows,
Along the street that was so familiar.
In the puddles I see the fear my imagination lets on,
The gutter is hiding the frightful images I dread so,
And as a gust of wind blows,
Paper flies by like ghosts.
I pick up my speed to reach the safety of home,
And feel relief at last,
I am home,
I lock the door!

Grafting
by Patricia A. Wessel

As in the "Grafting" of a rose bush
With the buds from other grown,
we all could live united,
grater beauty never known!

We all can live on common turf
and grow in harmony.
With the diversity of cultures,
enriched our lives would be!

If we traced our family tree,
we'd find we're all related,
as the one inside the greenhouse,
each seed, he equally created!

Just like the "Grafting" of the rose bush
Creates a blend of radiance!
Protect each seed, nurture the soil,
inspire peace rose continuance!

In this world, a flower bed,
a mixture of such crafting!
Each bud a beauty by itself,
grater beauty when there's "Grafting"!

This Imperfect World
by Rachael Wheat - age 12

In this imperfect world we have today
     things happen that we can't control.
Bombing,
Crashes,
some happen on accident,
some happen on purpose,
but, whatever they may be,
sadness happens in this world that
     shouldn't happen.

    I would like to dedicate this poem to
anyone in this world who has lost a family
member, friend, or suffered a loss.

Again The Bird Sings
by Patricia A. Wessel

If I were a bird on your shoulders I'd rest,
knowing full well with you...
I am safe as your guest.
Ever so gently, you stroke me on cue.

I've watched you from above as I'd fly overheard.
Feeling I knew you quite well;
although we've had no contact...no words ever said,
I injured my wing and beside you I fell.

When you saw I was injured...
you, with care, nursed my wound.
Then I grew hungry and thirst I incurred.
You gathered up water and food, hoping I could fly soon!

So attached and so caring of those you assist...
no confinement, restraining or cruel selfish things,
free to leave any time, you'd never resist!
Then in flight good as new, strongly..."Again The Bird Sings"!

That Same Appeal
by Patricia A. Wessel

Would things we shared and treasured
with each other mean so much,
if we would put our love on hold?
Will we lose or stay in touch?

For quite some time we wondered
how would we act and feel;
if we were to meet up again,
would there be "That Same Appeal"?

You gave to me, I gave to you,
space and time to feel like our oats,
get to find, know and like ourselves,
climb up mountains...sail the boats.

There are so many love affairs
that happen much too fast.
It's just infatuation...
all too often they don't last.

Nothing more to put on hold,
a deeper love we yield;
for all the future years ahead
we'll have "That Same Appeal"!

The Sentinel
by Dorothy Jean West

When the shadows, dark and cold
lay like a mist upon the night,
And the solstice winter storm
hides the moon's waning light
*In an old stone circle
the celts built long before
A Sentinel take his stand
to do battle once more.
*Against a back drop of thunder
in mortal combat, they clash
And the storm permeates them
with every lighting flash
*But every echo of time
brings the same defeat
The Sentinel survives
with his enemy at this feet
*The Sentinel stands alone
as the storm subsides
Then he walks into the night
where he and time abides.
*Now when the solstice storm comes
on a winter solstice night
They listen for the thunder
echoing the Sentinel's fight.

Computers
by Meghan Orelene West - age 14

He has a large square head,
And wakes when someone touches him on the front and back of
his head.
His arms are folded as they lay on a table,
And he makes different faces when touched at a certain
point.
He has arms and legs coming from his back hooked into a
wall.
The brain he carries may be small,
But it is full of tons of information.
When he gets sick,
He has what is called a Virus,
Which is contagious to others.
And when he gets hungry,
He eats food which is small, square, and flat,
Called disks.
He can have a choice of either hard or floppy disks,
And when he eats he is filled with even more knowledge.
Each of his generation becomes better and better,
Smarter and smarter.
Who knows how far they will go until they finally come to a
bitter destruction.

The Secret
by Marilyn West

We were young
innocent
and bold
we should of told...

Stolen childhood
broken dreams
to precious
so it seemed

Lost in my own thoughts
of all that we have lost...

there is no solace
or so it seems
only memories
of a dream

dust and ashes abound
in a world without boundaries
in a world without care
maybe it's time to share?

To tell the stories untold
how we stood out in the cold

Despair marking every step
The spirit moans and fails...
my body frail and pale
death knocking on the door
I think we have been here before

should we dare to dream again?
Do we dare to spread our wings and fly?
or is it too painful to even
try?

Four Horses
by Marilyn West

Flying over mountains covered with snow
Away to the North I go...

On wings of feathers white
Consumed by light of distant sun
For the glory of his son

Flying swiftly toward his voice
to trumpet calls and brothersong...
I am not worthy...yet still I go...
flying far above the world below...

To end the sorrow of long ago...

Wait..The sound of hoofbeats fills the air...
I turn and stare...
A horseman, a vision of white...
takes to flight...
prepared for battle..prepared to fight..
To fulfill Gods plan his only plight

Light flashes and the clouds fill with light
A fiery flash of an all red knight..Sword in hand no peace tonight
For the son of man there will be no sleep..
For the man of war awakens the beast...

The clouds swiftly darken so thick like smoke
A black horse rides out of the fire...
His hoofs pounding the earth with every stride
Bringing truth into the night...

Another now...The thunder rolls...
A pale horse now with blackened robes...
For death he brings to the son of man...
Our salvation is now at hand...

Polar Storm
by Rupert Westmaas

It was a dream; Intense; Alive;
The meaning of I often strive
On May the eighth in Ninety-four
'Twas a rounded grey-blue orb, I'm sure.
Like an eyeball, round, so it seemed,
with intelligence it so teemed.
Then a terrible storm in sky did trash
and I saw many a jagged lightning flash.
It struck a spot on Polar Cap
with very intense and terrible ZAP.
Though cap it was so many feet thick,
it shattered just like a blasted brick.
Big chunks were tossed wide here and there
as widening hole each flash did bare;
And sea, though cold, did boil and steam
like devil's cauldron it would seem;
Exposing grey-blue shiny sphere
which then began to gently veer
and it slowly to the right did slide
inside the chasm growing wide;
But strange! It seemed the globe was I
which slowly sank from view of sky.
Anxious then, I wished to see
and wondered where my family be.
With deep concern I suddenly awoke;
A wondering, very sad-heavy bloke.

Racism: It's A Big Deal
by Tina Westmeyer - age 14

White is the color of many things
and so is black
so why does the world have
to separate because of that.
People out there don't care
how each other feel
they only see color
and not what's real.
What's on the inside
is all that matters
not their appearance
or their clothes in tatters.
The world is full of racist thoughts
and this is the reason
for many fights fought.
And still to come
day by day
more racist feelings
or bad things to say,
unless we stop
we stop it now
and live the way God wants
the way he knows how!!!

Losing You
by Kristy Westphal

How reality can swiftly crumble
When your stability loses its foundation
Someone who is strong and loving
Turns frail, bitter and sad
It hurts to look at you like this
It makes me question The Plan
Life can change so quickly
In only the blink of an eye
I hope you make your peace soon
I hope that life will continue on
Your eternal reality is just beginning
Fear not
Hesitate not
Charge onwards with dignity
And know I will always love you

Mother
by Kristy Westphal

If there was one word for you
I would have a hard time finding it
So many wonderful words
Come to my mind when I think of you
Strength, hope
Love, caring
Kindness, courage
Friend...
You have always been there for me
You have inspired me to stretch
My mind, my emotions, my aspirations
What do you get in return?
Strength hope love caring kindness courage
From more people than you dreamed
We are all thankful
In ways you may never know

View
by Joshua L. Whetstine

a dead end path rising and falling, strewn with
 age of moderate use for old fashion life
serene, quiet
gravel paves the path,
the weeds and brush along the side are faded,
 covered with a light blanket of gray
wire laced over wooden post,
 gently hold the fields in place
green pastures are spotted
 with black and brown cows
farm houses lay low in the surroundings
 allowing the wires on the tall sticks to find their destinations
wind gently rustles the brush,
 giving rise to the sweet smell of warm summer grass
the air is fresh, full of the sounds of crickets
 and frogs in the stream nearby
calming, uplifting, energizing
the sun surrenders to dusk,
 a view ancient as Iowa.

Untitled
by Angela White - age 16

every night i pray for god to
make you mine
i wish you would realize it and
step across the line
i know you can see how much
i love you everytime you look in
my eyes
because every time you do my
heart is mesmerized
you are the one that visits me
in my sleep
i'll never let you go, your love is
here for me to keep
i love how your eyes are as bright
as the sky
your like a drug everytime i get you
it gets me high
every night you are the wish i
send up to a star
it's like your the one up there and
i keep reaching for you but your too
far
you say your heart is loving and full
your love is true
there;s always been something i've
wanted to say and that is i love you

It's Getting Better All The Time For Some People
by Morgan Whitehouse - age 16

It gets better all the time that's what the Beatles say is true for a lot of people but those people who they miss is just like one person in a million of people. They forget how one person can make so much difference in a lot of people's lives.

But a lot of people just don't give a damn about other people anymore it is like everyone is running a race to see who gets first and screw everybody else on there way.

Untitled
by Angela White - age 16

i scream out to the world but
nobody hears
these eyes aren't filled with joy
but pain and fear
i'm all by myself in this lonely
world
why do i feel like a frightened
little girl
every night, is spent looking at the
sky
sometimes i get so lonely i wish
i could die
i made a promise to myself not
ever to tell a soul
but everytime i do this i dig deeper
in my security hold
i feel like i'm just a portrait of
what everybody wants me to
be
i wish i was made of glass so
these feelings could be shown
and everyone could see

Dandelion, Dandelion
by Angela White - age 16

dandelion, dandelion, your pretty
as lace
dandelion, dandelion i wish i
could take your place
dandelion, dandelion you have a
love of your own
dandelion, dandelion your true
beauty is how it's shown
dandelion, dandelion i wish i
could join you in the fields
hide me from the world for your
love i cannot shield
dandelion, dandelion your the
only person that will listen
i love it when the sun hits you
because your petals sparkle and
glisten
dandelion, dandelion i wonder
where you are
dandelion, dandelion i try to reach
you but you are too far

Safe In The Arms Of Love
by Jody Widener

Whenever I'm about to
fall you catch me with your
arms of security. Whenever
I'm sad and lonely you comfort
me with your tender arms of
mercy, even while I cry.
Whenever I'm in a storm
your arms are like a refuge
in the night. No matter what I
go through, you are there, and
there for us all with your
sweet love and open arms.

Death of a Nun
by Phyllis White

Spirit ascending, removed from the glaciers
Hands crossed over white breasts below
I scent you with Devon Violet to dismiss
the desecration of mahogany: now more
than two of you gone.

Angels sing and wait, untroubled by mortality;
I feel a bitterness towards your Father: he is not mine.
Musing, I unleash your habit from the tattered clothesline,
where it once flapped, sun-blessed and fragrant, awaiting a novice,
perhaps me.

Now the heavens must contend with you and our favorite Cat,
Whose timely death was a sanction for your departure,
your funerals prophesizing my course in life;
How we laughed, mutually irreverent, as the chalice
spilled heavily from the lips of our only priest.

I may be a child, but I am no fool.
You chose your death; a child is not so fortunate.
Still I harken to the intrusiveness of angels,
their faces amorphous, unreal.

The Road
by Alexis Hunter Whitfield - age 14

As I make my way down the road,
to be the very best.
I try my very hardest,
and hope to have success.

Thanks to my mom,
She has taught me right.
I treat everyone equal,
and never start a fight.

If I get knocked down,
I just get back on my feet.
I know to never quit struggling,
even after a defeat.

I think about a lot of things,
such as my generation.
I am ready for the future,
because of proper education.

As I go down the road,
I will do my best.
I hope to be the very one,
to rise above the rest.

Unfamiliar Comfort
by Douglas Wiegand - age 20

The moonrays...
In through the window they caught her face
and held in it celestial purity.
Intense spell enhanced by soothing laughter...
Their glances were locked in silent unison.
Unwinding release--
They embrace.
The lad's emotions joined hands with his soul,
forming daisy chains which circled his heart with rhythmic chaos.
Unfamiliar comfort.
Concentrated hope.
She smiles in her sleep,
and forever inhabits his dreams.
I miss them both.

Your Love and My Means
by Kacie Wielgus - age 16

You may not feel for me as I for you-
but in your heart you know I will always be true.
It may hurt me greatly to be denied the feelings I have for you,
but I know you will always be there for me-and that my friend is
    the greatest love of all!

The love you offer cannot be denied, nor mistaken-
though I may still feel a bit neglected.
My friend the love we share is a bond that will last forever,
my heart is full of your smiles as yours of my happiness!

The Mystery Of Being Me
by Kacie Wielgus - age 16

What is the great mystery, you may kindly ask,
the response, is quite complex.
For to understand the great mystery of being me-
you must first understand who I am.
This could become quite complex, due to the fact I am not certain whom
I am.
Am, I happy, or sad, smiling or frowning, dictating or doing?
Those are all valid questions, but I cannot answer a one.
Reason being, being me is like reading a great mystery.
As one discovers something about me, so do I.
For I am a teenager, where the most simplistic things must be
rediscovered for oneself-
So I hope you now understand the greta mystery of being me.

Being Me Is Like Reading A Great Mystery
by Kacie Wielgus - age 16

Being me hurts-
Why? because deep within I do not know who I am.
Being inside my mind is like reading a great mystery, from the days of old.
I know in my heart that I will survive, or do I? I could always fold.
It is like all my previous certainties have become uncertainties.
My mind is like on constant rewind.
I find pleasure in the past; experience pain the present
Knowing for certain being a teenager is true hell.
Why, because there is no certainty, and definitely no freedom.
but tremendous responsibility, emotion,
pain and the necessity for independence.
When, will this all end, when my children are feeling as I do now.
The only thing I truly need is to be understood, and not belittled.
Is that so much to ask?

A Regretful Goodbye
by Lisa Wikoff - age 19

I am not trying to avoid you
    It just happens that we never meet.
It try my best to run into you where ever you are
    But there is always some obstacle that keeps me from you.
Whether it's of human decent or from Mother Nature,
    It seems that we're not meant to meet again,
Or to laugh with each other one more time.
    What a relief it would be to see your shinning face right now.
To feel your arms wrapped around me, keeping me
Warm and secure at this moment would be wonderful.
But this will never happen again for some reason.
    Maybe I was just being foolish
When we first met, to think there
Could have been something between us.
Now I see that it was never meant to be
For us to know one another better.
For we could never have made it through all the troubles
We'd have to face without hurting each other.
I guess what I am saying is that
I will always care for you with all of my heart
But I am so very sorry that I must tell you
Something that pains me so very much to say.
This decision does not come easy for me
Because in the future I know
That I am going to regret this
But in the present I have no other choices,
So I am afraid that this is my final Good Bye to you.

Govern My Thoughts
by Lillie D. Wilder

Govern my thoughts Lord,
Keep them honest and true.
Help me live by your guidelines.
Let me imitate You.

My heart feels much lighter,
Just knowing You're near.
To know when I pray to You,
That You'll always hear.

How blessed I feel that I can kneel,
And call upon Your name,
And claim your promises of old,
Which today are still the same.

You tell us not to worry,
That You'll be by our side.
I want to serve You with gladness,
Knowing You can turn the tide.

Judgements
by Judi Wild-Becker

    What Wisdom among us can expressly reveal
    The trials and the triumphs our brother can feel?

    We look and we ponder. It's a game as we whittle.
    Not a care or concern as our judgements belittle.

    But just let some potent and bigoted 'feller'
    Ever <u>dare</u> to pursue us; we'll respond with a 'yeller!'

    If we each would take notice, our own feelings aside,
    It's our difference that makes us just humans...with pride!

    So the next time you're tempted to disparage and rage,
    Try to tune in to Beauty with the thoughts of a sage.

The Small Brindle Cow
by Judi Wild-Becker

    Was a breeze on the meadow and a breeze crossed my brow
    The first time I saw her, the small brindle cow.
    So different she looked.

    Just minding her manners; her nose in the clover
    Other cows stood beside her, seldom cared to look over,
    So different she seemed.

    Her odd little coat with colors like marble
    Made me ask the next question: what mix caused the garble?
    How strange she did look.

    Does it go all way through? Does chocolate cream rise?
    Or is it quite true beneath color or size
    They're all just the same?

    Reminds me of people so different and such
    With colors and types we think <u>do not touch</u>
    So different they seem.

    But under the wrapper, beneath color and size
    When hearts rule brave heads; a new thought to the wise
    We're mostly the same.

    More alike than we're diffr'nt, although not quite like me.
    Like the small brindle cow, even though I can't see
    Underneath we're the same.

    Oh, I enjoy thinking different, I enjoy thinking free,
    I enjoy surprising those who dare snicker at me.
    I'm unique, I am me!

A Proposal
by Darryl Williams

My love I come now before you with God as my witness, asking you to share my life and make my love your own in a wedded bliss.

I don't have much to give you, and I come with only one promise to keep, to love you from when God opens my eyes in the morning until he lays me down to sleep.

Even though the sun will shine upon us, I know a little rain will also fall, I will love you with all the strength God has blessed upon me and lift my hands toward heaven for him to guide me through it all.

Marry me my love and accept this token to place on your finger, let it announce to the world that you are mine, and I am yours and that our love no longer has to linger.

Grandma
by Heather Willis - age 11

Dear Grandma I miss you
I have and always will

Whenever I see kids with
their grandmas I think about
you the whole day through

Why'd you have to go and
leave me all alone?

I miss you and love you
too

Inside Myself
by Cynthia Anne Wilson - age 20

From every corner and crack I feel a presence greater
than myself.
Outside the looking glass I see distorted colors and
visions of fallen angels
One by one they pick up their broken wings while walking
painlessly on broken glass
I have repeatedly created this warped reality.
The clock is growing louder now as the crowd gathers, or
do they?
With each passing minute it grows harder for me to
reality and fantasy
Temptation to step over to the dark side overwhelms my
slowly corrupting soul.
Shaking and screaming I break the walls which have held
me captive.
I feel no pain as the shattered glass carefully cuts
into my feet.
Slowly I pick up my broken wings simultaneously
contemplating which situation is worse
My protective walls keep me safe, but with this safety
I become a slave to all I try so desperately to keep out
Alone and defenseless, I break down all walls striving
to become who I am destined to be.
I picked my poison.

In The Dark
by D'Esta C. Wilson - age 20

Have you ever seen things in the dark?
In the dark?
What have you seen in the dark?
When the lights are all turned out,
When no one ever dared to shout,
When all the children sleeping out,
In the dark.
Have you ever been truly scared in the dark?
In the dark?
What have you been afraid of in the dark?
When the shadows are not what they seem,
When a faucet sounds like a stream,
When everything looks so very mean,
In the dark.
If you haven't, then you never will be afraid in the dark,
In the dark.
Then you know not what we fear in the dark.
You don't know what shape shadows take,
You aren't afraid that breathing aloud could be a mistake,
You don't know that what is real to us is really fake,
In the dark.

Companions
by Amanda Winger - age 15

The gushing wind grows stronger and stronger
against my cool face as I feel us
accelerating into our own world.

I look down into the cascading brown mane
of the horse flowing freely, and I too
turn free.

I feel as if nothing can stop this
journey to nowhere. Sure of this,
I smile to myself.

The faint sounds of hooves stampeding
over rolling hills ring through the night.

Though I cannot see, I trust the beast
I am riding because I feel what he
feels and he knows what I know.

Galloping under the pale light of the
moon, we are one. With us there is
no fine line between horse and rider.

    We are companions.

The Wanderer
by Rose Wiser - age 14

As I walk I see a dusty
dirt road covered with dark,
dead leaves.
While birds sing softly
with a mournful tune.
While trees stand bare and
silent, in the cold air.
Even the wind is silent,
as I wander alone.
Another lost and lonely
soul with no place to call home.

Morning Light
by Rose Wiser - age 14

As the dark clouds gather,
the sun breaks through
and lights up the dark clouds
with heavenly light.
While the sun rays shine
down with a silvery gold
light and the wind blows
cold. While trees shiver
and sway, and birds sing
to the light of the day.

Letting Go
by Brittany Wissler - age 17

How can you let go,
Of a loved one in your life?
Someone who touched your heart,
you have to say goodbye.
Will the pain ever cease?
Time is the only teacher.
Wanting to hold on
to the bitter sweet memories.
The only thing you have left to cling to.
Wishing you could hold them,
one last time.
Heavy barriers;
that can't be seen, or destroyed.

A Memory Is Born
by Larry Wnorowski

A memory is born and time is lost, and no matter what you do, today turns into yesterday.

Retrieval is impossible of the seconds, minutes and hours that are casually and nonchalantly thrown or washed away.

The present is inevitably the past, but will the feelings of today and the way we are last; last to be yesterday's history?

Will we let or make history repeat itself in our life or in the people who live around us?

One day, there will be no tomorrow, which means that today may be the last today, and if this is so, we will be judged by our yesterdays, which were at one time...today.

A Colorless World
by Lawrence Wnorowski

A man asked me a question today,
A question he asked to me.
He said, "In your own way,
What does it mean to be free?"

I answered with words of truth,
The truth I told to him.
"When everyone gets along, please,
Let me elaborate." Is what I told said to him.

"When I'm not white trash
And you not nigger.
When your not smaller
and I'm not bigger.

When your my friend
And my brother.
When all our races
can respect one and the other.

When your conscience is light
To let your child play with mine.
When all people live in peace,
and not just from time to time.

When you can walk the streets at night
Without having to watch your back.
When we are a color blind people
And violence is what we lack.

When we can relate to one another
Without color being the first we see.
When we can all hold hands and live in harmony...
That is the day that we are all truly free.

Day Dreaming
by Lawrence Wnorowski

As the flickering candle light waves in the salty sea breeze, it casts its shadow of all the features of her face making her appear, momentarily mortal. I am watching her lips moving and I'm listening to the words that she speaks, yet I hear nothing, and still I manage to respond with the appropriate words that she wants to hear without even really realizing it. I am entranced by her heart, soul, mind and beauty. I am hardly even aware that I'm still sitting at this table with this bottle of wine and this carnation that only seems to highlight her beauty. And as I watch the candle flicker in the reflection in her eyes, I am refreshingly awakened from the trance to the realization that this is no dream and that this woman is the woman that I want to spend the rest of my life with. I am suddenly aware that this is the real thing. I quietly say to myself, "So this is love. This is really love."

My Best Friend
by John Wolfgang - age 12

My best friend was a cat. He was a very special cat. His name was Crystal. He was all white with a brownish tint to his fur. Crystal and I would talk to each other. He wasn't like other cats. He did tricks. This story is dedicated to my dearest friend Crystal.

On a chilly night in November, when my new nanny and her cat, Crystal, came to live with us, I instantly fell in love with him. It blew my mind when I saw him unscrew the lid and open a jar to dig out kitty treats for himself. He was fifteen years old when I met him. My nanny had raised him since he was only six days old. I often stayed up late at night just holding and petting him. I spent most of my free time in his room enjoying his company. We were very close.

After Christmas he began to lose weight rapidly. We took him to the animal hospital, and the vet told us he had cancer. He told us Crystal must gain weight before he could have surgery. We took him home and fed him concentrated food, vitamins, and antibiotics. Still he continued to get skinnier and skinnier. He was unable to drink water, so we fed it to him in a straw.

Late one evening he started vomiting. First he vomited food. Then when there was no more food, he vomited bile. We sat up all night to hold him and rock him. In the morning he went into convulsions. He made one meek little mewing sound as if to say, "Please make the hurt go away." We put a soft blanket and his little pillow into his basket. We carried him through the rain and put him gently into the car for his last ride to the doctor's office.

I carried my friend through the waiting room full of sick animals that were going to be made well, and my heart started to break. We were led in an examining room and told, "The doctor will be with you soon." A few minutes later the doctor came into the room with a needle. We put Crystal on his soft blanket on the table. He was very calm, as if he knew that his suffering would soon be over. Nanny and I held Crystal lovingly as the doctor injected the fatal dose of pain-killer into the cat's leg. Crystal quietly quit breathing in just a few seconds. We held each other and cried for the loss of our loved one. Nanny carefully placed her companion of nearly sixteen years into his basket and covered him with his soft blanket.

We went to our friend's house to bury our cat beneath a banana tree. The rain hid our tears as we dug a deep hole to put Crystal's basket into. I miss him so much. It is not the same lying in the bed without his warm, furry body to pet.

I will never forget Crystal. I will always love him. What we had to do was hard, but there were no other choices to be made. We did the right thing... We did the only thing that could be done... I'm sure that Crystal knew that...

running gangly
by Wesley Wordsmith

bull-calf, knock-kneed child, arms flailing, wingtips flapping,
you take flight across the green horizon of your
spring and stop to pluck the golden lion's tooth. "here,
mommy, see, i have a nice surprise for you!" your
tiny fingers fondly place a flower's tender
touch upon your mother's hair. your sunday at the park
(as all things are for you) is marvelously
strange and staggered with anticipation. i watch

you from ancient eyes. i see your joy and feel your
trust, the hope, the majesty of my exiguous
self-god seed blooming forth as innocence ripens
into graceful summer. i remember my own
springtide (with it's misty, out-of-focus edges)
and i look away. off to my left, gathering
clouds observe a hoary sea endlessly licking
at the face of caustic earth. sandscabs hang in time...

Curiosity Killed The Cat
by Holly Wolford - age 12

He said he would have a few drinks then take me home.
I agreed......Jinx. Weaving in and out of all two lanes,
acting crazy like he had no brains, he swerved us into
the oncoming lane, my face went white then I felt lots
of pain.

Then we woke up smashed into a truck, lights blinking all
around us. Screaming sirens filled the night with sound,
with lots of people all around, looking at us with faces
filled with fright.

I saw a strong young man lift my body into a emergency
van. But the strange thing is, I didn't feel a thing.
That's when I saw a little girl, curled up so small in
a ball, I heard a EMT trying to comfort her. Why I wondered
what is wrong with her? That's when a young women came in
and said her parents were......dead.

I guess we killed them that's what she said massive injuries
to the head.

All of the sudden I woke on my back laying flat,
wondering soon if every thing would go all black.
I heard machines buzzing around my head wondering if soon
I would soon be dead.

My boyfriend said he wanted the rush of drinking to much,
he wanted to see how far he could drive that way and all
I have to say is............
CURIOSITY KILLED THE CAT

I Am With You Always
by Melva Mae Wong

I feel so very blessed, dear lord
On this glorious Easter Sunday;
As I watch the golden sunrise
Kiss our earth with warmth today.

The joy I feel within my heart
To know, you live for me;
Your gift of love, are rays of hope--
A promise...You'll always be with me.

Always
by Olivia H. Wong

Though day turns to night
And time passes on,
Remember I will love you
From dawn to dawn.

Though stars may fall
And clouds fill the sky,
Remember my love
Will continue, sublime.

Though the seasons go by
And blossoms fade,
Remember I will be constant
Till my dying day.

Though Earth spins on its axis
And the universe roams free,
Remember you are cherished
Beyond eternity.

Freedom
by Barbara Woodall - age 14

Another name goes on the wall,
A man who stood proud and tall.
He fought for liberty and for freedom,
It was for his family and his kingdom.
Families eyes are crying,
But people are still dying.
War is the reasoning,
It is human it is seizing.
Veterans who were lucky enough to live,
They go to the graves and give.
Give there soul and hearts,
No one ever wanted them to part.

Apocalypse Now
by TerRance Woodard - age 20

Where does life end and death begin?
Or does life begin at deaths end
Does anyone truly know which existence we inhabit?

Most believe in a Heaven and Hell, upon death where will I go?
However in my character this question does not show
I question this ideal and have come to a sure conclusion
This place I live is hell on earth and heaven is societies illusion
It would be hard to grow worse than this perverse realm of death in which
  I exist
I've witnessed friend die and families cry and looked death in the eye as
  trauma persist
My life has been short and filled with obstacles, but strength is what I need
I live my life for the moment and ignore death for this is how my soul will
  be freed
A vision of pearly white gates as thy enter the kingdom is expected
I remain a gondolier on the River Stix in Hades for those who are rejected

Don't think in apocalyptic terms, but this world is come to an end
We live and or die in a new realm of reality, soon to begin
Consequently, I inhabit a world of questions that begins only to end.

The Stick Pony & The Hobby Horse Ranch
by Doris Wood - age

Once upon a time, in a land far, far away. In the land of hush-a-bye, where fair tails are made. On top of a tall hill, stands a jolly little house. Where in it lives Wild Bill, a gentle little mouse. "Just who is Wild Bill?" you ask. You mean you really don't know? Why he takes care of stick ponies & hobby horses that boys & girls out grow. He gathers them together each night, and take them to his ranch. Where hobby horses can romp & rome, & stick ponies can prance. There's hills & valleys with lakes & lots or rich green grass. There's stick ponies of today & hobby of the past.
  Would you like to know how it got started & where Wild Bill fits in? It started with a stick pony badly in need of mend. Just how long ago it isn't easy to say, but that lonely sad stick pony badly needed to play. It stood in the back of a store clean out of sight, when a little mouse happened in, on a cold, wet dreary night. Wild Bill walked around just looking at all the toys. Thinking of all the fun for the little girls & boys. When he heard a whimper, a faint little cry, "please come & play with me," the stick pony sighed. Now Wild Bill was a cowboy, in bad need of a horse, but that stick pony needed Wild Bill even worse.
  "How did you get stuck back here Wild Bill ask the pony. The pony told Wild Bill of his sad & lonely story. The store owner had a son who used to play with me, & of all the fun they had. One day the boy stopped coming & had left him alone. He was told later, that the boy was grown.
  Wild Bill asked the pony to go with him to a ranch, he had heard of it in a story one night by chance. Like a flash they were gone, to the ranch in a land far far away, & each night Wild Bill & his stick pony go looking for hobby horses & stick ponies badly needing to play. They round them up, to take them to their ranch, where they romp, rome, run & even hobby horses prance.
  "Why haven't you heard of this ranch before?" you ask. Few people know, what happens to stick ponies & hobby horses, & where they go. Why, to a land far far away in the land of hush-a-bye where fairy tails are made.

Fantasy Child
by Marie Woods - age 19

So caught up in fantasy
She knew not what was true.
She believed the slightest bit of
Imagination, but threw away
All belief in truth.
She wanted to live a life,
A life no one else knew.
A dream world is what she
Wanted to come true.

Heart Scars
by Regina Woods

You try your best
to forget
but the scars
are still on your heart

Some heart scars
are short lived
others last for years

You never expected
the one you loved
and trusted
to be the one
to break your heart

At first it was painful
to accept
then the tears begin
the numbness set in

The promise wasn't kept
your heart wasn't protected
but betrayed
now breaking

My Kite
by Nancy Woolson

My kite is broken,
It will not fly;
The string is old,
Tattered and worn,
And the colors have faded;
The tail has fallen off,
The frame is cracked,
Old and warped,
It was caught in
The tree too often;
My kite has had its day;
There will never be another
Like my kite.

True
by Knoelle Higginson Wydro - age 12

When I am riding in a car
To someplace near or someplace far,
I think of how I used to be -
About when I was two or three

When I was just a little girl
My dad would give me a big twirl-swirl
He'd swing me high onto the bed
Someitmes he'd stand me on my head

We lived out where there was grass
and trees
Lots of flowers, birds and bees!
I used to chase the tennis ball
And jump in leaves when it was fall

Then I as big. I was in grade three
People asked me what I wnted to be
What I want to be is two or three
And find the key to the real, true me

Love Ya
by Lisa Yeager - age 13

I like ya,
I really do.
But I don't have the courage,
To say I love you.
This tears me up inside,
It really does, I swear.
I want so bad to tell you,
How much I really care.
I wish I had the courage,
To come up to you and say
I love you and I always will from this day
But I don't
So I'm writing this.
Someday if you read it.
Please don't laugh at my expense.
All I know is that I love you.
I hope to tell you some day.
That I can't live without you.
So please don't turn me away.

A Wish
by Chrissy Yee - age 12

> For every wish I make
> on a star,
> For every coin I throw
> in a pond.
> I wish you will come
> back in my life
> with tons of love!!

Angel In Disguise
by Krista Yelton - age 13

As I peered across the room and gazed into his eyes,
An angel I saw reflected in his face,
But then I looked deeper and to my surprise,
The incarnate devil had taken his place.
For behind I saw the raging fires of sin,
As before him I viewed my gullible mind,
He beckoned and told me to let him come in,
For I would be shocked at what I would find.
The Jesus appeared and took my hand,
And the devil soon followed the heavenly band,
As music surrounded my Savior and life,
The echo of sinful laughter only added to my strife.
Then flames surrounded me; left me standing there,
With only helpless tears to cry,
Then without thinking I fell down in prayer,
And time quickly passed by.
Years passed and once again I peered into his eyes,
An angel I then saw reflected in his face,
But then I, searchingly looked deeper and to my surprise,
He had regained all his beauty and grace.

Can't Understand
by Jamie Young - age 12

You feel so empty, your heart is breaking,
that is the risk you are taking
It's like you're on the outside, looking in,
yes... it has happened again
You're left out feeling sad and used,
as you watch the glistening dew
Other people are always in command,
that is why I can't understand
Living in this crazy world we see,
everyone is like you and like me
One is your enemy, one is your friend,
the way this life is going, that will never end
It will always be like that I guess,
you will eventually get in a mess
Well... if that is how the story ends,
then I can't understand

Untitled
by Amy Youngman - age 18

I watch the rain fall from the sky
   and think of the twinkle in your eye
The rain comes fast, the rain comes
   I think of the feeling locked and barred
The rain falls down like a sheet
   hiding everything underneath
The clouds are dark, the skies are black
   here comes the first attack
The lightening flashes, the thunder claps
   it's nothing like a pat on the back
Your words I can no longer hear
   because of all the fight and fear
Your arms won't reach me anymore
   because someone's closing the door
So reach out now if you want me
   and all the things were meant to be
Before someone locks the door
   and I won't see you anymore

Who
by Morgan Zerbe - age 15

She sits and she stares and
wonders, who?

Who are these people sitting next to me?
Who are these people saying hi?
What are they doing?
What are they saying?
Why don't I understand why I am here?

I sit and I stare and
wonder, is she better off not knowing?

Night Shadows
by Sylvia Ziegler

As night shadows creep over me
my one true love comes to me
Low and Behold
open wide the Portal of Time
as thirst beneath the Desert Sun
oh Spanish Moon
capture me, weave your spell
bind me, ever so tight
Vibrations of passion have come to light
as baying wolves and shadows form as ghosts
above the ground
the Full-moon beckons our love to flight
as it whispers a solemn good-night!

What is Love?
by Abby Zimmerman - age 17

Is love precious, is love kind,
Never once lift behind?
Is love awesome, is love cool,
Sitting by the ocean blue?
Sitting by the love who's meant to be,
thinking of what it all means to me.
Is love confusing?
I don't know.
Is it like the first fallen snow?
Does love make you happy,
Or make you feel down?
Does love make you hear most every sound?
The sound in my heart tells me love is good,
Is my heart being misunderstood?
What is love?
Please let me know,
If I'm in love, will it show?

My Valentine
by Casey Zollman - age 17

Never has my life been touched
by someone as wonderful as you.
Whenever a smile reaches my face
it makes our love feel brand new.
I wish to let you know
on this very special day.
That you have brightened my life
in so many precious ways!

Dreamer Lost
by Christopher Q. Zobrist - age 18

Dreamer, lost in a cold cruel world
Trying to find her way home
Dreamer, who's sail is always unfurled
Waiting for the wind to come

Dreamer, scorned and shunned by all
Dreaming of man's lone flight
Dreamer, still standing proud and tall
Standing by her silver line'd kite

Dreamer, unconcerned of her foundation
Building her castles in the sky
Dreamer, never once losing her concentration
Wanting, wishing, only to fly

Dreamer, gazing at the sky so blue
Seeing her only salvation from this land
Dreamer, her dreams had finally come true
Gliding through the clouds of heaven,
Guided by Death's cold hand.

"Death is not a dream, but a truth. One must live the dream of life, before realizing the truth of death."

Whispers Around The World

Whispers

Chapter Nine

About The Author

Selected biographies of competitors
and members of the National Authors Registry.

Ahearn, Geri - I was born and raised in New York living in Long Island, NY almost all my life. My husband and I are high school sweet-hearts. We were married in 1972. He became a police officer and I became a R.N. I graduated nursing school in 1974 having worked in hospitals, nursing homes, clinics and schools. We have two daughters, one seventeen and thirteen. We have a pet dog named Domino. He was adopted in New York when he was a small pup. Last June, we moved to Arizona. I celebrated my forty-fifth birthday in our new Arizona home. As of June 1996, we will have lived one year in the Southwest. It's quite an adventure, to have lived both in the northeast and southwest. We left behind us some good friends, back in the northeast. They are treasured memories that will last forever. But, one must move on in a life time. "Seek and you shall find." My motto certainly holds truth. In less than one year, we met several new friends. We enjoy southwest living, and adapted well to our new life. The difference in climate is a drastic change. I've live through cold, stormy winters, with plenty of snow to shovel. Now, we experience warm, hot, dry weather all year round. However, my family enjoys Arizona sunshine, including Domino. My three goals in life were: become a nurse, grow in happiness with my children, and become an author. My first goal was a success, because I worked in the field and enjoyed helping many people. Growing with my children has been a rewarding experience. Writing for children will be a new door I hope to open. My plans for the future include: exploring Arizona, gardening, and writing. There is much more to learn about the southwest. Gardening is my favorite hobby. Writing for children will be a challenge and an exciting journey into the future.

Alton, Pamela C.D. - Pamela is 23 years old. She was born and raised in Massachusetts, but now resides in New York. In December 1995, she graduated a member of Alpha Epsilon Rho, The National Broadcasting Honor Society, with a B.A. in Electronic Journalism from Hofstra University, in Hempstead, Long Island. On her road to breaking into the news media, she has had several newspaper articles published. Although her poem, "Déjà Vu" is her first poem published in a national anthology, she has also had a short story titled, "Catherine I was, Catherine I am," published in a college literary magazine. Pamela has kept a personal journal and has been writing short stories since she was twelve years old. Her number one passion in life is her drive to create the written word. She is particularly interested in writing short stores and poems surrounding the Supernatural, Reincarnation, ghosts and vampires.

Bard, Denise Marjory Newcombe - BORN: Denise Marjory Newcomb, October 3, 1928 in Houlton, Aroostook, Maine. PARENTS: Harold Lambert Newcomb (1907-1976), Muriel Florence Hayes (1905) divorced 1942. STEPFATHER: M. Arthur Boynton (1913-1995). SCHOOLING: Hallowell schools graduating in 1947 with honors, some home study in Law and Art. MARRIED: 1947, had two sons: Norman (1949-1985 died in auto accident); Samuel (1952). Divorced in 1953; married in 1962, widowed in 1970; Married Wesley Elton Bard 20 September 1981, an exceptionally talented musician. EMPLOYMENT: Secretary, State Department of Education retired in 1982. Soloist for weddings and church events, husband is pianist-organist, members of the L-D-S church where we use our talents. My wonderful talented parents saw my talents early. They taught me to sing many songs and organized my own radio program when I was three during which time many request were received. They also took me to sing on children's programs throughout Maine. Dad was pianist for silent movies in Houlton before I was born. He was radio announcer for the station in Augusta where he also had his own piano request program. He taught all musical instruments, taught music theories at several schools, played for dances and for dancing schools, and wrote music. Mother, a talented classical pianist chose to work for her father in his "Hayes Home Bakery" in Hallowell, later for State of Maine, then in stepfather's grocery store. She was also an accomplished ballroom dancer when young. When I was six Dad arranged for me to take dancing lessons in acrobatics, my favorite, toe, tap and ballet. I was asked to perform at scout benefits, church affairs and school minstrels. Poetry came naturally at about 12 as did piano at six having my own methods. At about 50 I started writing songs, patriotic and religious. Dad passed away before he could hear them.

Barkakati, Ivy - Ivy Barkakati has been an avid reader since she was only four years old. By the time she was nine, she was writing short stories and poems. She became a small-time published author by age ten when one of her short stories appeared in the *Kids Gazette*, a local North Potomac newspaper which contains children's pieces of writing and art. She has continued being published in the *Kids Gazette* and hopes to publish a children's novel in the future. Ivy is now nearly twelve years old and will be entering the seventh grade at Robert Frost Middle School in Rockville, Maryland. She resides in North Potomac, Maryland with her parents and two younger sisters, Emily, age ten, and Ashley, age five.

Berning, Marilyn Helen - (Pen name, Marilyn [Bublitz]) Berning). Address: Stewartville, MN. Date of Birth: July 27, 1938, Winona, MN. Parents: Donald & Helen Bublitz. Husband: William E. Berning. Married: Sept. 13, 1958. Children: Jeffrey & Jason Berning, Peggy Lynn Berning (Deceased). Memberships: International Society of Poets. I believe a good poem embellishes one's soul. I was born one-of-seven-daughters. My life started in Winona, Minnesota and later I moved to Spring Valley, MN. I graduated from Spring Valley, MN High School in 1956. Following I took some additional classes. I currently am a homemaker and co-owner in a used-car-sales business near Rochester, MN. I have lived in Stewartville, MN for approximately 23 years. I have three grandchildren Seth, Britini, and Luke Berning. I started writing poems last fall and have written approximately 300 since that time. I write something almost every day and usually more than one verse. I am also interested in drawing and getting into that field more seriously. I started writing about family members and then it took off from there about feelings, etc., till now I write almost every type of verse. I find it helps me cope with chronic pain I have and a good outlet for emotions of the soul. I couldn't give up writing now if I tried. It has become a part of me. I also am now having some songs I wrote recorded. Anything that is written and enjoyed is of worth.

Bond, Katherine L. - Born June 7, 1949 to parents Emma M. Clerk and William T. Coble in Sardis, Mississippi. Married July 27, 1969 to John R. Bond, IV. They have two daughters, Sonia L. O'Neal and Tasha M. Bond. A graduate of Joliet West High School, with some college background from Joliet Junior College and Northern Illinois University. Occupation: Medical Transcriptionist II at St. Joseph Medical Center. Memberships: The National Authors Registry, International Society of Authors & Artists, Poets' Guild, the National Poets' Association and the International Biographical Association. Honors and Awards: (5) Editor's Choice Awards through the national Library of Poetry and ISP, (4) Achievement of Merit Awards through Creative Arts & Science, Ent., International Poet of Merit 1995 & 1996 through the National Library of Poetry & ISP, President's Award for Literary Excellence through Iliad Press, Editor's Preference Award of Excellence, Diamond Homer Trophy through Famous Poets Society, Honorable Mention through Carlton Press and Who's Who is New Poets Spring 1996. Other Writings: Lord, The Rapture, Her Fight Our Reward, An Epitaph, Not Yet!, Immortal Man, Seasoned, and many others. Personal Note: God and prayer make it all possible. Proverbs 3:6 -- In all thy ways acknowledge Him, and He shall direct thy paths.

Heinze, George-Alicea (pen name), AKA D.H. Boyd. - Born in Santa Monica California. Studied art at Otis Art Institute, Art Center L.A. Several writing groups, Adult writing classes. Studied dramatics with Josephine Dillion. Private music lessons, piano. Photography awards, Tech. Art awards, Writing awards. Forty(40) years as artist Northrop Adv. Sys. My work dedicated to Father, mother, brother and wife. And dear friends Roy and Mazzie Holes. Love writing mysteries, children's fairy tale poems and stories, and especially poetry. Paint in water colors, oils, pastels, portraits and landscapes; sculptures. Seven(7) years Commissioner of Northrop Art Club. Played in small theater, did son WWII shows, TV commercials. Won several Suggestion Awards-job related. Retired as Creative Artist Designer. My pen name as above in memory of parents for their support in all my creative interests.

Boyette, Sandra - Ever since I learned how to read the printed word, I have found a key to unlock a magic kingdom to a bright place far from the happenings of the everyday and common-place. My early poetic influences were the more ancient Scot and Celtic poets, many who did not even leave their name behind on their poetry, but their works speak for them. My favorite Scottish poet is Robert Burns and my favorite modern poets are Robert Frost and Carl Sandburg. I am married, have two children still at home and live in Pearcy, AR. This is my first publication.

Braslavsky, Gela - Most people think that Europe is the most glamorous of places, but when you live in Russia for a while, glamorous would not be the describing word used. I was born in Kishenov, Russia in 1982. Because my family is Jewish, we dint' receive the best treatment from many people. So, my parents decided to move to America when I was eight years old. In the United States, it took me about two years to learn the language, but I like it much more than Russian. I had an interest in poetry before I even began writing, so I studied the work of many known poets. My own writing though, is mostly genetic, because my grandmother published two books of her poems. Other than poetry, my interests include: painting, sculpting, and especially acting. Although I devote the same amount of time to each activity, all the others just serve as inspiration for my poems. Some people might wonder why poems are so sad and angry. The reason for that is, I only write poems when I am upset or angry. They are my way of dealing with emotions. So far, poetry is just a hobby for me, but very soon I hope to turn it into a profession.

Brennan, Margaret A. - I was born on May 18, 1947 to Mary and Frank Harucki. Now, I reside in North Babylon, New York with my husband, Richard and my step-son Richard, Jr. I have a married step-daughter and two sons of my own, both, also, married. I am a high school and business school graduate. My current employment is that of a part-time accounting clerk. In addition to writing poetry and short stories, my interests are as follows: first aid, fire arms, fishing, boating, photography. My memberships include the NRA, Bay Area Poets Coalition, International Society of Poets, the National Authors Registry, North American Fishing Club, and America OnLine. I hold current cards for Public Notary, Certified First Respondent and CPR. I started writing poetry at age 16 but became more involved later on. My merits include: several published poems, Gold Poet awards, Silver Poet Award and Honorable Mention awards. In conclusion, I was awarded the Certificate of Poetic Achievement, in 1994, by the Amherst Society. My inspiration comes from life, itself. There are so many things happening around me that I never lack for subjects.

Buessing, Stacie Lynn - (I despise being called by my middle name because it always means I'm in trouble). I was born in Mesa, AZ and, though I have moved to Ahwatukee, have lived there all my life. I was born on March 1, 1981 and am now 15 yrs. old. This past year has been extremely difficult; I was diagnosed as a clinical depressive, meaning I get depressed for no reason. However, very recently, I have joined a teen chruch group and my life has turned around for the better, only with the help of God. I have the perfect family (mom, dad, and two sisters) who are supportive of all that I do. I'm involved in many clubs at school and feel honored to be nicknamed "The Sunshine Girl." (Even though I can't figure out my own problems nor take my own advice, I can always solve other people's problems. I suppose that's the way life is though.) Robert Frost is my inspirational writer and has given me a quote to live by, "I have three words to sum up everything I've learned about life. It goes on." This poetry contest has been a blessing to me and I hope that others who are going through what I went through find the good Lord and live by his wisdom and love. Thank you.

Bush, Gordon Lee - *Born*: in Miami, Florida January 36, 1948. Grew up living in Hialeah, Florida. Graduated Hialeah High School 1967. AA Degree Miami Dade Community Junior College. *Military Service*: 4 years U.S. Navy. Boot Camp in Great Lakes, IL. Engineman A School in Great Lakes, IL. Served 1½ years in Viet Nam on LST Jennings County 846. Returned to States, served remainder of tine in Key West assigned to Submarine Tender Howard W. Gilmore. *Married*: Joan Lorrain Puckett on August 1, 1970. *Children*: Blessed with one child, Christopher Lee Bush. Born: November 30, 1972. *Interest*: Outdoors and nature from mountains to the sea, writing poetry, riding motorcycle. *Employed*: Currently at Suwanee Valley Electric Coop as Meter Reader. *Other Published Works*: "Friend?" through National Library of Poetry in *Tapestry of Thoughts*; "The Oak" through National Library of Poetry in *Best Poets of the 90's*. *Seeks Inspiration*: One has but to look deep within, there is a wealth of untouched and untapped emotions there within us all. *Groups & Organizations*: Member of Free and Accepted Masons, Masonic Lodge #205, Princeton, FL and The National Authors Registry.

Bush, Lou Ethel Wade - (Pen name: Trudee Lee Bush). Born: January 4, 1952. Married: Arthur Bush, Jr. Education: W.H. Reed High-N.Y.C. Corps, Inc. Baton Rouge, Louisiana; Art Instruction School, Washington, D.C. Occupations: Writer, Income Tax Preparer, Bookkeeper, Artist. Poetry: "The Burning Bush,: book of poetry, first volume to be release 1997. Comments: We should take a stand for what is right and good; never violating God's law; living the laws of the universe we should; never causing flaw. Children: Shalonga Bush-Arthelius Bush, John Bush-Lotika Bush-Wendy Canada. Grandchildren: Davin J. Bush-Darien D. Trask-John Bush II.

Bush, Paul David - I am a very young person with quite an interesting perception of the world around me. I tend to see the good in others even when no one else can do so. I am from a family full of love and trust and I would not have wanted my life to be any differently. Others may see me as a dreamer but I see myself as a visionary because dreams are just ideas waiting to be put into motion. I have written poetry for many years already and see writing as the most impressive of arts. There is no other art form in which concepts can be so individual based on the observer. I am from a small town in Tennessee called Ashland City where I have lived my entire life. I hope that everyone experiences life in a small town because it is here that I found out what small, ordinary things are actually treasurers to be cherished.

Carey, Joyce B. - born in Orange, New Jersey and grew up in the North Jersey area. She attended elementary and high school there. She has lived in Massachusetts, Texas, Germany, and Arizona. She moved back to South Jersey in 1976 and resided in Medford Lakes for 11 years where most of her poetry was written. During the last five years she has lived in the Mount Holly area. She is currently residing in Lumberton. Her poetry has been published by Quill Books of Harlingen, Texas. She has been published in six consecutive years by this publisher as a Novice Poet. She is married to William M. Carey, a retired computer scientist. She has one daughter, Barbara, currently living in Nevada, with three children of her own, and a son Brian who lives in the Philadelphia area. In 1993, she and her husband retired to Nevada.

Caron, Kimberly L. One of my greatest desires in life has been to share my deepest thoughts and feelings with others. Through the magic of poetry, I can connect with others by the sharing of like experiences, which carries a healing power for me. Fragmented pieces of my life, shattered long ago, can be reexamined and, in many cases, come together again through the adhesive quality of poetry. Poetry allows me to explore some of my deepest and most hidden feelings--love, pain, sorrow, and yes, even anger, rage and incomprehension. Through my writing I am able to carve out answers for myself to some of life's most puzzling questions, and to explore the mysterious and the unknown, the shadow areas of my life which have never before been touched upon. Some of my favorite poems have been written during the moments in my life which have caused me the most pain. My poem, "Memories," for example was written for my only child, Michael, after my ex-husband was granted custody of him after our divorce. Through the writing of this poem, I was able to articulate the deep pain I was feeling and begin my grieving process. My emotions, sometimes as gentle as a teardrop, oftentimes as powerful as a waterfall, cry out to me to be examined, and through my poetry. I am able to explore and work through my feelings, rather than be paralyzed by them, which for me is the ultimate magic of poetry! I grew up and spent most of my life in the Bay Area. I attended San Jose State University, where I majored in English, and graduated from Sawyer College of Business in 1984. I now make my home in northern California, where I live with my boyfriend, Christopher. I have written numerous poems and short stories, and am currently working on my first fiction novel. My poem "Memories," which appears in this volume, marks my first publishing success, and I look forward to having many more such successes in the future.

Cedervall, Stephanie M. (Mrs. Tor) - B.A. cum laude, Marygrove College, Detroit Michigan; M.A. Sec. Ed., English certificate, Newark State College (now Kean College) in Union, NJ. Post-graduate courses in Shakespeare and Contemporary Drama, University of Michigan. Opera, creative writing at New School of Social Studies, NYC. Intensive private voice (singing and diction). Church soloist and choir member. Retired corporate executive son's business: Able Metro-North American Van Lines, South Plainfield, NJ. Previously senior copywriter for J.C. Penney Co, NYC, S. Klein, Metro Newspaper Service, Cox Adv. Agcy., Detroit, others. Widow of Tor Cedervall, former labor editor, *Record*, Retail Wholesale Department Store Union (RWDSU) NYC. With husband, published *Toledo* (Ohio) *Town Topics*, weekly entertainment magazine. Freelance advertising: Barton Alexander Advertising Agency; Toledo. Teaching: English, Diction. RE: poetry, interest from childhood. Editor: high school paper and year book. Co-editor college paper. Several poems published in the "Random Shots" column of *Detroit News*, several poetry magazines, local newspapers, church bulletins, special occasions, greeting card verse. One song published--full orchestration. Varied forms except free verse or blank verse. Preference: classical forms, especially sonnet. Experimented with haiku and other inventive forms...with rhyme. Aim: professional growth in retirement; compile own book of poetry. Varied background: academic, business, direct sales and sales training, homemaking, child care. Past president Rahway Woman's Club (GFWC-NJ State Federation of Woman's Clubs); charter member, past president Friends of the Rahway Public Library, Rahway Historical Society, others. Commercial writing: newsprint, magazine, radio, catalogs, business brochures, advertising copy and sales, etc. Positive poetic influence: exposure to art and sacred songs, popular ballads (no rock!), heightened awareness of word connotation and sound; strong sociological and philosophical background. Born, Hamtramck Michigan, Polish descent. Husband Swedish/Norwegian. Resides in Rahway, NJ at 521 Central Ave. 07065-3338. Two married sons: Paul Tor and Charles Frans Cedervall. Three grandchildren. Writes volunteer publicity for organizations; several photo and copy submissions each month. Cedervall comments: a poet can paint, sculpt, sing, amuse, censure, inspire, illuminate, console, share experience. "Obsessive verbiage can obscure communication, thereby serving self-indulgence rather than being all the more communicative precisely because the work is poetic!"

Celentz-Anderson, Karla - I started writing about 12 years ago thanks to a high school teacher and my father. I have received Third places with my work and an Honorable Mention and President's Award of Literary Excellence for my writing. People ask, "How do I do it?" I tell them I look into my heart and soul and I write what I see. I have three daughters: Elizabeth, Emily, and Danielle. Maybe one will take after me.

Chediak, Andria - a thirteen year old resident of Boca Raton, Florida where she lives with her mother, stepfather, her sister Sasha, and their two dogs and two cats. She attends St. Joan of Arc Catholic school where she is in the eighth grade. Andria has been writing poetry, stories, and song lyrics since she was nine years old. She writes in her spare time and shares her work mainly with her closest friends. Despite her young age, she has been very prolific in her writing. Andria also is skilled with the electric guitar and piano and loves writing music. She became interested in poetry when she discovered her favorite entertainers Kurt Cobain and Jim Morrison also wrote poetry. Andria aspires to be a great guitar player and songwriter when she grows up.

Cobb, Shané - I was born at 3:23 pm on Oct. 3, 1971. I've never called any one place home until now. In all honesty, I don't remember much about my life beyond six years ago. I do know that it was filled with heartache and tragedy, and I'm a lucky man to have survived it. I see my life in documentation. Some of the accomplishments are amazing to me. Although I do not care to discuss them, I am proud of what it seems I have done. I love to write. It is my one passion, that I can truly become engulfed. In time, I hope to be remembered for this love. Some day I hope to find a compliment to this life. Someone who wants to live life to the fullest on the spur of the moment. I think about marriage and the family, but that is a sacred partnership not to be entered into lightly. I can't say who influenced my style of writing, because I see so many different styles emerging. I think it could be best described as my heart's style. It was always said that I wore my heart on my sleeve, and in truth, I let my heart dominate everything I do. I don't care about proper form, or offending the offensive. I just want the passionate truth to always shine through. For my heart to always shine through.

Collins, L. George - born and raised in the then new land of Oklahoma. Most of his childhood and teen years were lived on the high prairie of the flint hills of the Osage nation, a land where limits did not intrude either on the land or the hearts of those who shared the fenceless horizons of the tall grass prairie. His first poem, "Faith," was published when he was in his teens. In 1935 he married Ruth Hamilton. The writing bug tugged at his heart, but making a living for a growing family during the depression years took priority. Then World War II came along. Though he and Ruth now had three children, he wanted to fly. He applied to take the Army Aviation Cadet Examination. Thirty sat for the examination. Twelve passed. He was one of the twelve. He graduated as a pilot in April 1944. After he and crew flew a new C-47 across the north Atlantic to England, he took up his combat assignment as pilot with the 87th Troop Carrier Squadron. Flying was in his blood now. He stayed in the United States Air Force for 21 years. Following that career his occupations included hotel manager, aircraft design engineer/planner, director of foreign student affairs, and running his own consulting business. During these busy years he also acquired his high school diploma, B.A. and M.A. degrees, and nominations for a Fullbright Scholarship and Woodrow Wilson Fellowship. Though leading a very busy life, he could not suppress the writing bug. This led to a top Freedom's Foundation award in 1962, as well as a national poetry award and a couple of national photography awards. He has been published, in magazines and newspapers and a couple of books - one of which he wrote. His work has appeared in, among others, *Air Force, Telescope-Messenger, Command, Practical Christianity, The World & I, The Jerusalem Times, The San Francisco Chronicle, The Tulsa Tribune*, and once nationally on the ABC Radio Network. He has now changed "writing" from an avocation to a vocation.

Crosby, Greg - born July 1953 and was soon being raised by loving grandparents in Raleigh, NC. He has lived in other cities, but finally settled back in his hometown of Raleigh. Greg is employed as an engineer with the state government and has worked there since 1976. His family is by far the most important part of his life. Crystal his wife works as a district manager for numerous apartment communities. His daughter Galadriel; named after an elf queen from *The Lord of the Rings*. Greg says of his daughter, "She inspires me with her common sense, kindness and a great sense of humor." Of his son Michael, Greg says, "My son has talent as an artist that keeps me humble in my attempts at writing poetry."

Dalrymple, Crystal - I'm the author of "For the Best?", I have lived near my family, friends, relatives, and church in Oklahoma City all of my life. I live with my eighteen year old brother, Andy; thirteen year old sister, Wendy; mother LaDonna; part Pekingese-Chihuahua-Beagle-Terrier-Dachshund mutt, Rozita; and part Cocker Spaniel-Pit Bull-Poodle puppy, Ace. Going to school at Western Heights is fun, yet challenging. In August of 1996 I'll start 10th grade (sophomore) and have more challenging classes. My friends at school, church, and other places encourage me in poetry. I have a God-child named April Durrand, I play the clarinet, and participate in volleyball and Upward Bound in my school. I love to sew cross stitch, read Stephen King, hang out with friends, swim, bicycle, and write poetry. My friends Shannon Scates, Lorrie Krupski, Sharon Shanderan, and my brother graduated. I go to church at Portland Avenue Chruch of the Nazarene with wonderful friends Courtney, Josh, Jeremy, Amber, Amanda, and Lisa. I like to babysit and/or mow lawns for money, especially my God-child April. I have done many things in my life, accomplishments and mistakes and have learned from every one of them. My accomplishments range anywhere from making A's and B's in school to winning a contest for memorizing the most lines of poetry, or making an honor band. Don't forget about my mistakes I make, and the many more I will make. I've lost my Grandpa, Grandma, and friend Triston Pope and have learned valuable lessons from them. Pretty soon I'm going to modeling school and in the future I plan to be certified as a obstetrician and EMT. I'm writing lots of other poetry and have some more I'm going to enter. So, keep looking for my name people, you'll probably hear from me again. I apologize to "some" friends for giving them a hard time. Hello to all my homeboys and homegirls out there, and hello to my best friend, Amber Chaney. Thanks for the puppy!

DePino, Louise - I was born in New Haven, CT and reside in New Haven. I come from a family of eight children, being the youngest. I am married and have four children, two boys and two girls. Three married children are married and one is single. I have nine grandchildren. I worked in an office, a nearby McDonald's and later I worked for the City of New Haven school system. While I was raising my children, I did not work. My husband worked and I hardly spent much time with him. My time was devoted mostly to my family, and I had many hard days growing the kids. We lived in a three-room apartment (my mother's house), which had no furnace and our apartment was heated by a gas stove, which did not give adequate heat. I am a faithful catholic and have a great faith in God. I like to hear daily mass, good music and like long walks. Mostly one of my pass times and hobbies is writing poetry. I enjoy reading verses and poems to family and friends. I wrote some poems and recited them at functions, like my birthday and anniversary. My utmost and fondest desire would be to see any one of my poems published and signed. That would be my dream come true. I appreciate the story, the lyrics and the rhymes. To me it's a work of art. A tremendous meaning from the heart. It was a great opportunity and a great pleasure introducing myself to you. Please read on, each foe and friend. Enjoy each word, to the very end.

Dethloff, John Joseph - born June 14, 1976 in New Orleans, LA. Resides at 3127 Silver Spring Ct. Missouri City, Texas 77459. Phone (713) 438-3177. *Education*: I am a junior in college. My majors are Literature and Psychology. *Career*: I want to be a poet, prose writer, and novelist. Comments: Writing is my *élan vital*. I murder words to give them life, with the intent to convey that life to people, while hopefully illuminating my audience's *anima* and turning them into a *res cogitans*.

Dia, Bocar - [d.b] August 25, 1960 [pl.b.] Dakar (Senegal) West Africa/living in the U.S. since 1991 [par.] Amadou Sada Dia and Fatou Aw Dia / single / 3 years of high school / electrician since 1982 / published and certified by Amherst Society, Poets' Guild, National Library of Poetry and others. Would like to share with the world of poetry some of my verse: "By the feather and the wisdom, knowledge is the real freedom."

Dimmick, Marianne - Born December 16, 1937 Marianne Rupsoff in Milwaukee, Wisconsin. Married.

Domsic, Melissa - I am thirteen years old, and am in eighth grade. I write poetry often and have a whole book of it. My favorite actress is Christina Ricci and my favorite actors are Tom Cruise and Bill Paxton. If I could have nay wish fulfilled I would be an actress. Author of "life is a game."

Dupont, Linda - born in a small village outside of Montreal, Quebec, Canada. At an early age, she displayed a keen interest in sports, becoming a team player in her high school track team. Later in life, she took an interest in karate, earning both a gold and a bronze medal in the inner-city championships. Her other love is the arts. Her interest in music led her to play in a rock band during high school and perform in variety shows at public schools and private parties. Finding she enjoyed the "blues", she sang and wrote songs with a group called "Dixie Lovin'". Having a penchant for writing, she has entered various contests and has since been published in a newspaper. With articles behind her, she decided to self publish a book of poems, "Inner Thoughts," promoting them in bookstores and handing them out to friends. She is now a resident in Chateauguay, Canada, with her husband, daughter and son. Volunteering some of her time to help troubled teens, she had the opportunity to put together a few short stories and articles on abuse. She has compiled a collection of poems which she hopes will one day be published.

Eicherlberger, Robert A. - I'm a twenty-one year old poet who hails from Lancaster, PA. I pass the time by listening to fine music, reading and writing poetry that comes from the heart, and searching for the largest fresh water fish I can catch with a rod and reel! I thank God for giving me the ability to write; and for making life full of love, sadness, joy, and most importantly, passion! I will arise and go now, for always night and day / I hear lake water lapping with low sounds by the shore; / While I stand on the roadway, or on the pavements grey / I hear it in the deep heart's core. -W.B. Yeats

Fansler, Harmony - I am fourteen years old, and a freshman in high school. I enjoy writing poems because they help me to clear my head, and all of my feelings. All of my poems are mostly centered around how I feel. I have been writing poems since I was about nine years old. I am very honored to be chosen to have one of my poems in this anthology. I believe that poetry has multiple meanings. I, and many others are grateful for publishing companies like these, to let our poems be displayed.

Garcia, Alegria - writer, dancer, pianist, and poet, was born and raised in San Antonio by Mexican-American parents. She studied Literature at the University of Texas at San Antonio and at the University of the Incarnate Word where she was also a featured piano soloist. She was a columnist and staff member with Bitter Magazine where she wrote articles ranging from Dance to Mexican history. Alegria has also been a featured poet for the Esperanza Peace and Justice Center and had her works on display there during Contemporary Art month. She has just completed a book of poetry and is at work on a novel. She expects to finish her Bachelor's Degree at the University of New Mexico.

Garcia, James - *Date of Birth*: June 27, 1961. *Place*: Woodland, California. *Marital Status*: Single. *Children*: Crystal Nicole, Joshua James. *Education*: Winters Joint Unified High School, Sacramento State University. *Current Occupation*: Nuclear Security Officer, Portland General Electric, Portland Oregon. *Memberships*: International Society of Poetry, Poets Guild and National Authors Registry. Other Writings: My poetry has been published by Quill Books, National Society of Poetry, Poets Guild, The Wexford Publishing Company and Iliad Press. *Personal Note*: I always strive to create the most heart felt poems possible. My greatest influence is my Heavenly Father, who continually fills my heart and mind, with eternal hope and prosperity for all mankind. *Address*: Longview, Washington 98632.

Gilbert, Tanya - I was born in Grand Junction, Colorado on June 27, 1985, the same day that my Great Grandma (Virginia McBride) was born on. She lives in Manzanola, Colorado with Grandpa John. I live in Ragely, Colorado, and go to school at Parkview Elementary. I have a Grandma and Grandpa Graham who live in Monte Vista, Colorado, and Aunt Jacque and Uncle Jim who live in Denver, Colorado, and Aunt Kathy, Uncle Terry, And Grandma Gilbert who live in Grand Junction, and Aunt Janie and Uncle Leo who live in Sierra Vista, Arizona, and of course my cousins Bead, Kari, who live in Sierra Vista, Arizona, James, Ben, and Sara who live in Grand Junction. I love to read, write poems, listen to music, swim, dance, go boating with my family, travel to new places, visit friends, spend time with my Grandma & Grandpa Graham, and I like to do art. I have my own business taking care of other people's animals while they are on vacation and I help my mom with her Mary Kay business. This fall I will be in the 5th grade with all my friends.

Givhan, Sherry Lynn - the author of several published poems. Born third of four children, December 20th 1957. Raised by both parents on Chicago's west side in the Garfield Park District. Completed thirteen years of school having graduated from Austin High School in 1976. Attended Wilber Wright College for three semesters. Sherry was employed ten years at a catholic hospital. Worked her way up from food service Pantry Hostess to licensed Pharmacy Technician. Simultaneously held other part time positions: Crowd Control Usher, Runner, Service Clerk. In recent years: Sales Associate (Venture Department Store) Temp. (Helpmate Temporaries Inc.) Currently interested in getting her first full length novel published. At thirty-eight, Sherry is a single, childless, ambitious African American woman with dreams of phenomenal success. Your correspondence is welcome. P.O. Box 408294, Chicago IL 60640.

Glentz-Anderson, Karla - I started writing about 12 years ago. Thanks to a high school teacher and my father. I have received Third Places with my work and Honorable Mention Presidential Awards for my words. People ask "How do I do it?" I tell them, "I look into my heart and soul and write what I see." I have three daughters, Elizabeth, Emily, and Danielle. Maybe one will take after me.

Gordon, Mary - I would like to introduce myself to you. I am Mary Gordon from West Chester, PA and college athletic coach (varsity volleyball and basketball). Also active in many church activities: Junior High Youth Advisor, committee member, Stephen Ministry leader; and Boy Scouts of America. I have been writing poetry since 1973. Writing poetry is one of my hobbies and I usually write when I am feeling worry, scared, happy or experiencing something in my life. I believe my writing of poetry is a gift by God. Poem title "Hope" was my first poem I ever wrote for a class. The words in the poem tells you there is hope in small and large things but the greatest hope is in God. Another poem titled "The Spirit of Christmas" explains all the things we do to make the season more jolly and happy for people around us. But the true meaning of Christmas which we should be celebrating is the birthday of our Lord Jesus and accept God's gift to everyone - His son.

Gregory, Grover Wayne II - lives in Wichita, KS with his cat Azriel. He was born in St. Louis, MO in 1972 and is a huge fan of gothic horror. Along with writing poetry he also is a singer/songwriter. His inspiration for writing is life itself, in all of its tragic glory and his work is untouched from the final pen-stroke, as you see it is how it came out. His favorite writers include Poe, Frost and Morrison (Jim). Currently he doesn't have anything published other than those you see here but hopes to put out a book sooner or later. Incidentally, "Traveling Trees" was written while on the phone with the young lady it was meant for, unknown to her at the time.

Harrison-Duke, Terry A. - Terry posses a double Bachelors of Arts degree from Spring Arbor College in Spring Arbor Michigan. The first is Management and the second is Family Counseling. She is presently working on her Masters in Administration from Central Michigan university. One of her main goals is to be able to assist young people that are under privileged in the community all over the state. Terry believes that if you take from the Community in which you live it is important to give something back. This will prevent the deplinishment of resources. She is single with a three year old son. She presently work for the Correctional System in Michigan as a prison counselor. She was born in cleveland, Ohio in 1960. Terry is presently working on a novel called "Scenes From A Womans Life". Her favorite readings are from Terry McMillens works and the V.C. Andrews Seris.

Heinze, George-Alicea - (Pen name, D.H. Boyd). Born in Santa Monica, California. Pen name is a combo of my parents names. I write in honor of them for they supported me in my creative interests and worked hard to help continue my time spent studying and working each of my interests. And humbly, I write for them and their memory, for my brother and sister-in-law, for my most dear friends, Roy and Mazzie Holes. Education: High school. Studied art at Otis Art Institute, Art Center, LA. Adult writing groups, private groups for writers. Comm. of Art Club for seven years. Studied dramatics with Josphene Dillion (Clark Gable's first wife). Made some TV commercials, small theater, some troop shows WWII. Studied music. Photography a couple of awards, and Tech Art awards. Several Suggestion awards on my job. 40 years on one job. Personal Thoughts: Hard work and dreams, do come true, we must open our hearts to let them come through. Our great country has one of the greatest sayings, "Do unto others as you would have do unto you." With that we can all live, love, build together a happy world. I try to make this real in my world and express it in work. For love is food and strength or all of us. I have enjoyed each of my interests mentioned above. They are all intertwined with one another, they go hand in hand throughout lives. Just as love, faith, believing is how we can, must survive, with all God's creatures one and all.

Blake, T.R. - has been writing poetry for 19 years. She is a native of California currently residing in the state of Washington. She is a graduate of Drury college from where she obtained an associate's degree in legal assistance and is currently serving in the US Army as a legal Noncommissioned Officer at Fort Lewis Washington. Her works have been published in the following books: *All My Tomorrows,* vol.II and *Echoes From The Silence*, vol.III with Quill Books, The National Library of Poetry *Tomorrow's Dreams* and with the *Northwest Guardian* (Military Local Paper). She's also the author of the book Meaningful Thoughts *Entangled Heart*, vol. I, Published by Brunswick Publishing Company. Blake also has two poems being set to music by Hilltop Records, one poem being set to music by Amerecord, one poem being set to music by Hollywood Artists Record Company and four poems being set to music by Tin Pan Alley, Inc. Blake is a new and Distinguished Member of the International Society of Poets, National Authors Registry (NAR), and with the Songwriters' Club of America (SCA). Blake has received honors and awards from The National Library of Poetry, Editor's Award. Blake and her husband Frank have three children.

Higgins, N. Loy Kuhn - (Pen name, LOY). *Born*: August 2, 1944 in Louisville, Kentucky; *Parents*: Arthur Louis Kuhn (deceased) and Nina Waller Kuhn. *Spouse*: Dr. David Michael Higgins, married November 27, 1990. *Education*: dupont Manual High School, Louisville, KY, Class of '62; Eastern Kentucky State College, Richmond, KY, '62-'64; Miami Dade Junior College, Miami, FL, '73-'74, AA Degree, Fine Arts/General; U of the State of New York, '86, AS Degree, Liberal Arts & General Studies (Regents Program), conferred Jan'87; Scottsdale Community College, Scottsdale, AZ, '95, Studio Recording & Electronic Music. *Current Occupation*: Writer, Musician, Teacher, Desktop Publisher. *Memberships*: International Society of Poets, National Authors Registry, Adult Recital Series of

AZ State Music Teachers Assn., Alliance Francais, Senior Friends. *Honors and Awards*: Honorable Mention, "Gamblers Choice," Pine Hills, NY Poetry Competition 1995; "Gamblers Choice," Iliad Press Fall 1995 Literary Awards Program; and two Editor's Choice Awards, "Silent Music" and "The Bar Mitzvah," The National Library of Poetry-1996; Superior & Excellent Awards, National Federation Junior Festivals '93, '94, '95; Special Commendation, National Guild of Piano Teachers '93, '94, '95, and membership in the National Fraternity of Student Musicians, Student Division of American College of Musicians and Piano Hobbyists; ASMTA, Central District, 43rd Piano Ensemble, '95. *Writing Credits*: "Silent Music," The National Library of Poetry, *A Voyage to Remember*, Spring 1996; "The Bar Mitzvah," Modern Poetry Society of Dunnellon, FL, *Mirrors of the Soul*, Spring 1996; "Reservation Request," The Mile High Poetry Society, *Muse*, April 1996; "The Bar Mitzvah," The National Library of Poetry, *A Muse to Follow*, Summer 1996; "Pursuit of Passion," The National Library of Poetry, *Amidst the Splendor*, Autumn 1996; "Gambler's Choice," Iliad Press, Chapter Two of *Crossings*, October 1996; "Ode to a Desert Rose Garden," Iliad Press, *Crossings*, October 1996; "The Weddin'," The National Library of Poetry, *The Best Poems of the '90's*, late Fall 1996; "Forgiving," The National Library of Poetry, *The Ebbing Tide*, Winter 1996; "A Marriage," The National Library of Poetry, *Memories of Tomorrow*, Winter 1996; "Silent Music," Iliad Press, *Whispers*, February 1997; "Quiet Rain," Iliad Press, *Whispers*, February 1997. *Writings & Recordings*: Poems, humorous short stories, songs, and lyrics. Writer & publisher of POETRY LINES series. Arranger and performer of several keyboard cassette recordings, recorded in my previous home studio in Scottsdale, AZ. *Hobbies*: Traveling and living abroad, reading and writing, playing piano, keyboard, and ukelele, beachcombing and shell collecting, studying and observing people, and enjoying all of the arts. *Personal Note or Philosophical Statement*: As many people sharing one world, we travel different pathways to one destination, using music, poetry, and the arts to communicate and express our emotions.

High, Sandra - Babes always helps me with my ideas for poems. Whenever I sit down at my desk and try to write a poem, it never works. Then Babes, with his motor running, jumps on to my lap and proceeds to take my mind off the matters at hand. All of a sudden, BOOM, an idea or even the first stanza for a poem pops into my head. Or I will get my ideas from something I see. When visiting a close friend in BC (British Columbia), I went walking in a thunder storm. I was up on a hill, watching the lake when slowly the words for "My Place" formed in my head. My family supports everything I do, even though there isn't a lot of us. My parents died in a car accident two years ago; so that left me with a brother an aunt, a cousin, and of course, a wonderful grandmother. My brother Scott and I live in a town house with our aunt Janet, cousin Rick, cat Babes, tarantula Crunch, snake Charles, and bunny, Greedy. Scott gave me the nickname "Smurf" because of my 5'2" height, and my petite build. Of course, my favourite colours (blue and white) didn't save me from that torture. Other than that, I am fairly mature for my age. I like swimming, even though I look more like a frog than a fish. I like to be in the outdoors; it's my favourite place to be. The next best thing to the outdoors, is helping my friend with ideas for his short stories, and proofreading his creations.

Hilko, Karen M. - I moved away from Clifton, New Jersey, where I lived all my life, when I was nineteen to attend Temple University in Philadelphia. I hope to graduate from Temple in the spring of 1997. When I graduate I will have a Bachelors in Music, with a concentration in jazz voice performance. When I came to Temple, I began writing poems. I fell in love with a wonderful guy three days before I moved to Philadelphia. We broke up after three months because he was moving to California. I had these feelings after he left, sadness, confusion, love, and anger. I did not know how to deal with them. I decided to let my true feelings come out in my poems. Now three years later whenever I feel the need to release what I'm feeling, or help someone else release a feeling, I write a poem. Most of the time I write sonnets. My mother, my best friend and my lost love have been the main inspirations to me. I am lucky to have such encouraging people in my life. Actually if it was not for my best friend I would not have even had the courage to let anyone else read my poems. A while ago I let a friend read a poem of mine and she laughed. Until a few months ago I never shared one poem. Now I am glad I let my friends enjoy them. It gives me a great sense of pride in my work to hear their positive comments and I hope they will be continually impressed. If they are not, I can still take pride because they have renewed my confidence in myself. I know writing makes me happy, and that is what is most important.

Hisaw, Betty L. Floyd - 2801 East 10th, Pine Bluff, AR 71601. *Place of Birth*: Cleveland County, Arkansas. *Married*: Samuel B. Hisaw on December 7, 1957. *Education*: Glendale High School, Glendale, AR. Graduated Valedictorian 1951; University of Arkansas at Monticello, Graduated 1954. Received a B.S.E. major Elementary Education with a double minor in English and History. Graduated with honors (Cum laude). *Special Studies*: I have 21 graduate hours in Elementary Counseling, Education and English. *Occupation*: I taught 38 years in Arkansas Public schools. I retired in May 1995. *Memberships*: The National Authors Registry. Past memberships include: AEA and NEA (Educational Associations), Southern Baptist Church, Phi Phi Phi Sorority, American Business and Professional Association. *Comments*: I have had no works published to date, I have only been submitting material since I retired. I have two children, Ken Hisaw and Lisa Hill and two grandchildren, Matthew and Sarah. My hobbies are: Reading, Wood Carving and Crafts.

Jackson, Robert - AGE: 23, *Born*: April 4, 1972. *Hometown*: Richmond, CA. *Education*: Santa Clara University; BA English-Creative Writing. *Publishing Notes*: Santa Clara Review, The Numbian, Praxis-Jersuit News Journal, Roots Magazine. *Reading Notes*: featured poet of the 1995 Multi-Cultural Extranvangaza on SCU Campus; Guest Poet at UC Davis African-American Writers Workshop (Sugar Shack); Guest Poet for "Bandele" (African-Freedom School Fund raiser); featured poet for Santa Clara Review Publication party; guest poet on Sally Baker's television program "Wee Poets". HONORS & ACCOLADES: 1995 African American Excellence in Literary Arts; one of three selected poets for 1994 Maya Angelou Bay Area Speaking Tour (Santa Clara County). *Personal Interest*: Football/Basketball-(coaching & commentary); Jazz Music; Nightlife; Camping. *Publishing Notes*: SANTA CLARA REVIEW, PRAXIS JESUIT INTERNATIONAL, ROOTS HIP-HOP and CULTURAL Magazine, NUBIAN AFRICAN AMERICAN JOURNAL. *Speaking Engagements*: Opening poet for Maya Angelou Bay Area Speaking Tour (1994); Keynote speaker for 1995 Martin Luther King, Jr., Celebration; Keynote speaker for African-American Woman Appreciation Day (1995); Opening poet for Multi-Cultural Extravaganza (1994); Selected reader for U.C., Davis Black Poetry "Sugar Shack" (1994); Selected reader for "Spoken Word" (1993). *Continuing Projects*: Co-author of a manuscript entitled "Fire & Ice"; started "Pieces of a Negro Man," not due until spring, 1996. *Other Accomplishments*: Three years Varsity Letterman for football at S.C.U., founder of the Urban Music Department at K.S.C.U. radio, Co-organizer of the Black Motivational Outreach Program for high schools.

Jean-Francois, Marie-Catheline - [b.] July 30, 1974, Brooklyn, N.Y.; [p.] Phinelie and Jeveille Jean-Francois; [ed.] The Mary Louis Academy, Hofstra University; [occ.] full-time college student with two part-time jobs; [memb.] National Library of Poetry, International Society of Poets, Hofstra Literary Magazine; [hon.] Dean's List at Hofstra, Editor's Choice Award, Eugene Schneider Prose Award; [oth. writ.] Several poems published by The National Library of Poetry and many short stories; [personal statement] I try to be inspirational with the work I produce, not only for myself, but for others who also share my love for poetry.

Joshi, Vishnu P. - Date of Birth: 05/08/34. Place of Birth: Burhanpur, M.P./India. Married, Spouse: Indu. Date of Marriage: 07/26/56. Education: Studied Electrophysics at Tenchnische Hochschule Munich, Germany, Graduated 1962. Studied Electronics, Computers and English at Middlesex Community College, Edison, NJ, USA, graduated 1991. Occupation: Worked with scientific institutions and industries. Presently working with computers. Membership: International Society of Poets, International Society of Authors and Poets, The Academy of American Poets, Poetry Society of America. Other Published Works (poetry): "Buddha In India," *The Voice Within*, The National Library of Poetry (Spring) 1996; "Human Soul," *A Muse To Follow*, The National Library of Poetry (Summer) 1996; "Human Doll," *Where the Dawn Lingers*, The National Library of Poetry (Summer) 1996; "Brahma," *The Best Poems of 90's*, The National Library of Poetry (Fall) 1996; "Brahma," *Whispers*, Iliad Press, (Spring) 1997; "My Only Wish," *The Best Poems of 96*, The National Library of Poetry (Spring) 1996. Awards Received: Editor's Choice Award (1996)-"Buddha In India;" Editor's Choice Award (1996)-"Human Soul;" Editor's Choice (1996)-Human Doll;" Editor's Choice (1996)-"My Only Wish;" Honorable Mention (1996)-"Brahma." Personal Comments: There is a minute difference in which the human cells in our brain rearrange to appreciate the Art and Science. But, like the day and night, that difference is necessary to explore the world within and around us.

Kahles, Christal Renee - born in Cincinnati, Ohio on May 6, 1982. Her early years of life were spent battling numerous health problems; a heart defect, asthma, and allergies to name just a few! Therefore, Christal had to spend many hours inside watching other children do what she could only hope to do someday. Determined to overcome, she decided to put all of her energy into positive outlets, and thus began her love of writing! At the age of 11, Christal began her first book about a handicapped young girl who became a missionary. At her present age, 14, she has completed poems, short stories, and begun her second book. Christal says that all of her inspiration comes from her love of God and His creation. She believes that this has been her source of healing and has allowed her to now participate in all those things that were once only a dream. She enjoys dancing, swimming, horseback riding, singing, and being an active member of the youth group in her local church along with her writing. As far as the future is concerned, Christal hopes "to become a missionary some day and use my writing to make a difference in the lives of those not yet aware that dreams really can come true!"

Kelly, Rex - Rex Kelly makes his home in Missouri where he worked as a musician and currently is employed by NU-TECH industries. Although he still enjoys music and is actively writing lyrics for the band Sapient (based in Austin Texas), in the last year his focus has changed to writing. Inspired by the works of R.A. Salvatore and Elaine Cunningham he is currently working on a fantasy novel. Poetry has always played an important part in his life and he is working to have a complete collection published. On his time off he enjoys indoor rock climbing, riding horses at his mother's farm and tending to the important things in life, like building sand castles with his daughter Suzie.

Kim, Elaine Ki Jin - born in Seoul, Korea on May 4, 1979, and after living in her home country for four years, she moved with her family to Los Angeles, California. Now she lives in Rancho Palos Verdes, California, with her parents and her four sisters--Joy, Janet, Grace, and Pearl. Joy is her older sister by one year, Janet and Grace are twins, and Pearl was born in 1990. Currently, Elaine, a junior at Peninsula High School, participates in the school dance team, National Honors Society, Spanish Honors society, Model United Nations, and Interact Club, the high school chapter of the Rotary Club. She also serves as the president of the Point-of-View Club, secretary of the Korean Culture Club, and bulletin editor for the school Key Club, the high school chapter of Kiwanis International. Elaine is very involved in community service, volunteering her time at the local food outreach center and soup kitchen and the Presbyterian church that she attends. She also boasts a 1550 SAT score, a 239 PSAT score, and a 3.9 GPA at one of the biggest public schools in the nation. Elaine's writing experience includes writing for the school newspaper and the inclusion of poetry and short stories in several literary magazines. Her work has been accepted by organizations such as Valory-Hetzel Publishing Co., Iliad Press, and Who's Who in New Poets. In April, 1996 Elaine received the opportunity to compete in the Writing Achievements sponsored by the National Council of Teachers of English. As a college student, Elaine plans to major in English, but whether or not she will utilize that knowledge in creative writing, education, or law, remains undecided. She hopes that she will be accepted to the school of her choice, which, at this point, are Yale University, Columbia University, and University of Pennsylvania. Elaine's family exerts the most influence on her life, her way of thinking, her writing. Growing up with four sisters has shaped her own personality, and that experience, she claims, has made her capable of juggling many responsibilities at one time while keeping a smiling face and a calm spirit.

Korer, Beth "freckles" Caroline - Ever since I was very little I wanted to be a writer. I come from a small family, my mother-Julie, father-Steven, and my little sister-Melanie. My goal in life is to become a successful writer. Everything I write I write for my best friend of many years Rebecca "Rebel" Lynn Krimm who was murdered this year-96. She gave me the strength to believe in what I write and to try and reach my goal no matter what stands in my way. I believe that writing brings out the real me and that nothing is really said until it is written down. I have had one poem published so far in one of the National Library of Poetry books. Right now I am thinking about which college I would like to attend in the summer of '97 where I hope to get a job as a journalist or poet. I go to Buffalo Grove High School in Buffalo Grove, Illinois where I attend as a senior-to-be, where I am working my way to my goal. Creative writing is my life.

Kuss, Nicole Marie - I am sixteen years old, and a native to Buffalo, New York. I have one brother, Eric, who is four years older than I am. I've written several poems concerning my relationship with him, and his with our father. I live with my mother, Marilyn, and her boyfriend, Tony. I've been writing poetry for several years. I started writing when I was in the sixth grade. I also experimented with short stories and haiku. The poetry I write is an expression of what I'm thinking or feeling. I started writing poetry to relieve the stress of everyday life, sort of as an outlet for my problems. Three people that have greatly helped me with my poetry are my mother, my dearest friend and counselor, Kari Jo, and one of my best friends and love, James Spence. They all supported me and it was with their pushing and persistence that I sent my poetry in for the first time.

Link, Sylvia Lynn - resides in Zion, Illinois with her husband James. She is the youngest daughter of Lucille Howe of Venice, Florida and Harold Teachenor, late of Chicago, Illinois. Ms. Link has a Bachelor of Science in Business Administration with high honors and is completing her Masters in Business Administration this year, also with high honors. Publications include "Show You Care" and "Justice" in *Treasured Poems of America*, 1996; "Show You Care" in *A Muse to Follow*, 1996; "Prejudice" and "Pages" in *Whispers*, 1996; "Weeds" in the *Best Poems of the 1990's*, 1996; and "Games" in *Best New Poems*, 1996. Personal outlook: Life is a never ending poem which, when we take the time to listen, reflects the true soul of mankind."

Lohman, Christopher Paul - Nature may be the answer. The awesome, unbelievable power, the absolute silences, the sheer size, and the gentle weaving of all of nature's children put nature on the path toward dominance. Love can be learned by simply watching a tree absorb the sun's rays and growing from the interaction. Hatred can be seen by studying the effects of an environmental disaster. Power and strength are cradled in the arms of a hurricane. A deer in a pair of headlights radiates the feeling of confusion. More often than not, nature can give you a demonstration of any feeling or reaction that you would like to learn about. I have allowed life to be ny educator. Most everything I write about I have experienced first hand, or I believe in deeply. I believe that a person's writing must deal with the subject that he believes in. The deeper the belief, the better the writing. The lack of belief on an author's part can be felt by the reader. It is as if the reader is reading a textbook by an unknowledgeable author. How long is it before the book is placed in the circular file? I grew up in a small town of fifty people in Northern California. Smartville was a mining community that turned into a ghost town and is now a textbook of nature. I left this fantasy-styled land only to attend college at California State University in Chico. After obtaining my BA in Accounting in 1990, I decided to forego the big city life, the "great" jobs, and the death of nature, to stay in the beautiful city of Chico. I have written many poems, short stories, and text papers over the last seventeen years. Some good writing, some not very good, but all increasing my knowledge. The year of 1996 is the year for me to test my writing ability. I am entering poem contests monthly, and I am working on my first fiction novel. Remember, don't strive to become the author, but rather strive to become the words.

Mabey, Amanda G. - Born: December 21, 1980 in SLC. Parents: Gun S. Mabey & Edward Milo Mabey. Citizenship: to America & Sweden. Education: Beginning second year of high school. Current home: 7525 E. Gainey Ranch Rd. #133, Scottsdale, AZ 85258, USA. Memberships: International Society of Poets. Published works: some poetry published in the National Library of Poetry's *A Moment in Time*, some in one of their 1996 anthologies, some in *Best Poets of the 90's*, and some on two audio cassettes from *The Sound of Poetry*. Some poetry published in Phoenix Country Day's *Write From the Heart* and *Daybreaks*. More poetry to be published in various anthologies from various companies. Other: I lived in Park City, UT until I was 2 years old, when I moved to Sweden. At 5 years of age I moved to Mijas Costa in Malaga, Spain, and at 10, when my father died, back to America to learn proper English. I am currently attending Phoenix Country Day High School in Arizona and can speak Swedish, English and Spanish. I am planning to study botany, biochemistry, and writing.

Alan, Robert - the pen name for Bob Margulies, grew up in Washington, D.C. and Maryland. He has lived in Southern California for many years. He is married to Holly Brooke Margulies and has three sons, Keith, Kevin, and Kraig plus a stepson, Tom, and a stepdaughter, Joanne. He has a Bachelor's degree and Masters degree and is a Senior Principal Specialist with McDonnell Douglas. His works have appeared in *Windows of the Soul, The Path Not Taken, The Rainbow's End, Poetic Voices of America, A Muse to Follow,* and *Spillway*. He is a member of the Los Angeles Poets and Writers Collective. Poetry allows him to express his experiences, observations, and perceptions about the past, present, and future.

Marquis, Brittanie L. - I was born in Aurora, Colorado February 6, 1983. The daughter of an Air Force instructor and his wife, I have also lived in Kansas City, Kansas and Cowgill, Missouri. I presently reside with my family on a farm near Parker, Kansas, about 75 miles southwest of Kansas City. I, along with my older brother, attend Prairie View High School near LaCygne, Kansas. I am a cheerleader and musician, with aspirations of becoming a corporate lawyer. In addition to my activities surrounding school, I help care for my invalid grandmother, who suffered a debilitating stroke in February 1995, and my 5-year-old brother, house work and farm chores. I also lend my full support to my older brother Kevin's high school athletic career. I began writing at age 11 as a means of relieving stress and emotions built up following the near-loss of my aunt Barbi, struck by a drunk driver in September 1994. With the support of my family and friends, I have recently entered my poetry in several contests. My father's work often takes him to all corners of the world, and I intend to include in future writings some of his more interesting experiences, until the time my own adventures are taking me to these places. When not studying, practicing cheers or music, or helping out at home, I enjoy rollerskating, swimming and horseback riding. I am also working toward my ultimate goal by improving my interpersonal skills, developing a more extroverted personality, and studying debate. I am looking forward to my 8th grade year, when I hope to add basketball to my already numerous activities. Of course, writing is something I hope I never have to give up.

Marshall, Andy - I was born in England with an identical twin, but after being bombed-and-dug-out in 1941, the remainder of the war years were spent at school in Northern Scotland. The education was spartan and thorough. We worked "on the land" to grow food for the cities, went to church every day and had a strong education in the Three R's. This was to give me a life-long love affair with writing and history. Later at London University I majored in Celtic Languages, before becoming an "Exchange Student" at Berkeley. I was probably the first "Drop Out" but how can one study Gaelic in California? Instead I turned to playing tennis, was sponsored by the Californian Tennis Association, and toured two years on the American Amateur Circuit, competing twice at Wimbledon and Forest Hills, with my twin sister. In due time I married a High School Teacher in Newton, Mass., and helped raise four wonderful kids (natch!) as well as being an unofficial "foster-home" to a score of mixed-up-kids of the 70's. During these years I remained active-up-to-the-elbows in neighborhood activities, that ranged from re-settling Cambodian refugees to weekly "adventures" when I took Boston-area children "exploring" their own historic city and the surrounding countryside. We retired to New Hampshire in 1981, after I had written several successful (but very trashy) Harlequin-type novels. I continue to send excerpts of a "White Mountain Diary" to several English magazines, even as I hone my skills into writing acceptable poetry. After a lifetime of writing "the old-fashioned-way," I find the free-for-all anything-goes Poetry of the 90's hard to put into shape. It takes working on (or perhaps it doesn't take any work at all?!). On the side, we tend a monster "veggie-patch" which sends produce to the local markets five months of the year, as I try and cope with the New England climate..."freeze and fry." It's a good life, and I'm lucky. I know it.

Martin, George W. - BORN: February 22, 1930 PLACE OF BIRTH: Trussville, Alabama; SCHOOLING: Newark High School, Newark, Arkansas; University of Chicago, School of Journalism AUTHOR CREDITS: Various Poetry Anthologies; a recently published book titled, *The Lay of Threll*, a fantasy told in rhyme with an additional collection of poetry. Have traveled extensively in the Orient and the United Kingdom. In the Orient (India, Japan, The Philippines, Okinawa, Guam, Korea) the travel was at the request of the United States Air Force! Took early retirement from the University of Missouri at Columbia, Mo. and have since lived a rather sedentary life of travel and occasional writing (mostly poetry, some short fiction). Favorite authors range through Science Fiction Azimov, Ellison, et al, to King, Dean Koontz and all the crazies.

Martinez, Julio Y. - Born December 20, 1924, Place Riverside California. Spouse: Florence C. Martinez. Date of Marriage: April 8. 1946. Children: two sons, Julio Jr. and Peter P. Education: Graduate San Bernardino Valley College, San Bernardino California, earned Teaching Credential at University of Los Angeles, California. Other writings: I have written numerous articles on veteran issues for *The Sun* newspaper, San Bernardino California, *The Redlands Daily Facts* newspaper, Redlands California. On September 8, 1955, my poem "What America Means To Me" was entered into the Congressional Record. Current Occupation: Instructor Youth Authority "RET". Memberships: I am a life member of the Veterans of Foreign Wars of the United States. Life member of The American Legion. I have served on numerous positions of leadership for U.S. Veteran organizations. Honors and Awards: I consider it an honor to have been recognized by the United States Congress as an American who loves his country. Philosophical Statement: Several years ago I met an ageless American Indian on the Montana Indian Reservation, who told me, when you write from the heart, people will listen to you. I strive to adhere to that philosophy.

Masek, Amelia - (Pen name: Amy). Parents: Anastacio and Elsie Laureano. Spouse: Brain Masek. Children: Brian Masek Jr. Education: Basic noncommissioned Officers School; Diploma United States Army Quarter Master Service School, Logistics; United States Army Adjutant Service School, Personnel Management; Aviation Logistics; Ft. McCoy, Logistic Management. Current Occupation: Active Duty Army (16yrs). Memberships: International Society of Poets, National Authors Registry. Honors and Awards: National Library of Poetry Editor's Choice Award; Army Achievement Medal; National Defense Service Medal; Armed Forces Reserve Medal. Other Writings: Published "The Creature" in the anthology *Songs on the Wind* by the National Library of Poetry. Personal Note: Normally I have written for my own enjoyment. Inspiration comes from own experiences and life realities. Thank you to my wonderful family whom without I could not get as far as I did. Dad I love you, and I only wish mom was here with us today. Thanks to my adoring brothers and sisters, Andy, Billy, Zoe, Zaida and Nancy Laureano, and to my wonderful son BJ and spouse Brian.

McAndrews, Journey W. - Born 1977, in Lexington, Kentucky, currently residing in Mount Sterling, Kentucky. A descendant of fiery ambition — a legacy the would mold the very soul of this destined writer. Observed to be a quiet, stubborn, and strong willed child, character traits that did not diminish with adulthood. While still a student at Christian Liberty Academy (which proved to be the only structure she would ever accept), she began writing poetry just as a means of expressing the sentiments her voice had locked deep within her soul. At age twelve she became interested in poetry and pursued to conquer the hidden secrets of William Shakespeare's works. Having done this at age fifteen, she began her personal quest of writing poetry. Being outspoken, highly opinionated, and stubborn, made her the constant victim of conversational reproach. Knowing this she began to write poetry just to spite those who wouldn't listen. And in the mist of her stubborn spite she fell in love with writing. Her thoughts, ideas, and inspirations came from William Shakespeare, Edgar Allan Poe, Emily Dickinson, and Sylvia Plath. Her most sorrowful poems were patterned after the works of Plath an Dickinson, as dedications to their poetical sorrow. The poems that express an abundance of sorrowful emotions, came from her awe and love for William Shakespeare. These poems were written in Elizabethan style poetry which is currently unacceptable in poetry contests and at publishing companies. The darkly destructive and malignant side of this young writer comes from her capability to derive from her own obscurity, and that of the majestic Edgar Allan Poem. Publishing was not a concern of hers until she was overcome by the urge to share her works with the world. Her first attempts at publishing were at Iliad Press, in Troy, Michigan. Since then she has become published in *Perspectives* (a 1995 Iliad Press anthology), upcoming *Achieving Excellence* (a 1996 Iliad Press anthology), and *Whispers* (a 1996 Iliad Press anthology). Winner of the 1996 President's Award for Literary Excellence for her poem "Utalume: The Return" a poem dedicated to Edgar Allan Poe's poem, "Utalume" (written in 1847). One of her greatest aspirations for the future is to find a publishing house for her forty books, which include more than twelve-hundred poems. The first book she wishes to publish is entitled *Burning a Paper Moon*. She is currently searching for a publisher for this book.

McKinnon, Chris - has attained her Master's in Secondary English Education and has taken post-graduate classes at Michigan State University and University of Wisconsin. Her BA is from MSU in English Education with a psychology minor. She has taught writing, humanities and communication at the college level for the last eight years in central Michigan. She has a strong commitment to writing and editing and has also taught business writing. Her personal writing has included poetry, short story and humorous essay. her short stories have appeared in *Midnight Zoo* and *Short Stories*, her poetry, in *Big Two-Hearted* and Australia's *Tirra Lirra*; short articles in *Being*, among other publications. Ms. McKinnon, a recent member of The National Authors Registry, belongs to the Academy of American Poets and the Poetry Society of America, along with the Modern Language Association.

McLean, Pamela Ann - I was born in Downers Grove, Illinois on June 16, 1985. I lived in the Chicago suburbs until May of 1988 when my family moved to Lafayette, Indiana. My parents are Hugh and Cheryl McLean. I have a brother, Dan, and a sister Katie. We have a dog, Missy and two hamsters. Kindergarten through fifth grade I attended Mintonye Elementary School. I wrote my first poem when I was in the second grade. Since then, I have won a local contest sponsored by Tri Kappa three years and written several poems for school. My fourth grade teacher, Mrs. Janice Garrett, has encouraged and supported my poetry since I was in her class. I enjoy writing poems for people as gifts, for example, my teacher at the end of the school year or the school nurse for Nurse's Day. Twice, once for Earth Day and once for Christmas, I read a poem that I had written at all-school assemblies. In the fall I will attend Southwestern Middle School. I attend Evangelical Covenant Chruch with my family. I enjoy writing poems about God and nature. A friend of my family, Mark Petri, enjoys photography. We have started working together by inspiring each other with our hobbies. In addition to my pets, I enjoy many sports. I have played on the girls baseball team that won the county championship twice and was runner-up a year ago. I enjoy playing tennis and basketball with my friends. Last fall I began taking flute lessons and enjoy that very much also.

Middlebrook, Wilda - I was born in our Iowa farm home to parents Ben and Selma Jacobson in 1923. In 1941 I graduated from Cresco High School with a degree in Normal Training. I married my high school sweetheart, Harlan Middlebrook, on June 3, 1945. We have four sons, namely: Kevin, Rodney, Steven, and Boyd, and five grandchildren: Jeb, Lia, and Hanna Middlebrook, and Lindsay and Drew Middlebrook. From 1968-1971 I attended Luther College in Decorah, Iowa, receiving a B.A. in Elementary Ed. I taught 23 years, 8 of which were in the rural one-room schools of Iowa before the births of our children. I am a retired teacher and farmer's wife who has taken up writing--mainly about nature and real-life situations involving our grandchildren and life on the farm. Stories and poetry telling of my experiences in the one-room schools are on file in the Iowa Women's Archives, University Libraries, University of Iowa, Iowa City, Iowa. Two of my recent poems appear in the Amherst Society's *American Poetry Annual*, published in 1995, "If You Would Write Poetry" and "The Gathering." In addition to writing, my other interests are in music, photography, and keeping records for my children and grandchildren. I am currently finishing the story of my life, growing up on an Iowa farm during the Great Depression, which will be published in the fall of 1996. I give full credit for my enthusiasm for writing to my Creative Writing instructor, author Evelyn Minshull of Mercer, PA through her tutelage at a writing seminar in Brookville, PA in October 1994.

Miller, Dolores M. - I am 45 years old. I have been married for twenty-three years. I have two beautiful children, Larry 20, and Michele 16. I am married to a wonderful and caring man. I run a small business in Richboro, PA. I am also an Adult Survivor of Childhood Abuse. In my writing, I wanted to convey the message of caring and courage. That no matter what life brings your way, with belief in God and yourself, you can rise above troubles. I strive to reflect the power of the human spirit, to overcome obstacles, the beauty of nature, and God's love. Finally, C.Hoppe has written exactly what I hope to strive for and achieve in my lifetime: "I hope my achievements in life shall be these that I will have fought for what was right and fair, that I will have risked for that which mattered, that I will have given help to those who were in need, that I will have left the earth a better place for what I have done and who I have been."

Minnifield, Robert Earl - (Pen name, Osaze). D.O.B. 1-31-64. Mother: Lola Mae Gray (Minnifield). Born in Birmingham, AL. Divorced. Three children, 2 girls & a boy: Imani Zalika Minnifield (5-8-90), Asia Sankofa Minnifield (6-11-95), & my son Jabari Diallo Minnifield (12-7-93). My father's name "Alpha & Omega." Education: Graduate Arlington H.S. Riverside, CA 1982, former H.S. Football Champion CIF 1981. Community College, U.S.A.F. 1 yr., currently enrolled a the Academy of Business College, Phoenix, AZ. Former SSGT U.S.M.F.-8 years. Currently employed as a T.S.P. for MCI Communications. Memberships: California's Writers Club, National Authors Registry, Poets' Guild, Famous Poets Society. Awards: Real Estate Principles, Lumbleau Real Estate School March 1993; Career Success School, Met Life May 9, 1992; Emergency Medical Technician, City Colleges of Chicago; Workcenter/Section Supervisor OJT Course, United States Air Forces, March 21, 1989; Installation Patrolman/Entry Controller, USAF-Europe, Dec. 22, 1988; Peacekeeper's Award for Exemplary professionalism in rendering emergency medical treatment, USAF-Europe, Dec. 2, 1988; Noncommissioned Officer in the grade of Sergeant, USAF, Dec. 1, 1986; NCO Preparatory Course, USAF-England, Aug. 2, 1985. Professional Licenses: Life Agent, State of California, Dept. of Insurance, March 19, 1992; Real Estate Salesperson, State of California, Dept. of Real Estate, July 10, 1993. Writing Credits: Iliad Press, *Whispers*, March 1997 Cader Publishing, Ltd. poem titles "I Believe," "Imani," and "Mustard Seed;" Sparrowgrass Poetry Forumn, 203 Diamond St. P.O. Box 193, Sistersville, WV 26175, *Treasured Poems of America*, poem title "I Believe" due out December '96; Poets Guild, P.O. Box 10900 Parkville, MD 21234, *Best New Poems*, poem title "I Believe;" Famous Poets Society, 1626 N. Wilcox Ave., Suite 126, Hollywood, CA 90028, *Famous Poems of the Twentieth Century*, poem title "Imani," Sept. 96. Hobbies: Camping, fishing, the Arts, traveling, reading, fine dining, going to plays. Personal Comments: Much praise to Angels our fellow servants! Someone once said a true patriot is someone who would protect their country even from the government. All good things come from God may his will be done on Earth as it is in Heaven and may the devil be shamed! We war not against flesh and blood! P.S. Osaze!

Mullins, Ronda Dee - P.O. Box 5554 / Athens, Ohio 45701. Born: July 8, 1957, Chanute Kansas to Richard and Donna Tripp. I have three younger brothers. Married: Roger Wayne Mullins, Dec. 5, 1990. My in-laws Victor and Barbara Mullins have been very supportive. Children: a son, Bryan Charles (Packard) Mullins, 18 who is a special needs child from a previous marriage; Roger Scott Mullins, Becky Mullins, Ryan Mullins. Four grandchildren: Jessica, Ryan, Dakota, Rowdie. My son, Bryan, has been an inspiration in much of my writing, developed as a result of the experiences of having a handicapped child. Education: Sign Language, Teacher's Aid Certificate, Desktop Publishing Diploma, Master Travel Diploma, Graduated from Chanute Senior High, 1975, studied English in college. My love of writing was instilled at age eleven when our class had to write poetry for an assignment. Job: Educational Aide with Athens City Schools. Awards, Publications: 16 Honorable Mentions, published in *The Ozarks Mountaineer*, *The Chanute Tribune*, *The Big Sandy* and *Hawkins Journal*, *The Post*, *Hill Country Courier and Trader*, as well as several anthologies. I have four books of poetry published. My latest being *Visionquest* and a cassette tape recording of my indian poetry called *Drumwake*. I also put out a quarterly poetry newsletter called *Pencil 'N Pen*, available by subscription for beginning and published poets. Hobbies: I am an avid collector of bells, postcards, angel memorabilia, inspirational books, the poetry of others and friends! I enjoy playing the keyboard, dulcimer, harmonica, as well as reading, writing, crocheting, being a mother, my job, and being able to travel. I wish to thank all my family and friends for being patient with me as I scribble on paper.

Nate, Patrick - Born April 28, 1940 in San Antonio, Texas. Patrick Nate has worked in many field for short periods of time, embracing many cultures and ideas. His hobbies include, photography, sculpting, painting, sailing, classic auto restoration, studying indigenous fish of Texas, West Texas and its unique culture. He also embraces Texana studies, plant and animal life of the desert, obscure characters in history who made a difference, studying underdogs, and most subjects of human interest. He has a background in creative writing and electronics, having spent 35 years in technocratic endeavors, (missiles, computers, research and development). Patrick has traveled extensively both in the United States, and abroad. He has traveled most of Europe, and has been to French Algiers, and has sailed to Greenland, up the Thames River to North Hampton, the North Sea, around the White Cliffs of Dover, and the Aegean Sea. He lived in Germany from '63 to '65. Patrick is the author of approximately 75 musical compositions. He is a full time novelist, having written the following novels, now represented under contract by A Rising Sun Literary Group, Savannah, Georgia: *Summertide 1959, Falcon Haynes, A Bridge To Tomorrow, A Mile Or More,* and is at present working on his fifth novel, *The Lord With No Name,* due to be completed in July. Exact dates of publication are pending. With great purpose he wished to capture the human spirit and emotions rather then the events in life. People are the main source of his work, and their value is paramount in each of his literary attempts. Patrick is working on a book of poetry and essays as the novels proceed, and hopes to have enough material by 1997 to seek publication of his first book of poetry, possibly from a university press.

Newman, Ruth Emily - Graduated from Florida Atlantic University, Boca Raton, Florida in 1982; taught elementary education ten years here in Belle Glade, Florida where I have resided for some 30 years; retired from my teaching career in 1992. I am quite active in the First Baptist Church's ministries where I have been a member for over thirty years. For the past year and a half, I have spent my spare time seeking God's direction in writing poetry. I have a great desire to one day soon have my, fifty some odd, sacred poems published in a chapbook. A member of The National Authors Registry, my literary works published during the past year and a half are as follows: two poems by Cader Publishing, Ltd., "Yes, He Really Cares," in *Perspectives*, "Life...A Gift of Love," in *Whispers*; "Only...By His Side," Quill Books, "Yes, He Really Cares," *The American Annual*, The Amherst Society. My last five poems (not in chronological order) were published by The National Library of Poetry: "Doctor," *Beneath the Harvest Moon*; "Use Me," *A Muse to Follow;* "If I Were a Poet," *Best Poems of the 90's*; "More Precious Than," *The Rippling Waters*; "Use Me," *Spirit of the Age*. Three awards I'm honored to have received are: Editor's Choice Award, 1996 The National Library of Poetry; Honorable Mention in the Longfellow Awards chapter, *Whispers*, Iliad Press' newest anthology for 1996 and lastly, nomination as one of the Poets of the Year for 1996, contest to take place during the sixth annual International Society of Poets Convention and Symposium in Washington, D.C. August 2-4. Closing remarks: "With special gratitude to my Lord for the encouraging and inspirational words He gives me to use in poetry writing, I pray HIS Presence will be very real and dear to each of the readers of this anthology!"

Nichols, T.G. - Ty Nichols was born in chattanooga, Tennessee. While his father was engaged in "The North Africa Campaign" of World War II, he was taken by his mother, Mrs. Aullie Jean Nichols, to live with his grandparents in the Sand Mountains of Alabama. He is now the father of five children: Michael, Sue, Tyra, Audra, and Tyson; he is also the grandfather of five: Tiffany, Matthew, Kristen, Sarah, and Nathan. He is now, and has been for thirty-four years, married to Mrs. Irma G. Nichols. Ty is currently enrolled in The University of Tennessee, studying english and American Literature, and Creative Writing. He has taken many such courses, and has had several short stories and poems published.

Ohno, Elizabeth - Date of Birth: October 18, 1980. Place: Honolulu, Hawaii. Parents: Young Hui Ohno (mother). Education: Student, Maryknoll High School (Honolulu, Hawaii). Honors & Awards: Scholar, National Young Leaders Conference (Washington, D.C.). Interests: Piano, Tennis.

Oots, Emily Katherine - The author and writer of the emotional poem, "The hero I never knew," is a nineteen year old college student form Kansas City Missouri named Emily Katherine Oots. Emily has been a fan of poetry since a young age and hopes one day to become a famous poem writer or journalist. She also dreams of one day turning her poetry into music, in which she has received numerous awards in vocalism in music in high school competitions and hopes to study it abroad in college. She has had the opportunity to reveal her artistic expressions by singing with her state winning choir, "The star spangle banner", at one of our local royal games, and competing in state regional music competitions. The poem is an actual inspired story about the long lost brother she never knew existed until it was to late. She hopes every one who has a long lost family member finds a small area of peace from reading her poem, and never gives up the search to find unforgotten relatives.

Parker-Courtier, Elaine - (Pen name: "Quanah Parker"). Elaine Parker-Courtier was born in 1945 in Nottingham, England. She earned a B.a. in English Literature from the University of Colorado. She also attended Harvard University and Bentley Business College in Waltham, Massachusetts. She has traveled extensively throughout the United States, Far East, Canada and Europe. She belongs to numerous writer's groups and workshops and has worked and written a variety of genres in the past twenty years. She has completed a manuscript for one novel and is at work on another. Her collection of new poetry is about 60. When the collection reaches about 100 poems, she plans to publish the collection as an anthology. She is retired and resides in Dana Point, California with her husband.

Pena, Anna - Hello readers. I am Anna Pena and I hope you enjoy the poems that I have written. To tell you about myself is not an easy one...I don't know where to begin. Let's see...I was born in Madison, WI. My parents are Pedro and Shirley Pena. I have many brothers and sisters, including a twin sister. I graduated from Memorial High School in Madison. I was an average student who loved to write stories or write poems or read books while the teacher was at the blackboard. After graduation, although I am not employed at this time, I had a variety of jobs. But it is the writing that I love best. I love to research for every story that I write. I hope that after having my poems published, I will be able to find a publisher that will publish my novels. It is my biggest dream to be able to walk into a bookstore and see one of my books in the store. I am sure every writer has this dream. Even though it is very hard to break into the field of publishing, I wish every writer the best of luck in seeing their dream fulfilled.

Peters, Ladonna S. - I turned 14 last December. I was born in California, but Colorado has been my home since I was 6 months old. I live in a quiet neighborhood on the out-skirts of Aurora, with my mother, step-father, and my two step-brothers. I have always had a love for horses, and like to spend most my free time with my horse "Little-girl," which is a two year old Quarter Horse, that is almost broke. When school times comes around, my free time that I used to spend with "Little-girl" is limited. This year I will be a Sophomore in High School, and I will still be the youngest in my grade. My peers find it hard to believe that I am only 14, but when I explain that I was moved up in the 6th grade, they congratulate me. Being younger doesn't make the school work any harder, it just gives me an edge over my peers. After school I like to hang out with my friends, or go see my horse. My friends always want to go see my horse, so we usually see her a lot. We're always finding things to do, like going to rodeos, horse back riding, or renting movies. I find that friends ave very important to me, and they have always been there to confide in or just have fun. My love for poetry began when I was 10 years old. While my parents were going through a divorce, I was very confused and feeling lost about what was happening to my family. My mother gave me a diary, she thought that it would help to write my thoughts down. But I thought a diary was too personal, so I found a different form to write my thoughts in, because this was saying the same thing in a different way. The true meanings of my poems are found between the lines. For the story behind poetry isn't always expressed through the words, but through the thoughts of the writer/reader. This creates the mysterious edge to poetry that I love.

Phipps, Brandi - I live in Tarpley, Texas. I am fifteen, and an only child. I am a Freshman at Utopia High School, and am active in several academic programs. A few of my outside interests include basketball, computers, drama, art, and the War on Drugs program. Along with these I am a National competitor in Barrel Racing Futurities and APHC shows around the country. I also enjoy writing very much. I have written quite a few poems, a couple of short stories, and I am in the process of writing my first novel. I have managed to have three of my poems published, I hope to have several more published, along with my novel. After graduation, I plan to attend college and seek a career in Criminal Law.

Radford, R.J. - (Pen name B.J. Radford) - Born in Seattle Washington on October 18, 1944. After graduating from high school, she attended Cosmetology School, and worked as a hairdresser for 20 years. She is married, and resides in Renton, a small town just south of Seattle. Her interests include, her family, especially her grandson Cody, writing, and painting. She and her husband Neil love to travel, and spend time in the great outdoors. She began writing poetry in her early twenties, but only recently began sharing her work with the outside world. Awards include: "Award of Merit" 1993 Longfellow Poetry competition, sponsored by Iliad press, for her poem "The Daylight Sips Away." Roberta's poem "The Beach" was published in an anthology titled *In The Desert Sun,"* The National Library of Poetry, 1993. She was also a semi-finalist in the 1993 North American Open Poetry contest. Roberta believes life is a dance and often tells her children; *"There is more to life than just stepping lightly here and there".....*

Ramsey, Glenda - *Date of Birth*: Feb. 12, 1947; *Place of Birth*: Tulsa, OK; *Spouse*: Albert Dale Ramsey; *Date of Marriage*: May 26, 1972; *Children*: Bryan Dale Ramsey, Bonita Kay Ramsey; *Education*: Davis High School, Davis, OK. West Texas State University, Canyon, TX, B.S. in Medical Technology; Northwest Texas Hospital, School of Medical Technology, Amarillo, TX, Registered Medical Technologist; University of Texas Medical Branch, School of Blood Bank Technology, Galveston, TX, Specialist in Blood Banking; *Occupation*: Supervisor of Bone Marrow Transplant Laboratory; *Memberships*: American Society of Clinical Pathologists, American Association of Blood Banks, Poets Guild; *Other Works*: Poem: "You Are Not Alone" to be published in the Winter 1997 Edition of *Treasured Poems of America*, Several other unpublished poems; *Comments*: I love writing Christian poems. I thank God for giving me the inspiration and talent to share the gospel through poetry.

Renner, Lisa Anna - I am fifteen years old. I was born May 23, 1981 in Amityville, New York. I have one sister and her name is Kritin Ellen Renner. Presently I live with both biological parents in Sorrento, Florida. My family and I relocated to Florida in January of 1988. I became fascinated with poetry at about the age of ten and began writing actively at about the age of twelve. I wish to continue writing as I find it a good way to express my inner feelings and it's nice when someone says they like what I write. I write many of my poems to help people to understand different aspects of life. I hope to one day see more of my poetry published so I may be able to feel that I have contributed to the society of mankind.

Riley, Virginia Nancy - Born: April 23, 1946. Father: Raymond Schuhriemen; Mother: Josephine Schuhriemen. Married: Robert Joseph Riley (DOB 2/10/44) Everett, Massachusetts. Children: Sandra Riley, Cynthia Riley. Education: William Cullen Bryant High, Biblical Educational Studies. Teaching Awards for Learning Disabled Children, three honor awards. International Poets Society Award. Occupation: Self Help full time Systemic Lupus, belong to Lupus Foundation of America. Published the poem "We" in *A Delicate Balance*, 1995; "Thank You for the Best" in *Treasured Poems of America*; published "A New Dawning," National Poetry of Congress, "A Dawning Memory." Thanks be to God for the patience of the loved ones who grow with us and care for us; Robert my beloved husband, my devoted children, Sandra and Cynthia Riley, my sisters Barbara Pasqua, Carole Miller, Joan Abbatepaolo - our little brother Richie, resting in peace. A special dedication to Brendan and Mary Riley, also Catherine (Riley) Boyan a wonderful humanitarian and great influence on this family, Edward and Bertha Riley, God Bless them. My friend and doctor Frederick Swerdlow, my friends in the Lord Annie, Louis Paul, Darlene, Denise, Debra, Ronnie, Bobby O' - Arthur Pasqua, Ruth, Helen P., Lou, Roy, Aunt Nancy, my mom, Grace Mangano. A special notice of gratitude to beautiful women, Dr. Dorothy Miro, Dorothy Dalheimer, Nettie Pasqua, the Lord has taken his child one day at a time. Thank you Lord. The motivation behind the poetic writings - the care of others - especially children and the ill. Our time is extremely short - and the love of others is extremely important- living in pain is hard, but living in pain with those who love you is a Blessing from God.

Roark, Sheila B. - I was born and raised in New York City, I have lived in Texas for over ten years. I am married to V. Gail Roark and have three grown children. Cyndee, my oldest is married and lives in New Jersey. I also have twins who are now twenty-six. Teri is married and lives in New York, and Meri who is single and lives in Texas. I attended Notre Dame school for twelve years and studied a college preparatory curriculum. Since graduating from high school, I have taken various courses over the years to expand my education--including some writing courses. I also learn a lot by reading. I have my own library and read an average of four books a week. I have been writing poetry for almost twenty years and enjoy every minute I write. I am also writing short stories and hope to have them published in the near future. I have been fortunate to have my work published in over thirty-five anthologies, several newsletters and in some literary magazines, among them *Tucumcari, House of White Birches, Oatmeal & Poetry* and *Explorer Magazine*. My poems has also won awards over the years including: World of Poetry - Certificate of Merit (6), Golden Poet Award (4); International Society of Poets, Poet of Merit (1995); Iliad Press, Honorable Mention (1995); National Library of Poetry, Editor's Choice Award (2); Arts & Science Accomplishment of Merit (1995); Drury's Publishing Achievement Award (1996). Poetry is a beautiful way to communicate with the world. My poems come from my heart and give me the means to share my love of the earth, people, life and God with those who read my work.

Rodriguez, Monica - My love for poetry began the first time I read *The Cat In The Hat*. I was fascinated with the rhyming verses so much, I memorized the whole book in just one day. Later in the years I discovered that rhyming wasn't used just to amuse children, but adults as well. That's when I discovered poetry. Ever since my life has changed. I had found a way to write down my feelings in a way that I could feel good, because rhyming can bring beauty to the ugliest passages, and everything I saw around me at those times was ugly. I grew up in a poor neighborhood and from abuse to crimes, I saw it. I was born in New York City (from Hispanic descendent), and was raised half my life in New York City and half in Puerto Rico; to which fact I owe greatly my fluency in both the English and Spanish languages. Some of my poems have been written in spanish. At present moment I am twenty-seven years old and mother to four beautiful daughters all who enjoy my poems, children books and novel. I am yet to publish. I'm presently enrolled in college to get my associates degree in liberal arts. I'm really excited with the idea of my literary works being published and being read by many. I give thanks deeply to the Iliad Press team, for having the courtesy of inviting my works for publication, and to all of you who will be reading them; may God provide you with the key to understand, but most importantly, to reflect upon these poems as I have as I've written them. To my family and special friends; you all know who you are, thank you for making me part of your lives. And to my daughters, Jamilette, Tatiana, Carol and Heavenly, I hope I have set an example for all of you on how dreams can be made true. God bless you all.

Ruiz, Jay - age sixteen, youngest out of four children. I was born and continue to live in Northern California with my sister and mother, both of who I care for dearly. My parents were divorced when I turned twelve, I lived with my father for three months and then he just go up and left me and my older sister, who at the time was working and trying to finish up high school. Once my father left my mother stepped into the picture and she has been here ever since. I am the writer behind the poem "Something." The reason I wrote this poems was because for sometime now I have been searching for the real me. (Surprise! A sixteen year old on a quest for his identity.) Cause I know that behind all the therapy and prescribed medication lays a sixteen year old with a bright future. The other reason why I needed to write this poems was because I am not the popular guy who gets invited to the cool parties, or gets to hang out with the best crowd, and in high school if you don't have a group that you can call your own then you are considered an outcast, and that is what I was. I found sanctuary in my writing and in music. I spent my whole lunch period writing about everything and anything, about class and about life in general. All my poems relate to something that occurred in my sixteen years here on earth. So much has happened in those years, from my parents getting a divorce to me having a nervous breakdown my freshman year in high school. Since then I have come to see my hidden talents emerge from the black tar that has covered my soul. My plans for the future are not set in stone quite yet. I want to finish high school and find my own place faraway from my hometown, pursue my acting career or fall back on my writing. I'd like to publish a book of poems so I can share my writing and prove that dreams really can come true.

Sanderlin, Brenda Carol Jones - born in Haywood County, Brownsville, Tennessee, May 28, 1952, to the parents of Mr. and Mrs. Leonard Lee Jones, who were farmers. I am the third child of nine. I graduated from Carver High School in 1970 with honors and worked from approximately five years at a local plant, tuning T.V. and radio tuners. In 1986 I married Richard J. Sanderlin and moved to Stanton, TN where I now live. Realizing that I needed more in life, I left the small city and attended the Art Institute Atlanta, Atlanta, GA where I received my Associates of Arts Degree in Fashion Merchandising. While working at the plant where I now work, I managed to go to West Tennessee Business College and there I obtained a Diploma in Word Processing in 1983. I worked in retail for about eight years and then went back to the factory where I am now. I write in my spare time and plan on publishing a book of poetry in the near future.

Saunders, Linda L. - (3-6-49). I was born in Deshler, Nebraska, Linda Youngblood. I graduated from Doane College in Crete, Nebraska with a B.A. in elementary education in 1971. I have taught school for 25 years. I have been writing poetry since I have been 7 years old. I have been happily married for 21 years. I am inspired by my tow children, Angel Lee who is 15 years old and John, who is 6 years old. I believe that life is an adventure and full of so many experiences that make each of us who we are. I believe that life is good and God has a special plan for each of us in this world. I believe that nothing is impossible. Poetry is one of my hobbies that releases and strengthens my soul. I use it with my children, both at home and at school. I write poetry for family and friends, it makes me unique. I believe everyone has the ability to write and give others a personal view into our hearts and souls.

Scavo, Theresa Marie - born on February 5th, is a 30 year old student teacher at Wheelock College and Co-President of *Self Help for the Hard of Hearing People Inc.* in Boston, Massachusetts. She resides in Salem with her husband Joseph, white Finch bird, known as "Bonnie," and Calico cat named, "Pumpkins." A transfer student from Gallaudet University, (the only university in the United States of the deaf) located in Washington, D.C.. Theresa has resided in Florida and Iowa during the last 3 years. She is a sponsor of World Vision for Bizunesh Sebba in Ethiopia as well as a "Big Sister" for Corey in Massachusetts. She has worked with children for the better part of her life, a Sunday school teacher as well as a teacher aide for the special children at the Development School in the North Shore. Her hobbies are: painting, sketching, gourmet cooking, swimming, bike riding and nature hiking. As a means of coping with her hearing loss, Theresa began writing poetry at the age of 12, has won three *Golden Poet Awards* and is currently writing her life story. She would like to share with others what it is like to grow up with a hearing impairment. "I've enjoyed reading the works of Edgar Allan Poe, Nathaniel Hawthorne, Emily Dickinson, Helen Keller and Robert Frost," quotes Theresa. "I also enjoy reading the works of new poets along with Fantasy/Fiction stories in my spare time." Theresa hopes to one day earn her Doctorate degree in teaching special needs children. Her future goals are to receive the *Teacher's Golden Apple Award* as well as many other poetry awards. Someday Theresa also hopes to publish a few children's books along with her biography.

Schlidt, Terri L. - I was born September of 1963 in California and lived there for nine years. I rodeoed all over the state of California. I was a Barrel Racer. I made it to the E.T.I. Convention. I then came to Colorado with my mom, at age 11, for the girl's rodeo. We never went back to California. At the age of 13, we moved to Wyoming where I stated high school. When I turned 15, I got married and my husband took me out of school, when I was only in the ninth grade. By the time I was 21, I already had three children, one boy and two girls. When I turned 23, I got a divorce. I raised by children by myself. I made the decision to go back o school and do something with my life, so I got my GED and then stared taking classes. I love art so much I made it my major. I never was too keen of college writing or English, but I love to write. I always wrote stories or poems; I didn't really have a clue if the grammar was correct. I actually didn't think that my work was good enough for public. It took a lot of people to convince me to submit some of it. I am remarried now and we moved into the city. I'm not crazy about city life but it will have to do for right now. I know someday I will be back in the country...

Schneider, Dixie Lee Honeycutt - I made my entrance into this world on May 2, 1943. I was born in the great town of Claremore, OK which was already made famous by the late great, Will Rogers. I graduated from N.S.U. in 1967 and worked as an elementary school teacher for over fifteen years. My talent as a writer was confined to the classroom where I liked to inspire creative thinking in my students by telling believe it or not stories. I am a mother of four children and a very proud grandmother. I felt a christian need in my life and community so I organized "The Potters Field Ministry," in October of 1994. I use poetry to tell my story and reach other people like myself who may have a little flaw or crack in their perfect vessel. Some of my poems are: "Breaking the Law," "Faith That Works," "Things Yet To Come," "Salvation Through Grace," "Pagan Holidays," "666," "Come Soon," "Confusion and Delusion," "Satan the Deceiver," "The Greatest Gift," "Perfect Love Casteth Out Fear," "Is Heaven Ready For You." I have just finished writing and illustration a short story about a family pet called, "Through Scouts Eyes." Hopefully you will be able to buy my work at your local bookstore in the very near future.

Schuster, Sylvia - I am a Professor in the R.I.S.E. (Reaching Individuals through Special Education) Department at the C.W. Post Campus of Long Island University. I am also the Assistant Director of the R.I.S.E. Department. I have also had the privilege of supervising Student Teachers of English and teaching English at various colleges and universities on Long Island. I have had my poetry published in numerous anthologies and wrote an anecdote for *Those Funny Kids* compiled by Dick Van Dyke. I am presently working a children's creative writing textbook. In addition to teaching and writing, I also have a passion for photography. I was selected as a winner in the 1992 American Photography Magazine Photojournalism Contest. Of all my accomplishments, my most important contribution to this world is my daughter, Maggie.

Sears, Debra A. - I was born on June 20, 1956 to Betty Miller, in Pottstown, PA. My birth name was Debra Jean Miller. At eight days old I went from the hospital to live with Howard and Marion Bartholomew, who later became my adopted parents. They named me Debra Ann Barthomomew. I was one of several children my natural mother gave up for adoption. The true nature of why we were all given up is unknown. My adopted parents divorced when I was 3½ years old. At age 6, I went to live in a foster home for a year. By age 7, I went to live with my adopted mom and new stepdad. In the years to follow there was a lot of abuse. That's what led me to start writing. It was a way for me to hope and dream of a better future. Mrs. Hill my eleventh grade English teacher at Woodrow Wilson High School inspired me the most. I left home at age seventeen and was married at age eighteen. My first son, Paul was born on April 12, 1975 and my second son, Michael was born on November 2, 1976. My first husband's name was Paul Ray Strayhorn. He was killed in an accident on the job on December 15, 1990. He was a good hearted person and we were the best of friends. I dedicate my poems to his memory. I remarried on January 28, 1994. My new name's, Debra A. Sears and my husband's name is Rodney. I have two precious guardians. They're Lee Anthony, age 8 and Tawana Marie, age 3. Rodney Sears and I separated on June 15, 1996 to be divorces in the future. My inspirations come from personal feelings about life, past loves, special friends, what I hope for in the future, and most importantly, from God. I love the country, horses, hiking, foraging, swimming, writing, playing with my children and grandchildren, and above all - enjoying life. I pray that somebody gathers some beauty of life and love out of my poems. I just enjoy writing with the hopes of touching somebody's life.

Short, Jennifer - I was born in Hazard, KY. I now live in Hindman, a small city in Knott County Kentucky. I never thought I would be a writer although I am becoming one. I live with my mom Carla and my pets. We have 18 German Shepards, one German Spitz, and one mixed dog. I have a black Persian cat and five tropical fish. I'm 13 years old and entering the eighth grade. I plan on studying law at the University of Kentucky and write in my spare time when I'm older. I play basketball for the Carr Creek Lady Indians. I'm also on the academic and drama teams. I'm dedicated to many other activities. I play the electric keyboard and take voice lessons. Last summer I won first place in a swimming competition at a camp. I've taken dance lessons and once won the county art contest. I love to read. In the first grade I won a contest at our local library for reading over 200 books in one summer. In now average 30 books a week or more. I began writing in the 7th grade and I was encouraged by my language arts teacher Ms. Paula Bates. I'll never forget what she wrote on a homework assignment, "You have found your true talent. With constructive criticism and your willingness to except you writing will become award winning." She was right! I've always been one to look at the other side of things, the side no one want to see. I've come to know through experience that something will go wrong every once in awhile. I have learned to except more than good events or occurrences. In doing so I can express it through writing. "Waiting in the Dark," is my favorite poem that I've written. I wrote if for all those people who have experiences any negative feelings. I want to thank my mom, my teacher, and my best friend for their encouragement.

Smith, Gloria J. - I have lived in North Bend, Oregon since 1976. I was born and raised in Sacramento, California. I have two daughters and six grandchildren. I have been widowed since 1989. In 1993 I started to take writing classes at Southwestern Oregon Community college. Writing has been something I have always wanted to do, and now have the time. I've had six poems published in the *Beacon* which is the college's literary magazine that is published twice a year. I have also had poems published in anthologies from Famous Poets Society and International Society of Poets, The National Library of Poetry which I won an Editor's Choice Award in 1995. My goal right now is: To compile enough poems of quality to eventually have a book of poems published.

Stenzel, Erika Ingeborg - (Pen name, E.I. Raddatz). Date of birth: January 4, 1934. Place: Poland. Parents: Friedrich Raddatz and his wife, Clara, nee Zinn. Spouse: Erich H. Stenzel. Children: Peter H. and Harold F.; Father, Arthur Bauer died 1972. Education: very limited, I learned English by reading the newspaper after I immigrated to Canada in 1953. Membership: Allied Arts, Crosnest Pass, AB, Canada; Lifetime member International Society of Poets. Honors and Awards: 1993: Editor's Choice Award, National Library of Poetry, USA; 1994: Poet of Merit Award, International Society of Poets; 1995: Editor's Choice Award, National Library of Poetry, USA. Other Writings: 1992: To commemorate Canada's 125th Birthday, "A Potpourri of Western Canadian History" and other poems; 1993: Prariegrass: *Poetic Expressions*, about Wild Flowers of North America; 1994: "Cowboy's Wit and Sorrow," *Cowboy Poetry*; "The Magic of Christmas: Christmas Poems" with illustrations. *Horst Du noch die Glocken lauten?* German, in memory of my mother's 90th birthday; 1995: 25 poems written for *Golden Glimpses,* author Tia Wever; "Autumn Leaves" dedicated to my husband's 70th birthday; "Only a City Cowboy," melody by Country Music USA, Nashville, TN; "When Horses Grew on Chestnut Trees," a short story, growing up with progress (unpublished); "Like a Weed, that blows in the wind," Memories about a family caught in war. Historical events on WWI and WWII (unpublished). Inspiration: I started to write January 14, 1991 with the threat of the Gulf War hanging over us. Personal Note: Speech, the greatest gift God gave man, don't abuse it.

Toussaint, Marcel - A French-American author. After his two children were grown there was a divorce and Marcel Toussaint found himself in control of his life the way he saw it best. He resumed writing, wanting to express his feelings and add on to the few poems he had already written and the essays that were turning yellow. In his free time he wrote 1000 poems, 500 occasional cards and 12 songs in three years and finished a novel not yet published, started a second one 80 percent done and has an entertaining "how to" about manners for children half way completed. He likes poetry: "A poem is a mini story by itself. I was not thinking of publishing anything until my friends kept on saying 'Are you published?' it was time to do something about it."

Suess, Angela - born on April 6th, 1975. I live in a small town in south central Minnesota. I am the youngest of five boys and four girls in my family. My favorite color is black. I'm a animal lover, I have a black lab named D.J. and a black cat named Moses. Being an Aries, I'm a headstrong person wanting to do things my own way. I don't like people telling me what to do or how to think. I'm a believer in astrology, psychic powers, and reincarnation. I started writing when I was younger, right around junior high. I had a hard time trying to express myself by talking so I started writing things in a journal. Later on I started writing poems as another form of expression. Writing has helped me in so many ways, when I'm depressed, angry, or just stressed out, I start writing what I'm feeling and I feel like I'm able to deal with life again.

Taylor, Velande - born in New York City in 1923, Velande Taylor (née Martha Pingel) holds the M.A. and Ph.D. in Philosophy. [In 1961, she married Bert Raymond Taylor, Jr.] A professor and writer-in-residence in America and overseas, she has lived in Seattle since 1985. Member of the American Philosophical Association and former member and officer, PEN International (Hong Kong), her publication credits include poetry, fiction, articles and essays. She also conducts writing retreats. She is listed in the *Directory of American Poets & Fiction Writers;* and in the Eighth Edition of the *International Who's Who in Poetry.* She is also a member of the Academy of American Poets. Her books include *An American Utilitarian* (1948); *Catalyst* (1951); *Icolog Concept-Training Cards* (1965); *Immortal Dancer* (1968); *Mode & Muse in a New Generation* (1978); *Fragments of a Broken Mirror* (1983), and *Homilies in the Marketplace: Parables for Our Time* (1996). *Copper Flowers* will be published this December; *ZBYX (Totems)* is tentatively scheduled for publication in September 1997.

Thomson, David C. - I was born July 8, 1943 in Warren, PA to David A. & Vernice M. Thomson where I have resided most of my life. I am a twice divorced grandfather of three grand-daughters and three daughters, the oldest being 33 and the youngest 17. I am currently receiving SSI disability because in November, 1989 I had two aneurysms removed from my brain; following the surgery I suffered a stroke (CVA). My last full-time employment was with the local aging office where I was a care manager. I graduated in 1961 from Warren Area High School and attended part-time Edinboro State University, Warren Off-campus Center in Warren declaring liberal arts as my major. I have been writing poetry most of my life. I recall writing a poem in 5th or 6th grade which was much too long. As for hobbies, I enjoy reading (especially poetry), playing with my grand daughters and gardening. I am in the middle of organizing all my previous work into a collection.

Tinsley, Jennifer - I am a 15 year old junior in high school. My hobbies are singing, dancing, roller blading, shopping, and writing short stories and poems. I also write songs. I have been a finalist three times in three different poetry contests over the past two years. I am a member of my church choir and have been for quite a while. As a Girl Scout, I am presently working on my badges. My goals after high school are to attend college and go through medical school. My career goals are to become a pediatrician, a pediatric cardiologist, or an ob/gyn. I presently reside in Dallas, Texas.

Tipps, Lou Ann, R.A. - (Pen name, Ellis) **Date of Birth**: February 2, 1949; **Parents**: Bill D. Ellis, Ph.D. and Mattie O. Ellis, M.Ed; **Married**: Ronnie R. Tipps, M.Ed. October 10, 1969; **Children**: Chad Eric and Rod Ryan; **Education**: Ardmore High School-Ardmore, OK, Southeastern Oklahoma State University, Durant, OK; **Occupation**: Executive Secretary; **Memberships**: ESPO/Educational Support Personnel Org., CASA/Court Appointed Special Advocate (for abused children), First Baptist Church-member and Youth Departmental worker, National Authors Registry; **Honors**: 1991 CASA of the Year, Recognized at Texas Instruments/TI for services to the United Way, Outstanding Worker at TI; **Other Writings**: *Treasured Poems of America*, Fall 1994, for "A Fire" and "October;" *Treasured Poems of America*, Winter 1995, "Child of a Darker World," which also received Honorable Mention in the spring Iliad Literary Awards Program, 1995 and will be published in *Voices; Inspirations* Fall 1995), "Synchronicity's Sonnet" (in final round of competition in Iliad Literary Awards Program); *Beyond the Stars*, (in the process of being published), "Quawpaw Tribal Powwow" (is a simi-finalist in North American Open Poetry Contest, Winter of 1995-96); **Philosophical Statement**: Writing is a release for me, but more than a personal satisfaction, I try to express thoughts that make a difference to someone else, or to paint a picture or express a feeling in words. I write in clear concise messages from the heart. I can see a poem in everything. I hope to some day write lyrics for songs and also enjoy writing short stories.

Valentine, Jessica J. - I was born on December 5, 1977, the only child of Daniel R. Valentine and Bonnie M. (Puckett) Valentine. My parents divorced when I was nine months old. My mother moved to Mt. Pleasant, Michigan, and began attending Central Michigan University. We lived there for five years. During that time my mother met a man named LeRoy Taglauer, when she graduated from college she married him, and we moved to Auburn, Michigan. I was diagnosed with osteogenic sarcoma (bone cancer) in September of 1989. I went through a year and a half of chemotherapy and had my right leg amputated at C.S.Mott Children's hospital in Ann Arbor, Michigan. During that time I attended Camp Catch-A-Rainbow for the first time. There I found a world where a little girl with cancer could just be a little girl. I met many wonderful people including my best friends Vickie, Isaac, Sara, and Jayme. A lot of the poems I have written have been for or about these incredible people. At eighteen years old, many people tell me I have been through more than my fair share of hard times. I have, however, learned a lot from my experiences, which I have only touched upon here. I would not change anything that has happened though. These events have only made me stronger. I began writing poetry in 1991 at the age of thirteen. Initially I only wrote funny poems or poems meant for one specific thing, like Halloween. It wasn't until my doctors discovered another tumor, in my left leg, in 1994 that I started to write serious poetry. The first poem of that nature that I wrote was "Childhood Cancer Revisited." Since then I have written more than forty poems. I have only recently begun to submit my poetry for publication. I had one poem, "The Stranger's Eyes" published in an anthology entitled *Echoes from the Silence* by Quill books. Three others, "Childhood Cancer Revisited," "Izzy," and "True Romance" are about to be published by the Iliad press in their forthcoming anthology *Whispers*.

Vanskiver, Colleen D. - "Battle Of The Soul," is a piece I am very proud of. It took many years to do this poem. I was very young when I lost my third son. He wasn't quite a year old when he died. I blamed God, and battled very hard to regain my faith. That battle was as hard almost as losing my son. I come from a God fearing family, and praying and God have always been part of my life. So when I couldn't pray anymore, it turned my world upside down. Just as losing my son did. I am happy to say God won the battle. I am a wife and the mother of five children and have three beautiful grandchildren. My family is my inspiration for writing. Reading Jack London's book "Call of the Wild," as a young girl, is I think what gave me the kick I needed to start writing. I remember thinking this man took blank paper, and words, and made you feel emotion. You cried for the dog Buck. I remember thinking wow! what a God-given talent to be able to make people cry or laugh with words. I am a student with the Institute of Children's Literature. I love writing for children. With any luck I will graduate this summer. Well getting married and having a big family put writing on the back burner for awhile. But I have always done birthdays and special cards for my family and friends. Whenever I needed to say something special, I would write it myself. I have always wanted to put things in my own words. My husband has always been very supportive and encouraging about my poems, and writing. He is the one who keeps after me to send my work out. Ever since I can remember, I have had a passion for writing. I have always wanted to move other people with words. To make someone else smile, or shed a tear. To take someone else far away from their life, and into your world with words. That is my dream, I hope I can make it come true.

Vaughan, Margaret L. (Maggie) - was born on Nov. 24, 1972. My poem "Fight Racism" was published by Cader Publishing in the *Perspectives* anthology last year. I was inspired by John Singleton's movie "Higher Learning". My poem "In Memory of Walter" was written after the loss of our assistant manager, Walter Crawford, where I work. His wife, Maggie Crawford, gave me the honor to read my poem at his final services. Thanks Maggie! It's very hard to lose someone you feel close to and writing this poem helped me deal with Walt's sudden passing. He did not die because the fond memories we have of him keep him very much alive. Walter used to say, "If I don't get nagged enough from Maggie at home, I can always come to work and get nagged by Maggie there." I am grateful that Maggie said it was okay for me to publish the poem, therefore I dedicate it to Walt's wife, Maggie, and to all of his family. I am lucky to have known Walter. I am still engaged to my loving fiance Jevon D. Lowe. We still have not set a date for our wedding. I hope everyone reads "In Memory of Walter" and feels the inspiration of God and Walter. I love and miss you Walt. I promise to keep in touch with Maggie and make sure she is doing okay.

Vaughn-Trader, Layla Beth - Twenty-one year old Layla Beth Vaughn-Trader has been writing short stories and poems since she was very young. An avid reader, Ms. Vaughn-Trader contends that she is very dramatic and has a vivid imagination. Although writing is a passion, she has always aspired to act and has won several beauty pageant titles. She also won "Actress of the Year" in her drama class her senior year in high school. Ms. Vaughn-Trader is married to her high school sweetheart, Justin Trader and has a little boy, Wyatt. Layla Beth Vaughn-Trader is a licensed cosmetologist and resides in Boardman, Oregon.

Vericella, Erica C. - I came into this world on November 15, 1975 in Ft. Pierce, Florida. I now reside in Sarasota, Florida. I work at the local animal shelter. I have one cat named Barlow.

Warner, Ruth - Born October 6, 1923, in Toledo, Ohio to parents David B. Edwards and Pearl (Beyer) Edwards. She married Neal E. Warner on October 27, 1945 and has a son, Craig A. Warner. She attended Woodward High School and Stautzenberger Secretarial School. She is a housewife and a former secretary. Her latest awards include (2) Editors' Preference Awards of Excellence from Creative Arts & Science Enterprises, (1995); a President's Award for Literary Excellence from the National Authors Registry (1995); (3) Editor's Choice Awards from The National Library of Poetry (1995); an Accomplishment of Merit Award form Creative Arts & Science Enterprises (1994). Her poem "Intensive Care Nurses" was published in *Treasured Poems of America* (1995) by Sparrowgrass Poetry Forum, Inc.,; "The Dog With Bloody Paws," "Take Stock," and "The Autumn of Our Years" were published in *Words on the Rising Wind* (1995) by Creative Arts & Science, Enterprises: "Which Mask" was published in *Celebrating Excellence* (1995) Cader Publishing, Ltd., "Amnesia Victim" was published in *Best Poems of 1995*, by the National Library of Poetry. Some of her hobbies include: collecting baseball cards, sports uniforms, postcards, figurines, and assembling and furnishing doll houses. She is a member of The International Society of Poets, International Society of Authors and Artists, and The National Authors Registry.

Wenman, Alexandra - born on the 26th of September, 1977, in Coffs Harbour, Australia. She began writing poetry and stories early in primary school and has continued to write throughout her teenage years. Her poetry has been entered in many competitions within Australia and awards include: The Sydney Morning Herald Young Writer of the Year Award (certificate of encouragement); First Place and the adjudicater's award for own composition in the Coffs Harbour annual eisteddfod (1988, 1989, 1991 and 1993); First Place for own composition in the Hastings District eisteddfod 1993) and Highly Commended for short story writing in the City of Grafton annual eisteddfod. Alexandra was educated at St. Augustine's Primary School, Coffs Harbour, where she was encouraged to write by her teachers and enrolled in both the Mitchellsearch and Scots College talented childrens' weekends for creative writing. Her high school years were spent at John Paul College, Coffs Harbour, before completing her final two years of high school as a boarder at S.C.E.G.G.S. Darlinghurst in Sydney. She is currently enrolled in a Bachelor of Arts Degree, majoring in English, at Sydney University, where she is also a keen member of the writers' society. The works of many other poets have influenced and encouraged Alexandra's writing. Some of them include: Sylvia Plath, Emily Dickinson, Rupert Brooke, and Judith Wright. Alexandra has completed many poetic works over the years and hopes, one day, to become a professional writer.

Wessel, Patricia A. - (Pen name, Patricia Fanning Avery Bawcum Wessel). Born May 11, 1942 in Weehawken, NJ. Parents: James J., and Elizabeth C. Fanning, Sr.(deceased). Step-mother, Marion Fanning (past 11 years). Married James R. Wessel in March 1989. Children: daughter, Deborah K. Avery O'Mara and son, Jayson Keith Bawcum. Education: St. Mary's High School Albuquerque, NM graduated 1960. Attended the University of New Mexico, Albuquerque, NM and Technical Vocational Institute, Albuquerque, NM. A retired Administrative Secretary currently working as a housewife. Memberships: The International Society of Authors and Artists, The National Authors Registry, International Society of Poets, and Songwriters Club of America. Honors and Awards: 4th Place Captured Moments through Creative Arts & Sciences, Ent. Honorable Mention from several books, Editor's Choice Awards-National Library of Poetry, Accomplishment of Merit from Creative Arts & Sciences. Other Writings: numerous poems in various anthologies by Creative Arts & Sciences, Ent., Sparrograss Poetry Forum, Inc., World Art Publishing, The Amherst Society, Iliad Press, Poets Guild, *Best New Poems* of 1995 and 1996, and *Who's Who in New Poets* of 1996. Personal Note: When I write poetry or song lyrics I try very hard to write about a subject matter that I feel will be of interest to the majority of readers or those who hear my songs. The majority of my writing tells a true story and is either about an experience I have had or an experience someone else has had. I write about my feelings, about issues within our society and my personal beliefs or someone else's beliefs. I write about life, both its happy and sad times in an effort to make the reader able to identify with what I am saying. As we all experience many of the same things or similar things. Any agreement with what I say is not important to me. It is the exchange of feelings, beliefs and experiences that is enjoyable and educational. Most importantly for all of us, we live in a country where we do have freedom of speech and the right to express our feelings and beliefs.

White, Phyllis Pearson - Born in Berkeley, California, Ms. White spent her formative years in the Santa Clara Valley. She has traveled extensively and is a graduate of the University of California at Davis. Her occupations have been multifarious ranging from working with autistic children to running a tax practice. She credits her father for her love of words. She started writing seriously in 1990.

Her favorite medium in poetry. Some of the poets who have influenced her writing are Plath, Sexton and e.e. cummings. About poetry, Ms. White has written: "Poetry is a dying art / generally disregarded / unless disguised / as a best selling novel// You can no longer leave / a scrap of paper / as Emily did / to secure her posthumous fame // in the nineties / poetry is a foreign affair / too high an art form / for most Americans //even if regarded domestically / it is only in bedrooms when / insides are turned outside / in perfect iambic pentameter // sometimes it is abided / if socially conscious / because war sells / and poetry stimulates / but what a selfish occupation / to be a soldier of thought / when all of life / crumbles around you/ poetry explains why / rain touches the spirit / or why you can't / get up in the morning // it is economical / transformational sincere / it makes the heart bleed / I'm just dying to write it..." Ms. White currently lives in Mendocino, California with her fianceé, eight-year-old son, Ian Alexander, and her three cats Rikkio, Beau and Lily.

Willet, Bill - I was born in Pittsfield, Illinois in 1949. I am presently divorced, father of four lovely daughters, all are grown and have blessed me with five (5) grandchildren: three girls, two boys. After high school I enlisted in the marine Corps and served nearly four months in Vietnam. Extensive injuries from shrapnel ended my tour of duty. I was honorable discharged on August 27, 1970. At the age of seventeen, my aunt siad I would become a writer. I didn't believe her until my incarceration in 1990. My decision to make something of my life began one evening in the quiet of my cell. Suffering from Post-Traumatic Stress Disorder, I devote most of my time writing. My poem "the Were Once The Same" was first published in 1992 in *Fires of Genius* Anthology by Fine Arts Press in Knoxville, Tennessee. It was published again in *ESC! Magazine* in Dekalb, Illinois. In spring of 1993 I was named "Poet Laureate" in *Verses* magazine for my poem "On A Carousel." I received the Iliad Press President's Award for my poem "Reminiscing," which appeared in *Perceptions* in April of '94. "Forever" also received Honorable Mention in the Spring '94 program and received the President's Award in *Celebrating Excellence* in May of '95. Other works include: "This Good Earth," *Farmer's Almanac* 1995; "Grant Me A Tomorrow," "The Silent Battle," "Soldier of War," "The Truth of War," have appeared in various anthologies by The National Library of Poetry. I am a working chef and one day would like to open a supper club, write poetry and short stories on the side and vacation in the Bahamas during the winter months. While incarcerated, I help teach a Vocational Food Service class to other inmates. I believe any man can change if he so desires.

Wise, Rose Anna - Age 14, born in Eagle Pass, Texas to Gaylord (deceased 1986) and Norma Wise. She lives with her mother and sister in the quiet Ozarks hills of Missouri. Rose attends Willow Springs Middle School. Rose sets her inspiration for her poems on the many trips she has taken to the middle and western states to visit her grandfather, Henry Croman who has been her best friend and supporter of all that she writes. Rose's hobbies include: collecting toy cars, reading, and enjoying Indian history and music.

Wong, Olivia H. - Born and raised in New York City. BA in Biology from New York University, New York, and DO degree from the University of Health Sciences College of Osteopathic Medicine, Missouri. Accepted into combined internal medicine/pediatrics residency program at Newark Beth Israel Medical Center, New Jersey. Instead, recently completed one year of rotating internship with special emphasis in pediatrics at NBIMC. Currently seeking employment in other areas of the health profession in New York City. First foray into writing competitions and publishing field: no formal training or background in the fine arts. Plans include future competitions.

Wordsmith, Wesley - born in Monterey, but grew up in the "projects" of the inner city in Southern California. Following High School, he enlisted in the United States Air Force, where he spent eight years as a photographer and photo journalist, including tours in Hawaii, Japan, and Vietnam. Severely injured in an industrial accident in 1979, he spent the following five years recuperating. In the fall of 1984, at the age of 40, he enrolled at Ventura Community College, earning an Associates Degree in English and a Certificate in Journalism. He earned his Bachelor of Arts Degree, in English, at the college of Creative Studies, University of California at Santa Barbara. While at California State University, Sacramento, where he spent two semesters pursuing a Masters Degree in English (writing emphasis), he was forced to interrupt his educational goals due to family illness. He has worked for several newspapers, and has published numerous articles in many others. His monthly column appeared in the *Hawaii Bowler* magazine for four years. Other published works include a dozen poems and two short stories. He is presently writing his first book, a fictionalized novel about mental illness, based closely on a real-life tragedy.

Whispers

Index

Alphabetical Index of Contributors

Arranged by last name.

Alphabetical Index by Author

A

Acree, Amanda 79
Adams, Debby J. 79
Adams, Elzbeth 207
Adams, R. Douglas 207
Adamson, Stephanie 79
Addeos, Danielle 79
Adesso, Jamie 207
Adesso, Joseph 79
Affinito, Meghan L. 207
Agbayani, Diana R. 25, 207
Agourias, Angela 207, 208
Aguon, Angela A. 79
Ahearn, Geri 208, 411
AHNA 210
Akers, Gregory 208
Alan, Robert 209
Alcala, Michael 80
Aldrich, Angela 80, 209
Aldrich, Rachel I. 6
Alfonsi, Lia-Maria 80, 208
Alholinna, Soili 25
Alicakos, Kara 80
Allard, Winifred 209
Alleman, Mariam Ann 209
Allen, Laurie 209
Allen, Nicole 80
Allen, Robert 25, 416
Allison, Vivian 25, 210
Almeda-Neville, Alice 210
Almeida, Ashlee 80
Almquist, Kristina Francia 80, 210
Alonso, Denise 81
Alton, Pamela C.D. 210
Ambion, Maria 81
Ameduri, Eric 211
Amerman, Shannon Joy 210
Amos, Heather O. 81
Anawati, Stout 81
Anderson, Bonnie J. 25, 211
Anderson, Ginger 211
Anderson, Stephanie 211
Andrews, Tanna B. 81
Angove, Jamie 81
Angulo, Gerardo L. 211, 212
Ankofski, Donald A. 26, 212
Anthony, Heather 82
Anthony, James A. 26
Antonuuci, Albert 212
Aragon, Shanna R. 213
Arbolino, Caryn E. 82
Arnone, Michael A. 82
Arthur, Teresa 82
Artley, Tiffany L. 82, 213
Aruldass, Vijaya Sebastian 26
Ashby, Melody 213
Ashton, Rita L. 27
Atkinson, Dianne 27
Atterberry, Thomas 27
Audino, Frank L. 213, 214
Auguste, Carlo 27
Austin, Chad 213, 214
Austrom, Dawn 6
Autry, Mary 83
Aylwin, Ashleigh Ann 83

B

Bachtell, Mary Tempest 28, 214
Badger, Sarah 214
Bahs, Elizabeth 6
Bahr, Jayme L. 212, 215
Baitakys, Lina 190
Baker, Chelsea 215
Baker, Lisa 26
Baker, Laura 215
Bakker, Vera Ogden 7
Balcer, Nicole 215
Baldesberger, Debbie 215
Baldwin, Susan 26
Ballance, Robert A. 215
Bard, Denise Marjory Newcom 216, 411
Barden, Angie 216
Barkakati, Ivy 83, 217, 411
Barnes, Jim 7
Barnes-Bourgillon, Juanita C. 217
Baron, Stephanie 217
Barr, Katie Chase 83
Barrick, B.A. 28
Barschdorf, Jayme 212
Barteau, Anthea 83
Barto, Marcy 217
Barton, Jr., Clyde J. 218
Barton, Mary Frances 218
Bartone, Heather A. 84
Bartz, William W. 219
Basham, Heather 213
Basher, Juliana 84
Bateman, Michael 84
Battaglia, Stephanie 84, 219
Bauer, Wendy 84
Baum, Erin 85
Beach, Sharon E. 219
Beahlen, Travis 85
Beausoleil, Brenda 6
Becker, Judi 76, 403
Becker, Shannon 218
Beckman, Andrea T. 85, 212, 219
Bedard, Gregory M. ,28, 219
Be'Dard, Monique 85
Beggs, Lacinda 28, 220
Beitler, Nikki 84, 220
Bellusci, Jennifer 220
Bender, Mandy 221
Bennett, Crystal 221
Bennett, Diana Colleen 220
Bentley, Robert 221
Berger, Alfred H. 29
Bergeron, Karl T. 29
Bermeo, Layla Ann 221
Bernard, Melissa 217
Berning, Marilyn Helen 411
Bernson, Teresa D. 222
Bertisch, Dana 85, 86
Bessman, Ben 30
Betz, Tonya 86
Biasetti, Tony 85, 218
Biccum, JoAnn 222
Biddle, Melissa 86, 222
Bigbee, Dominique Renee 87, 219, 222
Bindeman, Faith 218
Birk, Kristin 222
Birlin, Jamie 87
Biss, Stacy 222
Bitgood, Anna Lisa 223
Bittinger, Amanda 86
Bivens, Brishandra 223
Biviano, Kate Elizabeth 223
Bivona, Jennifer 86, 223
Black, Amy 218
Black, Christine J. 216
Blackshear, Helen F. 7
Blair, Laura Ellen 87
Blake, T.R. 286, 414
Blakeney, Brandy 217
Blakley, Pamela 87, 223
Blanch, Emma J. 197
Blank, Mandy 223
Blaszczyk, Darcy 224
Bledsaw, Mark Stephen 224
Blinn, Maryiln C. 195
Bliss, Ashley 87
Block, Tracy 88
Bloom, Jamie 224
Bluteau, Lisa 88
Bodine, Stacy D. 224
Boggs, Catherine Lynn 88, 224
Bolz, Tiffany 7
Bolles, Olivia 88
Bond, Emily 89
Bond, Katherine L. 30, 220, 225, 411
Bondurant, Melissa 89
Bonura, Jessica 225
Bonzil, Marjory 89
Boone, Lisa 31
Booster, Genery 89
Borges, Crissy 221
Boserman, Jennifer 89, 221, 225
Bost, Benjamin McIver 87
Bostic, Miranda 90, 225
Boswell, Katie 90
Bourke, Leslie 8
Bowe, Sarah 225
Bower, Tara 90
Bowins, Brenda Lee 226
Bowser, Jenifer 90
Boyd, Kitty 226
Boyette, Sandra 28, 226, 411
Boyle, Melissa Leigh 90
Boysen, V. Elizabeth 227
Bozak, Jennifer 89
Bradshaw, John Patrick 227
Brady, Laura 227
Brady, Peggy S. 29
Bramer, Rhonna 228
Brand, Adrienne 8
Brashears, Eva 227, 228
Braslavsky, Gela 90, 411
Brax, Najwa Salam 197
Brazee, April 8
Brazil, Cindy 31
Brazley, Marshetta Shavon 228
Bredemeyer, Abby 227
Breese, Stephanie 88
Brehm, Marilyn 32, 191, 197
Brennan, Margaret A. 197, 228, 411
Brewer, Doris Hartsell 27, 195
Brogan, Jim 229
Brokaw, Charity 8
Brooks, Dianne 8
Brooks, Tiffanie 91
Brown, Adriane 91
Brown, Elizabeth R. 91
Brown, Ella 229
Brown, Jackie 229
Brown, Lindsay Nicole 230
Brown, Rachel 88
Brown, Rachelle R. 230
Brown, Thomas A. 229
Brown, Tawanda 91
Brulotte, Tammy 91
Brunk, Jessie 230
Bryant, Fantei 230
Bryant, Mike 230, 231
Buckner, Steve 91, 231
Budzynski, Lindsey A. 92
Buessing, Stacie 92, 232
Buettner, Lisa M. 92, 232
Buff, Amanda M. 232
Bui, Hong D. 26
Bull, Jamie 232
Bunker, Jill L. 232
Burch, Jessica 92
Burden, Michele 27, 232
Burger, Bethany 92, 233
Burk, Catrina A. 92
Burkholder, Nicole 233
Burns, Liza 230
Burns, Rachel 92
Buro, Anais 233
Burris, Nick 93, 233
Burroughs, William Bedford 234
Burrowes, Adrian Lloyd 234
Burrows, Dr. Elizabeth M. 198
Burt, Rebecca L. 234
Bush, Ethel W. 235, 412
Bush, Gordon L. 234, 412
Bush, Paul David 203, 412
Busse, Krista 93
Busse, Ronlad A. 32
Butler, Sherry 231
Buttler, Jennifer Ayn 30
Buxton, Charissa M. 235
Buxton, Dana E. 93

C

Calhoun, Lorraine 195

Campbell,Beckie 93
Campbell,Laura 235
Campbell,Ramie 93
Campbell,Tanisha 94, 235
Campellone,Tina 236
Cappolla,Sandy 236
Capps,Sarah Elizabeth 236
Cardin,Kathryn 94
Cardo,Alida Rose 94
Carey,Elizabeth McNielly 32, 236
Carland, Milt 8
Carey,Joyce B. 32, 412
Carle,Mark 32
Carlson,Kathleen M. 94, 236
Carlson,Micah J. 94, 237
Carlson,Stephanie 94
Carney,Bettie G. 33
Caron,Kimberly 237, 412
Carpenter,Amy 237
Carpenter,Jacque 238
Carpenter,Rhiannon 238
Carrell,Amanda 95
Carsley,Rebecca 95
Carter,Jenn 95
Cartier,Joseph G. 31
Case, Gregory 9
Case,Tara 233
Casey,Sara 238
Casselman,Kate 94
Castillo,Maricris T. 237
Castle,Diana 195
Castle,Janie 95
Castro,Andorrea 32
Catanio,Jennifer 238, 239
Cedervall,Stephanie 33, 237, 238
Celentz-Anderson,Karla 412
Chaffee,Rachel Kimberly 93, 239
Chamberlain,David B. 96
Chambers,LaTanya N. 96, 234, 239
Chapa,Annette 239
Chapin,Debra 96
Chapman,Crystal 96
Chappell,Lindsay 93
Charles,Tresha 240
Chediak,Andria 240, 241, 413
Cheetham,William J. 95
Chen,Kathleen Chia-ling 97
Chini,Amy 97
Chinners,Jill 239
Chiodo, Kara 9
Chio,Daniel 97
Chmiel,Agata 97
Choe,Grace 98
Cholinthia 153, 347
Chou,Annie 241
Christensen,Amanda 240
Christensen,Amy 98, 234
Christie,Jennifer Lynn 241
Christianson,Sarah 98, 242
Christian,Lavon 241
Christmas,Amanda 98
Christopher,Anna 5
Christy,William J. 231, 242
Chumbley,Clayton E. 242
Churchey, Shannon 9
Cibarelli,Bill 33, 242
Cirulli,Liz 242
C.J. 378
Clark,Cynthia 98
Clark,Cory 240
Clark,Lenore Cooper 29, 243
Clark,Rhonda Sue 98
Clay,Ashley 99
Cleveland,Sommer 243
Cline,Starr 99, 242, 243

Cline,William M. 243
Clough,Katie 99
Cobb,Bethany 99, 243
Cobb,Shane 244, 413
Cobian,Jacqueline 99, 243
Cochran,Eric 244
Cochran,Sylvia Marie 33
Coffin,Elizabeth D. 100
Coffman, Susie 9
Cohen,Whitney 100
Cole,Stephanie 100
Coleman,Caytee 244
Collins,James E. 100, 244
Collins,W.L. George 34, 244, 413
Columbus,Kathleen A. 100
Conden,Julie 244
Conley,Alison 31
Conley,Angela Lynn 100
Connally,Lisa 241
Conner,Lillian Page 245
Conquer,Norman 101
Conrad,Donna 101
Consla,Ruth 101, 245
Constance,Rhonda 34
Contreras,David 101
Cook,Jennifer Lee 245
Cook,James Stuart 245
Corneau,Katie 102, 245, 246
Corduz,Geraldine 246
Cornelius,Franklyn C. 246
Cortez,Jodi Ann 246
Cosby,Angela 102, 246, 247
Cote, Shawn 9
Cotman,Jacqueline N. 29, 247
Courrejou,Jennifer 102
Couts,Erin KR 102, 246, 247
Coutts,Christy 240
Cowdrey,Dena 34
Cowgill,Stephanie 103, 247
Cox,Amy 247
Crabtree,Elizabeth H. 103, 248
Crabtree,Martha 10, 29, 248
Crawford,Patricia M. 6
Crissman,James W. 248
Crosby,Greg 31, 248, 413
Cross-Zepernick,Melissa 34
Crowley,April 102
Cruickshank,Emily A. 249
Cullen,Rebecca 190
Cunningham, Sarah 10
Cunningham,Kate 102
Cupini,Alison 103
Currier,Melissa 103
Curry,June L. 249
Curtis,Kelly 103
Cuth,Emese 103
Cyphert,Steve 104
Czapiewski,Summer 104, 249

D

D'Augostine,Heather 250
DeCosta,Wendy 252
Dafoe,Stephanie 104
Dalangauskas,Donna 104
Dalrymple,Crystal 104, 249, 413
Dalrymple,Heather 105
Dalvesco,Rebecca 35, 250
Daniels,Fawn G. 248
Danyow,Jill 105
Darnell,Katie 250
Das Neves, Nancy 105, 250
Davenport,Melinda 250
Davids,Teri 35

Davidson,Don W. 35
Davis-Carpenter,Arnetta F. 251
Davis,Craig Welch 250
Davis,Gwen 105
Davis, Jr.,Julius J. 35
Davis,Katie Mae 251
Davis,Lindsey 204
Davuis,Melissa 251
Davish,Kate 251
Davison,Jeanne B. 252
Dawson,Heather Marie 99
Day,Dora 35
Day,Lauri 105
DeFalco,Jessica 253
DeGrey,Krista 249, 251, 252
DeGroff,Michelle 106
DeLaFlor,Sarah 106
DePaulis,Melanie 106, 253
DePino,Louise 36, 413
De Shazo,Rois 254
DeStefano,Gina Marie 254
Dean,Angela Lynn 252
Dean,Rita 195
Dearth,Derek S. 252
Defere,Peter 248, 253
Degraffinreid,Tracy 105, 251
Dellinger,Sarah 253
Demanet,Mylene N. 253
Denney,John Michael 36
Depies,Mandy 106, 254
Dethloff,John 254, 413
Deutschmann,Beth Ann 106, 255
Dhanji,Samira Kathryn 255
DeGirolomo,Rachel 107
Diaz,Mara 255
DiMarco,Maria 256
Dia,Bocar 255, 413
Diaz,Rosa M. 254
Dick,Pamela Merrin 106
Dietzman,Cindy 36
Dilizio, Cherisse 10
Dimmick,Marianne 36, 413
Dino,Nichole Anna 256
Dinho, Scott 10
D.J.R.,Irish 358
Dodge,Kara E. 256
Dodson,Teresa Ann 107
Doede-Straubhaar,Janeta J. 256
Doffont,Lauren 249
Dolmer,Amy Shea 256
Dolphin,Charlotte 107
Domanek,Roxanne 247
Domsic,Melissa 107, 413
Dooley,Carolyn 257
Dou,Johney 108
Dowling,Sarah Marie 108, 257
Downs,Kathleen 257
DuBowy,Jennifer 258
Duarte,Christentany 257
Ducharme,Jessy 108
Dudley,Ann 37, 258
Due, Jr.,Lonny 258
Driggers, Jr.,W. Douglas 255
Dumlao,Maritoni 258
Dunaway,Alicia 108
Dupont,Linda 107, 413
Dupres,Deseree M. 255
Duperry,Jinger 258
Durante,Molly R. 36
Durbin,H.F. 37
Durden,Terri L 365
Duro,John S. 259
Dwyer,Jennifer 109
Dyer,Heather Jean 259

E

Earl, A. Katherine 11
Eastlick,Chasity 109, 258
Easto,Nancy 259
Eaton,Daniel J. 109, 260
Ebanks,Trevor D. 37, 259, 260
Ebert,Candice Patricia 260
Edgeman,Emily E. 109
Edwards,Christy L. 260
Edwards,David E 183, 395
Edwards,John 37
Eggers,Faith 109
Eichelerger,Robert 260
Elgers,Barbara 261
Eliason,Sarah 261
Eller,Mariah 259
Elliott,Jennifer 261
Elliott,Nicole 7
Elliott,Shannon 261
Ellis,Duane Norman 38
Ellis,Ronda 110, 261
Eng,Tammy 104
England,Kristel 261
Englehart,E. Jane 2
Engler,Elizabeth Koken 262
Enz,Dave 38
Eoff,Mauryah 108
Epstein,Melissa 110
Erdman,Lisa 110
Ernst,Jen 111
Erwin,Kelly 111, 262
Eskins,Mary Beth 262
Eslami,Elizabeth A. 262
Estrada,Kim 262
Estrela,Steph 262
Etue, Larry 11
Evans,Erica 111
Ezzell,Cin 38

F

Fairchild, Jr.,Andrew 263
Falconer,Nichole 31, 263
Fallis,Anna 108
Fansler,Harmony M. 110, 414
Farmer,Emily 5
Farris,Shena 263
Faught, Kimberly 11
Faustino,Patricia 112
Feinstein,Elizabeth 112
Fejes,Mike 38
Feldkamp,Arthur 263
Fellman,Stanley A. 263
Ferri,Crystal 112, 263
Ferry,Brittany 112, 264
Fink, Liz 12
Fillion,Kelly 264
Fisher,Jennifer Lynn 264
Fishman,Kathy 113
Fite,Renee 264
Flanagan,Jen 112
Flood,Brenna 113
Floyd,Leslie 264
Flynn,Billy 110
Fogarty,Mary 39
Foote,Tina 265
Ford,Colleen 38, 265
Forsyth,David A. 37, 265
Foulke,Heather Ann 265
Fournier,Christina Lynn 113
Frame, Alan 12, 191, 198

Fox,Brian A. 266
Francis,Jennifer 266
Franco,Sharon 266
Franz,Sarah K. 114
Frazier,Christopher 266
Frazier,Danielle 112
Frazier,Elizabeth 113, 267
Fredman,Erin 114
Freiberger,Elizabeth 111
French,Elisa 267
Friedman,Jean 12
Friis-Jensen,Nina 114
Fritz,Amanda 114
Fryer,Ron 267
Fuller,Jennifer 266

G

Gaffney,Tari 114
Gagnon,Mathieu 114
Gaken,Lindsay Rae 115
Galazyn,Mindy 265, 268
Galbraith,Rachel 115, 268
Gallagher,Shannon 115
Gallegos,Allison Joan 268
Gallerani,Gian-Mical 268
Gallo,Mike 269
Galloway,Sabrina 269
Ganaway,Andrew D. 115, 269
Ganz,Jason 115, 269
Garcia,Alegria 115, 269, 414
Garcia,James 268, 414
Garcia,Krisha 270
Gardiner,Nicholas 39
Garrido, Gabriel 13
Garrett-Bledsoe,Evelyn 25, 270
Garris,Christina L. 116, 270
Garst,Samantha 270
Gartman,Joanne S. 116
Garvey,Marianne 39, 270
Garvine,Laura 110
Gautney II, Carol L. 13
Gauvin,Terri Donna 111
Gay,Lacy 116
Geiger,Harley L. 271
Genoble,Amy 271
Genzlinger,Dawn K. 116
Germain,Danielle 271
Gerstman,Maria 272
Gianaskos,Maia 272
Gianneschi,Allison 116
Giddings,Annie 272
Gifford,Jessica 272
Gilbert,H.S. 39, 272
Gilbert,Tanya D. 116, 272, 414
Gilchrist,G.G. 40
Gill,Elizabeth S. 40
Givens, Stephanie 13
Givhan,Sherry Lynn 39, 414
Glentz-Anderson,Karla 271, 414
Goheen,Jenna 273
Goldman,Christine 117
Goldsmith,Lasondra Carol 273
Golley Jr,Howard 40
Gomez,Arthur Paull 111
Gomm,Emily Hope 117
Gonzalez,Angelina R. 117, 273
Gonzalez,Andrea 40
Gonzales,Heidi 273
Goodall,Elizabeth Ann 117
Gooden,Kimone 118, 274
Goodman,Michael 41, 274
Goodman,Shelly 113
Goodwin,Emily 274

Gordon,Darius K. 41, 275
Gordon,Mary 41, 267, 414
Gottfried,Jessica 275
Gould,Kimberly Anne 117
Grace,Cynthia 118
Grace,Laura J. 118
Graham,Summer Michelle 118, 271, 274
Grant,Barbara J. 275
Grant, Natasha 12
Grant,Lisa Marie 275
Grant,Nickie 276
Gray,Elizabeth D. 39, 276
Gray,Virginia 117
Grazulis,Linda C. 270
Green,Matilda 276
Green,Tina M. 276
Greenberg,Krista A. 41
Greer,Jill 277
Gregorio,Lisa 277
Gregory II,Grover Wayne 42, 277, 414
Gretch,Corinne 276
Grice,Christine 118
Gridley,Sarah 277
Griffin,Heather 278
Grimmon,Amanda 119, 278
Groom,Madonna N. 42
Gross,Amber 119, 278
Growder,Michael J 392
Grouzalis,Lisa Marie 278
Grube,Cassie 119
Gruber,Brenda 119
Gruss,Samson 191
Guastella,Angela M. 119
Guffey,Misty Leigh 119
Gunby,Caroline 120
Gurley,Candace 278
Gurney,Laurence T. 120
Guticrrez,Christian 279
Gutierrez,Wendy 279
Gygi,Laura D. 42

H

Habermann,Paul David 275, 279
Hagen,Mandy 280
Hagmaier,Jill 280
Hain,Amy 120
Halcomb,Sarah 280
Halfvarson,Laura L. 43
Hall,Erin Elizabeth 120
Hall,Heather 41
Hall,Mistie 280
Hallberg,Al 195
Haller,Marci A. 273
Hallman,Tami 280
Hamilton, Dianne 13, 198
Hamdan,Leila 120, 280
Hamilton,Lee 43
Hamilton,Nathan 281
Hamilton,Sheila T. 40
Hamlett,Brooke Meryl 120
Hamlin,Katie 281
Hammill,Jill 121
Hammond,Emily 121
Hampton,Janelle 121
Hamrick,Martha 281
Handel,Theresa 276
Hanebrink,Lisa A. 43, 198, 281
Hannah,Kim V. 282
Hansen-Blizzard,Lyn J. 44
Hansen,Stacey 121
Hapgood,Timothy 122

Harrington,Kairi 282
Harrington,Krystina A. 282
Harrison-Duke,Terry A. 282, 414
Hartle,Lisa M. 283
Harvath,Katherine Elizabeth 122
Harvey,Linda 44
Harville,Paul A. 44
Haserick,Beth 282
Hasledalen,Sara 122
Hatcher,Stephanie 122, 283
Hatfield,Brianne 283
Hausman,Kristi 123
Hawkins,Charlene Ann 123
Hawthorne,Kerry Jo 283
Hay,Jolene 121, 284, 285
Hayden,Melissa Anne 284
Hayes,Bonnie C. 42
Hayes,Lynne 45, 284
Haynes,Keith 123, 284
Hayslette,Cynthia 45, 281
Hebrank,Ashley 120
Heck,Carolyn 45
Heckman,Lucinda 123
Heimark,Anna 123
Heinze,Amanda 285
Heinze,George-Alicea 191, 411
Heise,David 285, 286
Hemmer,Stacy Dawn 122
Hendon,Stac-E 124, 286
Hennie,Rachel 284
Hensiak,Melanie Ann 124
Herber,Lori 286
Hernandez,Janice 45
Herring,Angela 287
Herring,Jennifer Kristina 124
Herron,Candice T. 283
Hester,Neil Shane 124
Higgins,N Loy 45, 287, 414
High,Sandra 415
Highley,Kathy 44, 287
Hiles, Williams J. 14
Hilgendorf,Rachelle 294
Hilko,Karen M. 288, 415
Hill,Amanda 288
Hill,Betty Jean 44
Hill,Cynthia Yvonne 287
Hill,Dawn 13
Hinrichs,Sarah 288
Hinton,Monica 288
Hipkins, Jr.,Robert A.278, 288
Hirsch-Tauber,Ethan 125
Hisaw,Betty L. Floyd 45, 415
Hissick,Toni Lynne 289
Hobernicht,Rachel 125
Hodgdon,Kristina 289
Hoffmeier,Christina 289
Hoheusle,Nicole 125
Holderfield,Andrea 285
Holland,Amy Lynne 125, 277
Holland,April Michelle 289
Holland,Dana 289
Holliday,Lori Ann 289
Holmes,Darcy 46
Holmes,Jeanette 290
Holmes,LaTisha 290
Holmes,Wendy 290
Holt,Jeanne 195
Honeycutt,Erin 290
Hooley,Marci'a D. 46, 290
Hopkins,Ann 291
Hopkins,Ashley Lauren 122
Hopkins,Heather 291
Horace,Erica 126, 291
Horwell,Patricia 126
Hoss,Maegan C. 291

Hotko,Melissa 290
Houser,Krista 126
Howard,Altiemeis 126
Howard,Jennifer 191
Howatt,Shaina 291
Howell,Raycendia 292
Hrinek,Samantha 127
Hubbard,Cassandra 123, 292
Hudepohl,Jasmine 127
Hudnell,Holly Michelle 292
Huff,Brandy Camille 127
Huggins,Linda 46
Hughes,Joseph A. 292
Hullum,Jeni Nicole 128
Hults,Corey 128, 292
Hunt, Joan E. 14
Hunt,Leslie G. 293
Hunter,T. 128, 292
Huntley,Robin 293
Hurber,Lori 291
Huso,Heidi 46
Hussey,Kaai 293
Huston, Nancy 14
Hutcheson,Carolyn P. 46, 293
Hutchinson,Aimee E. 293
Huynh,Nhuloan Le 293
Hylla,Gerald T. 294

I

Ibbotson,Justin 47
Inbar, Miriam 12
Ingalls,Katie W. 294
Irgens,Barbara 47
Irish,D.J.R. 358
Irwin,Sarah Elizabeth 128
Isa,Annet 129
Isham,Jennifer 129
Ivy,Keely 294

J

Jackson,Jenetra 295
Jackson,Robert 415
Jacob,Melinda 47
Jane,F 355
Janes,Tiffany 295
Jarvis,Helen J. 47
Jazon,Claudel 295
Jean-Francois,Marie Catheline 46, 415
Jefferies,William C. 129, 295, 296
Jeffries,Nicole Yasmin 296
Jett,Matthew T. 296
Jenkins,Marlene E. 125
Jessup,Melissa 296
Johansen,Kristin 129
Johnson,Julienne 48, 297
Johnson,Jennifer S. 297
Johnson,Marsha A. 48
Johnson,Toni 296
Johnson,William 129
Johnston,Jennifer A. 129
Jones,Alma LaRocque 297
Jones, Amy 14
Jones,BJ 297
Jones,Gene 297
Jones,Heather 130
Jones,Nicole E. 298
Jones,Nancy A. 298
Jones,Rachel 298
Jones,Stephanie Marie 130, 297
Jones,Yohnikka 130
Jose,Linda 42

Alphabetical Index by Author

Joshi, Vishnu P. 48, 299, 415
Joy, Gary M. 15
Joy, Joy Joy 299

K

Kaczenas, Estelle 42, 299
Kafantaris, Demetra 48
Kahles, Christal 130, 299, 415
Kahn, Matt 299
Kai, Cyrus 314
Kalican, Susan G. 299
Kalil, Amy Beth 130, 300
Kallas, Jason 130, 300
Kam, Christy 131
Karst, Josef 47, 300
Katac, Nikki E. 131
Kaup, Julienne N. 131, 300
Keehan, Kelly 124
Keen, Becca 301
Kell, Alice B. 301
Keller, Harry E. 301
Keller, Rebecca Lynn 195
Kelley, Brenda Darlene 49
Kelley, Darlene 49, 301, 302
Kelley, Kathy 132
Kelly, Amy L. 302
Kelly, Lisa 126
Kelly, Rex 15, 49, 302, 416
Kennard, Doris 199
Kennedy, Erinn 132
Kent, Patricia 1
Keothammakhoun, Susan 132
Kermane, Bruce Nassiri 49, 302
Kerr, Millie 190
Ketchum, Jennifer 132
Keyes, Erik 132
Khan, Zarina 303
McAndrews, Journey W. 145, 321, 417
Killingsworth, Ashley 133, 303
Kim, Elaine Ki Jin 303, 416
Kim, Patricia 133
Kimminau, Joan A. 49
Kindle, David 199
King, Candyce Seji 50
King, Joumana 303
King, Megan 303
Kiper, Kristina M. 133
Kirby, Angi 133
Kirkendoll, C. Jason 304
Kiss, Suzanne 127, 304
Klauk, Shirley J. 304
Klick, Leah 304
Klippstein, Abigail 134
Knell, Jonathan 134
Kneubuhler, Kara 50
Knight, Summer D. 134
Koch, Rachael K. 3, 50
Kolb, Daniel 50, 304
Koo, Grant 15
Kolinsky, Lee 305
Kopp, Cassandra 305
Korer, Beth 305, 416
Korschow, Vitaly 50
Kovacic, Kristina 134
Kramer, Kathy Ann 305
Krause, Kellee Carene 15
Krigbaum, Nickilou 124
Kuffler, Brandi 125, 305
Kuhn, Laura 135, 306
Kujawinski, Faaea Letuli 304
Kulla, Deborah 303
Kurtz, Heather 135

Kuss, Nicole 135, 416
Kowk, Michelle 306

L

LaFleur, Dalicia 307
LaPierre, Robert E. 205
LaRocque, Tiffanie 308
Labby, Jessica 306
Labeck, Emily 306
Laffan, Sara 131, 306
LaFrentere, Lester 51
Lamar, Cyriaque William 128, 306
Lamb, Robert M. 308
Lamb, Ruth Anne 307
Lambert, Amanda 307
Landry, Carrie 308
Lane, Rhonda 133
Lang, Diane 308
Langway, Erin 135
Lankford, Tarah 308
Larche,'Rida 51
Larson, Dara Rose 309
Larson, Heather 309
Law, Casey T. 309
Lawson, Amanda L. 127
Layson, Cherokee Leano 127
Layton, Arianna Shareen 136
LeBlanc, Carrie 136
Le, Syindie 137
Leath, Isaac 309
LeBelt, Sherry 136
Leckbee, Christine 51
Ladbetter, Janice G. 310
Lee, Emma 136
Lee, Meredith N. 136, 310
Lee, Patricia 310
LeeAnn, Janice 310
Lefever, Paul 16
Legan, Anne Marie 52, 195
Leinen, Anita 16
Leisey, Mary Jane 16, 52
Lemons, Jeanie 128, 311
Lenox, Carl 16
Leonard, Patricia V. 311
Leos, Brandi 311
Lerner, Pamela Dawn 311, 312
Leslie, Gerree 52
Leveille, Tammy L. 312
Levinson, Frances H. 195
Lewis, Daryl 52
Lewis, Tissy 135
Ley, Jennifer A. 130
Li, Jie 138
Libhart, Heather 137, 312
Licari, Meredith Jean 137
Lichtenstein, Steven 137
Liljegren, Airika L. 312
Lin, Alice & Verity, Compton 138
Lin, Anny 313
Linden, Sandi 138
Lindsay, Joy 17, 53
Link, Sylvia Lynn 313, 416
Linsmeier, Rebecca 307
Liu, Lei 138
Livingston, Angela 191
Llepes, Rachael Marie 139
Lohman, Christopher Paul 314, 416
Lomas, Stacie 308
Long, Katrina E. 139, 314
Lopez, Avelina Maria 314
Los, Michelle 312
Loucks, Sharon L. 50
Lovelace, Ami 134

Lovelett, Emily Ruth 131, 312
Low, Maggie 139
Lowe, Carrol C. 53, 315
Lowe, Sydney 139, 305
Lowerly, Lucas 224
Lowry, Charles A. 51
Lowry, Kelly M. 132
Lozano, Joseph R. 315
Lozoya, Deborah A. Hancock 315
Lueken, Jillian 139
Luna, Bonnie L. 53, 298, 315
Lund, Rosemary N. 133
Luoto, Michelle M. 140
Lupkes, Jackie 314
Lurie, Rita 192, 195, 199
Lurker, Jaclyn 140
Lynch, Collin R. 316
Lynch, Kathleen M. 140
Lyons, Whitney 49

M

Mabey, Amanda G. 140, 416
MacDonald, Michelle 141, 316
MacDonald, Stacey 141
MacIntosh, Robert 43, 316
MacLean, Brenna 141
Macaluso, David 316
Macias, Veronica 310
Mack, Bertha L. 53
Mackey, Kimberly 317
Maddux, Carrie 54
Mae, Tonya 34
Mahnke, Rachel 141
Maillet, Brenda A. 51, 317
Maisenhelder, Gwen 142, 317
Maiser, Sarah 141, 310
Malaske, Tamra Lea 318
Malcolm, Joy 54
Mally, Jessica Anne 142
Malon, Diana L. 199
Maloney, Annette 318
Maloney, Melissa 309
Manchester, Eric Travis 142, 318
Mangels, Kelly R. 142, 318
Manick, Cynthia 143, 319
Mannhardt, Jessica 316, 317
Manthey, Sara Ann 143
Manzanares, Faith 319
Mardis, Amy C. 143, 319
Maria, Av Santa 199
Marion, L. Marvin 319
Marquis, Brittanie L. 143, 319, 416
Marsh, Lorrin Anne 320
Marshall, Andy 192, 200, 416
Marshalek, Sara 143, 320
Martin, Alexandra 144, 320
Martin, Elizabeth M. 135, 320
Martin, Faith 144
Martin, George W. 17, 322, 417
Martinez, Julio Y. 321, 417
Martin, Katie 144
Martin, Klaire L. 14
Martinez, Eddie 320
Martinez, Isaiah B. 321
Martinez, Marina Luna 144
Masek, Amelia 322, 417
Maslow, Jamie 144
Mason, Jennifer 138
Masters, Tiffany Corine 321
Mastnak, Amanda 321
Masztak, Christine M. 322
Matthews, Talaina J. 145
Mayer, Cathy 145

Mayers-Hall, Misha 322
Mazur, Lisa 145, 323
McAllister, Katherine J. 313
McCall, Jenna 323
McCann, Brooke 323
McCarron, Carey 142
McCarthy, Amy K. 323, 324
McCauley, Caitlin 145
McCauley, Tiffany J. 145
McConnell, Amanda 316
McCormick, Andrea 315
McCrary, April 324
McCray, Ann 54, 324
McCreesh, Erin 144, 325
McCubbin, Jessica 145
McCullough, Sara 146, 325
McCumber, Marissa A. 325
McCusker, Sarah 146
McDonald, Shawn 146
McGill, Imo 54
McGill, Sue 325
McGonagle, Corinne R. 54
McGrath, Anne M. 324
McGregor, Nichole 324, 325
McGuan, Bridget 146, 326
McGuyer, Sara 146, 323
McKain, Crystal Ann 326, 327
McKasty, Barbara 146, 327
McKee, Jamie 17
McKenna, Lindsay 147
McKeown, Malea 147
McKinnon, Chris 55, 417
McKnight, Jennifer Marie 327
McLain, Kelley J. 327
Mclaughlin, Emi 138
McLean, Pam 147, 417
McLemore, Terry M. 328
McLuckie, Craig 55
McMillen, Charlene 328
McNeely, Robin Renee' 55, 328
McVicker, Amanda L. 328
Meadows, Norah 18
Medders, Karen 18
Meeker, Erin 323
Mefford, Daniel 147, 328
Meizinger, Katie 326
Melnyk, Christina 18
Mensen, Stormy 147
Meranus, Dara M. 18
Merhej, Suzanne 148
Mervish, Martha 55
Meyer, Crystal R. 140, 318, 326
Meyer, Samuel D. 329
Meyers, Steven 17
Michael, Dunya 43, 282
Michalski, Carol A. 192, 195, 200
Micheli, Julia 326
Middlebrook, Wilda 200, 417
Middleton, Wanda Lee 329
Miko, Donna Marie 148
Milbourne, Rebeekah L. 329
Mild, Krystal 141, 321
Milkovich, Scott 329
Miller, Amanda 148
Miller, D. 329, 330, 418
Miller-Degrave, Jackie 148
Miller, Jessica 327, 330
Miller, June 7
Miller, Kimberly A. 195
Miller, Melissa E. 56, 330
Miller, Sarah 148, 331
Miller, Willie 331
Millican, Debra 330, 331
Milstead, James E. 56, 331
Minnema, Debbie 56

Minnick, Natalie M. 148
Minnifield, Robert E. 53, 418
Minok, Heather 19
Minton, Jeffrey S. 57, 331
Mireles, Tristen Jean 332
Mitchell, Michael L. 56
Mizerka, Michelle 332
Mlady, Beth A. 332
Moeller, Mary L. 58
Mohr, Heather 147
Moncion, Elsie 317
Mondragon, Amber M. 318
Monteiga, Courtney 320, 330
Monti, Andrea 333
Moore, Icie 57
Moose, Natasia 149
Moreau, Joanne 332
Morey, Donald E. 329
Morgan, Billie 149
Morgan, Joyce 56
Morgan, Juli L. 56
Morgan, Sara 333
Morie, Morgen 149, 333
Morrison, Angela 149
Morrison, Jr., Eugene T. 333
Morrison, Steven 52
Morton, Dena A. 58, 334
Mosley, MaryAnn 77
Moss, Stephanie 149
Mouton, Alicia 149
Mowat, Becky 149
Muir, David Michael 150
Muller, Jennifer 334
Mullins, Amber 332
Mullins, Ronda D. 58, 334, 418
Mulraux, R.H. 267
Mulrava, R.H. 267
Mulvey, Valerie 19
Murachanian, Pamela J. 334
Murdaugh, Andrea N. 150
Murphy, Christopher M. 150, 331, 334
Murphy, Colleen 332
Murrie, Adam E. 150

N

Nagode, Mary E. 57, 335
Napper, Jessica 150, 335
Nash, Lara 150
Nate, Patrick 58, 418
Nave, Dwon 150
Naylor, Michelle 336
Naylor, Natalie 151
Negussie, Hawani 58
Nelson, Bruce E. 336
Nelson, Jessie 151
Nelson, Marilyn 336
Neuhauser, Kimberly Anne 59
Newman, Ruth Emily 200, 418
Newman, Rick 151, 336
Newton, Barbara Marie 57, 337
Ngov, Samantha 151
Nguyen, Anh-Thu 337
Nguyen, Tammii 334
Nichols, Mary 335
Nichols, T.G. 337, 418
Nies, Kaitie 151
Nix, Shawnie 152
Noggle, Shaina L. 152, 337
Noll, Samantha 152, 336, 337
Norris, Marnie 338
Norton, Michele 152
Novak, Joseph V. 57

Nowak, Jennifer 152
Nuwatanka 74, 392
Nwachku, Adaku 153
Nyberg, Sean 57, 338
Nzerem, Claire 201

O

O'Brien, Obie 59
O'Connor, Lisa 153
O'Connor, Paulline 59
O'Donnell, Marjorie A. 13, 338
O'Hare, Rebecca J. 338
O'Neal, Angela L. 339
O'Neill, Jennifer 153, 339
O'Neill, Stephanie A. 339
O'Rourke, Lindsey 339
O'Toole, Kelly 154
Obermiller, Katie 153
Odom, Cindy 59
Oglesby, Starr 338
Ohno, Elizabeth Kim 152, 336, 418
Olyan, Jason 339
Ong, Charlene 339
Oots, Emily Katherine 154, 418
Orkiszewska, Aleksandra 338
Ortona, Stephanie 154
Osborn, Amanda 339
Osborne, Robin Yvette 60, 340
Oshlick, Katie 340
Oslizlok, Magdalena 154
Ostrow, Andrea 154
Ottolini, Jessica M. 154
Owen, Jillian 155
Owen, Reba 60, 340

P

Palley, Beau 340
Palmonari, Anita Pat 60
Pao, Christina 142
Paquette, Susan M.V. 61
Park, Denise 155, 340
Parker, Billy Joe 61
Parker, Carol 61
Parker, Quanah 61
Parks, Kimberly Lynn 155
Parks, Melissa Sue 155
Parrish, Melissa Ann 155
Parsons, Jennifer 155, 340
Parsons, Kelly Lee 61
Parvin, Carly Mae 341
Pasket, Pamela Jean 341
Passmore, Kasandra 156, 341
Paster, Theodore 62
Patterson, Amy 342
Patterson, Sandra 156
Paul, Kristin 342
Payne, Terri 155, 341, 342
Payne, Yolanda Coney 342
Pears, Leslie 156
Peck, Maegan 343
Peckar, Carrie 156, 342
Pelfrey, Stan 60, 343
Pellegrini, Lisa 19, 343
Pelletier, Stefani 156
Pelman, Susan B. 62
Peltsch, Alicia 343
Penna, Anna 344, 419
Penix, Rachel 156, 343
Pepin, Natalie 344
Perez, Cally 344
Peters, Bret 344
Peters, Cynthia Ann 344

Peters, Katie Eden 157
Peters, Ladonna Sheriese 157, 344, 416
Peterson, Annamaria 345
Peterson, RN, Ronnie 62, 345
Petrovic, Katarina 62
Petruka, Andrea 157, 344
Petty, Tonya 157
Pfarr, Amanda 346
Pfarr, Maynerd 151
Phillips, Fred 63, 346
Phipps, Brandi Michelle 342, 419
Phipps, Gregory Richard 346
Photikarmbumrung, Elma Diel 19, 63
Piazza, Shellise 157, 346
Pienn, Rochelle Theo 20
Pierce, Gordon C. 63, 346
Pierson, Denise 60
Pikcilingis, Julie 158
Piner, Karen 346
Pinnix, Waynette 158
Piper, Marissa 158, 347
Platt, Jr., Richard 347
Plummer, Sharonda 347
Plummer, Stephanie Jean 347
Podszus, Deborah 63, 347
Pokryfky, Stephanie 153
Polensky, Lory 158
Pollard, Michael C. 63
Ponoski, Kristi 348
Pool, Henry 64
Poole, Amy 341
Poorian, Sarah 348
Porcaro, Stephanie 20
Porter, Anna 159
Porter, Katie Michelle 159, 348
Porter, Lori Beth 64
Posey, Rebecca 348
Powers, Brandi 348
Pratt, Alma K. 63, 349
Pray, Amy 159
Presto, Stephanie 159, 349
Prezioso, Debra Nicole 160, 349
Price, Jayme 160
Pritchett, Sarah 160
Procuk, Michael S. 160
Provence, Kristy 349
Prow, Abbey 160
Pryor, Emily 161
Pursley, Elizabeth 350
Purvis, Melissa Kathrine 161
Pusc, Nick 161
Putman, Tami 161, 349
Pyka, C.H. 61
Pyzynski, Carolyn L. 350

Q

Quan, Latricia M. 350
Queen, Angela 350
Quigley, Daniel J. 162
Quilty, Beth 351
Quinn, Jessica 351
Quinn, Kattie 351

R

Radcliffe, Jessica 162
Rademacher, Sarah 350
Rader, Christie 351
Radford, B.J. 352, 419
Radzak, Jessica L. 162

Raia, Shari R. 352
Ramer, Rachel 162
Rampton, Kathleen 64
Ramsey, Glenda 65, 419
Ramseyer, Loretta 20
Raskauskas, Carolyn 352
Rasmussen, Angela 352
Rathbun, Charles 64
Ratliff, Jessica 162, 353
Ray, Chevin 21
Ray, Elizabeth L. 65
Ray, Melissa 65
Raynes, Chandra 162, 353
Reavis, Valorie 353
Rector, Jessica Loren 163
Rector, Jennifer 352
Recupero, Anna A. 353
Reece, Shawna 163
Reed, Karen 353
Reed, Randy R. 65
Rees, Christine 163
Reese, Nicole 353, 354
Reeve, Kimberly 350
Reeves, Patrice DeeAnn 352, 354
Reeves, Rebecca 354
Remillard, Stacy Ann 163
Renner, Lisa A. 354, 419
Reynolds, Emily E. 164
Reynolds, Sally 21
Reynolds, Thomas 11
Reznik, Anna 354
Rhea, Mildred Bedinger 66
Rhodes, Hilary 355
Rhodes, Joseph 355
Rice, Jude 355
Richardson, Brandi 159
Richardson, Donald K. 355
Riden, Somer 355
Ridgway, Madeline Johnson 65
Ridley, Charity 356
Riedel, Cheri L.A. 164
Rieger, Susan 356
Rigg, Elizabeth Capron 356
Riley, Sasha 357
Riley, Virginia 66, 357, 419
Rinyu, Christina 164
Roach, Maryellen 356
Roark, Sheila B. 64, 192, 201, 357, 419
Robbins, Jr., Andee 358
Robbins, M.K. 356
Robbins, Rebecca Ann 164
Robbins, Williams 20
Roberge, Jessica C. 165, 358
Roberts, Emily 358
Robertson, Jennifer 165, 357, 358
Roberts, Jennifer 358
Roberts, Robin 67
Robinett, Valerie 357
Robinson, Jamie 157, 356
Robson, Shari 359
Rockstad, Danielle Lynn 165
Rodarte, Brenda 359
Rodriguez, Monica 67, 419
Roe, Kathleen F. 359
Roeder, Raye Carol 359
Rogers, Brooke 166
Rogers, Michael 166
Rogers, Patricia 166
Rogers, Raymond 196
Rohleder, Crystal 166, 359
Rold-Danner, Tamela 67, 360
Rose, Kim Aleta 360
Ross, Jeanne 192, 201
Roth, Karla 360

Alphabetical Index by Author

Rotmil, Jasmine Alowan 167, 357
Rottman, Cristine 360
Rowe, Marianne R. 360
Roxas, Karell 360
Rubin, Julia 167
Rud, Amanda 167, 361
Ruiz, Jay 168, 420
Rumala, Bernice 361
Rutten, Elizabeth 361
Rutter, Jo Ann Lynn 361
Rutter, Marilyn B. 361
Ryan, Brooke 362
Ryno, Megan 362

S

Sabat, Kimberly 363
Saffas, Andriana 168, 363
Saker, Cora 168
Salisbury, Allison 169
Salomone, Tony 68, 363
Sampson, Rhonda 363
Sanchez, Leticia 363
Sanderlin, Brenda C. 364, 420
Sanders, Erika 364
Sanders, Jennifer 220
Sanders, Susan 21
Sandlin, Tami 68
Sangisetty, Suma 364
Saunders, Linda L. 68, 420
Savage, Sarah 17
Savard, Mandy 169
Savic, Gerri 364
Saylor, Margret R. 169
Scavo, Theresa M. 365, 420
Schadler, Donna 365
Schilb, Amber Rose 365
Schlauch, Dina 168
Schlidt, Terri L. 420
Schmidt, Amanda 364
Schmitt, Colleen 169, 366
Schneider, April 366
Schneider, Dixie Lee 365, 366, 420
Schoenfelder, Erin 366
Scholl, Margaret 193
Scholleman, Maggie 169
Schuble, Alisha 367
Schumacher, Jamie L. 169
Schuster, Sylvia 68, 367, 420
Schweigert, Rhea 170
Scott, Danaera 165
Scott, Eva O. 367
Scott, Kristen Marie 165, 367, 368
Scott, Robyn 368
Scott, Rikki 167, 368
Scutro-Ward, Bonnie 368
Sears, Cheryl A. 368
Sears, Debra Ann 367, 368, 369, 420
Seastrom, Valerie Gail 369
Sellari, Louis P. 69
Sellars, Stephanie C. 170
Sellers, Shaun 69
Senger, Caroline 167
Serock, Erica 369
Serrano, Sheila Lynn 370
Serrata, Flor 370
Settergren, Nicole 370
Sexton, Ellie 370
Sgro, Kathleen 69
Shafaie, Atossa 369, 370
Shaffer, Ann E. 170
Shallcross, Wendy 170
Shams, Nicole S.K. 171

Shanahan, Tracie D. 69, 371
Shananhan, Kimberley 369
Shank, Jr., Barry Lee 371
Shannon, Paula Wiest 66
Sharp, Brouke 371
Shaver, Alexis 170
Shaw, Kristy 20
Shawn, Jr., Joseph J. 372
Shaw, Jennifer L. 371
Sheenan, Frank 372
Shelton, Cammy D. 171
Shelton, Jeanell 170
Sheridan, Lauren 166
Sherman, LaVeta B. 372
Sherrill, Lizabeth 372
Sherrod, Philip L. 372
Shih, Cynthia 21
Shiue, Eileen 373
Short, E.M. 11
Short, Jennifer 171, 373, 421
Shouse-Bland, Celena 112, 172
Shriver, Dorothy M. 22
Shubert, Becca 172
Shuler, Alexis 164
Sicking, Jessica 373
Sielaff, Amanda 161
Sierra, Nichole Kathleen 171
Siler, Elizabeth 373
Silken, Lindsey 373
Sillin, Sarah 64
Sills, Samantha J. 172, 373
Simmons, Danyal D. 374
Simoneaux, James 374
Simon, Jennifer 11
Simpson, Brooke 374
Sims, Ashia R. 374
Sims, Kathryn P. 164
Singer, Shereen 374
Sizer, Tina Marie 374
Skaggs, Hillary A. 375
Skalla, Elaine 375
Sklar, Elyse 172
Slater, Rachel Marie 375
Slininger, Maya 375
Smit, Marcy Dianne 377
Smith, Alicia M. 172, 375
Smith, Anne 166
Smith, Annie 375
Smith, Christy S. 375
Smith, Christina M. 68, 376
Smith, Gloria J. 70, 376, 421
Smith, Monica 172
Smith, Megan 168
Smith, Michael 173, 376
Smith, Nicole 173, 376
Smith, Shannon 376
Smith, Sandra G. 376
Smullin, Cayce 377
Smyth, Jenni 377
Snider, Shana 159, 377
Snow, Mary A. 377
Snyder, Eugene 377
Snyder, Katie R. 378
Sockwell, Cynthia 173
Soler, Dona K. 70, 193, 201
Song, Han-Na 173
Sorell, Tiffanie 378
Sorensen, Brenda 70
Sosko, Christine 378
Soto, Jessica 173, 379
Soule, Crystal 379
South, Michael L. 66
Spencer, Kathleen 379
Spencer, Virginia L. 174
Spessard, Heather 163

Spiegel, Emily J. 174
Spoor, Daniel E. 70
Sprague, Devon 23
Sprenger, Ana 171, 376, 379
Sroczymski, Jamie L. 168
St. George, Jenette 66, 382
St. Patrick, R.J. 33
Stacy, Jennifer Lynn 379
Staley, Tabitha L. 380
Stalts, Linda L. 70
Stancampiano, Robert 71, 380
Stanford, Amy 174
Stanford, Julie A. 174
Staniszewski, Heather L. 380
Starling, Renee' 380
Stathis, Marigo 71
Stebleton, Mira R. 163, 380
Steedman, Ashley 175
Steel, Vetta E. 66, 380
Steele, Judy 71
Steele, Kelly Lynn 175
Stenzel, Erika I. 201, 421
Stephan, Adrienne 175
Stetzler, Beth 174
Stevens, Benjamin 72, 381
Stevens, Karen 381
Stevens, Victoria 381
Stevenson, Vanessa 175
Stewart, Kristin 381, 382
Stewart, Sara E. 382
Stoll, Jesica 176
Stone, Alissa Patrice 4
Storney, Rachael 382
Stout, Andrea 176
Stowell, C.R. 382, 383
Strahan, Stephanie 383
Strawser, Emily 383
Streetman, Tabitha 161
Strickland, Michelle A. 176
Strohm, Gretchen 176
Strohmeyer, Tonia Louise 176
Studeman, Brooke 160
Suess, Angela 383, 421
Sugar, Pink 267
Sullivan, Brian Clement 384
Sullivan, Rebecca 175
Sumner, Susan Marleen 384
Swafford, Rebecca 384
Swann, Janet Nicholson 71
Swanson, Kerri 177
Swedberg, Amber 385
Sykes, Tammy Turale 385
Szentpetery, Sonya 385
Szpara, Danen D. 385
Szper, Laurie 385

T

Tacuyan, Naomi 176, 384
Tanzini, Elizabeth 177
Tarter, Robin 177
Tate, Lisa N. 384
Taylor, Amanda L. 386
Taylor, A. Arwer 22
Taylor, Jessica 386
Taylor, Rebecca 386
Taylor, Sheena K. 177
Taylor, Stasia 386
Taylor, Velande 196, 421
Teaster, Kristina 178, 386
Teeples, Daniel 178
Terrell, Connie L. 387
Terrillo, Tera 387
Teska, Nikki 169

Tew, Stephany 387
Therrien, Jay 178, 387
Thomas, Jamie 178
Thomas, Jeremy 239, 296, 387
Thomas, Melissa 388
Thompson, Heather 388
Thompson, Tonyce 388
Thomson, David C. 72, 421
Throsh, Kevin P. 179
Tilden, David 179
Timm, Robin E. 17
Tinsley, Jennifer 388, 421
Tipps, Lou Ann 388, 421
TLC 101
Tobin, Jennifer 179, 389
Tolliver, Sarah J. 72, 389
Torello, Jacqueline Marie 388
Torsney-Weir, Maggie 179
Tousaint, Marcel 389, 420
Townsend, Paula 180, 389
Toy, Connie J. 390
Traff, Darin 180
Trageser, Amy 390
Trajceski, Cammie 67
Trinkle, Jo Anne 196
Trojan, Toni L. 390
Troxle, Rachel Dawn 180
Tucker, Jameson 22
Turek, Jaime Marie 181, 386
Turnbough, Bobbye Lee 390
Tyson, Christine 181

U

Udland, Abby M. 390
Uhrich, Jodi L. 72
Underwood, Patricia 181
Urbina, Rebecca L. 390

V

Vader, LaDonna 391
Valentine, Jessica J. 181, 391, 421
VanCamp, Linda 73
Van Note, Roberta 391
Van der Wal, Crystal 180
Van Gundy, Annamarie 182
Vanskiver, Colleen 73, 422
Vaughan, Margaret L. 392, 422
Vaughn, Harriette 73
Vaughn, Jeannie 73
Vaughn-Trader, Layla Beth 74, 422
Vegter, Jocelyn 179
Vericella, Erica C. 392, 422
Vernon, Kristy 182
Villavicencio, Ricardo A. 74
Vinneau, Melissa Ann 69
Vogel, Jessica L. 182, 392

W

Wade, Daylin 392
Wade, Rikki Renee 393
Wager, Blythe A. 389
Wagner, Rhonda 393
Waite, Catherine 182
Walits, Melanie Elizabeth 393
Walker, Addrean 182
Walker, Kathryn 180, 385, 393
Wallace, Doris Yates 394
Wallace, Michelle 393
Walsh, Jennifer 394

Walston,Joey 183
Walter,Jeremy 183
Wang,Latisha Lea 177
Wangberg,Elizabeth L. 74, 394
Ward,Morris Eldon 394
Ward,Paula 183
Ware,Marianne 395
Warner,Ruth 395, 422
Warren,Charles E. 395, 396
Wasson,Lori 183
Waters,Carrie 174
Watkins,Tamara 396
Watson,Lori Lynne 19
Watson,Rhae 182
Watt,Amy 396
Weaver,April 184, 396
Weber,Molly 184, 396
Weekley,Stacy 396
Weese,Constance M. 75
Weetz,Elizabeth 396
Weidlein,Cheri 397
Weisenfeld,Lindsey 397
Weiss,Cecelia 397
Weiss,Francesca 397
Wellman,Jaime 184
Wenman,Alexandra 422
Weppener,Barbara S. 75, 196
Werling,Amy 184
Wernio,Monica K. 184
Werntz,Tamara 398
Wert,Jessi 398
Wessel,Patricia A. 398, 399, 422
West,Dorothy Jean 399
West,Marilyn 399, 400
West,Meghan Orelene 185, 398, 399
Westmaas,Rupert Harry Desmond 75, 400
Westmeyer,Tina 400
Westphal,Kristy M. 400
Wheat,Rachael 398
Whetstine,Joshua L. 401
Whiskeyman,Maria 185
White,Angela 185, 401
White,Mallory Beth 184
White,Phyllis 75, 402, 422
Whitehead,Eva 185
Whitehouse,Morgan 401
Whitesell,Connie M. 185
Whitfield,Alexis 402
Whittredge,Ashley 186
Wick,Alex Jarrod 186
Widener,Jody 401
Wiegand,Douglas 402
Wielgus,Kacie 402
Wikoff,Lisa 75, 403
Wilder,Lillie D. 403
Wiley,Megan 186
Wilhelm-Norton,Wanda 22, 76
Willett,Bill 76, 423
Williams,Darryl L. 403
Williams,Karen 3
Williams,Lindsey Renee 186
Williams,Maureen 16, 190
Williamson,Markella 186
Williams,Pauline 77
Willis,Heather L. 404
Wilson,Cynthia Anne 404
Wilson,D'Esta C. 186, 404
Wilson,Eddie 23
Wilson,Nadia Lynn 187
Winger,Amanda 187, 404
Winslow,Janet 69
Winston,Tridaugh 187
Winter,Dianne 183

Wirth,Jared B. 187
Wiser,Rose 178, 404, 423
Wissler,Brittany 187, 404
Wnorowski,Lawrence 405
Wohlwend,Sarah L. 187
Wolc,Natalie 188
Wolf,Jessica 188
Wolf,Rackelle White 394
Wolfgang,John 405
Wolford,Holly 406
Wolfram,Jennifer 189
Wong,Melva Mae 406
Wong,Olivia H. 406, 423
Wood,Doris A. 406
Woodall,Barbara 406
Woodard,Susan 188
Woodard,TorRanee 406
Woods,Gail 23
Woods,Regina 407
Woods,V. Marie 407
Woolson,Nancy L. 407
Wordsmith,Wesley 24, 77, 405, 423
Wydro,Knoelle Higginson 407

Y

Yager,Debra L. 76
Yeager,Lisa 407
Yee,Christina F. 407
Yee,Elmer 23, 77
Yelton,Krista 408
Yoder,Suzanne Y 189
Yoder,Sharon 77
Yoshioka,Malia 189
Young,Allen 189
Young,Christina 24, 189
Young,Jamie L. 408
Youngman,Amy 408

Z

Zappone,Dona Samson 73
Zerbe,Morgan 408
Ziegler,Sylvia 408
Zimmerman,Abby 408
Zobrist,Chris 188, 409
Zollman,Casey 409